Scots Criminal Law

SCOTS CRIMINAL LAW

Fourth Edition

Sheriff Andrew M Cubie

Sheriff of Glasgow and Strathkelvin at Glasgow
Deputy Director of the Judicial Institute for Scotland

Bloomsbury Professional

Bloomsbury Professional Limited, Maxwelton House, 41–43 Boltro Road, Haywards Heath, West Sussex, RH16 1BJ

© Bloomsbury Professional Limited 2016

Bloomsbury Professional is an imprint of Bloomsbury Publishing plc

Reprinted 2019

A CIP Catalogue record for this book is available from the British Library.

ISBN: 978 1 78043 867 2

Typeset by Phoenix Photosetting, Chatham, Kent
Printed and bound in Great Britain by CPI Group (UK) Ltd, Croydon, CR0 4YY

Contents

Preface		*vii*
Tables of cases		*ix*
Table of statutes		*xxxiii*
List of abbreviations		*xli*

Part I	**General Principles**	**1**
1	The sources of Scots criminal law	3
2	Principles of liability	23
3	Strict liability offences	45
4	Corporate criminal liability	55
5	Causation	63
6	Parties to crime	75
7	Inchoate crimes	93
8	Defences	109

Part II	**Offences Against the Person**	**135**
9	Assault	137
10	Homicide	153
11	Sexual offences	175

Part III	**Social Protection Offences**	**191**
12	Social offences	193
13	Road traffic offences	207

Part IV	**Property Offences**	**223**
14	Theft/Reset	225
15	Robbery	251
16	Fraud/uttering	255
17	Embezzlement/extortion and bribery	269
18	Malicious mischief	281

Part V	**Offences Against the State and Administration of Justice**	**291**
19	Offences against the state	293
20	Offences against the administration of justice	301

Index	**311**

Preface

Five years have elapsed since the last edition and the landscape keeps changing. Breach of the peace has been effectively usurped by statute as the public order offence most usually charged; the evolution of that crime is addressed in Chapter 12. That is part of a trend towards statutory regulation of areas where the common law had previous dominion, an ongoing development of concern to academics and others. There is still no criminal code for Scotland, although the work of the authors of the Draft Criminal Code has been mentioned with approval in the High Court

Again it has been a pleasure and a privilege to be able to contribute to the analysis and, hopefully, understanding of the developments in Scots criminal law. An environment where almost all cases, journal articles, and text books, can be accessed through the internet remains a significant advantage which I enjoyed over my predecessors. Any errors are of course my responsibility.

I have received assistance and support from a number of people. Paula O'Connell and Jane Bradford at Bloomsbury were as ever courteous, helpful and understanding. Thanks to Andrew Devine for his considerable work in final copy editing, both quickly and thoroughly, at a busy time of the year. And particular thanks to my father, John P Cubie, who read through the whole text checking for intelligibility and grammatical errors, and to my wife Joan, who proof-read everything, when there were many more attractive things to do, and without whose encouragement and support this task would not have been possible.

Andrew M Cubie
Glasgow
January 2016

Table of cases

[*references are to paragraph numbers*]

A

Abbas v Houston 1993 SCCR 1019... 13.12
Adair v McKenna 1951 SLT (Sh Ct) 40 .... 13.21
Adcock v Archibald 1925 JC 58, 1925 SLT 258 .... 16.9, 16.10, 16.11
Ahmed v MacDonald 1994 SCCR 320, 1995 SLT 1094.................................... 3.8
Alex Carr (1854) 1 Irv 464 .... 8.22
Alex Findlater and Jas McDougall (1841) 2 Swin 527...................................... 9.8
Alex Bannatyne (1847) Arkley 361 .... 16.16
Alex Gilruth Fleming (1885) 5 Coup 552.. 17.2, 17.4
Alex Macdonald (1826) Alison I, 282 .... 14.21, 14.24, 14.29
Alex Mitchell (1874) 3 Coup 77.. 17.4
Alex Robertson (1867) 5 Irv 480... 14.4
Alexander Mitchell (1833) Bell's Notes 90.. 9.12
Alister v The Queen (1984) 154 CLR 404, Aust HC... 7.10
Allan Lawrie (1837) 2 Swin 101.. 14.24
Allan v HM Advocate 1995 SCCR 234.. 15.1
Allan v Milne 1974 SLT (Notes) 76 .... 12.5
Allan v Patterson 1980 JC 57, 1980 SLT 77..................................... 2.25, 13.12, 13.15,
16.13, 18.6
Allenby v HM Advocate 1938 JC 55, 1938 SLT 150 .... 17.5
Allison v HM Advocate [2010] UKSC 6, [2010] All ER (D) 103 (Feb)........... 1.5
Alphacell v Woodward [1972] AC 824, [1972] 2 WLR 1320, [1972] 2 All ER
475, HL 3.4, 3.6, 3.7
Alston and Forrest (1837) 1 Swin 433... 14.22
Amato (Antony) v Walkingshaw 1990 JC 45, 1990 SLT 399, 1989 SCCR 564,
HCJ 12.6
Ames v McLeod 1969 JC 1 .... 13.2
AMT, Petitioners. *See* T, Petitioner
Anderson v HM Advocate 2001 SLT 1265, 2001 SCCR 738............................. 11.11
Anderton v Ryan [1985] AC 560, [1985] 2 WLR 968, [1985] 2 All ER 355,
HL... 7.11
Andrew Lyall (1853) 1 Irv 218 .... 11.13
Andrew Steuart (1874) 2 Coup 554... 18.6
Angus McKinnon (1863) 4 Irv 398 .... 14.5, 14.8
Angus Sutherland (1874) 3 Coup 74 .... 14.22
Angus v HM Advocate (1905) 13 SLT 507, 4 Adam 640.................... 18.7, 18.9, 18.11
Angus v HM Advocate 1935 JC 1, 1934 SLT 501.. 20.2
Anwar, Respondent [2008] HCJAC 36, 2008 SLT 710 .... 20.4, 20.5
Armstrong v Clark [1957] 2 QB 391, [1957] 2 WLR 400, [1957] 1 All ER 433,
DC... 13.18
Arthur v Anker [1997] QB 564, [1996] 2 WLR 602, [1996] 3 All ER 783,
[1996] RTR 308, CA... 14.9
Atkins v London Weekend Television Ltd 1978 JC 48, 1978 SLT 76................ 20.6
Atkinson v HM Advocate 1987 SCCR 534 .... 9.2
Attorney General v Able [1984] QB 795, [1983] 3 WLR 845, [1984] 1 All ER
277.. 6.14, 6.15, 10.2

Attorney General v English [1983] 1 AC 116, [1982] 3 WLR 278, [1982] 2 All
ER 903, HL 20.6
Attorney General v MGN Ltd and Others [1997] 1 All ER 456, [1997] EMLR
284, QBD 20.6
Attorney General's Reference (No 1 of 1975) [1975] 1 QB 773, [1975] 3 WLR
11, [1975] 2 All ER 684, CA 6.3
Attorney General's Reference (No 2 of 1999) [2000] 3 All ER 182, [2000] 3
WLR 195, [2000] 2 Cr App R 207 .... 4.8

B

B v Harris 1990 SLT 208; sub nom C v Harris 1989 SC 278, 1989 SCLR 644.... 9.3
B v HM Advocate [2015] HCJAC 56, 2015 SLT 476, 2015 SCL 663, 2015
SCCR 281, 2015 GWD 21-369 .... 14.4
B v R 2010 SLT (Sheriff Court) 20.4
Backhurst v McNaughum 1981 SCCR 6 .... 14.26, 14.29
Bain v HM Advocate 1992 SCCR 705, 1992 SLT 935 .... 12.5
Balmer and others v HM Advocate [2008] HCJAC 44, 2008 SLT 799, 2008
SCCR 765 .... 4.3
Barbour v HM Advocate 1982 SCCR 195 .... 11.14
Barile v Griffiths 2010 SLT 164 .... 2.20, 2.21, 11.18
Barile v Procurator Fiscal Dundee [2009] HCJAC 88 .... 9.3
Batty v HM Advocate 1995 SCCR 525, 1995 SLT 1047 .... 11.20
Bean v Sinclair 1930 JC 31 .... 3.9
Beck (1989) 43 A Crim R 135, Queensland CA 2.11
Beckford v R [1988] AC 130, [1987] 3 WLR 611, [1987] 3 All ER 425, PC 8.28
Benton v Cardle 1987 SCCR 738, 1988 SLT 310 .... 13.23
Bernard Greenhuff (1838) 2 Swin 236 .... 1.7
Bett (Robert John) v Brown; *sub nom* Bett v Hamilton 1997 SLT 1310, 1997
SCCR 621, HCJ Appeal 18.4
Bird v HM Advocate 1952 JC 23, 1952 SLT 446 .... 5.6, 10.13
Black and Penrice v Carmichael 1992 SLT 897, 1992 SCCR 709 .... 14.6, 14.7, 14.9,
14.12, 14.13, 14.14, 14.15,
14.16, 17.6, 17.7, 17.8, 17.9
Black v Allan 1985 SCCR 11 .... 18.6
Black v HM Advocate 1974 SLT 247 .... 3.3
Blane v HM Advocate 1991 SCCR 376 .... 8.6, 18.7, 18.8, 18.9, 18.11
Bocking v Roberts [1974] QB 307, [1973] 3 WLR 465, [1973] 3 All ER 962,
DC 12.6
Bonar v Macleod 1983 SCCR 161 .... 2.14, 6.10, 9.4
Bowers v Tudhope 1987 SCCR 77, 1987 SLT 748 .... 20.7
Boyne v HM Advocate 1980 SLT 56 .... 6.20
Brennan v HM Advocate 1977 JC 38, 1977 SLT 151 .... 2.27, 8.11, 8.12, 8.13,
8.19, 8.20, 10.6, 10.10
Britten v Alpogut [1987] VR 929 .... 7.14
Broadley (Rose) v HM Advocate [2005] HCJAC 96, 2005 SCCR 620 .... 2.28, 5.16
Brown and Lawson (1842) 1 Broun 415 .... 9.12
Brown v Braid 1984 SCCR 286, 1985 SLT 37 .... 13.6
Brown v Hilson 1924 JC 1, 1924 SLT 35 .... 9.8
Brown v HM Advocate [2010] HCJAC 66 .... 10.11
Brown v HM Advocate 1993 SCCR 382, HCJ 6.7
Brown v Orr 1994 SCCR 668, HCJ 13.12
Brown v Stott 2000 SLT 379, 2000 SCCR 314, 2000 JC 328 .... 1.10
Brown v Stott 2001 SC(PC) 43, 2001 SLT 59, PC 2.12

Brown v W Burns Tractors Ltd 1986 SCCR 146.. 4.5
Bruce (Allan) v McLeod 1998 SCCR 733, 1998 GWD 40-2044, HCJ Appeal.... 11.7
Brunton v Lees 1993 SCCR 98, HCJ... 13.12
Bryans v Guild 1989 SCCR 569, 1990 JC 51, 1990 SLT 426........................... 9.4
Burns v HM Advocate 1995 JC 154, 1995 SLT 1090, 1995 SCCR 532 .... 8.27
Butterworth v Herron 1975 SLT (Notes) 56 .... 20.4
Byrne v HM Advocate 2000 JC 155, 2000 SCCR 77, 2000 SLT 233 .. 18.7, 18.9, 18.11

C

C v Harris. *See* B v Harris
C v HM Advocate 1987 SCCR 104 .... 11.14
C v HM Advocate 2009 SLT 707, 2009 SCL 863, 2009 SCCR 606 .... 8.24
Cameron (Allen Gordon) v Maguire 1999 JC 63, 1999 SLT 883, 1999 SCCR
  44, HCJ Appeal 2.25, 10.15
Cameron v HM Advocate 1971 JC 50, 1971 SLT 202 .... 14.10, 15.4
Cameron v HM Advocate 2008 SCCR 669 .... 15.2
Cameron v Orr 1995 SLT 589, 1995 SCCR 365 .... 20.4
Campbell and Cosans v United Kingdom (1982) 4 EHRR 293, ECHR............. 9.3
Campbell v HM Advocate 1942 JC 86 .... 17.10
Campbell v MacLennan (1888) 1 White 604, 15 R (J) 55.............................. 14.5, 14.8
Campbell v McKenzie 1982 JC 20, 1981 SCCR 341 .... 13.25
Cannon v HM Advocate (Unreported) 6 October 1999, HCJ............................. 6.20
Capuano v HM Advocate 1984 SCCR 415, 1985 SLT 196............................... 6.5
Cardie v Mulrainey 1992 SCCR 658, 1992 SLT 1152 .... 2.9, 8.20
Carmichael v Ashrif 1985 SCCR 461 .... 11.9
Carmichael v Boyle 1985 SCCR 58, 1985 SLT 399.. 2.7
Carmichael v Hannaway 1987 SCCR 236.. 13.8
Carmichael v Kennedy 1992 SLT 583, 1991 JC 32, 1991 SCCR 145.............. 17.10
Carr v HM Advocate 1995 SLT 800, 1994 SCCR 521 .... 18.8, 18.9
Carrington v HM Advocate 1994 JC 229, 1995 SLT 341, 1994 SCCR 567....... 2.9
Carruthers v HM Advocate (Unreported) 14 December 1999, HCJ................... 6.15
Cartmill v Heywood 2000 SLT 729 .... 13.20
Cawthorne v HM Advocate 1968 JC 32, 1968 SLT 330.................. 7.8, 7.9, 7.10, 10.7
Chandler v DPP [1964] AC 763, [1962] 3 WLR 694, [1962] 3 All ER 142, HL.. 19.5
Chas Sinclair (1794) 23 St Tr 777.. 19.4
City and Suburban Dairies v Mackenna 1918 JC 105, 1918 2 SLT 155 .... 3.10, 4.4
Clark v Clark 1940 SLT (Sh Ct) 68 .... 13.21
Clark v HM Advocate 1965 SLT 250, CCA 14.28, 14.29
Clark v HM Advocate 1968 JC 53, 1969 SLT 161 .... 2.23, 3.3
Clark v Syme 1957 JC 1, 1957 SLT 32.. 8.2
Clydebank Co-operative Society v Binnie 1937 JC 17, 1937 SLT 114............. 4.5
Clyne v Keith (1887) 1 White 356, 14 R (J) 22... 14.5
Cochrane v HM Advocate 2001 SCCR 655, HCJ 8.35
Codona v Cardle 1989 SCCR 287, 1989 SLT 791 .... 9.4
Codona v HM Advocate 1996 SCCR 300, 1996 SLT 1100, HCJ Appeal 6.20
Connelly v HM Advocate 1990 JC 349, 1990 SLT 397, 1990 SCCR 504 ..... 8.23, 8.24
Conner v HM Advocate 1995 SCCR 719 .... 7.16
Connor v Jessop 1988 SCCR 624... 9.5
Cornelius O'Neil (1845) 2 Broun 394 .... 14.6, 14.22
Cosgrove v HM Advocate 1990 JC 333, 1991 SLT 25, 1990 SCCR 358.... 10.17, 10.18
Crampton v Fish [1970] Crim LR 235, (1969) 113 SJ 1003, DC...................... 6.10
Crawford v HM Advocate 1950 JC 67, 1950 SLT 279........................ 8.8, 8.26, 8.27,
                                                                                         8.28, 9.9, 11.16

Crichton v Burrell 1951 JC 107 .... 13.20, 13.21
Crofter Hand Woven Harris Tweed v Veitch 1942 SC (HL) 1, [1942] AC 435,
    [1942] 1 All ER 142, HL... 7.16
Cromar v HM Advocate 1987 SCCR 635.. 15.2
Crooks [1981] 2 NZLR 53 .... 2.24
Cummings v HM Advocate [2009] HCJAC 55, 2009 SCL 1195 .... 16.5
Cunliffe v Goodman [1950] 2 KB 237, [1950] 1 All ER 720, 66 TLR (Pt 2) 109,
    94 SJ 179, CA 2.22
Curlett v McKechnie 1938 JC 176, 1939 SLT 11 .... 20.7

D

D Stanton & Son Ltd v Webber [1972] Crim LR 544, [1973] RTR 87, (1972)
    116 SJ 667, DC 6.14, 6.21
Dalton v HM Advocate 1951 JC 76, 1951 SLT 294 .... 20.7
Daniel Taylor (1853) 1 Irv 230 .... 16.16
Davey v Lee [1968] 1 QB 366, [1967] 3 WLR 105, [1967] 2 All ER 423, DC 7.3
David Keay (1837) 1 Swin 543... 9.1
David Monro (1831) Bell's Notes 48, Alison I, 451, Macdonald p 84............. 18.3
Davidson v HM Advocate 1990 SCCR 699, HCJ 12.5
Dawes v Cardel 1987 SCCR 135... 20.4
Dawson v Dickson 1999 SCCR 698, HCJ.. 8.34
Dean v John Menzies (Holdings) Ltd 1981 JC 23, 1981 SLT 50 .... 4.6, 4.7
Dennis v Plight (1968) 11 FLR 458, Aus 6.10
Derrett v Lockhart 1991 SCCR 109, HCJ 8.26, 9.4, 12.8, 12.10
Dewar (1777) at Burnett p 115 .... 14.18
Dewar v HM Advocate 1945 JC 5 .... 14.4, 14.7, 14.20
Dewar v HM Advocate 2009 JC 260 .... 9.4
Dickson v HM Advocate 2001 JC 203, 2001 SCCR 397 .... 12.4
Dickson v National Bank of Scotland Ltd 1917 SC (HL) 50, 1917 1 SLT 318 .... 4.3
Dilks v Bowman-Shaw [1981] RTR 4, DC.. 13.17
Dingwall (1867) 5 Irv 466.. 8.22
Docherty v Brown 1996 JC 48, 1996 SCCR 136, 1996 SLT 325, HCJ
    Appeal 13.4, 7.6, 7.13, 7.14, 7.15, 12.3, 14.4
Docherty v HM Advocate 1945 SLT 247, 1945 JC 89 .... 6.4
Docherty v Stakis Hotels Ltd 1992 SLT 381, 1991 SCCR 6 .... 4.6
Donald Kennedy (1838) 2 Swin 213... 8.32
Donnelly (Stephen) v HM Advocate 2009 SCCR 512, 2009 GWD 20-338,
    HCJ 12.13
Donnelly v Dunn; Walsh v Dunn [2015] HCJAC 35, 2015 JC 266, 2015 SCL
    555, 2015 SCCR 214, 2015 GWD 13-229, HCJ 1.10
Donnelly v HM Advocate 1984 SCCR 419 .... 12.4, 12.7
Doris v HM Advocate 1996 SCCR 854, 1996 SLT 996 .... 11.16
Douglas v Phoenix Motors 1970 SLT (Sh Ct) 57 .... 4.3
Downie v HM Advocate 1984 SCCR 365 .... 14.4
DPP v Beard [1920] AC 479, 89 LJKB 437, 122 LT 625, 84 JP 129, HL.......... 8.11
DPP v Bedder [1954] 1 WLR 1119, [1954] 2 All ER 801, (1954) 38 Cr App
    Rep 133, HL.. 10.18
DPP v Daley [1980] AC 237, [1979] 2 WLR 239, [1979] Crim LR 182, (1979)
    69 Cr App Rep 39, (1978) 122 SJ 861, PC.. 5.15, 10.14
DPP v Harris [1995] 1 Cr App Rep 170, [1995] RTR 100, [1995] Crim LR 73,
    QBD 13.15
DPP v Hastings [1993] RTR 205, (1994) 158 JP 118, (1994) 158 JPN 10, DC.... 13.1

DPP v K (a Minor) [1990] 1 WLR 1067, [1990] 1 All ER 331, (1990) 91 Cr
App R 23, [1990] Crim LR 321, DC 9.5
DPP v Majewski [1977] AC 443, [1976] 2 WLR 623, [1976] 2 All ER 142,
HL 8.11, 8.13
DPP v Merriman [1973] AC 584, [1972] 3 WLR 545, [1972] 3 All ER 42,
HL 6.3
DPP v Morgan [1976] AC 182, [1975] 2 WLR 913, [1975] 2 All ER 347,
(1976) 61 Cr App Rep 136, HL 8.9, 11.16, 11.17, 14.20
DPP v Newbury [1977] AC 500, [1976] 2 WLR 918, [1976] 3 All ER 365, HL .. 10.14
DPP v Ray [1974] AC 370, [1973] 3 WLR 359, [1973] 3 All ER 131, HL ... 16.2, 16.7
DPP v Stonehouse [1978] AC 55, [1977] 3 WLR 143, [1977] 2 All ER 909,
HL 7.5, 7.7
DPP for Northern Ireland v Maxwell [1978] 1 WLR 1350, [1978] 3 All ER
1140, (1978) 68 Cr App R 128, HL 6.13, 6.14
Druce v Friel 1994 SLT 1209, 1994 JC 182, 1994 SCCR 432 .... 14.26
Drury v HM Advocate 2001 SLT 1013, 2001 SCCR 583 .... 9.9, 10.6, 10.18,
10.19, 10.21
Du Cros v Lambourn [1907] 1 KB 40, 76 LJKB 50, 95 LT 782, DC 6.10
Duffy (James) v HM Advocate [2015] HCJAC 29, 2015 SCL 544, 2015 SCCR
205, 2015 GWD 11-188 .... 8.26, 9.9, 10.17, 10.21
Duffy v Tennant 1952 JC 15 .... 3.10
Duguid v Fraser 1942 JC 1, 1942 SLT 51 .... 3.2, 4.4
Dunne v Keane 1976 JC 39 .... 13.6
Duxley v Gilmore [1959] Crim LR 454, DC 6.10
Dyer v Watson [2002] UKPC D 1, [2004] 1 AC 379, [2002] 3 WLR 1488,
[2002] 4 All ER 1, PC 1.15

E

Eaton v Cobb [1950] 1 All ER 1016, 114 JP 271, 48 LGR 528, DC 3.3
Ebsworth v HM Advocate 1992 SLT 1161, 1992 SCCR 671 .... 2.9
Edgar v McKay 1926 JC 94, 1926 SLT 446 .... 17.2, 17.4, 17.5
Elizabeth Edmiston (1866) 5 Irv 219, LJC 9.14
Elizabeth Muir (1830) Alison I, 469–470 .... 20.1
Elliott v HM Advocate 1987 JC 47, 1987 SCCR 278 .... 8.28
Empress Car Co (Abertillery) Ltd v National Rivers Authority [1999] 2 AC 22,
[1998] 2 WLR 350, [1998] 1 All ER 481, [1998] Env LR 396, [1988] EHLR
3, [1998] EG 16 (CS), (1998) 95(8) LSG 32, (1998) 148 NLJ 206, (1998)
142 SJLB 69, [1998] NPC 16, HL 3.4, 3.6

F

F v West Berkshire Health Authority [1990] 2 AC 1, [1989] 2 WLR 1025,
[1989] 2 All ER 545, [1989] 2 FLR 376, HL 9.4
Farrell v Stirling 1975 SLT (Sh Ct) 71 .... 2.7, 13.3, 13.26
Farquarson (1854) 1 Irv 512 .... 14.21
Fenning v HM Advocate 1985 JC 76, 1985 SCCR 219 .... 2.6, 8.30, 10.17
Ferguson and Edie (1822) Hume I, 237 .... 9.12
Ferguson v HM Advocate 2009 SCL 250 .... 10.12
Ferguson v Normand 1994 SCCR 812, 1994 SLT 1355 .... 20.4
Finegan v Heywood 2000 JC 444, 2000 SLT 905 .... 2.5, 2.8, 2.9
Finegan v Heywood 2000 JC 444, 2000 SLT 905, 2000 SCCR 460 .... 13.3
Finlayson v HM Advocate 1979 JC 33, 1978 SLT (Notes) 60 .... 5.1, 5.10, 5.11, 10.4
First Quench Retailing Ltd v McLeod 2001 SLT 372, 2001 SCCR 154 .... 3.8

Flynn v HM Advocate 1995 SCCR 590, 1995 SLT 1267 .... 15.2
Forbes v HM Advocate 1994 SCCR 471, 1995 SLT 627 .... 14.30
Fowler v O'Brien 1994 SCCR 112 .... 14.14, 14.16
Frail v Lees 1997 JC 203, 1997 SCCR 354, 1997 GWD 15-653, HCJ Appeal.. 14.24
Frame v Kennedy 2008 HCJAC 25, 2008 JC 317, 2008 SCCR 382 .... 2.13, 12.14
Frame v Lockhart 1985 SLT 367 .... 13.12
Frank v HM Advocate 1938 JC 17, 1938 SLT 109 .... 16.3, 16.16
Fraser (1847) Arkley 280 .... 11.15
Fraser v Lockhart 1992 SCCR 275, HCJ 13.12
Friel v Docherty 1990 SCCR 351, HCJ 14.29, 14.30

G

Gair v Brewster 1916 JC 36, 1916 1 SLT 380 .... 4.4
Galbraith v HM Advocate (No 2) 2002 JC 1, 2001 SLT 953, 2001 SCCR
   551 .... 8.24, 10.20
Gammon (Hong Kong) Ltd v Attorney General for Hong Kong [1985] 1 AC 1,
   [1984] 3 WLR 437, [1984] 2 All ER 503, PC 3.5
Gant v HM Advocate [2009] HCJAC 84, 2010 SC 95, 2009 SCCR 929 .... 12.3
Gay v HM Advocate [2015] HCJAC 125 .... 6.11
Gellatly v Laird 1953 JC 16, 1953 SLT 67 .... 11.9
Geo Macbean (1847) Arkley 262 .... 18.9
George Brown (1839) 2 Swin 394 .... 14.1, 14.6
George Kerr (1871) 2 Coup 334 .... 2.10, 6.11
Gibson v National Cash Register Co Ltd 1925 SC 50, 1925 SLT 377 .... 16.5
Gilbert McCawley (July 1959, unreported), HCJ 14.28
Gilchrist and Hislop Bell's Notes 34 .... 14.22
Gill v Lockhart 1987 SCCR 599, 1988 SLT 189 .... 12.7
Gillick v West Norfolk and Wisbech Area Health Authority [1986] 1 AC 112,
   [1985] 3 WLR 830, [1985] 3 All ER 402, HL 6.15
Gillon v HM Advocate 2007 JC 24, 2006 SLT 799, 2006 SCCR 561 .... 9.9, 10.18, 10.21
Gilmour v McGlennan 1993 SCCR 837, HCJ 2.18, 15.3
Giorgianni v The Queen (1985) 156 CLR 473 .... 6.14
Gizzi v Tudhope 1982 SCCR 442, 1983 SLT 214 .... 2.25, 9.11
Glasgow Corpn v Hedderwick & Sons 1918 SC 639, 1918 2 SLT 2 .... 20.6
Gloag v Perth and Kinross Council 2007 SCLR 530, Sh Ct 9.4
Gorman v HM Advocate (unreported) 6.11
Grainger v HM Advocate 2006 JC 141, 2005 SLT 184, 2005 SCCR 175 .... 11.18
Grant v Allan 1987 SCCR 402, 1988 SLT 11 .... 1.8, 14.3, 17.1
Grant v McHale [2005] HCJAC 86, 2006 JC 81, 2005 SLT 1057, 2005 SCCR
   559, 2005 GWD 27-535 .... 13.5
Grant v Wright (1876) 3 Coup 282, 3 R (J) 28 .... 3.3
Gray v Hawthorn 1964 JC 69 .... 9.3
Grieve v Macleod 1967 JC 32, 1967 SLT 70 .... 12.13
Griffen v HM Advocate 1940 JC 1, 1940 SLT 175 .... 16.15
Griffiths v Hart 2005 JC 313, 2005 SCCR 392 .... 11.7
Guild v Lees 1994 SCCR 745, 1995 SLT 68 .... 16.2, 17.4
Gunnell v DPP [1994] RTR 151, [1993] Crim LR 619, DC 13.2

H

H L Bolton Engineering Co v T J Graham & Sons Ltd [1957] 1 QB 159, [1956]
   3 WLR 804, [1956] 3 All ER 624, CA 4.6
H v Griffiths 2009 SLT 199, HCJ 3.2, 7.11

H v Lees; D v Orr 1993 JC 238, 1994 SLT 908, 1993 SCCR 900 .... 2.23, 3.3
HM Advocate v Airs 1975 SLT 177 .... 20.3, 20.5
HM Advocate v Aitken (1902) 4 Adam 88 .... 8.22
HM Advocate v Aldred (June 1921, unreported), Glasgow HC 19.4
HM Advocate v Allan (1873) 2 Coup 402 .... 1.13
HM Advocate v Al-Megrahi (No 1) 2000 JC 555, 2000 SLT 1393, 2000 SCCR
    177 .... 7.16
HM Advocate v Anderson 1928 JC 1, 1927 SLT 651 .... 7.12, 7.13
HM Advocate v Baillie (David Axl) [2012] HCJAC 158, 2013 SCL 550, 2013
    SCCR 285, 2013 GWD 17-356 .... 9.14, 15.3, 17.6
HM Advocate v Baxter (1908) 5 Adam 609, (1908) 16 SLT 475 .... 6.12, 7.4
HM Advocate v Beggs (opinion no 2) 21 September 2001 .... 20.6
HM Advocate v Blake 1986 SLT 661 .... 8.23
HM Advocate v Bradbury (1972) 2 Coup 311 .... 1.13
HM Advocate v Browne (1903) 6 F(J) 24, 11 SLT 353 .... 14.28
HM Advocate v Cairns 1967 JC 37, 1967 SLT 165 .... 20.2
HM Advocate v Callander 1958 SLT 24 .... 10.19
HM Advocate v Camerons 1911 SC (J) 110, 1911 2 SLT 108, 6 Adam 456 ... 7.6, 16.9,
    16.10
HM Advocate v Campbell 1993 SCCR 765, 1994 SLT 502 .... 13.9
HM Advocate v Carson (Darren Charles) 1997 SLT 1119, 1997 SCCR 273,
    1997 GWD 12-498, HCJ Appeal 2.20
HM Advocate v Carson 1964 SLT 21 .... 9.4
HM Advocate v City of Glasgow Bank Directors (1879) 4 Coup 161, 6 R (J)
    19 .... 16.4, 17.5
HM Advocate v Coulson [2015] HCJ 49, 2015 SCL 606, 2015 SCCR 254,
    2015 GWD 19-316 .... 20.2
HM Advocate v Crawford (Alex M) (1850) J Shaw 309 .... 17.6, 17.7, 17.8, 17.9
HM Advocate v Cunningham 1963 JC 80, 1963 SLT 345 .... 2.6, 2.7, 2.8, 8.22
HM Advocate v Currie (December 1962, unreported), Glasgow High Ct 7.9
HM Advocate v Dewar (1777) 14.3
HM Advocate v Dickie 2002 SLT 1083, 2002 SCCR 312 .... 20.4
HM Advocate v Doherty 1954 JC 1, 1954 SLT 169 .... 8.29
HM Advocate v Donoghue 1971 SLT 2 .... 17.6
HM Advocate v Ferreira (April 1976, unreported), Glasgow Sh Ct 12.4
HM Advocate v Finlayson 1979 JC 33, 1978 SLT (Notes) 18 .... 9.12, 10.14
HM Advocate v Forbes 1994 SLT 861, 1994 SCCR 163 .... 14.21
HM Advocate v Fraser and Rollins 1920 JC 60, 1920 2 SLT 77 .... 10.11
HM Advocate v Graham [2010] HCJAC 50 .... 1.5
HM Advocate v Grainger and Rae 1932 JC 40, 1932 SLT 28 .... 11.15
HM Advocate v Greig (May 1979, unreported), HCJ 10.20
HM Advocate v Hardy 1938 JC 144, 1938 SLT 412. .... 16.14
HM Advocate v Harris (Andrew) 1993 JC 150, 1993 SCCR 559, 1993 SLT
    963 .... 9.5, 9.10, 9.11, 13.17
HM Advocate v Harris (September 1950, unreported), Glasgow HC 6.20
HM Advocate v Hartley 1989 SLT 135 .... 10.13
HM Advocate v Hill 1941 JC 59, 1941 SLT 401 .... 10.19
HM Advocate v Jean Crawford (1847) 1 Arkley 394 .... 9.12
HM Advocate v John Smith (1887) 1 White 413 .... 17.1
HM Advocate v Johnstone 1926 JC 89, 1926 SLT 428 .... 6.15
HM Advocate v Kay and Strain (May 1952, unreported), Glasgow HC 6.12, 7.17
HM Advocate v Kerr (Gareth) [2011] HCJAC 17, 2011 SLT 430, 2011 SCL
    485, 2011 SCCR 192, 2011 GWD 8-201 .... 7.9

HM Advocate v Kidd 1960 JC 61, 1960 SLT 82 .... 8.19, 8.20
HM Advocate v Laing (1891) 2 White 572 .... 17.4, 17.5
HM Advocate v Lappen 1956 SLT 109 .... 6.1, 6.19
HM Advocate v Lawrence (1872) 2 Coup 168 .... 17.4
HM Advocate v Livingston (1888) 1 White 587, 15 R (J) 48 .... 16.1, 16.2, 16.4
HM Advocate v Logan 1936 JC 100, 1937 SLT 104 .... 11.14
HM Advocate v Lourie 1988 SCCR 634 .... 10.13
HM Advocate v MacAlister (November 1953, unreported), HCJ 19.4
HM Advocate v Mackenzie 1913 SC (J) 107 .... 7.4, 14.3, 14.11
HM Advocate v Mannion 1961 JC 79 .... 20.4
HM Advocate v Martin (1886) 1 White 297 .... 9.8
HM Advocate v Martin 1956 JC 1, 1956 SLT 193 .... 20.8, 20.9
HM Advocate v McAdam (July 1950, unreported), Glasgow HC 7.9
HM Advocate v McCarron (February 1964, unreported), Perth High Ct;
    approved on appeal, March 1964 .... 10.9
HM Advocate v McGuinness 1937 JC 37 .... 10.8
HM Advocate v McKean (Vikki Lynne) 1996 JC 32, 1996 SLT 1383, 1996
    SCCR 402, HCJ 10.19
HM Advocate v Mclean 2010 SLT 73, 2010 SCL 166 .... 1.5
HM Advocate v McLeod 1956 JC 20 .... 8.11
HM Advocate v McPhee 1935 JC 46, 1935 SLT 179 .... 2.12
HM Advocate v Millbank 2002 SLT 1116, 2003 SCCR 771 .... 11.11
HM Advocate v Miller and Denovan (December 1960, unreported), HCJ 10.11
HM Advocate v Parker and Barrie (1888) 2 White 79, (1888) 16 R (J) 5 .... 5.4
HM Advocate v Pattisons (1901) 3 Adam 420 .... 16.4, 16.5, 16.9
HM Advocate v Pawn and McNab (1845) 2 Broun 525 .... 10.15
HM Advocate v Phipps (1905) 4 Adam 616 .... 9.5
HM Advocate v Purcell 2008 JC 131, 2008 SLT 44, 2008 SCL 183, 2007
    SCCR 520 .... 1.3, 7.9, 8.12, 8.13, 9.11, 10.11
HM Advocate v Raiker 1989 SCCR 149 .... 2.8
HM Advocate v Ritchie 1926 JC 45, 1926 SLT 308 .... 2.6, 2.8
HM Advocate v RK 1994 SCCR 499, HCJ 11.9, 11.20
HM Advocate v Robertson and Donoghue (August 1945, unreported), HCJ 5.3, 10.8,
                                                                                          10.9, 10.14
HM Advocate v Ross 1991 SCCR 823, 1991 SLT 564 .... 2.6
HM Advocate v Rutherford 1947 JC 1, 1947 SLT 3 .... 2.18, 5.6, 10.14
HM Advocate v Rutherford 1998 JC 34, 1998 SLT 740, 1997 SCCR 711 .... 10.19
HM Advocate v Robertson (1870) Coup 404 .... 20.4
HM Advocate v Savage 1923 JC 49 .... 8.22, 8.23, 8.24
HM Advocate v Scotsman, The and others 1999 SLT 466, 1999 SCCR 163,
    HCJ 20.6
HM Advocate v Semple 1937 JC 41 .... 7.14
HM Advocate v Smith & Wishart (1842) 1 Broun 342 .... 17.1
HM Advocate v Smith (1887) 1 White 413 .... 17.3
HM Advocate v Smith (1893) 1 Adam 6 .... 16.16
HM Advocate v Smith (May 1975, unreported), Glasgow High Ct 7.16
HM Advocate v Smith (unreported, noted Gordon p772) 10.18
HM Advocate v Smith 1934 JC 66, 1934 SLT 485 .... 20.1, 20.2
HM Advocate v Stewart and Walsh (1856) 2 Irv 359 .... 18.2, 18.5
HM Advocate v Sweenie (Charles) (1858) 3 Irv 109 .... 11.15
HM Advocate v Tannahill and Neilson 1943 JC 150, 1944 SLT 118 .... 6.12, 7.4
HM Advocate v Tarbett 2003 SLT 1288 .... 20.4
HM Advocate v Thompson 2010 SLT 509 .... 1.3

HM Advocate v Thorn (1876) 3 Coup 332 .... 9.8
HM Advocate v Walsh 1922 JC 82, 1922 SLT 443 .... 19.4
HM Advocate v Welsh and McLachlan (1897) 5 SLT 137 .... 6.4
HM Advocate v Wilson 1983 SCCR 420 .... 1.3
HM Advocate v Wilson, Latta, and Rooney (February 1968, unreported), HCJ
  Glasgow 7.16
HM Advocate v Wishart 1975 SCCR Supp 78 .... 16.9, 17.2, 17.3, 17.4
HM Advocate v Wormald (1876) 3 R (J) 24 .... 17.2, 17.3
Haggard v Mason [1976] 1 WLR 187, [1976] 1 All ER 337, [1976] Crim LR
  51, DC 12.4
Haines v Roberts [1953] 1 WLR 309, [1953] 1 All ER 344, 117 JP 123, DC.... 13.20
Hall v Associated Newspapers Ltd 1979 JC 1, 1978 SLT 241 .... 20.6
Hamilton v Fife Health Board 1993 SLT 624, 1993 SC 309, 1993 SCLR 408,
  IH 13.10
Hamilton v Friel 1994 SCCR 748 .... 14.31
Hamilton v Mooney 1990 SLT (Sh Ct) 105 .... 14.4
Hamilton v Wilson 1994 SLT 431, 1993 SCCR 9 .... 14.4
Harris v HM Advocate [2009] HCJAC 80, 2009 SLT 1078, 2010 SCL 56 ... 9.14, 12.9,
                                                                                                                         15.3, 20.9
Harrison v Jessop 1992 SLT 465, 1991 SCCR 329 .... 15.1
Hassan v Scott 1989 SCCR 49, 1989 SLT 380 .... 13.25
Heinrich Heidmeisser (1879) 17 SLR 266 .... 5.11
Hemming v Annan 1982 SCCR 432 .... 12.13
Henderson and Marnoch v HM Advocate [2005] HCJAC 47, 2005 SCCR 354: 17.6
Heriot v Auld 1918 JC 16, 1917 2 SLT 178 .... 4.4
Herron v Best 1976 SLT (Sh Ct) 80 .... 14.12
Herron v Diack & Newlands 1973 SLT (Sh Ct) 27 .... 14.2, 14.7, 14.10
Herron v Latta (1968) 32 JCL 51, (1967) SCCR Supp 18 .... 14.30
Hill v Baxter [1958] 1 QB 277, [1958] 2 WLR 76, [1958] 1 All ER 193, DC... 2.5
Hill v McGrogan 1945 SLT (Sh Ct) 18 .... 17.8, 17.9
Hillan v HM Advocate 1937 JC 53 .... 9.9
Hipson v Tudhope 1983 SCCR 247, 1983 SLT 659 .... 14.29
Hogg v Macpherson 1928 JC 15, 1928 SLT 35 .... 2.3
Hogg v McLeod 1983 SCCR 161 .... 2.11
Hogg v Nicholson 1968 SLT 265 .... 13.6
Holmes and Lockyer (1869) 1 Coup 221 .... 1.7
Hood v Young (1853) 1 Irv 236 .... 16.8
Howarth v HM Advocate (No 2) 1992 SCCR 525 .... 12.3
Howman v Russell 1923 JC 32, 1923 SLT 336 .... 3.7
Hoy v McFadyen 2000 JC 313, 2000 SLT 1060, 2000 SCCR 875 .... 13.2
Hugh Mitchell (1856) 2 Irv 488 .... 2.3

I

Indedon v Watson (1862) 2 F&F 841 .... 16.5
Inglis and Colvilles (1784) Hume I, 237 .... 9.12
Ingram v Macari 1983 JC 1, 1982 SCCR 372 .... 11.7

J

Jackson and Hodgetts v R (1989) 44 A Crim R 320 .... 10.16
James Kinnison (1870) 1 Coup 457 .... 2.23, 3.3
James Paton (1858) 3 Irv 208 .... 16.3, 16.8
James Williamson (1866) 5 Irv 326 .... 5.11
James Wilson (1838) 2 Swin 16 .... 5.11

Jamieson v HM Advocate 1994 JC 88, 1994 SLT 537, 1994 SCCR 181 .... 7.10, 8.9,
 11.16, 11.17, 11.18
Jas Cairns (1837) 1 Swin 597 .... 9.1
Jas Davidson (1841) 2 Swin 630 .... 14.22
Jas Devlin (1828) Alison I, 402 .... 16.14, 16.16
Jas Hall (1849) Shaw 254 .... 16.15
Jas Miller (1862) 4 Irv 238 .... 9.14, 15.3, 17.6
Jas Scott (1853) 1 Irv 132 .... 8.22
Jessop v Johnstone 1991 SCCR 238 .... 2.4
JM (a Minor) v Runeckles (1984) 79 Cr App R 255, DC 8.25
JM v Locality Reporter, Glasgow [2015] CSIH 58, 2015 SLT 543, 2015 Fam
 LR 81, 2015 GWD 23-412 .... 2.23, 3.3
Jobsin Co UK Plc (t/a Internet Recruitment Solutions) v Department of Health
 [2001] EWCA Civ 1241, [2002] 1 CMLR 44, [2001] EuLR 685 .... 8.3
John Baird (1820) Hume I, 522 .... 19.2
John Carrigan and Thos Robinson (1853) 1 Irv 303 .... 14.22
John Duncan (1843) 1 Broun 512 .... 19.2
John Grant (1848) 17 Shaw 50 .... 19.4
John Hall (1881) 4 Coup 438, 8 R (J) 28 .... 16.6
John Henderson (1830) 5 Deas & And 151 .... 16.15
John Jaffray (1815) Hume i, 44 .... 9.14
John Murdoch (1849) J Shaw 229 .... 18.3
John Robertson (1854) 1 Irv 469 .... 5.16
John Smith (1838) 2 Swin 28 .... 14.1, 14.6, 14.7, 14.8, 14.9
John Smith (1871) 2 Coup 1 .... 16.16
John Thomas Witherington (1881) 4 Coup 475, (1881) 8 R(J) 41 .... 1.12, 1.13
Johns v The Queen (1980) 143 CLR 108 .... 6.20
Johnson v Youden [1950] 1 KB 544, [1950] 1 All ER 300, 48 LGR 276, DC ... 6.21
Johnston (William Love) v HM Advocate [2009] HCJAC 38, 2009 JC 227,
 2009 SLT 535, 2009 SCL 737, 2009 SCCR 518, 2009 GWD 18-289 .... 5.12, 6.4
Jolly (Andrew) v HM Advocate [2013] HCJAC 96, 2014 JC 171, 2013 SLT
 1100, 2013 SCL 832, 2013 SCCR 511, 2013 GWD 29-576 .... 12.11
Jones v Brooks (1968) 52 Cr App Rep 614, [1968] Crim LR 498, (1968) 112 SJ
 745, DC 7.3
Jones v HM Advocate 1989 SCCR 726, 1990 SLT 517, 1990 JC 160 .... 8.26, 8.27,
 8.28, 10.21
Jones v State 220 Ind 384, 43 NE 2d 1017 (1942) 5.16
Joseph and Mary Norris (1886) 1 White 292 .... 5.16
Joyce v DPP [1946] AC 347, [1946] 1 All ER 186, 174 LT 206, 62 TLR 208,
 31 Cr App Rep 57, [1946] WN 31, HL 19.1, 19.3

K
Kaur (Dip) v Chief Constable of Hampshire [1981] 1 WLR 578, [1981] 2 All
 ER 430, (1981) 72 Cr App R 359, CA 16.5
Kaur v The Lord Advocate 1981 SLT 322 .... 1.5
Keane v Gallacher 1980 JC 77, 1980 SLT 144 .... 12.6
Keane v HM Advocate 1986 SCCR 491, 1987 SLT 220 .... 20.6
Keaney (James) v HM Advocate [2015] HCJAC 3, 2015 JC 259, 2015 SLT 102,
 2015 SCL 316, 2015 SCCR 81, 2015 GWD 3-64 .... 8.8
Kelly v Hogan [1982] RTR 352, [1982] Crim LR 507, DC 13.4
Kelso v HM Advocate 1998 SLT 921, 1998 SCCR 278, HCJ Appeal 13.20
Kennedy v HM Advocate 1944 JC 171, 1945 SLT 11 .... 8.11, 10.8
Kenny v HM Advocate 1951 JC 104, 1951 SLT 363 .... 9.14, 17.6, 20.9

Kenny v Tudhope 1984 SCCR 290.. 13.18
Kent v HM Advocate 1950 JC 38, 1950 SLT 130 .... 17.2, 17.3, 17.4
Kerr v Hill 1936 JC 71, 1936 SLT 320.. 16.11, 20.7
Kerr v HM Advocate 1986 SCCR 91... 9.8
Khaliq v HM Advocate 1983 SCCR 483, 1984 JC 23.................... 1.7, 5.13, 6.15, 9.6,
9.12, 9.13, 14.9
Kidston v Annan 1984 SCCR 20, 1984 SLT 279 .... 14.13
Kimmins v Normand 1993 SCCR 476, 1993 SLT 1260.................................... 2.14
King v Lees 1993 JC 19, 1993 SCCR 28, 1993 SLT 1184.............................. 13.25
King v Webster [2011] HCJAC 109, 2012 SLT 342, 2012 SCL 207, 2012
SCCR 59, 2011 GWD 36-738 .... 3.2
Kinnaird v Higson 2001 SCCR 427, HCJ 12.10
Kivlin v Milne 1979 SLT (Notes) 2 .... 14.14, 14.16, 14.17
Knewland and Wood Hume I, 108 .... 15.3
Kokkinakis v Greece Series A No 260–A, (1994) 17 EHRR 397, ECHR.......... 1.10
Kwok Chak Minh (No 1) v The Queen [1963] HKLR 226 .... 13.10
Kyprianou v Cyprus (No 2) (2007) 44 EHRR 27, ECHR 20.3

L

Laing (1891) 2 White 572.. 17.3, 17.4
Laird v HM Advocate 1984 SCCR 469, 1985 JC 37....................................... 1.12
Lamont v Strathern 1933 JC 33, 1933 SLT 118 .... 7.12
Langman v Valentine [1952] 2 All ER 803, [1952] 2 TLR 713, 116 JP 576,
DC 13.21
Latta v Herron (1967) SCCR Supp 18... 2.24
Leach v Evans [1952] 2 All ER 264, 116 JP 410, DC 13.21
Lennon v HM Advocate 1991 SCCR 611....................................... 10.17, 10.21
Lieser v HM Advocate [2008] HCJAC 42, 2008 SLT 866, 2008 SCL 1050,
2008 SCCR 797 .... 8.8, 8.9, 8.26, 8.28
Lilburn (David) v HM Advocate [2011] HCJAC 41, 2012 JC 150, 2011 SLT
861, 2011 SCL 678, 2011 SCCR 326, 2011 GWD 14-333 .... 8.18, 8.24
Lim Chin Aik v The Queen [1963] AC 160, [1963] 2 WLR 42, [1963] 1 All ER
223, PC.. 3.4, 3.6
Lindsay (James) v HM Advocate 1996 SCCR 870, 1997 SLT 67, 1997 JC 19,
HCJ Appeal 8.18, 8.22, 8.24
Linton v Stirling (1893) 1 Adam 61, (1893) 20 R (J) 71 .... 4.4
Lloyd v DPP [1992] 1 All ER 982, [1992] RTR 215, [1991] Crim LR 904, DC: 14.9
Lockhart v National Coal Board 1981 SLT 161, HCJ 3.4, 3.7, 3.10, 13.8
Lockwood v Walker 1910 (J) SC 3 .... 11.11
London and Globe Finance Corpn, Re [1903] 1 Ch 728, 72 LJCh 368, 88 LT
194... 16.2
Lord Advocate v Scotsman Publications Ltd 1989 SLT 705, [1990] 1 AC 812,
[1989] 3 WLR 358, [1989] 2 All ER 852, HL... 19.4
Lord Advocate v University of Aberdeen 1963 SC 533, 1963 SLT 361............ 14.5
Lord Advocate's Reference (No 1 of 1985) 1986 JC 137, 1986 SCCR 329,
1987 SLT 187... 20.1, 20.2
Lord Advocate's Reference (No 1 of 1994) 1995 SCCR 177, 1995 SLT 248....... 5.5, 5.5,
5.14, 9.13, 10.3, 10.14
Lord Advocate's Reference (No 1 of 2001) 2002 SLT 466, 2002 SCCR 435.... 7.10, 8.8,
11.14, 11.15, 11.16, 11.17, 11.13
Lord Advocate's Reference (No 2 of 1992) 1993 JC 43, 1992 SCCR 960, 1993
SLT 460... 2.18, 9.5, 9.6

Lord Advocate's Reference (No 2 of 1992) 1993 JC 43, 1992 SCCR 960, 1993 SLT 460 .... 9.6
Lord Advocate's Reference (No 1 of 2000) 2001 JC 143, 2001 SLT 507, 2001 SCCR 296 .... 2.18, 2.21, 8.2, 8.32, 8.34, 8.35, 8.36, 18.5, 18.6
Low v HM Advocate 1988 SLT 97, 1987 SCCR 541 .... 20.2
Lunn (Laura) v HM Advocate [2015] HCJAC 103, 2016 SCL 36., 2015 GWD 38-600 .... 12.13

M

M v HM Advocate (No 2) [2013] HCJAC 22, 2013 SLT 380, 2013 SCL 361, 2013 SCCR 215, 2013 GWD 8-170 .... 20.2
MacAngus v HM Advocate; Kane v HM Advocate [2009] HCJAC 8, 2009 SLT 137 .... 2.18, 5.14, 6.15, 9.13, 10.14
Macara v Macfarlane 1980 SLT (Notes) 26 .... 20.4
MacDonald (Gordon) v HM Advocate (No 2) 1996 SLT 723, HCJ Appeal... 16.1, 16.2
MacDonald v HM Advocate [2006] HCJAC 89, 2007 SCCR 10 .... 2.28, 5.15, 6.2, 9.1, 9.7
MacDonald v HM Advocate [2008] HCJAC 5, 2008 JC 262 .... 12.9
MacDonald v Howdle 1995 SLT 779, 1995 SCCR 216, HCJ 3.10
Macdonald v Provan Ltd 1960 SLT 231 .... 14.10
Macdonald v Tudhope 1983 SCCR 341, 1984 SLT 23 .... 16.14
MacDougall v Yuk-Sun Ho 1985 SCCR 199 .... 18.6
Mackay Bros & Co v Gibb 1969 JC 26, 1969 SLT 216 .... 4.3, 4.5
Mackay v Hogg (11 May 1973, unreported), HCJ 12.7
Mackinnon v Douglas 1982 SCCR 80, 1982 SLT 375 .... 20.4, 20.6
Maclachlan v Harris 2009 SLT 1074, 2009 SCL 1271, 2009 SCCR 783 .... 4.3
Macleod v Ken 1965 SC 253, 1965 SLT 358 .... 14.10
MacLeod v Napier 1993 SCCR 303, HCJ 2.9
Macleod, Re (1970) 12 CRNS 193, 1 CCC (2d) 5 (Canada) 6.12
MacMillan v Lowe 1991 JC 13, 1991 SCCR 113 .... 14.8
MacNeill v Dunbar 1965 SLT (Notes) 79 .... 13.6
Macpherson v Beath (1975) 12 SASR 174 .... 9.2
McGuire v Higson 2003 SCCR 440, 2003 SLT 890 .... 12.14
McArthur v Valentine 1990 SLT 732, 1990 JC 146, 1989 SCCR 704 .... 13.2
McAvoy v Jessop 1989 SCCR 301 .... 12.8
McBrearty v HM Advocate 1994 SCCR 122 .... 8.29
McBurnie v McGlennan 1991 SCCR 756 .... 14.24
McCallum v Hamilton 1986 JC 1, 1986 SLT 156 .... 13.12
McCluskey v HM Advocate 1959 JC 39, 1959 SLT 215 .... 8.27, 8.28, 8.32
McCluskey v HM Advocate 1988 SCCR 629, 1989 SLT 175 .... 10.1, 13.10
McConnachie v Scott 1988 SCCR 176, 1988 SLT 480 .... 13.23
McCrone v Normand 1989 SLT 332, 1988 SCCR 551 .... 13.16
McCrone v Riding [1938] 1 All ER 157, 158 LT 253, 102 JP 109 .... 13.15
McCue v Currie 2004 JC 73, 2004 SLT 858 .... 2.13
McCue v Currie 2004 JC 73, 2004 SLT 858, 2004 SCCR 200 .... 18.10
McDermott v HM Advocate 1973 JC 8, 1974 SLT 206 .... 10.19
McDonald (Felix Charles) v HM Advocate [2006] HCJAC 89, 2007 SCCR 10 .. 6.2, 9.8
McDonald (Niall Duncan) v HM Advocate 2004 SCCR 161, HCJ 9.6, 11.18
McDonald v Heywood 2002 SCCR 92, HCJ 12.10
McDonald v McEwen 1953 SLT (Sh Ct) 26 .... 13.6
McEachran v Hurst [1978] RTR 462, [1978] Crim LR 499, DC 13.5

McEwan v Higson 2001 SCCR 579, HCJ 13.18
McFadyen v Annan 1992 JC 53, 1992 SLT 162, 1992 SCCR 186..................... 1.15
McInnes v HM Advocate [2010] UKSC 7, [2010] All ER (D) 101 (Feb)........... 1.5
McIntyre v Nisbet [2009] HCJAC 28, 2009 SCL 829..................................... 12.9
McKay v HM Advocate 1992 SLT 138, 1991 JC 91, 1991 SCCR 364............. 10.19
McKearney v HM Advocate 2004 JC 87, 2004 SLT 739, 2004 SCCR 251 .... 11.16
McKenzie v HM Advocate 1988 SCCR 153, 1988 SLT 487............................. 16.11
McKenzie v Skeen 1983 SLT 121... 12.5, 12.6
McKenzies 1913 SC (J) 107 .... 14.13
McKinnon v HM Advocate (No 2) 2003 JC 29, 2003 SLT 281, 2003 SCCR
  224... 6.7, 10.11
McLaughlan v Boyd 1934 JC 19, 1933 SLT 629................. 1.8, 11.8, 11.10
McLaughlan v HM Advocate 1991 SLT 660, 1991 SCCR 733....................... 6.16
McLaughlin v Stewart (1865) Macq 32... 14.8
McLean v McCabe 1964 SLT (Sh Ct) 39 .... 13.5
McLeod v Mason 1981 SCCR 75, 1981 SLT (Notes) 109 .... 14.16, 14.19, 14.24
McLeod v Mathieson 1993 SCCR 488, Sh Ct.................................... 2.9, 13.3
McLeod v McDougall 1988 SCCR 519, 1989 SLT 151 .... 13.26
McManimy and Higgins (1847) Arkley 321... 2.12
McNab v Guild 1989 SCCR 138 .... 13.26
McNairn v HM Advocate [2005] HCJAC 112, 2005 SCCR 741 .... 11.15
McNeil v HM Advocate 1968 JC 29, 1968 SLT 338................... 14.28, 14.29
McNeil v HM Advocate 1986 JC 146, 1987 SLT 244, 1986 SCCR 288........ 6.17, 12.3
McNeill v Fletcher 1966 JC 18.. 13.20
McPhail v Clark 1982 SCCR 395, 1983 SLT (Sh Ct) 37 .... 2.13, 9.11, 13.17, 18.4
McQuaid v Anderton [1981] 1 WLR 154, [1980] 3 All ER 540, [1980] RTR
  371, DC... 13.2
McShane v Pawn 1922 JC 26, 1922 SLT 251.. 9.3
Maidstone Borough Council v Mortimer [1980] 3 All ER 522, (1982) 43 P&CR
  67, [1981] JPL 112, DC 3.3
Mallin v Clark 2002 SLT 1202, 2002 SCCR 901 .... 2.14, 9.11
Maloco v Littlewoods Organisation Ltd 1987 SC (HL) 37, 1987 SCLR 489,
  1987 SLT 425.. 5.9
Malone (Andrew Stewart) v HM Advocate 1988 SCCR 498, HCJA 5.12
Marchbank v Annan 1987 SCCR 718.. 9.4
Margaret Robertson or Brown (1886) 1 White 93 .... 8.11
Marion Macdonald (1879) 4 Coup 268 .... 17.6
Marr v HM Advocate 1996 JC 199, 1996 SCCR 696, 1996 SLT 1035, HCJ
  Appeal... 11.18
Marshall v Osmond [1983] QB 1034,[1983] 3 WLR 13, [1983] 2 All ER 225,
  CA... 13.15
Mather v HM Advocate (1914) 7 Adam 525, 1914 SC (J) 184 .... 16.12
Mathieson and Murray v HM Advocate 1996 SCCR 388, HCJ Appeal............. 6.20
Mathieson v HM Advocate 1981 SCCR 196... 10.14
Maxwell v HM Advocate 1980 JC 40, 1980 SLT 241 .... 7.12, 7.16
Maxwell v Pressdram Ltd [1987] 1 WLR 298, [1987] 1 All ER 621, (1987) 131
  SJ 327, CA 20.5
Mayer v HM Advocate 2004 SCCR 734, 2005 JC 121, 2004 SLT 1251 .... 20.4
MD v PF Falkirk 2009 SLT 476 .... 8.34
MD v Procurator Fiscal Falkirk [2009] HCJAC 37 .... 13.26
Meek v HM Advocate 1982 SCCR 613, 1983 SLT 280................. 1.5, 8.8, 8.9, 11.16,
                                                          11.17, 14.20
Melvin v HM Advocate 1984 SCCR 113, 1984 SLT 365............... 6.7, 10.11

Meridian Global Funds Management Asia Ltd v Securities Commission [1995]
    2 AC 500, [1995] 3 WLR 413, [1995] 3 All ER 918, [1995] 2 BCLC 116,
    PC 4.7
Merrin v S 1987 SLT 193 .... 8.25
Milburn 1946 SC 301, 1946 SLT 219 .... 20.4
Miller (1848) Arkley 525 .... 18.3
Milne and Barry (1868) 1 Coup 28 .... 9.12
Milne v Tudhope 1981 JC 53, 1981 SLT (Notes) 42 .... 14.3, 14.5, 14.10, 14.11,
    14.12, 14.13, 14.15, 14.16, 14.18, 14.19
Mingay v Mackinnon 1980 JC 33 .... 12.5
Monk v Strathern 1921 JC 4, 1920 2 SLT 364 .... 9.8
Monro of Auchinbowie, Hume I, 122 .... 18.2
Montes v HM Advocate 1990 SCCR 645 .... 12.1, 12.3
Moore v HM Advocate [2010] HCJAC 26, 2010 SCL 843, 2010 SCCR 451,
    2010 GWD 11-189 .... 17.4, 17.5
Moore v MacDougall 1989 SCCR 659 .... 8.30
Morrison (Rory Connell) v HM Advocate [2010] HCJAC 16, 2010 JC 174,
    2010 SLT 571, 2010 SCL 679, 2010 SCCR 328, 2010 GWD 7-119 .... 15.2
Morrison v Robertson 1908 SC 332, (1908) 15 SLT 697 .... 16.3
Morrison v Smith 1983 SCCR 171 .... 12.7
Morrison v Valentine 1991 SLT 413, 1990 SCCR 692 .... 13.26
Morton v Confer [1963] 1 WLR 763, [1963] 2 All ER 765, 61 LGR 461, DC .. 13.22
Morton v Henderson 1956 JC 55, 1956 SLT 365 .... 7.4, 7.16
Morton v HM Advocate 1986 SLT 622 .... 6.4
Moss v Howdle 1997 JC 123, 1997 SLT 782, 1997 SCCR 215, HCJ Appeal ... 3.7, 8.33,
    8.34, 8.35, 8.36, 13.26
Mousell Bros Ltd v London and NW Railway [1917] 2 KB 836, 87 LJKB 82,
    118 LT 25, 81 JP 305 .... 3.9
Mowles v HM Advocate 1986 SCCR 117 .... 10.13
Moynagh v Speirs 2003 SLT 1337, 2003 SCCR 765, HCJ Appeal 11.11
Muirhead v Douglas 1979 SLT (Notes) 17 .... 20.4
Murray v MacPhail 1991 SCCR 245, HCJ 12.5
Murray v Muir 1950 SLT 41 .... 13.20
Murray v O'Brien 1994 SLT 1051 .... 18.6
Murray v Robertson 1927 JC 1, 1927 SLT 74 .... 14.19

N

National Coal Board v Gamble [1950] 1 QB 11, [1958] 3 WLR 434, [1958] 3
    All ER 203, 42 Cr App R 240, DC 6.3
Neish v Stevenson 1969 SLT 229 .... 13.22
Newberry v Simmonds [1961] 2 QB 345, [1961] 2 WLR 675, [1961] 2 All ER
    318, DC 13.5
Nisbet v HM Advocate 1983 SCCR 13 .... 14.30
Niven (1795) 21 December, Hume I, 23 .... 10.10
Norman v Smith 1983 SCCR 100 .... 9.4
Normand v Morrison 1993 SCCR 207, Sh Ct 2.14
Norris v Macleod 1988 SCCR 572 .... 12.10

O

O'Brien v Strathern 1922 JC 55, 1922 SLT 440 .... 14.6, 14.7, 17.4
O'Moran v DPP; Whelan v DPP [1975] QB 864, [1975] 2 WLR 413, [1975] 1
    All ER 473, DC 19.8
O'Neill v HM Advocate 1934 JC 98, 1934 SLT 432 .... 14.22, 15.1, 15.2

O'Toole v McDougall 1986 SCCR 56.. 13.12
Orr v Annan 1987 JC 38 .... 20.4
Orr v K 2003 SLT (Sh Ct) 70, 2003 Fam LR 26... 14.4
Owens v HM Advocate 1946 JC 119, 1946 SLT 227............................... 8.8, 8.27, 8.28

P

Pagan v Ferguson 1976 SLT (Notes) 44 .... 13.12, 13.15
Palazzo v Copeland 1976 JC 52... 2.20
Parker, ex parte [1957] SR (NSW) 326.. 6.10
Parr v HM Advocate 1991 JC 39, 1991 SLT 208, 1991 SCCR 180 .... 10.19,10.20
Paterson (Tate Wilson) v Lees 1999 JC 159, 1999 SCCR 231, 1999 GWD
 9-414, HCJ Appeal... 11.9
Paterson v Harvie [2014] HCJAC 87, 2015 JC 118, 2014 SLT 857, 2014 SCL
 606, 2014 SCCR 521, 2014 GWD 26-517 .... 12.11
Paterson v HM Advocate (1901) 3 Adam 490, 4 F (J) 7...................................... 14.8
Paterson v HM Advocate [2008] HCJAC 18, 2008 SLT 465............................. 12.9
Paterson v Ogilvy 1957 JC 42, 1957 SLT 354.. 13.6
Paton v HM Advocate 1936 JC 19... 2.25, 2.27, 9.10, 10.15
Patrick Slaven (1885) 5 Coup 694 .... 5.15
Patterson v Landsberg (1905) 7 F 675, 13 SLT 62 .... 16.4, 16.5
Pawn v HM Advocate 1936 JC 19, 1936 SLT 298 .... 2.25, 9.10
Peebles v McPhail 1989 SCCR 410, 1990 SLT 245... 9.3
People v Goodman (1943) 44 NYS 2d 715 .... 9.1
Perka v The Queen [1984] 2 SCR 232, 55 NR 1, Canadian SC......................... 8.35
Peter Alston and Alex Forrest (1837) 1 Swin 433 .... 14.21
Petto (Samuel) v HM Advocate [2011] HCJAC 80, 2012 JC 105, 2011 SLT
 1043, 2011 SCL 850, 2011 SCCR 519, 2011 GWD 26-585, HCJ 1.1, 1.3, 1.5,
 7.9, 8.6, 10.6, 10.11, 18.8
Petto v HM Advocate [2009] HCJAC 43, 2009 SLT 509, 2009 SCL 842.... 10.6, 10.10,
 10.11
Pharmaceutical Society of Great Britain v Storkwein Ltd [1986] 1 WLR 903,
 [1986] 2 All ER 365, (1986) 83 Cr App Rep 359, HL..................................... 3.3
Piracy Jure Gentium, Re [1934] AC 586, 103 LJPC 153, 152 LT 73, 51 TLR 12,
 78 Sol Jo 585, PC.. 15.4
Pirie v Hawthorn 1962 JC 69, 1962 SLT 291 .... 20.4
Pountney v Griffiths [1976] AC 314, [1975] 3 WLR 140, [1975] 2 All ER 881,
 [1975] Crim LR 702, HL 9.4
Procurator Fiscal Edinburgh v Riordan (2007) 4 September, Edinburgh Sh Ct... 20.6
Pryde v Brown 1982 SCCR 26, 1982 SLT 314 .... 13.7
Purcell Meats (Scotland) Ltd v McLeod 1986 SCCR 672, 1987 SLT 528......... 4.6
Purcell v HM Advocate [2007] HCJ 13, 2007 SCCR 520, 2008 JC 131, 2008
 SLT 44, 2008 SCL 183 .... 6.15, 8.46, 10.3, 10.10, 10.11, 18.9

Q

Quinn v Cunningham 1956 JC 22, 1956 SLT 55..................... 2.25, 9.10, 10.15, 13.17
Quinn v Lees 1994 SCCR 159, HCJ... 2.18

R

R v Ahlers [1915] 1 KB 616, CCA.. 19.3
R v Aitken [1992] 1 WLR 1006, [1992] 4 All ER 541, (1992) 95 Cr App R 304,
 (1992) 136 SJLB 183, Cts-Martial App Ct.. 9.6
R v Allan [1966] AC 1, [1965] 1 QB 130, [1963] 2 All ER 897, CCA 6.11

R v Ancio (1984) 10 CCC (3d) 385 .... 7.10
R v Anderson; R v Morris [1966] 2 QB 110, [1966] 2 WLR 1195, [1966] 2 All
  ER 644, CCA 6.3
R v Andrew Hardie (1820) 1 St Tr (Notes) 609 .... 19.2
R v Andrew's-Weatherfoil Ltd [1972] 1 WLR 118, [1972] 1 All ER 65, 56 Cr
  App R 31, CA 4.7
R v Asbury [1986] Crim LR 258, CA 8.28
R v Austin [1981] 1 All ER 374, (1981) 72 Cr App Rep 104, CA 6.6
R v Bagshaw [1988] Crim LR 321 .... 14.19
R v Bainbridge [1960] 1 QB 129, [1959] 3 WLR 656, [1959] 3 All ER 200,
  CCA 6.13, 6.14
R v Baker (1909) 28 NZLR 536, [1909] 1 All ER 277, CA 6.15
R v Barnard (1837) 7 C & P 784 .... 16.3
R v Becerra; R v Cooper (1975) 62 Cr App Rep 212, CA........................... 6.18
R v Beck (Valmae) (1989) 43 A Crim R 135, Qld CCA............................. 6.11
R v Bettles [1966] Crim LR 503, CCA.. 6.13
R v Bland 1988] Crim LR 41, (1987) 151 JP 857, (1987) 151 JPN 825, CA 6.11
R v Blaue [1975] 1 WLR 1411, [1975] 3 All ER 446, (1975) 61 Cr App Rep
  271, CA 5.6, 5.16
R v Bottrill, ex parte Kuechenmeister [1947] KB 41, [1946] 2 All ER 434, 115
  LJKB 500, CA 19.3
R v Bourne (1952) 36 Cr App Rep 125, CCA 6.5
R v Boyle and Boyle (1986) 84 Cr App Rep 270, [1987] Crim LR 111, CA..... 7.7
R v Broughham (1986) 43 SASR 187 .... 2.10
R v Brown (Anthony) [1994] 1 AC 212, [1993] 2 WLR 556, [1993] 2 All ER
  75, (1993) 97 Cr App R 44, HL 9.6, 11.18
R v Bunn (1989) Times, 11 May 5.16
R v Burgess [1991] 2 QB 92, [1991] 2 WLR 1206, [1991] 2 All ER 769, (1991)
  93 Cr App R 41, CA.. 2.5
R v C [2009] UKHL 42, [2009] 4 All ER 1033.. 11.2
R v Carver [1978] QB 472, [1978] 2 WLR 872, [1978] 3 All ER 60, CA 12.6
R v Casement [1917] 1 KB 98, 86 LJKB 467, 115 LT 267.............................. 19.3
R v Caunt (17 November 1947, unreported), Assizes..................................... 19.4
R v Chenjere 1960 (1) SA 473 (Sup Ct of the Federation of Rhodesia and
  Nyasaland) 6.16
R v Cheshire [1991] 1 WLR 844, [1991] 3 All ER 670, (1991) 93 Cr App Rep
  251, [1991] Crim LR 709, CA 5.12
R v Church [1966] 1 QB 59, [1965] 2 WLR 1220, [1965] 2 All ER 72, CCA... 10.14
R v Clarkson [1971] 1 WLR 1402, [1971] 3 All ER 344, 55 Cr App R 445, Cts-
  Martial App Ct 2.10, 6.11
R v Clear [1968] 1 QB 670, [1968] 2 WLR 122, [1968] 1 All ER 74, CA 17.7
R v Coffey [1987] Crim LR 498, CA 14.12
R v Cogan; R v Leak [1976] QB 217, [1975] 3 WLR 316, [1975] 2 All ER
  1059, CA 6.4, 6.6
R v Collingridge (1976) 16 SASR 117 .... 7.14
R v Commissioner of Metropolitan Police, ex parte Blackburn (No 2) [1968] 2
  QB 150, [1968] 2 WLR 1204, [1968] 2 All ER 319, CA 20.4
R v Conway [1989] QB 290, [1988] 3 WLR 1238, [1988] 3 All ER 1025,
  [1989] RTR 35, CA.. 13.26
R v Coughlan, ex parte Evans. *See* Evans v Pesce and Attorney General for
  Alberta
R v Court [1989] AC 28, [1988] 2 WLR 1071, [1988] 2 All ER 221, HL 2.20
R v Cox and Hodges (1982) 75 Cr App Rep 291, [1983] Crim LR 167, CA..... 3.3

R v Crisp & Homewood (1919) 83 JP 121, CCC 19.6
R v Croft [1944] KB 295, [1944] 2 All ER 483, (1944) 29 Cr App Rep 169,
 CA 6.12
R v Crooks [1981] 2 NZLR 53, NZCA 2.23
R v Croucamp 1949 (1) SA 377 .... 7.7
R v Cummerson [1968] 2 QB 534, [1968] 2 WLR 1486, [1968] 2 All ER 863,
 CA 3.3
R v Dammaree and Purchase (1710) 15 St Tr 52 .... 19.2
R v Delgado [1984] 1 WLR 89, [1984] 1 All ER 449, (1984) 78 Cr App R 175,
 CA 12.4
R v Dica [2004] EWCA Crim 1103, [2004] QB 1257, [2004] 3 WLR 213,
 [2004] 3 All ER 593 .... 9.13
R v Dix (1972) 10 CCC (2d) 324, Cananda 9.6
R v Donovan [1934] 2 KB 498, [1934] All ER Rep 207, 25 Cr App Rep 1,
 CCA 9.6
R v Doot [1973] AC 807, [1973] 2 WLR 532, [1973] 1 All ER 940, HL 1.13
R v Doran (Robert) [2015] EWCA Crim 384, CA 12.1, 12.6
R v Dudley and Stephens (1884) 14 QBD 273, 54 LJMC 32, 52 LT 107, 49 JP
 69, 33 WR 347, 1 TLR 118, 15 Cox CC 624, CCA 8.36
R v Evans (1976) 64 Cr App Rep 237, [1977] Crim LR 233, CA 12.3
R v Farrance [1978] RTR 225, [1978] 67 Cr App Rep 136, [1978] Crim LR
 496, CA 13.4
R v Fell [1963] Crim LR 207, 107 SJ 97, 113 LJ 580, CCA 19.6
R v Fletcher and Zimnowodski [1962] Crim LR 551, 106 SJ 554, CCA 6.18
R v Flynn (1867) 16 WR 319 .... 5.16
R v Forman and Ford [1988] Crim LR 677 .... 6.10
R v Gibbins and Proctor (1918) 13 Cr App Rep 134 .... 10.15
R v Gladstone Williams [1987] 3 All ER 411, (1984) 78 Cr App Rep 276,
 [1984] Crim LR 163, CA 8.28
R v Gnango (Armel) [2011] UKSC 59, [2012] 1 AC 827, [2012] 2 WLR 17,
 [2012] 2 All ER 129, [2012] 1 Cr App R 18, (2012) 109(2) LSG 16, (2011)
 155(48) SJLB 31, SC 2.3, 6.16
R v Harding [1976] VR 129 .... 6.14
R v Harris [1964] Crim LR 54, CCA 6.10
R v Harry [1974] Crim LR 32 .... 17.7
R v Hennigan [1971] 3 All ER 133, [1971] RTR 305, (1971) 55 Cr App Rep
 262, CA 13.10
R v HM Advocate 1988 SCCR 254, 1988 SLT 623 .... 11.8, 11.20
R v HM Advocate 2003 SC (PC) 21, 2003 SLT 4, 2003 SCCR 19 .... 1.15
R v HM Coroner for East Kent, ex parte Spooner (1987) Cr App Rep 10, 152
 JP 115, [1987] BCC 636, QBD 4.5
R v Holland 174 ER 313, (1841) 2 Mood & R 351, Ct of KB 5.16
R v Holmes [1976] Crim LR 125, DC 12.4
R v Howe [1987] AC 417, [1987] 2 WLR 568, [1987] 1 All ER 771, HL 8.36
R v Instan [1893] 1 QB 450, [1891-94] All ER Rep 1213, CCR 2.15, 10.15
R v Jakeman (1982) 76 Cr App Rep 223, [1983] Crim LR 104 .... 12.3
R v Jenkins (Nathan) [2015] EWCA Crim 105, [2015] 1 Cr App R (S) 70,
 [2015] RTR 16, [2015] Crim LR 467, CA 13.11
R v Jordan (1956) 40 Cr App Rep 152, CCA 5.11
R v Kennedy (No 2) [2007] UKHL 38, [2008] 1 AC 269, [2007] 3 WLR 612,
 [2007] 4 All ER 1083 .... 5.14
R v Khan [1990] 1 WLR 813, [1990] 2 All ER 783, 91 Cr App R 29, 154 JP
 805, (1990) Independent, 31 January, CA 7.10

R v Komaroni and Rogerson (1953) 103 LJ 97 .... 7.7
R v Konzani [2005] EWCA Crim 706, [2005] 2 Cr App R 14 .... 9.13
R v Kopi-Kame [1965–66] P&NGLR 73 .... 7.7
R v Krause (1902) 66 JP 121 .... 6.12
R v Lankford [1959] Crim LR 209, CCA 7.7
R v Larsonneur (1933) 149 LT 542, 29 Cox CC 673 .... 2.4
R v Lawson and Forsyth [1986] VR 515 .... 8.31
R v Linekar [1995] QB 250, [1995] 2 WLR 237, [1995] 3 All ER 69, [1995] 2
  Cr App R 49, CA 11.15
R v Lloyd [1985] QB 829, [1985] 3 WLR 30, [1985] 2 All ER 661, (1985) 81
  Cr App Rep 182, CA 14.19
R v Loukes [1996] 1 Cr App Rep 444, [1996] RTR 164, [1995] Crim LR 341,
  CA 13.9
R v Lynch [1903] 1 KB 444, 72 LJKB 167, 88 LT 26, 67 JP 41, 51 WR 619, 19
  TLR 163, 20 Cox CC 468 .... 19.1
R v MacGrowther (1746) 18 St Tr 391 .... 19.3
R v Mackie (1973) 57 Cr App Rep 453, [1973] Crim LR 438, CA 5.15
R v Maginnis [1987] AC 303, [1987] 2 WLR 765, [1987] 1 All ER 907, HL ... 12.4, 12.7
R v Malcherek; R v Steel [1981] 1 WLR 690, [1981] 2 All ER 422, (1981) 73
  Cr App Rep 173, CA 5.10
R v Malcolm [1951] NZLR 470 .... 6.18
R v Marison [1996] Crim LR 909, [1997] RTR 457, (1996) 93(29) LSG 29,
  CA 13.3
R v Martyn [1967] NZLR 396 .... 6.15
R v Mayberry [1973] Qd R 211 .... 6.14
R v McDonagh [1974] QB 448, [1974] 2 WLR 529, (1974) 59 Cr App Rep 55,
  CA 13.2
R v McEnery 1943 SR 158 .... 5.15
R v McNamara (1988) 87 Cr App R 344 .... 12.6
R v Mgxwiti 1954 (1) SA 370 (A) 6.16
R v Miller [1983] 2 AC 161, [1983] 2 WLR 539, [1983] 1 All ER 978, HL.. 2.13, 18.4
R v Morris (David) [1983] QB 587, [1983] 2 All ER 448, CA; [1984] AC 320,
  [1983] 3 All ER 288, HL 14.7, 14.16, 16.5
R v Most (1881) 7 QBD 244, 50 LJMC 113, 44 LT 823, 45 JP 696, 29 WR 758,
  14 Cox CC 583, CCR 6.12
R v Mtembu 1950 (1) SA 670 (A) 6.16
R v Mubila 1956 (1) SA 31 (Southern Rhodesia) 5.16
R v Nbakwa 1956 (2) SA 577 (Southern Rhodesia) 10.3
R v O'Donovan and Vereker (1987) 29 A Crim R 292 .... 6.15
R v Page [1933] VLR 351 .... 7.7, 7.8
R v Paget and Pemberton (1983) 76 Cr App Rep 279, (1982) 4 Cr App R (S)
  399, [1983] Crim LR 274, CA 5.9
R v Papadimitropolous (1957) 98 CLR 249 .... 11.15
R v Parrot (1913) 8 Cr App Rep 186 .... 19.6
R v Peverett 1940 AD 213 (SA) 10.3
R v Roberts (1972) 56 Cr App Rep 95, [1972] Crim LR 27, (1971) 115 SJ 809,
  CA 5.15, 9.1
R v Russell [1933] VLR 59 .... 2.14
R v S [2005] EWCA Crim 819 .... 10.3
R v Shivpuri [1987] AC 1, [1986] 2 WLR 988, [1986] 2 All ER 334, (1986) 83
  Cr App R 178 .... 7.11, 7.13, 7.14, 12.3
R v Slack [1989] QB 775, [1989] 3 WLR 513, [1989] 3 All ER 90, (1989) Cr
  App R 252, CA 6.20

R v Smith (David) [1974] 1 QB 354, [1974] 2 WLR 20, [1974] 1 All ER 632, CA 18.5

R v Smith [1959] 2 QB 35, [1959] 2 WLR 623, [1959] 2 All ER 193, Cts-Martial App Ct 5.1, 5.11, 5.8

R v Smith [1960] 2 QB 423, [1960] 2 WLR 164, [1960] 1 All ER 256, CCA... 3.3

R v Spratt [1990] 1 WLR 1073, [1991] 2 All ER 210, (1990) 91 Cr App Rep 362, CA 9.5

R v Steane [1947] KB 997, [1947] LJR 969, [1947] 1 All ER 813, CCA 19.3

R v Stone and Dobinson [1977] 1 QB 354, [1977] 2 WLR 169, [1977] 2 All ER 341, CA 2.15

R v Taaffe [1983] 1 WLR 627, [1983] 2 All ER 625, (1983) 77 Cr App R 82, CA 12.3

R v Taylor (1859) 1 F & F 511, 175 ER 831 .... 7.7

R v Thornton (Sara Elizabeth) (No 2) [1996] 1 WLR 1174, [1996] 2 All ER 1023, [1996] 2 Cr App R 108, CA 10.20

R v Treacy [1971] AC 537, [1971] 2 WLR 112, [1971] 1 All ER 110, HL 1.13

R v Tyrrell [1894] 1 QB 710, [1891–94] All ER Rep 1215 .... 6.8

R v Vaughan (1696) 13 St Tr 485, 2 Salk 634 .... 19.2

R v Vilinsky 1932 OPD 218, S Africa 7.7

R v Wakely [1990] Crim LR 119, CA 6.20

R v Wall [1974] 1 WLR 930, [1974] 2 All ER 245, (1974) 59 Cr App Rep 58, CA 12.3

R v Warner [1969] 2 AC 256, [1968] 2 WLR 1303, [1968] 2 All ER 356, HL.. 3.1, 12.6

R v Watkins (Richard Alan) [2010] EWCA Crim 2349, CA 6.4

R v West (1848) 2 Cox CC 500, 175 ER 329 .... 13.10

R v White [1910] 2 KB 124, 102 LT 784, [1908-10] All ER Rep 340 .... 7.5

R v Whitefield (1984) 79 Cr App Rep 36, [1984] Crim LR 97, (1983) 80 LS Gaz 3077, CA 6.18

R v Whitehouse [1977] QB 868, [1977] 2 WLR 925, [1977] 3 All ER 737, CA 6.8

R v Wilcox [1982] 1 NZLR 191 .... 7.7

R v Williams [1923] 1 KB 340, 92 LJKB 230, 128 LT 128, 87 JP 67, 39 TLR 131, 67 Sol Jo 263, 27 Cox CC 350, 17 Cr App Rep 56 .... 11.15

R v Williams [1965] Qd R 86 .... 7.7

R v Wills [1983] 2 VR 201 .... 10.14

R v Wilson (Alan) [1997] QB 47, [1996] 3 WLR 125, [1996] 2 Cr App R 241, CA 9.6

R v Wright [1976] Crim LR 248 .... 12.7

R (on the application of Anderson) v Home Secretary [2002] UKHL 46, [2003] 1 AC 837, [2002] 4 All ER 1089, [2002] 3 WLR 1800 .... 1.5

R (on the application of Pretty) v DPP [2001] UKHL 61, [2002] 1 AC 800, 63 BMLR 1, [2002] 1 All ER 1, [2001] 3 WLR 1598 .... 10.3

R (on the application of Nicklinson) v Ministry of Justice [2014] UKSC 38, [2015] AC 657, [2014] 3 WLR 200, [2014] 3 All ER 843, [2014] 3 FCR 1, [2014] HRLR 17, 36 BHRC 465, (2014) 139 BMLR 1, SC 10.3

R (on the application of Purdy) v Director of Public Prosecutions [2009] UKHL 45, [2010] AC 345, [2009] 3 WLR 403, [2009] 4 All ER 1147 .... 2.20, 10.3

Rankin v Murray 2004 SLT 1164 .... 19.8

Rattray v Colley 1991 GWD 1–71 .... 13.12

Reader's Digest Assoc v Pirie 1973 JC 42, 1973 SLT 170 .... 4.5

Reid v HM Advocate 1999 SLT 1275, 1999 SCCR 19, 1999 SC(JC) 54, HCJ 6.6

Reid v Nixon 1948 JC 68 .... 13.18

Rendal Courtney (1743) Hume I, 99.. 14.22
Reynolds v Austin (GH) & Sons Ltd [1951] 2KB 135, [1951] 1 All ER 606, 49
  LGR 377, DC.. 3.6
RHW v HM Advocate 1982 SCCR 152, 1988 SLT 42................................. 9.10, 9.11
Richards v HM Advocate 1971 JC 29... 2.2, 16.6, 16.7
Robert Stirling (1821) Alison, 487.. 20.2
Robert v Agnes Black (1841) Bell's Notes 46... 14.26
Roberts v Hamilton 1989 SLT 399, 1989 SCCR 240..................................... 8.6, 9.5
Roberts v Local Authority for Inverness (1809) 2 White 385........................... 8.4
Robertson v Hamilton 1987 SCCR 477, 1988 SLT 70, 1987 JC 95............ 16.11, 20.7
Robertson v HM Advocate 1987 SCCR 387 .... 11.11
Robertson v HM Advocate 1994 JC 245, 1994 SLT 1004, 1994 SCCR 589 ... 9.9,10.21
Robertson v HM Advocate; Gough v HM Advocate 2007 SLT 1153, 2008
  SC 1.. 20.3, 20.4
Robertson v Klos [2005] HCJAC 136, 2006 SCCR 52 .... 13.17
Robson v United Kingdom (1996) Application no 25648/94............................ 1.5
Rodger v Normand 1995 SLT 411, 1994 SCCR 861...................................... 13.6
Ronald v Duke of Buccleuch [2014] CSOH 101, 2014 GWD 21-392.............. 17.9
Rooney v Brown [2013] HCJAC 57, 2013 SCL 615, 2013 SCCR 334, 2013
  GWD 17-354.. 12.11
Ross (Robert) v HM Advocate 1991 SCCR 823, 1991 SLT 564....... 2.7, 2.8, 8.11, 13.3
Ross v Lord Advocate [2015] CSOH 123, 2015 SLT 617, 2015 GWD 30-503 .. 1.8,
                                                                                                                10.1, 10.4
Royle v Gray 1973 SLT 31 .... 20.3
Rubie v Faulkner [1940] 1 KB 571, [1940] 1 All ER 285, KBD 6.10

S

S v Daniels 1983 (3) SA 275 .... 5.10
S v Magxwalisa 1984 (2) SA 314... 7.7
S v Thomo 1969 (1) SA 385... 6.16
Salduz v Turkey (2009) 49 EHRR 19, ECHR 1.5
Salmon v HM Advocate 1991 SCCR 628, HCJ... 20.9
Salmon v HM Advocate 1999 JC 67, 1999 SLT 169, 1998 SCCR 740, HCJ
  Appeal... 12.4, 12.5, 12.6
Saltman v Allan 1989 SLT 262,1988 SCCR 640, HCJ.................................... 12.10
Samuel Smith (unreported), noted Gordon para 21–10, n 30........................... 17.8
Samuel Tumbleson (1863) 4 Irv 426 .... 16.16
Sandlan v HM Advocate 1983 SCCR 71 .... 14.11, 14.13, 14.15
Sarwar (Athif) v HM Advocate [2011] HCJAC 13, 2011 SCCR 159, [2011]
  Lloyd's Rep FC 244, 2011 GWD 7-182.. 2.12
Sayers v HM Advocate 1981 SCCR 312, 1981 JC 98................................ 2.22, 7.16
Scott (George) v HM Advocate [2011] HCJAC 110, 2012 SCL 153, 2012
  SCCR 45, 2011 GWD 37-757 .... 2.19, 5.14, 9.6, 9.13, 10.10
Scott v Dunn [2014] HCJAC 134, 2015 SCL 201, 2015 GWD 1-12 .... 20.4
Scott v Everitt (1853) 15 D 288.. 14.4
Scott v HM Advocate [2015] HCJAC 57... 2.9, 2.19
Scott v Smith 1981 JC 46... 11.6
Serious Fraud Office v Standard Bank plc (30 November 2015, unreported) ... 4.2,
                                                                                                                17.11
Shannon v HM Advocate 1985 SCCR 14... 14.30
Shaw v DPP [1962] AC 220, [1961] 2 WLR 897, [1961] 2 All ER 446, HL..... 1.8
Siddique v HM Advocate [2010] HCJAC 7... 19.8
Silverstein v HM Advocate 1949 JC 160, 1949 SLT 386............. 17.6, 17.7, 17.8, 17.9

Simon Fraser (1859) 3 Irv 467.. 16.15
Simon Fraser (1878) 4 Coup 70.. 2.5
Simpson v Gifford 1954 SLT 39.. 4.4
Simpson v Peat [1952] 2 QB 24, [1952] 1 WLR 469, [1952] 1 All ER 447,
    DC... 13.15, 13.16
Simpson v Tudhope 1987 SCCR 348 .... 20.1
Skinner v Robertson 1980 SLT (Sh Ct) 43 .... 9.4
Smart v HM Advocate [2006] HCJAC 12, 2006 JC 119, 2006 SCCR 120 .... 11.7
Smart v HM Advocate 1975 SLT 65, 1975 JC 30........... 6.8, 9.5, 9.6, 9.7, 11.18, 14.9
Smith (Hugh Ian) v HM Advocate 1996 SCCR 49, 1996 SLT 1338, HCJ
    Appeal.. 3.5
Smith of Maddiston Ltd v Macnab 1975 JC 48, 1975 SLT 86 .... 2.24, 3.10, 13.8
Smith v Donnelly 2002 JC 65, 2001 SLT 1007, 2001 SCCR 800.................. 1.10, 12.9
Smith v Jenner [1968] Crim LR 99, 112 SJ 52, DC 6.14, 6.21
Smith v Watson 1982 JC 34, 1982 SCCR 15.................................... 14.29, 14.32
Sommerville v Tudhope 1981 JC 58, 1981 SLT 117................................ 11.6
Sorley v HM Advocate 1992 SLT 867, 1992 JC 102, 1992 SCCR 396 .... 2.9
Southern Water Authority v Pegrum and Pegrum [1989] Crim LR 442, (1989)
    153 JP 581, (1989) 153 LG Rev 672, DC...................................... 5.8
Spendiff v HM Advocate [2005] HCJAC 68, 2005 1 JC 338, 2005 SCCR 522 .. 11.15,
                                                                               11.16
Staffordshire Chief Constable v Lees [1981] RTR 506, DC............................ 13.7
Stallard v HM Advocate 1989 SCCR 248, 1989 SLT 469.............................. 1.3, 11.13
State v Mitchell (1902) 170 Mo 633, 71 SW 175, Supreme Court of Missouri.... 7.14
Stebbings v Westwater 1991 GWD 1–55...................................... 13.16
Stephenson v State (1933) 205 Ind 141, 170 NE 633................................ 5.16
Steuart v Macpherson 1918 JC 96, 1918 2 SLT 125 .... 16.3
Stewart v Jessop 1988 SCCR 492.. 12.10
Stewart v Nisbet [2012] HCJAC 167, 2013 SCL 209, 2013 GWD 2-70....... 9.7, 11.18,
                                                                               14.9
Stewart v Thain 1981 JC 13, 1981 SLT (Notes) 2 .... 2.21, 11.18
Stirling v Associated Newspapers 1960 JC 5, 1960 SLT 5............................... 20.6
Stobbs v HM Advocate 1983 SCCR 190...................................... 10.18
Strachan v HM Advocate 1994 SCCR 341, 1995 SLT 178 .... 7.6
Strathern v Fogal 1922 JC 73, 1922 SLT 543........................... 16.4, 16.12
Strathern v Seaforth 1926 JC 100, 1926 SLT 445 .... 1.8, 14.15, 14.18, 14.19
Streatfield (1991) 53 A Crim R 228.. 10.16
Stuart (1829) Bell's Notes 22.. 14.23
Sugden v HM Advocate 1934 JC 103... 1.14
Sunday Times v United Kingdom (1979) 2 EHRR 245, ECHR..................... 1.10
Sutherland v HM Advocate 1994 SCCR 80, 1994 SLT 634......... 2.25, 9.12, 14.9, 18.7
SW v The United Kingdom (1996) 21 EHRR 363, [1996] 1 FLR 434, [1996]
    Fam Law 275, ECHR... 1.10
Sweeney v X 1982 SCCR 509, HCJ.. 11.15
Sweet v Parsley [1970] AC 132, [1969] 2 WLR 470, [1969] 1 All ER 347, HL... 3.2, 3.5
Sykes v DPP [1962] AC 528, [1961] 3 WLR 371, [1961] 3 All ER 33, HL 19.4

T

T, Petitioner; *sub nom* AMT, Petitioners 1997 SLT 724, 1996 SCLR 897,
    [1997] Fam Law 225, 1 Div.. 1.5
Tail v Lees 1991 GWD 2–122.. 13.16
Tapsell v Prentice (1910) 6 Adam 354, 1911 SC (J) 67............................... 16.8, 16.12
Templeton v HM Advocate 1988 JC 33, 1988 SLT 171, 1987 SCCR 693......... 6.21

Tesco Supermarkets v Nattrass [1972] AC 153, [1971] 2 WLR 1166, [1971] 2
All ER 127, HL 4.6, 4.7
Thomas Muir's Case (1793) 23 St Tr 118 .... 19.4
Thompson v Crowe 1999 SLT 1434, 1999 SCCR 1003, HCJ Appeal 20.2
Thomson v HM Advocate 1983 JC 69, 1983 SCCR 368 .... 8.34
Thomson v HM Advocate 1985 SCCR 448, 1986 SLT 281 .... 10.18, 10.19
Thos Mackenzie (1878) 4 Coup 50 .... 16.15
Transco v HM Advocate (No 1) 2004 JC 29, 2004 SLT 41, 2004 SCCR 1 .... 4.6, 4.7,
4.8, 10.15
Trippick v Orr 1994 SCCR 736, 1995 SLT 272 .... 13.12
Tuck v Robson [1970] 1 WLR 741, [1970] 1 All ER 1171, 114 SJ 191, DC 6.10
Tudhope v Every 1976 JC 42 .... 13.5
Tudhope v Grubb 1983 SCCR 350, Sh Ct 3.7, 13.26
Tudhope v McKee 1987 SCCR 663, 1988 SLT 153 .... 12.4
Tudhope v O'Neill 1982 SCCR 45 .... 12.12
Tudhope v Robertson 1980 JC 62, 1980 SLT 60 .... 12.4
Turnbull v HM Advocate 1953 JC 59 .... 20.8
Twycross v Farrell 1973 SLT (Notes) 85 .... 9.8

U
Ulhaq v HM Advocate 1990 SCCR 593, 1991 SLT 614 .... 5.13, 9.12, 9.13
Urquhart (Robert) v HM Advocate [2015] HCJAC 101, 2015 SLT 853, 2016
SCL 53, 2015 GWD 37-592 .... 12.11
Usman v HM Advocate 2007 JC 111, 2007 SCCR 106 .... 3.5

V
Valentine v MacBrayne Haulage Ltd 1986 SCCR 692 .... 13.8
Vaughan v HM Advocate 1979 SLT 49 .... 6.8, 6.21

W
Wade (Philip) v HM Advocate [2014] HCJAC 88, 2014 SCL 680, 2014 GWD
25-481 .... 20.9
Wali v HM Advocate [2007] HCJAC 11, 2007 JC 111, 2007 SCCR 106 .... 12.5
Walker v HM Advocate 1985 JC 53, 1985 SCCR 150 .... 6.20
Wallace v Major [1946] KB 473, [1946] 2 All ER 87, 175 LT 84, 110 JP 231,
KBD 13.2
Wallace v McLeod 1986 SCCR 678 .... 13.18
Ward v Robertson 1938 JC 32, 1938 SLT 165 .... 18.5
Warner v Metropolitan Police Commissioner [1969] 2 AC 256, [1968] 2 WLR
1303, [1968] 2 All ER 356, HL 12.5, 12.6
Watson v HM Advocate (1978) SCCR Supp 192 .... 13.10
Watt v Annan 1978 JC 84, 1978 SLT 198 .... 11.8, 11.10
Watt v Home (1851) Shaw 519 .... 17.1
Webster v Dominick 2005 1 JC 65, 2003 SLT 975, 2003 SCCR 525 .... 1.3, 1.8, 11.2,
11.6, 11.10, 11.11, 11.20, 11.17
Welham v DPP [1961] AC 103, [1960] 2 WLR 669, [1960] 1 All ER 805,
HL 16.2, 16.9
West v HM Advocate 1985 SCCR 248 .... 7.16
White v Ridley (1978) 21 ALR 661, 52 ALJR 724 .... 6.18
Wightman v Lees 2000 SLT 111, 1999 SCCR 664 .... 9.4
Wilcox v Jeffrey [1951] 1 All ER 464, [1951] 1 TLR 706, 115 JP 151, DC .. 2.11, 6.11
William Fraser (1847) Arkley 280 .... 1.7, 16.11
William Hardie (1847) Arkley 247 .... 2.14

Wilson v Brown 1982 SCCR 49, 1982 SLT 361 .... 12.8
Wilson v HM Advocate 1983 SCCR 420, 1984 SLT 117 .... 18.1, 18.2, 18.3,
18.4, 18.5
Wilson v Macphail 1991 SCCR 170, HCJ 13.15, 13.15, 13.17
Wilson v Procurator Fiscal Aberdeen [2009] HCJAC 30 .... 14.24
Windsor v United Kingdom (1988) Application no 13081/87 (14 December
1998, unreported) 1.5
Winkle v Wiltshire [1951] 1 KB 684, [1951] 1 All ER 479, [1951] 1 TLR 368,
DC 3.3
Winter v Morrison 1954 JC 7 .... 13.21
Winzar v Chief Constable of Kent (1983) Times, March 28, DC 2.4
With v O'Flanagan [1936] Ch 575, [1936] 1 All ER 727, CA 16.5
Wither v Adie 1986 SLT (Sh Ct) 32 .... 18.11
Wm v HM Advocate [2010] HC JAC 75 .... 9.14
Wm Wilson (1882) 5 Coup 48 .... 14.10
Wm Anderson (1840) Bell's Notes 199 .... 14.22
Wm Mann (1877) 3 Coup 376 .... 16.15
Wm Jeffrey (1842) 1 Broun 337 .... 16.16
Woodage v Jones (No 2) [1975] RTR 119, (1975) 60 Cr App Rep 260 .... 13.21
Woods v Heywood 1988 SLT 849, 1988 SCCR 434 .... 12.12
Woodward v James Young (Contractors) Ltd 1958 JC 28, 1958 SLT 289 .... 13.5
Wylie v HM Advocate 1966 SLT 149 .... 20.3
Wyness v Lockhart 1992 SCCR 808, HCJ 12.9

Y

Yates v Murray 2004 JC 16, 2003 SLT 1348 .... 13.6
Young v Armour 1921 1 SLT 211 .... 20.6
Young v Carmichael 1993 SLT 167, 1991 SCCR 332 .... 13.6
Young v Heady 1959 JC 66, 1959 SLT 250 .... 12.9
Young v HM Advocate 1932 JC 63, 1932 SLT 465 .... 6.5, 6.21
Young v McGlennan 1991 SCCR 738, HCJ 11.18

Z

Zecevic v DPP of Victoria (1987) 71 ALR 641 .... 8.28

Table of statutes

[references are to paragraph numbers]

A

Anatomy Act 1984	10.4
Aviation and Maritime Security Act 1990	
s 9	15.4

B

Bankruptcy Acts	16.4
Bribery Act 2010	17.11
s 1, 2	17.11
6, 7	17.11
13	17.11
18	17.11
British Nationality Act 1948	
s 3	19.1

C

Carrying of Knives etc (Scotland) Act 1991	12.14
Children and Young Persons Act 1933	
s 50	8.25
Children and Young Persons Act 1963	8.22
Children and Young Persons (Scotland) Act 1937	
s 12	3.3
Children's Hearings (Scotland) Act 2011	8.25
Civic Government (Scotland) Act 1982	11.7, 12.10
s 46–56	12.10
48	12.10
51	11.6
51A–51C	11.6
52	11.7
(1)(2A)	11.2
52A	11.7
52B	11.7
57(1)	14.24
67–75	14.9
67(6)	14.9
Communications Act 2003	
s 127	11.6
Companies Act 1967	
s 68(5)	4.2

Computer Misuse Act 1990	1.1
Constitutional Reform Act 2005	1.5
Consumer Rights Act 2015	14.4
Contempt of Court Act 1981	20.6
s 2(1), (2)	20.6
3	20.6
4	20.6
(2)	20.6
5	20.6
10	20.5
Sch 1	
para 14	20.6
Corporate Manslaughter and Corporate Homicide Act 2007	4.6, 4.8, 10.5
s 1(4)(b), (c)	4.8
2	4.8
(5)	4.8
Sch 1	4.8
Counter Terrorism Act 2008	19.8, 19.11
Counter Terrorism and Security Act 2015	19.8
Courts Reform (Scotland) Act 2014	
s 46–62	1.4
Crime and Courts Act 2013	
s 45	4.2, 17.11
Crime and Disorder Act 1998	
s 96	1.6
Criminal Attempts Act 1981	7.2
s 1	7.11
Criminal Justice and Licensing (Scotland) Act 2010	4.8, 4.9, 8.22, 8.25, 12.9
s 26	1.6, 8.10
38	1.1, 12.11
(1), (2)	12.11
39	4.8
49	16.13
(1), (3), (5)	16.13
52	8.25
53	4.9
Sch 5	20.1
Criminal Justice (International Co-operation) Act 1990	1.13

Criminal Justice (Scotland) Act
1949
s 31 .... 6.21
Criminal Justice (Scotland) Act 1980
s 78 .... 18.6
   (1) 18.6
Criminal Justice (Scotland) Act
2003
s 51 .... 9.3
74 .... 1.6
Criminal Law (Consolidation)
(Scotland) Act 1995 .... 6.8, 11.19,
                11.14, 11.16
s 1 .... 11.19
2 .... 11.20
3 .... 11.20
7(2)(a) 11.14
   (b) 11.15
  (3) 11.15
11(1) 6.6
   (a) 6.6
47 .... 12.12
  (1) 12.12
49 .... 12.14
52 .... 18.6
Criminal Procedure (Scotland)
Act 1887
s 56 .... 18.7
61 .... 16.14
Criminal Procedure (Scotland)
Act 1995 .... 8.18
s 11A 1.13
27 .... 1.6
41 .... 8.22
41A 8.25
51A 8.21
51B 8.24
52–52U 8.18
53–53D 8.18
54 .... 8.17
54–57 .... 8.18
57 .... 8.17
70 .... 4.3
136 .... 1.15
143 .... 4.3
293(1) 6.6
328 .... 8.21
Sch 3 .... 14.10
  para 8(2) 14.26
     (3), (4) 17.4
Customs and Excise Consolida-
tion Act 1976
s 42 .... 11.6

Customs and Excise Management
Act 1979 .... 12.1
s 170 .... 12.1
  (2) 12.3

D

Damages (Scotland) Act 1976 .... 13.10
Dangerous Drugs Act 1920 .... 12.1
Dog Fouling (Scotland) Act
2003 .... 12.10

E

Education (No 2) Act 1986
s 48 .... 9.3
Education (Scotland) Act 1980
s 48A 9.3
Emergency Workers (Scotland)
Act 2005 .... 9.7
End of Life Assistance (Scotland)
Bill 2010 .... 2.19, 10.3

F

False Oaths (Scotland) Act 1933
s 7(1)(b) 20.1
Firearms Act 1968 .... 3.5
s 16 .... 12.10

H

Health and Safety at Work Act
1974
s 37 .... 4.9
Hijacking Act 1971
s 1 .... 15.4
Human Organ Transplants Act
1989 .... 1.1
Human Rights Act 1998 ..... 1.5, 1.8, 1.10
s 2 .... 1.5, 1.10
  (1)(a) 1.5
4 .... 1.10
Human Tissue Act 1961 .... 10.4

I

Incest Act 1567 .... 6.8, 6.21
Incest and Related Offences
(Scotland) Act 1986 .... 6.8, 11.20
s 1 .... 6.8

J

Judges Act 1540 .... 20.4

K

Knives Act 1997 .... 12.14

L

Land Reform (Scotland) Act 2003.............................. 9.4
Legal Aid, Sentencing and Punishment of Offenders Act 2012.............................. 13.11
Licensing (Scotland) Act 2005
  s 102.............................. 3.8
    141A.............................. 3.8

M

Marriage and Civil Partnership (Scotland) Act 2014 .... 14.32
Medicines Act 1968 .... 3.3
Mental Health (Care and Treatment) (Scotland) Act 2003
  s 311.............................. 9.16, 11.16
    315.............................. 9.4
Mental Health (Scotland) Act 1960
  s 107.............................. 9.4
Mental Health (Scotland) Act 1984
  s 102.............................. 11.16
    122.............................. 9.4
Misuse of Drugs Act 1971 .... 1.1, 12.1, 12.6
  s 3(1).............................. 12.3
    4.............................. 12.4
    (3)(b).............................. 12.5
    5.............................. 12.5, 12.7
    (3).............................. 12.4
    (4).............................. 12.7
    20.............................. 12.3
    28.............................. 12.4
    37(1).............................. 12.4
  Sch 2.............................. 12.2

O

Offences (Aggravation by Prejudice) (Scotland) Act 2008.............................. 1.6
Offensive Behaviour at Football etc (Scotland) Act 2012
  s 1.............................. 1.10
Official Secrets Act 1911
  s 1.............................. 19.5, 19.6
    (2).............................. 19.5
    2.............................. 19.6
    (2).............................. 19.7
    3.............................. 19.5
    5.............................. 19.7

Official Secrets Act 1911 – *contd*
  s 5(2).............................. 15.7
    7.............................. 19.7
Official Secrets Act 1920 .... 19.5
  s 1.............................. 19.7
    3.............................. 19.7
    7.............................. 19.7
Official Secrets Act 1989
  s 1.............................. 19.6
    (1).............................. 19.6
    (3)–(5).............................. 19.6
    (9).............................. 19.6
    2, 3.............................. 19.6

P

Partnerships (Prosecution) (Scotland) Act 2013.............................. 4.3
Police and Fire Reform (Scotland) Act 2012
  s 90.............................. 9.8
Police (Scotland) Act 1967
  s 41.............................. 9.8
Postal Services Act 2000
  s 85.............................. 11.6
Prevention of Corruption Act 1906.............................. 6.21, 17.10, 17.11
  s 1(1).............................. 17.10
Prevention of Corruption Act 1916.............................. 17.11
Prevention of Crime Act 1953 .... 12.12
Prevention of Terrorism Act 1974.............................. 19.4, 19.8
Prevention of Terrorism Act 2005.............................. 19.4, 19.11
Proceeds of Crime Act 2002 ... 2.12, 12.1
  s 328.............................. 2.12
Protection from Harassment Act 1997.............................. 1.2
Protection of Children and Prevention of Sexual Offences (Scotland) Act 2005 .... 1.13, 11.7
  s 1.............................. 1.13
    10–12.............................. 11.7
Public Bodies Corrupt Practices Act 1889.............................. 17.11

R

Rent (Scotland) Act 1971
  s 101, 102.............................. 17.8
Rent (Scotland) Act 1984
  s 22(2) 17.8

Rivers (Prevention of Pollution)
Act 1951
s 2(1)(a)... 3.4
Road Safety Act 2006 .... 13.1, 13.13
s 30... 13.13
Road Traffic Act 1960
s 257(1)..................................... 13.6
Road Traffic Act 1972.............. 2.7, 13.1
s 1... 10.1
6(1)...................................... 3.7
Road Traffic Act 1988............ 8.11, 8.30,
10.1, 13.1
s 1–5................................. 13.1, 13.9
1........................... 13.9, 13.10, 13.15
1A... 13.11
2..................................... 13.12, 13.15
2A....................................... 13.9, 13.10
(3)...................................... 13.10
2B... 13.13
3........................... 13.12, 13.15, 13.17
3A.................................. 13.13, 13.14
3ZA................. 13.13, 13.15, 13.17
(2)–(4)........................... 13.13
4... 13.25
(1)................... 13.18, 13.19, 13.24
(2)...................................... 13.20
(3)....................... 13.22, 13.24
(5)...................................... 13.18
5...............8.11, 13.23, 13.25, 13.26
(1)...................................... 13.23
(b)...................................... 13.24
(2)...................................... 13.24
6(1), (2)................................ 13.23
7... 13.23
8(2)... 13.23
11(2)........................... 13.18, 13.23
15(2)..................................... 13.23
38(7)..................................... 13.16
170.. 13.7
172........................... 1.10, 2.12
178... 14.19
(2)(b)................................ 14.15
185(1)...................................... 13.5
192(1)...................................... 13.6
Road Traffic Act 1991.......... 13.1, 13.12
s 1.. 13.9
3..................................... 13.13, 13.14
4.. 13.5
Road Traffic Offenders Act 1988: 13.1
s 15(2)..................................... 13.25
34... 13.26
(1)...................................... 8.11
44(2).. 8.11

Roads (Scotland) Act 1984
s 151.. 13.6

S

Scotland Act 1998.............. 1.5, 1.8, 1.10
s 57(2).................................. 1.15, 1.10
98...................................... 1.5
Sch 6................................. 1.5
Sexual Offences Act 2003.......... 11.2
s 67, 68...................................... 11.4
Sexual Offences (Scotland) Act
2009..................... 1.1, 6.8, 8.25, 11.1,
11.2, 11.12, 11.13,
11.20
Pt 1 (ss 1–11) 11.2
s 1–3... 11.3
9.. 11.14
Pt 2 (ss 12–16) 11.2
s 12... 11.2
13..................................... 11.2, 11.4
14..................................... 11.2, 11.4
15... 11.4
Pt 3 (s 17)................................. 11.2
Pt 4 (ss 18–41) 11.2
Pt 5 (ss 42–47) 11.2
s 52... 11.2
Social Work (Scotland) Act 1968
Pt III... 8.25
Standards in Scotland's Schools
Act 2000
s 16... 9.3
Suicide Act 1961 .... 10.2
s 2(1)..................................... 6.14

T

Terrorism Act 2000 .... 19.8
s 11... 19.8
12... 19.8
13... 19.8
15–18.............................. 19.9, 19.10
19................................... 2.12, 19.10
20................................... 2.12, 19.10
54... 19.8
54–58A.............................. 19.8
57... 19.8
Sch 3A.................................. 19.10
Terrorism Act 2006 .... 19.8
s 1... 19.8
2... 19.8
Terrorism Prevention and Investigation Measures Act 2011....... 19.11
Theft Act 1968 .... 16.9
s 6(1)..................... 14.12, 14.19

Theft Act 1968 – *contd*
s 15(1) 16.8
21 .... 17.7
21(1) 17.9
34 .... 17.9
Trade Descriptions Act 1968
s 1(1) 16.8

Trade Descriptions Act 1968 – *contd*
s 24 .... 3.8
Transport Act 1981
Sch 8 .... 13.25
Treason Act 1351 .... 19.2
Treason Act 1708
s 1 .... 19.1

List of abbreviations

Case reports

A Crim R	Australian Criminal Reports
AC	Law Reports, Appeal Cases (House of Lords and Privy Council) 1890–
ALJR	Australian Law Journal Reports
ALR	Australian Law Reports
All ER	All England Law Reports 1936–
Arkley	Arkley's Justiciary Reports 1846–48
Broun	Broun's Justiciary Reports 1842–45
C & P	Carrington and Payne's Reports (England) 1823–41
CCC	Canadian Criminal Cases
CLR	Commonwealth Law Reports (Australian)
CR	Criminal Reports (Canada)
Coup	Couper's Justiciary Reports 1868–85
Cox CC	Cox's Criminal Cases (England) 1843–1941
Cr App Rep	Criminal Appeal Reports (England) 1908–
Crim LR	Criminal Law Review
DLR	Dominion Law Reports (Canada)
Dears & B	Dearsly and Bell 169 English Reports 1856–58
Deas & And	Deas and Anderson's Decisions (Court of Session) 1829–32
EHRR	European Human Rights Reports 1979–
ER	English Reports 1220–1865
F	Federal Reporter (USA) 1880–1924
F & F	Foster and Finlayson 171–3 English Reports 1856–67
F(J)	Justiciary Cases in Fraser's Session Cases 1898–1906
GWD	Green's Weekly Digest 1986–
HKLR	Hong Kong Law Reports
Irv	Irvine's Justiciary Reports 1851–68
JC	Justiciary Cases 1917–

KB	Law Reports, King's Bench Division (England) 1900–52
Macq	Macqueen's House of Lords Reports 1851–65
Med LR	Medical Law Reports
Mo	Missouri Reports (USA)
NBR	New Brunswick Reports
NE	North Eastern Reporter (USA)
NYS	New York State Reports
NZLR	New Zealand Law Reports 1883–
P & NGLR	Papua and New Guinea Law Reports
QB	Law Reports, Queen's Bench Division (England) 1891–1901, 1952–
R(J)	Justiciary Cases in Rettie's Session Cases 1873–98
RTR	Road Traffic Reports 1970–
SA	South African Law Reports 1947–
SASR	South Australian State Reports
SCCR	Scotish Criminal Case Reports 1981–
SCCR Supp	Scotish Criminal Case Reports Supplement (1950–80)
SCL	Scottish Criminal Law 2007–
SCLR	Scottish Civil Law Reports 1994–
SCR	Supreme Court Reports (Canada)
SLR	Scottish Law Reporter 1865–1925
SLT	Scots Law Times 1893–1908, and 1909–
SR	Southern Rhodesia Reports
SR (NSW)	State Reports (New South Wales)
So	Southern Reporter (USA)
St Tr	State Trials 1163–1820
Swin	Swinton's Justiciary Reports 1835–41
Tas SR	Tasmanian State Reports
VLR	Victorian Law Reports (Australia)
VR	Victorian Reports 1870–72, and 1957–
WLR	Weekly Law Reports (England) 1953–
WR	Weekly Reporter (England) 1852–1906
White	White's Justiciary Reports 1885–93

Journals

BMJ	British Medical Journal
Br J Crim	British Journal of Criminology
Camb LJ	Cambridge Law Journal
Can Bar Rev	Canadian Bar Review
Col LR	Columbia Law Review
Crim LJ	Criminal Law Journal (Australia)
Crim LQ	Criminal Law Quarterly
Crim LR	Criminal Law Review
Edinburgh LR	Edinburgh Law Review
ICLQ	International and Comparative Law Quarterly
JCL	Journal of Criminal Law
JLSS	Journal of the Law Society of Scotland
JR	Juridical Review
LQR	Law Quarterly Review
LS Gaz	Law Society's Gazette (England) 1903
Med Sci Law	Medicine, Science and the Law
NILQ	Northern Ireland Law Quarterly
NLJ	New Law Journal
SALJ	South African Law Journal

Textbooks

Alison: Archibald Alison *Principles and Practice of the Criminal Law of Scotland* (2 vols, 1832 and 1833)

Burnett: J Burnett *A Treatise on Various Branches of the Criminal Law of Scotland* (1811)

Gane and Stoddart: CHW Gane, CN Stoddart and J Chalmers *A Casebook on Scottish Criminal Law* (4th edn, 2009, W Green)

Gordon: GH Gordon *The Criminal Law of Scotland* (3rd edn and supplement, edited by Michael G A Christie, 2001, W Green)

Hume: David Hume *Commentaries on the Law of Scotland Respecting the Description and Punishment of Crimes* (2 vols, 1797) (reprinted 1986, Butterworths)

Macdonald: George Macdonald *Practical Treatise on the Criminal Law of Scotland* (1867) (5th edn, 1948, by J Walker and DJ Stevenson)

List of abbreviations

Mackenzie: George Mackenzie *Laws and Customs of Scotland in Matters Criminal* (1678–99)

Smith and Hogan: D Ormerod *Smith and Hogan Criminal Law* (13th edn, 2011, OUP)

Wheatley: A Brown *Wheatley's Road Traffic Law in Scotland* (5th edn, 2014, Bloomsbury Professional)

Part I
GENERAL PRINCIPLES

Chapter 1

The sources of Scots criminal law

1.1   The criminal law of Scotland is a combination of common and statutory law. Many crimes are still based on common law, this being the case with
serious crimes (such as murder) as well as with the less serious crimes (such as
breach of the peace). Common law has tended to be a more important source
of criminal law in Scotland than it has been in England. In most jurisdictions in
which the criminal law is uncodified there is a draft code available for discussion
and possible enactment. There is no official draft criminal code in Scotland,
although in 2003 a group of distinguished academics, with the encouragement
of the Scottish Law Commission, produced a draft criminal code[1], which has
been mentioned with approval by the High Court[2]. Scotland remains one of
the very few jurisdictions in which an uncodified system of criminal justice
is applied. The growing number of statutory offences touch upon areas previously exclusively governed by the common law[3]. Some new statutory offences
are of course completely novel, particularly where the criminal law addresses
a problem thrown up by changed social habits or by advances in technology.
The Misuse of Drugs Act 1971, along with its predecessor Acts, deals with a
problem which criminal lawyers of the nineteenth century simply would not
have recognised. Similarly, the Human Organ Transplants Act 1989 and the
Computer Misuse Act 1990 create offences which for obvious reasons had no
equivalent in the common law. Some concern has been expressed that the period
since 2000 has seen an unnecessary increase in legislation[4], with Scotland in
particular seen as introducing a disproportionate amount of criminal offences[5].

1 See www.scotlawcom.gov.uk/files/5712/8024/7006/cp_criminal_code.pdf See also Clive; Codification of Scots Criminal Law 2008 SCL 747.
2 See *Petto v HMA* 2012 JC 105, where the Lord Justice Clerk said in connection with the mental
   state required for murder 'In recent years, the authors of the draft Criminal Code for Scotland
   have greatly assisted our thinking on the matter'.
3 Examples include legislation on sexual offences (the Sexual Offences (Scotland) Act 2009) and
   legislation dealing with conduct also covered by the common law crime of breach of the peace
   (The Criminal Justice and Licensing (Scotland) Act 2010, s 38).
4 Article; The drafting of criminal legislation – need it be so impenetrable?' Professor JR Spencer
   2008 Camb LR 585.
5 'Scotland: twice as much criminal law as England', Chalmers and Leverick 2013 Edin LR 376.

1.2   The preponderance of common law offences in Scots criminal law
was regarded as one of its strong points. The fact that certain offences in Scots
law are broadly defined and are not constrained by the language of statute
could mean that the courts were able to deal with novel issues in a flexible and
responsive way. But the supposed advantage of responsiveness must be set
against the argument that the broad definition offends the principle of legality,
that principle which requires that there be a clear statement in advance of what
conduct is criminal, a principle that is enshrined in the European Convention
on Human Rights under Article 7, discussed later. The broader the definition,

3

or the fuzzier its borders, the greater the potential doubt as to the precise ambit of the criminal law. Scots law did not actually require that criminal conduct be specifically labelled with a *nomen iuris*, or the name of a crime. Some forms of conduct were criminal even if they had no special name; all that was required was that the conduct be clearly enough described in the indictment in which the nature of the alleged infraction of the criminal law was set out for the information of the accused person and the court[1].

The common law of crime is based on custom, as embodied in the decisions of the criminal courts. Romano-canonical sources were important in the development of Scots criminal law, with the criminal courts making frequent references to texts of Roman law and to the works of jurists in the European civilian tradition. By the end of the eighteenth century, however, such sources were of secondary importance, domestic Scottish authorities being considered more pertinent. The earlier influence of Roman law was sufficient to place pre-eighteenth century Scots law in a reasonably close intellectual relationship with its continental counterparts, but this proximity was irretrievably shattered by the movement to criminal law codification which occurred in the nineteenth century. As a result of this, Scots criminal law cannot easily be classified in comparative terms. It is not a typical system of the Anglo-American tradition (where codification is now the norm); nor has it much in common with the codified criminal law systems of civil law countries in Europe and elsewhere. In some respects it is close to English criminal law, particularly where UK statutes are involved, but there are nonetheless substantial differences between the criminal law of the two jurisdictions, and superficial similarities may be misleading. The Scots law of murder, for example, differs markedly from its English law counterpart in the way in which the *mens rea* requirement is defined. The end result may be very similar in many cases, but the process by which a conclusion is reached may be very different.

1 For discussion, see 7 *Stair Memorial Encyclopaedia* para 24.

1.3   For practical purposes the starting point for any investigation of modern Scots criminal law must be the work of the eighteenth-century jurist, David Hume[1]. Hume's *Commentaries on the Law of Scotland Respecting the Description and Punishment of Crimes* was first published between 1797 and 1800, although the commonly used edition is that which appeared in 1844[2]. The particular importance of Hume's treatise lies in the fact that it was written at the end of a period of considerable development in the criminal law and represents a systematisation of an area of the law which had not benefited from the same degree of conceptual organisation as had civil law. Hume was not the first legal writer to turn his attention to the criminal law of Scotland: Sir George Mackenzie's *Laws and Customs of Scotland in Matters Criminal*, which appeared between 1678 and 1699, and William Forbes' *Institutes of the Law of Scotland*, published in 1730, both set out to provide a complete account of the criminal law, but both, for different reasons, had outlived their usefulness by the late eighteenth century.

The authority enjoyed by Hume's work was considerable, both during the nineteenth and twentieth centuries, and into the twenty-first century; it is still not uncommon for it to be cited before the courts today. It is important to bear in mind that although Hume is considered an institutional writer, his work is no more than a statement of the law as it was at the time of his writing, and his views do not have the weight of statute. The courts are therefore prepared to depart from his interpretation of the law, as was the case in *Stallard v HM Advocate*[3], in which the High Court held that social conditions had so changed as to make Hume's views on the subject of the marital exemption in rape unacceptable. Yet the authority which the *Commentary* still enjoys is undoubted, particularly when an issue arises for which there is no modern precedent and which requires court to address a fundamental issue of principle, illustrated for example by reference to Hume in both *Webster v Dominick*[4] (looking at shameless indecency) and *HM Advocate v Purcell*[5] (wicked recklessness), and even in relation to more procedural questions; see *HM Advocate v Thompson*[6] in relation to the requirement for an indictment to call in court.

1 For an account of Hume's legal career, see DM Walker *The Scottish Jurists* (1985, Edinburgh) p 316 et seq. Quotations from Hume have been literally set in stone, in a frieze designed by Gary Breeze which decorates the balcony of the High Court extension in Glasgow.
2 A reprint of this edition was published in 1986: Law Society of Scotland, Edinburgh.
3 1989 SCCR 248, 1989 SLT 469. See also *HM Advocate v Wilson* 1983 SCCR 420 (Hume's views on malicious mischief departed from).
4 2005 1 JC 65, 2003 SLT 975, 2003 SCCR 525; see also *Petto v HMA* 2012 JC 105 at para [19].
5 2008 JC 131, 2008 SLT 44, 2008 SCL 183, 2007 SCCR 520.
6 2010 SLT 509.

1.4   Subsequent writers on the criminal law are cited before the courts, although there is none with the authority of Hume. Archibald Alison's *Principles and Practice of the Criminal Law of Scotland*, published between 1832 and 1833, is referred to from time to time, but is not considered a work of major significance. There has been great reliance on John Macdonald's *Practical Treatise on the Criminal Law of Scotland*, which ran to many editions from the time of its first publication in 1867. The edition currently used by the courts is the fifth edition, which appeared in 1948. In spite of its limitations, this work has had an undoubted status as the *vade mecum* of practitioners for over a century, and is still extensively referred to. Sir Thomas Smith's *Short Commentary on the Law of Scotland*, which was published in 1962, was primarily concerned with civil law, but dealt with criminal matters as well, and played a major part in reawakening interest in theoretical aspects of Scots criminal law. But the real credit for this must go to Sheriff Gordon's magisterial work, *The Criminal Law of Scotland*[1]. This book, which is in the highest traditions of criminal law scholarship, is in daily use in Scottish criminal courts and law practices and also enjoys a considerable reputation not only within the High Court of Justiciary but in the supreme courts of other jurisdictions. *The Laws of Scotland: Stair Memorial Encyclopaedia*, an ambitious survey of the entire sweep of Scots law also contains an important modern statement of criminal law[2] and may usefully be a first port of call to those seeking authoritative commentary and citations to a wide range of criminal law sources.

The real source of the law, of course, is not the textbook but the decisions of the courts. The common law of crimes is located in the judgments of the High Court and, to a lesser extent, those of sheriff courts. To these sources

will be added decisions of the Sheriff Appeal Court, an innovation introduced by the Courts Reform (Scotland) Act 2014 which came into being on
22 September 2015 to deal with all summary criminal appeals[3]. There is a
wealth of criminal law decisions to quarry, but in practice it is unusual for
a modern court to go back to decisions which were made earlier than the
nineteenth century. On most issues, where relevant Scottish precedents are
to be found, these will occur in twentieth-century reports, although it may
sometimes be necessary to refer to decisions made in the late nineteenth
century. This is not to say that older authorities are irrelevant; much will
depend on the subject matter. On a question of statutory liability, for example,
the relevant decisions will inevitably be modern, the reason for this being
that the issue of strict liability has only been discussed by the courts since
an appreciable body of statutory criminal law came into existence during
the twentieth century.

1   (3rd edn, 2001) edited by Michael Christie. Sheriff Gordon is rightly regarded as significant
    in the development of Scots Criminal Law. His contribution was marked by the publication of
    Essays in Criminal Law in his honour, Edinburgh University Press 2010.
2   There is also an ongoing commentary on the law and practice arising from articles appearing in
    publications such as SLT, SCL, Edin LR and JLSS, together with case commentaries or com-
    ments in SLT, SCCR and SCL which, although without the authority of *Gordon*, help inform and
    enlighten the courts.
3   Sections 46–62.

1.5   The influence of English sources on Scots law generally has been the
subject of some controversy. Scots criminal law was not historically subject to
appeal to the House of Lords, and was not therefore subject to interpretation
by English judges. However, the availability of the Judicial Committee of the
Privy Council (a jurisdiction now assumed by the Supreme Court) as a court of
appeal in relation to devolution issues has meant that Scottish Criminal procedure and practice, and even the substantive law have been subject to scrutiny[1].
Criminal law has also been, by its very nature, more local in character, and the
mercantile influences which tend to uniformity in commercial law, do not operate in this area. At the same time, there has always undoubtedly been a degree
of English law influence, both terminological and substantive, a matter upon
which Hume himself expressed concern. Scots lawyers use the terms *mens rea*
and *actus reus*, as do their counterparts in systems based on English law, and
the old Scots equivalent of *mens rea*, dole, seems largely to have disappeared[2].
In matters of substance there have been instances in which the courts have
imported English legal decisions into Scots law, occasionally somewhat controversially, as in the case of *Meek v HM Advocate*[3], where Scots law was said
to be the same as English law in respect of error in rape, a position which conflicted with a well-established body of Scottish decisions on the requirements
of error[4]. In the Supreme Court decision of *McInnes v HM Advocate*[5], the court
had to consider the question of whether the failure to disclose information
gave rise to unfairness. Lord Brown, an English member of the court said,
after discussing the facts: 'This, I apprehend, would be the position in English
law (both as to the test to be applied – in England as to whether the conviction
under appeal is unsafe – and as to the decision being one for the appeal court
itself) and I can see no good reason why it should be any different under Scottish law.'

Standing these comments and having regard to the decision of the Supreme Court in *Allison v HM Advocate*[6] concern has been expressed that more recent cases have shifted the constitutional position, and that the Supreme Court has consolidated a general appellate jurisdiction in the Supreme Court[7]. The decision in *Cadder v HMA*[8] seemed to fortify that trend. The Supreme Court overturned a decision of a seven-judge bench in connection with the safeguards available to an accused.

The comparative self-sufficiency of Scots law in relation to criminal law sources does not preclude the need to refer to cases from other jurisdictions. The ingenuity of criminal accused – or their solicitors or counsel – means that novel points will always arise. Such issues may be settled on the basis of pure principle, or on the basis of authority, and a precedent-based system invariably looks to the latter. A small jurisdiction will have a relatively limited range of criminal decisions to which reference might be made, and in these circumstances the decisions of other jurisdictions will be useful. Most frequent reference is made to English decisions, for reasons of convenience, but there is no reason why the decisions of other Commonwealth jurisdictions should not carry weight. This is particularly the case with Canadian and Australian decisions, where a great deal of judicial attention has been paid to the principled development of the criminal law. Examination of the decisions of other jurisdictions may also assist to identify areas where one's own laws are defective or in need of reform. The usefulness of such comparators was emphasised by the Lord Justice Clerk in *Petto v HMA*[9] when he said:

'It is regrettable that in this appeal, heard by five judges, in which the Crown sought to establish an important principle, the Advocate-depute relied almost exclusively on Scottish sources, referred briefly to some English case law and failed to refer us to any decisions on this familiar fact-situation in other English speaking jurisdictions … From my own researches … I have the impression that other English-speaking jurisdictions may have attained greater maturity in their jurisprudence on this topic than Scotland has. In Scotland we have a definitional structure in which the mental element in homicide is defined with the use of terms such as wicked, evil, felonious, depraved and so on, which may impede rather than conduce to analytical accuracy[10].

The courts have additionally now to take account of any judgment, decision, declaration or advisory opinion of the European Court of Human Rights, in terms of s 2 of the Human Rights Act 1998. This applies where a court is determining a question which has arisen in relation with a right relating to the European Convention on Human Rights (ECHR). Given the spread of the convention rights and the need for the courts and the prosecuting authorities to comply with the convention, together with the need for national courts to refrain from interpreting the criminal law to the detriment of accused, the reference to such case law is an important component in the courts' general interpretation of the law.

The courts in Scotland had been reluctant to consider ECHR case law as an aid to interpretation of the law. In *Kaur v The Lord Advocate*[11] (a case challenging a deportation order), Lord Ross held that, as the ECHR was not part of the municipal law of the United Kingdom, the Scottish courts were not entitled to have regard to it, either as an aid to construction or otherwise. However, in *T Petitioner*[12] (a case involving an application to adopt by a homosexual male), the Lord Justice General said that Lord Ross's opinion 'had been increasingly outdated ... and ... it is time that it was expressly departed from'. He held that it was appropriate to use the ECHR as an aid to construction in areas of ambiguity. The Scotland Act 1998 required the Scottish Government to act in a way compatible with the ECHR; finally on 2 October 2000, the Human Rights Act 1998 came into force, imposing the s 2 obligation.

The Scottish approach was originally described as follows in *Mclean v HMA*[13] at paragraph [29]:

'Section 2(1)(a) of the Human Rights Act 1998 requires us to "take into account" judgments of the Court. It has been observed that the House of Lords, sitting as a final court of appeal in an English process of judicial review, "will not without good reason depart from the principles laid down in a carefully considered judgment of the [European] court sitting as a Grand Chamber" (*R (Anderson)* v *Home Secretary* [2003] 1 AC 837, per Lord Bingham of Cornhill at para 18) ... In the present case the United Kingdom was not a party to the process in *Salduz v Turkey* [2009 49 EHRR 19]. Although a British judge was a member of the Grand Chamber, there is no suggestion in any of the opinions that either he or any of his fellow judges had brought to their attention any features of Scottish criminal procedure – although the Scottish system had previously been examined by the Commission without adverse comment (*Robson* v *United Kingdom* (1996) Application no 25648/94; *Windsor* v *United Kingdom* (1988) Application no 13081/87). The implications for that system cannot be said to have been "carefully considered". In these circumstances we are of opinion that, while the judgment in *Salduz* commands great respect, we are not obliged to apply it directly in Scotland'.

However, that seven-judge decision was comprehensively overturned in *Cadder*[14]; and the observations in Mclean must be seen in that light. In determining that the Strasbourg jurisdiction was clear, Lord Rodger said:

'A right of access to a lawyer, which is implied in order to protect a right at the heart of the notion of a fair procedure under Art 6, must itself lie near that heart. For this reason, in my view there is not the remotest chance that the European Court would find that, because of the other protections that Scots law provides for accused persons, it is compatible with Art 6(1) and (3)(c) for the Scottish system to omit this safeguard – which the Committee for the Prevention of Torture regards as 'fundamental' – and for suspects to be routinely questioned without having the right to consult a lawyer first. On this matter Strasbourg has spoken: the courts in this country have no real option but to apply the law which it has laid down.'

The comments fortify the need for Scottish courts to give the appropriate weight to Strasbourg jurisprudence.

1   The Scotland Act 1998, s 98 and Sch 6 as amended by the Constitutional Reform Act 2005.
2   See Shiels, 'The unsettled relevance of dole 2010' SCL 421.

3 1982 SCCR 613, 1983 SLT 280.
4 The Scottish courts will also take into account English decisions in sentencing matters where there is an overlap in the crimes concerned. A good example is *HM Advocate v Graham*, [2010] HCJAC 50 in which substantial reference was made to the English approach to sentencing in the making of indecent images of children.
5 [2010] UKSC 7.
6 [2010] UKSC 6.
7 See article by Aidan O'Neill QC 'End o' anither auld sang?' JLSS March 2010.
8 2011 SC (UKSC) 13.
9 2012 JC 105, 2011 SLT 1043, 2011 SCL 850; 2011 SCCR 519.
10 2012 JC 105.
11 1981 SLT 322 at 330.
12 1997 SLT 724.
13 2010 SLT 73, 2010 SCL 166.
14 At para [93].

THE ROLE OF CRIMINAL STATUTES

1.6   Although Scots criminal law may be predominantly of a common law nature, statutes nevertheless play an increasingly major part in the criminal law, even, it has been argued, a disproportionate amount[1]. There has been some debate as to the precise place of minor statutory offences in the scheme of the criminal law: are such breaches of the law to be considered crimes (in the true sense of the word) or are they merely 'non-criminal offences'? There certainly exists a moral distinction in the minds of most people between those acts which are intrinsically and profoundly wrong – such as murder – and those acts which are either trivial or technical breaches of the law – such as parking offences. This distinction is certainly mirrored in the sentencing patterns of the courts, but it is not necessarily reflected in the way in which crimes are classified or described in the law. There is a tendency to describe minor infringements of the law as 'offences' rather than as crimes, but the term 'offence' is also used in relation to serious breaches. Nor will the seriousness of an infringement be determined by whether or not it is punished by common law or statute. Many statutory offences involve morally reprehensible conduct, and may anyway be based on earlier common law crimes. This is the case, for example, with some of the offences specified in sexual offence legislation.

On balance, it is preferable to describe as crimes only those infringements of the criminal law which attract moral opprobrium. This would mean that the stigma which goes with conviction of a crime is reserved for those who really deserve it. The term 'offence' will probably continue to be used indiscriminately, but it only acquires real moral force in the appropriate context, when it is linked with a morally reprehensible act (such as assault, theft, murder and the like).

For a considerable period there was a marked tendency in English-speaking jurisdictions to interpret penal statutes restrictively, that is, in favour of the accused. The origins of this are to be found in judicial attempts during the nine-teenth century to limit the Draconian effects of laws which provided for the death penalty for even comparatively minor infringements of the criminal law. Penal statutes are now interpreted according to the same canons of construction as are applied to other statutes, but if, at the end, there remains an element

9

of doubt as to whether the conduct of the accused falls within the scope of the statute, this doubt will be resolved in favour of the accused. In every case the question will be whether the conduct of the accused can reasonably be said to have infringed the law according to the ordinary meaning of the language used in the statute. The courts will not speculate on what the intention of the legislature must have been: the test is what the legislature actually said in the statute.

It should be noted that on occasion the common law and statutory provisions overlap. The most obvious is the charging of an accused with a common law offence which is aggravated by his being on bail, in terms of s 27 of the Criminal Procedure (Scotland) Act 1995. Other forms of aggravation have been established by statute. Accordingly an offence such as assault can be charged as aggravated under s 96 of the Crime and Disorder Act 1998 (racially aggravated offences); under s 74 of the Criminal Justice (Scotland) Act 2003 (religiously aggravated offences); and aggravations relating to disability, sexual orientation and transgender status under the Offences (Aggravation by Prejudice) (Scotland) Act 2008. The effect of all of these is to allow the aggravation to be formally reflected in conviction and sentence.

1 'Scotland: twice as much criminal law as England, Chalmers and Leverick' 2013 Edin LR 376.

THE DECLARATORY POWER

1.7 A historical source of criminal law was the declaratory power of the High Court. This was the power vested in the High Court to declare conduct to be a crime, even if it has not previously been considered to be criminal. This power was exercised retrospectively; it was therefore possible that a person could act on sound legal advice that what he was doing was not criminal, only to discover subsequently that he was to be penalised. The extent to which this infringes the principle of legality is self-evident, and will be discussed further below.

The *locus classicus* of the declaratory power in the nineteenth century is the case of *Bernard Greenhuff*[1]. Greenhuff had been convicted of running a gaming house in which cards were played, a form of conduct which clearly offended at least some moral sensibilities at the time. There was one strong dissenting opinion in this case, but for the majority of the judges there was no question but that this was conduct which implied the greatest social danger and which therefore justified the invocation of the declaratory power. It was accepted, though, that this power should be used sparingly. As one of the judges, Lord Mackenzie, put it, 'In order to bring any act within the jurisdiction of this court, as a crime … the act must either in itself be so grossly immoral and mischievous on the face of it, that no man can fairly be ignorant of its nature, or it must have been settled by a course of experience, and become notorious, that such is its nature'[2]. In no other nineteenth-century case is the declaratory power used so openly. The bounds of criminal liability were, of course, extended, but this tended to be achieved through the technique of bringing novel forms of criminal conduct within the categories of existing offences[3]. Bringing the facts of conduct within the ambit of existing criminal offences is an unexceptionable procedure, and necessary if the criminal law is to avoid an undesirable status.

This was emphasised in the case of *Khaliq v HM Advocate*[4] in which Lord Justice-General Emslie quoted with approval the dictum of Lord Cockburn in his dissenting judgment in *Greenhuff*: 'An old crime may certainly be committed in a new way; and a case, though never occurring before on its facts, may fall within the spirit of a previous decision, or within an established general principle'[5]. There are nevertheless limits to this process. In particular, it should not result in unforeseeable criminal liability. If it does, it is subject to precisely the same criticisms as is the declaratory power.

1 (1838) 2 Swin 236.
2 At 268.
3 See William Fraser (1847) Arkley 280 in which the accused faced a fraud charge of obtaining sexual intercourse by pretending to be the victim's husband. See also *Holmes and Lockyer* (1869) 1 Coup 221. There is a discussion of this and other nineteenth-century cases in Gordon para 1–24.
4 1983 SCCR 483, 1984 JC 23.
5 1984 JC 23 at 32.

1.8   The existence of the declaratory power was reasserted in the twentieth century, most unambiguously in the case of *Grant v Allan*[1] but the court nevertheless declined to use the power. In a number of modern cases the courts have in effect created new crimes, but have not done so on the basis of the declaratory power. Two cases in particular demonstrate this: *Strathern v Seaforth*[2] and *McLaughlan v Boyd*[3]. In *Strathern* the crime of the clandestine taking and using of another's property was created, the grounds for this being the adverse social consequences of failing to punish such conduct; in *McLaughlan*, a case which for some time left a much more significant mark on the law, the crime of shameless indecency was recognised by the court. In the latter case, Lord Justice-General Clyde pointed out that it would be a mistake:

> '... to imagine that the criminal common law of Scotland countenances any precise and exact categorisation of the forms of conduct which amount to crime. It has been pointed out many times in this Court that such is not the nature or quality of the criminal law of Scotland. I need only refer to the well-known passage of Baron Hume's institutional work, in which the broad definition of crime – a doleful or wilful offence against society in the matter of "violence, dishonesty, falsehood, indecency, irreligion" is laid down'[4].

This set remarkably broad boundaries for the criminal law. Although it is clear that precise definition is an unrealistic goal in criminal law and that some offences must be broadly stated (as is the case with theft or assault)[5], it is quite another thing to use broad moral categories, such as dishonesty or falsehood, as the basis of criminalisation. In *Webster v Dominick*[6] a bench of five judges 'put right' the law by disapproving of the crime of shameless indecency and re-categorising it as public indecency; in doing so they were critical of both the decision and thought processes of *McLaughlan,* describing it as introducing a 'confusion of ideas', as 'misguided', 'surprising' and asserting that 'The Lord Justice-General wrested the statement [by Hume] from its context as a basis for a general proposition that was insupportable.' However, the potential difficulty arising from such broad categories has been materially affected by the passing of the Human Rights Act 1998 and the Scotland Act 1998. The principle of non-retroactivity of criminal law finds expression in Article 7(1) of the European Convention on Human Rights discussed below.

The clearest modern recognition of the continued existence of the declaratory power is found in the judgment of Lord Justice-Clerk Ross in *Grant v Allan*[7]. The accused, who was employed by a commercial firm, abstracted computerised information relating to clients of the firm and then offered this for sale to a commercial competitor. He was charged with the theft of this information, but objections to the relevancy of the charge were sustained. The court declined to exercise the declaratory power in this case, citing in support of this position Lord Reid's observations in *Shaw v DPP*[8] to the effect that the place to decide on the punishment of immoral acts is Parliament. The judgment made it clear, nonetheless, that the power continued to be available at that time.

1 1987 SCCR 402, 1988 SLT 11.
2 1926 JC 100 1926 SLT 445.
3 1934 JC 19, 1933 SLT 629.
4 1934 JC 19 at 22.
5 But see *Gordon Ross Petitioner* 2015 SLT 617, where Lord Doherty in making the distinction between the criminal law and prosecutorial guidelines said '[T]he certainty required of prosecutorial policy is of a lesser, more indicative, order than the certainty required of provisions which create or identify criminal offences.'
6 2005 1 JC 65, 2003 SLT 975, 2003 SCCR 525.
7 1987 SCCR 402, 1988 SLT 11.
8 [1962] AC 220 at 275.

1.9   But there always were powerful arguments against the continued existence of the declaratory power. There is no doubt that in the formative period of the criminal law, a law-making power on the part of the courts is necessary, especially in the absence of a tradition of legislative activity in this area. That time has long since passed. Parliament can address the new forms of criminality which will require to be considered. This is particularly so now that Scotland has a permanent law reform body, the Scottish Law Commission, which can address in-depth controversial areas of criminal law and make recommendations to the legislature.

The declaratory power always offended the basic legal principle that there should be no criminal offence without clear prior prohibition – *nullum crimen sine lege*. It must be implicit in any acceptable system of rules that what is not prohibited is permissible. If the criminal law does not explicitly prohibit certain forms of conduct, then such conduct may properly be taken to be permitted. It is not open to the courts subsequently to withdraw this implied permission to act once an action has been performed.

If there ever was any argument in favour of it, it was that it prevented serious wrong-doing, in the sense of grossly immoral conduct, from going unpunished, and thereby preserved public confidence in the willingness and ability of the courts to punish wrongdoers. It also served to satisfy the retributive principle; the immoral actor can be said to deserve (in the moral sense) his punishment. Yet the value of the principle of legality outweighs both of these considerations, both of which are open to capricious abuse. Finally, the declaratory power so starkly conflicted with the legal principles which lie at the heart of criminal jurisprudence in the western tradition that its continued existence had become anomalous in a modern legal system. Article 7 renders the declaratory power redundant.

THE HUMAN RIGHTS ACT AND SCOTS CRIMINAL LAW

1.10   The European Convention of Human Rights ('ECHR') was introduced into Scots law by the Scotland Act 1988 and the Human Rights Act 1998. By reason of devolution, from 20 May 1999 the powers of the Scottish Executive or Government were limited by s 57(2) of the Scotland Act 1998, in that they could not perform acts which were incompatible with the ECHR. The Lord Advocate is a member of the government; accordingly any decision to prosecute a case is theoretically challengeable. The Human Rights Act 1998 came into force on the 2 October 2000, imposing responsibility on the courts to act compatibly with the ECHR. Commentators quickly realised that certain offences under Scots criminal law would be susceptible to challenge[1].

The Human Rights Act directly incorporated the ECHR into Scottish law and, as discussed above, in s 2 imposed an obligation on the courts to have regard to the jurisprudence of the European Court of Human Rights. It also provided for declarations of incompatibility in s 4 in the event of any actings by the Executive.

As has been recognised above, Article 7 also affects the substantive law. Article 7 of the Convention provides:

'1. No one shall be held guilty of any criminal offence on account of any act or omission which did not constitute a criminal offence under national or international law at the time when it was committed. Nor shall a heavier penalty be imposed than the one that was applicable at the time the criminal offence was committed.

2. This article shall not prejudice the trial and punishment of any person for any act or omission which, at the time when it was committed, was criminal according to the general principles of law recognised by civilised nations.'

In *SW v The United Kingdom*[2] the European Court of Human Rights said at paragraph 34 and following:

'The guarantee enshrined in Article 7, which is an essential element of the rule of law, occupies a prominent place in the Convention system of protection, as is underlined by the fact that no derogation from it is permissible under Article 15 in time of war or in other public emergency. It should be construed and applied, as follows from its object and purpose in such a way as to provide effective safeguards against arbitrary prosecution, conviction and punishment.'

Accordingly, as the court held in its *Kokkinakis v Greece* judgment of 25 May 1993 ((1994) 17 EHRR 397), Article 7 is not confined to prohibiting the retrospective application of the criminal law to an accused's disadvantage: it also embodies, more generally, the principle that only the law can define a crime and prescribe a penalty (*nullum crimen nulla poena sine lege*) and the principle that the criminal law must not be extensively construed to an accused's detriment, for instance by analogy. From these principles, it follows that an offence must be clearly defined in the law. In its aforementioned judgment the court added that this requirement is satisfied where the individual can know from the wording of the relevant provision and, if need be, with the assistance of the courts' interpretation of it, what acts and omissions will make him criminally liable. The court thus indicated what when speaking of 'law' Article 7 alludes to the very same concept as that to which the Convention refers elsewhere when using that term, a concept which comprises written as well as unwritten law and implies qualitative requirements, notably those of accessibility and foreseeability.

However clearly drafted a legal provision may be, in any system of law, including criminal law, there is an inevitable element of judicial interpretation. There will always be a need for elucidation of doubtful points and for adaptations to changing circumstances. Indeed, in the United Kingdom, as in the other Convention States, the progressive development of the criminal law through judicial law making is a well-entrenched and necessary part of legal tradition. Article 7 of the Convention cannot be read as outlawing the gradual clarification of the rules of criminal liability through judicial interpretation from case to case, provided that the resultant development is consistent with the essence of the offence and could reasonably be foreseen. This was referred to with approval by the High Court in *Smith v Donnelly*[3].

Article 7 has as its primary concern the retrospective imposition of criminal liability. In the first place, it is apparent that the declaratory power of the High Court discussed above at paragraph 1.9 would not conform to Article 7. However, Article 7 extends further than either retrospective criminal liability or the declaration of new crimes. It also has been interpreted as requiring crimes to be clearly defined in law. The law has to be accessible and must be formulated with enough precision to enable citizens to foresee and consider the consequences which a given action might entail[4].

Accordingly, common law crime must be accessible, intelligible and foreseeable. The excellent *Guide to Human Rights Law in Scotland*[5] should be consulted for further study.

The substantive criminal law was discussed in *Brown v Stott*[6]. In that case the challenge was to s 172 of the Road Traffic Act 1988 whereby a person questioned by the police has an obligation to name the driver of a vehicle. This was challenged under Article 6 of the Convention which provides a right against self-incrimination. It was argued that such a right precluded the use of any admission under s 172. This matter was eventually decided by the Privy Council who determined that an admission obtained under s 172 did not breach an Article 6 right, since the right against self-incrimination was not an absolute right and had to be balanced against clear public interest, in this case the enforcement of the road traffic legislation in order to address the high incidence of death and injury on roads caused by the misuse of motor vehicles. The Privy Council emphasised that a trial judge maintained the right to exclude admission where there were suggestions of unfairness or coercion or oppression. Essentially, s 172 was part of a regime which was a proportionate response to the problems of maintaining road safety and anyone who owned or drove a car knowingly subjected themselves to that regime.

The crime of breach of the peace had been seen by some as ripe for consideration when seen through the prism of the ECHR[7]. The High Court considered
the matter in *Smith v Donnelly*[8]. The accused was charged with a breach of the
peace by lying in front of a military convoy, impeding its passage. She argued
that the definition of the crime had been developed and expanded to the point
that it was a meaningless charge and incompatible with Article 7. The court
reviewed a number of authorities, deciding that the definition of the crime
found in the principal authorities met the requirements of the ECHR. However,
in recognising the new era of ECHR compatibility, the court concluded: 'We
would add that it seems to us that … it will normally be proper, now that regard
must be had to the Convention, to specify the conduct said to form the breach
of the peace in a charge …'.

In *Donnelly and Walsh v PF Edinburgh*[9], the accused were convicted after
singing a sectarian song at a football game; the High Court dealt with an appeal
about whether their rights under Article 7 had been infringed, not by reason of
the definition of the offence (under s 1 of the Offensive Behaviour at Football
etc (Scotland) Act 2012), but rather because the accused did not know that their
rendition of a particular song could be offensive. The Lord Justice Clerk dealt
with Article 7 referring to *SW v United Kingdom*[10] as follows:

'Article 7 "embodies the principle that only the law can define a crime and
prescribe a penalty"… An offence must be clearly defined. This requirement
is satisfied where the individual can know from the wording of the relevant
provision and, if need be, with the assistance of the court's interpretation
of it, what acts and omissions will make him criminally liable … Judicial
interpretation to produce clarity is legitimate if the resultant development
"is consistent with the essence of the offence and could reasonably have
been foreseen" (SW para 36).'

So, it can be seen that if the provisions of an act have been subject to interpretation, an accused is deemed to know that. In the circumstances of Donnelly, the
particular song had been deemed as potentially criminal in an earlier case; the
court held the accused must be taken to be aware of that.

1   See article by Timothy Jones 2000 SLT (News) 95 for general observations, and article by
    Pamela Ferguson 'Breach of the peace and the ECHR' 2001 Edin LR 5 for a detailed critique
    of the crime and its apparent incompatibility with the Convention. See Chapter 12 for further
    discussion.
2   (1996) 21 EHRR 363.
3   2002 JC 65, 2001 SLT 1007, 2001 SCCR 800.
4   *Sunday Times v United Kingdom* (1979) 2 EHRR 245, para 49.
5   *Reed and Murdoch* (3rd Edition, 2011) Bloomsbury Professional.
6   2000 SLT 379.
7   See article by Pamela Ferguson 'Breach of the peace and the ECHR' 2001 Edin LR 5.
8   2002 JC 65, 2001 SLT 1007, 2001 SCCR 800.
9   2015 HCJAC 35.
10 (1996) 21 EHRR 363.

THE CLASSIFICATION OF CRIMES

1.11   There is no officially endorsed classification of crimes in Scots criminal law. *Hume* follows no particular overall system, while *Macdonald's* princi-

pal distinction is between those offences which may attract a capital or prison sentence and those offences which are 'not truly crimes' (welfare or regulatory offences). The latter are inevitably statutory, but it is unhelpful to make a firm distinction between statutory and common law offences in that the subject matter of each category may overlap. There are certain statutory offences which deal with topics traditionally dealt with by the common law. Similarly, the mental requirement in statutory and common law offences may be the same: not all statutory offences are offences of strict liability. For this reason, any classification may include offences of either type within the same category.

The following classification takes into account the nature of the interest which the criminal law seeks to protect:

(1) Crimes against the person. The highest value which the law seeks to protect is that of human life. Crimes against the person range from minor assaults to murder.

(2) Crimes against property. This is a broad category, including not only those crimes in which the property of others is wrongfully appropriated by another, but also those crimes which entail the wrongful destruction of property.

(3) Crimes against the state. The interests protected by this category of crimes are state interest in security and good government.

(4) Public order and public morality crimes. No single personal interest may be compromised by such crimes, but the community as a whole may be said to be harmed by criminal activity of this nature.

(5) Regulatory offences. These offences (rarely called crimes) are those which infringe laws required for the administration of a complex modern society. They include pollution and factory regulations, road traffic law, and other similar material. The breach of such regulations may be minor, or it may have profound adverse consequences (as in a serious pollution offence, which may have a major effect on the property of others and on the environment in general).

The classification of crimes according to the interests protected is the scheme which has been favoured, in one form or another, by both civilian jurists and those in the Anglo-American tradition. Roman law tended to classify crimes more on the basis of which harm was perpetrated than on the basis of the harmed interest, but by the time of jurists such as Voet and Matthaeus, the focus had shifted to interests. The classifications of English law have ranged from the terse, tripartite system of JF Stephen's *History of the Criminal Law of England*[1] (offences against the persons of individuals; offences against the property of individuals; and offences against public rights) to the ten-part scheme of *Russell on Crime*[2]. Most modern penal codes in the continental tradition favour a classification not dissimilar to that proposed above, although it is not unusual to find categories of offence which have no direct counterpart in the English-speaking world. An example is the category of 'crimes against the family', found as a separate category in the Italian and related codes[3].

1 1883.
2 JWC Turner (ed) (12th edn, 1964).
3 *Codice Penale*, arts 556–574 (Italy).

THE TERRITORIAL SCOPE OF CRIMINAL LAW

1.12   Scots criminal law observes the territorial principle. This means that the courts are principally concerned with crimes which are committed within Scotland; criminal acts committed elsewhere are not normally the concern of the Scottish courts. Difficult issues may arise, however, in the following circumstances: where an act is committed in Scotland which takes effect outwith Scotland; or where an act committed abroad takes effect in Scotland.

An act performed in Scotland which has criminal consequences in another country may in certain circumstances be triable in Scotland. If the act itself amounts to a criminal offence according to the law of Scotland, then that criminal offence will of course be triable in Scotland. If the act performed in Scotland does not of itself amount to an offence, then the Scots courts would still have jurisdiction, provided that the 'main act' element of the offence has been performed in Scotland.

The term 'main act' appears in *Hume* in a discussion of cross-border crimes.

'If one compose and print a libel in England and circulate it here, or if one forge a deed abroad and utter it here, certainly the proper Courts for the trial of such a case are those of this country, since it is here that the main act is done which completes the crime .... it may plausibly be argued that he shall be subjected to the same course of trial who shall write an incendiary letter in England, and put it in a course of conveyance, thence by means of which it is received by the person to whom it is addressed in Scotland'[1].

The meaning of 'main act' seems clear enough in the context of the first two examples; the accused performs within Scotland those acts which constitute the definitional elements of the offence. Hume goes further than this, stating that a person who acts outwith Scotland, but whose act takes effect within Scotland, may still be triable before a Scottish court. In such a case, of course, no 'main act' is done within Scotland, unless 'main act' is taken as being synonymous with 'main effect'. Certainly Hume accepts that there will be jurisdiction where a crime takes effect, as the passage quoted above demonstrates. In *John Thomas Witherington*[2] it was held that the High Court had jurisdiction in a case where a fraudulent order for goods was written in England and posted to Scotland, where it was acted upon. The ratio of this decision is the fact that the effect of the fraud was felt in Scotland; it was there that the victim acted upon the representation and there that the damage occurred. Hume's 'main act' passage was referred to, but it is clear that the court was more concerned with the issue of where the crime is completed. This would appear to be a 'taking effect' theory rather than a 'main act' theory.

The 'main act' theory is supported by Macdonald[3], and was specifically approved by the Court of Criminal Appeal in *Laird v HM Advocate*[4]. In *Laird* the accused had been convicted of fraud in respect of a scheme which they had concocted in Scotland but which involved the making of fraudulent representations in England. The exchange of the goods which formed the basis of the fraudulent scheme, together with the payment of the purchase price, took place in England, both of which facts were taken into account in holding that the 'main act' was located in Scotland. There is no confusion in this case of notions of 'main act' and 'main effect', but the court nonetheless appeared to take a broad view of what amounts to a 'main act'. Indeed, one of the judgments in *Laird* goes so far as to suggest that the taking of an initial step in Scotland would be sufficient to establish jurisdiction for the Scottish courts.

1 II, 54.
2 (1881) 4 Coup 475, (1881) 8 R(J) 41.
3 *Macdonald* p 191. For discussion, see *Gordon* para 3–43, and PW Ferguson 'Jurisdiction and criminal law in Scotland and England' 1987 (32) JR 179.
4 1984 SCCR 469, 1985 JC 37.

1.13   The root of the problem for Scots law here is that the term 'main act' is used loosely by Hume, and later by Macdonald, both of whom seem to consider it to be equivalent to, or at least not exclusive of, 'main effect'. The main act theory provides a theory of jurisdiction which is not incompatible with the principle of territoriality, but it cannot be combined with a main effect theory without implying concurrent jurisdiction. The main act may be committed in country **A** and the main effect felt in country **B**. If both theories are applied, then jurisdiction may be exercised by the courts in both **A** and **B**, which offends the principle of territoriality.

There is ample Scottish authority for the proposition that jurisdiction lies where the criminal act has its effect. This is the tenor of Hume's approach, and this finds judicial support in *HM Advocate v Allan*[1], *HM Advocate v Bradbury*[2], and *Witherington*[3]. In the English courts, where the issue has received close judicial attention, there has been a consistent application of the rule that jurisdiction is to be exercised where the crime takes effect[4]. This approach may place certain limitations on the ability of the courts to punish acts which cause harmful consequences abroad, but it at least avoids difficulties that may arise out of the differences which exist between substantive systems of criminal law. A person may perform in Scotland an act which takes effect abroad, but the effect abroad might not amount to a crime in the law of Scotland. Is he then to be charged with an offence which forms no part of Scots law? This would be unacceptable. It could be argued, however, that the main act theory applies only in relation to those crimes which are crimes under Scots law. This certainly deals with the objection, but the theory is still open to the charge that it potentially busies the Scottish courts with crimes which are primarily the concern of another jurisdiction. It may be that a conscientious state has this obligation, but if this is so, it is an obligation which has in the past received only very cautious recognition, and any extension of the obligation should arguably be achieved through the statutory development of extra-territorial jurisdiction. This has been achieved in the case of terrorist, drug and aviation offences, and it may be that international fraud is an appropriate case for similar treatment[5].

One statue gives an example of the requirement for a more outward looking approach; the Protection of Children (Scotland) Act 2005 provides that it is an offence for a person who has met or communicated with a child before, to intentionally meet or communicates with, or travel to meet, or arrange to meet, the child with intention to either engage in sexual activity with the child, or in the child's presence. There must be a 'Scottish connection', which is met if a meeting or travelling or making of arrangements or any part of it takes place in Scotland[6]. Similarly, s 11A of the Criminal Procedure (Scotland) Act 1995 provides that conspiracy in Scotland to commit an offence outwith the United Kingdom is in itself an offence, so long as the purpose of the conspiracy would itself constitute an offence in the place intended as the site.

1 (1873) 2 Coup 402.
2 (1972) 2 Coup 311.
3 (1881) 4 Coup 475.
4 *R v Treacy* [1971] AC 537, [1973] 1 All ER 940; *R v Doot* [1973] AC 807.
5 For drug trafficking, see W Gilmore 'Combatting international drugs trafficking: the 1988 UN Convention against illicit traffic in narcotic drugs and psychotropic substances' (Commonwealth Secretariat, 1991, London). Under the Criminal Justice (International Co-operation) Act 1990, the Scottish courts have jurisdiction in respect of drugs being smuggled on foreign vessels on the High Seas.
6 Section 1.

THE TEMPORAL SCOPE OF THE CRIMINAL LAW

1.14   Many legal systems provide for the prescription of many, even if not all, criminal offences after a specified period of time has elapsed from the commission of the offence. Scots criminal law has no such period in respect of common law crimes[1], and it is therefore open to the courts to convict a person of crimes committed decades before the framing of any indictment or complaint, a matter which has been reflected in the preponderance of historic sexual abuse cases with which the High Court deals[2]. A major difficulty with prosecutions brought in respect of crimes committed many years previously is that of obtaining reliable evidence. One justification for prosecuting what offences of this nature lies in the significance which the victims of such offences attach to the bringing of the perpetrator to justice. Against that, in the overwhelming majority of legal systems, the principle adopted is that most crimes, with the exception of homicide, prescribe – sometimes within fairly brief periods.

1 *Sugden v HM Advocate* 1934 JC 103.
2 According to Scottish Government statistics 'Sexual crimes increased by 12%, from 7,693 in 2012–13 to 8,604 in 2013–14. Sexual crimes have been on an upwards trend since 2008–09, However this increase is likely due to an increase in reporting, including reporting of historic crimes, as victims find the courage to come forward and report such crimes to the police.' See http://news.scotland.gov.uk/News/Recorded-Crime-in-Scotland-2013-14-129d. aspx#downloads.

1.15   An important qualification to the principle of the non-prescription of common law offences existed; the trial judge had a discretion to bring a halt to a prosecution if the lapse of time between commission and prosecution seems oppressive to the accused person[1]. The introduction into Scots Law of the ECHR brought a sharper focus to the issue. Article 6 of the Convention provides that accused persons are entitled to a trial within a 'reasonable time'. There was a flurry of cases after the introduction of this provision seeking to challenge delays in the prosecution system; one example will suffice. In *R v HM Advocate*[2] the question of delay culminated in a reference to the Privy Council (now the Supreme Court). The accused was charged with offences of indecency. There had been delays in the prosecution. The Privy Council held that by virtue of the Scotland Act 1998, s 57(2) the Lord Advocate had no power to do any act incompatible with the Convention rights of an accused. Therefore, once it was established that there had been an unreasonable delay in the prosecution of the case against an accused, the court had no discretion; it was obliged to dismiss the charges from the indictment. The rights enshrined in Article 6(1), including the 'reasonable time' guarantee, covered all stages of proceedings from the laying of the charge to its determination. Although the threshold for determining an unreasonable delay was high[3], once it had been crossed it was inevitable that the proceedings should be terminated. On the facts in *R*, there had been a delay of about five years for which there was no reasonable explanation.

Statutory offences may specify a prescriptive period after which a prosecution may not be brought. If there is no such period stated, and the offence is one which is triable summarily, then the prescriptive period is six months[4].

1 *McFadyen v Annan* 1992 JC 53; 1992 SLT 162, a decision of a bench of five judges.
2 2003 SC (PC) 21; 2003 SLT 4; 2003 SCCR 19.
3 *Dyer v Watson* [2002] UKPC D 1.
4 Criminal Procedure (Scotland) Act 1995, s 136.

CRIMINAL LAW AND MORALITY: THE LIMITS OF INTERVENTION

1.16 One of the most important issues in criminal law theory is that of the proper scope of the criminal law. The positivist would argue that the boundaries of the criminal law are determined by those acts which are actually punishable by the courts. That action is criminal, then, which breaches a provision of the criminal law, whether statutory or common law in origin. All other acts, no matter how immoral they may be, are not criminal. This points to a fundamental fact which any analysis of criminal law must acknowledge: criminal law and morality are two quite distinct concepts. The rules of criminal law may reflect the morality of the society which they regulate, but this coincidence is not a necessary one. A society may be governed by certain criminal law rules which many people may find abhorrent, but this moral objection does not diminish the legal validity of the rules. Such laws may properly be called unjust or immoral, but unless a natural law position is adopted, they are still appropriately described as laws.

The acceptance of a possible dichotomy between criminal law and moral rules does not necessarily preclude the use of moral principles as a basis for the development of criminal law. Rules of morality are the foundation of criminal law; many crimes exist because of the moral conviction of legislators or the courts that the conduct in question is morally wrong. Yet the moral wrongfulness of an act is not, by itself, a sufficient ground for the criminalisation of that conduct. Some acts may be considered immoral but do not necessarily deserve to be treated as criminal – a breach of a promise, the telling of a lie, or the sexual or emotional exploitation of another are all examples of immoral conduct, but they are not usually punished by the criminal law.

The characteristic which attracts the attention of the criminal law is harm to a specific interest which is recognised as being of such weight as to merit criminal law protection. Some of these interests are social in nature – such as the interest which society has in protecting public order; others are private – such as the interest which the individual has in his physical integrity or property. Faced with these numerous and varied interests, the draftsman of the criminal law must decide what principle is to govern the selection of some interest for criminal law protection and the rejection of others. For example, everybody has an interest in his reputation, but should the criminal law make it an offence to defame another? The answer in Scots law is that it should not; in other legal systems certain forms of defamation are treated as criminal. Or should it be a crime to display pornography openly? This may be criminal in Scotland, but in certain other jurisdictions the interest which the community at large has in being protected from possible offence of this nature is not given legal recognition.

A principle which attracts considerable support amongst legal and social philosophers holds that the criminal law should be invoked only in those cases where conduct causes or threatens a real degree of harm to the welfare of others. This limitation was expressed by John Stuart Mill in the nineteenth century[1], and has been echoed in the works of a number of twentieth-century writers[2]. It was the philosophy which underpinned the Report of the Wolfenden Committee[3] (which recommended the liberalisation of the law in relation to prostitution and homosexual offences) and to a very great extent it represents the consensus in modern criminal jurisprudence. According to this approach, private consensual acts are not the concern of the criminal law, provided that there is no substantial harm caused to the participants. The possession and enjoyment of pornography should therefore fall outwith the scope of the criminal law, as should all sexual acts conducted in private between consenting adults.

The attraction of such a philosophy of criminal law is that it maximises individual freedom, which is seen to be a good. At the same time it is open to the criticism that the libertarian position frequently overestimates the extent to which acts are private. In his celebrated debate with HLA Hart, the English judge, Lord Devlin, argued that many private acts are, in fact, capable of causing harm to the 'fabric of society'[4]. Indeed, it was Lord Devlin's belief that any act of immorality weakened society in some way, even if there was no apparent individual victim. This argument has found little support, although it is certainly possible to argue that mere knowledge of the fact that certain forms of conduct are being perpetuated may combine to a process of 'moral blunting' or 'moral brutalisation', the ultimate effect of which may be felt by society in general or by individual victims. The mere knowledge that women are being subjected to insult and degradation in pornography causes understandable distress to many women (and men), and this distress may exist irrespective of the consensual status of the participants. It may also be felt that this mere knowledge could somehow embolden potential abusers of women to translate fantasy into reality, or just not to bother about women's feelings; this could perhaps provide an additional argument in favour of the criminalisation of pornography.

1 *On Liberty* (1859).
2 A major contemporary statement of the liberal vision of criminal law is to be found in Joel Feinberg's four-volume work, *The Moral Limits of the Criminal Law* (1984–88).
3 *Report of the Committee on Homosexual Offences and Prostitution* (1957) (Cmnd 247).
4 *The Enforcement of Morals* (1965) ch 1.

1.17   The danger with such arguments lies in the fact that they readily lead one into a position in which virtually any form of immoral conduct becomes a candidate for criminalisation. Such a position would be intolerable because of the restriction of freedom it would involve and also because of the extent to which it would damage respect for the criminal law. The criminal sanction is an extreme one, to be used as sparingly as possible. For most forms of day-to-day immorality, moral disapproval and informal social sanctions must suffice, and only when crucial state or individual interests are at stake should the criminal law intervene. Such techniques may be shown to fail, of course, and in such cases criminal sanctions may properly be used, provided that the harm threatened is sufficiently grave. Race relations legislation is a useful example here. The distress caused by racial insult, and the social dislocation which racial tension causes, are such that what might normally be a matter of moral censure or exhortation becomes, quite properly, a matter for concern on the part of the criminal law.

Chapter 2

Principles of liability

2.1   Before a person can be convicted of a criminal offence, it must be established (1) that he committed a criminal act or omission and (2) that his conduct was accompanied by a 'guilty' state of mind. This is usually expressed as the requirement that there be an *actus reus* (a wrongful act) and *mens rea* (a wrongful state of mind). There is an important exception to this proposition, however, in the case of certain offences created by statute. These may be offences of strict liability, which do not require *mens rea* on the part of the accused. They are discussed separately below.

The following example illustrates the dual requirement. **X**, while shooting on a shooting range, sees what he takes to be the target appearing. In fact, it is a hiker who has ignored the warning notices. **X** fires and the hiker is fatally wounded. **X** has committed the *actus reus* of a criminal offence (he has shot the victim), but there is no *mens rea* (because of **X**'s excusable error). There is therefore no criminal liability.

THE *ACTUS REUS* REQUIREMENT

2.2   The criminal law does not punish mere intentions[1]: there must be an overt action or an omission to act before liability is attributed. Acts may consist of a single event or of a series of events. The striking of another is an example of a single event, which amounts, in fact, to the *actus reus* of assault. Other acts may be more complex, involving one or more actions on the part of the actor, followed by certain consequences. The act of defrauding another may consist of the writing of a misleading statement, the issuing of the statement to another, and the recipient's acting upon the statement. The act of murder consists of the physical harming of the victim followed by a necessary consequence: the victim's death. Single event crimes have been referred to as 'conduct crimes'; crimes requiring more than one event have been referred to as 'result crimes'. This division of crimes is of practical importance, in that it may be necessary to prove *mens rea* in relation to both circumstances and consequences, and therefore each element in such crimes must be clearly identified.

1 But see *Richards v HM Advocate* 1971, JC 29, where Lord Justice-Clerk said in connection with an allegation of fraud, 'A man's present intention is as much a fact as his name, or his occupation, or the size of his bank balance'.

The voluntary act requirement

2.3   When the *actus reus* takes the form of an act rather than an omission, this act must be voluntary. The meaning of the term 'voluntary' is very specific here, and must be distinguished from the concept of voluntary action as being that which one positively wishes to do. A reluctant conscript may join the armed services involuntarily; a taxpayer may pay his taxes involuntarily – in both of these cases the actor would rather not do what he does. In the context of the criminal law, however, the term voluntary refers to action which is performed under the control of the actor. Involuntary acts are therefore those which the actor does not know he is performing or acts which he cannot stop himself from performing. Awareness or control may be absent where:

(i) The criminal state of affairs results from external events beyond the control of the actor

The classic example of this is where an external force is responsible for what happens. This external force may take the form of a natural phenomenon (for example, a gust of wind) or of human intervention. In *Hogg v Macpherson*[1] the accused's car collided with a lamp standard as a result of a heavy gale, and there was therefore no liability. Similarly, in *Hugh Mitchell*[2], where a man attacked a woman carrying a child, forcing her to squeeze the child, responsibility for the death rested with the man and not the woman. If, therefore, **A** seizes **B** and, taking hold of his hand, forces him to strike **C**, **B** cannot be said to have assaulted **C** – there was no voluntary act on his part. If the accused's actings have contributed to the criminal state of affairs, even if the external event causing a death was beyond his control, he may still be criminally liable. In *R v Gnango*[3] the accused became involved in a shoot-out as a result of which a passer-by died. The fatal shot had not come from the accused; the perpetrator escaped. The Supreme Court held that the accused bore criminal responsibility[4].

1 1928 JC 15, 1928 SLT 35; interestingly, the accused was charged with breaking the gas lamp 'through accident' and failing to pay for the damage.
2 (1856) 2 Irv 488.
3 [2012] 1 AC 827.
4 See commentary by R Craig Connal QC, 'The escape of bandana man; guilty of not firing the fatal bullet' 2012 JR 305.

2.4 There is a curious category of cases which would appear to be an exception to this fundamental requirement of a voluntary act. This is the category of the so-called 'status offences', in which the gravamen of the charge is not what the accused is alleged to have done but what he was at a particular time. For example in *R v Larsonneur*[1], the accused, a Frenchwoman, was arrested by the Irish police and taken to Britain, where she was convicted of the offence of being an alien 'found' in the United Kingdom without permission. In *Winzar v Chief Constable of Kent*[2] the accused had been brought to hospital, where he was found to be drunk. The police were called, and they removed him to their car, which was parked on the road. The accused was then convicted of being drunk on the highway. In both of these cases, the offence was based on the status of the accused at a particular time, rather than anything they were alleged to have done. It might be argued that there was some degree of culpability in the case of *Winzar* in that he had allowed himself to become intoxicated, but he could only be called to account for the eventual public drunkenness if it could be shown that he could have foreseen the possibility of being removed and put in a public place; in the absence of such foreseeability a person in his position is surely blameless.

(ii) *The criminal state of affairs results from a reflex action on the part of the accused*

There are some movements which may be performed in a state of consciousness but which are nevertheless not under the control of the actor. These movements – commonly known as reflex actions – are not actions in the full sense of the word (not being willed by the actor) and they should not therefore attract criminal liability. A person whose arm jerks in a sudden, uncontrolled movement, causing him to knock over a person standing next to him, should not be convicted of assault; he has not chosen to strike his victim, nor could he have stopped himself from doing so[3].

1 (1933) 149 LT 542, 29 Cox CC 673.
2 (1983) Times, March 28; discussed by CMV Clarkson and HM Keating *Criminal Law: Text and Materials* (1990), p 122.
3 In *Jessop v Johnstone* 1991 SCCR 238 a boy struck a teacher with a rolled-up jotter. The teacher responded by punching him, a response which the sheriff accepted as being a reflex action. The High Court did consider it to be such, but Lord Justice-Clerk Ross observed: 'We appreciate that there may be cases where a person instinctively reacts to violence in a reflex way, such as if a person is suddenly and without warning struck and turns round sharply so that he comes into contact with his assailant ...' (at 240), although the High Court held that a conviction should have followed as a result of a blow struck after the spontaneous reaction.

2.5   Involuntariness was raised more successfully, however, in *Hill v Baxter*[1] where the accused was acquitted of a driving offence on the grounds that he had lost control of his car when a swarm of bees had entered it by a window and he had instinctively moved his arms to protect himself.

(iii) *The criminal state of affairs has been produced by the action performed during unconsciousness*

Acts performed in a state of unconsciousness, or during a state of grossly impaired consciousness, are known as automatic acts, the person performing them being, temporarily, an automaton. This can arise in a number of ways, amongst which are: through somnambulism; as a result of concussion caused by physical blow to the brain; through the presence of abnormal sugar levels in the blood; or during or shortly after an epileptic seizure. More controversially, it is apparent that a state of dissociation can develop as a result of extreme psychological stress and that this may result in action which has many of the features of automatism.

Somnambulism. Somnambulism, or sleep-walking, occurs during slow-wave sleep, when the body is capable of fairly complex movement. Somnambulistic violence is rare, but there is fairly general agreement among psychiatrists that it is quite possible for a sleeping person to commit assault or even homicide in a state of complete unconsciousness and to have no waking recollection of what has been done[2]. In such a case, there is clearly no voluntary act and therefore it could be argued that there can be no *actus reus*.

There are comparatively few decisions on this point[3], although one of the earlier reports is a Scottish one, the case of *Simon Fraser*[4]. Fraser had killed his eighteen-month-old son and claimed that he had done this during his sleep. The jury was directed that if this was so, then he was not responsible for what happened, a view which they were prepared to accept. In the event, Fraser agreed to sleep alone in future, a precaution which is mirrored in modern medical advice to those who have been troubled by aggressive behaviour during sleep. In *R v Burgess*[5] the Court of Appeal in England held that somnambulistic automatism was a form of insanity and should therefore be treated as insane automatism. The implications of this are discussed below. In *Finegan v Heywood*, the accused was convicted of a drink driving offence committed whilst in a state of parasomnia; the condition had been brought on by his drinking. In refusing the appeal, the court seem to give tacit approval to the approach taken in *Burgess*, in that sleepwalking, as a manifestation of an internal factor, whether functional or organic, was a disease of the mind; this would rule out non-insane automatism as a defence[6].

1 [1958] 1 QB 277, [1958] 1 All ER 193.
2 For a full discussion, see C Shapiro and A McCall Smith (eds) *Forensic Aspects of Sleep* (1997).
3 The dearth of authorities is referred to in *Finegan v Heywood* 2000 JC 444 at p 447.
4 (1878) 4 Coup 70.
5 [1991] 2 QB 92, [1991] 2 All ER 769.
6 2000 JC 444 at 447.

2.6   Other forms of automatism.   Somnambulistic automatism may come before the courts fairly rarely, but this is not so with certain other forms of automatism, notably automatism induced by epilepsy or diabetes. Although there is no particular association of epilepsy with violence, epileptics may occasionally commit violent acts in the post-ictal stage (that is, in the immediate aftermath of a seizure). These acts are clearly beyond their control, and, if the voluntary act requirement were to be applied, there would be no *actus reus*. Until the decision in *HM Advocate v Ross*[1], which recognised a defence of non-insane automatism, the effect of the decision in *HM Advocate v Cunningham*[2] was to deny the possibility of acquittal on the grounds of automatism, while leaving open the possibility in such cases of a defence of insanity. In *Cunningham* the accused, who was charged with certain driving offences, claimed that he was acting in a state of temporary dissociation resulting from an epileptic fugue or 'other pathological condition'. The court ruled that any 'mental or pathological condition short of insanity – any question of diminished responsibility owing to any cause, which does not involve insanity' was relevant only to the question of mitigating circumstances and sentence. The court in *Cunningham* expressly disapproved the earlier decision of Lord Murray in *HM Advocate v Ritchie*[3], in which it had been accepted that if a person is not 'master of his own actions' (through the operation of some temporary overcoming factor, in this case toxic fumes), the presumption of responsibility may be overcome and a special defence succeed. *Cunningham's* rejection of this placed persons who act automatically in an invidious position; they could assert their non-responsibility, but only through the defence of insanity, which involved the prospect of compulsory hospitalisation. Even if an epileptic could be described as insane in terms of the Scots law on the subject – which requires a total and non-temporary alienation of reason – the question remained as to what was the point of sending or admitting an epileptic or a diabetic to a psychiatric hospital? The only justification can be that of public safety, and such considerations should be applied only where there are clear grounds to suggest that there is a possibility of a recurrence of the violent behaviour in question.

1 1991 SCCR 823, 1991 SLT 564. For discussion, see G Laurie 'Automatism and insanity in the law of England and Scotland' 1995 JR 253.
2 1963 JC 80, 1963 SLT 345.
3 1926 JC 45, 1926 SLT 308.

2.7   The reaction to the decision in *Cunningham* was overwhelmingly negative, and indeed in a number of cases lower courts appeared to have ignored the decision and acquitted in cases involving automatism. In *Farrell v Stirling*[1] the accused, a diabetic, was charged with an offence under the Road Traffic Act 1972, and claimed to have been suffering from hyperglaecemia at the time of the offence. The sheriff sought to distinguish *Cunningham* and held that the movements of the accused's hands, body and legs were involuntary and 'wholly uncontrolled by any conscious effort of will on his part'. This approach was not endorsed, however, in *Carmichael v Boyle*[2] when the High Court upheld a Crown stated case appeal from a sheriff court which had acquitted a diabetic who had committed assault in a state of hypoglycaemia. The High Court emphasised that *Cunningham* unambiguously excluded any defence of automatism in such a case and that this must remain the position until the legislature decided otherwise or until a larger court overruled the decision.

The opportunity arose in *Ross (Robert) v HM Advocate*[3]. In this case the accused had been convicted of attempted murder and assault in respect of a frenzied knife attack which he carried out on a number of strangers in a public place. The accused contended that the can of lager which he had been drinking had, without his knowledge, been adulterated with Temazepam and LSD, and that he had therefore been acting as an automaton and should be acquitted. This defence was successful, the court overturning rejection of non-insane automatism in *Cunningham* on the grounds that in such a case there was no question of *mens rea:*

> 'In principle it would seem that in all cases where a person lacks the evil intention which is essential to guilt of a crime he must be acquitted ... So if a person cannot form any intention at all because, for example, he is asleep or unconscious at the time, it would seem impossible to hold that he had *mens rea* and was guilty in the criminal sense of anything he did when he was in that state. The same result would seem to follow if, for example, he was able to form intention to the extent that he was controlling what he did in the physical sense, but had no conception whatever at the time that what he was doing was wrong. His intention, such as it was, would lack the necessary evil ingredient to convict him of a crime. Insanity provides the clearest example of this situation, but I do not see why there should be no room for the view that the lack of evil intention in cases other than insanity, to which special considerations apply, should not also result in an acquittal. Indeed, since it is for the Crown to prove *mens rea* as well as the *actus reus*

27

of the offence, it would seem logical to say that in all cases where there is an absence of *mens rea* an acquittal must result'[4].

1 1975 SLT (Sh Ct) 71.
2 1985 SCCR 58, 1985 SLT 399.
3 1991 SCCR 823, 1991 SLT 564.
4 1991 SCCR 823 at 829, per Lord Justice-General Hope.

2.8 In his survey of the cases, Lord Justice-General Hope noted that *Cunningham*, although hitherto binding, was contradicted by the decision in *Ritchie* and by dicta of Lord McCluskey in *HM Advocate v Raiker*[1], and that it was also fundamentally out of step with English and Commonwealth decisions. *Cunningham* was seen as a policy-influenced decision, based on a fear that 'laxity or confusion' would result if the court were to admit such a defence; a fear which the Lord Justice-General saw as misplaced.

The decision in *Ross* is limited to those cases where automatic behaviour is not self-induced[2], and where the factor which produces it is not the result of 'continuing disorder of the mind or body which might lead to the recurrence of the disturbance of ... mental faculties'[3]. Where automatism is so produced, *Cunningham* stands, and the only defence will be that of insanity. As a result of this, Scots law is now essentially the same as English law on this point and automatism may be divided into non-insane and insane categories, the implications being the same in both jurisdictions.

The court spent some time on two further points. It was argued by the Crown that, by analogy with the defence of insanity, the burden of proof of non-insane automatism should rest on the accused. This was rejected, the court pointing out that non-insane automatism does not involve the rebuttal of any presumption of insanity; the issue at stake is one of responsibility. A further contention of the prosecution – that the defence should be a special one, requiring written notice – was considered by the court, but opinion was reserved.

1 1989 SCCR 149.
2 See for example *Finegan v Heywood* 2000 JC 444; 2000 SLT 905, distinguishing *Ross*, which expressly excluded the defence if a condition (in this case parasomnia) is induced by alcohol and the accused knew that fact.
3 1991 SCCR 823 at 829.

2.9 The implications of the decision in *Ross* soon came to be tested. In *Sorley v HM Advocate*[1] the appellant had been convicted of a breach of the peace which he alleged was committed only because the can of lager given to him by another contained three sleeping tablets and two LSD tablets inserted without his knowledge. The court stressed that the defence of automatism required that three elements be present: (1) that the automatic state should result from an external factor which was not self-induced; (2) that this factor must be one which the accused was not bound to foresee; and (3) that it should have resulted in a total alienation of reason causing a complete loss of self-control[2]. In the case under consideration, the court held that although there was an admission by the person who had given the appellant the can of lager that he placed the drugs in it, there was no other evidence of the fact that the accused was suffering from a total alienation of reason. For this, clear evidence was required, and this would usually involve the giving of opinions by experts, which may help to corroborate the evidence of those who observed the accused's conduct at the time. It is evident, then, that the courts will need considerable convincing of a total alienation of reason, and that nothing short of expert medical evidence is likely to satisfy them. Decisions following *Sorley* have similarly taken a relatively cautious view of the defence. The absence of medical evidence was fatal to the defence in *MacLeod v Napier*[3], and in *McLeod v Mathieson*[4] the loss of control through hypoglycaemia was held to be foreseeable and therefore culpable. In *Ebsworth v HM Advocate*[5] the appellant had consumed grossly excessive quantities of pain-killing drugs which had been prescribed following an injury. After the ingestion of these drugs, he committed criminal acts in a state of automatism, but was denied the defence on the grounds that his 'alienation of reason' was produced by his own deliberate or reckless act. In *Finegan v Heywood*[6], the accused suffered from parasomnia; he argued that as he was suffering from non-insane automatism, he should be acquitted regardless of the circumstances leading to the condition. The High Court disagreed, holding that a person who consumes intoxicants voluntarily, whether or not their effect was foreseeable, could not rely upon the defence of automatism. In *Scott v HMA*[7], the High Court affirmed the three elements of the test adding the following observations on the means of establishing the defence:

> 'First ... depending on the facts of each case there may be cases where adequate evidence of the appropriate state of mind may be available without the necessity of the accused giving evidence. And, secondly, in this particular case, the proposed expert witness ... did not have before him the primary facts upon which he could assist the jury with his expert opinion as to the state of mind of the appellant at the relevant time'.

1 1992 SCCR 396.
2 On the requirement of a total alienation of reason, see *Cardie v Mulrainey* 1992 SCCR 658, 1992 SLT 1152 see also *Carrington v HM Advocate* 1994 JC 229; 1995 SLT 341.
3 1993 SCCR 303.
4 1993 SCCR 488.
5 1992 SLT 1161, 1992 SCCR 671.
6 2000 JC 444; 2000 SLT 905.
7 [2015] HCJAC 57.

Omissions

2.10   In the majority of cases the *actus reus* consists of an act rather than an omission to act. The criminal law is generally reluctant to impose liability on the basis of an omission, although in certain circumstances this may happen. This reluctance is attributable in part to conceptions of causation which tend to downplay the causative potency of omissions and in part to a desire to limit the extent of criminal liability. While everybody can appreciate the causal link between positive acts and their consequences, the equivalent link between omissions and their consequences tend to be less readily acknowledged. The person who pushes another into a river may be said to have caused his victim's drowning; the person who, being able to rescue a swimmer whom he sees drowning, but who fails to take any steps to do so, is less likely to be identified as the cause of the swimmer's death. As far as the limitation of criminal liability is concerned, liability for omissions is inherently more open-ended, and even uncertain, than is liability for positive acts. In the example used above, if a general liability for failure to rescue is accepted, where does the duty to rescue begin and end? Is a person to be liable for failing to call the police if he hears violence being perpetrated next door? Is he liable for the violence he hears being perpetrated in the next street? It is precisely this sort of difficulty which has resulted in the restriction of omission liability to those cases where one or more of a small number of special factors is present.

Is there a duty to prevent the commission of a crime?

There is Scottish authority to the effect that a person who fails to take steps to prevent a crime does not thereby commit an offence. In *George Kerr*[1] several accused who looked over a hedge while a rape was being committed in a field were acquitted on a charge of art and part guilt of rape, a decision which demonstrates the offensive results to which the principle of non-responsibility for omissions can give rise. A similar outcome occurred in *R v Clarkson*[2] and *R v Broughham*[3]. In *Clarkson* it was held that the mere presence of the accused, a soldier, as a spectator of a barrack-room rape perpetrated by his fellow soldiers, was not enough to secure his conviction for aiding and abetting the offence – a result which, once again, will strike many as shocking.

1 (1871) 2 Coup 334.
2 [1971] 3 All ER 344.
3 (1986) 43 SASR 187.

2.11   Mere presence on the scene of a crime may result in criminal liability if there is some factor, in addition to presence, which justifies the inference of a duty to act in some way. In *Wilcox v Jeffrey*[1] the accused attended (as a journalist working for the sponsoring magazine) an illegal concert; it was held that his presence, in the circumstances, amounted to an encouragement of the illegality – liability therefore could only have been avoided by efforts made to stop the performance or by walking out. The question of whether the mere presence of the accused amounted to encouragement will depend on all the circumstances. Fortuitous presence will clearly not be sufficient to give rise to a duty to act, but, as pointed out by the Queensland Court of Appeal in *Beck*[2], 'a calculated presence or a presence from which opportunity is taken can project positive encouragement and support for the principal offender'. It is probably the case then in Scots law that a person who realises that his presence is lending support to another in a criminal act, is under a duty to withdraw from the scene of the crime if he wishes to avoid criminal liability. In *Hogg v McLeod*[3] a prisoner was assaulted by a police officer; another, more senior, police officer was present but did nothing to disassociate himself from the assault. The High Court held that he was art and part guilty of the assault, his position being a *fortiori* of that of an official standing by and allowing a breach of law, although the court also took into account that he had taken an active part by 'fast marching' the complainer.

1 [1951] 1 All ER 464.
2 (1989) 43 A Crim R 135 at 142.
3 1983 SCCR 161.

2.12   In a small number of cases, statute imposes an obligation to act in respect of the commission of a crime by another. Under s 172 of the Road Traffic Act 1988, a person who is required by the police to give information as to the identity of a driver suspected of committing certain offence under the Act commits an offence if he fails to give that information. That provision was challenged as being incompatible with Article 6 of the European Convention on Human Rights (the right to a fair trial). The Privy Council held that since there was a clear public interest in the enforcement of road traffic legislation, an admission secured under s 172 of being the driver could be used against a person without undermining the right to a fair trial[1]. The duty to act imposed by the Terrorism Act 2000 is even more rigorous, imposing a duty on certain persons to disclose suspicions about the behaviour of others[2]. Similarly, the Proceeds of Crime Act 2002 provides that a person commits an offence if he enters into or becomes concerned in an arrangement which he knows, or suspects, facilitates (by whatever means) the acquisition, retention, use or control of criminal property by or on behalf of another person[3].

The categories of omission liability

In spite of the fact that omissions are less likely to attract criminal liability than positive acts, there are certain circumstances in which the courts are prepared to treat an omission as criminal. These are:

(1) Where there have been prior dangerous actings on the part of the accused.   A person who creates a situation of danger for another may be held liable for any injury that ensues if he fails to avert the danger he has created. In a sense, such situations do not entail pure omission liability, as there is an earlier act on the part of the accused. This act, however, may not be a wrongful one itself, and any wrongfulness must therefore be located in the omission.

Several cases are concerned with a victim who is placed in a situation of danger and then abandoned. In *McManimy and Higgins*[4] two lodging-house keepers were convicted of culpable homicide after they had removed an ill guest and left him out in the street, where he died. In *HM Advocate v McPhee*[5] the exposure of an assaulted victim was similarly at issue, although in a case of this type the death of the victim can be seen as much as a consequence of the assault as of the abandonment to the elements.

1 *Brown v Stott* 2001 SC (PC) 43; 2001 SLT 59.
2 Sections 19 and 20.
3 Section 328; see *Sarwar v HMA* 2011 SCCR 159.
4 (1847) Arkley 321.
5 1935 JC 46, 1935 SLT 179.

2.13   The decision in *McPhail v Clark*[1] demonstrates how an innocent situation may later become dangerous through the operation of natural forces. In this case the accused had set fire to straw in a field, something which he was entitled to do, but then failed to extinguish the fire after it had spread and the smoke had begun to cause a danger to passing motorists. This failure to act, once he had become aware of the danger, was held to amount to a culpable omission and he was convicted of recklessly endangering the lives of car occupants. The English case of *Miller*[2] is to similar effect. Here a squatter had inadvertently set fire to a mattress in the house he was occupying, and rather than extinguish the flames he had merely moved to another room. The appellant's conviction of causing reckless damage was upheld by the House of Lords in a decision which can be interpreted in more than one way. In one view the ratio of *Miller* is that a prior dangerous act imposes liability to act[3]; in another, liability in *Miller* is based on the 'continuing' act theory which sees the initial causing of the fire and the subsequent attitude of recklessness towards it as being part of one overall continuing act[4]. Whichever view is taken, the result is the same; the first explanation, however, has the advantage of avoiding the necessity of treating what are clearly discrete events as being a single act. *Miller* was cited in the case of *McCue v Currie*[5]. The accused had broken into a caravan to steal from it. He inadvertently started a fire and left it to take effect. He was convicted of culpable and reckless fire raising and appealed. The court allowed the appeal, holding that accidental fire raising was not a crime; they dealt with *Miller* as follows:

> '*R v Miller* ... is cited in a footnote at para 3.34 of Gordon[6]. In the paragraph that case is given as authority for the statement: "Where a person by his actings has created a situation of danger, he has a duty to do what he can to avert the danger he has created". It is to be noted, however, that the case of *Miller* was concerned with the interpretation of an English statutory provision which has no counterpart in Scots law. Counsel submitted that, for that reason, the case does not support the conclusion set out in Gordon, and that it is not of assistance in determining the present appeal. We, for our part, are disposed to agree with that: and it is to be noted that the Advocate-depute did not seek to rely on *Miller* as supporting the sheriff's conclusion in the present case'.

Accordingly, Gordon's assertion cannot be regarded as reflecting the current law.

The control of dangerous things may be treated as an instance of prior act responsibility in that the acquisition of such control, or its continuance after there has been a realisation of dangerousness, amounts to a prior dangerous act. There is no Scottish authority on this point, but it is submitted that the person who willingly takes control of a dangerous thing of whatever nature (whether it be animate or inanimate) will be liable for the damage caused by that thing, provided that he is negligent in failing to prevent that damage. The degree of negligence manifested must be such as to amount to the reckless indifference referred to in *McPhail v Clark*[7] and in other cases in which criminal liability is imposed for negligent conduct[8]. On this basis, the owner of a dangerous building might be held criminally liable for injury caused by the collapse of the building if he has failed to take steps to prevent such injury and if this failure amounts to recklessness. The custodians of dangerous animals might be convicted of recklessly endangering the lives and safety of others if they fail to take suitable steps to prevent such danger.

1 1982 SCCR 395, 1983 SLT (Sh Ct) 37.
2 [1983] 2 AC 161, [1983] 1 All ER 978.
3 See JC Smith [1982] Crim LR 527.

4 See Glanville Williams [1982] Crim LR 773.
5 2004 JC 73 at page 77–78; 2004 SLT 858; the failure of the court to clarify the criminal law on omissions was lamented by James Chalmers in 'Fire-raising by Omission' 2004 SLT (Notes) 10.
6 *Gordon* para 3–34 footnote 12.
7 1982 SCCR 395, 1983 SLT (Sh Ct) 37.
8 See the discussion of negligence liability at p 43 below.

2.14 Failure to warn another of a danger which one has created oneself may be charged as a form of reckless conduct[1]. Cases in this category include those in which police officers have been exposed to the risk of needle-stick injury in the course of searching suspects. In *Normand v Morrison*[2] the accused, who was convicted of culpable and reckless conduct, was silent as to the presence of an unprotected needle in her handbag and did nothing to prevent the searching officer from being injured. In *Kimmins v Normand*[3] there was a positive denial of the presence of a needle, and again a conviction of culpable and reckless conduct was obtained. However in *Mallin v Clark*[4], the High Court quashed a similar conviction for culpable and reckless conduct on the basis that, on the particular facts, and the terms of the charge, no proper basis for a duty of disclosure on the accused had been established.

(2) Where the status of the accused is such that he has a duty to act. A person who occupies a public office or a position of responsibility of some sort may have a duty to act to prevent the occurrence of harm and may be criminally liable if he fails to do so. Liability for culpable homicide may result where death has resulted from the accused's failure to discharge the duties imposed by his position[5]. The life-guard who culpably fails to make any effort to rescue the swimmer in distress may be liable for his omission, as may the prison warder who stands by and allows an unpopular prisoner to be fatally assaulted. In other cases there may be art and part liability, as in *Bonar v Macleod*[6], where the accused, a police officer, failed to intervene to prevent the assault of a person in police custody by an officer junior to himself.

(3) Where a close relationship exists between the accused and a person who suffers harm which the accused has failed to prevent. The existence of a relationship of dependence between two persons may give rise to a duty to act to prevent harm. The Scottish courts have not addressed the issue, but are likely to infer the existence of such an obligation in the case at least of parent and minor child, and possibly in other cases. It might be that a duty is owed to a spouse to prevent harm, and the same view might today be taken of unmarried persons living together. It is not the family relationship which matters in these cases, but the fact that the parties are members of the same household. The essence of the obligation is the dependence which normally follows such a close relationship. The failure of a householder to summon medical help for a long-term lodger who is gravely ill gives rise to the same form of moral disapproval as the failure of a parent to do the same thing for a minor child living in his household[7].

1 See discussion in Chapter 9.
2 1993 SCCR 207, Sh Ct.
3 1993 SCCR 476, 1993 SLT 1260.
4 2002 SLT 1202, 2002 SCCR 901.
5 *William Hardie* (1847) Arkley 247: failure of an Inspector of Poor to deal with an application for assistance.

6 1983 SCCR 161.
7 One of the few cases involving a failure to rescue family is the Australian case of *R v Russell* [1933] VLR 59. In this case, the accused failed to take steps to prevent his estranged wife from jumping into a swimming pool with his two young children. He was convicted of the manslaughter of all three, although his conviction in respect of the wife's death was based on the criminality, at that point, of suicide. If events were repeated in the same jurisdiction today, there would be no conviction on those grounds. See P Brett, L Waller and CR Williams *Criminal Law* (6th edn, 1989), p 507.

2.15   A legally recognised relationship of dependence may come into existence through the assumption of a duty. A number of cases involve a failure to provide care and attention for elderly people for whom the accused assumed responsibility. In *R v Instan*[1], for example, the accused lived with an aged aunt whom she neglected in the last twelve days of the aunt's life, failing to call medical help to deal with the gangrene which the aunt had developed. The decision in *R v Stone and Dobinson*[2] was to similar effect. In this case the accused persons failed to look after the frail sister of one of them whom they had admitted to live in the house: they were held liable for manslaughter after she died from neglect[3].

(4) Where an obligation is imposed by contract.   A person may have an obligation to act imposed upon him by contract. Failure to perform his duties under the contract may result in the imposition of criminal liability. If A agrees to watch B's children, and fails to do so, he or she may be liable for the culpable homicide of one of the children if that child falls into a river and drowns.

1 [1893] 1 QB 450.
2 [1977] 1 QB 354, [1977] 2 All ER 341.
3 For criticism of the decision, see Glanville Williams 'What should the Code do about omissions' (1987) 7 *Legal Studies* 92.

MENS REA

2.16   The commission of an act prohibited by the criminal law, an *actus reus,* will not be sufficient ground to criminal liability unless a necessary mental element is present. This is the general rule, to which there is an important category of exceptions: offences of strict liability[1]. Except in cases of strict liability, the prosecution must prove that the accused acted with a culpable state of mind, now generally known as *mens rea* (a guilty mind). The objective of this requirement is the limitation of criminal liability to those cases in which the accused committed a prima facie wrongful act in a wrongful cast of mind. In theory, therefore, the *mens rea* requirement should exculpate those who are morally innocent. In practice, the outcome may be different, and it has been said that all the *mens rea* requirement achieves is the identification of those states of mind which the law regards as appropriate for conviction.

1 Discussed below at Chapter 3.

Mens rea **and dole**

2.17   *Mens rea* is the modern term used most frequently in Scots law; in the older cases, and in *Hume,* the equivalent term was dole, a word possibly derived from the Latin expression dolus (evil). The classic definition of dole is drawn from *Hume*, who describes it as 'that corrupt and evil intention which is essential (so the light of nature teaches, and so all authorities have said) to the guilt of any crime'[1]. *Hume* also speaks of the *malus animus* necessary for conviction of crime. This, he says, is 'vice or corruption of purpose which has the effect of 'fixing' an 'evil character' on a deed[2]. Both of these definitions focus on the specific state of mind of the accused in respect of the criminal act; *Hume* also seems prepared to take into account the broader mental attitude of the accused, stating that the act 'must he attended with such circumstances as indicate a corrupt and malignant disposition, a heart contemptuous of order, and regardless of social duty'[3]. In modern law, the character of the accused is irrelevant, except perhaps in determining punishment. Criminal guilt is not determined by the extent to which one's outlook on the world is malicious or anti-social, but by the intention with which one performs such acts as come under the scrutiny of the courts. The criminal law does not therefore punish a malignant disposition; it punishes malignantly conceived acts.

1 I, 21.
2 I, 23.
3 I, 22.

The differing *mens rea* requirement of individual crimes

2.18   There is no single, universal form of *mens rea* which will suffice for all crimes. Each crime has its own *mens rea* requirement, and in order to be convicted of that crime the accused must have demonstrated that particular mental state on committing the crime. Another way of approaching this is to say that the state of mind of the accused person must fit the outlines of the *actus reus*. Murder requires that the accused either intended the death of his victim or that he acted with wicked recklessness. Theft requires that the accused should have intended to deprive the owner of his property, usually, but not always, permanently. Assault requires that the accused should have inflicted force or the threat of force with *evil intent* (that is, with the intent of causing the victim harm). The *mens rea* requirement of these three common law crimes is therefore different, although there may be elements, such as intention, which are common to all of them.

Legislation may define a *mens rea* requirement very specifically. For example, a statute may read: Any person who makes a false statement to a returning officer with the intention of causing a false return to be made, commits an offence. Here the *mens rea* requirement of the statutory offence is not met if the accused has made a false statement unknowingly and therefore without any intention of causing a false return to be made.

Mens rea and motive

2.19   In the statutory example cited above, the motive with which a person acts is relevant to determining whether mens rea is present. This type of case is exceptional; in general, motive does not affect mens rea. A motive provides the reason for which an act is performed, and in most cases this is not taken into account by a court in determining guilt[1].This issue has been focused in the context of a death occasioned by the administration of a controlled drug. In *MacAngus v HM Advocate*[2] the High Court determined that a charge of culpable homicide in the context of the supplying or administration of a controlled drug was relevant only if the Crown offered to prove that the supplying or administration was in the circumstances reckless. The act of supplying could not of itself be regarded as an offence against the person supplied, in the context of culpable homicide, The motive of simple supply could not form the basis of a culpable homicide charge. Administration of the drug might. This was addressed in *Scott v HMA*[3] thus:

> 'In cases where drug abusers give mutual assistance to inject the drugs, it is conceivable that there may be no intention to harm. Indeed that may be fairly common. It is notorious that drug addicts may on occasions suffer more from the lack of a fix than they might from receiving an injection. It will therefore always be a matter of circumstances whether injecting another who wishes to be injected amounts to assault. It is entirely understandable that the Crown have generally elected to proceed by way of charges of culpable and reckless conduct. In the hazy and shady world of drug abuse, securing reliable evidence to establish the *mens rea* for assault may often prove difficult. On the other hand the risks associated with abuse of Class A prescribed drugs are so notorious that assisting another to abuse the drug may readily be seen as culpable and reckless conduct.'

A claim that an overtly criminal act was carried out for a jesting motive was considered by the High Court in *Lord Advocate's Reference (No 2 of 1992)*[4]. In this case, the accused had been acquitted of assault after he had pointed a toy gun at a shop assistant and had announced his intention of robbing the shop. He later claimed that the whole incident had been a joke – a claim which was accepted by the jury. The High Court ruled that even if he had acted in jest, that motive was irrelevant, as there had still been the necessary *mens rea* of assault (evil intent). When the accused pointed the gun at the assistant, he had intended that she should be frightened, even if this was for purposes of jest. The harm, therefore, had been done. Subsequent cases have confirmed this approach. In *Quinn v Lees*[5] the accused had set his dog on three boys and later claimed that this was only a joke. The High Court pointed out, however, that even if this had been his motive, the dog could not have been expected to understand the joke[6]. In *Lord Advocates Reference No 1 of 2000*[7] the court discounted the motives of the accused who claimed that they had destroyed property for a purported greater good. The accused had vandalised a submarine with a view to preventing the deployment of nuclear weapons. The court rejected the notion that their motive negated the *mens rea* of the offence of malicious mischief.

1 *HM Advocate v Rutherford* 1947 JC 1 at 6, per Lord Justice-Clerk Cooper.
2 2009 SLT 137.
3 [2011] HCJAC 110.
4 1993 JC 43, 1992 SCCR 960, 1993 SLT 460.
5 1994 SCCR 159.
6 See also *Gilmour v McGlennan* 1993 SCCR 837.
7 2001 JC 143; 2001 SLT 507.

2.20   Motive may play a role in mitigating punishment, but this occurs after the essential question of criminal liability has been decided. Theft committed with a motive of giving the proceeds to the poor may strike some as an act performed with a laudable motive, especially if the property is stolen from a heartless and impersonal corporation. This motive, however, has no bearing on the *mens rea* requirement of theft, which does not look to the reasons for which property is taken. In *Palazzo v Copeland*[1] the accused had fired a gun to scare off a group of drunken and abusive youths. His appeal against a conviction for breach of the peace was rejected on the grounds that although his motive was the 'sound one' of trying to stop a breach of the peace on the part of the youths, this was irrelevant. This decision may be contrasted with the decision of the English Court of Appeal in *R v Court*[2]. The appellant here had been convicted of indecent assault, having confessed to the police an indecent motive for touching a young girl. It was observed that motive often throws a light on intention and is therefore generally admissible in the proving of intention. Evidence of motive may be relevant, as was pointed out in *HM Advocate v Carson*[3]. In this case the accused was charged with breach of the peace after he had been seen taking photographs of children in public. He was found to be in possession at home of pornographic material detailing his interest in the commission of sexual offences against children, evidence of which, if admitted would clearly portray outwardly innocent conduct in a criminal light.

In practice, too, motive may play an important role in determining whether a prosecution is instituted or deciding the nature of the offence. Mercy killing provides an instance of this. A distressed relative, who kills a dying person in order to relieve the victim of further suffering, generally attracts sympathy. Here the unselfish motive of the avoidance of suffering may incline the prosecution to accept a plea of diminished responsibility, even on slender medical evidence, with a view to avoiding conviction of murder. Following a number of high-profile cases, most notably *R(on the application of Purdy) v Director of Public Prosecutions*[4], which required the DPP 'to clarify what his position is as to the factors that he regards as relevant for and against prosecution' (paragraph 55) in cases of encouraging and assisting suicide, in February 2010 the Director of Public Prosecutions in England introduced guidelines in relation to assisted suicide[5]. There is no Scottish equivalent although two separate attempts have been made to have the Scottish Parliament address the matter[6].

In *Barile v Griffiths*[7] the High Court took the unusual step of expressing a view about the decision to prosecute. The accused was a teacher who was accused of assaulting pupils. After describing their behaviour as provocative and disgraceful, Lord Kingarth giving the opinion of the court concluded as follows:

'[The sheriff] informs us that he observed, when sentencing the appellant, that had he not been a teacher it was unlikely that he would have been prosecuted. Not only do we entirely agree with these observations, but we have to say that, even allowing for the fact that the appellant was a teacher, given the extreme provocation which he faced in the form of the complainers' disgraceful behaviour and given the relatively insignificant nature of his physical response, it is, on the face of it, difficult to understand why it was thought to be in the public interest, looking at the offences of which he was convicted alone, to bring criminal proceedings at all, whatever actions others might have wished to take'.

1 1976 JC 52.
2 [1989] AC 28, [1988] 2 All ER 221.
3 1997 SCCR 273.
4 [2009] UKHL 45.
5 Available at www.cps.gov.uk/publications/prosecution/assisted_suicide_policy.html.
6 The End of Life Assistance (Scotland) Bill in 2010 and the Assisted Suicide (Scotland) Bill 2015; see also Gordon Ross Petitioner [2015] CSOH 123.
7 2010 SLT 164.

2.21   Motive also plays a part in determining whether certain defences of justification are available. A person who destroys property in order to prevent the occurrence of a greater harm, may be able to claim the defence of necessity. In such a case, the motive with which he acts is central to the availability of the defence[1]. The same is true of the defence of coercion, which may be available to one who commits a criminal offence in order to avoid a threat of severe physical harm to himself. It is implicit in this defence that the motive with which he acts must be one of avoiding the harm to himself, and inquiry may be directed towards determining just that. A further example of circumstances in which motive may determine the wrongfulness or otherwise of an act is that of the doctor examining a patient. If the doctor conducts an intimate examination in order to reach a diagnosis, his therapeutic motive justifies the touching involved. If, however, his motive is not therapeutic, and he conducts the examination for improper reasons, the touching becomes an indecent assault. In *Stewart v Thain*[2] the motive of a schoolmaster in chastising the naked buttocks of a boy was taken into account in determining whether the chastisement was a lawful application of discipline or a sexual assault. The finding of a disciplinary motive was sufficient in this case to justify the act. This was considered in *Barile v Griffiths*[3]. Interestingly the court, having concluded in their initial opinion that it was difficult to see the public interest in the prosecution being brought, granted an absolute discharge in reviewing the sentence.

1 The Lord Advocate's Reference (No 1 of 2000) 2001 JC 143; 2001 SLT 507.
2 1981 JC 13, 1981 SLT (Notes) 2.
3 2010 SLT 164.

The constituent elements of *mens rea*

2.22   *Mens rea* may be inferred if the accused person acts (1) with the requisite intention; (2) recklessly; or (3) negligently. As has already been pointed out, different offences will require different forms of *mens rea* and whichever of these three states of mind needs to be proved will depend on the way in which the *mens rea* requirement is phrased in relation to the offence in question. For murder, for example, the third of these states of mind – negligence – will not be sufficient to establish *mens rea*. The same is true of theft: one cannot steal property negligently.

Intention

The intentional commission of a crime provides us with the classic case of criminal liability. If **A** aims a blow at **B**, he intends to commit assault, and the culpability of such intentional action is beyond controversy. Yet there are many cases in which the intentionality of an act will be less evident, particularly where the focus of attention is, as in murder, not so much the act itself but a consequence which follows upon that act. Such cases have given rise to much jurisprudential debate, criminal law in this area providing rich pickings for the philosophers. The discussion has proved particularly intense in systems such as English law, which define murder entirely in terms of intention to kill or to cause grievous bodily harm. In Scots law, the definition of murder encompasses recklessness, and hence the need for close analysis of the concept of intention in this context has not been pressing. Intention, however, does feature in judicial pronouncements on *mens rea* in Scots law and therefore requires analysis.

A useful starting point may be to define intention in terms of what it is not. The antithesis of intentional action is accidental action. The difference between dropping a thing to the floor and throwing it down is clear enough; in the first case the actor does not direct any action towards the achievement of the result, whereas in the second case he performs an act which has the objective of the thing's landing on the floor. In the first case therefore the fall of the thing is unintentional, or accidental, while in the second it is intended. As a minimum, then, we can exclude from our account of intentional action those events which are properly considered to be accidents.

To act intentionally is to act with a view to bringing something about. An intended event is **wanted** by the actor, although he may not want it for itself but as a means to a further end. If **A** wishes to inherit his elderly relative's money and kills her for this reason, he intends her death. It may be that his real want is the money; it may even be that he very much dislikes the idea of his relative dying. If, however, he is sufficiently motivated by the thought of the ultimate reward he may accept the killing of the relative as a necessary evil to be borne in order to achieve the further ambition. The fact that the death is not wanted for its own sake does not make the relative's killing any the less intentional. Something which is not wanted may therefore still be intended.

Difficulties arise in cases where a person wants **X** to occur but where consequences **Y** and **Z** also result from his bringing about of **X**. Are these consequences to be considered to have been intended by the actor? **A** may leave rat poison in his shed with the aim of killing a troublesome rat. If the rat poison is eaten by a young child, **B**, who dies as a result, is **A** to be held to have intended the death of the child? The answer is surely no. Yet a different reply might be given in a case where **A** has set fire to his neighbour's house with a view to driving him out of the neighbourhood. **A** may believe the house to be empty, or may think that the blaze will not approach that part of the house where the neighbour is sleeping, and yet in one view the death of the neighbour may be regarded as having been intended by **A**.

The issue here is one of foresight of consequences and the effect which foresight has upon intention. The matter has not been explored in detail In Scotland. In *Sayers v HM Advocate*[1] Lord Ross endorsed the definition of intention propounded by Asquith LJ in the civil case of *Cunliffe v Goodman*[2]:

> 'An intention ... connotes a state of affairs which the party "intending" ... does more than merely contemplate; it connotes a state of affairs which, on the contrary, he decides, so far as in him lies, to bring about, and which, in point of possibility, he has a reasonable prospect of being able to bring about, by his own act of volition'.

1 1981 SCCR 312 at 318.
2 [1950] 2 KB 237 at 253.

2.23 The use in statutes of terms such as 'wilfully' has been interpreted as requiring a particular form of intention on the part of the accused. To perform an act wilfully is to act voluntarily rather than involuntarily, but this is not the meaning attributed to the term by the courts. In *Jas Kinnison*[1] it was held that 'wilfully' in a statute meant that the act should be done with the intention of doing the thing which was prohibited, an interpretation which would exclude acts done under a misapprehension of the nature of what was being done. In *Clark v HM Advocate*[2], in which the appellants had been charged with the wilful neglect of their children, the defence argued that the reason for the neglect was fecklessness rather than malice and that the requirement of wilfulness was not met. This was rejected, the requirement of wilful neglect being taken as synonymous with intentional or deliberate neglect, which was present in spite of the motive which lay behind it. The matter was further considered in *H v Lees* and *D v Orr*[3] where the High Court confirmed that wilfulness could be established by deliberate acts giving rise to a consequence that was foreseeable if not intended; it is not the outcome that requires to be intended, but the behaviour leading to that outcome, if the outcome is foreseeable. In *JM v Locality Reporter, Glasgow*[4] the Second Division of Court of Session examined the definition of 'wilful' in the context of an offence against a child; Lord Carloway, the Lord Justice Clerk concluded:

> 'The character or quality of conduct that will constitute ill-treatment is a matter to be determined objectively. The addition of the term "wilful" does not import a subjective element to that assessment. The proper threshold of criminal liability is fixed also by reference to the likelihood of sufficiently grave consequences arising from deliberate or voluntary action or inaction. The term "wilful" necessarily serves to exclude accidental or inadvertent conduct, as opposed to the accidental or inadvertent consequences of deliberate conduct, from the scope of the offence. It is unnecessary, and contrary to the statutory purpose, to restrict the scope of the offence by reference to the subjective awareness of the individual of the harmful nature of the conduct in question.'

Intention and knowledge

Whether or not action is intentional may depend on a person's knowledge of surrounding circumstances. Certain offences may require knowledge as to the identity of some other person or thing: a person does not act with the intention of assaulting a police officer if he is not aware of the fact that the person whom he is assaulting is a member of the police force. The intention necessary for reset is absent if the person does not know that the goods he is buying have been stolen.

1 (1870) 1 Coup 457.
2 1968 JC 53, 1969 SLT 161.
3 1993 JC 238; 1994 SLT 908.
4 2015 CSIH 58.

2.24   A state of wilful blindness may be taken as the equivalent of knowledge. Wilful blindness occurs when a person deliberately refrains from finding out whether a state of affairs exists because he does not wish to inform himself of the truth. In order to be wilfully blind in relation to a fact, there must be a belief in the possibility of the existence of that fact. This is distinct from a mere suspicion, which may be a suspicion as to a remote possibility[1]. Scottish decisions appear to accept that wilful blindness may exist even where the accused's state of mind falls short of an actual belief in the likelihood of the existence of a fact, although there is a dearth of cases meaning there has been limited judicial scrutiny of the point. Effectively, if **A** does not inquire about a fact because he cannot be bothered to do so, or because he negligently fails to consider the need to inquire, then he may be considered to be wilfully blind as to that fact. A broad interpretation of the concept has been favoured by the Scottish courts in cases such as *Smith of Maddiston Ltd v Macnab*[2]. In that case, which dealt with an offence of causing and permitting an illegal use of a vehicle, the court held that guilt could only follow if the person who caused the use knew or should have known about the contravention; the Lord Justice General said the following 'a charge of permitting the use in contravention imported a state of mind and required knowledge on the part of the person who permitted not only the use of the vehicle but of its use in contravention. Knowledge in this connection includes the state of mind of a man who shuts his eyes to the obvious and allows another to do something in circumstances where a contravention is likely, not caring whether a contravention takes place or not.' In *Latta v Herron*[3] the court did not interfere with the sheriff's conclusion that a wilful blindness to an inescapable inference could constitute the required knowledge and that a negligent or reckless failure to make inquiry may amount to wilful blindness. In *Latta* the test of wilful blindness is clearly objective, the court inferring from the surrounding facts that the accused 'must have wilfully blinded himself' to the fact that property was stolen.

Recklessness

The definition of recklessness in Scots criminal law is not straightforward; it has been productive of much academic discussion, with suggestions that the notion of recklessness gives rise to a subjective rather than an objective standard and to a number of sub-categories of recklessness, so that different criteria should be applied depending on the nature of the crime[4].

Conventionally, to act recklessly is to act without regard to the consequences of one's actions. A person who throws a burning cigarette out of a car window while driving though a dry forest is reckless with regard to the possibility of fire, if he knows that there is a risk that he will start a fire (as he surely does), but who does not care whether this happens or not. Such a person is indifferent to the risk, and acts as he does in spite of his awareness of what might happen[5].

Recklessness requires that the actor should have been aware of the existence of the risk, or that the existence of the risk should have been foreseeable. The risk must be a possible consequence of the action. Recklessness deservedly attracts criminal liability, whereas negligence will usually not be punishable.

1 See the case of *Crooks* [1981] 2 NZLR 53 for an example of judicial consideration of this matter.
2 1975 JC 48, 1975 SLT 86.
3 (1967) SCCR Supp 18.
4 See for example Stark, 'Rethinking recklessness' 2011 JR 163; Barton, 'Recklessness in Scots criminal law: subjective or objective?' 2011 JR 143; Ferguson, 'The mental element in Scots criminal law' 2010 *Essays in Criminal Law* (EUP).
5 See for example 'Culpable and reckless conduct – irresponsible prank with serious consequences' Graeme Brown 2014 *Crim LB* 8, reporting on a case where the accused set the victim's homemade sheep costume on fire.

2.25 The concept of recklessness in Scots criminal law is an objective one. There is a preponderance of case law supporting the objective test. Phrases such as 'criminal indifference to consequences', 'utter disregard of what the consequences of the act in question may be', 'obvious and material dangers', 'clearly a risk', 'recklessness so high as to involve an indifference to the consequences for the public generally' appear in the reported cases[1]. The accused need not have 'adverted to' or made 'desiderative' choices about the consequences. If a reasonable person in the position of the accused would have been aware of the existence of a risk, and if to proceed to act in the face of this risk would be considered to demonstrate indifference to the consequences, then recklessness exists. In *Gizzi* v *Tudhope*[2] the accused used guns for practice shooting in a place where any reasonable person would have expected people to be. This fact was sufficient to justify a finding of recklessness even if the accused in question had not themselves been aware of the risk of harm to others. Similarly, in *Allan v Patterson*[3] the High Court supported an objective view of recklessness, although this case was concerned with the statutory offence of reckless driving, and the court based its decision on the absence of any requirement in the legislation that there should be any inquiry into the state of knowledge of any particular driver. Further support for the objective view of recklessness was to be found in a number of decisions concerned with wicked recklessness in murder, which is looked at in more detail in Chapter 10.

Negligence

Negligence exists where there is a failure to act in accordance with an expected standard of conduct. The standard in question is usually that of the reasonably competent person, and this, again, is an objective standard. Although a person who does his best may not be morally culpable if that best is not good enough, the law has found no difficulty in holding him to account for such conduct. Liability, though, is usually limited to civil liability, as negligent conduct does

not normally evince that degree of culpability which is deemed necessary for
criminal liability.

1 *Sutherland v HMA* 1994 JC 62, 1994 SLT 634, 1994 SCCR 80; *Paton v HMA* 1936 JC 19; 1936
 SLT 298; *Quinn v Cunningham* 1956 JC 22, 1956 SLT 55; *Cameron v Maguire* 1999 JC 63,
 1999 SLT 883, 1999 SCCR 44; *Allan v Patterson* 1980 JC 57, 1980 SLT 77.
2 1982 SCCR 442, 1983 SLT 214.
3 1980 JC 57, 1980 SLT 77.

2.26   During the nineteenth century the courts were prepared to impose
liability for negligent conduct as a means of regulating transport and
industrial activity. This regulatory role, however, was to be taken over by
specific legislation and the readiness of the courts to treat negligent conduct
as criminal accordingly diminished. Gross negligence, however, continued
to be punishable, principally in the context of culpable homicide, although
prosecutions were rare. Today the causing of death through gross negligence
may result in conviction for culpable homicide, or, in road traffic cases, for
the statutory offence of causing death through dangerous driving or through
careless driving, arguably diluting the high standard of negligence required.
The standard of negligence required for dangerous driving is high. In *Paton v
HM Advocate*[1] the degree of negligence required was defined as being 'gross, or
wicked, or criminal negligence, something amounting, or at any rate analogous,
to a criminal indifference to consequences'. The accused must therefore have
fallen considerably below the level of competence expected and he must have
failed to take precautions or to carry out steps which would have been very
obviously necessary to any reasonably competent person. Even applying this
standard, however, an argument may be made out for the non-punishability of
negligence, however gross. As long as the negligent actor is unaware of a risk
of harm to others, he is arguably morally unaccountable for that harm. Once
he becomes aware of the risk of harm, he stands to be considered reckless, and
this may quite properly give rise to criminal liability.

The coincidence of the *actus reus* and *mens rea*

2.27   The attribution of criminal liability normally requires that the commission of an *actus reus* be accompanied by *mens rea*. This rarely gives rise
to difficulty, but in some cases the courts have accepted that an *actus reus* and
mens rea may not coincide in the temporal sense, and that a wrongful state
of mind at an earlier time may still influence an *actus reus* committed at a
later stage. The classic example of this approach in Scots law is that of *Brennan v HM Advocate*[2] where the accused had manifested a wrongful state of
mind (recklessness) before becoming intoxicated, and this was held to justify
conviction in respect of an *actus reus* committed at a time when he would not
have been capable of forming the necessary *mens rea*. The opinion of the court
concluded:

> 'Self-induced intoxication is itself a continuing element and therefore an
> integral part of any crime of violence, including murder, the other part being
> the evidence of the actings of the accused who uses force against his victim.
> Together they add up or may add up to that criminal recklessness which it is

the purpose of the criminal law to restrain in the interests of all the citizens of this country.'

1   1936 JC 19, 1936 SLT 298.
2   1977 JC 38, 1977 SLT 151.

2.28   In *Broadley v HM Advocate*[1] the accused was convicted of murdering the deceased by causing her to fall from a window. The deceased had been seen by witnesses falling to the ground. No-one else was seen and only the deceased's fingerprints were found on the windowsill. The High Court quashed the conviction on the basis that there was no evidence to support the Crown's speculation that the accused had been ordered to jump; absent the means whereby the accused caused the deceased to go through the window, there was no basis in the evidence for any involvement between the accused and the death. In *MacDonald v HM Advocate*[2], the court again had to consider a charge of causing the deceased to fall from a window. The deceased had been assaulted and then locked in his flat. He was found the following day outside the window of his kitchen. It was not disputed that the accused left the flat between five and thirty minutes before the fall. The trial judge in his report considered that it was open to the jury to conclude that after the assault, the deceased had tried to escape. The court considered that the matter was properly one for the jury, putting particular emphasis on the short time between the conclusion of the attack and the fall; the jury was entitled to reach the decision that but for the locking of the door in the context of the assaults, the deceased would have lived.

1   2005 SCCR 620.
2   [2006] HCJAC 89.

Chapter 3

Strict liability offences

3.1   Although *mens rea* will normally be required for conviction of a crime, a number of statutory offences may not require it in relation to one or more elements of the offence. These are known as strict liability offences and, to a great extent, they are limited to those day-to-day regulations which are needed for the ordering of a complex industrial society. Strict liability in this context originated in the nineteenth century and the number of offences in this category has grown markedly since then[1]. Most courts and at least some criminal law commentators accept them as a necessary evil[2].

1 For an historical survey, see L H Leigh *Strict and Vicarious Liability* (1982).
2 In *R v Warner* [1969] 2 AC 256 at 272, [1968] 2 All ER 356 at 360, Lord Reid said of strict liability in relation to regulatory offences '… [it] may well seem unjust but it is a comparatively minor injustice'.

3.2   The argument in favour of dispensing with a *mens rea* requirement in the case of at least some statutory offences rests on the proposition that without strict liability it would be impossible adequately to control certain forms of anti-social activity. If *mens rea* had to be proved in the case of every vehicle regulation, for example, the task of the authorities would become impossible. Similarly, in the case of industrial and pollution regulations, the difficulties of rebutting defences based on lack of knowledge or error would make successful prosecution rare and the level of protection afforded to society by such legislation would be reduced. These pragmatic arguments have considerable force, especially if discretion is shown in the decision to prosecute. Not every infringement of a strict liability provision will result in criminal proceedings.

The starting point in any inquiry as to whether a statutory offence involves strict liability is the presumption in favour of *mens rea*. It is to be assumed that a statutory offence requires proof of mens rea unless the contrary intention can be ascertained. This was stated by Lord Justice-Clerk Cooper in the following terms in *Duguid v Fraser*[1]:

'Our reports already contain many examples of cases in which it has been held that a *malum prohibitum* has been created by statutory enactment in such terms and under such circumstances as to impose an absolute obligation of such a kind as to entail this wider liability. In all such cases it has, I think, been the practice to insist that the Crown should show that the language, scope and intendment of the statute require that an exception should be admitted to the normal and salutary rule of our law that *mens rea* is an indispensable ingredient of a criminal or quasi-criminal act; and I venture to think that it would be misfortune if the stringency of this requirement was relaxed.'

The same presumption has been emphasised in other decisions. In the important case of *Sweet v Parsley*[2] Lord Reid stressed the moral significance of the presumption when he said:

> '…there has for centuries been a presumption that Parliament did not intend to make criminals of persons who were in no way blameworthy in what they did. That means that whenever a section is silent as to *mens rea* there is a presumption that, in order to give effect to the will of Parliament, we must read in words appropriate to require *mens rea*…'[3].

This presumption may, however, be rebutted in favour of strict liability, each case being determined according to guiding principles which the courts have identified over the years.

The High Court had the opportunity to consider the application of *Sweet* in *H v Griffiths*[4]. The accused had sexual relations short of intercourse with a girl under the age of sixteen. He thought that she was over sixteen. If they had had intercourse, he could have taken advantage of a statutory defence on the basis of a reasonable belief. No such defence was available. He argued that he did not have the necessary *mens rea*. The court affirmed that the starting point 'must be the presumption that *mens rea* is required for all the elements of a statutory offence, unless that requirement is excluded by express words in the legislative provision in question or by necessary implication'[5]. This was emphasised in *King v Webster*[6]. Here, the accused was convicted of racially aggravated conduct. She had used racially offensive terms in a telephone conversation. She had not intended that the victim hear the insults; the phone call was put on loudspeaker, whereby the victim overheard.

The court held that the issue was not whether mens rea was required; there was clear authority from *Sweet* and *Griffiths* that there is a presumption in favour of a mens rea requirement, but the cases did not provide material assistance on the question of what that requirement was. They each concerned knowledge, in *Sweet* in the context of being concerned in the management of premises, and in *Griffiths* in the context of sexual offences and belief as to the age of the girl. Neither the position of the landlord subletting premises, in relation to the knowledge of their use, nor the position of a man who believes that he is having intercourse with a consenting adult, could reasonably be compared with a person making a foul-mouthed racist remark about a person in the belief that that person will not hear it. In these cases, standing the landlord's knowledge and the man's belief, there is nothing in the behaviour that could be considered reprehensible, whereas in the latter, even where there was a belief that the remark would not be heard by the subject, there may remain significant elements of the behaviour indicative of evil intent, specifically the malicious expression of ill will.

Accordingly even if there is a presumption of *mens rea*, consideration must be given to the nature of that requirement.

1 1942 JC 1, 1942 SLT 51.
2 [1970] AC 132, [1969] 1 All ER 347, HL.
3 [1970] AC 132 at 148, HL.
4 2009 SLT 199.
5 Paragraph [21].
6 2012 SLT 342.

WHERE THE STATUTE USES WORDS IMPLYING *MENS REA*

3.3　　The use of certain words may point to a legislative intention to require *mens rea*. If a statute requires that an act be done 'wilfully' this suggests that there must have been knowledge of the material elements of the offence and an intention to achieve the prohibited results[1], or at least the act is done in a way which leads to the prohibited results. An example will assist. The word 'wilful' appears in s 12 of the Children and Young Persons (Scotland) Act 1937 in the context of ill-treatment of children. In *JM v Locality Reporter, Glasgow*[2], the Court of Session (dealing with the question of whether an offence had been established in the context of proceedings in relation to the welfare of a child) held that 'wilful' ill-treatment required deliberate or intentional conduct; it involved intention. But in holding that it was not intention as to outcome, the court adopted remarks from *Clark v HMA*[3] where the then Lord Justice Clerk (Grant) said:

> 'As the Sheriff-substitute pointed out, "neglect is the want of reasonable care, that is the omission of such steps as a reasonable parent would take, such as are usually taken in the ordinary experience of mankind. That is what neglect is, but before you can bring a criminal charge, you have got to prove that it was wilful in the sense of being deliberate or intentional, but ... without necessarily having any intent to harm the child" [original emphasis]. In other words, while proof of wilfulness is essential to establish head (a), the test under head (b) is an objective one. That test is whether the neglect was "in a manner likely to cause ..." and not whether it was "in a manner intended to cause ... " The absence of such intention where, as is said to be the case here, the actings or omissions are due ... to fecklessness and incompetence is ... no defence.'

In *JM* the Lord Justice Clerk (Carloway) added:

> 'What is required, first, is that the conduct be deliberate. Secondly, the court must be able to categorise the conduct as "ill-treatment", in the sense of involving what can reasonably be described as cruelty. The character or quality of conduct that will constitute ill-treatment is a matter to be determined objectively. The addition of the term "wilful" does not import a subjective element to that assessment. The proper threshold of criminal liability is fixed also by reference to the likelihood of sufficiently grave consequences arising from deliberate or voluntary action or inaction. The term "wilful" necessarily serves to exclude accidental or inadvertent conduct, as opposed to the accidental or inadvertent consequences of deliberate conduct, from the scope of the offence. It is unnecessary, and contrary to the statutory purpose, to restrict the scope of the offence by reference to the subjective awareness of the individual of the harmful nature of the conduct in question.'

So wilfulness, at least in this context, looks to the actions, or omissions, rather than the consequence of these actions or omissions.

'Knowingly' implies that there must be awareness of such facts as are material to the offence; in possession cases, for example, where the statute refers to

47

one who 'knowingly possesses', there must be knowledge of the nature of the substance or object possessed, not just knowledge of the fact that the item is in one's possession. In *Black v HM Advocate*[4] where the offence charged was that of possession of explosives, the court held that it had to be proved that the accused knew of the character of the substances stored in his house; mere knowledge that they were there was insufficient. Where mere possession, as opposed to knowing possession, is at issue, knowledge of the character of the item may not be necessary[5]. Other words sometimes used to import a *mens rea* requirement are: 'fraudulently'[6] and 'maliciously'. The word 'falsely' does not suggest that *mens rea* is required[7], nor does the term 'corruptly'[8].

The stipulating of a *mens rea* requirement in one or more sections of a statute and not in others may be taken to suggest that *mens rea* is not required in the latter. In *Pharmaceutical Society of Great Britain v Storkwein Ltd*[9], the fact that the Medicines Act 1968 stipulated for *mens rea in* some sections but not in the section under consideration was taken as grounds for concluding that Parliament intended strict liability.

1 *James Kinnison* (1870) 1 Coup 457. See also Lord Young's definition of 'wilfully' in *Grant v Wright* (1876) 3 Coup 282, 3 R (J) 28. As *Gordon* points out (para 8–18) there is little Scottish authority on the significance of the use of 'wilfully' in a statute. The English courts have not been entirely consistent in their interpretation of this term: cf *Eaton v Cobb* [1950] 1 All ER 1016 with *Maidstone Borough Council v Mortimer* [1980] 3 All ER 522.
2 [2015] CSIH 58.
3 1968 JC 534.
4 1974 SLT 247.
5 Eg *Winkle v Wiltshire* [1951] 1 KB 684, [1951] 1 All ER 479.
6 *Cox and Hodges* (1982) 75 Cr App Rep 291.
7 *R v Cummerson* [1968] 2 QB 534, [1968] 2 All ER 863.
8 *Smith* [1960] 2 QB 423, [1960] 1 All ER 256.
9 (1986) 83 Cr App Rep 359, HL.

WHERE THE STATUTE IS SILENT AS TO *MENS REA*

3.4   In the absence of any specific mention of a *mens rea* requirement the court will still apply the presumption in favour of *mens rea*. In deciding on the rebuttal of the presumption courts have taken into account the following factors:

(i)   The regulatory nature of the statutory provision

Statutory provisions intended to regulate the day-to-day functioning of society may be considered regulatory offences, which do not require *mens rea*. The main examples of these offences are traffic offences, pollution offences, and trading offences. The common characteristic of these offences is their importance for the protection of the public – strict liability, it is felt, is justified in the interests of public safety. This rationale is explicitly endorsed in *Alphacell v Woodward*[1], in which a company was convicted of causing pollution to enter a river[2] in spite of the absence of evidence of knowledge of the pollution or negligence on the company's part. In his judgment in this case Lord Salmon said:

'It is of the utmost importance that rivers should not be polluted ... The offences created by the Act of 1951 seem to me to be prototypes of offences which "are not criminal in any real sense, but are acts which in the public interest are prohibited under a penalty" ... I can see no valid reason for reading the word "intentionally", "knowingly" or "negligently" into section 2(1) (a) ... This may be regarded as a not unfair hazard of carrying on a business which may cause pollution ... If ... it were held ... that no conviction could be obtained ... unless the prosecution could discharge the often impossible onus of proving that the pollution was caused intentionally or negligently, a great deal of pollution would go unpunished and undeterred ...'[3].

In *Lockhart v National Coal Board*[4], the High Court approved the approach in *Alphacell*. The accused were accused of polluting water after the conclusion of the operation of a coal mine. The court held that the prosecution must prove that the accused carried out some active operation, or chain of operations, the natural consequence of which was that polluted matter entered a stream; that knowledge and foreseeability were not matters which required to be proved; and that neither negligence nor *mens rea* need be established.

1 [1972] AC 824, [1972] 2 All ER 475.
2 Under s 2(1)(a) of the Rivers (Prevention of Pollution) Act 1951.
3 [1972] AC 824 at 848, [1972] 2 All ER 475 at 490, 491. For a similar justification of strict liability in terms of social interest, see *Lim Chin Aik v The Queen* [1963] AC 160 at 174, [1963] 1 All ER 223 at 228, PC, per Lord Evershed.
4 1981 SLT 161, and see *Empress Car Co (Abertillery) Ltd v National Rivers Authority* [1999] 2 AC 22.

(ii) Is the offence a real crime?

3.5   'Real crimes' and regulatory offences are to be contrasted in that the former involve moral opprobrium and the possibility of a high penalty, and therefore require *mens rea*[1]. The distinction is not a clear one, as there are cases in which strict liability has been imposed in spite of the moral opprobrium surrounding the offence and the provision of a possible prison sentence for the offence. Conviction for unlawful possession of a firearm under the Firearms Act 1968 has the whiff of traditional criminality about it and also involves a maximum penalty of three years' imprisonment; yet in *Smith v HM Advocate*[2] the High Court ruled that conviction of possessing a firearm did not require that the accused should know that the item which he had in his possession was, in fact, a firearm, thereby endorsing a strict liability approach to this category of offences. To similar effect is *Gammon (Hong Kong) Ltd v Attorney General for Hong Kong*[3] a Privy Council decision, in which the court held that the mere fact that a severe penalty was provided for in the legislation did not preclude strict liability.

'... there is nothing inconsistent with the purpose of the ordinance in imposing severe penalties for offences of strict liability. The legislature could reasonably have intended severity to be a significant deterrent, bearing in mind the risks to public safety arising from some contravention *of* the ordinance[4]'.

The ease with which courts have recently been prepared to accept strict liability in the case of offences involving either moral opprobrium or a severe sentence (or both) points to a weakening of the principle proposed in *Sweet v*

49

Parsley[5], that moral opprobrium requires moral guilt. It is submitted, therefore, that this test must now be considered an unreliable one, although its usefulness in combatting the over-extension of strict liability offences is evident.

1 The modern *locus classicus* of the 'real crime' concept remains *Sweet v Parsley* [1970] AC 132, [1969] 1 All ER 347 in which the House of Lords reversed a tendency to allow strict liability convictions for drug-related offences, in this case the offence of being concerned in the management of premises used for the purpose of smoking cannabis.
2 1996 SCCR 49, 1996 SLT 1338 applied in *Usman v HM Advocate* 2007 JC 111; 2007 SCCR 106.
3 [1985] 1 AC 1, [1984] 2 All ER 503, PC.
4 [1985] 1 AC 1 at 17, PC.
5 [1970] AC 132, [1969] 1 All ER 347, HL.

(iii)   Could the accused have done otherwise?

3.6   From time to time the courts have acknowledged the pointlessness of punishing those who could have done nothing to avoid the occurrence of an *actus reus*. It was stated in *Reynolds v Austin & Son Ltd*[1] that 'as a safe general principle ... where the punishment of an individual will not promote the observance of the law either by that individual or by others whose conduct he may reasonably be expected to influence, then, in the absence of clear and express words, such punishment is not intended'. In that context, was there any way, for example, whereby the company convicted of polluting the river in *Alphacell v Woodward* could have done more to prevent the offence from occurring? The answer perhaps lies in *Empress Car Co (Abertillery) Ltd v National Rivers Authority*[2] in which the House of Lords held that an act causing pollution did not have to be the immediate cause of the escape; so keeping a tank containing a noxious substance was doing something even if the immediate cause of the pollution was lack of maintenance, a natural event or a third party; the fact that something else had caused the pollution did not preclude a finding that the defendant had caused it as well. If the defendant had created a situation in which the substance could escape, but a prerequisite of the escape was the act of a third party or a natural event, the question was whether the act or event was something normal or extraordinary. An ordinary event or act would not nullify the causal effect of the defendant's acts, but in the case of an extraordinary act or event, the court could conclude that the defendant had not caused the pollution.

In practice, there will be very few cases in which an accused will be able to claim that there was nothing more which could have been done to prevent the occurrence of the *actus reus*. In food hygiene offences, for instance, samples can always be taken for analysis and more sophisticated and persistent checks on staff adherence to hygiene regulations could be insisted upon, even if these would have the effect of making businesses impossibly slow and unprofitable. In most cases, then, it will not be open to the accused to make the argument that there was no possibility of his having avoided committing the offence.

(iv)   The effectiveness argument

The fact that a statutory provision can only be given effect to if *mens rea* requirements are dispensed with is another ground upon which the courts may opt for a strict liability interpretation[3].

1 [1951] 2KB 135, [1951] 1 All ER 606 at 612, per Lord Devlin.
2 [1999] 2 AC 22.
3 *Lim Chin Aik v The Queen*, above; *Alphacell v Woodward* [1972] AC 824, [1972] 2 All ER 475.

Defences

3.7   It is not clear which defences are available in a strict liability offence, although it is likely that insanity[1], automatism[2], and nonage would be accepted as defences in this context. Error, by contrast, would not, as error affects *mens rea* which is irrelevant in strict liability offences

Necessity and self-defence should, in theory, be available as defences on the grounds that they are justificatory defences, the effect of which is to lead to the conclusion that the accused's act was not criminal. It was accepted in *Tudhope v Grubb*[3] that necessity was available as a defence to a strict liability offence under section 6(1) of the Road Traffic Act 1972, an approach which was endorsed in the subsequent decision of the High Court in *Moss v Howdle*[4]. Acts of third parties or natural events ('acts of God') may be defences although there is scant Scottish authority on this point. In *Howman v Russell*[5] the effect of a gale on the lights of a car was not taken into account, but in *Alphacell Ltd v Woodward*[6] the court clearly considered that there would be circumstances in which a defence based on third-party intervention would be available. In *Lockhart v NCB*[7] the court did accept that consideration had to be given to such things as natural forces, the act of a third party or an act of God, if the evidence justified the bringing of such matters into consideration.

1 *Gordon* para 8–28 expresses the view that it is 'almost inconceivable' that insanity would not be available as a defence in a strict liability offence.
2 RS Clark 'Automatism and strict liability' (1968) 5 Victoria University of Wellington Law Rev 12.
3 1983 SCCR 350, Sh Ct.
4 1997 SCCR 215.
5 1923 JC 32, 1923 SLT 336.
6 [1972] AC 824 at 834, 840, 845, 847–848, [1972] 2 All ER 475.
7 1981 SLT 161.

3.8   In an increasing number of statutes the possibility of a defence is being written into the statute. These provisions may require the accused to prove that he used all due diligence to avoid the occurrence in question. Section 102 of the Licensing (Scotland) Act 2005 prohibits the admission to licensed premises of those under eighteen but allows for a defence under s 141A if the accused had exerted 'all due diligence' to prevent the admission of such persons. This is not an impossibly high standard to meet, although it may not be enough merely to instruct staff accordingly. In *Ahmed v MacDonald*[1] the accused satisfied the court that he had exercised all due diligence, having employed a doorman to exclude under-age persons and having had regular briefing sessions with staff to instruct them in the need to comply with the statutory restrictions. By contrast in *First Quench Retailing Ltd v McLeod*[2] the accused was convicted of selling alcohol to a person under the age of 18 through the actions of an employee. The accused appealed on the basis that their employees had undergone a degree of training. The High Court considered that the court had been entitled to reject a 'due diligence' defence holding that, in the particular circumstances of the case, an employer exercising due diligence would have implemented and monitored an effective training scheme.

Statutes may also allow a defence of third-party intervention, or, where knowledge of a state of affairs is required, the statutory defence may simply allow acquittal if the accused satisfies the court that he did not have the necessary knowledge and could not, with reasonable care, have acquired this knowledge[3]. There may be a defence of 'reasonable excuse', for example, in the possession of an offensive weapon[4].

1 1994 SCCR 320, 1995 SLT 1094.
2 2001 SLT 372; 2001 SCCR 154.
3 Trade Descriptions Act 1968, s 24.
4 See Chapter 12.

VICARIOUS LIABILITY

3.9   Vicarious liability for crime offends the normal principle that a person is not to be held accountable for the actions of another. The attribution of vicarious liability, however, is accepted in limited circumstances, particularly in offences relating to sale to the public and in licensing cases. As is the case with strict liability regulatory offences, these offences do not involve 'true criminality', a fact which goes some way towards justifying the notion of vicarious liability.

Vicarious liability may be expressly provided for in a statute or it may be inferred from the nature of the statutory provision. If a statutory provision regulates an activity which normally involves employees, then the courts are likely to impose vicarious liability. For example, if a statute provides that it is an offence for a trader to sell any item without an appropriate licence, then the fact that sales are frequently conducted by employees justifies an inference of vicarious liability[1]. *Mens rea* on the part of the accused is not required, and therefore it makes no difference if an employer had no knowledge of the fact that his employee was, for example, carrying out a prohibited transaction. If the offence itself is described as requiring *mens rea*, then it is not clear whether the intent of the employee can be attributed to the employer. For example, if a statute makes it an offence 'knowingly to sell' a particular item, can an employer be convicted provided that his employee had the necessary knowledge? There is English authority suggesting that an employer is liable in such a case[2], and this would probably be followed in Scotland[3].

1 *Bean v Sinclair* 1930 JC 31.
2 *Mousell Bros Ltd v L and NW Railway* [1917] 2 KB 836.
3 For discussion, see *Gordon* para 8–58.

3.10   Vicarious liability requires that the offence should have been committed by the employee acting within the scope of his employment[1], but an act will not be removed from the scope of employment merely because it breaches general instructions given by the employer. In order to avoid vicarious liability in such a case, an employer must give highly specific instructions, the breach of which effectively puts the employee outside the scope of his employment[2]. The fact that an employer exercised all due diligence in the hiring, training and supervision of staff will not be a defence to vicarious liability, except where a statute specifically allows for this.

1 *City and Suburban Dairies v Mackenna* 1918 JC 105.
2 *Duffy v Tennant* 1952 JC 15.

CAUSING AND PERMITTING OFFENCES

A statute may make it an offence to 'cause or permit' a prohibited occurrence. After a period of inconsistency in the interpretation of such provisions, it is now clear that in certain circumstances no *mens rea* is required where the charge is one of causing something to happen[1]; permitting, by contrast, requires knowledge on the part of the accused that the prohibited act is taking place. In some cases, knowledge of the illegality will be inferred where the accused manifested wilful blindness to the possibility of the illegality[2]. On the other hand, in *McDonald v Howdle*[3], a conviction was quashed in circumstances where the accused knew that her car was not covered by her insurance to allow another driver, but gave permission on the basis of his assurance that he was insured. The High Court held that no permission was given unless the second driver had insurance to cover his use. Permission subject to an unfulfilled condition was no permission at all.

1 *Lockhart v National Coal Board* 1981 SLT 161. Cf *Smith of Maddiston Ltd v Macnab* 1975 JC 48, 1975 SLT 86. Whether 'causing' requires knowledge may eventually depend on the context of the provision and the presence elsewhere in the statute of qualifying words. See paragraph 2.23
2 *Smith of Maddiston Ltd v Macnab* 1975 JC 48, 1975 SLT 86.
3 1995 SLT 779, 1995 SCCR 216.

Chapter 4

Corporate criminal liability

4.1   A great deal of crime is committed in the context of companies or corporations, which are the dominant forces in modern commercial life. Prosecution authorities may still proceed against individuals within companies, and always charge them personally with the crimes they have committed, but to do so may obscure the real actor behind the criminal conduct – the company itself. This is open to the obvious objection that the real culprits, those who sought to profit by the crime, may escape prosecution, while the minor official bears the brunt of the blame. It may also be difficult to identify within a company those who have actually committed a criminal offence. This will be particularly so where a company is a large multinational one, with complex and possibly impenetrable corporate structures. It is clearly simpler in such a case to prosecute the company.

Opposition to the idea of corporate liability for crime historically focused on the alleged inherent impossibility of a company committing a crime[1]. How can a company, which is a metaphysical entity, form a criminal intention and perpetrate an offence? Both the intention and the perpetration are referable to human actors, and it is they who should be punished. This view, of course, ignores the reality of corporate action. It is widely accepted that corporations act in the real world, and the law acknowledges this by allowing companies to enter into contracts and by requiring them to answer for their negligence. If no conceptual difficulties occur in this context, then why should a company not be capable of criminal conduct? It is only if one subscribes to the teleological view that criminal conduct lies quite outside the range of competence of a corporation that one must reject the possibility of corporate crime. Yet a corporation can be used as a criminal instrument. It is possible to imagine the whole point and ethos of a company being criminal, as where the company is set up with the specific purpose of perpetrating fraud.

1 For discussion, see P French, *Collective and Corporate Responsibility* (1984) p 31 et seq.

4.2   A further, pragmatic objection founds on the pointlessness of convicting companies of criminal offences. According to this argument, individuals can be punished for their crimes but companies cannot. A company has no conscience to shame and no physical person to detain. A company cannot be sent to prison[1], nor can it feel the consequences of a fine. When a company is fined it is the shareholders, and indirectly the employees, who feel the consequences of the penalty. The company itself does not suffer.

These objections are based on an unrealistic notion of corporate identity. Companies do respond to threats and sanctions, and indeed negative publicity[2]. A company will tailor its actions according to the consequences, as demonstrated by the assiduity with which companies will avoid bad publicity. Companies are in many respects similar to human actors, with a sense of identity, a sense of purpose, and a responsiveness to surrounding circumstances. It is true that these objectives and corporate 'state of mind' may be experienced and expressed collectively, but this does not diminish their reality. Collective interest may exist quite independently of the interests of those who make up the collectivity.

1 Although this fact appeared to have escaped the attention of Parliament when it enacted the Companies Act 1967, s 68(5) of which provided: 'An insurance company which contravenes ... shall be guilty of an offence and liable on conviction on indictment to imprisonment for a term not exceeding two years', although this was repealed in 1973.
2 This was manifest in the first deferred prosecution agreement (DPA) in the UK, *SFO v Standard Bank plc* EWHC Crim 30 November 2015. A DPA is only available against a body corporate, a partnership, or an unincorporated association, not an individual. See s 45 of the Crime and Courts Act 2013. This applies to England and Wales only.

WHO MAY BE LIABLE?

4.3   Procedures exist for the prosecution, on indictment, of any 'body corporate'[1] and, on summary complaint, 'a partnership, association, body corporate or body of trustees'[2]. In summary proceedings, any partner, manager or the person in charge or locally in charge of its affairs (in the case of a partnership or firm), or the managing director or the secretary or other person in charge or locally in charge of its affairs (in the case of an association or body corporate), may be dealt with 'as if he was the person offending'.

In *Balmer and others v HM Advocate*[3], the issue of the status of a dissolved partnership was considered. This was an application to the Nobile Officium by three former partners of a partnership which had owned and run a nursing home. The home had suffered a fire in which fourteen residents died and criminal proceedings on indictment were raised against the partnership. It had been dissolved. The former partners sought a declarator that the indictment was incompetent. The High Court held that the dissolved partnership did not have any continuing legal personality following dissolution and the indictment was incompetent. They also rejected the Crown's alternative argument that the partners of the former firm retained responsibility for the criminal liabilities of the partnership; that would require an indictment directed against the partners of the former firm and it was clear that the former partners were not parties to the indictment. The court observed that, in principle, there was either a person or there was not a person, and personality, whether natural or juristic, was not created or extinguished in slices or instalments. The structures and principles of the law relating to the creation and extinction of legal personality could not lightly be departed from. A person, in all respects having died or ceased to exist, could not be deemed to be alive or extant as a person who could receive and accept service of an indictment and instruct entry of a plea and conduct a defence. The court did recognise that a partnership could possibly elide criminal responsibility by dissolution, which was undesirable, but considered that in the case of most common law crimes and many statutory offences the individual partner responsible for the act or omission would be readily identifiable and could be prosecuted in a personal capacity.

The issue canvassed was the effect of the dissolution of a partnership on the criminal liability of the partnership and the individual partners. The failure of the prosecution led to a Scottish Law Commission report[4]. Following consultation, the Partnerships (Prosecution) (Scotland) Act 2013 was enacted, effective from 26 April 2013. The Act allows prosecution of a partnership within five years of dissolution, dis-applies provisions which require fines levied on a partnership to be paid from partnership assets, provides that a change in membership has no effect on the prosecution of the partnership or the partners, and that dissolution is no bar to proceedings against any individual partner[5].

1 Criminal Procedure (Scotland) Act 1995, s 70. A body corporate includes a partnership: *Mackay Bros & Co v Gibb* 1969 JC 26, 1969 SLT 216; *Douglas v Phoenix Motors* 1970 SLT (Sh Ct) 57.
2 Criminal Procedure (Scotland) Act 1995, s 143. See *Maclachlan v Harris* 2009 SLT 1074; 2009 SCL 1271; 2009 SCCR 783 for an example of s 143 and its interaction with other statutory provisions.
3 2008 SLT 799, see also *Dickson v National Bank of Scotland* Ltd 1917 SC (HL) 50.
4 SLC, Criminal Liability of Partnerships (2011), Scot Law Com No 224.
5 See article, 'The criminal liability of partnerships and partners' JBL 2014 585.

STATUTORY OFFENCES
(1) Strict liability offences

4.4   Little difficulty has been experienced by the courts in holding a company liable for statutory offences of strict liability. The basis of this is that the company is vicariously liable for the acts of its employees, the general presumption against vicarious liability in the criminal law being rebutted either by the wording of the statute or by the implication that without vicarious liability the statute could not be applied[1]. The act of the employee must, of course, occur within the context of his employment in order for the company to be held liable on those grounds[2]. A company should not be held criminally responsible for the acts of employees who are pursuing their own private ends[3], but it will not always be a defence for a company simply to argue that the act was committed in defiance of instructions[4]; the company must show that the instructions were express and specific[5].

1 *Gair v Brewster* 1916 JC 36, 1916 1 SLT 380; *Duguid v Fraser* 1942 JC 1, 1942 SLT 51.
2 See discussion of vicarious liability at p 55, above.
3 *Heriot v Auld* 1918 JC 16, 1917 2 SLT 178; *City and Suburban Dairies v McKenna* 1918 JC 105, 1918 2 SLT 155.
4 *Linton v Stirling* (1893) 1 Adam 61, (1893) 20 R (J) 71; *Simpson v Gifford* 1954 SLT 39.
5 See *Gordon* para 8–104.

(2) Statutory offences requiring *mens rea*

4.5   Where the statutory offence requires *mens rea*, as is the case with the 'permitting' offences, the question is whether the knowledge of an individual employee or director can be imputed to the company. The Scottish courts have been prepared to make this imputation. In *Clydebank Co-operative Society v Binnie*[1] the knowledge of the company's transport manager that an unlicensed vehicle was being used in the business was 'brought home' to the company. Other decisions are to the same effect: in *Mackay Brothers & Co v Gibb*[2] the court held that the firm had knowledge of the fact that vehicle types were in an illegal condition, this knowledge being brought home to it by the knowledge of the firm's garage controller. In *Brown v W Burns Tractors Ltd*[3] a clerical assistant was aware of the fact that company drivers were driving illegally and this knowledge was attributed to the company.

Who must have knowledge within the company? Will the fact that any employee knew what was happening justify the conclusion that the company knew? Differing views have been expressed on this issue. In *Mackay Bros* the Lord Justice-Clerk suggested that the knowledge of any employee would suffice; Lord Wheatley and Lord Milligan, however, thought that there must be knowledge on the part of an employee in respect of those matters delegated to him. In *Brown*, the clerical assistant who knew what was happening was the person to whom day-to-day responsibility for the relevant matters had been delegated by the company. The tendency, then, is to require that the knowledge be possessed by one who is responsible for the relevant area of the company's operations[4]. Knowledge on the part of an employee who is in no position to change working practices will not suffice. The fact that a receptionist happens to observe another junior employee perpetrating an offence in the works yard, and is the only person (other than the perpetrator) who knows of the offence, will not mean that the company can be held to be permitting the conduct in question.

1 1937 JC 17, 1937 SLT 114.
2 1969 JC 26, 1969 SLT 216.
3 1986 SCCR 146.
4 *Reader's Digest Assoc v Pirie* 1973 JC 42, 1973 SLT 170.

(3) Common law offences

4.6   There is now no doubt that a company may be convicted of a common law offence in Scots law, although it is clear that there are some offences, such as murder[1], which a company lacks the capacity to commit[2]. The basis on which Scots law attributes corporate liability for common law crime was resolved in *Transco v HM Advocate (No 1)*[3]. In *Dean v John Menzies (Holdings) Ltd* it had been accepted that such liability could exist, although the majority declined to identify the juristic basis of it and excluded its operation in a case of shameless indecency. The dissenting judgment of Lord Cameron in this case, however, and Lord Ross's judgment in *Purcell Meats (Scotland) Ltd v McLeod*[4] both appeared to point to an acceptance of the 'controlling mind' fiction; effectively its application was assumed. That fiction was first advanced by Lord Denning in *H L Bolton Engineering Co v T J Graham & Sons Ltd*[5] and further developed in *Tesco Supermarkets v Nattrass*[6].

In *Bolton*, Lord Denning used the metaphor of the human body when he said:

'A company may in many ways be likened to a human body. It has a brain and nerve centre which controls what it does. It has also hands which hold the tools and act in accordance with directions from the centre. Some of the people in the company are mere servants and agents who are nothing more than hands who do the work and cannot be said to represent the mind or will. Others are directors and managers who represent the directing mind and will of the company and control what it does. The state of mind of those managers is the state of mind of the company and is treated by the law as such'[7].

1 *Dean v John Menzies (Holdings) Ltd* 1981 JC 23, 1981 SLT 50. In this case, Lord Stott firmly excluded the possibility of corporate liability for murder, but the Corporate Manslaughter and Corporate Homicide Act 2007 meets this criterion. See para 4.7.
2 There may be cases in which even a statutory offence may require individual human agency. In *Docherty v Stakis Hotels Ltd* 1991 SCCR 6 a company was charged with an offence under the Food Hygiene (Scotland) Regulations 1959, which placed a duty on the 'owner or other person having the management and control of a food business'. It was held that the company could not be considered as having management and control for the purposes of the regulations: '… such a corporate cannot for the purposes of this regulation have management control. A limited company can only act through its employees or servants' (at 14).
3 2004 JC 29.
4 1986 SCCR 672, 1987 SLT 528.
5 [1957] 1 QB 159, [1956] 3 All ER 624.
6 [1972] AC 153, [1971] 2 All ER 127.
7 [1956] 3 All ER 624 at 630.

4.7   In *Tesco Supermarkets* an attempt was made by the House of Lords to answer the question as to who may be considered to be the controlling mind of the company, but no single criterion emerged. Various approaches were favoured, varying from the fairly formal test as to who is designated by the articles of association to exercise power on behalf of the company[1], to the functional view of Viscount Dilhorne, who was of the opinion that the directing mind of the company was to be found in those persons who have actual control of the company's affairs and who are not subordinate to another in the exercise of this control.

The allegation of vagueness is still levelled at the controlling mind test in spite of efforts to clarify matters on the part of the House of Lords[2]. Attempts had been made to develop further leeway in the determination of who could be the 'mind' of the company[3]. None of the criteria suggested in *Tesco* really seem to draw a clear line between those who make up the directing mind and those who are no more than employees. There is also the objection that the ratio in *Tesco* allows a company to escape liability if its day-to-day managers are subject to a board-level veto[4]; this was inconsistent with the earlier Scottish authority discussed above, the tendency of which is to ask whether there was a de facto delegation of responsibility.

In *Transco*, the court accepted that Scots Law (like English Law) makes corporate liability depend upon an identifiable human agent's criminal responsibility for both the *actus reus* and the *mens rea*; accordingly it would not be enough for various people to have had particular knowledge and done nothing. The knowledge cannot be aggregated[5]. Much of the usefulness of corporate criminal liability lies in its ability to ensure compliance with regulations intended to control commercial and industrial life. The real blameworthiness of offending companies may lie, therefore, in the fact that their system of internal control is insufficient to supervise properly the activities of employees. This fault can realistically be pursued by the prosecution of the company, and it is perhaps here that prosecution resources are best directed.

1 See the judgments in this case of Lord Pearson and Lord Diplock.
2 Eg by Lord Maxwell in *Dean v John Menzies* 1981 JC 23, 1981 SLT 50.
3 See *Meridian Global Funds Management Asia Ltd v Securities Commission* [1995] 2 AC 500.
4 This is an aspect of the *Tesco* decision which has been played down in a number of subsequent cases: *R v Andrew's Weatherfoil Ltd* [1972] 1 All ER 65, [1972] 1 WLR 118.

5 For an analysis of Transco see 'Corporate culpable homicide'; article by PW Ferguson 2004 SLT 97.

Corporate Manslaughter and Corporate Homicide Act 2007

4.8 Many of the issues considered in *Transco* relating to the issue of corporate culpable homicide have been addressed by this act; it was promulgated following a long period of consideration. Concerns had been expressed by Lord Justice Rose in *Attorney General's Reference (No 2 of 1999)*[1] echoed (although not referred to) by Lord Osborne in *Transco plc v HM Advocate*[2] as follows:

'[If] Parliament considers that a corporate body should be subjected ... to the opprobrium attaching to a conviction for culpable homicide, then it must legislate[3].'

The Law Commission in England had proposed a statutory offence of 'corporate killing' as far back as 1996.[4] The Law Commission's report, including its proposals on corporate killing, provided the basis for the Government's subsequent consultation paper in 2000. A draft Corporate Manslaughter Bill (Cm6497) was published in March 2005 which became the 2007 Act.

The new Act introduced the crime of corporate homicide in Scotland. There is provision for prosecuting companies and other organisations[5] where there has been a gross failing, throughout the organisation, in the management of health and safety with fatal consequences. An organisation whose gross breach of a relevant duty of care leads to death will face criminal prosecution for corporate homicide.

The relevant duty of care is defined in section 2 and derives that definition from the law of negligence. Whether a particular organisation owes a duty of care to a particular individual is a question of law, requiring the judge to make findings of fact as necessary to decide that[6]. Guilt can only arise if the way in which the organisation's activities were managed or organised by senior management was a substantial element in the gross breach of the relevant duty. A gross breach arises if the conduct falls far below what can reasonably be expected of the organisation in the circumstances[7]. Senior management means persons who play significant roles in either the decision making, or the actual management of an organisation.[8] It is not clear, given the limited application of the Act so far, whether the interpretation of 'senior management' will be more extensive than the common law predecessor of 'controlling mind'. If a finding of guilt follows, a company will be liable for an unlimited fine[9].

1 [2000] 3 WLR 195.
2 (No 1) 2004 JC 29; 2004 SLT 41; 2004 SCCR 1.
3 Paragraph [25].
4 Law Commission's report *Legislating the Criminal Code: Involuntary Manslaughter* (Law Com 237).
5 Various government departments and bodies, contained in Schedule 1 of the Act, police forces, together with partnerships, trades unions, and employers' associations provided that they are employers.
6 Section 2 (5).
7 Section 1(4)(b).

8 Section 1(4)(c)
9 For a useful critique of the Act see Field and Jones; 'Five years on: the impact of the Corporate Manslaughter and Corporate Homicide Act 2007: plus ca change?' 2013 ICCLR 239.

Liability by individual directors or partners

4.9   The Criminal Justice and Licensing (Scotland) Act 2010 established a consistent provision for individual criminal liability of partners for offences committed by Scottish partnerships. The policy memorandum for the Bill recognised that although many statutes which create criminal offences provide for the individual liability of directors of corporate bodies, where the body corporate is found guilty and there has been consent or connivance or neglect[1], there was no consistent equivalent provision for partners in Scottish partnerships. The introduction of s 53 deals with this by determining that wherever a statute provides for individual liability for directors, there will be equivalent individual liability for partners in a Scottish partnership. Similar provisions are in place for Limited Liability Partnerships[2].

1 See for example Health and Safety at Work Act 1974, s 37.
2 Limited Liability Partnerships (Scotland) Regulations 2001, SSI 2001/128 at para 6.

Chapter 5

Causation

5.1   Criminal liability for a result depends upon the accused person having caused that result. This requires the making of a satisfactory link between the act of the accused and the event in question; in the absence of such a link the criminal result is not attributable to the accused – it is not his responsibility. In most cases, causation will not be an issue, as the link between actor and result will be self-evident. In some cases, however, the liability of the accused for a result may be placed in question by causal doubts. For example, in *R v Smith*[1] the appellant stabbed the deceased, a soldier, who was then carried to the casualty station by a fellow soldier, who dropped him twice on the way. At the casualty station, the victim was administered oxygen, which was an inappropriate and dangerous treatment in the case of a lung injury, and he died. Had the victim been correctly treated, his chances of recovery were estimated to be as high as 75%, and on these grounds the appellant argued that his act of stabbing was not the cause of death.

The accused's appeal against conviction was unsuccessful, but what would have been the result had the victim been transported to the casualty station by an ambulance which had crashed *en route*, causing him fatal head injuries? Alternatively, what would have been the result if, after the initial stabbing by Smith, the victim had been shot in the heart by another, dying immediately after the shooting? Or, to compound the complication, who would have been responsible for his death if the victim, after being stabbed by Smith, shot by another, dropped twice by his rescuer, was connected to an artificial respirator in hospital, which was then switched off by a nurse who had formed the (correct) impression that the victim was not going to survive more than a few hours[2]?

1 [1959] 2 QB 35, [1959] 2 All ER 193.
2 *Finlayson v HM Advocate* 1979 JC 33, 1978 SLT (Notes) 60.

5.2   Although few cases will involve as many possible causes as the last example, there will be circumstances in which a court has to select, from amongst a number of candidates, those events which are of special causal significance. This process of selection really amounts to an attribution of blame, and may therefore be affected by policy considerations. To identify conduct as the cause of an event entails the judgment that the person responsible for that conduct has to *answer* for a particular result, a decision which may clearly be influenced by notions of blameworthiness. Causation can therefore be viewed as a moral question, and causal decisions may be affected more or less explicitly by considerations of policy[1].

1 See eg DH Sheldon 'Dole, Directness and Foresight in Causation' 1996 JR 25.

SUFFICIENT LEGAL CAUSATION

5.3   Criminal responsibility for a result requires that the act of the accused be a sufficient legal cause of the event in question. This may be stated in the following rule: *the act of the accused must have been sufficient in itself to produce the result, provided that the result was not too remote from the original act.* If this criterion is met, then the accused's act may safely be considered to be the legal cause of the result.

'Sufficient in itself'

5.4   An act will only be a cause of an event if it is *causa sine qua non;* that is, if the event would not have occurred without it, or 'but for' the act, the event would not have occurred. If **A** stabs **B**, who bleeds to death, the result (**B**'s death) would not have occurred but for **A**'s act of stabbing. The stabbing is therefore a *causa sine qua non*. But if **A** stabs **B**, and **B** while in hospital receiving treatment for the stab wound, dies of a wholly unconnected illness, **A**'s stabbing is not a *causa sine qua non* as **B**'s death would have occurred without it.

An exception must be made in relation to concurrent causes. If **A** and **B** both shoot **C** at the same time, each shot being sufficiently serious to cause death, then we can see that **C**'s death would have occurred without **A**'s act, yet **A** will still be held to have caused the death[1].

1 *Gordon* para 4–29, citing the authority of *HM Advocate v Parker and Barrie* (1888) 2 White 79, (1888) 16 R (J) 5.

5.5   It should be noted, however, that while it is (generally[1]) necessary that the accused's actions should be a *sine qua non* of the relevant result, it is not always sufficient. The actions of the accused must be a material cause of death, and they must be a proximate cause; that is, they must not be too remote from the result which actually occurs. A father who fails to strap his son into a child-seat for a car journey may feel responsible if the child is killed in an accident caused by the dangerous driving of another. But in law it is the other driver, and not the child's father who is responsible for the child's death, even if it can be shown that the child would have survived the accident had he been strapped in.

1 Cf Lord Advocate's Reference (No 1 of 1994) 1995 SCCR 177, 1995 SLT 248, which should be viewed with caution. See discussion at para 5.9.

Existing conditions

5.6   An act is sufficient in itself even if it achieves its causal potency only because of an existing state of affairs. This is the so-called 'Thin Skull' rule which requires an accused person to take the victim as he finds him. The rule applies both in relation to the circumstances surrounding the victim at the time of an assault and in relation to the victim's personal condition (bad health, anatomical peculiarities, etc). The rule was stated by Lord Justice-Clerk Cooper in the following terms:

'It would never do for it to go forth from this court that house-breakers or robbers, or others of that character, should be entitled to lay violent hands on very old or very sick or very young people, and, if their victim died as a result, to turn around and say that they would never have died if they had not been very weak or very old or very young. That is not the law, and I think you will agree with me that it is not common sense ...'[1].

If, therefore, the accused has stabbed the victim in a vital organ, with fatal results, it will be no defence to argue that the victim's organs were abnormally positioned and that such a stabbing would not have resulted in death in a normal person. A slight wound may lead to the death of a haemophiliac, and this will be homicide even if the accused did not know of his victim's abnormal condition. Psychological or religious characteristics are also irrelevant in this context. In *R v Blaue*[2] the victim, a Jehovah's Witness, declined an operation to treat a stab wound she had received at the hands of the accused, and the court observed:

'It has long been the policy of the law that those who use violence on other people must take their victim as they find them. This in our judgment means the whole man, not just the physical man. It does not lie in the mouth of the assailant to say that his victim's religious beliefs which inhibited him from accepting certain kinds of treatment were not reasonable'[3].

1 *HM Advocate v Robertson and Donoghue* (August 1945, unreported), HCJ; Gane and Stoddart p 183. See also *HM Advocate v Rutherford* 1947 JC 1, 1947 SLT 3; *Bird v HM Advocate* 1952 JC 23, 1952 SLT 446.
2 [1975] 3 All ER 446, (1975) 61 Cr App Rep 271.
3 [1975] 3 All ER 446 at 450.

INTERRUPTION OF CAUSATION: THE *NOVUS ACTUS INTERVENIENS*

5.7 An act will not be a sufficient cause of a result if the link between it and the result is interrupted by an intervening event, a *novus actus interveniens* or *nova causa interveniens*. This intervening event must be significant enough to acquire causative potency for itself. An act which is an expected or 'regular' part of the sequence of events will not usually be treated as sufficient to interrupt the causal link between the original act and the result.

A *novus actus interveniens* may fall into any of the following categories:

(1) An 'act of God'

5.8 A natural event, outside human agency, may be a *nova causa interveniens*. The injured victim who is fatally struck by lightning on the way to hospital, will not be regarded as having been killed by the original assailant, even if the stab wound was potentially lethal. An 'act of God' is, however, something quite unpredictable; predictable natural events, such as a river spate or a high tide, will not amount to interrupting events[1].

1 *Southern Water Authority v Pegrum and Pegrum* [1989] Crim LR 442.

(2) An act of a third party

5.9 Third party acts may amount to a *novus* actus *interveniens* unless such acts are foreseeable and accepted as being 'within the risks' of the original act[1]. The basis for recognising such an act as a *novus actus interveniens* is the general presumption that voluntary human actions are not caused and that therefore the occurrence of a voluntary human action will interrupt a causal link[2]. A simple illustration demonstrates this principle: if **A** leaves a knife on the table which is then picked up by **B** and used to kill **C**, the link between **A**'s act of leaving the knife and **C**'s death is interrupted by **B**'s intervening voluntary act.

The issue of third party intervening action arose in the unusual case of *R v Pagett*[3] in which a girl used as a human shield by the accused was fatally wounded by bullets fired by police officers. The appellant argued that the action of the police officers in firing the shots amounted to a *novus actus interveniens*, but this argument was rejected. In its decision, the Court of Appeal in England placed some weight on the view that third-party action would not amount to a *novus actus interveniens* where it was either involuntary or performed in the course of official duty[4].

1 In civil cases, the actions of the third party must be foreseen as being 'highly probable' before causation can be established – see Lord Mackay in *Maloco v Littlewoods Organisation Ltd* 1987 SC (HL) 37, 1987 SCLR 489, 1987 SLT 425.
2 Discussed by J Feinberg in *Doing and Deserving* (1970) p 152.
3 (1983) 76 Cr App Rep 279.
4 The Court of Appeal placed some store by the opinion expressed by HLA Hart and AM Honore in *Causation in the Law* (1st edn, 1959) p 299.

5.10 It is not settled whether a criminal act on the part of another person may amount to a *novus actus interveniens* if the original act may have had fatal results anyway. **A** shoots **B** wounding him in a way which would prove fatal after thirty minutes, whatever happened. **C** then happens upon the scene and takes the opportunity himself to shoot **B**; if **B** dies immediately after being shot by **C** (as a result of **C**'s shot and **C**'s shot alone), is **A**'s act of shooting to be considered a cause of **B**'s death? *Macdonald* takes the view that it should not, but there is no clear authority for this[1], and it would be open to a court to espouse a contrary view. Such examples, of course, appear highly artificial and unlikely until they actually occur, as happened in *S v Daniels*[2]. Here **A** shot **V**, inflicting injuries which were likely in the circumstances to be fatal. **B**, acting independently of **A**, came upon the scene and shot **V** in the ear, as a consequence of which **V** died. Two of the five judges hearing **A**'s appeal against conviction for murder, were of the view that **A**'s act was a cause of **V**'s death. They refused to accept that the 'proximate' cause of the victim's death – **B**'s shot – had to be regarded as the sole cause, and could see no policy reasons for limiting the liability of **A**[3].

Malregimen

Medical mishaps may substantially worsen the condition of a victim and may therefore interrupt the causal link between act and result. The action of a doctor will not normally amount to a *novus actus interveniens* provided that the doctor is not departing unduly from what is medically expected in the circumstances. In *Finlayson v HM Advocate*[4] the switching off by doctors of a mechanical ventilator was not treated as an interrupting cause. The decision to discontinue artificial ventilation was not treated as unwarrantable; it was, in fact, described by the court as a perfectly reasonable course of conduct, not something ultroneous or unforeseeable. In *R v Malcherek; R v Steel*[5] the Court of Appeal in England addressed the question of brain death in two cases in which the victims were declared brain dead while respiration was still being maintained artificially. The court declined to hold that switching off of the machines constituted a *novus actus interveniens:*

> 'Where a medical practitioner adopting methods which are generally accepted comes bona fide and conscientiously to the conclusion that the patient is for all practical purposes dead, and that such vital functions as exist – for example, circulation – are being maintained solely by mechanical means, and therefore discontinues treatment, that does not prevent the person who inflicted the initial injury from being responsible for the victim's death'[6].

1 *Gordon* (para 4–32) points out that the passage of *Hume* I, 181 cited by *Macdonald* in support of his proposition does not in fact provide the necessary authority, as *Hume* is dealing with a case where the original wounding is not clearly fatal.
2 1983 (3) SA 275.
3 For two of the other judges, the causal issue did not need to be decided, as they took the view that **A** and **B** were acting in concert, a conclusion which would anyway justify both being convicted of **V**'s murder. For discussion, see CR Snyman *Criminal Law* (2nd edn, 1989), p 72.
4 1979 JC 33, 1978 SLT (Notes) 60.
5 (1981) 73 Cr App Rep 173, [1981] 2 All ER 422.
6 (1981) 73 Cr App Rep 173 at 181.

5.11 Apart from the discussion in *Finlayson v HM Advocate*[1], there is little modern Scots authority on the causal significance of intervening medical treatment. Earlier authority must be treated with some caution, given the scientific uncertainties of the times and the difficulty medical witnesses would have experienced in attributing death to a particular cause. In *James Williamson*[2] Lord Justice-Clerk Inglis accepted that the 'unskilful and unjudicious treatment' of a 'simple and early cured wound' could interrupt the causal link, and this was also accepted, more cautiously, in *Heinrich Heidmeisser*[3]. The problem is really the same as that of criminal acts by third parties, however. An English case, *R v Smith*[4], has been extremely influential in a number of jurisdictions and has proved to be persuasive in a Scottish decision on this matter. In *Smith*, the facts of which have been outlined above[5], Lord Parker CJ expressed the *novus actus interveniens* principle as follows:

> 'Only if it can he said that the original wounding is merely the setting in which another cause operates can it be said that the death does not result from the wound. Putting it another way, only if the second cause is so overwhelming as to make the original wound merely part of the history can it be said that death does not flow from the wound'[6].

1 1979 JC 33, 1978 SLT (Notes) 60.
2 (1866) 5 Irv 326.

3 (1879) 17 SLR 266.
4 [1959] 2 QB 35, [1959] 2 All ER 193.
5 [1959] 2 QB 35 at 58, [1959] 2 All ER 193 at 198.
6 [1959] 2 QB 35 at 43. Cf the old Scottish case of *James Wilson* (1838) 2 Swin 16. The ruling in *Smith* might be contrasted with the less stern view expressed in *R v Jordan* (1956) 40 Cr App Rep 152, a case in which the inappropriate administration of an antibiotic to a patient with an intolerance for that antibiotic was held to be palpably wrong and therefore a *novus actus interveniens*.

5.12   The approach recommended in *Smith* has been endorsed in subsequent decisions. In *R v Cheshire*[1], the Court of Appeal in England stressed that, in order to amount to a *novus* actus *interveniens* the negligent treatment must be so independent of the accused's acts, and so potent in causing death, that what the accused did pales into insignificance. The original wounding does not therefore have to be the *only* cause of death; it must, however, be a significant cause of death. This test is not favourable to an assailant: only rarely will medical negligence be of such a nature as to overshadow the accused's causal contribution to the victim's death. This approach was referred to by the High Court with approval in *Johnston v HMA*[2] where, after considering a series of cases including Smith and Cheshire, Lord Reed said:

> 'The English decisions which we have cited are consistent with the approach to the law of causation adopted in the case of *Malone*[3]. We also respectfully agree with their emphasis upon the importance of avoiding undue elaboration in the directions on causation that are given to a jury. Although the correct identification of the causal connection required by the law can in some contexts be a matter of difficulty (as has been illustrated, for example, by cases in the law of negligence concerned with industrial diseases), in the present context the law's requirement – that the wrongful act of the accused should have materially contributed to the death of the deceased – is not in doubt. Whether that causal connection has been established in a particular set of circumstances is a question to be determined by the jury, applying common sense.'

1 [1991] 3 All ER 670, [1991] 1 WLR 844.
2 2009 JC 227.
3 1988 SCCR 498.

(3)   An act of the victim himself

5.13   The victim may himself make a causal contribution to the criminal result, but this need not amount to an interruption of causation. Once again, it seems that the test is whether the victim's act is of a spontaneous voluntary or unreasonable nature, or is, on the other hand, an entirely foreseeable result of the accused's conduct.

(i)   The supply cases

In *Khaliq v HM Advocate*[1], the accused was charged with endangering the lives of certain young persons who had bought 'glue sniffing kits' from him.

The fact that the purchasers of the solvents had ingested them voluntarily was held not to break the chain of causation. Lest it be thought that this decision was dependent on the age of the 'victims' in *Khaliq*, it should be noted that in the subsequent and similar case of *Ulhaq v HM Advocate*[2], the High Court specifically held that the age of the purchasers was irrelevant. Another difference between *Ulhaq* and *Khaliq* was that the charge was one of simple supply of solvents rather than in the form of 'kits' designed to make for easier abuse. Lord Justice General Hope at p 615 said that:

> 'The essence of the charge … was that the appellant knew that the purpose of the acquisition of the solvents was their abuse and that the supply of them to their recipients was a cause of that abuse. That is sufficient for the conduct to be criminal, because once that is established then there is no material distinction between the supply of the solvents and the direct administration of their fumes to the purchasers which, it was accepted, would plainly be criminal. So neither the age of the purchaser nor the supply of kits to assist inhalation is essential. As the learned advocate-depute put it, they do not provide the measure of the offence. They are simply factors, whose weight will vary with the circumstances. Their presence may make it easier to draw the inference that the supply was a cause of the abuse, but their absence does not mean that that inference cannot be drawn. In our opinion the sheriff was right to … leave it to the jury to decide whether, on the evidence, the supply was conducted in this case in the knowledge that the substances would be abused and was therefore not merely to be the occasion of the abuse but its cause'.

1 1983 SCCR 483.
2 1990 SCCR 593, 1991 SLT 614.

5.14   So if the accused knows the use to which a substance, or, presumably, an article, is to be put, then he can be liable for the consequences of that use. In *Lord Advocate's Reference (No 1 of 1994)*[1] a young man supplied a girl with amphetamines. She selected the amount she wished to take and voluntarily ingested the drug, as a result of which she died. The supplier was charged with culpable homicide. He was acquitted by the trial judge on the ground that the voluntary act of the 'victim' was a *novus actus* which broke the chain of causation. On a reference to the High Court by the Lord Advocate, however, it was held that there was no such break in the chain of causation, provided that the supplier knew that the drugs were supplied for the purpose of abuse. Accordingly the mere supplying of the drug was equiparated with culpable and reckless conduct; and the act of supplying regarded as sufficient to satisfy the *mens rea* for the offence of culpable homicide.

That is no longer the case. In *MacAngus v HM Advocate*[2] at paragraph [29] the Lord Justice General (Hamilton) stated;

> 'With the possible exception of the *Lord Advocate's Reference (No 1 of 1994)*, where the view of the court is open to interpretation, there appears to be no support for the view that unlawful act culpable homicide can be made out except where, as in assault or analogous cases, the conduct is directed in some way against the victim.'

The opinion in *MacAngus* cannot be reconciled with that in the *Lord Advocate's Reference (No 1of 1994)*, and the latter should probably be regarded as an incorrect assessment of Scots criminal law.

MacAngus (heard along with the case of *Kane*) was another case concerned with the supply of controlled drugs leading to the death of some of those ingesting them. The cause of death was intoxication by the controlled drug. The Lord Justice General continued at paragraph [30]:

> 'We are satisfied that a charge libelling culpable homicide in the context of supply (or the administration of) a controlled drug is relevant only if the Crown offers to prove that the supplying (or the administration) of the drug was in the circumstances reckless'.

The court, having reviewed a comprehensive list of authorities, concluded at paragraph [42];

> 'These ... authorities tend to suggest that the actions (including in some cases deliberate actions) of victims, among them victims of full age and without mental disability, do not necessarily break the chain of causation between the actings of the accused and the victim's death. What appears to be required is a judgement (essentially one of fact) as to whether, in the whole circumstances, including the inter-personal relations of the victim and the accused and the latter's conduct, that the conduct can be said to be an immediate and direct cause of the death'.

In *Scott v HMA*[3], the High Court had occasion to re-visit the topic of the supply and administration of illicit drugs, where the ultimate user died. After refusing the appeal, on being satisfied that the accused had been reckless (taking into account factors including that the drugs were known to be particularly strong, and that the victim was not a user of the drug in question), the court addressed the question of the complicity of the victim as follows:

> '[I]n cases involving injection of prescribed drugs, the relevance of consent depends upon the circumstances. In cases where drug abusers give mutual assistance to inject the drugs, it is conceivable that there may be no intention to harm. Indeed that may be fairly common. It is notorious that drug addicts may on occasions suffer more from the lack of a fix than they might from receiving an injection. It will therefore always be a matter of circumstances whether injecting another who wishes to be injected amounts to assault. It is entirely understandable that the Crown have generally elected to proceed by way of charges of culpable and reckless conduct. In the hazy and shady world of drug abuse, securing reliable evidence to establish the *mens rea* for assault may often prove difficult. On the other hand the risks associated with abuse of class A prescribed drugs are so notorious that assisting another to abuse the drug may readily be seen as culpable and reckless conduct.'

This is to be compared with the position in England. In *R v Kennedy (No 2)*[4]. In that case the accused had filled a syringe with heroin and passed it to the victim who ingested it and then died of opiate intoxication, The Court of Appeal considered a manslaughter charge was open to the jury. The matter went to the House of Lords in the form of a question to the Lords as follows: 'When is it appropriate to find someone guilty of manslaughter where that person has been involved in the supply of a class A controlled drug, which is then freely and voluntarily self-administered by the person to whom it was supplied and the administration of the drug then causes his death?'.

The speech given by Lord Bingham of Cornhill, delivering the unanimous opinion of the Lords was unequivocal in answering the question. 'In the case of a fully informed and responsible adult, never'[5].

1 1995 SCCR 177, 1995 SLT 248.
2 2009 SLT 137.
3 2012 SCL 153.
4 [2007] UKHL 38, [2008] 1 AC 269, [2007] 3 WLR 612, [2007] 4 All ER 1083.
5 Paragraph [25].

(ii)   The escape cases

5.15   A number of cases involve victims who have caused injury to themselves in an attempt to escape from a situation of danger created by the accused. Such an attempt will not generally be a *novus actus interveniens*, unless the attempt at escape is so utterly unreasonable that it could not be foreseen[1]. In *R v Roberts*[2] the appellant made sexual advances to a female passenger in his car. The passenger jumped out of the moving car and received injuries as a result; the appellant argued (unsuccessfully) that these injuries flowed from a novus *actus interveniens* on the victim's part. *R v Mackie*[3] also involved an attempt at escape, in this case by a three-year-old boy who fell downstairs, sustaining fatal injuries, while fleeing the appellant's physical ill-treatment. Once again, conduct resulting from the well-founded fear of the escapee did not amount to a *novus actus interveniens*[4]. In *MacDonald v HM Advocate*[5], the High Court had to consider a charge of causing the deceased to fall from a window. The deceased had been assaulted and then locked in his flat. He was found the following day outside the window of his kitchen. It was not disputed that the accused left the flat between five and thirty minutes before the fall. The trial judge in his report considered that it was open to the jury to conclude that after the assault, the deceased had tried to escape. The High Court considered that the matter was properly one for the jury, putting particular emphasis on the short time between the conclusion of the attack and the fall; the jury were entitled to reach the decision that but for the locking of the door in the context of the assaults, the deceased would have lived.

1 There are few cases of escape which have been found to be unreasonable. However, see *R v McEnery* 1943 SR 158 – a jump from a train to avoid assault at the hands of an unarmed drunk.
2 (1972) 56 Cr App Rep 95.
3 (1973) 57 Cr App Rep 453.
4 *DPP v Daley* [1980] AC 237, (1979) 69 Cr App Rep 30 (PC): the victim's fear of being hurt must be reasonable and must be caused by the conduct of the accused. See also, *Patrick Slaven* (1885) 5 Coup 694. For discussion, see DW Elliott 'Frightening a person into injuring himself' [1974] Crim LR 15.
5 [2006] HCJAC 89.

(iii)   The victim's feckless conduct

5.16   *Hume* is of the view that the exacerbation of a slight injury 'through the obstinacy and intemperance' of the victim, or through his application of 'rash and hurtful applications' will interrupt causation[1]. The decision in *Joseph and Mary Norris*[2] is to like effect, the victim in this case having drunk alcohol and removed a bandage from a minor wound inflicted by the accused. Courts in other jurisdictions have been unwilling to conclude that the causal link is broken in such cases[3]. It is surely foreseeable that the victim of an assault will neglect to seek treatment (which is not unusual), or will fail to comply with medical instructions. A downright refusal of medical treatment, whether on religious or other grounds, is also not unforeseeable, and was held in *R v Blaue*[4] not to amount to a *novus actus interveniens*.

1 I, 182.
2 (1886) 1 White 292.
3 *R v Holland* (1841) 2 M & Rob 351, 174 ER 313; *Flynn* (1867) 16 WR 319 (Ireland); *R v Mubila* 1956 (1) SA 31 (Southern Rhodesia).
4 [1975] 3 All ER 446, (1975) 61 Cr App Rep 271.

(iv)   The victim's suicide

Suicide by the victim of an assault may raise the question of whether the original assailant caused the victim's death. The issue is alluded to obiter in *John Robertson*[1], in which the court expressed the view that suicide following immediately upon an attack might 'come very near' to culpable homicide, but apart from this dictum there is no Scottish authority on this point. *R v Bunn*[2] involved a murder charge in a case where the victim committed suicide three-and-a-half months after an assault, but the prosecution was abandoned on the grounds of doubts as to causation. Courts in other jurisdictions have adopted a less cautious attitude. In the American case of *Stephenson v State*[3] a homicide conviction was returned in respect of the suicide of a girl who had been raped and held captive by the accused[4], and in *Jones*[5] a rapist was convicted of murder after his victim jumped into a river. In both these cases, of course, the suicide follows hard upon the assault; a different decision may have been reached if some time had elapsed between the original wrongful act and the commission of suicide. The only relatively recent Scottish case which considered that matter has been *Broadley v HM Advocate*[6]; the accused was convicted of murdering the deceased by causing her to fall from a window. The deceased had been seen by witnesses falling to the ground. No-one else was seen and only the deceased's fingerprints were found on the windowsill. The High Court quashed the conviction on the basis that there was no evidence to support the Crown's speculation that the accused had been ordered to jump; absent the means whereby the accused caused the deceased to go through the window, there was no basis in the evidence for any involvement between the accused and the death. The opinion of the court concludes:

> 'In most, if not all, cases where confessions or admissions by an accused have been held to be virtually sufficient and requiring very little corroboration, the Crown has already established that the relevant crime has been committed, the issue being by whom. They do not achieve that position in this case, as we have discussed, since there is no direct evidence or even inferential evidence to support the view that the deceased was the victim of a murderous attack by one means or another when she came through the

window. If one stands back and looks at the evidence as a whole as listed ... it seems to us that, on balance, the more legitimate inference to draw is that the deceased committed suicide'[7].

No exploration was made of whether the accused's actions might have prompted the suicide, on the basis that there was no evidence of the necessary *mens rea*.

The real obstacle which the prosecution will have to overcome in a suicide case is the usual presumption that a voluntary act is not treated as having been itself caused by another act. It is only if the act of suicide is closely connected with the original assault, or other wrongful act, that its presumed status as a *novus actus interveniens* can be overcome. Evidence of significant depression on the victim's part, as a result of the attack, may help to establish this; as might evidence of predisposition to suicide, since the attacker must take the victim as he finds him.

1 (1854) 1 Irv 469.
2 (1989) Times, 11 May.
3 (1933) 205 Ind 141, 170 NE 633.
4 See discussion of the special factors in this case: *Gordon* para 4–52.
5 43 NE 2d 1017 (1942).
6 2005 SCCR 620.
7 At para [8].

CONCLUSIONS

5.17   It is difficult to summarise the law on causation since so much appears to depend upon the circumstances of a particular case. Certain principles can be articulated in determining legal causation in the criminal law – the need for an action to be at least a *sine qua non* of the prohibited result; the need to show that that the action is a proximate and a material cause of the outcome; the need to show that no fresh cause intervened in the causal mechanism, unless that fresh cause was an entirely predictable or foreseeable adjunct to the original action. It seems, however, that none of these principles taken in isolation can be relied upon completely to produce a predictable legal result. As noted earlier, the most important factor would appear to be the extent to which the accused can and should be held responsible for his involvement in the outcome.

Chapter 6

Parties to crime

6.1　A criminal offence may be committed by a person acting on his own, or by one who acts in concert with others. In the latter case, there may be a number of persons each of whom plays a different role in the commission of the offence, including the instigation of the crime, the provision of technical assistance for its commission (for example, the provision of firearms or keys), and actual participation in the carrying out of the crime (as a principal actor or as, for example, the lookout). Each of these persons is equally responsible for the crime even if there is only one principal actor who eventually performs the *actus reus* of the crime[1]. The term used in Scots law to describe this form of guilt is 'art and part' guilt; other terms used include 'complicity in crime', 'accession to crime', or 'ancillary responsibility'.

1 *Hume* I, 264; *HM Advocate v Lappen* 1956 SLT 109.

THE JUSTIFICATION OF ART AND PART GUILT

6.2　The fact that the criminal law treats all participants in a criminal offence as equally guilty may strike some as unduly harsh, given different degrees of participation on the part of those involved. The actions of a look-out man who warns of the approach of the police may seem less reprehensible than those of the person who actually commits a robbery. Similarly, the person who provides details of another's movements in order to allow him to be set upon and killed, may in one view seem less blameworthy than the murderer who actually strikes the blows. Such intuitions, however, are open to criticism on the grounds that they fail to give adequate weight to the social danger which an accomplice represents. One who advises another to commit a crime is actually as much of a threat to society as the person who commits it: one who provides the explosives for the terrorist is as dangerous as the terrorist himself. The social danger view, then, suggests that the reason why we hold accomplices responsible for crimes lies in the positive contribution they make to criminal conduct. The doctrine of art and part involvement is limited; where two or more people embark upon a common criminal purpose 'they will normally be responsible for what happens in the execution of that purpose. It is the unexpected and unforeseen, going clearly outwith the parameters of the joint purpose, for which art and part liability is elided[1].'

1 *McDonald v HM Advocate* 2007 SCCR 10 at para [18].

6.3　This view of the accomplice as a danger to society raises the question of whether the attribution art and part guilt can be justified on causal grounds. Is the accomplice causally responsible for the commission of the crime and therefore legally responsible too? This analysis has been advanced by some criminal law commentators, and has been approved in a number of cases in other jurisdictions, but has not been discussed by the Scottish courts. In some judgments causation is depicted as an essential element of accomplice liability[1], but the theoretical objections to requiring a causal link between the accomplice's act and the eventual commission of the crime will be considerable. This is particularly so in the case where the secondary party did no more than instigate a crime. It will be effectively impossible to link the giving of advice to the actual commission of the crime, as there is no means of establishing that the action of the perpetrator resulted from the instigation rather than from a determination on his own part to go ahead with the crime. A similar difficulty is encountered in cases involving the provision of assistance, as demonstrated in the following example: **A** decides to help **B** to break into a house. He leaves a ladder by the side of the house, intending that **B** should use it to enter an upstairs window. **B**, in fact, enters by forcing the front door. In this case **A**'s act has not played a causal role in the entry to the house, but it is likely that he would still be considered art and part guilty of the burglary.

1 *Dicta* to the effect that a causal link is required: *NCB v Gamble* [1950] 1 QB 11 at 20. See also *Anderson and Morris* [1966] 2 QB 110 at 120; *DPP v Merriman* [1973] AC 584 at 592 and 607; *Attorney General's Reference (No 1 of 1975)* [1975] 1 QB 773.

FORMS OF ART AND PART LIABILITY

6.4   Art and part liability may arise where there is one of the following: (1) joint commission of a crime; (2) the commission of a crime through innocent agency; or (3) associate liability.

(1)   Joint commission

Joint commission occurs where two or more parties both perform acts which constitute an *actus reus*. An example is where **A** and **B** contemporaneously assault **C**, both striking blows. **A** and **B** have jointly committed an assault on **C** in this case. Where **A** acts as a lookout while **B** robs a bank, both **A** and **B** have jointly committed robbery of the bank.

The parties must act in concert. This may be inferred from prior agreement between them, or on the basis of spontaneous actings. If concert cannot be established, then each person is liable only for what he is proved to have done. This principle may give rise to difficulties in cases where there has been an attack on a victim by a number of persons but it is not clear what each person did. If the attack results in the death of the victim, and the prosecution cannot establish concert nor establish who struck the fatal blow, then there is no alternative but to acquit all the participants of murder (although all those who were shown to have actually struck the victim in any way could be convicted of assault). Authority for this is to be found in *Docherty v HM Advocate*[1], *HM Advocate v Welsh and McLachlan*[2] and in *Morton v HM Advocate*[3]. In *Johnston v HMA*[4] the court re-affirmed that principle, saying, 'At a later point, the judge raised the possibility that the jury might conclude that the deceased had been killed by only one of two people, but were unable to decide which of the two. In that situation, the jury were directed to acquit both people unless they found concert to be established. That was a correct direction'. Interestingly, in *Johnston* the two accused were convicted of murder on the basis that each, by reason of individual assaults they had carried out on the victim, was guilty of murder. The verdicts, by implication, rejected the Crown's contention that the accused had acted in concert.

The application of the art and part doctrine to murder is not without difficulty. *Gordon* at paragraph 5.42 comments; 'An accused might be convicted of an offence he neither contemplated nor desired. This applies whether the allegation is of joint criminal enterprise or spontaneous concert, and is emblematic of the general unsatisfactory nature of Scottish law on the mental element in homicide'[5].

1 1945 SLT 247, 1945 JC 89.
2 (1897) 5 SLT 137.
3 1986 SLT 622
4 2009 JC 227, 2009 SCL 737.
5 See also Leverick, 'The (art and) parting of the ways: joint criminal liability for homicide' 2012 SLT 227.

(2) Innocent agency

Innocent agency is involved where **A** uses **B** to commit a crime, **B** being either unaware of some material factor or being innocent on other grounds, such as coercion. *R v Cogan and Leak*[1] provides an example of this. In this case, Leak forced his wife to have intercourse with Cogan, who believed that she was consenting (Leak knew that she did not consent). Leak was convicted of aiding and abetting a rape, while Cogan was acquitted, the court regarding this as an instance of the commission of a crime through innocent agency. The decision has been subject to criticism and comment[2] and may not, according to the Court of Appeal, still be regarded as good law[3].

1 [1976] QB 217, [1975] 2 All ER 1059.
2 Smith and Hogan on Criminal Law p 221.
3 *R v Watkins* [2010] EWCA Crim 2349.

(3) Associate liability

6.5   Art and part liability may be seen as a form of associate liability. Associate liability may be attributed to an accused who does not himself perform an *actus reus*, but who is art and part guilty because of an *actus reus* performed by another. His liability derives from that of the main perpetrator, with whose actions he has associated himself and this gives rise to a number of questions, including the following.

(i) Can there be liability where the person committing the actus reus is himself acquitted?

The acquittal of an actual perpetrator may result in a number of ways. There may be inadequate evidence against the perpetrator, or the actual perpetrator

77

may have a defence (such as insanity or coercion[1]) which exculpates him. It is quite competent in Scotland for an accessory to be convicted of an offence in respect of which another has been acquitted, provided that he was capable of being convicted of the offence himself. In *Young v HM Advocate*[2] the appellant had been charged with fraudulent offences in relation to company dealings. The directors and secretary of the company were acquitted, and it was held that the appellant could not in such circumstances be convicted as he himself, not being a director or secretary of the company, could not commit the offence in question. His liability therefore was entirely derivative upon that of his co-accused. By contrast, in *Capuano v HM Advocate*[3] the appellant's conviction was upheld in the face of the acquittal of his co-accused on the grounds that the latter were not adequately identified. The distinction to be made here is that in *Capuano* the appellant was capable of committing the offence of assault himself; his fault in no sense depended on the fault of his co-accused. Stones were thrown by members of a group while he was a member; the fact that the appellant's co-accused were not satisfactorily identified as members of the group was held not to detract from the appellant's own participation in the criminal activities in question.

1 In *R v Bourne* (1952) 36 Cr App Rep 125 the accused had forced his wife to have sexual connection with a dog. The Court of Appeal rejected the argument that the husband could not be guilty of aiding and abetting something which by virtue of the fact that the wife had a defence of duress, was not a criminal offence.
2 1932 JC 63, 1932 SLT 465.
3 1984 SCCR 415, 1985 SLT 196.

6.6   It must be shown, however, that a prima facie criminal act was committed by some person. If, in the case of murder, it cannot be shown that a murder was committed by somebody (even a person unknown), then there can be no conviction of an accused person on art and part grounds. This does not exclude liability where the perpetrator of the act is not punishable, for reasons of excuse or for some technical legal reason, such as an evidential one. Conviction of the accessory may be achieved in such a case by the operation of the doctrine of innocent agency (discussed above). In *Cogan and Leak*[1] there was, technically, no rape because Cogan was not aware of the victim's lack of consent. This, however, did not prevent conviction, on the grounds that the offence was committed through innocent agency. In *R v Austin*[2] the accused was convicted of aiding and abetting child stealing by encouraging the father of the child to snatch the child from its mother. The latter could not be convicted of child stealing, but this did not deter the court from convicting the accessory of the offence. In *Reid v HM Advocate*[3], the accused, a female, was charged with living on the earnings of prostitutes. This was an offence under s 11(1) of the Criminal Law Consolidation (Scotland) Act 1995. That section provides that it is an offence for a 'male person' to live off the earnings of prostitutes. She challenged the indictment on the basis of impossibility further arguing that if it had been intended that a female person could be charged under subsection 11(1), the subsection would not have been confined to male persons. In refusing the appeal, the High court said:

'We are not persuaded that this argument is sound. Section 293(1) of the Criminal Procedure (Scotland) Act 1995, on which the sheriff had founded his decision, provides:

"A person may be convicted of, and punished for, a contravention of any enactment, notwithstanding that he was guilty of such contravention as art and part only".

That provision is expressed in general terms and is not stated to be subject to a contrary intention appearing in the terms of any statutory offence. [Counsel for the accused] accepted that, on the basis of art and part, a woman could be convicted of rape .... If the mischief to which section 11(1)(a) is directed is the living of a male person on the earnings of prostitution, there is no reason to suppose that the guilt of a female person on the basis of her acting art and part is excluded. The submission that section 11 contains within it a structure which determines the gender of the person who can competently be convicted is attractive at first sight, but we do not consider that it has substance, when regard is had to the terms of section 293(1) to which we have referred.'

It can be argued that there is no theoretical problem for Scots law here. Scots law makes no distinction between principal and secondary offenders – all those involved in the crime are equally guilty[4]. This means that the innocence of the person who commits the *actus reus* is irrelevant, and all that matters is that the accused should by his actions have associated himself in some way with the commission of the crime. This approach achieves much the same result as a doctrine of innocent agency, although the doctrine of innocent agency might provide a more readily understood explanation of art and part liability in such cases.

1 [1976] QB 217, [1975] 2 All ER 1059.
2 [1981] 1 All ER 374, (1981) 72 Cr App Rep 104.
3 1999 SLT 1275.
4 As suggested by *Gordon* para 5–04.

(ii)   *In respect of the same act, can A be convicted as being art and part guilty of one offence while his co-accused is convicted of another?*

6.7   In *Melvin v HM Advocate*[1] the appellant was convicted of murder while his co-accused was convicted only of culpable homicide in respect of the same incident. It was argued on behalf of the appellant that the verdict of murder was inconsistent with that returned in respect of the co-accused, as they had both acted in concert. This argument was rejected; the court held that it was open to the jury to consider the actings of art and part actors and to assess the degree of their guilt according to the extent to which their individual actings demonstrated wicked recklessness or otherwise. As Lord Stott observed:

'Where two are charged with murder the actings of the one may display such utter recklessness as to require a verdict of guilty as libelled, without it being a necessary corollary that the actings of another who is art and part in the homicide must be taken to infer the same degree of recklessness'[2].

A similar issue arose in *Brown v HM Advocate*[3], in which two persons, a man and a woman, acting in concert, attacked a third person. On the way to the *locus* of the crime one of them (the man) picked up an iron bar, which was used as a weapon in the attack. A knife was also produced by the man, who used it to stab the victim fatally through the heart. It was held by Lord Justice-General Hope that the woman could not be convicted of murder unless she had known that a weapon would be used either with intent to kill or with such a degree of viciousness as to justify a finding of wicked recklessness. In other words, she would have to have known that the man with whom she was acting in concert would act with the *mens rea* of murder.

Both of these cases were considered and qualified by the decision in *McKinnon v HM Advocate (No 2)*[4] in which appeals were dismissed. The accused had been part of a group which had gone to carry out a robbery. The victim died as a result of an assault by stabbing. The High Court held, dismissing the appeals, that the courts had historically approached the establishment of guilt on the basis of concert by taking an objective rather than a subjective approach. The court asked, in the case of the individual accused, what was foreseeable as likely to happen. *Brown* and *Melvin* could be distinguished, as *Brown* did not adequately address the issue of antecedent conduct and should not be regarded as authoritative, and *Melvin* could not be regarded as a catalyst for the approach in *Brown* as it was clearly not a case of antecedent concert. The court considered that if the relevant concert was established, there was no separate question as to whether the individual accused had the necessary criminal intent, the guilt of the individual depending on whether there was a common criminal intent and its scope. The court found that an accused was guilty of murder art and part where, first, by his words or actions he actively associated himself with a common criminal purpose which was, or included, the taking of human life, or carried the obvious risk that human life would be taken, and secondly, in the carrying out of that purpose, murder was committed by someone else. Further they held that where the accused was proved only to have participated in some less serious common criminal purpose in the course of which the victim died, he might be guilty art and part of culpable homicide, whether or not any other person was proved guilty of murder. In the circumstances of the case they held that if the jury were satisfied that an individual accused was aware that knives were being carried and liable to be used, the inference, that there was an obvious risk that they might be used to commit murder in pursuing the criminal purpose of robbery, was virtually inevitable.

1 1984 SCCR 113, 1984 SLT 365.
2 1984 SCCR 113 at 118.
3 1993 SCCR 382.
4 2003 JC 29, 2003 SLT 281, 2003 SCCR 224.

THE VICTIM AND ART AND PART GUILT

6.8 Unwilling victims of criminal offences are clearly not art and part guilty of the offence perpetrated upon them. Willing 'victims' raise difficult questions: is the consenting victim of an assault art and part guilty of the assault, or is the girl under the age of consent who consents to sexual intercourse art and part guilty of an offence? As far as assault is concerned, the issue has not been decided by the courts, but in principle there is no reason why in a case such as *Smart v HM Advocate*[1] where consent was held to be no defence, the victim should not be art and part liable[2]. The situation in respect of sexual offences is probably not so straightforward, and the question of art and part guilt probably depends on the purpose of the offence, that is whether it is intended to protect vulnerable persons or to prevent the commission of certain wrongful acts, irrespective of the age of the parties. Those offences which are designed to protect young or otherwise vulnerable persons probably do not entail the attribution of art and part guilt to the willing victim. There is no Scottish authority on this point, but it is likely that a Scottish court would follow the decision in *R v Tyrrell*[3] and *R v Whitehouse*[4]. If this view was to be accepted, there would be no art and part liability for the willing victim in the common law offence of lewd practices. The Sexual Offences (Scotland) Act 2009 introduced offences where each party may be seen as both victim and perpetrator[5].

The position is different in relation to incest, and public indecency, which share the feature of being offences directed against morality in general rather than being offences directed against particular victims. The offence of incest is committed by both parties, although the Incest and Related Offences (Scotland) Act 1986 introduced the rule that there is no criminal liability on a girl under the age of 16 involved in an incestuous act[6]. *Vaughan v HM Advocate*[7] established that an adult, who is not within the prohibited degrees can be guilty art and part in relation to the commission of an offence under the relevant Act (in that case the Incest Act 1567).

1 1975 SLT 65.
2 B Fisse *Howard's Criminal Law* (5th edn, 1990) p 352 takes the same view.
3 [1894] 1 QB 710, [1891–94] All ER Rep 1215.
4 [1977] QB 868, [1977] 3 All ER 737.
5 See chapter 11.
6 1986 Act, s 1. The provisions of this Act are now re-enacted in the Criminal Law (Consolidation) (Scotland) Act 1995. See Chapter 11.
7 1979 SLT 49.

BILATERAL REGULATORY OFFENCES

6.9   Some statutes may make it an offence, for example, to sell or trade in certain conditions and the question then arises as to whether a purchaser or customer is art and part guilty of the offence committed by the vendor or trader. These statutes are not protective in their purpose, and the protection principle referred to above, which would exclude art and part guilt, does not therefore apply. *Gordon* suggests that there should be no liability on a purchaser in such a case, as the statutory restriction of liability to the seller indicated parliamentary intention that the purchaser should not be penalised[1].

1 At para 5–06.

WHEN ART AND PART LIABILITY WILL OCCUR
(1) Doing nothing: the mere presence cases

6.10   A person who witnesses the commission of a crime does not become art and part guilty of that crime by the mere fact of being present. There is no general duty to intervene to prevent the commission of a crime, but art and part liability may result if there is some special factor of status or relationship which (i) imposes a duty to act on one person who is present at the commission of the crime; or (ii) if the mere presence of the accused amounted to active encouragement of the offence.

(i) In *Bonar v Macleod*[1] a police officer was held art and part liable for an assault committed in his presence, by a policeman who was junior to him. The duty of an employee to prevent theft of his employer's property gave rise to accomplice liability in *Ex parte Parker*[2], and in a series of cases courts have accepted that the owner of a car may be an accomplice to a driving offence committed by a person driving his car in his presence if he fails to take steps to prevent the commission of the offence[3]. The licensee of licensed premises may be art and part liable to be convicted of the offence of illegal consumption of alcohol if he remains passive in the presence of such after-hours drinking on his premises[4].

1 1983 SCCR 161. See also *Forman and Ford* [1988] Crim LR 677.
2 [1957] SR(NSW) 326.
3 *Du Cros v Lambourne* [1907] 1 KB 40; *Harris* [1964] Crim LR 54; *Crampton v Fish* [1970] Crim LR 235; *Rubie v Faulkner* [1940] 1 KB 571; *Dennis v Plight* (1968) 11 FLR 458. The driver cases are discussed by D Lanham 'Drivers, control and accomplices' [1982] Crim LR 419.
4 *Tuck v Robson* [1970] 1 All ER 1171, [1970] 1 WLR 741. Cf *Duxley v Gilmore* [1959] Crim LR 454.

6.11   (ii) Mere presence at the scene of a crime was not sufficient for art and part guilt in *Geo Kerr*[1], but in more recent English and Commonwealth cases the courts have accepted that there might be accessory liability when mere presence amounts to encouragement. In *Allan*[2] the Court of Criminal Appeal in England accepted that mere presence at a fight could result in accomplice liability provided that the spectator knew that his presence encouraged the offender. In *Clarkson*[3], soldiers who passively witnessed a barrack-room rape were held liable to conviction as accomplices, although their conviction was quashed on the grounds that the trial judge had not informed the jury of the requirement that the accused should have ***intended*** their presence to encourage the offender in the carrying out of the rape[4]. The Queensland Court of Criminal Appeal has stated the matter as follows in *Beck*[5]:

> 'Voluntary and deliberate presence during the commission of a crime without opposition or real dissent may be evidence of wilful encouragement or aiding. It seems that all will depend on a scrutiny of the behaviour of an alleged aider and the principal offender and on the existence which might appear of bond or connection between the two actors and their actions. The fortuitous and passive presence of a mere spectator can be an irrelevance so far as an active offender is concerned. But, on the other hand, a calculated presence or a presence from which opportunity is taken can project positive

encouragement and support to a principal offender. The distinction between a neutral and a guilty presence of a person at the scene of a crime will be for the jury to assess. Proof of guilt of the crime of aiding and abetting will not ordinarily be established by mere presence if no telltale acts are performed by the alleged aider but the intention behind and the effect of the presence of the additional person at the scene may be established by other evidence from which it is possible to say that a case of intentional encouragement or support of the principal offender is made out'[6].

So mere presence may itself be evidence of an intention to encourage, but whether it is sufficient evidence of such an intention will depend on the circumstances. In *Gorman v HM Advocate*[7], one of the accused was convicted of murder on the basis that he had refused to let others go for help despite the fact he had not participated in the murderous assault. In *Gay v HMA*[8] the High Court upheld a conviction where the jury deleted an allegation that the accused had 'instructed' other participants to assault the complainer. It was argued that, in the absence of an allegation of express instruction, there could be no concert. The Court said that concert can 'depending on the circumstances proved, comprise not only words uttered but also acts carried out and attitudes adopted by those involved'. The court continued '[The jury] were further entitled to conclude that the appellant's failure to prevent the more serious assault, together with his giggling and laughing as he filmed the incident … his behaviour and words towards the complainer after the incident, and his subsequent showing of the video to another person, amounted to his active association with the escalated level of criminality of the spontaneous common criminal purpose of the group.' Although the case turns to an extent upon its own facts, the court's observations are interesting in their inclusion of behaviour which takes place after the incident giving rise to criminality; the active association at the time of the offence can be fortified by behaviour afterwards.

1 (1871) 2 Coup 334.
2 [1965] 1 QB 130, [1963] 2 All ER 897.
3 [1971] 1 WLR 1402, [1971] 3 All ER 344.
4 See also *Wilcox v Jeffrey* [1951] 1 All ER 464, [1951] 1 TLR 706 (mere presence as a spectator at an illegal jazz performance); *Bland* [1988] Crim LR 41 (no liability where the accused merely shared accommodation with a drug dealer).
5 (1989) 43 A Crim R 135.
6 At 142, per Macrossan CJ.
7 See http://news.bbc.co.uk/go/pr/fr/-/1/hi/scotland/glasgow_and_west/8357245.stm.
8 [2015] HCJAC 125.

(2) Counselling and instigating an offence

6.12   To counsel an offence is to advise on the commission of an offence. There may be no encouragement that the offence be committed, as long as mutual counselling takes place. To instigate an offence is to urge or encourage its commission. It is not instigation to express a desire that a crime be committed; there must be words or action directed towards achieving that end. Nor need the instigator give directions as to how the offence is to be committed, provided the mind of the other person is turned by him to the thought of committing the crime.

There is no instigation unless the perpetrator of the crime was, in fact, influenced by the words or actions of the instigator, although an unsuccessful instigation may be charged as attempted instigation[1]. Instigation requires that the words or action were actually communicated to the perpetrator[2], but it is not necessary that the instigation should have been directed against a particular person[3]. The withdrawal of instigation after it has been made will not affect the art and part guilt of the instigator[4], although it is possible that he will cease to be regarded as an instigator if he has done everything in his power to stop his instigation being acted upon[5]. In *R v Croft*[6] the accused had entered into a suicide pact with the deceased. The deceased shot herself, causing a wound, and then asked for assistance. The accused left her in order to secure assistance. His conviction of murder was upheld on the grounds that he had not done anything to remove from the deceased's mind the effect of the counsel which he had previously given her.

(3) Supply of materials or information

The provider of materials or information for the purposes of committing a crime is art and part guilty of that crime. This obviously does not apply to an innocent provider – to the taxi driver, for example, who unaware of the fact that his passenger is bent on murder, drives him to his victim's house. Some knowledge of the recipient's criminal purpose is required, although the precise extent of this knowledge may be difficult to quantify. Is it enough, for instance, that the provider entertained a suspicion that the materials may be used for the furtherance of a criminal purpose? Does the provider have to know exactly what crime the recipient has in mind, or is it sufficient if he knows that a crime of some sort will be committed?

1 *HM Advocate v Tannahill and Neilson* 1943 JC 150, 1944 SLT 118; *HM Advocate v Kay and Strain* (May 1952, unreported), Glasgow High Court: discussed by *Gordon* at para 6–73.
2 *R v Krause* (1902) 66 JP 121 (accused acquitted of soliciting murder as the prosecution had not proved that the letters in which he mentioned murder had been received by the person to whom they were addressed).
3 *Re Macleod* (1970) 12 CRNS 193, 1 CCC (2d) 5 (Canada) (publication of an article giving detailed instructions on the growing of cannabis plants held to amount to counselling the growing of cannabis); *R v Most* (1881) 7 QBD 244 (conviction upheld in which an article urged readers in general to resort to violence).
4 *Hume* I, 279–280.
5 There is a suggestion to this effect in *HM Advocate v Baxter* (1908) 5 Adam 609, (1908) 16 SLT 475, supported by *Gordon* para 5–24 et seq. Withdrawal of encouragement is discussed (*inter alia*) in *White v Ridley* (1978) 21 ALR 661. For further discussion, see the general treatment of withdrawal at para 6.16 below.
6 (1944) 29 Cr App Rep 169.

6.13   There is no clear Scottish authority on this question, but the issue has been dealt with in a number of English and Commonwealth cases. In *R v Bainbridge*[1] the accused had obtained welding equipment for a man who, he knew, would be using it for a criminal purpose. It was held that there would be no accessorial liability if there was knowledge that there was some illegal venture contemplated; there had to be knowledge of the 'type' of offence which was to be committed. The apparent helpfulness of this ruling was, however, illusory, as the notion of 'type' remained undefined. It was clear that there had to be knowledge of at least some specific features. In *Bettles*[2] knowledge of the fact that there was a 'dishonest and unlawful purpose' did not amount to knowledge of the type of offence.

Further clarification of the issue came in the decision of the House of Lords in *DPP for Northern Ireland v Maxwell*[3] In this case the accused was convicted of being an accessory to an explosives offence, after he had directed members of a terrorist organisation to their target. He had known that the offence contemplated was one of violence, but he claimed not to know of the fact that explosives would be used. His appeal was rejected on the grounds that all that was required was that the offence actually be committed within the range of possible offences which he had foreseen. *DPP for Northern Ireland v Maxwell* does not overrule *Bainbridge*, and the type test may therefore be taken, in English law at least, as continuing to be available alongside the foresight test suggested in *Maxwell*. It would be open to a Scottish court to resort to either formulation, and it is suggested that given the 'range test' applied in other contexts, there may be a preference for the straightforward *Bainbridge* approach.

1 [1960] 1 QB 129, [1959] 3 All ER 200.
2 [1966] Crim LR 503.
3 [1978] 1 WLR 1350, [1978] 3 All ER 1140.

6.14   An adoption of *Bainbridge* will not, of course, dispel uncertainties. There will still be awkward cases, as illustrated in the following example. **A** gives to **B** a jemmy which he is to use for housebreaking on a target which they have both identified. Shortly before the planned housebreaking, **B** is arrested for another offence and sentenced to two years' imprisonment. On his release, without any further contact with **A, B** carries out a housebreaking on a different target, but using the jemmy supplied by **A**. In such circumstances the type test may appear to be satisfied, while a foresight test would fail. Or can it be that a burglary committed on another target is not an offence of the same type as that committed on an originally agreed target? The lapse of time in itself makes a difference. *Hume* states that art and part guilt requires that there is assistance for an *immediate* crime; there will be no art and part liability in respect of crimes that are remote, in temporal terms, from the act of assistance[1]. This proposition has the authority of *Hume*, although it is difficult to see why in principle the lapse of time should make a difference. A delay in the commission of the crime is nothing to do with the person who furnishes assistance, and his liability should be capable of continuity until he has countermanded or otherwise negatived the effect of his assistance[2].

Does the accused have to have actual knowledge of the fact that an offence is to be committed, or will some lesser mental state such as negligence or recklessness, suffice? If **A** gives **B** a knife, knowing that there is a possibility that the knife will be used for an attack on **C**, is he art and part to the subsequent attack on the grounds of recklessness? There is no Scottish authority on this point, but the view of the House of Lords in *Maxwell* was that awareness of a **probability** was sufficient to establish guilt. That view would be likely to find favour in the Scottish courts, which may also be prepared to impose liability where there is no more than a possibility of a crime being committed[3]. Wilful blindness would probably amount to actual knowledge, and thus attract art and part liability.

85

Negligence is another matter altogether, and it is unlikely that this state of mind could justify a holding of art and part guilt. The issue has been discussed at length by the Australian High Court in *Giorgianni v The Queen*[4] in which the court overturned the appellant's conviction for complicity in the offence of culpably causing death by failing to make himself aware of the dangerous state of a truck of which he was owner but not driver. The High Court took the view that nothing short of knowledge was sufficient for complicity and that even recklessness as to the possibility of an offence being committed was insufficient[5]. In Scots law negligence is almost certainly an insufficient basis for art and part guilt[6], but a Scottish court would be unlikely to follow the *Giorgianni* decision and exclude recklessness, as to do so would be to severely limit the scope of art and part guilt.

1 *Hume* I, 276; *Burnett* p 269.
2 The elapse of time was considered to be significant in *Attorney General v Able* [1984] QB 795, [1984] 1 All ER 277 where it was held that the publishers of a booklet detailing methods of committing suicide would be liable for aiding and abetting a suicide under s 2(1) of the Suicide Act 1961 (which does not apply in Scotland) where 'a long period of time' has elapsed between the issuing of the booklet and the act of suicide or attempted suicide.
3 *Mayberry* [1973] Qd R 211 (accessorial liability when accused knew that offence 'might be committed'); *R v Harding* [1976] VR 129 (held to be irrelevant that accused believed that murder might not take place on account of a possible change of mind by the perpetrator).
4 (1985) 156 Crim LR 473.
5 Two of the judges were prepared, however, to hold that wilful blindness amounts to knowledge (at 482, 495).
6 *D Stanton & Son Ltd v Webber* (1972) Crim LR 544; *Smith v Jenner* [1968] Crim LR 99.

6.15   The provision of materials used for the commission of a crime may occur in the course of the provider's legitimate business, in which case the provider will not normally be art and part liable for the subsequent criminal use of the materials. It will be different, though, if he has knowledge of the illegal purpose; liability here will be determined according to the normal principles covering art and part guilt. The reckless selling of an item which might be used for criminal purposes may lead to conviction, provided there was something in the circumstances which pointed to a high degree of probability that the item sold will be used for the commission of an offence. For example, the trader who sells a weapon to a customer whom he knows to have a record of offences of violence, may be deemed to be reckless, although action is likely to be taken only against those who persist in such sales, in the face of very clear warnings[1]. The legitimacy of the provider's conduct may be a factor to be taken into account, as in *Gillick v West Norfolk and Wisbech Area Health Authority*[2].

The giving of information used to facilitate the commission of an offence may lead to art and part liability if all that is done is to impart what *Hume* terms 'naked advice'[3]. In *HM Advocate v Johnstone*[4] the accused gave a woman the name of an abortionist who was not known personally to her (that is, to the accused). This did not lead to art and part guilt in the offence of abortion as there was no connection between the abortionist and the provider of the information. This seems to be a very restrictive decision as it would exclude liability in a case where **A**, planning to kill **B**, asks **C** for the name of a person prepared to carry out a contract killing. **C**'s facilitation of the murder of **B** is surely culpable, as without this information, the killing may never have taken place[5]. It is submitted that the authority of *Johnstone* is weakened by the fact that it was concerned with abortion, a crime which even at that time did not necessarily attract the same degree of opprobrium as many other offences. It is difficult to see the same view being taken if the advice concerned murder or robbery.

(4) Assisting the perpetrator in the commission of the crime

Involvement in a criminal offence may result from prior agreement or may be spontaneous. Where there is agreement this may be explicit or implicit. In the case of spontaneous participation, there may be no agreement between the parties, as the original perpetrator may not welcome the involvement, and this may mean that he may not be considered art and part guilty of what the new participant does. If **A** joins **B** in an assault upon **C**, and **B** does not welcome or endorse this participation, then **B** will not be art and part guilty if he detaches himself from the assault. If, however, he continues, his mental reservation as to **A**'s participation will be irrelevant – he associates himself, albeit unwillingly, with **A**'s actions. In *Carruthers v HM Advocate*[6], the accused was found guilty of murder. He appealed *inter alia* on the basis that no reasonable jury would have convicted the appellant of murder in the light of his evidence that he had only punched the deceased twice at the outset of the incident. There was an absence of evidence of any further physical contact between the deceased and the appellant. The co-accused was more clearly implicated given the extent of the co-accused's clothing being contaminated with the deceased's blood, the presence of the co-accused's blood-stained fingerprint on the bedroom cupboard door and the evidence that the co-accused had said to the police when he was apprehended, that the appellant had not been involved in the crime of murder. The jury were apparently satisfied that the co-accused was the principal actor; he was also convicted of this murder. The court declined to allow the appeal holding:

> 'Nevertheless these factors do not detract from the fact that, on the evidence to which we have referred, the jury were entitled to reach the view that the appellant was ***present throughout the whole of these activities and was taking an active part in at least some of them.*** Accordingly we see no substance in this ground of appeal.' (emphasis added)

1 As in *Khaliq v HM Advocate* 1984 JC 23, 1983 SCCR 483, although see the cases of *Purcell v HM Advocate* 2008 SLT 44, where recklessness in some contexts requires an intention to cause physical harm, and *MacAngus v HM Advocate* 2009 SLT 137, where a charge of culpable homicide in relation to supplying controlled drugs was only relevant if the Crown can prove that the supply was reckless.
2 [1986] 1 AC 112, [1985] 3 All ER 402, HL (discussed, in its criminal aspects, by JC Smith [1986] Crim LR 166); *O'Donovan and Vereker* (1987) 29 A Crim R 292.
3 *Hume* I, 278.
4 1926 JC 89, 1926 SLT 428.
5 Cf *Attorney General v Able* [1984] QB 795, [1984] 1 All ER 277. Cf the law in New Zealand: *Martyn* [1967] NZLR 396; *Baker* 28 NZLR 536, [1909] 1 All ER 277: accused held guilty of counselling a crime when he told a friend how to blow open safes.
6 Unreported High Court of Justiciary 14 December 1999.

6.16   There is a potentially difficult problem if the person who joins in an assault on another does so after the fatal blow has been struck: does such a person become guilty of the culpable homicide or murder of the victim? The issue was clarified in *McLaughlan v HM Advocate*[1] in which the High Court ruled that when a person joins in an already existing criminal enterprise, there was no question of his adopting what happened before he joined in; his responsibility is limited to that which occurs after he joins in. The question of cumulative effect is not dealt with in this case, and so it remains unclear what the position will be if the accused's acts combine with what has happened before he has joined in to produce the final effect. It is submitted that in a case of homicide or assault this will be determined by the application of the rule that one takes one's victim as one finds him. If the position of an already wounded victim is exacerbated by the accused's subsequent assault, then the accused should be responsible for whatever is the outcome. A person who sees that his victim is already injured arguably demonstrates wicked recklessness in assaulting him further and may therefore be convicted of murder[2].

In an unusual case from England, *R v Gnango*[3], the accused became involved in a shoot-out with another individual (referred to as 'bandana man') in a car park. A passer-by was shot dead. The fatal bullet had not come from the accused, but the Supreme Court held that there was criminal responsibility, notwithstanding the lack of responsibility for the fatal shot.

1 1991 SLT 660, 1991 SCCR 733.
2 The problem of joining in has been discussed elsewhere, notably in the South African courts: *R v Mtembu* 1950 (1) SA 670 (A); *R v Mgxwiti* 1954 (1) SA 370 (A); *R v Chenjere* 1960 (1) SA 473 (Supreme Court of the Federation of Rhodesia and Nyasaland). For discussion, see R Whiting 'Joining in' 1086 SALJ 38; *S v Thomo* 1969 (1) SA 385.
3 [2012] 1 AC 827.

WITHDRAWAL

6.17   A participant in a criminal enterprise cannot escape art and part liability merely by dissociating himself from the actions of his co-participants. Dissociation may be relevant in determining whether there is concert between the parties, but once the commission of the crime has commenced, dissociation is no defence. In *McNeil v HM Advocate*[1] an attempt was made to raise a defence of dissociation on the part of a member of the crew of a ship which had been used to transport a cargo of controlled drugs to the United Kingdom. The accused alleged that he had only become aware of the nature of the cargo once at sea, and left the ship at a port before reaching Britain. On the issue of dissociation, Lord President Emslie observed:

'If a crime is merely in contemplation and preparations for it are being made, a perpetrator who then quits the enterprise cannot be held to act in concert with those who may go on to commit the crime because there will be no evidence that he played any part in its commission. If on the other hand, the perpetration of a planned crime or offence has begun, a participant cannot escape liability for the completed crime by withdrawing before it has been completed unless, perhaps, he also takes steps to prevent its completion'[2].

1 1986 JC 146, 1987 SLT 244, 1986 SCCR 288.
2 At 318.

6.18 This leaves open the question of whether a defence of withdrawal will be successful if the accused makes an attempt to stop the completion of the crime. The question is left undecided. Guidance is available from common law jurisdictions in which this issue has been considered, and where withdrawal has, in certain circumstances, been accepted by the courts as a defence. These decisions show, first of all, that the withdrawal should be voluntary: the abandonment of a criminal project rings insincere if it takes place in the face of imminent detection[1] or if it stems from a sense of squeamishness rather than from moral disapproval of the crime[2]. The giving of an instruction that the crime should not proceed may not be enough to relieve the accused of accessorial liability although it will, in general, be a minimum requirement of a defence of withdrawal or dissociation. Any countermand must be timely[3] and should be backed by other action directed to preventing the crime from proceeding. In *R v Becerra and Cooper*[4] Becerra knew that Cooper was carrying a knife on the burglary on which they were mutually engaged. Cooper produced the knife when they were disturbed, whereupon Becerra shouted 'Come on let's go'. Becerra argued that he had withdrawn from the common purpose by the time the stabbing occurred, but the Court of Appeal took the view that this withdrawal was ineffective. The court did not say that Becerra should have attempted to take the knife from Cooper, although it may have had in mind steps such as the shouting of a warning to the victim or the use of language more clearly indicative of an intention to withdraw[5].

1 *White v Ridley* (1978) 52 ALJR 724: abandonment of a drug importation after the suspicions of Customs officials had been aroused.
2 *R v Malcolm* [1951] NZLR 470.
3 *White v Ridley* (1978) 21 ALR 661, per Gibbs J: 'Where the accused has requested a person who is of sound and mature mind to do an act which the accused knows, but the agent does not know, is illegal, the accused will not be liable if he has given timely countermand of his request. The countermand must have been manifested by words or conduct sufficiently clear to bring it home to the mind of the agent that the accused no longer desires the agent to do what he was previously asked to do; a vague, ambiguous or perfunctory countermand would not be enough. And the accused must have done or said whatever was reasonably possible to counteract the effect of his earlier request'.
4 (1975) 62 Cr App Rep 212.
5 Verbal withdrawal unaccompanied by physical steps, was said by the Court of Criminal Appeal in England to be acceptable in *Fletcher and Zimnowodski* [1962] Crim LR 551. See also *Whitefield* (1984) 79 Cr App Rep 36. The issue of withdrawal in general is discussed by D Lanham 'Accomplices and withdrawal' (1987) 97 LQR 575.

THE SCOPE OF ART AND PART LIABILITY: THE PROBLEM OF UNINTENDED CONSEQUENCES

6.19 When two or more persons act together in the pursuit of a criminal objective, they are said to be acting for a **common purpose** and each party will be art and part liable for what is done by the other in pursuit of that purpose. There is a clear modern statement of this in Lord Patrick's direction to the jury in *HM Advocate v Lappen*[1]:

'... if a number of men form a common plan whereby some are to commit the actual seizure of the property, and some according to the plan are to keep watch, and some according to the plan are to help carry away the loot, and

89

some according to the plan are to help dispose of the loot, then, although the actual robbery may only have been committed by one or two of them, every one is guilty of the robbery, because they joined together in a common plan to commit the robbery. But such responsibility for the acts of others under the criminal law arises if it had been proved affirmatively beyond reasonable doubt that there was such a common plan and that the accused were parties to that common plan. If it has not been proved that there was a common plan, or if it had not been proved that the accused were parties to this previously concluded common plan, then in law each is only responsible for what he himself did, and bears no responsibility whatever for what any of the other accused or any other person actually did'.

The scope of the common plan therefore determines liability: those acts which are part of the plan will be attributed to all the accused involved in the plan; those acts which fall outwith the plan will be attributed to the individual actor. The question in each case will be whether an act may be regarded as part of the plot, a matter which will be determined by the agreement, express or implied, between the parties. What is implicitly agreed will depend on the circumstances: an agreement to commit a robbery involves an agreement to use at least some degree of force; an agreement to break into a building involves implicit agreement to damage property in the course of gaining access.

1 1956 SLT 109.

6.20 On occasion a party to a joint criminal offence may depart from a previously agreed plan and do something which was not in the contemplation of his accomplices. In such a case art and part liability will depend on whether the act in question was foreseeable to the accomplices[1]. If the act in question was foreseeable, then all parties may be art and part answerable for it; if it was unforeseeable, and was committed by one of the participants for reasons of his own, then there will be no art and part liability in respect of it[2]. For example, **A** and **B** agree to break into a bank and, in the course of the break-in, **B** fires a gun at and kills a security guard. If **A** was unaware of the fact that **B** was carrying a gun and there was no agreement that violence be used against anyone they might encounter, then the killing is an unintended consequence as far as **A** is concerned. The question of **A**'s art and part liability for homicide will then depend on an objective test of foreseeability; that is, on the answer to the question; would the reasonable person in **A**'s position have foreseen that **B** might have a gun which he might use during the course of the break-in[3]?

In an attack on another, the production by one participant of a weapon may have the effect of ending the common plot if the others then desist from the attack. Those who desist will be art and part liable for what went before, but will not be liable for the consequences of the use of the weapon – provided, of course, its use went beyond what had been agreed upon. If they continue with their own part of the attack, they will be deemed to endorse the use of the weapon and will be responsible for the consequences of its use. In *Mathieson and Murray v HM Advocate*[4] the appellants participated in an attack with three other men. One of the other three produced a knife, with which he inflicted several wounds on the victim. The appellants continued to kick the victim while this was being done (and the court held that they must have witnessed the use of the knife). In these circumstances they were held to be art and part liable for the infliction of the stab wounds.

In *Mathieson and Murray* the appellants became aware of the murderous nature of the attack and were therefore liable for the death of the victim. Where there is no awareness of this, a person who participates at the beginning and then stands by is not necessarily art and part liable for what transpires to be murder. An example of this is *Codona v HM Advocate*[5], in which the appellant, a fourteen-year-old girl who kicked the victim at the outset of an attack and then stood by while three young men carried out a vicious assault, was held not to be art and part guilty of murder. In *Cannon v HM Advocate*[6] a robbery had been in contemplation, encouraged and instigated by the accused. His co-accused had gone into the locus to steal a purse. The intended victim had been asleep but had woken up and resisted; the co-accused struck her with a candle-stick. The accused was convicted of assault and robbery. He appealed, accepting that there was evidence of theft, but none which would allow a conviction of assault or robbery even on an art and part basis. The High Court allowed the appeal holding that even if the accused was actually in the house or running out of the house when the assault and robbery took place:

> 'His mere proximity to the events could not, however, in itself permit the jury to infer his participation in them. Nor, as the Sheriff appears to have thought, could the appellant's recent possession of the proceeds of the crime be a basis upon which his complicity in robbery rather than theft of those proceeds could be inferred.'

1 *Boyne v HM Advocate* 1980 SLT 56.
2 *HM Advocate v Harris* (September 1950, unreported), Glasgow High Court, discussed by Gordon para 5–40.
3 In *Walker v HM Advocate* 1985 JC 53, 1985 SCCR 150, the court appeared to accept that there could be art and part liability for a stabbing if the accused knew or should have known of the presence of a knife. Recent English cases focus on the 'tacit agreement or understanding' of the parties rather than on an objective test of foreseeability: *Slack* [1989] 3 All ER 90, [1989] QB 775; *Wakely* [1990] Crim LR 119. (Subjective foresight leads to an acceptance of the risk that violence may be used.) Australia adopts a subjective view, requiring foresight of the possibility that the consequence in question might ensue: *Johns v The Queen* (1980) 143 CLR 108.
4 1996 SCCR 388.
5 1996 SCCR 300.
6 Unreported High Court of Justiciary 6 October 1999.

ART AND PART GUILT AND STATUTORY OFFENCES

6.21   There is no bar to art and part guilt when the offence committed is a statutory offence[1]. In the past it was not possible for a person to be convicted on an art and part basis if the statutory offence was one which he was incapable himself of committing (on the grounds that he lacked special capacity)[2]. Legislation has now removed this objection. This can be seen in *Vaughan v HM Advocate*[3] (art and part guilt in relation to the Incest Act 1567, although the accused was not in the forbidden degrees) and *Templeton v HM Advocate*[4] (art and part guilt under the Prevention of Corruption Act 1906, although the accused was not an 'agent'). If the statutory offence is one of strict liability, the art and part offender will nonetheless require to have the normal *mens rea* needed for art and part guilt[5].

1 *Hume* II, 239; W J Dobie 'Art and part in statutory offences' (1944) 56 JR 89. Section 31 of the Criminal Justice (Scotland) Act 1949 removed doubts as to the possibility of art and part conviction in relation to statutory offences.
2 *Young v HM Advocate* 1932 JC 63, 1932 SLT 465.
3 1979 SLT 49.
4 1988 JC 33, 1988 SLT 171, 1987 SCCR 693.
5 There is no Scottish authority on this, but the point is well established in English law: *Johnson v Youden* [1950] 1 KB 544, [1950] 1 All ER 300; *Smith v Jenner* [1968] Crim LR 99; *D Stanton & Son v Webber* [1972] Crim LR 544.

Chapter 7

Inchoate crimes

7.1   Inchoate crimes are crimes which are not complete. There are three forms of inchoate crime: attempt, conspiracy, and incitement.

ATTEMPT

Not all criminal activity succeeds. The shot which misses its target, the bank robbery which is interrupted by the timely arrival of the police, or the fraudulent misrepresentation which fails to induce its recipient to act – all these are examples of attempted crimes. In such circumstances, no overt damage may be done to the community. The victim of attempted murder may not even be aware, at the time, of the poison in his tea cup, although the subsequent realisation of the fact that he has been the object of homicidal intentions may have a profoundly disturbing effect. In many cases, though, the actual deleterious consequences of an attempted crime may be negligible. No great harm is caused by the would-be bank robbers who are arrested by the police on their way to the bank.

There are three main issues to be considered in relation to attempts:

(1)   Should attempted crimes be punishable in the same way as completed crimes?
(2)   When does conduct amount to an attempt?
(3)   Should attempts to do the impossible be punished?

(1)   The punishment of attempts

Attention has been paid to the fundamental question of whether attempts should be punished to the same or a lesser extent as completed crimes, or, indeed, whether they should be punished at all. The argument for the total non punishment of attempts is not convincing. An attempted crime constitutes a threat to social peace and a challenge to the legal order. To ignore attempted criminal activity is tantamount to condonation, and therefore a legal response to attempted crime is both justified and necessary. Yet this response must be a measured one, and should reflect the actual gravity of what has been done by the accused.

There is an argument – and a fairly convincing one at that – for the proposition that no distinction should be made in terms of punishment between attempts and completed crimes. If criminal law is concerned with the moral assessment of conduct, then it should not distinguish on the grounds of arbitrary factors, such as result. On this view, there is no moral difference between the person who fires a gun at his victim, intending to kill him, but who misses, and the person who, with the same intention, fires and succeeds in hitting the victim. Each is equally guilty from the moral point of view: all that distinguishes the two cases is what philosophers have termed 'moral luck'[1]. All that prevents the unsuccessful murderer from being a successful murderer may be a chance factor, such as a gust of wind which deflects the bullet from its course.

While this argument has its undoubted appeal, its application in criminal law is generally thought to be inappropriate. Criminal law is concerned with result – inevitably so – and there are clear reasons why the law should focus on what actually happens in the physical world rather than what might have happened. Realised events provide the basis of criminal law intervention, and even if this may involve a morally arbitrary choice, it nonetheless provides a practical means of limiting intervention by the criminal law[2]. Attempts are therefore less serious because they fail to satisfy the necessary requirements for the full criminal sanction. In addition to this, attempts are treated less seriously because they involve less real damage. An attempted murder causes less harm than a completed murder, and the same is true of an attempted robbery. A reaction to harm, rather than a reaction to interior malevolence, is a proper function of the criminal law, especially in a liberal theory of justice which seeks to limit the extent to which the criminal law interferes in the lives of people.

1 B Williams 'Moral Luck' (1976) 50 Proceedings of the Aristotelean Society 115; T Nagel *Mortal Questions* (1979) p 24 et seq.
2 The nineteenth-century jurist, Stephen, sees emphasis on result coming from the sense of public outrage that accompanies serious consequences: 'If two persons are guilty of the very same act of negligence, and one of them causes thereby a railway accident, involving the death and mutilation of many persons, whereas the other does no injury to anyone, it seems to me that it would be rather pedantic than rational to say that each had committed the same offence, and should be subjected to the same punishment. In one sense, each has committed an offence, but the one has had the bad luck to cause a horrible misfortune ... Both certainly deserve punishment, but it gratifies a natural public feeling to choose out for punishment the one who actually has caused great harm ...' *History of the Criminal Law* III, 311.

(2) What conduct amounts to an attempt?

7.2   Efforts to identify a wholly satisfactory answer to this question have been conspicuously unsuccessful. A range of theories is on offer, many of them aimed at providing a theoretical structure to the sometimes inconsistent and varying approach of the courts. In many jurisdictions in the common law world, legislation defines the point at which a punishable attempt is committed; this is the case in both England and the United States, where the Criminal Attempts Act 1981[1], and the Model Penal Code, require that the accused should have gone beyond mere preparation for the commission of an offence; continental penal codes similarly set out criteria of varying precision as to when an attempt occurs. Scotland, however, has no legislation on the question, and a degree of uncertainty hangs over the question of what conduct amounts to an attempt.

The nature of the problem

The difficulties inherent in deciding when an attempt occurs are illustrated in the following hypothetical sequence:

(1)   **A** decides to rob a bank.
(2)   He purchases a map of the town in which the bank is situated.
(3)   He visits the town and walks past the bank to view it from the outside.
(4)   He enters the bank and discreetly sketches the layout on a piece of paper.
(5)   He buys a gun with a view to using it on the robbery.
(6)   He sets out from his house, armed with the gun, a face mask, and a bag for the money.
(7)   He enters the bank wearing the mask but not yet pointing the gun or making any demands.
(8)   He points the gun at the teller and asks for the money.
(9)   The teller presses an alarm button. **A**, losing his nerve, runs out and returns home.

1 Sections 1(1) and 1A.

7.3   There is little doubt that at some point in the series of events, **A** may be said to have attempted to rob the bank. Yet the point at which the attempt actually occurs is not clear. If **A** were to be interrupted and arrested at point (1), thereby being unable to proceed further, would an attempt have been committed? The answer must be an unequivocal 'no'. Criminal law does not recognise 'thought crimes'. A person may form all sorts of criminal schemes in his mind, but provided he proceeds no further than that, he commits no crime. It is equally clear that by point (8) an attempted crime has been committed; yet, between these extremes, the position may be less certain. Some may regard (6) as marking the watershed between preparatory action and attempt; others may feel that it would be premature to infer an attempt even at this point. It would, for example, be very difficult to frame an appropriate and sufficiently precise charge since, at this stage, **A**'s target is unclear.

It is useful to distinguish what is an attempt from what is not. An attempt is not a completed act; equally it is not mere preparation. It strains language to suggest that those acts which precede an attempt in themselves constitute an attempt. A prospective purchaser of an item does not attempt to purchase the item when he consults an auction catalogue or inspects the item at a viewing. It can be said, however, that an attempt is made to purchase the item once a bidding instruction is given or an actual bid is made. The acts which precede that are preparations for the actual making of the attempt; they are not sufficiently close to the completed action to be categorised as attempts.

Much has been made of the difficulty inherent in distinguishing between preparation and attempts. There may well be a grey area in which preparations and attempts blur, but this is not fatal to the whole concept of the distinction. Preparatory acts may be fundamentally different in nature from attempts, in that they are not unequivocally referable to the *actus reus* of a crime. The purchase of the map in the example above is not unequivocally referable to the commission of a robbery; entering the bank with a firearm is. Moreover, the idea that preparation does not amount to an attempt allows the law to recognise the valuable possibility of withdrawal from a criminal plan at an early stage. It seems right and sensible that the law should, so far as is consistent with public safety, encourage repentance before matters proceed too far.

There may also be a temporal reason for the distinction. An act which precedes the commission of the final act by a considerable period may be considered mere preparation on those grounds. It simply confounds our intuitive sense of the temporal boundaries of acts to say that an act performed well before the point at which the completed act would be performed amounts to an attempt. Attempts normally occur reasonably shortly before the completed act could be anticipated[1].

Reliance on the distinction between mere preparation and attempt allows considerable leeway in determining just when an attempt is committed. This may be a disadvantage, as it could be argued that the criminal law should reveal more clearly the boundaries between criminal and non-criminal conduct. Yet the selection of more exact criteria may mean that one has to opt for either an earlier or later cut-off point than might be desired. For example, in the sequence above, if one were to apply a last act theory (which holds that an attempt occurs only after the actor has performed the last act necessary to achieve the result) an attempt would only be committed after he had pointed a gun at the teller and asked for the money – stage (8). Stage (7) would not be an attempt, under this theory, as the demand remains to be made; yet the distinction, in terms of social dangerousness, between stages (7) and (8) is extremely slight. Similarly, if one applies the unequivocal act theory, which holds that an attempt is committed when an act is unequivocally referable to the commission of a crime, attempt liability potentially comes into play at stage (4), which would seem excessively early[2].

1 Temporal proximity was a factor in *Davey v Lee* [1968] 1 QB 366, [1967] 2 All ER 423, and in *Jones v Brooks* (1968) 52 Cr App Rep 614. In the latter case, the court referred to 'sufficient proximity' between the act and an expressed intention to commit a crime.
2 Although this example reveals the weakness of the theory, since it is difficult to define precisely when one act is unequivocally referable to another. Sketching the layout of the bank, for example, could be referable to a planned robbery, an architectural design project, or merely idle doodling.

7.4   A potentially useful way of distinguishing between preparatory acts and attempts is to ask whether the accused was, at the point in question, '*trying* to do **x**' (**x** being the crime). If the answer is yes, then he has gone beyond the point of preparation; if the answer is no, then he is merely preparing. The athlete who buys a new pair of running shoes is not trying to break the record at that precise point. Nor is he trying to break the record when he is on the track, training. He may be 'planning' to break the record, or 'hoping' to break the record, but this is not the same thing as 'trying' to break it. Once he walks up to the start line, however, we may be readier to say that he has reached the stage of 'trying'. 'Trying' would appear to involve action directed towards a desired result, and very closely linked with the possible achievement of that result. A person who tries to do something has normally embarked on a very specific course of action and has reached the stage of commitment to his objective. A person who is preparing has not necessarily reached the stage of commitment. It could be argued that this amounts to no more than substituting one vague term for another; yet the term 'to try' is perhaps more familiar in everyday usage than the term 'to attempt', and as such may be a better guide to the moral intuitions underlying the attribution of responsibility in this quarter.

The position in Scots law

Scottish authorities have been inconsistent on the issue of what constitutes an attempt. Some of the cases point to a 'last act' theory, and some suggest that an attempt occurs when matters proceed beyond the point at which a person can intervene to stop what he has set in motion[1]. The latter theory restricts liability to a very late stage in events, and is undesirable for that reason. The last act theory, which enjoys more support, holds that an attempt is committed once the accused has done everything required of him to commit the crime. Attempted murder therefore exists once the parcel bomb is posted to its victim, or once the shot is fired. Of course, the 'last act' theory, and the 'possible intervention' theory may give the same result in some cases, but in others may produce different outcomes. For example, where the accused is said to have attempted murder by poisoning, the last act which the accused can do to complete the crime is the placing of the poison in the victim's drink. But although there is nothing further he can do to complete the crime, he can still repent and, at the last moment, remove the food before the victim can consume it.

1 For an example, see *HM Advocate v Baxter* (1908) 5 Adam 609; in *HM Advocate v Mackenzie* 1913 SC (J) 107 Lord Justice-Clerk Macdonald talks of a requirement of an 'irrevocable act of commission or attempt'; in *HM Advocate v Tannahill and Nelson* 1943 JC 150, 1944 SLT 118 it was stated that an attempt required 'some overt act, the consequences of which cannot be recalled by the accused'. See also *Morton v Henderson* 1956 JC 55, 1956 SLT 365.

7.5   The authority of *Hume* has been claimed for the last act theory, but there must be some doubt as to whether this was, in fact, his view. The relevant passage states that there is an attempted crime '… if there has been an inchoate act of execution of the meditated deed; if the man have done that act, **or part of that act**, by which he meant and expected to perpetrate his crime, and which, if not providentially interrupted or defeated, would have done so …'[1]. It has been argued[2] that this represents an endorsement of the last act theory, but the words 'or part of that act' present some difficulty. *Gordon* suggests that it is not clear what these words mean; their meaning, though, will be that any act of perpetration, rather than the last act, will suffice. This is subject, of course, to the proviso as to providential interruption or defeat, which would seem to impose liability only where the act of perpetration is a reasonably advanced one. On a strict last act theory the person arrested when beginning to pick the lock of a house does not commit attempted burglary as he has not yet committed the last act, which arguably would be actually to gain access. Applying *Hume's* passage, however, the picking of the lock would certainly be attempted burglary, and rightly so. *Alison*, by contrast, is unambiguously in favour of a last act approach, requiring that the accused should have done 'all that in him lay' to effect the crime[3].

1 I, 27.
2 *Gordon* para 6–38 to 6–43.
3 I, 165.

7.6   Whatever the theoretical attractiveness of the last act theory, the weight of opinion now seems to be in favour of a preparation/perpetration test[1]. Judicial support was voiced for this approach in *HM Advocate v Camerons*[2] in which a husband and wife who had conceived a plan to defraud an insurance company staged a fake robbery. The prosecution failed to prove that a claim had actually been made to the insurance company, but this did not prevent the couple's conviction for attempted fraud. In his instruction to the jury, Lord Dunedin stressed that the essence of the question was the determination of the point at which preparation ended and perpetration began. This, he said, was a question of degree which fell to be determined by the jury. In the important case of *Docherty v Brown*[3] the High Court gave obiter support to perpetration test, but gave little guidance as to determining when a sufficiently advanced stage of perpetration is reached. Applying the test tentatively formulated above, it seems reasonable to say that **A**, does not *try* to rob the bank at least until stage (7) and possibly even stage (8). In a case involving the use of a firearm, for example, it would seem difficult to say that there has been attempted murder at least until the weapon has been pointed, and possibly even until the weapon is actually fired. But much will depend upon the context and the circumstances. A person who points a gun at the bank teller in the course of a robbery may well be guilty of attempted robbery, but almost certainly not attempted murder. On the other hand, a person who emerges from a crowd of onlookers and aims a gun at a visiting dignitary might well be regarded as having made an attempt on his life. In *Strachan v HM Advocate*[4], the accused's conviction of attempted murder was upheld by the High Court where he had brandished a machete at police officers, threatened to kill them, made to strike them with the machete, and struggled with them. A reference in the indictment to the accused repeatedly striking the officers with the machete had been deleted by the jury. Although there is little discussion of the matter by the court, it seems that in the circumstances, it was clear that the accused was actively *trying* to kill the officers. In summary, it may be that in some cases, an approach close to adopting a last act theory may be appropriate; in others, it may seem right to categorise acts as an attempt at a rather earlier stage. The great advantage of the perpetration theory is that it gives the court the flexibility to take this approach.

1 See *Gordon*, eg, para 6–43 who reluctantly accepts the perpetration test as the test most likely to be endorsed in the future.
2 1911 SC (J) 110, 1911 2 SLT 108.
3 1996 JC 48, 1996 SCCR 136, 1996 SLT 325, discussed below.
4 1994 SCCR 341, 1995 SLT 178.

7.7   The popularity of the test in other jurisdictions means that some judicial guidance is available as to when acts may be considered to progress beyond mere preparation, although in each case it will be for the jury to decide whether the accused has gone far enough. In some of the decisions the courts seem willing to categorise fairly 'advanced' acts as no more than preparatory. Travelling to the scene of an intended crime, armed to carry it out, but being arrested half a mile before reaching the destination was not sufficient to constitute an attempt in the New Zealand case of *Wilcox*[1]. Examining stolen clothes with a view to purchase has been held not to be an attempt to purchase stolen property[2], and trailing a lorry for over a hundred miles in the hope of having the chance to steal it has similarly been held not to amount to an attempt[3].

The following are examples of conduct which courts have held to amount to more than preparation:

(1) breaking down a door with a view to entering premises to steal[4];
(2) arranging inflammable material in a building intending to burn the building down[5];
(3) faking death with a view to allowing one's spouse to claim under a life insurance policy[6];
(4) assaulting a victim with the intention of committing rape[7].

Abandonment

Scottish courts have yet to pronounce on the effect of voluntary abandonment of efforts to commit a crime, and it is not clear whether this would constitute a defence.

1 [1982] 1 NZLR 191. In *Kopi-Kame* [1965–66] P&NGLR 73 the accused was arrested outside his wife's house armed with a loaded shotgun: no attempt. Another case involving travelling to the scene of the crime is *S v Magxwalisa* 1984 (2) SA 314 in which again there was said to be no attempt.
2 *R v Croucamp* 1949 (1) SA 377.
3 *Komaroni* (1953) 103 LJ 97.
4 *R v Boyle and Boyle* (1986) 84 Cr App Rep 270.
5 *R v Vilinsky* 1932 OPD 218 (see also *R v Taylor* 175 ER 831 (1859): striking a match in order to set fire to a haystack).
6 *DPP v Stonehouse* [1978] AC 55, [1077] 2 All ER 909.
7 *Williams* [1965] Qd R 86. *Quaere:* would it be attempted rape if the accused is interrupted before he seeks to effect insertion? The Queensland court appeared to accept that this could be so.

7.8   Arguments in favour of a defence of voluntary abandonment stress the inappropriateness of punishing one who has shown himself to be no further danger to society. It should also be borne in mind that by allowing a defence of this nature, the law encourages people to abandon criminal plans, thereby reducing the incidence of completed crime[1]. Against these factors is to be weighed the difficulty of establishing that the abandonment was, in fact, voluntary. This was alluded to in the Australian case of *R v Page*[2], where the court stressed that in almost every case there would have to be an assessment 'whether the accused desisted from sudden alarm, from a sense of wrongdoing, from failure of resolution, or from any other cause'. Even if a defence of abandonment were to be allowed, it is likely that it would be relatively easy for the prosecution to persuade jurors as to the involuntariness of the accused's desisting. It will of course weigh in any sentencing if there has been a voluntary abandonment of the criminal plan.

The mental element

To attempt to do something is to act with a view of bringing about a desired result. This has been taken to imply that there can be conviction for assault only where the accused intended the *actus reus*, and not where he was reckless or negligent. This raises difficult questions in relation to attempted murder. Murder can be committed recklessly, but does attempted murder require a frustrated intention to kill? If one who was only reckless can be convicted of attempted murder, then a person who at no point had any intention of killing is labelled as having tried to kill. This is seen by some as misleading and illogical.

The issue was considered for Scots law in the case of *Cawthorne v HM Advocate*[3]. Cawthorne fired two shots through the door and window of a room in which he knew four people to be sheltering. The bullets did not hit anybody directly, although one of the occupants of the room was slightly grazed. Cawthorne was convicted of attempted murder and appealed against the conviction on the grounds of misdirection of the jury: the jury should have been told that attempted murder required intention to kill on the part of the accused. The appeal failed, the court being firmly of the view that the *mens rea* of murder and of attempted murder are the same. Lord Justice-General Clyde said:

> 'In my opinion attempted murder is just the same as murder in the eyes of our law, but for the one vital distinction, that the killing has not been brought off and the victim has escaped with his life. But there must be in each case the same *mens rea*, and that *mens rea* in each case can be proved by evidence of a deliberate intention to kill or by such recklessness as to show that the accused was regardless of the consequences of his act, whatever they may have been'.

1 See M Wasik 'Abandoning criminal intent' [1980] Crim LR 785.
2 [1933] VLR 351.
3 1968 JC 32, 1968 SLT 330.

7.9   Prior to the decision in *Cawthorne*, there had been a degree of judicial disagreement as to the role of intent in attempted murder. Intent to kill had been recognised in *HM Advocate v McAdam*[1] but wicked recklessness sufficed in *HM Advocate v Currie*[2], a case which demonstrates precisely the sort of circumstances in which an attempted murder charge might be thought warranted: the accused, in the course of a police car chase, had swerved their car into the path of a police car which was pursuing them and had thrown objects into the path of the police vehicle. *Cawthorne* appeared to settle the issue, but caused a degree of concern. In particular it has been suggested that *Cawthorne* opens the way to charges of attempted murder in cases which are not sufficiently serious to warrant such a charge[3]. The matter is affected by the decision in *HM Advocate v Purcell*[4]. The accused was driving a car. He was chased by police officers in their own vehicle. During the chase the accused struck and killed a ten year old boy who was crossing the road legitimately at a controlled crossing. Purcell was charged with *inter alia* murder. The High Court held that the Crown can establish 'wicked recklessness' only by showing an intention 'to cause physical injury' while 'displaying a wicked disregard of fatal consequences'[5]. *Cawthorne* has been taken to stand for the proposition that the *mens rea* for an attempt is the same as that for a completed offence, even if that was constituted by recklessness; *Cawthorne* suggests that, since murder can be committed recklessly, so can attempted murder. *Purcell* undermines this, as there cannot be murder, or attempted murder, absent an intention to cause physical harm[6]. In *Petto v HMA*[7], a five-judge court again looked at the matter; the court considered that wilful fire-raising in an urban tenement provided sufficient intent for the crime of murder. It was not an exception to the principle that murder

100

requires a deliberate attack intended to cause injury. Rather, the fire-raising itself would have merited a charge of assault on the inhabitants, even if the fire-raiser had not known the specific locations or identities of those inhabitants. This appears to further undermine the proposition purportedly derived from Cawthorne.

In *HMA v Kerr*[8], the court looked at attempted murder through the prism of diminished responsibility and provocation. The court held that where evidence of diminished responsibility or provocation was accepted by a jury, then the necessary mens rea for murder was absent; accordingly it was held to be unjust and illogical to convict of attempted murder when the accused could not have been convicted of murder if the victim had died. So, in a case of attempted murder where diminished responsibility or provocation was established, the appropriate verdict was guilty of assault.

The main argument in favour of restricting attempted murder to those cases where there was intent is that of protecting the integrity of the concept of murder. The term 'murderer' means, to the public mind, a person who has set out deliberately to take human life. It is arguable that the person who assaults his victim, not caring whether the latter lives or dies, is equally morally culpable whether the victim in fact lives or dies. Certainly, from the point of view of punishment objectives, it is difficult to distinguish between them.

1 (July 1950, unreported), Glasgow High Court.
2 (December 1962, unreported), Glasgow High Court.
3 This criticism, along with others, was addressed by the Scottish Law Commission in *Attempted Homicide* (Consultative Memorandum no 61, 1984).
4 2008 SLT 44.
5 Paragraph [16].
6 See 'Foreseeing the consequences of Purcell' article by Plaxton 2008 SLT 21 for an analysis of Purcell, and the requirements to reconsider other 'seminal cases' the interpretation of which is affected by the decision.
7 2012 JC 105.
8 2011 SLT 430, 2011 SCL 485, 2011 SCCR 192.

7.10   In *R v Khan*[1] the Court of Appeal in England upheld a conviction of attempted reckless rape, stating:

'... the intent of the defendant was precisely the same in rape and in attempted rape, and the *mens rea* was identical, namely an intention to have intercourse plus the knowledge of or recklessness as to the woman's absence of consent. No question of attempting to achieve a reckless state of mind arose; the attempt related to the physical activity; the mental state of the defendant was the same'.

The *Lord Advocate's Reference (No 1 of 2001)*[2] dealt with the issue of reckless-ness so far as it applies to rape under Scots Law. The court approved the dicta in *Jamieson v HM Advocate*[3] as follows:

'[T]he question is whether he genuinely or honestly believed that the woman was consenting to intercourse. It will not do if he acted without thinking or was indifferent as to whether or not he had her consent. The man must have genuinely formed the belief that she was consenting to his having intercourse with her. But this need not be a belief which the jury regards as reasonable, so long as they are satisfied that his belief was genuinely held by him at the time.'

Thereafter, the opinion continued:

'It may be noted that the implication of the court's decision in *Jamieson* was to distinguish between the man who failed to think about, or was indifferent as to, whether the woman was consenting (which might be described as subjective recklessness); and the man who honestly or genuinely believed that the woman was consenting but had failed to realise that she was not consenting when there was an obvious risk that this was the case.'

The latter might be described as objective recklessness, concluding at paragraph [44]: 'Standing the decision in *Jamieson* and in the absence of discussion of this topic in the present reference, "reckless" should be understood in the subjective sense to which I have referred earlier in this opinion'.

Accordingly, recklessness in rape will be established if the perpetrator failed to think about, or was indifferent to, whether the woman consented. This would seem to allow an offence of attempted rape, where the perpetrator was reckless.

Statutory offences

The Scottish courts have yet to address the issue of whether *mens rea* is required where the accused is charged with attempting to commit an offence of strict liability[4]. The following hypothetical example illustrates the problem: the legislature has created an offence of strict liability, making it an offence for a pharmacist to sell a particular drug. A, a pharmacist, who has inadvertently mistaken the regulated drug for an innocent one, is arrested shortly before he is going to sell the drug to a customer. Is his lack of *mens rea* a bar to conviction of an attempted breach of the regulation? The decision in *Cawthorne* suggests that there is no reason why there should not be a conviction in such a case. *Gordon* points out that the antipathy of the courts to strict liability offences might incline them to require *mens rea* here[5], a view which has attracted some judicial support in other jurisdictions[6]. Against this view it can be argued that the justification of strict liability lies in the prevention of certain forms of conduct which could not practically be prevented if *mens rea* were to be required. This justification applies equally to attempted strict liability offences[7].

1 [1990] 1 WLR 813.
2 2002 SLT 466, 2002 SCCR 435.
3 1994 JC 88, 1994 SLT 537, 1994 SCCR 181.
4 See Chapter 3 for consideration of *mens rea* in the context of strict liability.
5 At para 7–82.
6 *R v Ancio* (1984) 10 CCC (3d) 385. See also dicta in *Alister v The Queen* (1984) 154 CLR 404, 421–122. For support, see Glanville Williams *Criminal Law: The General Part* (2nd edn) pp 618–620; [1962] Crim LR 300.
7 JC Smith [1962] Crim LR 143.

7.11   As in the case of attempted murder, the real problem lies in the apparent illogicality of saying that a person has attempted to perform an act, when he was perhaps ignorant of those features of the act which make it a crime.

(3)   Impossible attempts

Impossibility may be factual or legal. An attempt to do the factually impossible is made when a person tries to achieve a goal by means which are physically incapable of bringing about his desired result, or where the facts are such that the desired result could not possibly be brought about. The classic example of the former would be an attempt to poison another through the use of a substance which is, in fact, not poisonous; a common example of the latter is where the accused attempts to import a controlled drug when in fact the white tablets he possesses are nothing more potent than indigestion pills. Legal impossibility exists where a person attempts to do something which is not criminal; that is, where the intended end does not amount to a criminal offence. An example of legal impossibility would be where a person, falsely believing that the making of homemade wine is an offence, sets out to make wine under the impression that in doing so he is breaking the law. A great deal of confusion surrounds the notions of factual and legal impossibility. The distinction is stated by Hall thus[1]:

> 'The rules attach liability to attempts which failed because of 'factual impossibility' but they exculpate where the attempt failed because of 'legal impossibility'. The rationale of the latter is that since the defendant would not have committed any crime even though he had done everything he intended to do, *a fortiori* he cannot be guilty of a criminal attempt if he did less than that ... In sum ... (1) unless the intended end is a legally proscribed harm, causing it is not criminal; hence any conduct falling short of that is not, a criminal attempt (ie the principle of legality); and (2) if the intended end is a legally proscribed harm, the failure to effect it because of a factual condition necessary to its occurrence is no defence (ie factual impossibility)'.

It is arguable that much of the difficulty over impossible attempts has arisen from the linguistic difficulties inherent in this distinction. The confusion is perhaps demonstrated by the *volte face* conducted by the House of Lords in the cases of *Anderton v Ryan*[2], and *R v Shivpuri*[3]. In Anderton, the defendant was charged with the attempted reset[4] of a video recorder which she incorrectly believed to have been stolen. Having bought the recorder in the belief that it was stolen, she had accomplished all that she had set out to do. At no point could the completed act have amounted to a crime, however, since the video recorder was not stolen property. The House of Lords upheld an appeal against conviction by the defendant by invoking the concept of 'objective innocence'. What she had done did not, and could not, amount to a crime, and therefore she was objectively innocent[5]. However, this was overturned at the first opportunity in *R v Shivpuri*. The accused had imported substances which he thought were illegal drugs; in fact they were harmless vegetable matter. The House of Lords held that on the true construction of s 1 of the Criminal Attempts Act 1981 the *actus reus* of the statutory offence of attempt required an act which was more than merely preparatory to the commission of an offence, and which the defendant did with the intention of committing an offence, notwithstanding that the commission of the actual offence was, on the true facts, impossible. The appellant had on the facts of the case been rightly convicted; the distinction which the House of Lords had previously drawn in regard to s 1 between acts which were 'objectively innocent' and those which were not, could not be maintained. *Anderton v Ryan* had been wrongly decided and, since it was indistinguishable from the present case, would be departed from.

1 *General Principles of Criminal Law* (2nd edn, 1960), p 586.
2 [1985] AC 560.
3 [1987] AC 1, [1986] 2 WLR 988, [1986] 2 All ER 334, (1986) 83 Cr App R 178.
4 Reset requires that the accused has knowingly taken possession of stolen goods: see Chapter 14 below.
5 [1985] AC 560.

7.12   The Scottish position on attempts to do the impossible was unclear for a number of years. The difficulty sprang from the irreconcilability of the earlier decisions on the matter: *HM Advocate v Anderson*[1] held that attempted abortion is not committed by one who administers abortifacient drugs to a woman who is not pregnant, while *Lamont v Strathern*[2] held that it *is* attempted theft to try to pick an empty pocket. It is difficult to see any meaningful distinction between the act in each case: the non-pregnancy of the woman is a question of fact, as is the emptiness of the pocket. In *Maxwell v HM Advocate*[3] the court considered the question of a factual impossibility in the context of conspiracy, and took the view that it was irrelevant. The conspirators in this case had conspired to bribe members of a licensing board, but at the time of the offence the board would have been incapable of doing what the conspirators wished, as the matter was then under appeal to the sheriff. It was held that this did not affect guilt, as the whole essence of the offence of bribery was the giving of the bribe, not whether the recipient subsequently manages to arrange what the conspirators wish to achieve. Although *Maxwell* did not resolve the issue of the conflict between *Anderson* and *Lamont*, it provided support for the view that factual impossibility should be no defence to a charge of attempt[4].

1 1928 JC 1, 1927 SLT 651.
2 1933 JC 33, 1933 SLT 118.
3 1980 JC 40, 1980 SLT 241.
4 'The argument that because of the accident of events or physical causes beyond or outwith the control or even the knowledge of the corrupting agent, the ultimate objective of the plan to corrupt or attempt to corrupt cannot be achieved, is itself enough to deprive what otherwise is a completed criminal act of its criminal quality appears on the face of it somewhat startling. If sound, this could place criminal responsibility at the whim of extraneous events wholly divorced from the criminally directed actions of the participants themselves': *Maxwell* 1980 JC 40 at 44, per Lord Cameron.

7.13   The issue of impossibility in Scotland was resolved by a bench of five judges in the High Court. *Docherty v Brown*[1] holds that factual impossibility is never a bar to criminal liability. Thus, an accused will be convicted unless either (a) he knows of the impossibility of what he is attempting, or (b) the crime which he believes himself to be attempting does not exist in the law – in other words if there is legal impossibility in the sense described above. According to the High Court, there is an attempt whenever there is an 'inchoate act of execution of the meditated deed; if the man had done that act, or a part of that act, by which he meant and expected to perpetrate his crime, and which, if not providentially interrupted or defeated, would have done so'[2]. Since a man may be defeated by the fact that his intended object is impossible, the High

Court drew the conclusion that such impossibility is no bar to laying a charge of attempt. The court held further that *Anderson* was wrongly decided and that comments in *Semple* implying otherwise were unsound[3]. The decision is based on basic principles of the law of attempts and essentially followed the approach in English law[4]. All that is required to constitute an attempt is an act more than merely preparatory to the commission of the crime, carried out with an intention (or, in Scotland, perhaps with recklessness) to bring about the prohibited result or act involved in the completed crime.

1 1996 SCCR 136, 1996 SLT 325.
2 *Hume* I, 27, approved by Lord Justice-General Hope in *Docherty v Brown* 1996 SCCR 136 at 142; Lord Justice Clerk Ross at 146–147; Lord Cameron of Lochbroom at 158.
3 1996 SCCR 136, per Lord Justice-General Hope at 142; per Lord Justice Clerk Ross at 149–150; per Lord Sutherland at 154.
4 See further *R v Shivpuri* [1987] AC 1, [1986] 2 WLR 988, [1986] 2 All ER 334, (1986) 83 Cr App R 178; and DH Sheldon 'Impossible attempts and other oxymorons' (1997) 1 Edinburgh LR 250.

7.14   The following further examples demonstrate the implications of the decision in *Docherty v Brown*:

(1)   The accused fires a shot into an empty room, believing that his intended victim is within. This is a matter of factual impossibility, and the accused may be charged with attempted murder[1].

(2)   The accused, wanting to kill **A**, sticks pins into a doll representing **A** in the belief that this will lead to **A**'s death. It is factually impossible to bring about death in this way, but strictly speaking this is nonetheless attempted murder. It would be risible to prosecute such an attempt, although *Gordon* points out that such a person could still be dangerous, and might progress from factually impossible means of procuring death to more objectively dangerous means[2].

(3)   The accused wishes to poison his victim. He places poison in the victim's food, but the quantity is insufficient to bring about death. This may be considered factual impossibility, in the sense that such a dose of poison is incapable of causing death, but in another view it is not so much factual impossibility as *insufficiency of means*[3]. Perhaps oddly, this has never been considered a bar to conviction of attempt in Scots law, in spite of doubts over other types of impossibility[4].

(4)   The accused, while on holiday abroad, buys a bag of white powder which he is informed is cocaine. He hides the bag in his luggage and is apprehended on entering the United Kingdom and charged with attempting to import a controlled drug. The powder is, in fact, a harmless substance. The accused in this case intends to commit an offence, and once again has performed actions which clearly cross the line between preparation and perpetration, although it is impossible to complete the offence in question by importing harmless white powder. This is factual impossibility and he would now be guilty of an attempt, both in Scotland and England – these are essentially the facts of both *Docherty v Brown* and *R v Shivpuri*[5].

(5)   The accused attempts to commit a crime which can be committed only by members of a special class of persons (for example, by company direc-

tors), of which he is not a member. In Docherty the court reserved its opinion on whether (where a crime could be committed only if a person was within a class of persons, such as licensees) it was relevant to libel an attempt to commit such a crime by someone who merely believed himself to be within that class. Although an example of a legal impossibility, there may be an attempted crime[6].

(6)   The accused attempts to commit a crime which does not exist (for example, the accused attempts to commit the 'crime of adultery'). Once again, this is legal impossibility and cannot amount to an attempted crime.

1 As was the case, in such circumstances, in *State v Mitchell* (1902) 170 Mo 633.
2 At para 6–50. Cf Glanville Williams *Criminal Law, The General Part* (2nd edn, 1961) p 652.
3 Cf *R v Collingridge* (1976) 16 SASR 117: attempt to murder wife by throwing a live wire into the bath. The current was insufficient to kill her (unless she actually touched the live wire). This was held to be attempted murder (by insufficient, rather than impossible means).
4 See *HM Advocate v Semple* 1937 JC 41.
5 [1987] AC 1. Cf also the Australian case of *Britten v Alpogut* [1987] VR 929.
6 But see *Gordon* para 6–52.

7.15   It can be seen that the rule in *Docherty v Brown* would justify prosecution in some rather absurd and trivial cases, in which no harm is done, or indeed ever could be done. On the face of it, it seems unsatisfactory that, although the rule may produce absurd results, no better rule can be produced.

CONSPIRACY

7.16   The crime of conspiracy is committed by two or more persons who agree together to carry out a criminal purpose, whether that criminal purpose is an end in itself or a means to a further end. What is essential is that this purpose 'be one which if attempted or achieved would itself constitute a crime by the law of Scotland'[1]. That essence was refined further in *HM Advocate v Al-Megrahi (No 1)*[2], proceedings against the man accused of the Lockerbie bomb. The accused was charged with murder and conspiracy to murder. He argued that as a conspiracy was complete as soon as agreement was reached, and the only locations specified in the conspiracy charge were outwith Scotland, no part of the conspiracy took place in Scotland and Scottish courts had no jurisdiction. The High Court held that conspiracy was a continuing crime until abandoned or completed, and if such a purpose included offending against the peace of Scotland, it was justiciable in Scotland.

The crime is committed once the agreement is reached; overt acts in pursuit of the conspiracy merely provide evidence of the fact that a conspiracy has been entered into[3]. It is not a conspiracy to put forward or discuss an idea for consideration with a view to possible future agreement[4].

While the existence of a conspiracy may be proved by or inferred from the actings of the accused persons – and indeed will usually have to be proved in that way[5] – there does not have to be evidence of specific verbal or written agreement. In *West v HM Advocate*[6] the conduct of the accused in loitering outside premises armed with a scissor blade and an open razor, was sufficient together with additional evidence to justify the inference that there was a conspiracy to assault and rob[7].

The criminal means which the accused conspired to use must be specified. It is not sufficient for the prosecution merely to allege that the accused agreed to further a criminal purpose, or to use unspecified criminal means[8]. Both conspiracy and the commission of the completed offence may be charged, although it must be emphasised that there is no need to prove completion of the offence, or even an attempt to commit it, in order to prove the conspiracy. Acquittal of the completed offence does not therefore preclude conviction of conspiracy, and the acquittal of one conspirator will not preclude the conviction of others[9]. In *Al-Megrahi*, the accused had argued that it was incompetent to charge conspiracy and murder cumulatively. The High Court observed that the practice of using conspiracy charges with other substantive charges was now a regular practice and not incompetent, though the practice might cause confusion.

1 *Maxwell v HM Advocate* 1980 JC 40 at 43, per Lord Cameron.
2 2000 JC 555, 2000 SLT 1393, 2000 SCCR 177.
3 *Crofter Hand Woven Harris Tweed v Veitch* 1942 SC (HL) 1 at 9, 10, 1943 SLT 2 at 5, per Viscount Simon; *HM Advocate v Wilson, Latta, and Rooney* (February 1968, unreported), HCJ; *Gane and Stoddart* p 203.
4 *HM Advocate v Smith* (May 1975, unreported), Glasgow High Court: *Gordon* para 6–56.
5 See Lord Justice Clerk Grant in *HM Advocate v Wilson, Latta and Rooney*, above.
6 1985 SCCR 248.
7 Cf *Conner v HM Advocate* 1995 SCCR 719, in which the accused's conviction for possession of a firearm with intent to rob, along with another person, was upheld in spite of his being acquitted by the jury on a charge of conspiracy with that other person to commit robbery.
8 *Sayers v HM Advocate* 1981 SCCR 312, 1981 JC 98.
9 *HM Advocate v Wilson, Latta, and Rooney*, above.

INCITEMENT

7.17   The offence of incitement or attempted conspiracy is committed by one who invites another to enter a criminal conspiracy or commit a crime. Attempted incitement may be charged if the person approached declines to join the conspiracy or commit the crime[1], although there is no reason in principle why incitement should not be charged in such a case, as the *actus reus* of the offence is complete once the invitation is made. The acceptance or otherwise of the invitation is irrelevant. It would be attempted incitement where **A** writes to **B**, urging him to commit a crime, but where the letter is intercepted and never reaches **B**.

1 *HM Advocate v Kay and Strain* (May 1952, unreported), Glasgow High Court: *Gordon* para 6–77; *Morton v Henderson* 1956 JC 55, 1956 SLT 365.

Chapter 8

Defences

ERROR

8.1   Subject to certain significant limitations, a person who acts in error may lack the *mens rea* necessary for conviction. Certain forms of error, however, are irrelevant as far as criminal liability is concerned, and a person who acts under such an error may still be convicted in respect of his mistaken actings.

Errors of law

8.2   An error of law is to be distinguished from an error of fact, the former being generally irrelevant to the guilt of the accused. An error of law arises when the accused has reached a false conclusion as to the state of the law[1]. An error of fact, by contrast, entails a false conclusion as to a state of affairs in the physical world. If I believe that I am legally entitled to drive at 80 miles per hour on a motorway, I make an error of law. If I believe that I am driving at 60 miles per hour, when in reality I am driving at 80 miles per hour, my error is an error of fact. Again, if I believe that I am entitled to shoot on sight any intruder I find on my property at night, my error is one of law. If I believe that the dark shape at which I shoot at night is a dog about to molest my sheep, whereas in reality it is a person who is crawling through the undergrowth, my error is factual rather than legal.

Errors of law may be divided into errors as to the general state of the criminal law and errors of civil law. The former do not constitute a defence to a criminal charge, whereas the latter may do so, principally in the context of offences of dishonesty.

1 *Clark v Syme* 1957 JC 1, 1957 SLT 32, followed as recently as The *Lord Advocate's reference (No 1 of 2000)* 2001 JC 143; 2001 SLT 507.

8.3   Irrelevant errors of law.   One of the most unbending maxims in the criminal law is *ignorantia iuris neminem excusat*: ignorance of the law is no excuse[1]. Ignorance of the law is an error of law in that the accused is unaware of the fact that his actions contravene a provision of the criminal law. Thus, if **A** does not know that it is a crime to marry more than one wife, his ignorance of the law of bigamy will be no defence. A more likely example would be that of a statutory offence. If **A** does not know that Parliament has enacted legislation making it illegal to operate a vehicle without a certain form of emission control device, his ignorance of the law will be irrelevant. This will be the case even if the legislation is recent, and even if **A**, having been out of the country at the time of the enactment of the provision, could not reasonably be expected to have been aware of it. In each case the person's ignorance of the law would be likely to inform the sentencing.

The notion that everybody may be presumed to know the law may have been a realistic one in a simpler age. The complexities of modern life have added a substantial corpus of criminal provisions which simply cannot be inferred through the exercise of moral intuitions or, indeed, on the basis of an ordinary understanding of society. As a result of this, ignorance of much of the criminal law is not only a possibility – it is probably also a widespread reality.

The main objection to the admission of ignorance of the law as a defence is a pragmatic one: the defence could be raised unmeritoriously and a great deal of court time wasted as a result. There are also considerations of fairness; the ignorant would be acquitted, while those who bothered to acquaint themselves with the law would be penalised. In certain contexts this could lead to unacceptable results. For example, **A** and **B** both engage in a specialist trade, which is regulated by complex rules contained in statutory instruments. **A** takes the trouble to acquaint himself with the rules, fails to comply with a provision of one of them and is punished. **B** decides deliberately to ignore all the rules and unknowingly infringes one. If an unqualified defence of ignorance of the law was available, **B** would be acquitted, although his conduct is clearly equally as culpable as **A**'s.

1 *Hume* I, 26. In *Jobsin Co UK plc (t/a Internet Recruitment Solutions) v Department of Health* [2001] EWCA Civ 1241 at para 33 Dyson LJ said 'although the maxim "**ignorance** of the **law** is no excuse" is not a universal truth, it should not in my view be lightly brushed aside'.

8.4   Even if the door is kept firmly closed to the reception of any ignorance of the law defence, there is one area in which reform might be effected without risking a wave of unmeritorious defences. If a person seeks official advice as to his position and then acts upon it in good faith, it seems harsh to convict him of an offence should the advice in question prove to be misleading. The cautious acceptance of this defence elsewhere has succeeded in mitigating the effects of an otherwise uncompromising rule.

There is no substantial Scottish authority in favour of the proposition that reliance on official advice is a defence. In *Roberts v Local Authority for Inverness*[1] a man who acted in accordance with official advice was held to have 'lawful authority or excuse' in terms of the statute which created the offence. This is unlikely to be generalised beyond the narrow confines of statutes with an equivalent form of wording.

1 (1809) 2 White 385.

8.5   Relevant errors of law. A person who mistakenly believes that he is acting under an entitlement of civil law may be acquitted on the grounds that he does not manifest the wrongful intent required for conviction of the offence[1]. Thus if A takes property mistakenly believing he has a legal right to do so (for example, believing that the property is his by right of succession), he does not commit theft. His error, however, must be a reasonable one[2]. This defence is also known as the 'claim of right defence'.

1 *Hume* I, 73.
2 *Hume* I, 74.

Irrelevant errors of fact

Error as to the object of the crime

8.6 An error as to the object of the crime is irrelevant to the question of criminal guilt. If **A** steals a car believing that it belongs to **B**, he will still be guilty of theft if it transpires that the car belonged to **C**. Similarly if **A** shoots at and kills **B**, believing him to be **C**, he will be guilty of murder even if he had no intention of killing **B**. This is a mistake of transferred intent, which has now been clearly recognised as a feature of Scots law in the decision in *Roberts v Hamilton*[1]. This doctrine of transferred intent is criticised by *Gordon* paragraphs 9–10, but its acceptance by the courts is now clear, at least in relation to assault: in *Blane v HM Advocate*[2] it was held that transferred intent did not apply to wilful fire-raising. The accused in this case had set fire to bedclothes and the fire had spread to the building. The principal objection to the doctrine is that it applies the doctrine of *versari in re itticita*, under which the accused is held liable for the unforeseen 'side effects' of illegal conduct on his part. Following *Purcell v HM Advocate*[3] and *Petto v HM Advocate*[4], the doctrine is now more limited in its application, to murder at least. These cases recognised the need for an intention to cause physical harm.

Error as to the identity of the victim may be relevant when the identity of the victim forms part of the definition of the offence. For example, if **A** makes a mistake as to the identity of **B** and assaults him in ignorance of the fact that **B** is a policeman, his error as to identity will be a defence to a charge of assaulting a policeman.

1 1989 SLT 399, 1989 SCCR 240. Discussed further at para 9.5.
2 1991 SCCR 376.
3 2008 SLT 44.
4 2012 JC 105; 2011 SLT 1043; 2011 SCL 850; 2011 SCCR 519.

Error as to method

8.7 An accused may intend to commit a crime by means **x** but as events transpire he in fact commits it by means **y**. This is an error as to mode and will, in general, be irrelevant. If **A** assaults **B** by kicking him and then stabbing him, intending to kill him by the stabbing, and if **B** then dies from the injuries received in the kicking rather than from the stab wounds, this is an error as to mode and does not affect **A**'s liability for the death of **B**. An error as to mode may be relevant, however, when the method by which a crime is committed is a 'definitional element' in that crime, that is, a particular method is required for that particular *actus reus*. If a statute provides that it is an offence to do **x** by doing **y**, a person who does **x** by doing **y** but under the erroneous belief that he is doing **x** by doing **z**, a defence may be open to him, provided, of course, the statutory offence is not one of strict liability.

Relevant errors of fact

8.8 The general principle in relation to relevant errors of fact is that the accused is judged on the facts as he thought them to be. The existence of an error as to fact may mitigate: if **A** gives **B** a pill which he takes to be a painkiller but which is in reality poison, his poisoning of **B** is unintentional. He therefore does not have the *mens rea* of murder. An erroneous belief may be arrived at recklessly, in which case there may be liability in those cases where reckless-ness is a sufficient *mens rea* for the crime in question. A man who wrongly believes that a woman consents to intercourse, and reaches this belief reck-lessly, cannot rely on his error to negate the *mens rea* of rape[1].

There is not a great deal of authority on whether the error needs to be rea-sonable, although two well-established self-defence cases point to a require-ment of reasonableness. In *Owens v HM Advocate*[2] Lord Normand held that a mistaken belief that the accused was being threatened would not exclude the defence of self-defence provided that such a belief was held on reasonable grounds. 'Grounds for such a belief may exist,' he said, 'although they are founded on a genuine mistake of fact'[3]. This amounts to a requirement that the reasonable person in the accused's position could have reached the con-clusion that he was threatened by the victim. In *Crawford v HM Advocate*[4], the court returned to the issue of reasonableness in another self-defence case. The main issue in this case was whether self-defence was justified in the cir-cumstances, but the court expressed the clear view that 'where self-defence is supported by a mistaken belief rested on reasonable grounds, that mistaken belief must have a purely objective background and must not be purely sub-jective or of the nature of a hallucination'[5]. In *Lieser v HM Advocate*[6], the High Court took the opportunity to confirm that there was longstanding and binding authority that a person who claimed he acted in self-defence, or was provoked, because he believed he was in imminent danger, had to have rea-sonable grounds for his belief[7].

1 *Meek v HM Advocate* 1982 SCCR 613, 1983 SLT 280. See also The *Lord Advocate's reference (No 1 of 2001)* 2002 SLT 466, 2002 SCCR 435. See also *Keaney v HMA* 2015 SLT 102 at para [12]
2 1946 JC 119, 1946 SLT 227.
3 1946 JC 119 at 125, 1946 SLT 227 at 230.
4 1950 JC 67, 1950 SLT 279.
5 1950 JC 67 at 71, per Lord Cooper.
6 2008 SLT 866, 2008 SCL 1050, 2008 SCCR 797.
7 At para [7].

8.9   The test is different in relation to rape cases, where the belief has to be honestly held but need not be reasonable. The matter was considered in *Meek*[1]. The High Court accepted in this case that '... an essential element in the crime of rape is the absence of honest belief in the consent of the woman ... The absence of reasonable grounds for such an alleged belief will, however, have a considerable bearing upon whether the jury will accept such an "honest belief" was held'[2]. Subsequently, in *Jamieson v HM Advocate*[3] the High Court settled doubts which had arisen in relation to *Meek*, confirming that an unreasonable error as to consent will be a defence to a charge of rape. If **A** therefore believes **B** to be willing to have intercourse, this belief will exclude the *mens rea* of rape **even if no reasonable man in his position would have believed similarly.** Only if he is reckless in reaching this belief will he be liable, recklessness being a sufficient *mens rea* for the crime of rape.

It is clear from the decision in *Jamieson* that the proposition is to be limited to rape cases and that in other areas a requirement of reasonableness will be insisted upon. In principle, the rule that a genuine, though unreasonable belief, should exclude *mens rea* is preferable, on the grounds that only the subjectively guilty should be punished[4]. In practice such a rule could be kept under control by the good sense of jurors who, as Lord Emslie suggests in *Meek*, would be disinclined to believe that the accused genuinely held a mistaken belief which is grossly unreasonable.

There is an apparent irreconcilability between the two treatments in *Lieser* and *Meek/Jamieson* of assessing the reasonableness of the belief; one must be reasonable, the other need not be This can be dealt with by limiting the reasonableness requirement to those cases where the accused is attempting to justify his conduct, as he is in cases of self-defence, coercion, or necessity. These defences amount to an assertion on the accused's part that what he did was right, and it is not unreasonable therefore to require that this assertion of right be objectively supportable. In other circumstances, the error affects intention, and reasonableness can play no appropriate justificatory role. In such cases the accused is not saying 'What I did was right' he is merely saying 'I did not intend to do that with which I am now charged'. On this account, there is no conflict between *Lieser* and *Meek/Jamieson* and genuine but unreasonable error might have the effect of excluding *mens rea*.

1 1982 SCCR 613, 1983 SLT 280.
2 1982 SCCR 613 at 618, per Lord President Emslie, following *DPP v Morgan* [1976] AC 182, [1976] 61 Cr App Rep 136.
3 1994 SCCR 181, 1994 SLT 537.
4 There is an extensive literature on the subject of the reasonableness requirement in cases of error. Examples include: P Alldridge 'Mistake in criminal law – subjectivism reasserted in the Court of Appeal' (1984) 35 NILQ 263; NJ Reville 'Self-defence: courting sober but unreasonable mistakes of fact' (1988) 52 JCL 84.

INTOXICATION

8.10   Intoxication may occur as a result of the ingestion of alcohol or drugs, the legal implications of either form of intoxication being the same. In practice, the courts will be concerned almost exclusively with alcoholic intoxication, the salient effects of which are to reduce inhibitions, interfere with physical control of the body, impair awareness and, in some cases, induce amnesia[1]. Excessive drinking over a prolonged period may also result in organic brain damage of a degree sufficient to have serious behavioural implications, as in Korsakoff's Psychosis, an alcohol-related dementia which has a significant effect on memory and certain social functions.

The close association of alcoholic intoxication with criminal conduct is a matter borne out by the everyday experience of the courts. There is a range of views on the implications of intoxication, varying from the view that intoxication should be neither an excuse nor a mitigating factor, to the view that it should be a complete defence to a criminal charge. The former position may be based on the notion that the decision to become intoxicated is a voluntary one and that the consequences of this decision are quite appropriately referable to the drinker. Alternatively, even if it is accepted that some people cannot control their drinking, intoxication may still not be treated as an exculpating factor on the grounds that an impossibly high proportion of offenders would thereby be acquitted, to the clear distress of the victims of their crimes. Certainly, this accords with our intuitions as to how people would respond to the information that the person who assaulted them was to be acquitted on the grounds that he was drunk at the time. In the Stage 1 Report of the Justice Committee of the Scottish Parliament on the Criminal Justice and Licensing Bill[2], the committee said 'The Scottish Government considers that there 'is a very strong link between alcohol and offending', but that intoxication can often be presented by the defence as 'an excuse or reason for offending behaviour'; despite the Committee's reservations about the need to make statutory provision, the Government enacted s 26 of the Criminal Justice and Licensing (Scotland) Act 2010 which provides that a court, in sentencing an offender in respect of an offence, must not take into account by way of mitigation the fact that an offender was, at the time of the offence, under the influence of alcohol as a result of having voluntarily consumed alcohol.

1 For an account of the implications of alcoholic intoxication, see CN Mitchell 'The intoxicated offender – refuting the legal and medical myths' (1988) 11 *International Journal of Law and Psychiatry* 77.
2 18th report 2009 (session 3).

8.11 On the other hand, the inappropriateness and harshness of attributing full responsibility to the intoxicated offender may in many cases be equally apparent. *Gordon* raises the example of the young man who drinks excessively at his first alcoholic party and who offends as a result[1]. To regard such a person as a deliberate criminal seems, he says, unduly harsh. What, though, would be the position if the act he committed in his state of 'blind drunkenness' was to point a loaded gun at another guest and pull the trigger? Is he to be considered a murderer, or is the offence to be reduced to culpable homicide, or is he to be acquitted altogether? The more serious the offence becomes, the less appealing becomes the prospect of amelioration of the offence and yet, at the same time, the more Draconian seems that approach which would exclude any room for mitigation in such a case. Obviously there is a world of difference between the young drunken killer and the man who shoots his victim in cold blood; yet the mandatory life sentence for murder allows little room for this difference to be acknowledged. These considerations of policy form the background against which the criminal law's response to intoxication is to be approached.

The Scots law on intoxication took some time to crystallise. Nineteenth-century cases reveal a willingness to take intoxication into account in the reduction of murder to culpable homicide, although it was not accepted as a complete defence[2]. In *Kennedy v HM Advocate*[3] a full court adopted the rule of the English case of *DPP v Beard*[4] with the result that intoxication, if capable of preventing the formation of the necessary intent for murder, would reduce murder to culpable homicide. The law remained in that state until the landmark decision in *Brennan v HM Advocate*[5], in which a full court rejected any defence of intoxication at least in relation to murder. The decision in *Brennan* leaves a number of issues unresolved, but the following examples demonstrate the law as it stands at present:

(1) (a) **A** is given a drink which he believes to be non-alcoholic; in fact it contains a substantial amount of vodka. **A** unwittingly becomes intoxicated and commits an assault.

A's intoxication in this case is involuntary and provided that the intoxication is of such a degree that he cannot form the intent necessary for assault, he should be acquitted[6]. If the alcohol merely disinhibits him then he may still be responsible for his acts, although the effect of the alcohol might possibly mitigate punishment.

(b) **A** becomes involuntarily intoxicated in circumstances identical to those in (a) above. In his state of intoxication he then launches into a vicious knife attack on **B** and kills him.

The decision in *Brennan* was entirely concerned with what the court termed 'self-induced' intoxication and the effect of this on the *mens rea* of murder. The fact that the court ruled out such intoxication as a defence may be taken as an indication that involuntary intoxication should be a defence in such a case, but the decision cannot properly be taken that far. On the strength of Lord McCluskey's dicta in *Ross*[7], involuntary intoxication (of a sufficient degree) should exclude the *mens rea* of murder and assault without distinction between them, and **A** should be acquitted.

(c) **A** becomes involuntarily intoxicated as in (a) and (b), but on this occasion rather than committing an attack on another, he gets into his car and drives away. He drives erratically, is found to be driving with an excess of alcohol in his blood, and is charged with an offence under the Road Traffic Act 1988.

This example illustrates the non-application of a defence of intoxication in relation to a strict liability offence. Liability under s 5 of the Road Traffic Act 1988 is strict and **A** would therefore have no defence. The fact, though, that he was involuntarily intoxicated may be a special reason for the court not to order endorsement or disqualification[8].

(2) **A** takes alcohol voluntarily and in an intoxicated state he assaults **B**.

In *Brennan* the court stated that '… in crimes of basic "intent" we understand the law of England to be at one with the law of Scotland in refusing to admit self-induced intoxication as a defence of any kind'[9]. The English law approach thus adopted excludes intoxication as a defence in those crimes which do not require a specific intent. In English law, assault is one such crime and the court in *Brennan* was evidently of the view that assault in Scots law likewise required only basic intent. The difficulty with this view is that assault in Scots law, at least at that time, required 'evil intent' which is probably rather more than basic intent. There is also the objection that the specific/ basic intent distinction is not part of Scots law. In spite of these doubts, however, the court's intention was clear: intoxication should not be a defence in a case of assault.

115

(3) **A** takes alcohol voluntarily and becomes chronically intoxicated. He then kills **B**.

This example is squarely covered by the decision in *Brennan*. **A**'s recklessness in becoming intoxicated was seen as justifying conviction in this case, the court pointing out that:

> 'There is nothing unethical or unfair or contrary to the general principle of our law that self-induced intoxication is not by itself a defence to any criminal charge including in particular the charge of murder. Self-induced intoxication is itself a continuing element and therefore an integral part of any crime of violence, including murder, the other part being the evidence of the actings of the accused who uses force against his victim. Together they add up or may add up to that criminal recklessness which it is the purpose of the criminal law to restrain.'[10].

(4) **A**, having become voluntarily intoxicated, takes **B**'s gold pen from **B**'s desk and slips it into his pocket. The next day he has no recollection of what happened the previous evening and the pen lies unnoticed in his coat pocket.

If *Brennan* allows a defence of intoxication in a case where the crime is one requiring more than a 'basic intent', then **A** has a defence to a charge of theft in that he did not have the necessary *mens rea* of theft at the time at which he took the pen; that is, he did not intend to deprive **B** of his property. The sheriff would have to believe, however, that he did not form this intention and the question he may well raise is: what **did A** have in mind when he put the pen in his pocket if it was not an intention to deprive the owner of the pen of his property?

(5) **A**, intending to kill **B**, drinks alcohol to build up 'Dutch courage'. He carries through his plan, doing so in a state of intoxication.

This is an instance of *actio libera in causa* and it is clear that intoxication would be no defence here, even if *Brennan* did not exist. This is the strongest case, perhaps the only case, in which in an ideal system of criminal justice, intoxication would have no bearing at all on criminal liability.

1 At para 12–01.
2 Margaret Robertson or Brown (1886) 1 White 93. Hume is firm in his rejection of intoxication as a complete defence.
3 1944 JC 171, 1945 SLT 11; although see *HM Advocate v McLeod* 1956 JC 20, where Lord Hill Watson had said, charging a jury, 'If a man is not shown by the evidence to be within the category of one with diminished responsibility when sober, he cannot place himself within the category ... by taking drink.' This observation was approved in *Brennan*.
4 [1920] AC 479.
5 1977 SLT 151.
6 The judgment of Lord McCluskey in *Ross (Robert) v HM Advocate* 1991 SCCR 823, 1991 SLT 564 provides the sole Scottish authority for the principle that involuntary intoxication may be a defence: '... one can see at once that the "evidence of mens rea" referred to [in Majewski and in *Brennan*] is wholly lacking in the case where the intoxicant has been administered to a person without his knowledge and consent' (at 840).
7 *Ross (Robert) v HM Advocate* 1991 SCCR 823, 1991 SLT 564.
8 Road Traffic Offenders Act 1988, ss 34(1), 44(2).
9 1977 JC 38 at 47, 1977 SLT 151 at 155.
10 1977 JC 38 at 51, 1977 SLT 151 at 158.

A critique of the law

8.12   The decision in *Brennan* is essentially hostile to any defence of intoxication. The policy arguments against recognising this defence are fairly persuasive, as indeed the restrictions on using voluntary intoxication as a mitigating factor confirm. The drunken assault cannot he condoned, and even if the accused has acted out of character and demonstrated remorse for what he has done, this cannot amount to a complete defence. However *Brennan* must be considered along with the decision in *Purcell*[1], which was to the effect that wicked recklessness could only be a basis for guilt if it is allied with an intention to cause physical injury and displaying a wicked disregard of fatal consequences. The accused in *Purcell* knocked over and killed a child whilst fleeing from the police in a car. The High Court held that for a charge of murder, there must be evidence of intention to cause physical harm. It may be too much to rely on a legal hypothesis that every person who becomes voluntarily intoxicated intends to cause physical harm[2].

1   *HM Advocate v Purcell* 2008 SLT 44.
2   See 'Foreseeing the consequences of Purcell' by Plaxton, article 2008 SLT 21.

8.13   The approach currently applied in English law is under *DPP v Majewski*[1]. The House of Lords held that while intoxication does not affect crimes of basic intent, in relation to crimes of specific intent it may be relevant. Where homicide is involved, the effect of intoxication may be to reduce the offence from murder to manslaughter (culpable homicide). This was much commented upon[2]. Scots law formerly had the latter option open to it. This was apparently removed by *Brennan*; whether *Purcell* allows a measure of re-instatement remains to be seen. But the antipathy to treating the effects of alcohol or substance abuse as a means of excusing behaviour is confirmed in the legislative measures dealing with diminished responsibility.

1   [1976] 2 All ER 142, [1977] AC 443.
2   See eg A Dashwood 'Logic and the Lords in *Majewski*' [1977] Crim LR 532, 591; E Colvin 'A theory of the intoxication defence' (1981) 59 Can Bar Rev 850; A Ashworth 'Reason, logic and criminal liability' (1975) 91 LQR 102. R Williams 'Voluntary intoxication – a lost cause' LQR 2013 129 (April) 264–289.

INSANITY AND DIMINISHED RESPONSIBILITY

8.14   The effect of mental abnormality on criminal responsibility is one of the more controversial questions in criminal jurisprudence. At one extreme is the view that many instances of criminal behaviour are directly attributable to some psychopathology of the offender and that the proportion of criminals fully responsible for their actions is actually fairly low. Directly opposed to this is the argument that even those who are mentally abnormal are still, in the vast majority of cases, answerable for what they do. Adherents of this position tend to be sceptical when confronted with psychiatric explanations of anti-social behaviour.

Whatever role criminology may attribute to mental abnormality in the aetiology of crime, systems of criminal justice have long recognised that at least some forms of mental abnormality will exculpate an accused person. This occurs through the operation of (1) the defence of insanity, and (2) the plea of diminished responsibility, the effect of which is to reduce a charge of murder to one of culpable homicide. In addition account must be taken of automatism, which may have a psychiatric explanation (fully discussed above in the context of *actus reus)*, and the plea in bar of trial, which prevents criminal trial on the grounds of the inability of the accused to understand the proceedings and to instruct counsel.

Mental abnormality and crime

8.15   The criminal law presupposes rationality and individual moral responsibility. The rational person acts in accordance with a view of the world which is shared by other rational agents, and behaves in a way which enables him to achieve those goals which he has identified as desirable. Such a person is usually capable of controlling himself, conforming to social norms, and of understanding the reason for such restrictions as may be placed on his behaviour.

A mentally disturbed person may not be capable of acting rationally in accordance with the criteria outlined above. This may be because of some limitation of his understanding (a defect in his cognitive capacities), or it may arise from a volitional disability. In the latter case the person is quite capable of understanding the world about him, but cannot help himself from acting in a particular way. In either case the moral responsibility of the mentally abnormal person may be affected. Defects in cognition have an exculpatory effect because one should not be held accountable for what one does not know; defects in volition may have a similar effect on the grounds that one is not to blame for that which he cannot help himself from doing.

Mental abnormality does not give rise to blanket exculpation: some mentally disturbed persons will not be so affected by their condition as to be considered non-responsible. For this reason psychiatric evidence will need to focus on the clinical features of the condition from which such a person suffers, and it is then for the jury to determine whether this satisfies the tests for responsibility which the law has set in this area. Psychiatric expertise provides an insight into the way the mind of a mentally disturbed person may be affected by his psychiatric condition.

8.16   Psychiatric conditions range from the relatively benign (mild neuroses) to the florid and debilitating (functional psychoses and organic disorders). While the former are unlikely to affect responsibility to an appreciable extent, the latter may well be so disabling as to justify exculpation.

The connection between mental abnormality and crime

8.17   The diagnosis of a psychiatric condition does not necessarily provide an explanation as to why a person has committed a criminal offence: the vast majority of mentally ill persons never commit an offence. Yet in some cases the fact that a mentally abnormal person has committed an offence seems very clearly attributable to the mental illness itself. There are many forms of crime in which the insights of psychiatry may play an important explanatory role without necessarily providing grounds for exculpation. Sexual offences are an example: the psychological profile of those who engage in certain forms of sexual offence, such as paedophiliac offences or offences involving, say, sado-masochistic or necrophiliac elements, is likely to deviate substantially from the norm. Such information can inform not just liability, but also sentencing, looking at risk and treatment.

The criminal law's response to mental abnormality

(a) Informal measures. The mentally disturbed offender who commits a minor offence may be informally dealt with by the police, or procurator fiscal, with health service involvement. The support of psychiatric services in the disposition of such cases without resort to court appearances saves the time of the criminal courts and provides a more humane means of dealing with those who do not pose any considerable threat to society.

(b) The plea in bar of trial. The accused's mental (or physical) health can be brought to the attention of court at any stage of the proceedings. The matter is regulated by s 54 of the Criminal Procedure (Scotland) Act 1995, applying to both solemn and summary proceedings. If the court is satisfied that a person charged with an offence is unfit for trial, so that a trial cannot commence or continue, the court must make a finding to that effect and state the reason for so finding. The matter then proceeds to an examination of facts. If satisfied that certain medical conditions are met, the court may make an order authorising the person's removal to and detention at a hospital. An examination of facts follows the procedure of a summary trial: it can result in an acquittal, but it cannot result in a conviction. The court is limited to making a finding that the accused did the act, or made the omission, complained of which must be established beyond reasonable doubt. The court must then consider whether, on a balance of probabilities, there are grounds for acquittal (that is, that he was not criminally responsible at the time of the offence). The disposals are contained in s 57 of the 1995 Act).

8.18 The Criminal Procedure (Scotland) Act 1995 also makes provision for procedures if a person charged with an offence appears to have a mental disorder. These are complex but essentially provide a mechanism whereby such a person can be subject to assessment and treatment. Powers to instigate such orders lie with the prosecutor, the Scottish Ministers and the court *ex proprio motu*. The complexity of the provisions is shown in the fact that they extend from s 52 to s 52U and s 53 to s 53D. A successful plea in bar of trial does not bar the Crown from bringing criminal proceedings if the accused is subsequently found to be fit to face trial.

(c) The insanity defence. The defence of insanity is a special defence, requiring prior notice to the Crown which, if successfully raised, results in the special verdict of not guilty on the grounds of insanity. Prior to the Criminal Procedure (Scotland) Act 1995 it was an inevitable consequence of this verdict that the accused should be detained in psychiatric hospital as a restricted patient. The courts now have discretion in such cases and can make a variety of disposals, including supervision and treatment orders, compulsion orders and restriction orders[1].

The burden of proof in respect of an insanity plea rests upon the defence. This is in contrast to the normal requirement that the burden of proof in a criminal trial rests upon the prosecution. In *Lindsay v HM Advocate*[2] the High Court confirmed that the burden of proving diminished responsibility also rests on the defence. This was re-asserted in *Lilburn v HMA*[3] where a five-judge bench of the High Court affirmed that there was a legal onus on the accused not only to raise, but to establish on a balance of probabilities, any plea of diminished responsibility.

1 1995 Act, s 57.
2 1996 SCCR 870.
3 2012 JC 150, 2011 SLT 861, 2011 SCL 678, 2011 SCCR 326.

The criteria of insanity in Scots criminal law

8.19   *Hume* states that the defence of insanity requires that there should be an:

> 'absolute alienation of reason[1] … such a disease as deprives the patient of the knowledge of the true aspect and portion of things about him – hinders him from distinguishing friend or foe, and gives him up to the impulse of his own distempered fancy'[2].

This wording is echoed in the modern cases, the most important of which are *HM Advocate v Kidd*[3] and *Brennan v HM Advocate*[4]. In *Kidd*, Lord Strachan said in his instructions to the jury:

> 'First, in order to excuse a person from responsibility for his acts on the grounds of insanity, there must have been an alienation of the reason in relation to the act committed. There must have been some mental defect, to use a broad neutral word, a mental defect by which his reason was overpowered and he was thereby rendered incapable of exerting his reason to control his conduct and reactions. If his reason was alienated in relation to the act committed, he was not responsible for that act, even though otherwise he may have been apparently quite rational'.

1 The role played by concepts of reason in the plea of insanity in Scotland dates back to at least the sixteenth century: H Arnot *A Collection and Abridgement of Celebrated Criminal Trials in Scotland 1536–1784* II (1833 edn) Part 2, p 363: trial of *Jaspar Lauder*. '… the said Jasper has been furious and wanted the use of resoune …'. Discussed by N Walker *Crime and Insanity in England* (1968) 1, p 138.
2 I, 37.
3 1960 JC 61, 1960 SLT 82.
4 1977 JC 38, 1977 SLT 151.

8.20   In *Brennan*, in which the accused's plea of insanity was based upon his extreme degree of intoxication at the time of the offence, a Full Bench of the High Court approved *Hume's* conception of insanity, explaining that:

'Insanity in our law requires proof of total alienation of reason in relation to the act charged as the result of mental illness, mental disease, or defect or unsoundness of mind and does not comprehend the malfunctioning of the mind of transitory effect ...'[1].

The direction in *Kidd* resolved the uncertainties which had crept into this area of the law since *Hume* In *Cardle v Mulrainey*[2], Lord Justice-General Hope explained a total alienation of reason in terms of a lack of knowledge of the nature of the act, or a lack of knowledge of the fact that it is wrong; it is not simply an inability to exercise control. Scots law has hitherto avoided exclusively cognitive tests in this area; but the definition of insanity proposed in *Kidd* and *Brennan* still raised a number of significant problems. What is meant by an 'alienation of reason' or a 'complete alienation of reason'? Is it merely an old-fashioned way of referring to what would now be considered substantial impairment of cognitive ability?

1 1977 JC 38 at 45, 1977 SLT 151 at 154.
2 1992 SCCR 658.

8.21   The criminal responsibility of persons with mental disorder is now regulated by s 51A of the Criminal Procedure (Scotland) Act 1995, which provides that a person is not criminally responsible for conduct constituting an offence if the person was at the time of the conduct unable by reason of mental disorder to appreciate the nature or wrongfulness of the conduct; but if the mental disorder consists only of a personality disorder characterised solely or principally by abnormally aggressive or seriously irresponsible behaviour.

This provision implemented a report from the Scottish Law Commission. There must be a mental disorder and it must have had a specific effect on the accused. The exclusion is aimed at psychopathic personality disorder, so other forms of personality disorder may give rise to a defence. Only the accused can raise the defence, and must establish the defence on a balance of probabilities

For the purposes of the defence, mental disorder is defined in s 328 of the 1995 Act and excludes dependence on alcohol or drugs, and acting as no prudent person would. Expert evidence will be inevitable so that the jurors can address the issue of whether the accused was unable to appreciate the nature or wrongfulness of the conduct.

Diminished responsibility

8.22   The effect of diminished responsibility in Scots law is restricted to a reduction of a charge of murder to one of culpable homicide[1]. It is therefore not a defence but a mitigating plea, akin in its effect to the plea of provocation[2].

The origins of the doctrine precede its recognition in the important case of *Dingwall*[3] a decision which is commonly regarded as its foundation in modern practice. *Mackenzie* argues for the moderation of the punishment for those who are not 'absolutely mad yet are hypochondrick and melancholy to such a degree that it clouds their reason ...'[4]. *Hume,* however, was less enthusiastic:

'As to the inferior degrees of derangement, or natural weakness of intellect, which do not amount to madness and for which there can be no rule in law: the relief of these must be sought either in the discretion of the prosecutor, who may restrict his libel to an ordinary pain, or in the course of application to the King for mercy …'[5].

In a number of nineteenth-century cases the accused's mental state was accepted as grounds for recommendations for mercy[6], but it was not until the decision in *Dingwall*[7] that the practice was established of returning a verdict of culpable homicide rather than murder in those cases in which responsibility was thought to be diminished. Although the courts were generally sympathetic to the concept of diminished responsibility, by the beginning of the twentieth century a degree of judicial scepticism had set in[8]. In *HM Advocate v Savage*[9] the High Court gave a direction on the nature of diminished responsibility which has come to be regarded as the authoritative statement of the modern law:

'… it has been put in this way: there must be aberration or weakness of mind; that there must be some form of mental unsoundness; that there must be a state of mind bordering on, though not amounting to, insanity; that there must be a mind so affected that responsibility is diminished from full responsibility to partial responsibility – in other words, the prisoner in question must only be partially accountable for his actions. And I think one can see running through the cases that there is implied … that there must be some form of mental disease'.

1 There had been some disagreement as to whether it was available in other cases: T B Smith 'Diminished responsibility in Scots law' [1957] Crim LR 354, reproduced in *Studies Critical and Comparative*, p 241. See, however, N Walker *Crime and Insanity in England* I, 144. Lord Clyde put the matter beyond doubt, at least for modern law, in *HM Advocate v Cunningham* 1963 JC 80, 1963 SLT 345, when he said '[diminished responsibility] is not open in the case of a lesser crime such as culpable homicide'.
2 See *Lindsay v HM Advocate* 1997 JC 19, at p 21 where giving the opinion of the court, Lord Justice General Hope said 'it appears to us that it is more accurate to regard diminished responsibility as a mitigating factor.'
3 (1867) 5 Irv 466.
4 *The Laws and Customs of Scotland in Matters Criminal* I, 1–8.
5 I, 44.
6 Eg *Jas Scott* (1853) 1 Irv 132; *Alex Carr* (1854) 1 Irv 464. For further instances and comment, see *Gordon* paras 11–11 and 11–12.
7 (1867) 5 Irv 466.
8 Eg *HM Advocate v Aitken* (1902) 4 Adam 88.
9 1923 JC 49 at 51 approved in *Lindsay v HM Advocate* 1997 JC 19.

8.23 Subsequent cases confirmed the *Savage* definition. In *HM Advocate v Blake*[1] Lord Brand said in his instructions to the jury:

'A man may suffer from some infirmity or aberration of mind or impairment of the intellect to such an extent as to render him not fully accountable in law for his actions. Such a man is described as being a man of diminished responsibility. If he has not been fully responsible for what he has done, he is guilty not of attempted murder but of assault ….

A man is not of diminished responsibility unless there is aberration or weakness of mind. There must be some unsoundness of mind bordering on but not amounting to insanity. There must be some sort of mental illness.

Any slight departure from the normal make-up of a man will not do. One must distinguish between something in the nature of a mental disease and a vicious tendency, between the mentally sick and the morally bad'[2].

The requirement that there must be some form of mental illness before diminished responsibility can be established was considered at length in *Connelly v HM Advocate*[3]. None of the psychiatrists who gave evidence in this case were able to diagnose any form of mental illness, although one called for the defence was of the view that the accused suffered from a personality disorder. It was argued for the defence, however, that the criteria suggested in the instruction of Lord Alness in *Savage* (excerpted above) should be read as alternatives rather than cumulatively. The Lord Justice General said:

'[I]t would be quite wrong, as I think counsel was suggesting, to isolate one part of Lord Justice-Clerk Alness's description in *Savage* as expressing the concept and to discard the others, or to treat his description as listing four criteria which can be regarded as alternatives so that if one only – and in particular the last – is met that is enough. This would be to place far too much emphasis on one phrase which is, as it happens, the least helpful of all those in the description because it is so obviously tautologous. The passage must be read as a whole with all its elements, and it must be read together with the remark at the end that running through all the cases one can see that there must be some form of mental disease'.

This proposition for the defence, which the court so clearly rejected, would have had the effect of allowing diminished responsibility when it could be established that there is 'a mind so affected that responsibility is diminished from full responsibility to partial responsibility'. Evidence from a defence psychiatrist had been rejected by the court as worthless, on the grounds that he was expressing himself on precisely the matter which it was for the jury to decide.

1 1986 SLT 661.
2 At 662.
3 1990 JC 349, 1990 SLT 397, 1990 SCCR 504.

8.24   In suggesting the interpretation of *Savage* discussed above, counsel for the accused in *Connelly* had argued for a re-assessment of the law of diminished responsibility arguing that it was out of touch, founded as it was in a decision from 1923 (*Savage*). The court had declined to re-assess the law, recognising that a much closer examination of the matter was required. There was another attempt to revisit the issue in *Lindsay v HM Advocate*[1] but the court declined holding that the law had been stated clearly and consistently. However, the opportunity for a 'closer examination' arose in *Galbraith v HM Advocate (No 2)*[2], when the issue was considered by a bench of five judges. The accused was tried for the murder of her husband. She raised the issue of diminished responsibility. The trial judge had charged the jury on the basis of *Savage* and *Connelly*. In a detailed opinion, the court reached a number of conclusions. The court held that *Savage* did not require that a jury be satisfied that the accused's state of mind satisfied all of the tests set out in that case (that is: 'aberration or weakness of mind'; 'mental unsoundness'; 'a state of mind bordering on, though not amounting to, insanity'; and 'a mind so affected that responsibility is diminished from full responsibility to partial responsibility'); rather, these were examples of the sort of thing that was necessary for a finding of diminished responsibility. They held that the court in *Connelly* were wrong to insist that *Savage* required all the criteria to be met, and overruled *Connelly*.

They further held that the phrase 'mental disease' as used in *Savage* should not be interpreted in a narrow sense, and had been interpreted too strictly in later cases. The issue was that the jury must be satisfied that, by reason of the abnormality of mind in question, the ability of the accused, as compared with a normal person, to determine or control his actings was substantially impaired. They held that diminished responsibility did not come into play unless the effect on the accused's mind was substantial, but that it did not have to border on insanity; the abnormality of mind might take various forms, but had to be one that was recognised by the appropriate science. Such an abnormality could be congenital, or derive from an organic condition, from some psychotic illness, or from the psychological effects of severe trauma; it might mean that the accused perceived physical acts and matters differently from a normal person, or might affect his ability to form a rational judgment as to whether a particular act was right or wrong, or to decide whether to perform it.

Significantly, the Lord Justice General observed that the remarks made in *Galbraith* (regarding the underlying principles of the law of diminished responsibility) were tentative, and may have to be modified or refined in the light of subsequent cases. He emphasised that there were limits to the class of states of mind which comprise diminished responsibility, and that in particular no mental abnormality short of actual insanity, which is brought on by the accused himself taking drink of drugs or sniffing glue, will fall within this class; specifically the condition of psychopathic personality disorder does not fall within this class. He concluded that where the accused lodged a special defence of insanity at the time of the killing, it might well be appropriate to direct the jury that if they find that the accused was not insane, they should nevertheless go on to consider whether his mental state bordered on insanity.

It will not therefore be enough for an accused to be described as immature, inadequate, or lacking in self control. In the absence of clear evidence of a mental disorder or mental disease, the criteria stated in *Savage* will not be met. Although this clarifies the situation, in that it indicates the minimum that psychiatric witnesses will be required to assert, it leaves the boundaries of the defence unclear as it does not define mental disorder or disease. *Galbraith* was considered in *C v HM Advocate*[3], where a plea of diminished responsibility was rejected. The court held that that abnormality of the mind, where established to the court's satisfaction, could properly be taken into account as a mitigating factor. In principle, there was no reason why it could not be taken into account in a case where a plea of diminished responsibility had been rejected by the jury, or where the issue arose in connection with the punishment part of a life sentence.

1 1997 JC 19.
2 2002 JC 1, 2001 SLT 953, 2001 SCCR 551.
3 2009 SLT 707, 2009 SCL 863, 2009 SCCR 606.

The common law, as desiderated in Galbraith, formed the basis for the introduction of a statutory provision, being s 51B of the 1995 Act. The statutory test provides that a person who would otherwise be convicted of murder is instead to be convicted of culpable homicide if the person's ability to determine or control conduct was substantially impaired by reason of abnormality of mind, including mental disorder. The section specifically excludes being under the influence of drugs, alcohol or other substance as constituting, of itself, abnormality of mind, although it does not prevent abnormality being otherwise established. In all cases where diminished responsibility is claimed, the onus of proof is on the accused, who must establish the defence on a balance of probabilities[1].

1 *Lindsay v HM Advocate* 1997 JC 19 at p 22, affirmed by a five-judge bench in *Lilburn v HMA* 2012 JC 150.

Nonage

8.25   There is an irrebuttable presumption that a child under the age of eight cannot be guilty of a criminal offence[1]. This age seems remarkably low[2], but the apparent severity of the law was mitigated by the requirement that the Lord Advocate should consent to the prosecution of any child who has reached the age of eight but who is not yet sixteen. Offenders under the age of sixteen are normally dealt with under the children's hearing system[3].

If an offender under the age of sixteen is prosecuted, his youth should be taken into account in determining *mens rea* questions[4]. This might have a bearing not only on whether he was capable of forming the necessary intention for the commission of the crime, but also on matters such as error.

The concern about the age at which children could be prosecuted was met in the Criminal Justice and Licensing (Scotland) Act 2010, s 52 added a new provision, s 41A of the Criminal Procedure (Scotland) Act 1995 which increases the age at which a child can be prosecuted to twelve; this follows a Scottish Law Commission report '*Report on Age of Criminal Responsibility*[5]' which recommended that restriction be placed on the prosecution of children under twelve. The recommendation to abolish the irrebuttable presumption in relation to children under eight was not taken forward[6].

1 Criminal Procedure (Scotland) Act 1995, s 41; *Merrin v S* 1987 SLT 193.
2 In England the age of criminal responsibility is ten: Children and Young Persons Act 1933, s 50 as amended by the Act of the same name of 1963. In English law, a child aged ten but under fourteen is rebuttably incapable of the *mens rea* necessary for any offence: *J M (A Minor) v Runeckles* [1984] Cr App Rep 255. In Germany the age of criminal responsibility is fourteen; in France, thirteen.
3 Established under the Social Work (Scotland) Act 1968, Pt III, and now governed by the Children's Hearings (Scotland) Act 2011. These proceedings are not criminal prosecutions.
4 As suggested by *Gane and Stoddart* p 284.
5 See http://www.scotlawcom.gov.uk/downloads/rep185.pdf.
6 See the Policy Memorandum to the Bill at http://www.scottish.parliament.uk/s3/bills/24-Crim JustLc/b24s3-introd-pm.pdf.

SELF-DEFENCE

8.26 The special defence of self-defence is available for acts which are done in defence of self, of others[1], and, in some cases, of property. The basic principle here is that a person is entitled to use force to prevent harm to interests and that the use of force, if it falls within the boundaries of the defence, is justified. Self-defence is therefore a matter of justification rather than excuse. The defence is broad in its scope. Most of the cases are concerned with homicide, but the plea has been recognised as a defence to a charge of assault and, to breach of the peace, although the libel of that offence was of engaging in a fight[2]. The effect of a successful defence of this nature will be the complete acquittal of the accused.

For a long period Scots law was plagued by confusion between provocation and self-defence, and it was necessary for the courts to spell out the distinction, first in *Crawford v HM Advocate*[3], and again in *Fenning v HM Advocate*[4]. The origins of this confusion are to be found in *Hume's* division of self-defence into those situations where the accused was responding to an unprovoked attack and those situations where the accused was involved in a quarrel[5]. In many cases, of course, counsel may wish to advance both provocation and self-defence as alternative pleas. This might be desirable where the accused has responded to an attack on himself with excessive force. Self-defence may be ruled out in such a case on the grounds of, for instance, the accused's ability to retreat from the threat, but the original attack may still constitute the basis of a successful provocation plea. In such a case, however, the issues of self-defence and provocation must be considered by the jury as separate matters. In *Lieser v HM Advocate*[6], the court considered the interaction between the two concepts. They held that there was longstanding and binding authority that a person who claimed he acted in self-defence, or was provoked because he believed he was in imminent danger, had to have had reasonable grounds for his belief, that it was essentially for policy reasons that the law chose to require certain conditions to be present in relation to provocation and self-defence and that self-defence and provocation were conceptually to be seen, where relevant, as relating to the primary question of whether the accused could be said to have had *mens rea* for murder; but the court emphasised that there was no reason to alter the accepted and well-recognised boundaries of the defences. However, the interaction does not remain free from difficulty. In *Duffy v HMA*[7] the High Court held that even where self-defence was pled, and provocation not mentioned by the Crown or defence, the court had a responsibility to direct the jury about the availability of provocation, saying that it was a matter for the jury, unless the court concluded that no reasonable jury could reach the view that there was provocation.

1 *Jones v HM Advocate* 1989 SCCR 726 at 738, 1990 SLT 517 at 524, per Lord Justice-Clerk Ross: 'Self-defence covers the situation where a man acts in order to defend his own person or in defence of persons other than himself'.
2 *Derrett v Lockhart* 1991 SCCR 109.
3 1950 JC 67, 1950 SLT 279.
4 1985 JC 76, 1985 SCCR 219.
5 For discussion, see PW Ferguson *Crimes Against the Person* (1990) p 48.
6 2008 SLT 866; 2008 SCCR 797; 2008 SCL 1050.
7 2015 HCJAC 29.

Killing in self-defence: the requirements of the defence

8.27   The defence will be available in a charge of murder or culpable homicide provided the following requirements are met:

(1)   There must be an imminent danger to life

The courts have consistently stressed that if self-defence is to be allowed the accused must have been faced with a threat to his life or, in the case of a woman, a threat of rape[1]. The requirement that life be threatened will mean that the defence will not be available where the accused has taken life in the belief that he is physically threatened but that he is not in danger of death[2].

There are obvious policy reasons why self-defence should be excluded where the accused has intentionally taken his attacker's life merely to avoid some relatively slight harm to himself, but these reasons do not apply with the same force to one who intentionally kills in order to avoid serious physical harm. The current formula, of course, may allow this by permitting any serious injury to be considered a threat to life. Any use of a weapon, for example, is potentially life-threatening, and an accused would normally, be justified in thinking his life to be in danger if an attack involved the use of a knife[3]. Even a party who kills someone in a quarrel which he himself started may plead self defence in relation to any retaliation faced. The question is whether the retaliation is such that the accused is entitled to protect himself. That will depend upon whether the retaliation is out of proportion to the initial attack, giving rise to a reasonable apprehension of immediate danger from which there is no escape. The violence must be no more than necessary to preserve life or protect himself from serious injury[4].

It is clear that the requirement that there should have been a threat to the accused's life cannot apply in cases of culpable homicide. If **A** is attacked by **B** and strikes him to ward off what is obviously no more than a minor attack, and if **B** then falls and strikes his head on the concrete (with fatal results), it would be unacceptable to deny **A** the defence.

The threat must be an immediate one rather than one which is to be put into effect at some vague point in the future. The notion of a pre-emptive blow is probably inapplicable in this context, as in such situations the person under threat will normally be able to avoid the danger by retreating or by reporting the threat to the authorities.

1 *Crawford v HM Advocate*, above; *Jones v HM Advocate*, above. See also 'Fatal self defence against rape; a call for clarification in Scots Law', 2012 JR 111, reflecting on the fact that rape is no longer gender specific.
2 Lord Clyde was adamant on this point in *McCluskey v HM Advocate* 1959 JC 39, 1959 SLT 215 where he stated: '... I can see no justification at all for extending this defence to a case where there is no apprehension of danger to the accused's life'.
3 *Owens v HM Advocate* 1946 JC 119 at 125, 1946 SLT 227; cf *Jones v HM Advocate* 1989 SCCR 726 at 738, 1990 SLT 517 at 524.
4 *Burns v HM Advocate* 1995 JC 154 at 158; 1995 SLT 1090.

(2) An erroneous belief that life is threatened

8.28   A person who is subjected to an attack may reach the conclusion that life is threatened although, in reality, it is not. The issue arose in *Owens v HM Advocate*[1] in which the appellant had been convicted of the murder of an attacker whom he mistakenly believed to be armed with a knife. The court held that the essential question in such a case was not whether the attacker was really armed with a knife but whether the appellant genuinely believed that he was so armed. The belief, although mistaken, must he based on reasonable grounds. In *Crawford*[2] the court reiterated the requirement of reasonableness, pointing out that 'when self-defence is supported by a mistaken belief rested on reasonable grounds, that mistaken belief must have an objective background and must not be purely subjective or of the nature of an hallucination'[3]. A similar endorsement of the subjective requirement is made in *Jones*, where self-defence was held to be justifiable if 'reasonably apprehended'[4]. The test is therefore whether a reasonable person in the position of the accused would have concluded that his life was in danger. An erroneous conclusion that the attacker is concealing a weapon, or an erroneous conclusion of homicidal intent will not preclude the defence, provided that there are reasonable grounds for the reaching of these conclusions. In Lieser (above), the High Court concluded that there was binding authority to the effect that 'a person, who claims he acted in self-defence because he believed that he was in imminent danger, must have had reasonable grounds for this belief'.

There is an argument for abandoning the requirement that the accused's belief in the danger to his life should be reasonable, as the person who acts under genuine, though unreasonable, error is as morally blameless as one who draws an erroneous, but still reasonable conclusion[5].

Scots law allows self-defence where a woman kills in defence against rape. This appears in *Hume*[6] in *Alison*[7], and was endorsed by Lord Clyde in *McCluskey v HM Advocate*[8]. The exception does not extend to threatened sodomy – the point at issue in *McCluskey* – even if it appears outdated and illogical to allow killing to prevent one form of non-consensual penetration but not another[9].

1 1946 JC 119, 1946 SLT 227.
2 1950 JC 67, 1950 SLT 279.
3 1950 JC 67 at 71.
4 1989 SCCR 726 at 740, 1990 SLT 517 at 525, per Lord Wylie.
5 See Leverick; 'Unreasonable mistake in self-defence' 2009 Edin LR 100.
6 I, 218.
7 I, 132.
8 1950 JC 39, 1959 SLT 215.
9 The decision in *McCluskey* was followed in *Elliott v HM Advocate* 1987 SCCR 278, where the accused alleged that he killed his victim to protect himself against a homosexual assault. The alteration of the offence of rape to include homosexual rape under the Sexual Offences (Scotland) 2009 is likely to extend the applicability of this defence, but so far this has not happened; see article by McPherson, 'Fatal self defence against rape' 2012 JR 111.

(3) The danger must have been inescapable

8.29   *Hume* states that self-defence is available where 'the party has other ways of escape from the assault, or some sure and easy means of putting an end to it; but where, out of pride, or humour, or some false notion of dishonour in the thing, he chooses rather to stand and repel the violence'[1]. This possibility of retreat was discussed in *HM Advocate v Doherty*[2] where the accused had an open door and stairs behind him but made no effort to use them. The means of escape, of course, must be reasonably available and not involve the accused in exposing himself to undue danger[3].

(4)   The force used must not be excessive

A person who comes under attack from another is entitled to use only that degree of force which is reasonably necessary to repel the attack. A person who is the victim of an attack will not be able to judge to a nicety the degree of violence that is used, and the courts will take into account the exigencies of the situation when assessing the reaction of an attack. In *HM Advocate v Doherty* for example, Lord Keith instructed the jury: 'You do not need an exact proportion of injury and retaliation; it is not a matter that you weigh in too fine scales …'[4]. An accused person may therefore use excessive force not because he wishes to do undue harm to his assailant but because he has, in the heat of the moment, miscalculated the amount of force required to protect himself.

1 I, 226.
2 1954 JC 1, 1954 SLT 169.
3 See *McBrearty v HM Advocate* 1994 SCCR 122 at 126.
4 1954 JC 1 at 4, 1954 SLT 169 at 170.

8.30   The use of grossly excessive force, or a 'cruel excess' will exclude self-defence[1]. In *Fenning v HM Advocate*[2] the accused was convicted of murder. He appealed arguing that murder might be reduced to culpable homicide if, whilst initially justified, there had been unnecessary violence or the violence continued after the danger had passed. Lord Cameron, giving the opinion of the court held:

> 'It is … clearly the duty of the judge to explain to the jury that the benefit of the defence is lost where the force used to repel the attack is excessive, and in my opinion where, as here, the language is precise and positive, and the degree of excess characterised, which will elide the defence, is specifically stated to be "cruel", then it is not mandatory for the judge to illustrate by examples the meaning of these words'.

It may be that in such a case provocation will be found which has this effect, but the issue of provocation is to be judged separately from that of self-defence.

1 *Moore v MacDougall* 1989 SCCR 659: the accused stabbed the victim in the buttocks with a pair of scissors after he (the victim) had assaulted her. It was held that this was excessive, given the moderate nature of the assault.
2 1985 SCCR 219, 1985 JC 76.

Self-defence and lawful force

8.31   A person is not entitled to defend himself against lawful force. The defence is therefore not available to one who defends himself against lawful arrest or against any other application of lawful force by officers of the law.

The fact that the accused started a quarrel will not mean that the defence is not available to him. For example, if **A** insults **B**, who then picks up a weapon and threatens **A** with it, **A** is entitled to defend himself against **B** although he has brought the attack upon himself. The same would apply if **A** struck **B**, provoking him to retaliate. The situation is different, however, if **A** assaults **B**, who then uses force to defend himself against **A**'s attack. **A** is not entitled to defend himself against **B**'s act of self-defence unless **B**'s response is excessive, in which case **B** is no longer acting in self-defence.

One might think that such situations rarely come before the courts, but one did so in *R v Lawson and Forsyth*. Here **L** and **F** were convicted of shooting **V** after **L** had approached **V**, carrying a shotgun. **V**, who had good reason to fear that **L** intended to kill him, drew a revolver and fired a number of shots. **L** argued that he had killed **V** in self-defence, having abandoned any homicidal intention towards **V**. This argument was rejected on the grounds that a change of mind on **L**'s part would need to have been unambiguously signalled to **V** before **L** would be entitled to act in self-defence; at the time of the killing of **V**, **L** was still the aggressor.

Defence of property

8.32   There is scant Scottish authority on the legitimacy or otherwise of the use of force in defence of property[1]. In principle, the use of moderate force to prevent damage to one's property or to prevent it being stolen, should be acceptable. It is difficult to imagine a court convicting of assault one who pushes away a thief who tries to steal his wallet. Similarly, a person who hits out at a robber who attempts to snatch his watch off his wrist should not be held to have committed assault. Such cases must be distinguished, however, from a situation where a householder, on surprising a housebreaker in his house, assaults him severely with a golf club or other weapon. This is immoderate force, more than is required to defend property, and should rightly be treated as assault.

Killing in defence of property is implicitly excluded by the judgment in *McCluskey v HM Advocate*[2] which limits homicide in self-defence to those cases where life is threatened. The setting of a man-trap for housebreakers would therefore not be permissible, no matter what the frequency of housebreakings suffered by the householder has been. It is submitted, though, that it should not be culpable homicide if the accused has caused the death of another as a result of the moderate use of force in the defence of property.

1 *Donald Kennedy* (1838) 2 Swin 213 at 231–232. Bell's *Principles* p 2032. *The Lord Advocate's Reference* (No 1 of 2000) supports the existence of a defence of self defence in relation to a charge of malicious mischief (paragraph [34]). For English law, see *Smith and Hogan* p 246. Some writers suggest that the use of force is particularly justified if the aggressor enters one's home: A Ashworth *Principles of Criminal Law* (1991), p 118. For general discussion, see D Lanham 'Defence of property in the criminal law' [1966] Crim LR 368, 426.
2 1959 JC 39, 1959 SLT 215.

NECESSITY AND COERCION

8.33   These have traditionally been considered to be two separate defences, but with the decision of the High Court in *Moss v Howdle*[1] the distinction between the two defences has been eroded. The defence of necessity has traditionally been applied in circumstances where the accused has performed a criminal act because it is the lesser of two evils with which he is faced. In such cases the evil with which he is confronted could result from some outside force (for example, a natural disaster) or from some other person. The usual case of coercion arose where the accused was threatened by another that he would be subjected to physical violence unless he committed some criminal offence. If **A** releases the water from a dam in order to prevent the dam wall from bursting, he acts in necessity, and might plead necessity as a defence if, as a result of his releasing the water, he endangers the lives of those downstream. If **A** is threatened by **B** that he will be killed unless he joins in an attack on **C**, he may claim coercion as defence to the charge of assault.

1 1997 SCCR 215.

8.34   The decision in *Moss v Howdle* rejects this division and treats both situations as aspects of the defence of coercion. It is a curious case in that the two concepts are treated as synonymous. This departs from the previous practice of the courts, which have recognised the existence of both coercion and necessity, and also differs from the views expressed by criminal law writers; for example, *Gordon* considers necessity and coercion to be separate defences. Necessity would now seem to be an aspect of coercion, possibly to be described as *coercion of circumstances*.

There are relatively few authorities on the subject in Scots law. In a number of cases concerning road traffic offences, sheriff courts recognised the availability of the defence of necessity, but the law was far from clear and there remained some doubt as to the general availability of the defence[1]. That doubt is now resolved by *Moss v Howdle*: there is a defence of necessity in Scots law (even if it is to be known as coercion). The requirements of the defence of coercion are set out in *Moss v Howdle*; it is only available if the accused had no real choice but to do what he did. This will arise only if the choice is either to do what the accused did or to face an immediate danger of death or great bodily harm. No other circumstances will be recognised as giving rise to such a limitation of choice. The duress must have dominated the mind of the accused at the time of the act, and the act must have been committed by reason of that domination; 'the defence only arises where there is a conscious dilemma faced by a person who has to decide between saving life or avoiding serious bodily harm on the one hand, and breaking the law on the other'[2].

This requirement adequately covers most cases which fell under the separate defence of coercion, that is, those cases in which there is an order followed by a threat[3]. It will also cover those cases in which the accused has broken the law in order to save himself or another from death or harm from whatever quarter, whether it be a natural force or another person. That definition did not appear

131

to cover cases – previously covered by the defence of necessity – in which a person commits a crime against property in order to save property. If I destroy your property in order to prevent greater harm, there can be no defence of coercion, as I have not acted in order to prevent bodily harm or death. This was resolved in *The Lord Advocate's Reference (No 1 of 2000)*[4]. In that case the accused had vandalised a submarine at the Faslane naval base. The sheriff upheld a submission of no case to answer. The Crown referred the matter to the High Court, which held that the defence of necessity was available in relation to danger to persons and property.

1 For discussion see P Ferguson 'Necessity and duress in Scots law' [1986] Crim LR 103.
2 *Dawson v Dickson* 1999 SCCR 698 at 703; see also *MD v PF Falkirk* 2009 SLT 476.
3 The requirements of coercion were discussed in *Thomson v HM Advocate* 1983 JC 69, 1983 SCCR 368.
4 2001 JC 143, 2001 SLT 507, 2001 SCCR 296.

8.35 The test of whether the accused was coerced into acting as he did is an objective one, and it is therefore not enough if the accused thought that he had no choice when, viewed objectively, he could have done otherwise. This is made clear in *Moss v Howdle*, the facts of which were that the accused drove along a highway at over 100 miles per hour, thus breaching strict liability provisions of the Road Traffic Act. He claimed that his passenger had uttered a cry of pain and, believing him to be in need of assistance, he drove as quickly as he could to the nearest service area. In the view of the court, however, this was not a situation in which the accused had no choice: it would have been possible for him to draw over and stop his vehicle with a view to summoning help. In emphasising this aspect of choice, the High Court quoted with approval the *dictum* of Dickson J. In the Supreme Court of Canada decision in *Perka v The Queen*[1]:

'If there is a reasonable legal alternative to disobeying the law, then the decision to disobey becomes a voluntary one, impelled by some consideration beyond the dictates of "necessity" and human nature'.

The decision in *The Lord Advocate's Reference (No 1 of 2000)* elaborated upon some of the issues affecting necessity. Lord Prosser gave the opinion of the court, saying at paragraph [42]:

'The [accused] must have good cause to fear that death or serious injury *would* result unless he acted; that cause for fear must have resulted from a reasonable belief as to the circumstances; the [accused] must have been impelled to act as he did by those considerations; and the defence will only be available if a sober person of reasonable firmness, sharing the characteristics of the [accused], would have responded as he did'.

In *Cochrane v HM Advocate*[2], the court considered the objective nature of the test. The accused had been involved in the commission of a robbery. He claimed that he had only done so as a result of threats made to him. He led evidence from a chartered psychologist about a degree of mental impairment and that the accused was unusually compliant. He was convicted and appealed. The High Court refused the appeal. The Lord Justice General (Rodger) held at paragraph [19]:

'In the first place, the objective test ... goes some way to ensuring a consistency of approach in dealing with accused persons. It is also designed to keep the defence of coercion within fairly strict bounds. Coercion or compulsion is not a defence which the law regards with particular favour ... by applying the objective test the law ensures that people who are, by definition, responsible for their acts under our criminal law cannot use the defence to avoid the consequences of those acts, simply because of some failing in their personality or make-up which they should, in fact, be striving to master.'

It is likely that an accused who acts under coercion because he has wrongfully placed himself in a position where he is likely to be subjected to pressure will not be able to claim the defence. Thus, one who joins a criminal gang and is then coerced into committing a crime will be denied the defence.

1 [1984] 2 SCR 232 at 252.
2 2001 SCCR 655.

8.36   It is also likely that the defence will not be available to one who takes the life of another in order to save his own. This issue has not been resolved in Scotland; *Ferguson* has argued that *Hume* denies that the defence will be available where the crime committed is an 'atrocious' one. The opposite reading of the relevant passage of *Hume* is possible, however, and certainly in *Moss v Howdle* the High Court suggested, obiter, its availability in armed robbery. Other jurisdictions differ in their approach, with some not excluding the defence in homicide cases and with others denying its availability in such circumstances. As far as the defence of necessity is concerned, the *locus classicus* of the discussion for English law is the remarkable nineteenth century case of *R v Dudley and Stephens*[1] in which two ship-wrecked sailors killed and ate a cabin-boy in order to save themselves from starvation; necessity did not save them from conviction for murder, even if it did save them from the normal penalty for murder. In less dramatic circumstances, the House of Lords addressed the issue for English law in the decision in *R v Howe*[2] and concluded that the defence of duress is unavailable in a charge of murder, and it is likely that the Scottish courts would follow a similar approach; *R v Howe* was viewed with favour – although not in the context of homicide – in both *Moss and The Lord Advocate's Reference (No 1 of 2000)*.

1 (1884) 14 QBD 273. The case, and its background, is discussed by AWB Simpson *Cannibalism and the Common Law* (1984).
2 [1987] AC 417, [1987] 1 All ER 771. For discussion, see P Alldridge 'Duress, murder and the House of Lords' (1988) 52 JCL 186; L Walters 'Murder and duress and judicial law-making in the House of Lords' (1988) 8 *Legal Studies* 61.

Part II
OFFENCES AGAINST THE PERSON

Chapter 9

Assault

9.1   The crime of assault consists of an attack on the person of another. An attack is an application of force which may involve (i) a direct physical onslaught, involving the use of the body or a weapon; or (ii) the use of indirect means; or (iii) the use of physically threatening gestures.

Most assaults fall into the first category. Examples would be administering blows with the fists, beating with a weapon of some sort, kicking, stabbing etc[1]. The degree of violence used may be slight, and it is not necessary that any appreciable degree of injury be caused. Spitting at a person is an assault[2], as would the directing at another of a high-pressure air or water hose.

Indirect assaults occur when events are deliberately set in motion with the intention of causing harm or fear of harm. In *David Keay*[3] the accused whipped a pony being ridden by the victim, causing the pony to rear up and throw its rider. This was considered an assault. If injury is caused by the victim's response to some wrongful action on the part of the accused, then that is assault. A person who sets a dog on another can be guilty of assault, through the agency of the dog. A person who seeks to escape from a situation which he considers threatening, and who causes himself injury in the course of the escape, may be considered to have been assaulted by the person who caused the attempt at escape[4].

1 *Hume* refers to the various colourful terms used in his time, including: invasion, beating and bruising, blooding and wounding, stabbing, mutilation, and demembration (I, 328).
2 *Jas Cairns* (1837) 1 Swin 597 at 610.
3 (1837) 1 Swin 543.
4 *R v Roberts* (1971) 56 Cr App Rep 95; *People v Goodman* (1943) 44 NYS 2d 715 – discussed by HLA Hart and AM Honore *Causation in the Law* (2nd edn, 1985), pp 330–331; and *MacDonald v HM Advocate*, [2006] HCJAC 89. The victim had been left locked in a flat and the accused was charged with murder by causing the deceased to fall from a window in the course of trying to escape.

9.2   The use of physically threatening gestures is an assault. The victim must anticipate harm to himself, and this anticipation must be reasonable. The shaking of a finger at another is unlikely to cause fear or alarm in a reasonable person, and is therefore not an assault[1]. A balled fist may do so; it will depend on the circumstances. At the other end of the scale, the pointing of a gun will have precisely that effect[2], arguably unless the victim knows that the weapon is unloaded or is an imitation firearm. Even then an unloaded weapon or imitation firearm can cause some apprehension, and it is possible to imagine circumstances in which the brandishing of an unloaded firearm is alarming[3].

In *Atkinson v HM Advocate*[4], the appellant had been found guilty of jumping over the counter in a shop, wearing a face mask. Lord Justice-Clerk Ross held that this was sufficient to constitute an assault:

'Assault may be constituted by threatening gestures sufficient to produce alarm. For someone with his face masked to come into a shop and jump over a counter towards the cashier in the shop, in our opinion, could constitute assault according to the law of Scotland ...'[5].

It is not clear whether the victim has to be aware of the threatening gesture. It has been suggested that pointing a gun at another's back should be assault[6]; this is not, however, a 'threatening gesture sufficient to produce alarm', at least not at the time at which the gun is pointed. Is subsequently experienced, or delayed alarm, experienced later, sufficient? If the victim learns ten minutes afterwards that A pointed a gun at his back, he may well experience fear or alarm, even though the danger has passed. Certainly the impact to his psyche may be as great as if he had witnessed it personally. The same question arises in relation to threatening gestures directed towards a sleeping person.

The use of threatening words is not in itself sufficient to constitute an assault. Threats are discussed further below[7].

1 It may be different if the accused knew of the undue timorousness of the victim: *Macpherson v Beath* (1975) 12 SASR 174 at 177.
2 *Hume* I, 443.
3 Even if this were not to be directed at any particular person, such actions might well constitute a breach of the peace. See Chapter 12, below.
4 1987 SCCR 534.
5 At 535.
6 *Gane and Stoddart*, p 385.
7 See para 9.14 below.

LAWFUL FORCE

9.3   Not all applications of physical force amount to an assault. Force will be lawful in the following circumstances, provided always that it is reasonable and not excessive.

(1)   Lawful chastisement

The law in Scotland has historically been that parents are entitled to apply moderate and reasonable force[1] to their young children in order to control and discipline them[2]. This is not an unfettered right. Section 51 of the Criminal Justice (Scotland) Act 2003 provides that where a person claims that something done to a child was a physical punishment carried out in exercise of a parental right, in determining any question as to whether what was done was a justifiable assault, a court must have regard to certain factors, including the nature of what was done, any effect which it has been shown to have had on the child; the child's age; and the child's personal characteristics. But if what was done included or consisted of a blow to the head, shaking, or the use of an implement, the court cannot find that it was a justifiable assault unless some other ground justifies such a finding.

A school teacher had a common law right, indeed part of the parent's right[3], to chastise children within a school. As a result of the decision in *Campbell and*

Cosans v United Kingdom[4] corporal punishment gradually disappeared from Scottish schools. The Standards in Scotland's Schools Act 2000 provided specifically that corporal punishment cannot be justified[5].

Corporal punishment of a child for the purpose of sexual gratification will constitute an assault, as will excessive punishment, or excessive force used in the control of a child. In *Gray v Hawthorn*[6] a teacher was convicted of assault after a series of slaps with a leather belt administered to a young boy over the course of a school day in circumstances redolent of what the court described as 'unjust persecution'.

1 A parent has no right to use excessive force: *Peebles v McPhail* 1989 SCCR 410, 1990 SLT 245: child of two slapped on face and knocked over – excessive. The fact that the mother acted in anger was taken into account in inferring evil intent. See also *B v Harris* 1990 SLT 208.
2 A right which survived the European Court of Human Rights decision in *Campbell and Cosans v United Kingdom* (1982) 4 EHRR 293, although as recently as 27 April 2010 the Council of Europe were calling for the UK to abolish that right as one of very few countries who have not abolished or committed to the abolition of corporal punishment for children; see http://www.coe.int/t/dc/files/pa_session/april_2010/20100427_news_fessee_en.asp?
3 *McShane v Pawn* 1922 JC 26, 1922 SLT 251; this was given qualified support in *Barile v PF Dundee* 2010 SLT 164 at paras [8] and [9].
4 (1982) 4 EHRR 293. This decision of the ECHR provided that parental rights under the European Convention of Human Rights are violated by the infliction of corporal punishment on their children against their (the parent's) wishes. See also Education (No 2) Act 1986, s 48, enacting a new s 48A of the Education (Scotland) Act 1980.
5 Section 16; see *Barile v PF Dundee* 2010 SLT 164 for a discussion about the interaction of the statute with the common law.
6 1964 JC 69.

(2) Force in restraint of others

9.4   Reasonable force may be used on others by those whose position requires them to use such force for the securing of a necessary degree of compliance. The prison officer who uses force to prevent a recalcitrant prisoner from blocking a gangway does not thereby commit an assault, and force may be required to be used by staff of psychiatric hospitals to protect patients or secure compliance with treatment[1]. The latter case poses particularly difficult issues. In general, it is clearly undesirable for nurses in psychiatric hospitals to use force on their patients, and yet there may be circumstances in which a slight degree of force may be needed to break a cycle of hysterical behaviour or to prevent further disruption[2]. This was recognised in *Skinner v Robertson*[3], although it is clear that the court was concerned strictly to limit the extent of this right. In that case the justification for allowing such force was held to be s 107 of the Mental Health (Scotland) Act 1960[4]. The behaviour of the accused would in the twenty-first century be seen as more likely to attract criminal sanction particularly having regard to s 315 of the Mental Health (Care and Treatment) (Scotland) Act 2003, which prohibits ill-treatment or wilful neglect. The principle of necessity might be involved in these cases; this principle was given significant endorsement by the House of Lords in *F v West Berkshire Health Authority*[5], a case concerned with the circumstances in which mentally handicapped patients may be treated without their consent. It is likely that force cannot be used on an informally admitted patient in a psychiatric hospital, the proper response to disruptive behaviour being to ask him or her to leave the hospital[6]. This remedy is clearly unavailable in the case of patients detained under the provisions of the Mental Health (Care and Treatment) (Scotland) Act 2003.

1 *Skinner v Robertson* 1980 SLT (Sh Ct) 43; *Norman v Smith* 1983 SCCR 100.
2 *Poutney v Griffiths* [1976] AC 314, [1975] 2 All ER 881.
3 1980 SLT (Sh Ct) 43.
4 Which became s 122 of the Mental Health (Scotland) Act 1984, now itself repealed and replaced by the Mental Health (Care and Treatment) (Scotland) Act 2003; that Act has no direct equivalent of section giving protection for acts done in pursuance of the Act; instead it provides (at s 315) specifically that it is an offence for anyone providing care and treatment to ill-treat or wilfully neglect a mentally disordered person.
5 [1990] 2 AC 1, [1989] 2 All ER 545.
6 B Hoggett *Mental Health Law* (3rd edn, 1990) p 217.

(3) Defence of self, others, or of property

Force used to protect one's own person or the person of another is not assault[1]. The force must not be excessive, and there must be no alternative means of avoiding the danger[2]. The use of force to protect property may be lawful, but only within very narrow limits. The owner or occupier of property is probably entitled to use reasonable force to eject a trespasser from the property, although there is little modern authority on this issue[3]. It may be possible to plead self-defence in the context of a charge of breach of the peace, although that may depend on whether the libel includes taking part in a fight[4].

1 *HM Advocate v Carson* 1964 SLT 21.
2 The absence of an escape route is to be considered differently if the force is used to protect another; see *Dewar v HM Advocate* 2009 JC 260. The matter is discussed at greater length at paragraph 8.29 above.
3 See *Gloag v Perth and Kinross Council* 2007 SCLR 530, especially paras [20] and [21] for some observations on the removal of an unwanted visitor to property. The matter is potentially complicated by the Land Reform (Scotland) Act 2003
4 *Derrett v Lockhart* 1991 SCCR 109.

(4) The prevention of crime

Police officers may use force to effect an arrest or prevent the commission of a crime. The amount of force used must be reasonable in the circumstances[1]. Persons other than police officers are entitled to use reasonable force to detain those whom they see committing serious crimes. There must be good grounds for the making of a so-called 'citizen's arrest'[2] and mere suspicion that another has committed an offence will not be sufficient, although in *Wightman v Lees*[3] the High Court held that it would not unduly extend the 'mere suspicion' rule where a citizen had a 'moral certainty' that a particular crime had been committed and a particular individual had committed it.

1 *Marchbank v Annan* 1987 SCCR 718; *Bonar v McLeod* 1983 SCCR 161.
2 *Codona v Cardle* 1989 SCCR 287, 1989 SLT 791. The court in this case approved of the statement in Renton and Brown *Criminal Procedure According to the Law of Scotland* (5th edn, 1983) para 5–19: 'A private citizen is entitled to arrest without warrant for a serious crime he has witnessed, or perhaps where, being the victim of the crime, he has information equivalent to personal observation, as when the fleeing criminal is pointed out to him by an eye-witness'. See

also *Bryans v Guild* 1989 SCCR 569, 1990 JC 51, in which the appellant twisted the arm of a youth he mistakenly took to have been a member of a group throwing objects at his house.
3 2000 SLT 111, 1999 SCCR 664.

THE *MENS REA* OF ASSAULT

9.5   The accidental application of force to another is not assault. Conviction for assault requires that the accused should have been motivated by 'evil intent'[1] towards the victim. 'Evil intent' has been described as an 'intention to do bodily injury'[2] or 'an intent to injure and do bodily harm'[3]. It is clear that assault cannot be committed negligently or recklessly[4], although the reckless conduct causing potential or actual harm to others is itself an offence and can be prosecuted as such[5]. In *Connor v Jessop*[6], the High Court did allow a conviction for assault where there was no intention to injure the particular victim, but where, arguably, recklessness was present. In that case the accused was charged with assaulting his victim by throwing a tumbler at her. The tumbler had, in fact, been thrown at another person, but had missed the intended victim and hit a bystander. The accused's conviction for assault was upheld on the grounds that the outcome was something which was 'likely to occur' as a result of the accused's action; it is perhaps better viewed as an endorsement of the doctrine of transferred intent. In *Roberts v Hamilton*[7], in which *Conner* was approved, the accused was charged with assaulting **A** by hitting him with a stick. She had, in fact, intended to hit **B**, but missed. This was therefore another classic case of *aberratio ictus*, or deflection of the blow. In upholding the conviction for assault, the High Court referred to Hume's comments on *aberratio ictus* in murder: 'If John make a thrust at James, meaning to kill, and George, throwing himself between, receive the thrust, and die, who doubts that John shall answer for it, as if his mortal purpose had fallen on James'. This could be applied equally, the court said, to assault[8], the doctrine of transferred intent being applicable even in respect of crimes which can only be committed intentionally.

The doctrine of transferred intent has been the subject of some criticism. The principle objection is because it involves convicting the accused of something which he did not intend to do: if **A** is convicted of assaulting **X** (his blow having been directed at **Y**) then the inference is that he bore evil intent towards **X** (which is not the case). 'Transferred intent' looks much more like recklessness in relation to **X**'s fate. This may indeed be misleading, but equally **A** is not being convicted, in such circumstances, of a crime any greater than that which he intended to commit. There is a difference between intending to assault someone, missing and hitting someone else and, for example, throwing a bottle out of a window, with no regard to the consequences. A charge of culpable and reckless conduct would follow from the latter act. In any event, *HM Advocate v Harris*[9] makes clear that in practice, the option of charging reckless conduct or causing reckless injury is always open to a prosecutor in these circumstances.

1 *Macdonald* p 115.
2 *HM Advocate v Phipps* (1905) 4 Adam 616.
3 *Smart v HM Advocate* 1975 SLT 65.
4 *Lord Advocate's Reference (No 2 of 1992)*, 1993 JC 43, 1992 SLT 460, 1992 SCCR 960. Reckless assault was recognised in English law in *DPP v K (a minor)* [1990] 1 All ER 331, [1990] 1

WLR 1067: the accused poured acid into a hot air drier, not with the intention of causing harm to any person but in order to hide the acid. See, however, *R v Spratt* [1990] 1 WLR 1073, (1990) 91 Cr App Rep 362.

5 See also *HM Advocate v Harris* 1993 JC 150, 1993 SCCR 559, 1993 SLT 963.

6 1988 SCCR 624.

7 1989 SCCR 240, 1989 SLT 399.

8 For criticism see 'Assault and recklessness' (contributed) 1989 SLT 357. The author points out that it is not apparent that the relevant passage from *Hume* applies to crimes requiring intention: transferred intent in relation to murder may be unobjectionable on the grounds that recklessness may be a sufficient *mens rea* for murder anyway.

9 1993 JC 150, 1993 SCCR 559, 1993 SLT 963.

CONSENT

9.6   Subject to certain limitations, consent to the application of force will normally be a defence to assault. Thus, an arm-wrestling contest over a table will not be an assault, nor will a physical embrace between two consenting partners. Consent to the infliction of physical harm, however, is a different matter, as demonstrated in the decision in *Smart v HM Advocate*[1]. The appellant and his victim agreed to fight one another (to have a 'square-go'), and during the course of the fight the victim was punched, beaten, kicked and bitten. The court rejected the contention that a person may consent to the infliction of a certain degree of violence, holding that there is no justification for distinguishing between serious and minor assaults. The real test is whether there is evil intent; once there is intent to injure and do bodily harm then the consent of the victim is irrelevant.

The court accepted that there will be circumstances in which the application of force will be legitimate:

'If **A** touches **B** in a sexual manner and **B** consents to him doing so (and there is nothing else involved which would constitute a crime under statute or at common law) there is no assault because there is no intention to attack the person of **B**. So, too, if persons engage in sporting activities governed by rules, then, although some form of violence may be involved within the rules, there is no assault because the intention is to engage in the sporting activity and not evilly to do harm to the opponent. But where the whole purpose of the exercise is to inflict physical damage on the opponent in the pursuance of a quarrel, then the evil intent is present, and consent is elided'[2].

Smart was seen as a problematic decision, in that its scope is potentially very wide[3]. It would seem that in Scotland consent will be irrelevant in assault, even where a very minor degree of force is employed, as long as there is an intention to harm[4]. The reference to the context of a quarrel, though, could be restrictive. Does this limit the principle to those situations where the parties have quarrelled, or are quarrels merely illustrative of the sort of circumstances in which an intent to cause harm may arise? The latter interpretation seems more likely, in which case any violence, other than in recognised sports amounts to assault. Sado-masochists, who deliver and receive pain for purposes of sexual gratification, almost certainly commit assault according to the decision in *Smart*, although, in practice, prosecutions in Scotland would be unlikely except when the degree of pain inflicted is excessive and involved a severe beating, mutilation, or wounding[5]. In this context, the court's reference to violent sporting activities, such as boxing, presents another difficulty. In the case of sexually motivated violence, one might argue (by analogy with boxing), that the participants' intention is not evilly to injure and do bodily harm, but rather to give sexual pleasure. This argument however, confuses intention with motive, an error which the High Court has itself subsequently criticised[6]. In *McDonald v HM Advocate*[7], the High Court declined to reach a concluded view as to whether, in an appropriate case, notwithstanding consent to the infliction of pain in a sexual context, an intention to cause pain could justify a conviction for assault in the absence of an intention to cause actual physical injury. The accused had claimed that the victim died as a result of consensual sexual activity, but the court held that his actions had extended beyond the infliction of pain to an intention to cause injury.

In *Scott v HMA*[8], the High Court dealt with an appeal against a conviction for murder where the accused had administered a fatal dose of heroin to the victim. Reference was made to *Khaliq v HMA*[9] where the Lord Justice General said 'Upon the matter of consent of the victim to conduct causing injury to him or his death, the law is perfectly clear. Clear consent on the part of the victim – even instigation by the victim – is of no importance at all.'

There is no doubt, however, that sporting violence *is* acceptable – provided it occurs within the rules of the particular sport. In most sports, violence will be incidental to the main aim of the game but boxing and wrestling are anomalies, and their exception from the normal rule can probably be justified as such only on the ground that they are part of a long-accepted sporting and social tradition. The main point of boxing is to strike the opponent, preferably hard enough to render him unconscious or incapable. By contrast, a football player who punches a member of the opposing team during the course of a game, commits an assault on the grounds that such an assault is quite outside the rules of the game.

1 1975 SLT 65.
2 1975 SLT 65 at 66.
3 See GH Gordon 'Consent in assault' (1976) 21 JLSS 168. Moreover, its attempts legally to justify the exclusion of sporting contests from the general rule appear to confuse intention and motive, the very trap against which the High Court has recently warned: see *Lord Advocate's Reference (No 2 of 1992)* 1993 JC 43.
4 In the Canadian case of *R v Dix* (1972) 10 CCC (2d) 324 a 'fair fight' consented to by the participants was held not to involve assault.
5 In the English case of *Donovan* [1934] 2 KB 498, [1934] All ER Rep 207 the accused was convicted of assault after caning a 17-year-old girl. *R v Brown* [1994] 1 AC 212, [1993] 2 All ER 75, concerned sado-masochistic violence of an extreme sort, which resulted in conviction. The consent of the participants was irrelevant. An interesting contrast to this case is provided, however, by the cases of *R v Aitken* [1992] 4 All ER 541, [1992] 1 WLR 1006, and *R v Wilson (Alan)* [1997] QB 47, [1996] 3 WLR 125. In the latter case, the defendant was acquitted of assault where his wife had consented to having his initials branded onto her buttocks; in the former, a number of RAF officers were acquitted of assault, having deliberately set fire to a sleeping colleague's flying suit. Although the victim suffered life-threatening burns, his friends escaped liability because of his consent to the 'horse-play' which gave rise to his injuries.
6 In *Lord Advocate's Reference (No 2 of 1992)* 1993 JC 43, 1992 SCCR 960, 1993 SLT 460.
7 2004 SCCR 161.
8 2012 SCL 153.
9 1984 JC 23, 1984 SLT 137.

'REASONABLE BELIEF IN CONSENT

9.7   There is no defence of having reasonable belief in the consent of the victim. In *Stewart v Nisbet*[1], the accused appealed against a conviction for assaulting the victim by wrapping sticky tape around her head, causing her breathing to be restricted. He had attended at the victim's place of work in the course of his duties as a police officer, and while there had handcuffed her to a window in a crucifix position before committing the assault of which he was convicted. He gave evidence that he had been engaging in 'banter' with the victim, and that she had been laughing and encouraging him. In rejecting the appeal and holding that there was no evidence of consent, the court said:

> 'Despite the route which the law in relation to sexual offences may have taken, there is no defence of "reasonable" or "honest" belief on the part of an attacker about his victim's state of mind in the context of assault. Indeed, as the law stands at present, even if the complainer had in fact consented, it is doubtful whether that would have amounted to a defence (*Smart v HM Advocate* (above), Lord Justice Clerk Wheatley). Be that as it may, whether the appellant thought he was engaging in "banter" or "horseplay" with the complainer, and no matter how he thought the complainer would react to his actions, what he did was deliberately attack the physical person of the complainer. That constitutes the crime of assault.'

1 2013 SCL 209.

AGGRAVATED ASSAULTS

9.8   Assaults may be rendered more serious by the presence of an aggravating factor. Aggravation of assault may occur as a result of:

(1)   The way in which the assault is committed

An assault with a weapon is more serious than an assault with bare hands. The nature of the weapon may make a difference to the severity of the sentence; assaults with firearms are particularly serious.

(2)   The consequences of the assault for the victim

It is an aggravation to assault the victim to his severe injury, or to his permanent disfigurement or impairment, or to the danger of his life[1].

(3)   The nature of the victim

Assaults on elderly or infirm victims or on children are aggravated by the victim's nature, as are assaults on the Sovereign, judges, sheriffs, and justices of the peace. It is aggravated assault to assault officers of the law in the execution of their duty[2]. The common law was supplemented by s 41 of the Police (Scotland) Act 1967, now s 90 of the Police and Fire Reform (Scotland) Act 2012. Such statutory protection was extended to others under the Emergency Workers (Scotland) Act 2005. The assault will be aggravated only if the accused knew of the nature of his victim[3].

(4) Breach of trust

An assault is aggravated by a person who is in a position of trust over his victim[4].

(5) The place of the assault

The fact that an assault is committed in the High Court or Court of Session may be an aggravating factor. Assaults committed where the attacker forces entry and then assaults the victim within the victim's own home, are known as hamesucken, and treated as aggravated. The term hamesucken has been said to have fallen into disuse, but it is still mentioned from time to time in the courts[5].

(6) An intention to commit another crime following upon the assault

Assault with intent to commit rape, or assault with intent to rob are examples of aggravated assaults in this category.

1 Conviction of assault to the danger of life is competent even if the victim's life was not, in fact, in danger: *Kerr v HM Advocate* 1986 SCCR 91. See also *HM Advocate v Thorn* (1876) 3 Coup 332.
2 *Monk v Strathern* 1921 JC 4, 1920 2 SLT 364; *Twycross v Farrell* 1973 SLT (Notes) 85.
3 *HM Advocate v Martin* (1886) 1 White 297.
4 *Brown v Hilson* 1924 JC 1, 1924 SLT 35 (teacher); *Alex Findlater and Jas McDougall* (1841) 2 Swin 527 (officer of law on prisoner).
5 See for example *McDonald v HM Advocate* 2007 SCCR 10.

MITIGATION OF ASSAULT

9.9   The seriousness with which an assault is viewed may be mitigated by the fact that the accused was provoked. *Hume* suggests that provocation could be a complete defence to a charge of assault[1], and this view of the matter was endorsed in *Hillan v HM Advocate*:[2] '... where the provocation is of such a kind as to justify the retaliation, the panel is entitled to be acquitted ...'. *Hillan* has attracted no subsequent judicial support, and was criticised in *Crawford v HM Advocate*[3]. Accordingly, provocation will not be accepted as a complete defence to a charge of assault[4], but may only serve to mitigate sentence.

As to what constitutes provocation in this context, the courts are unlikely to depart from the standard adopted in homicide cases. The provocation would therefore have to be recent and to have been of a nature which would have caused a reasonable person in the position of the accused to have lost control.

The High Court has given this matter considerable attention with no fewer than two five-judge bench decisions. In *Drury v HM Advocate*[5] the court held that a person who killed under provocation was to be convicted of culpable homicide rather than murder. This was because, even if he intentionally killed his victim, he did not have the wicked intention required for murder. This reflected the fact that while, as a matter of policy, Scots law admitted the plea of provocation only where the accused had been assaulted and there had been substantial provocation, it also admitted an exception by recognising that violence due to a sudden and overwhelming indignation caused by the discovery of sexual infidelity, was not committed with the wicked state of mind required for murder. In *Gillon v HM Advocate*[6] the court had been asked to reconsider *Drury*, and in particular the proportionality test, but declined. The court held that there were no good reasons to effect an alteration in the criterion of 'reasonable proportionality' currently applied in relation to provocation in the context of violence. The court approved Lord Justice Clerk Ross's statement in *Robertson v HM Advocate*[7] as follows:

> 'It is by now well established that loss of control is not the only element in provocation. Although provocation does involve the loss of control, there must be a reasonably proportionate relationship between the violent conduct offered by the victim and the reaction of the accused'.

It is possible to argue provocation in the context of a special defence of self-defence. Although not immediately obvious alternatives, the High Court has held that they are not mutually exclusive. In *Duffy v HMA*[8], the court said:

> 'Whether the use of a knife in what appeared to be a fist-fight is disproportionate will generally, in our view, depend upon the particular facts of the case. There may be circumstances in which a reasonable jury might conclude that the use of a knife was not grossly disproportionate, and accordingly that if the other three elements of provocation (namely physical attack, loss of self-control, and immediate retaliation) were proved to their satisfaction, the rider of provocation should be added. It is very much a question for the jury.'

1 I, 334. Yet he contradicts himself on this point: see discussion of *Hume's* views in *Gordon* para 29–44.
2 1937 JC 53 at 57, per Lord Justice-Clerk Aitchison.
3 1950 JC 67, 1950 SLT 279.
4 Cf R Scott 'The defence of Provocation' 1969 SLT (News) 193, supporting *Hillan. Gordon* para 29–45 and 46. *Gane and Stoddart* p 440: '… it is not immediately clear why provocation ought not to provide a complete defence to minor assaults – apart from difficulties of categorising assaults as "minor" or "serious"'.
5 2001 SLT 1013, 2001 SCCR 583.
6 2007 JC 24, 2006 SLT 799, 2006 SCCR 561.
7 1994 SCCR 589 at p 593F.
8 2015 SCL. 544.

CAUSING OR RISKING INJURY TO OTHERS

9.10   Culpable and reckless acts which cause injury to others, or which create a risk of injury, are punishable as criminal offences[1]. The *mens rea* requirement is that the accused manifested 'an utter disregard of what the consequences of the act in question may be so far as the public are concerned'[2]. It is clear, therefore, that the degree of reckless required is high. In *HM Advocate v Harris*, Lord Murray said[3]:

> 'In my opinion the court in *Quinn v Cunningham* were right to emphasise the high degree of culpability required to be averred and proved before reckless conduct as a crime at common law could be established. Carelessness, negligence or even recklessness in general are not enough. There must, I think, be conduct deliberately done in [the face] of potential danger to another or others in complete disregard of the consequences for him or them. ... But that quality of recklessness may be inferred from averments that the reckless conduct in fact caused substantial injury to another person.'

1 *HM Advocate v Harris* 1993 JC 150, 1993 SCCR 559, 1993 SLT 963.
2 *Quinn v Cunningham* 1956 JC 22 at 24, 1956 SLT 55 at 56, per Lord Clyde; approved in *RHW v HM Advocate* 1982 SCCR 152, 1988 SLT 42. See also *Paton v HM Advocate* 1936 JC 19. It should be noted that *Quinn* was over-ruled by *HM Advocate v Harris*, above, in so far as it required a charge under this head to libel that the reckless conduct was 'to the danger of the lieges'.
3 1993 SCCR 559 at 566 also reported at 1993 JC 150, 1993 SLT 963.

9.11   Accordingly, while there is no need for proof that the conduct led to severe injury, or indeed any injury at all, such proof will doubtless make it easier to establish a charge of culpable and reckless conduct. In *Harris*, the accused was a nightclub bouncer who ejected a woman from the premises by throwing her down some stairs and into a road where she was struck by a car and severely injured. This conduct was said to be reckless in relation to the injuries received, and his conviction for recklessly causing injury was upheld even although the initial 'assault' may well have been justified or at any rate was committed without the necessary *mens rea* for that offence[1]. It will also assist the prosecution case to show that the accused was aware of the risks involved. But such awareness or foresight is not necessary. In *RHW v HM Advocate*[2] the reckless behaviour consisted of the throwing of a bottle from the fifteenth floor of a block of flats, causing severe injury to a person on the ground below. The accused was aware of the risk, and had been warned not to throw the bottle; in *Gizzi v Tudhope*[3], in which the charge was one of recklessly discharging firearms, the risk of injury to others may not have been so self-evident, but it satisfied the test for recklessness laid down in *Allan v Patterson*[4], which is an objective one. The test must therefore be whether the risk would have been apparent to the reasonable person in the position of the accused. This means that there may be liability for recklessly endangering others even if the accused was subjectively unaware of the risk created by his conduct. Lord Prosser said in *Harris*[5] that:

> 'Analysis probably becomes unreal; but I think that one can say that in deciding that some conduct has been reckless, one will always be at least very close to saying that it involved a failure to pay due regard to foreseeable consequences of that conduct, which were foreseeably likely to cause injury to others, and which could correspondingly reasonably be called dangerous in relation to them.'

147

The implications of this are significant. If **A** leaves a garden rake lying upside down on his path and this rake is then stepped on by the postman, to his injury, **A** may be liable for recklessly causing injury if the reasonable person would have been aware of or foreseen the risk posed to others by leaving the rake lying on the path, although it is subject to the test that it could reasonably be called 'dangerous'. If **A** was not aware of this obvious risk, he is subjectively innocent and should arguably not be punished for an offence of this seriousness, but the objective nature of the foreseeability gives rise to liability. This is subject, of course, to the 'utter disregard' test, and it is possible that the threshold of recklessness in this context will be kept sufficiently high to prevent inappropriate convictions. The issue of recklessness as it applies to murder was addressed in *HM Advocate v Purcell*[6], the High Court holding that an accused acts with wicked recklessness only if there is an intention to cause physical injury while displaying a wicked disregard of fatal consequences.

1 See, however, Lord McCluskey's dissenting opinion 1993 SCCR 559 at 566.
2 1982 SCCR 152, 1988 SLT 42. See also: *Macphail v Clark* 1982 SCCR 395, 1983 SLT (Sh Ct) 37: farmer by culpable negligence caused danger to the lieges by setting fire to straw in a field, thereby causing smoke to drift over and obscure a public road.
3 1982 SCCR 442, 1983 SLT 214.
4 1980 JC 57, 1980 SLT 77; although see *Mallin v Clark* 2002 SLT 1202; 2002 SCCR 901 for limitations.
5 1993 SCCR 559 at 574.
6 2008 SLT 44; see discussion at Chapter 10.

Administration or supply of noxious substances

9.12   It has long been the law that the deliberate administration of noxious substances to another is punishable as a form of culpable and reckless endangerment, or reckless injury, provided that the accused demonstrated the requisite degree of indifference to the consequences of his actions[1]. It was probably not necessary for the accused actually to force the victim to ingest the substance, provided that the latter did not know the nature of the substance being given[2], or was not in a position to refuse it[3]. In *Milne and Barry*[4], two men were accused of 'wickedly and feloniously' administering jalap, a strong purgative, to the victim, who was injured by it. The High Court held that the absence of concealment, malice and the possibility that it was administered with consent supported the defence, that the victim had ingested it with consent, and in the knowledge of its dangerous properties.

As the law has developed, however, the question of the victim's consent remains an uncertain matter as a defence to a charge of causing real injury or endangering health through the administration of noxious substances.

In the case of *Khaliq v HM Advocate*[5], Lord Justice-General Emslie peremptorily rejected a defence argument based on consent[6]. In that case the accused was said to have supplied solvents to a number of young people, in such a form as to make it easy for them to abuse the substances. The substances were not directly administered to the 'victims', and the victims clearly knew what the substances were and took them voluntarily. Nevertheless, it was held that the conduct of the accused was in this case equivalent to direct administration, given his knowledge of the purpose to which the victims intended to put them.

In the subsequent case of *Ulhaq v HM Advocate*[7], in which the accused supplied solvents to adults, it was made clear that the decision in *Khaliq* did not turn upon the age of the victims, but rather on the knowledge of the accused that the substances were to be used for 'no proper purpose'. Moreover, in *Ulhaq*, it was said to make no difference that the substances were not supplied in 'kit' form, as they were in *Khaliq*. Again, the only factor of importance was said to be the state of the accused knowledge about the purpose for which the substance was supplied. The Lord Justice General (Hope) said:

> 'The essence of the charge ... was that the appellant knew that the purpose of the acquisition of the solvents was their abuse and the supply of them to their recipients was the cause of that abuse'[98].

1 See the cases of *Alexander Mitchell* (1833) Bell's Notes 90; and *Ferguson and Edie* (1822) and *Inglis and Colvilles* (1784) *Hume* I, 237.
2 See *Milne and Barry* (1868) 1 Coup 28.
3 See *Brown and Lawson* (1842) 1 Broun 415; *HM Advocate v Jean Crawford* (1847) 1 Arkley 394.
4 *Milne and Barry* (1868) 1 Coup 28. See also *HM Advocate v Finlayson* 1978 SLT (Notes) 18. The case proceeded upon a number of concessions by the Crown, however, and is probably a rather dubious authority.
5 1983 SCCR 483.
6 Arguably in doing so, he misread the authorities, or at any rate expanded them unwarrantably, given that all the Scots authorities for his decision were either assault or homicide cases which turned on the intention of the accused; cases more in point, such as *Milne and Barry*, above, point in the opposite direction. This does not seem to be a stateable argument in the current state of the law however – see in particular *Sutherland v HM Advocate* 1994 SCCR 80.
7 1990 SCCR 593, 1991 SLT 614.
8 1991 SLT 614 at 615.

9.13   These cases raised a number of issues. They appeared to overlook the voluntary acts of the 'victims'. They equate supply with administration[1]. Even if supply is equivalent to administration, as these cases hold, they ignore the consent of the victim to that administration.

In spite of such observations, the cases of *Khaliq* and *Ulhaq* were adopted in, and formed the basis for, the decision in *Lord Advocate's Reference (No 1 of 1994)*[2], in which it was held that an accused person who has supplied controlled drugs to another, who then dies as a result of voluntarily ingesting them, is guilty of culpable homicide. Lord Ross, the Lord Justice Clerk, said:

> 'It is clear from what is said in the reference and in the trial judge's report that [the accused] supplied a quantity of the controlled drug to a number of people including the deceased and that that the purpose of that supply was so that the deceased and others could take doses of the drug. In our opinion, such conduct on the part of [the accused] is the equivalent of culpable and reckless conduct.[3]'

The indictment nowhere libelled that the accused's conduct had been culpable and reckless, merely that the supply of the drugs was unlawful. Accordingly, *Lord Advocate's Reference (No 1 of 1994)* seemed to have taken the law relating to real injury a step further by removing the need to prove recklessness altogether in certain types of case. The supply of controlled drugs was apparently in itself a sufficiently reckless act to remove the need to libel the specific consequences in relation to which the accused is said to have been culpably indifferent[4]. The case gave rise to what was described as a 'perception' that an accused who supplied an individual with a controlled drug for ingestion, which ingestion then caused death, was guilty of culpable homicide[5]. This perception was addressed in *MacAngus v HM Advocate*[6] at paragraph [29] where the Lord Justice General (Hamilton) stated:

> 'With the possible exception of the Lord Advocate's Reference (No 1 of 1994), where the view of the court is open to interpretation, there appears to be no support for the view that unlawful act culpable homicide can be made out except where, as in assault or analogous cases, the conduct is directed in some way against the victim.'

The opinion in *McAngus* cannot be reconciled with that in the *Lord Advocate's Reference (No 1 of 1994)*, and the latter should be regarded as an incorrect assessment of Scots criminal law[7] In *Scott v HMA*[8], the accused was convicted of murder by injecting heroin into the victim; the accused argued that the victim had consented to the injection and consent was a defence. The court rejected that argument, observing that in the circumstances of the case, the only reasonable inference was of intent to cause harm; the circumstances included the facts that the heroin was strong and the victim had not previously abused heroin, facts known to the accused. The court did observe that:

> '... In cases involving injection of prescribed drugs the relevance of consent depends upon the circumstances. In cases where drug abusers give mutual assistance to inject the drugs, it is conceivable that there may be no intention to harm. Indeed that may be fairly common. It is notorious that drug addicts may on occasions suffer more from the lack of a fix than they might from receiving an injection. It will therefore always be a matter of circumstances whether injecting another who wishes to be injected amounts to assault. It is entirely understandable that the Crown have generally elected to proceed by way of charges of culpable and reckless conduct. In the hazy and shady world of drug abuse, securing reliable evidence to establish the *mens rea* for assault may often prove difficult. On the other hand the risks associated with abuse of class A prescribed drugs are so notorious that assisting another to abuse the drug may readily be seen as culpable and reckless conduct.

Another difficulty concerns the liability of someone who recklessly exposes others to the risk of infection, particularly to the risk of HIV infection. Such conduct could well be prosecuted in Scotland as culpably risking injury to others, although it is unclear precisely what state of knowledge on the part of the accused would have to be proved in such a case[9].

1 See DH Sheldon 'Dole directness and foresight in causation' 1996 JR 25.
2 1995 SCCR 177, 1995 SLT 248.
3 1996 JC 76 at p 81; 1995 SLT 248 at p 253.
4 See Sheriff Gordon's commentary to the case in 1995 SCCR 177 at 186.
5 *McAngus v HM Advocate* 2009 SLT 137 at para [9].
6 2009 SLT 137.
7 See article 'Causation drugs and culpable homicide in the High Court' by Stephen, 2009 SLT 27.
8 2012 SCL 153, 2012 SCCR 45.
9 See *R v Dica* [2004] EWCA Crim 1103, [2004] QB 1257, [2004] 3 WLR 213, [2004] 3 All ER 593; *Konzani* [2005] EWCA Crim 706, [2005] 2 Cr App R 14 for recent English consideration of the point.

THREATS

9.14　The making of threats to another, oral or written, can constitute a criminal offence. The threat may be to do violence to the recipient, to destroy his property, or indeed in any way to menace or intimidate him[1]. A threat to do serious injury to a person, whether oral or written, is criminal in itself. This was the view taken in *James Miller*[2], where the Lord Justice Clerk explained (pp 244–246) that there were two classes of threats: first, those which involved 'grievous bodily harm, or to do any serious injury to his property ...'; and, secondly, those in a 'much larger class' which contemplated lesser or vaguer harms. Only the former were criminal *per se*, while the latter might acquire criminal status if they were used for an unlawful purpose, such as extortion or robbery. It is not criminal, of course, to threaten to do something which one is entitled to do, unless such a threat is made in an improper context (such as threatening an officer of the law with an adverse consequence should he discharge his duties). In *Harris v HM Advocate*[3], the accused had been charged with a breach of the peace. The High Court held that the charge was irrelevant because the threats (made to a police officer) were not capable of breaching the public peace. The court did however conclude that, given the conduct, the common law of threats might have been invoked[4].

The matter was examined in *Baillie v HMA*[5] where the High Court confirmed the approach to be taken, saying, 'For the crime to be completed, it is not enough that the threat simply be spoken or written. It must be communicated to a third party' (Macdonald (above) p 128). However, it is not a requirement that the threat be conveyed directly to the party threatened. Communication to a third party will suffice (*John Jaffray* (1815) Hume i, 441, footnote 2).

The court went on:

> 'As with almost all common law crimes, the act must be done deliberately. The accused must have intended to do the act. Threatening a person is no doubt, in the ordinary case, motivated by a desire to cause that person, or a third party to whom the threat is communicated, fear and alarm and/or to do something which he would not otherwise have done. However, it is not necessary, for a libel to meet the test of relevancy, that it specify either motive or result. Unlike breach of the peace, where the acts may not be unlawful when looked at in isolation, the communication of a threat of serious harm to the potential object of the harm or to a third party, is itself unlawful. The necessary criminal intent is inferred from the carrying out of the act itself (*Elizabeth Edmiston* (1866) 5 Irv 219, LJC (Inglis) at 223). It is no defence that, for example, the act was intended to amuse in a situation where, objectively, it was likely to cause fear and alarm.'

1　See *inter alia Jas Miller* (1862) 4 Irv 238; *Kenny v HM Advocate* 1951 JC 104; Macdonald: *Criminal Law* (5th edn) p 128; Hume: *Commentaries* i, 439–440; Alison: *Principles* 579.
2　(1862) 4 Irv 238.
3　[2009] HCJAC 80, 2009 SLT 1078, 2010 SCL 56.
4　Paragraph [23]. See also *WM v HM Advocate* [2010] HC JAC 75.
5　2012 HCJAC 158.

Chapter 10

Homicide

10.1   Human life is afforded protection by the criminal law from the moment of conception to the moment of death. The protection given to the human fetus in its earliest stages will be theoretical rather than real, given the difficulties of proving pregnancy at that stage, but once pregnancy is established the fetus is protected by the criminal law relating to abortion. This protection is qualified of course: medically authorised abortion is not an offence.

Abortion, however, is not homicide, and the law of homicide only applies once the child is born. *Macdonald* defines homicide as the destruction of 'self-existent human life'[1], a state which he regards as coming into existence once breath has been drawn. Injuries inflicted on children *in utero* may cause the death of the fetus and subsequent miscarriage. This is not homicide, as self-existent life has not been destroyed. But what is the position if a child is born alive but then dies from injuries sustained *in utero? Hume* did not rule out the possibility of homicide being committed in such circumstances[2]. In *McCluskey v HM Advocate*[3] the accused was convicted of the statutory offence of causing death by reckless driving[4] in respect of injuries caused to a child *in utero* who was born prematurely and died as a result of those injuries.

1 Page 87.
2 I, 187.
3 1988 SCCR 629, 1989 SLT 175.
4 Under s 1 of the Road Traffic Act 1972 (now Road Traffic Act 1988).

SUICIDE

10.2   Suicide is not a crime in Scots law and it is therefore not a criminal offence to attempt suicide[1]. Encouraging or assisting another to take his own life is another matter, as the sympathy which the law has for the suicide does not necessarily extend to those who facilitate suicide. There is no Scottish authority on this issue; in other jurisdictions it is not unusual to find statutory provisions which penalise the provision of any assistance to the would-be suicide[2].

The giving of advice on the best methods of taking one's life raises interesting issues of criminal liability. In the English case of *Attorney General v Able*[3] the court held that the provision of a booklet detailing means of committing suicide could amount to aiding and abetting suicide, provided that the connection between the provision of the booklet and the suicide or attempt at suicide was close enough[4].

1 *Gordon* para 23–01 suggests that attempted suicide may be prosecuted as breach of the peace. Suicide was said to be a crime by *Alison* (1, 1) and also by Mackenzie *Laws and Customs of Scotland in Matters Criminal* (1678–99) (I, 13).

2 In England the Suicide Act 1961 decriminalised suicide but preserved the offence of aiding and abetting a suicide.
3 [1984] QB 795, [1984] 1 All ER 277.
4 The court stressed temporal closeness; see criticism in KJM Smith *A Modern Treatise on the Law of Criminal Complicity* (1991), p 57.

10.3 The position in England in relation to assisting suicide has been the subject of significant judicial scrutiny. In *R (On the application of Pretty) v DPP*[1], the House of Lords dismissed an appeal against the refusal of the DPP to grant an immunity from prosecution to the husband of a terminally ill woman who wished to end her life but required her husband's assistance so to do. In *R (On the application of Purdy) v DPP*[2], the applicant was in a similar position; she was terminally ill and wished her husband to assist her in her suicide, She sought an order that the DPP set out the factors to be taken into account in deciding whether it was in the public interest to prosecute someone who assisted in the suicide. The House of Lords held that the code of practice which existed at that time was insufficient. They required the DPP 'to clarify what his position is as to the factors that he regards as relevant for and against prosecution'[3]. In February 2010 the DPP issued 'Policy for Prosecutors in Respect of Cases of Encouraging or Assisting Suicide'[4], thus providing some clarity for the English approach. The matter was canvassed again in *R (On the application of Nicklinson) v Ministry of Justice*[5]. The Supreme Court declined to make a declaration of incompatibility, nor to dictate the DPP code of practice.

But the offence is governed by statue in England. In Scotland there is no specific crime of assisting a person to commit suicide, so the Lord Advocate will not issue equivalent guidelines. The English developments and the uncertainty about the attitude of the Scottish prosecution authorities contributed to the introduction of two Bills to the Scottish Parliament; The End of Life Assistance (Scotland) Bill, rejected by Parliament in December 2010, and the Assisted Suicide (Scotland) Bill, the principles of which were defeated in May 2015. There is neither statutory regulation, nor specific guidelines from the Lord Advocate[6].

The matter has been subject to judicial scrutiny, albeit in a civil context. In *Gordon Ross Petitioner*[7], the petitioner sought an order that the Lord Advocate adopt and publish a policy in relation to the criteria for the prosecution in Scotland of person who helped another to commit suicide. Lord Doherty held that the court could review the legality of the Lord Advocate's policy, but not dictate the content. The prosecutorial policy need only be indicative, in contrast with the certainty required of provisions which created (or identified) criminal offences. He held that the Crown policy was accessible, as the code (and related statements) was published; he considered that there was no evidence of arbitrary or inconsistent behaviour on the part of the Crown, and their published policy was in accordance with the law.

So, in the absence of legislation making it an offence to assist suicide, the issue would have to be determined according to common law principles, having regard to the published criteria by the Crown; it is submitted that in Scotland the following possibilities exist:

(1)   The giving of advice on suicide, or indeed the provision of means to commit suicide would not give rise to criminal liability on the grounds that the act of the suicide or would-be suicide constituted a *novus actus interveniens* interrupting the causal link between the accused's act and the final result[8].

(2)   The act of the providing of advice or practical means for the commission of suicide constitutes the offence of recklessly endangering life. A strong case for conviction of this offence would be where **A** gives **B** a gun, knowing him to be depressed and knowing him to be contemplating suicide[9].

(3)   The provision of advice on suicide or the practical means of committing suicide amounts to the offence of recklessly endangering life and this, if acted upon and resulting in death, constitutes the basis of culpable homicide. There has been an unlawful act (recklessly endangering life) followed by death, and this is sufficient for conviction of culpable homicide. This option would require the act of the deceased to be disregarded as a *novus actus interveniens*[10].

(4)   The provision of advice on suicide or the practical means of committing suicide amounts to murder on the grounds that the person assisting manifests wicked recklessness, one of the forms of the *mens rea* of murder[11].

Of the above possibilities, the most appropriate one, should the prosecution authorities wish to proceed in these circumstances, would be the second one. This would avoid any difficulties that might be posed by the *novus actus interveniens* doctrine.

1   [2001] UKHL 61, [2002] 1 AC 800.
2   [2009] UKHL 45, [2009] 4 All ER 1147.
3   At para [55] of Purdy.
4   Available at http://www.cps.gov.uk/publications/prosecution/assisted_suicide_policy.html.
5   [2014] UKSC 38, [2015] AC 657, [2014] 3 WLR 200, [2014] 3 All ER 843.
6   Although there has been discussion; see Chalmers, Assisted Suicide 2010 ELR 295; for the prosecution code, see http://www.copfs.gov.uk/images/Documents/Prosecution_Policy_Guidance/Prosecution20Code20_Final20180412__1.pdf
7   2015 SLT 617. An appeal was in anticipation at the time of writing.
8   *R v Peverett* 1940 AD 213 (SA) (act not a *novus actus*); Cf *R v Nbakwa* 1956 (2) SA 557 (Southern Rhodesia) (accused had suggested to his mother that she kill herself and upbraided her for not doing so: deceased's act was held to be a *novus actus interveniens*).
9   See *R v S* [2005] EWCA Crim 819 where the accused was convicted of aiding and abetting suicide by encouraging his girlfriend to jump to her death.
10   Cf *Lord Advocate's Reference (No 1 of 1994)* 1995 SCCR 177, 1995 SLT 248; this seems most consistent with *Purcell v HM Advocate* 2008 SLT 44 where the recklessness has to be in conjunction with an intention to cause physical harm.
11   See the discussion on wicked recklessness at para 10.7.

THE DEFINITION OF DEATH

10.4   It hardly needs saying that homicide requires a live victim to be killed; the dead are protected against physical insult or indignity[1], but they are beyond the protection of the criminal law of homicide. Death is undefined in Scots criminal law, but requires, beyond doubt, the cessation of cardio-respiratory functions. Developments in medical technology enable respiration and circulation to be maintained beyond the point at which brain death occurs, but persons in this position must still be considered alive. It is submitted, then, that any unlawful act directed towards the stopping of cardio-respiratory activity in such a person would amount to homicide, at least in terms of *Macdonald*'s definition as the destruction of human life.. The intentional switching off of an artificial ventilator by one not medically authorised to do so may amount to murder; medically indicated cessation of ventilation is on a par with other medical cessation of treatment in such circumstances and does not constitute a *novus actus interveniens*[2].

Spontaneous heartbeat and respiration may survive the death of the higher parts of the brain, resulting in a person being irreversibly comatose. Such persons may present no signs of cortical activity, but are still given the full protection of the criminal law. It would undoubtedly be homicide to kill such a person[3] (for the reasons stated above in relation to the killing of an artificially ventilated person).

The fact that a person is on his death bed when he is killed in no way mitigates the seriousness of killing him. If **A** is about to die of natural causes, and **B**, wishing to spare him the last few moments of suffering, smothers him, this is homicide[4]. In *Ross Ptnr*, the court recorded the Crown's published position, that there is a 'high interest in prosecuting all aspects of homicide where there is sufficient available evidence'; and that 'it is difficult to conceive of a situation where it would not be in the public interest to raise a prosecution, but each case would be considered upon its own facts and circumstances'[5].

1 Interference with dead bodies after burial, or other storage, is the common law crime of violation of sepulchres: *Hume* I, 85; *Gordon* para 42–01. The implication of the Anatomy Act 1984 and the Human Tissue Act 1961 are discussed by PDG Skegg 'Criminal liability for the unauthorised use of corpses for medical education and research' (1992) 32 *Med Sci Law* 51.
2 *Finlayson v HM Advocate* 1979 JC 33, 1978 SLT (Notes) 60.
3 The position of the irreversibly comatose person is discussed by P Skegg 'Irreversibly comatose individuals: alive or dead' (1974) 33 *Camb LJ* 130.
4 *Gordon* para 23–08.
5 See the observations about assisted suicide *above*.

THE CATEGORIES OF HOMICIDE

10.5   There are three categories of homicide: non-criminal homicide, murder, and culpable homicide.

NON-CRIMINAL HOMICIDE

Non-criminal homicide may be **casual** or **justifiable**. Casual homicide is accidental homicide committed by a person who is not engaged at the time in unlawful activity. The category of casual homicide does not include those cases where death has been caused by culpable negligence[1].

Justifiable homicide consists of killing in circumstances where, in the eyes of the law, the taking of life is a right and proper thing to do. Killing in self-defence is justifiable homicide, as is a soldier's killing of the enemy in battle.

Hume states that a magistrate is entitled to order life to be taken to suppress a riot, but different considerations may apply to such a situation today[2]. The question of whether necessity justifies homicide is unresolved in Scots law, although it is submitted that it should[3]. If a security guard discovers an unexploded bomb in a room full of people and, unable to evacuate the room, he throws the bomb out of the window, he should not be punished for the killing of the person whom he sees in the street outside and who, he knows, may be killed by the explosion. The choice he made was justified: it was the right thing to have done.

1 Arguably this has been altered by the Corporate Manslaughter and Corporate Homicide Act 2007, where a gross breach of a relevant duty of care can found a conviction for culpable homicide.
2 *Gordon* para 23–34. Cf PW Ferguson *Crimes Against the Person* (1990) p 13.
3 The defence of necessity is discussed at greater length at para 8.33 above.

MURDER

10.6 Murder was defined by a bench of seven judges in *Brennan v HM Advocate*[1] as follows; 'In the law of Scotland ... the crime of murder is constituted by any wilful act causing the destruction of life, whether intended to kill or displaying such wicked recklessness as to imply a disposition depraved enough to be, regardless of the consequences. Our definition of murder includes the taking of human life by a person who has an intent to kill or to do serious injury, or whose act is shown to have been wickedly reckless as to the consequences'. The case of *Drury*[2] refined this by stating that the intention had to be wicked. Therefore, murder consists of the unlawful killing of another by a person who either (1) has a wicked intention to kill, or who (2) acts in a way which manifests 'wicked recklessness' as to whether or not his victim lives or dies.

1 1977 JC 38 (at p 47), 1977 SLT 151 (at p156). See also *Drury v HM Advocate* 2001 SLT 1013.
2 2001 SLT 1013, 2001 SCCR 583.

(1) Intentional killing

There is intention to kill where the accused directs his action to the attainment of the desired goal, namely the death of the victim. A clear example of intentional killing is the pointing of a rifle at the victim and the pulling of the trigger in the knowledge that the gun is loaded, and with the desire that death should result. The victim's death may not be wanted as an end in itself, rather as a means to another end; this, of course, is still intentional killing.

The intention of the accused may be gathered from his actings; in most cases there will be no other direct evidence of intention. In assessing what a person intended, the jury will take into account its own experience of human behaviour and motivation.

The Scots doctrine of wicked recklessness[1] has meant that Scottish courts have not been exercised over the question as to whether acts done in the knowledge that there is a high degree of probability that a particular consequence will ensue will amount to an intention to achieve that consequence.

(2) Wicked recklessness

This form of possible *mens rea* for murder enables the Scots courts to convict of murder those who kill in morally reprehensible circumstances but who do not necessarily have any intention to kill. *Alison* states that murder is an act which flows from 'a deliberate intention to kill, or to inflict minor injury of such a kind as indicates an utter recklessness as to the life of the sufferer, whether he live or die'[2]. *Macdonald*'s statement, which has provided the basis of modern judicial instructions on this matter, is as follows: 'Murder is constituted by any wilful act causing the destruction of life, whether intended to kill, or displaying such wicked recklessness as to imply a disposition depraved enough to be regardless of the consequences ...'[3].

However, any analysis of wicked recklessness must be made against a background of the words of the then Lord Justice Clerk, Lord Gill, in *Petto v HMA*[4]; after disposing of the appeal (of which more later), he made the following observations

> 'Since this appeal can be decided on the narrow basis as to the meaning of intent in the clear-cut circumstances of the case, it is unnecessary for us to explore the greater profundities of the mental element in murder and culpable homicide in contemporary Scots law. The discussion of that subject in *Gordon* (paras 23.10–23.22) should suffice to persuade any reader that the subject is in need of a thorough re-examination.
>
> From my own researches on the point, pursued in response to the Crown submission, I have the impression that other English-speaking jurisdictions may have attained greater maturity in their jurisprudence on this topic than Scotland has. In Scotland we have a definitional structure in which the mental element in homicide is defined with the use of terms such as wicked, evil, felonious, depraved and so on, which may impede rather than conduce to analytical accuracy. In recent years, the authors of the draft Criminal Code for Scotland have greatly assisted our thinking on the matter; but we remain burdened by legal principles that were shaped largely in the days of the death penalty, that are inconsistent and confused and are not yet wholly free of doctrines of constructive malice.
>
> My own view is that a comprehensive re-examination of the mental element in homicide is long overdue. That is not the sort of exercise that should be done by ad hoc decisions of this court in fact-specific appeals. It is pre-eminently an exercise to be carried out by the normal processes of law reform.'

The uncertainty of terms such as wicked and evil has been subject to comment[5]. The comprehensive re-examination is still awaited.

---

1 See comments by Lord Goff, at p 178, n 1, below.
2 *Alison* I, 1. *Gordon* para 23–18, points out that 'minor injury' in this context means 'non-fatal injury'
3 Page 89.
4 2012 JC 105, 2011 SLT 1043, 2011 SCL 850, 2011 SCCR 519.
5 See for example McDiarmid 'Something wicked this way comes', 2012 JR 283.

10.7   In one view wicked recklessness itself is not sufficient justification for conviction of murder; all that it does is to point to the presence of intention to kill. This interpretation was supported in some of the judgments in *Cawthorne v HM Advocate*[1], but is at odds with the view espoused by *Alison*, for example, that wicked recklessness is the equivalent of intention to kill[2]. The modern consensus, however, appears clear: wicked recklessness stands on its own as sufficient *mens rea* for murder.

1 1968 JC 32, 1968 SLT 330.
2 *Alison* I, 163: 'In judging of the intention of an accused who has committed an aggravated assault, the same rules are to be followed as in judging of the intent in actual murder, viz, that a ruthless intent, and an obvious indifference to the sufferer, whether he live or die, is to be held as equivalent to an actual attempt to inflict death'. Endorsed by Lord Cameron in *Cawthorne* 1968 JC 32 at 39.

What constitutes wicked recklessness

10.8   The presence of wicked recklessness will be inferred from all the circumstances of a case. Usually it will be the severity of the assault which will entitle the jury to conclude that the accused was indifferent as to the fate of his victim, although the condition of his victim (his age, evident infirmity, etc) may render a moderate assault wickedly reckless. In *HM Advocate v Robertson and Donoghue*[1] it was pointed out by Lord Justice-Clerk Cooper that 'much less violence if applied to a feeble, old man, to a person whom the assailant must have known was a feeble, old man – if you think he must have known it – may suffice to justify an inference of wicked recklessness to consequences'.

The fact that a weapon was used in an attack has been taken as conclusive of wicked recklessness. This was so in *HM Advocate v McGuinness*[2] where Lord Justice-Clerk Aitchison said:

'People who use knives and pokers and hatchets against a fellow citizen are not entitled to say "we did not mean to kill", if death results. If people resort to the use of deadly weapons of this kind, they are guilty of murder, whether or not they intended to kill'.

A similar view was expressed by Lord Carmont in *Kennedy v HM Advocate*[3], but it goes too far to hold that the use of weapons will inevitably point to wicked recklessness: the fact that a weapon was used will be one of the factors to be taken into account, but will not of itself settle the matter[4].

1 (August 1945, unreported), HCJ; *Gane and Stoddart*, p 497.
2 1937 JC 37 at 40.
3 1944 JC 171 at 174.
4 *Attempted Homicide* (Scot Law Com Consultative Memorandum no 61) (1984), p 18; PW Ferguson *Crimes Against the Person* (1990), p 20.

Wicked recklessness: subjective or objective?

10.9   Can conduct be described as reckless if the accused had no knowledge of the risks it entailed? Theoretically, it cannot; nor *a fortiori* may conduct be described as 'wickedly reckless' if there was ignorance of the risks – the terms 'wicked' or 'wickedly' imply a cast of mind which, in the absence of such knowledge, simply is not there. A subjective test of recklessness in this context would therefore require an awareness of a risk of death, and if a jury were to be satisfied that the accused genuinely did not appreciate the risk, even if it would have been apparent to the reasonable person in his position, it would be entitled to acquit. The test in Scots law, however, is in practice objective. The issue is whether the conduct of the accused manifested wicked recklessness, and this will be decided according to objective criteria. Conduct which, in its externals, is wickedly reckless, justifies an inference of wicked recklessness on the part of the accused. Not caring whether one's victim lives or dies, then, would seem not to require any awareness of the risk of death. For those purposes, a person may be said not to care even if he has not addressed his mind to the risks entailed in his conduct[1].

Yet subjective factors may not be entirely irrelevant. The accused's assessment of his victim, for example, would appear to be relevant; at least this would appear to be so according to Lord Cooper's instruction in *Robertson and Donoghue*, quoted above[2]. It would be open to a future court to introduce further subjective considerations to take into account the rare case where objectively reckless conduct does not reflect subjective recklessness. Certainly there is nothing in such an approach which contradicts accepted statements of the law, including *Macdonald*'s widely used definition, and this would mean that an assailant of limited intelligence, who just does not understand the risks of his conduct, might be convicted of culpable homicide rather than murder.

Wicked recklessness and intention to inflict harm

An act may be wickedly reckless and may lead to loss of life, but may nonetheless involve no intention to cause harm to any person. *Gordon* suggests that such an act will not amount to murder[3], and cites in support of this proposition Lord Wheatley's direction to the jury in *HM Advocate v McCarron*[4] that if the accused had fired a shot at his victim 'not intending to kill or injure her but merely to frighten her, but acted with gross and wicked negligence that he in fact killed her, the crime could be culpable homicide and not murder'. It should be noted that Lord Wheatley referred to gross and wicked negligence rather than recklessness; negligence does not require acceptance of risk to life which is of the essence of recklessness.

1 Cf Lord Goff's comment on wicked recklessness in Scots law 'I think it important to observe that the principle so stated does not necessarily involve a conscious apprehension of the risk of death at the relevant time. This is of importance, because we can think of many cases in which it can be said that the accused acted regardless of the consequences, not caring whether the victim lived or died, and yet did not consciously appreciate the risk of death in his mind at the time – for example when a man acts in the heat of the moment, as when he lashes out with a knife in the heat of a fight … I cannot see that the fact that, in consequence, he did not have the risk of death in his mind at the time should prevent him from being held guilty of murder': 'The mental element in the crime of murder' (1989) 104 LQR 30 at 55.
2 *Gane and Stoddart* p 497.
3 *Gordon* para 23–17.
4 (February 1964, unreported), Perth High Court; approved on appeal, March 1964.

10.10 *Gordon's* contention finds no support from *Hume*, who states that murder may be committed even when there is no animus directed towards any particular person:

'... it is not even indispensable, that the malice be directed against any one in particular. If a man fire at random among a multitude, or if he wilfully turn loose a mad dog into the street, at a time when it is full of passengers, and a person perish in consequence of this brutality; surely any difference between such a case of indiscriminate malice, and one of special hatred to an individual, is all to the disadvantage of this offender ... Of this sort, in some measure, was the charge brought against James Niven, 21st December 1795, in that having loaded a small cannon with powder, and a bit of iron, and having pointed it up a lane or street of common passage, he then fired it off, at a time when two persons were standing in the direction of the piece, and several others were passing along the lane; whereby one of the persons first mentioned was killed ... It was held on the Bench, that ... he was guilty of no lower crime than murder ...'[1].

However, with customary prescience, Sheriff Gordon seemed to have anticipated the way the law developed (or, perhaps, recorded correctly what it was all the time). His contention found favour in the case of *Purcell v HM Advocate*[2] in which *Gordon* was quoted with approval.

The accused was being chased by police officers whilst he was driving. In his flight he knocked over and killed a child. He was charged with murder. Unusually, during the trial, the High Court convened a court of three judges to deal with the issue of the relevance of the charge of murder. The court held that wicked recklessness could not be established in the absence of an intention to cause physical harm[3]. This was revisited in the case of *Petto v HM Advocate*[4]. The accused there had murdered someone and in order to cover his tracks, set fire to the flat where the body had been left. The fire took effect in the block of flats resulting in the death of another occupant. The case was remitted to a court of five judges to determine whether the circumstances could justify a charge of murder because of the absence of authority about these matters. The full bench had little difficulty in determining that the appropriate charge was murder, holding that it was not an exception to the rule from *Purcell* requiring intention to injure, because the driver losing control of his car, which mounts the pavement and kills a pedestrian cannot be said to have intended to drive onto the pavement or to injure the victim. Fire-raising is, however, a wilful act; as Lord Gill said:

'Where a person starts a major fire on the ground floor of such a building, the inevitable conclusion is, in my view, that he does so in the certain knowledge that those who are in the building, and especially those in the upper floors, will be at a grave risk of being killed or seriously injured in consequence of the fire. While there may be no desiderative element in the mind of such a person, his appreciation of the virtual certainty that such a risk will eventuate and his deliberate acceptance of it should, in my opinion, be rightly equiparated with an intention that such consequences should occur.'

So the pouring of petrol into a letter box of a house, for example, and its subsequent setting alight appears to amount to wicked recklessness, even if the accused's desire is to harm property rather than an individual, or destroy evidence. If somebody is killed in the resultant blaze, even if it is somebody whom the accused did not know was there, this could be murder rather than culpable homicide, although it will depend on whether the presence was foreseeable; as Lord Gill said in *Petto*:

> 'There could be a case where one who deliberately set fire to a building had no reason to know that there was someone inside; for example where a tramp was sleeping inside a ruined barn. I do not accept that in such a case Scots law should recognise an exception to the general principles of *mens rea* on which *HM Advocate v Purcell* was decided.'

The current position was summarised in *Scott v HMA*[5], a case arising from the supply and administration of a fatal dose of heroin, as follows:

> 'As was fully explained in the recent Full Bench case of *Petto v HM Advocate*, a wilful act such as injecting another with heroin can amount to murder as long as it is shown to be committed with intent to kill or with such a degree of wicked recklessness as to amount to reckless indifference to the consequences.'

1 I, 23.
2 2008 JC 131, 2008 SLT 44, 2008 SCL 183.
3 The decision elicited some comment; see 'The true meaning of "wicked recklessness"' by James Chalmers 2008 Edin LR 298, (which observes that surprisingly no reference was made to *Brennan v HM Advocate* 1977 JC 38); and 'Foreseeing the consequences of Purcell' by Michael Plaxton 2008 SLT (News) 21.
4 2009 SLT 509; 2009 SCL 842; Five Judge Bench 2012 JC 105, 2011 SLT 1043, 2011 SCL 850, 2011 SCCR 519.
5 2012 SCL 153, 2012 SCCR.

Homicide and robbery

10.11   Homicide committed during the course of a robbery was treated as murder rather than culpable homicide, even if there is no intention to kill and no wicked recklessness. Thus if **A**, while robbing his victim, gave him no more than a moderate blow, he may be held to have murdered him should the victim die as a result of this assault. Support for this rule was said to be found in *HM Advocate v Miller and Denovan*[1], and *Melvin v HM Advocate*[2]. However as discussed below, this can no longer be regarded as sound law.

It was difficult to see any justification for treating as murder any homicide committed in the course of a robbery, and there has been persistent criticism of similar rules elsewhere. In *McKinnon v HM Advocate*[3] the court considered the matter in the context of a conviction on an art and part basis for murder, which had happened in the course of a planned robbery. The court held that an accused was guilty of murder art and part where, first by his conduct, he actively associated himself with a common criminal purpose which was or included the taking of a human life, or *carried the obvious risk that human life would be taken*, and secondly, in the carrying out of that purpose, murder was committed by someone else. They held that, where the accused was proved only to have participated in some less serious common criminal purpose in the course of which the victim died, he might be guilty art and part of culpable homicide, whether or not any other person was proved guilty of murder. But if the jury were satisfied that an individual accused was aware that knives were being carried and liable to be used, the inference that there was an obvious risk that they might be used to commit murder in pursuing the criminal purpose of robbery was virtually inevitable. Whilst these observations were obiter, as the matter was concerned with art and part guilt, it is submitted that they carry some weight. In *Purcell*, the court considered that the amount of recklessness required may vary and approved McDonald's observation that 'If in perpetrating or attempting another crime a person uses serious and reckless violence which may cause death, without considering what the results may be, he is guilty of murder if the violence results in death although he had no intention to kill' commenting that for such analysis to apply, the court would have to be satisfied '... in the cause of death ensuing in the course of the commission of another crime what [he] has in mind is the use of serious and reckless violence during that other criminal enterprise'[4].

It might be argued that the mere fact of carrying out a robbery could amount to wicked recklessness, on the grounds that robberies can, and do, lead to unexpected deaths, but this extends the concept of wicked recklessness unduly, particularly in the light of *Purcell* and *Petto*. A more likely rationale for the rule – that it deters the use of weapons during the course of a robbery – may have been persuasive in days of capital punishment for murder but current penalties for a serious armed robbery are not necessarily so much lower in real terms than the period of imprisonment involved in a life sentence. *McKinnon* undermines the previous certainty that homicide during a robbery was murder; the issue will be whether the obvious risk that human life would be taken arises. *Brown v HM Advocate*[5] appears to dispense with that certainty. In *Brown* the accused had struck the complainer on the head with a bottle, allegedly in the course of a robbery. The complainer died without regaining consciousness. The trial judge, on the basis of *Miller and Denovan,* directed the jury that a finding of culpable homicide was not open to them if the element of robbery was proved. The appeal court, while not requiring to consider the matter in detail (the Crown conceding that culpable homicide was the appropriate verdict) said '... in this day and age *Miller and Denovan* cannot be regarded as good law'[6].

1 (December 1960, unreported), HCJ; *Gordon* para 23–26 et seq; Gane and Stoddart p 500. Cf *HM Advocate v Fraser and Rollins* 1920 JC 60, 1920 2 SLT 77.
2 1984 SCCR 113, 1984 SLT 365.
3 2003 JC 29, 2003 SLT 281, 2003 SCCR 224.
4 *HM Advocate v Purcell* 2008 JC 131, 2008 SLT 44 at para [9].
5 [2010] HCJAC 66
6 Paragraph [11] of the Lord Justice Clerk's opinion.

10.12 The relationship between murder and culpable homicide in the context of a trial was considered in *Ferguson v HM Advocate*[1]. The accused was convicted of murder by stabbing his victim once in the context of an assault. In his charge to the jury the trial judge did not advise the jury that it was open to them to return a verdict of guilty of culpable homicide, as it was not raised expressly or by implication by either Crown or the accused, and he considered it to be unfavourable to the accused.

The High Court held that the court had a responsibility in certain murder trials to raise with a jury the issue of culpable homicide. That responsibility arises where the potential alternative verdict emerges from the evidence in a realistic way. Lord Osborne put it thus at para [35]:

> 'While … it is not for the trial judge to place before the jury the option of a verdict which would not be justified upon a reasonable view of the evidence before them it was erroneous to suggest that the way in which the case was presented by the parties was in some undefined way necessarily determinative of the options available to the jury'.

Accordingly whether the parties raise the matter or not, there is a responsibility upon a court to consider *ex proprio motu* whether the evidence could reasonably give rise to a verdict of culpable homicide. Failure to so direct the jury could result in a miscarriage of justice.

1 2009 SCL 250.

CULPABLE HOMICIDE

10.13   There are two forms of culpable homicide: involuntary culpable homicide and voluntary culpable homicide. The first category encompasses those cases where an unintended death occurs as a result of an assault or other criminal act or as a result of culpable negligence; in the second category are those cases where death results from an intentional or reckless act but where, because of provocation or diminished responsibility, the offence is reduced from murder to culpable homicide.

Involuntary culpable homicide

Involuntary culpable homicide more commonly entails the commission of an assault on the victim. The assault need not be a serious one: all that is required is that the act causing death should satisfy the legal definition of assault. The pointing of a firearm at another may amount to an assault[1], as may a push, shove, or light slap. In such a case, if the victim were to stumble and strike his head on the ground, the assailant could be liable for culpable homicide[2]. Causing death by fright may be culpable homicide, even if there has been no physical contact between assailant and victim. In *HM Advocate v Lourie*[3] there was no challenge to the relevance of an indictment for culpable homicide in a case in which two youths caused the death by shock of a householder from whom they were committing a theft. The fact that there was no allegation of physical contact between the accused and the deceased did not deter the bringing of the charge.

1 In *Mowles v HM Advocate* 1986 SCCR 117 the accused pointed a firearm at another believing that it was unloaded. The gun was grabbed and fired as a result, killing a person other than the person at whom it had been pointed. It was held that the initial unlawful act of assault justified a finding of culpable homicide.
2 *HM Advocate v Hartley* 1989 SLT 135.
3 1988 SCCR 634. See also *Bird v HM Advocate* 1952 JC 23.

10.14 The fact that death is caused by some particular weakness or peculiarity on the part of the victim is irrelevant. The rule that you take your victim as you find him means that it is culpable homicide to cause death by a minor punch to the abdomen of one who, unknown to you, has a misplaced spleen. As Lord Clyde said in *HM Advocate v Rutherford*[1]: 'It is no answer for an assailant who causes death by violence to say that his victim had a weak heart or was excitable or emotional ... He must take his victim as he finds her'[2]. This may be seen as a logical corollary to *Robertson and Donoghue*[3].

Unlawful acts other than assault

Although the courts have stressed that deaths which result from any unlawful act is culpable homicide, the reported cases are almost exclusively concerned with situations in which there has been an intention to cause harm to the person. *Lourie*[4] is a possible exception to this, as is *Mathieson v HM Advocate*[5]. In the latter case the accused was convicted of culpable homicide after he had unlawfully started a fire which subsequently caused the death of a number of victims. It is clear then, that any unlawful act directed against property which is capable of causing physical injury, could be culpable homicide. Interference with the mechanism of a lift would be an example, as might be vandalism which impedes the use of fire-fighting apparatus.

It may be culpable homicide to provide another – illegally – with a substance which one knows to be harmful and which then causes death. This was the result of the ruling in *Lord Advocate's Reference (No 1 of 1994)*[6] in which it was held that the provider of illegal drugs could be convicted of culpable homicide even the recipient administers them himself. However, in *MacAngus v HM Advocate*[7], the court rejected that conclusion holding that there was '... no support for the view that unlawful act culpable homicide can be made out except where, as in assault or analogous cases, the conduct is directed in some way against the victim.'

The court went on to hold at paragraph [30]: '... A charge libelling culpable homicide in the context of supply (or the administration of) a controlled drug is relevant only if the Crown offers to prove that the supplying (or administration) was ... reckless.[8]'

It is more doubtful whether culpable homicide is committed where the unlawful act is not one normally associated with the risk of injury. In *HM Advocate v Finlayson*[9] the prosecution argued that any act 'tainted' by illegality will be sufficient, but the point did not require to be decided. There is no authority in Scots law for the proposition that the unlawful act requires to be dangerous[10], but it is submitted that such a limitation is desirable. If there is no such requirement, then there could be liability for culpable homicide when death is quite 'incidental' to the unlawful activity. For example, if a person stealing a bicycle knocks over a child who suddenly appears in the path before him, this death would be culpable homicide, even if entirely fortuitous.

A court would have to decide on the degree of dangerousness required. Differing standards have been applied in those systems recognising such a test, with some courts requiring a risk of serious injury[11] and others being satisfied with even a slight risk of harm[12]. There is a strong argument for requiring a risk of serious injury, and for requiring, too, that the injury should have been foresee-able by the accused; this is on a par with the standard required for conviction for culpable homicide on the grounds of negligence. Any lower standard might extend the boundaries of liability too far: virtually any conduct is statistically capable of causing a slight degree of harm. It is technically dangerous to drink alcohol, for example, as there is a remote risk that one might cause injury to oneself while intoxicated. Should it be culpable homicide if a person who irre-sponsibly laces another's drink with a small amount of alcohol thereby causes the other to trip over and fall downstairs, with fatal results?

1   1947 JC 1 at 3, 1947 SLT 3 at 3.
2   For criticism of this rule, see *Gordon*, para 26–18 et seq.
3   See para 10.8
4   1988 SCCR 634.
5   1981 SCCR 196.
6   1994 SLT 248.
7   2009 SLT 137.
8   See Chapter 5 at 5.14 for further discussion.
9   1979 JC 33, 1978 SLT (Notes) 18.
10 English law requires an 'unlawful and dangerous' act for commission of manslaughter: *DPP v Newbury* [1977] AC 500, [1976] 3 All ER 365.
11 Eg *R v Wills* [1983] 2 VR 201.
12 *Church* [1966] 1 QB 59, [1965] 2 All ER 72; *DPP v Daley* [1980] AC 237, (1979) 69 Cr App Rep 39.

Omissions

10.15   If an omission to perform a legal duty leads to death, this is usually culpable homicide rather than murder. The neglect of a dependant and vulner-able person provide examples of such liability[1]; if a person fails to provide food or medical support for a person in his care who needs them, then the omission may amount to an unlawful act.

There is no general duty to rescue in Scots law. This means that a person who fails to take steps to help another in obvious peril commits no offence, unless, of course, he has a legal duty to act. Such a legal duty would exist only where there is a relationship between the parties; where the accused is obliged to act by virtue of the position he occupies; or where the peril has been created by the accused's own actings.

Involuntary lawful act homicide

During the nineteenth century culpable homicide was frequently charged where negligence in the course of employment led to death[2]. This has virtually disappeared in the twentieth century, owing to the fact that statutory controls exist to police dangerous practices in the workplace. Twentieth-century cases of lawful act culpable homicide are therefore rare, and almost entirely con-cerned with causing death on the roads. At the same time, there is a growing view that homicide prosecutions should follow upon certain acts of negligence, particularly where companies are alleged to have been negligent in relation to safety matters[3]. The issue of involuntary culpable homicide by a company was considered in *Transco (No 1) v HM Advocate*[4]. The accused company was charged with culpable homicide in relation to a gas explosion which resulted in the destruction of a house and the death of the four occupants. The court determined that as a company had no mind, it could not have a guilty mind; accordingly the *mens rea* required could not be established without the identification of a directing mind[5].

The court looked at the development of the definition of culpable homicide, approving of the formulation in *Quinn v Cunningham*[6], adopted in *Cameron v Maguire*[7]. Lord Hamilton in *Transco* noted that the law had developed into requiring a greater degree of culpability. In *Transco* the common law prosecution had proceeded on the basis of lawful but reckless conduct.

The *mens rea* of involuntary culpable homicide in this context was negligence of a particularly high degree. Ordinary negligence, of the sort which gives rise to civil liability, was insufficient. Until *Transco*, the case of *Paton v HM Advocate*[8], was regarded as giving a classic definition of involuntary culpable homicide, that is, 'gross, or wicked, or criminal negligence, something amounting to, or at any rate analogous, to a criminal indifference to consequences'. However that description was described as circular (in the use of the word criminal) and confusing (by use of the term 'negligent') in *Transco* at para [4] of Lord Osborne's opinion. The preferred test is whether there is a completer disregard of potential dangers and of the consequences to the public, 'an utter disregard' or 'recklessness so high as to involve an indifference to the consequences for the public generally.[9]' Criminal negligence is not quite wicked recklessness, and therefore falls short of the *mens rea* of murder.

1 *R v Instan* [1893] 1 QB 450; *R v Gibbins and Proctor* (1918) 13 Cr App Rep 134.
2 The cases are surveyed by *Gordon* para 26–04 et seq. See eg *HM Advocate v Pawn and McNab* (1845) 2 Broun 525.
3 The question of corporate liability for homicide formerly attracted considerable attention. See eg HJ Glasbeek and S Rowland 'Are injuring and killing at work crimes?' (1979) 17 *Osgoode Hall Law Journal* 506; GL Mangum 'Murder in the workplace: criminal prosecution and regulatory enforcement' (1988) 39 *Labor Law Journal* 220; B Fisse *Howard's Criminal Law* (5th edn, 1990), p 608 et seq.
4 2004 JC 29, 2004 SLT 41.
5 See Chapter 4 for more about corporate responsibility and the Corporate Manslaughter and Corporate Homicide Act 2006.
6 1956 JC 22, 1956 SLT 55.
7 1999 JC 63, 1999 SLT 883.
8 1936 JC 19 at 22.
9 *Transco plc v HM Advocate* (No 1) at para [4] of Lord Osborne's opinion.

10.16   In deciding whether conduct is reckless or sufficiently indifferent for these purposes, a jury will probably be guided by its sense of outrage.

Practical jokes or pranks which go wrong may amount to culpable homicide if the victim is killed and if the conduct of the accused is considered to be so risky as to amount to gross negligence[1].

1 In the Australian case of Jackson and Hodgetts (1989) 44 A Crim R 320 the putting of meat preservative in a can of soft drink was held to be a 'classic example' of conduct amounting to criminal negligence. In *Streatfield* (1991) 53 A Crim R the accused's act of pointing a gun (which he thought to be unloaded) at his wife and pulling the trigger was described by the court as an 'act of monumental stupidity', justifying conviction of negligent manslaughter and (on appeal) a sentence of five years' imprisonment.

Voluntary culpable homicide

10.17 Intentional or reckless killing may be reduced from murder to culpable homicide if there is either diminished responsibility or provocation[1].

Provocation

Provocation exists where, in response to conduct on the part of the deceased the accused loses his self-control and takes life[2]. Provocation is frequently pleaded alongside self-defence, but is to be distinguished from self-defence, which is a complete defence which leads to acquittal[3]. The effect of a successful plea of provocation being to reduce murder to culpable homicide, provocation only has a mitigating effect.

The theory underlying provocation is that allowance should be made for the effect of anger and that people are not to be held fully accountable for what they do in 'a blind rage'[4]. Although this accords with our intuitive understanding of human behaviour, the reluctance of the courts to apply the plea in anything but the most limited circumstances is understandable. The criminal law expects self-control, and indeed is based on notions of individual responsibility and self-restraint. Concessions made to ill-temper and anger are concessions to human frailty, are potentially anarchic, and can result in unacceptable notions of the non-punishability of the 'crimes of passion'. For this reason the courts maintain a delicate balance between sympathy for those who have been pushed to the limit of human forbearance, and concern at the potentially anarchic implications of allowing passionate action to go unpunished. As a number of the cases discussed below indicate, this balance is frequently difficult to achieve.

1 Diminished responsibility is discussed in conjunction with the insanity defence, above.
2 *Macdonald* defines provocation as follows: 'Being agitated and excited, and alarmed by violence, I lost control over myself and took life, when my presence of mind had left me, and without thought of what I was doing': p 94. It was approved in terms in *Cosgrove v HM Advocate* 1990 JC 333.
3 The difference between provocation and self-defence was stressed in *Fenning v HM Advocate* 1985 SCCR 219 at 225. They are not mutually exclusive. See *Duffy v HMA* 2015 SCL 544.
4 Provocation should not be viewed as being based on the notion that the deceased 'deserved it'. This idea sometimes creeps into jury directions: see, for example, the trial judge's instructions in *Lennon v HM Advocate* 1991 SCCR 611 – 'A man has perhaps the right to revenge himself against an aggressor who attacks him, when the retaliating blow is struck in the heat of the moment, in the heat of blood...'. Thus no reference to revenge should appear in relation to either self defence or provocation.

The requirements of provocation

10.18 There must have been a physical attack, a loss of self-control, a response immediately following the provocation and a proportionate response.

Physical attack. Scots law is unlike English law and related systems in that it requires that there should have been a serious assault committed by the victim on the accused. (There is one exception, that of a confession of adultery or unfaithfulness, discussed below.) The rejection of verbal provocation is well-established and consistent. *Hume* said that 'no provocation of words, the most foul and abusive, or of signs or gestures, however contemptuous or derisive soever, is of sufficient weight in the scale'[1], and *Macdonald* is similarly unambiguous: 'Words of insult, however strong, or mere insulting or disgusting conduct, such a jostling or tossing filth in the face, do not serve to reduce the crime from murder to culpable homicide'[2].

Conduct can, of course, be highly provocative (in the non-legal sense of the word), even if it entails no physical violence. Sexual taunts[3], drawing attention to and mocking physical infirmities, and racial insults can all be extremely provocative, and it is not difficult to imagine loss of self-control when a particular raw nerve is touched by the insult. The court in *Cosgrove v HM Advocate*[4] ruled that the classic definition put forward by *Macdonald* constituted a proper jury instruction on the matter and that it will not amount to a misdirection if the judge excludes verbal provocation. Whether or not conduct short of an assault can be considered to be provocation depends entirely upon the trial judge's view as to its seriousness.

Conduct not amounting to an assault was accepted as potentially provocative in *Stobbs v HM Advocate*[5], but a background of business arguments and minor assault was considered not to amount to provocation in *Thomson v HM Advocate*[6], and in *Cosgrove* a confession of indecency was similarly rejected. In *Drury v HM Advocate*[7] a bench of five judges considered the issue; although it was done in the context of the unfaithfulness exception, the court took the opportunity of affirming the limitation on the availability of provocation and approving the test in *Cosgrove*, whilst reserving their opinion about proportionality of response (Lord Cameron at paragraph [5] of his opinion).

There was explicit approval in another five-judge case *Gillon v HM Advocate*[8], where at paragraph [19] the court said 'Before us there was little controversy over the state of the existing law in relation to provocation taking the form of the infliction of actual violence. In *Thomson v HM Advocate*[9], Lord Justice-Clerk Ross said (p 284):

'A minor assault of that kind, whether or not one also takes into account the history of the business dealings, is clearly insufficient to found a plea of provocation which would palliate the taking of the deceased's life by stabbing. Where the victim has used force, there must be some relation between that force and the violence of the retaliation'.

In *HM Advocate v Smith* (unreported on this point but referred to in *Gordon*, page 772), the Lord Justice-General told the jury:

'It takes a tremendous amount of provocation to palliate stabbing a man to death. Words, however abusive or insulting are of no avail. A blow with a fist is no justification for the use of a lethal weapon. Provocation, in short, must bear a reasonable relation to the resentment which it excites'.

1 I, 247.
2 Page 93.
3 *DPP v Bedder* (1954) 38 Cr App Rep 133.
4 1990 SCCR 358.

5 1983 SCCR 190.
6 1985 SCCR 448, 1986 SLT 281.
7 2001 SLT 1013.
8 2007 JC 24, 2006 SLT 799.
9 1986 SLT 281, 1985 SCCR 448.

10.19   The unfaithfulness exception. A confession of adultery by a spouse has long been accepted as an exception to the assault requirement. The rule was originally restricted to cases in which the spouse is discovered in the act of committing adultery[1], but it later came to be extended to cover confession of adultery[2]. In *HM Advocate v Callander*[3] the court allowed provocation to be raised when the sexual unfaithfulness involved a wife and a lesbian lover, and the courts have recently accepted that the principle applies equally when the relationship between the parties is not based on marriage but is an informal equivalent[4]. The high-water mark of judicial liberalism in this area, however, is the decision in *HM Advocate v McKean*[5] in which the provocation took the form of a disclosure by the victim of sexual intimacy between himself and the lesbian lover of the female accused. A discovery of unfaithfulness, or its confession, must still occur in such circumstances as to give rise to a loss of self-control. In *McKay v HM Advocate*[6] the confession came at a time when the couple had already been separated and after a lengthy period during which the accused had known that the deceased had been associating with other men. In this context provocation was not accepted. In *Drury* , the court considered a number of examples including *HM Advocate v Rutherford*[7] (where the court held that the deceased's giving of a fresh account of her infidelity to the accused, two days after first informing him of it, could in itself have caused a reaction of sudden and overwhelming indignation which was separate from any reaction to the original account) concluding that 'What all these cases had in common was the concept of sudden and overwhelming indignation as a reaction to the discovery of sexual infidelity' Lord Cameron at para [7]. It should be noted however that the relationship in *Drury* (where the parties had lived together from August 1995 until December 1996; the relationship continued until March 1998; the accused contended that thereafter they continued to see one another and have a sexual relationship until the time of the acccused's attack on the victim) was ultimately challenged by the Crown. They sought at the appeal before five judges to argue that the relationship was not of a kind to give rise to a plea of provocation; the court declined to allow such argument holding that it came too late.

The response must follow upon the provocation. The accused's act must follow immediately upon the provocation offered by the deceased; a lengthy delay between the provocative act and the response will preclude provocation[8]. What constitutes an unacceptable delay will depend on the circumstances, but it is probably the case that a delay of more than a few minutes will be considered sufficient time for the accused to have recovered his self-control[9]. As *Alison* puts it:

> 'The defence of provocation will not avail the accused, if the fatal acts are done at such a distance of time after the injury received as should have allowed the mortal resentment to subside, or with such weapons, or in such a manner, as indicates a desire of unmeasured revenge'[10].

Similarly MacDonald put it thus:

'Provocation although great will not palliate guilt if an interval has elapsed between the provocation and the retaliation' (Approved in *Parr*[11]).

1 *Hume* I, 245.
2 *HM Advocate v Hill* 1941 JC 59, 1941 SLT 401.
3 1958 SLT 24.
4 *McDermott v HM Advocate* 1973 JC 8, 1974 SLT 206, *McKay v HM Advocate* 1991 SCCR 364.
5 1996 SCCR 402.
6 1991 SCCR 364.
7 1998 JC 34, 1998 SLT 740, 1997 SCCR 711.
8 *Thomson v HM Advocate* 1985 SCCR 448, 1986 SLT 281, *HM Advocate v Hill* 1941 JC 59, 1941 SLT 401, *Parr v HM Advocate* 1991 JC 39, 1991 SLT 208, 1991 SCCR 180.
9 Cf P Brett 'The physiology of provocation' [1970] Crim LR 634.
10 Alison p 8; Macdonald p 94.
11 1991 JC 39, 1991 SLT 208, 1991 SCCR 180.

10.20   There has been some judicial sympathy in the past for the doctrine of cumulative provocation, which would allow the plea where the response is not to a recent assault but occurs after a long history of unreasonable and violent behaviour. In *HM Advocate v Greig*[1], the accused killed her husband while he was sitting asleep in his chair. Although the trial judge could find no evidence of recent provocation, the issue was nevertheless left to the jury, who duly accepted it in view of the deceased's past violent behaviour. This decision was welcomed by those who considered the criminal law to be insufficiently sympathetic towards the plight of victims of domestic violence; despite a growing recognition of the dynamics of domestic abuse, there has yet to be a clear identification in Scotland of the precise approach to be adopted in dealing with homicide as a response to domestic violence. The issue arose in *Galbraith (No 2) v HM Advocate*[2], but was considered in the context of diminished responsibility. The accused in that case had shot her husband whilst he slept. She claimed years of abuse. She led evidence from two psychologists that she suffered from a form of post-traumatic stress disorder. She was convicted of murder, but the appeal was on the basis that the trial judges had misdirected the jury about the requirements of diminished responsibility. In *Parr v HM Advocate*[3] provocation was excluded when the accused had killed his mother by whom he had in the past been slapped on the face and with whom he had endured arguments. The court pointed out that there was no evidence of provocative conduct on the deceased's part on the day of the killing; and indeed the court observed that there was no compulsion on him to go on living with his mother and to endure the arguments they had with one another.

Parr is a very weak case of cumulative provocation. It may be possible that future cases of severe domestic provocation will incline the courts to relax the immediacy standards, but judicial opinion has been slow to change, and the approach taken by the accused in *Galbraith* may point to the future direction taken by those advising parties suffering at the hands of such cumulative conduct. There are cases in which those who are provoked in circumstances of domestic violence are treated leniently by the courts; such victims can by no means rely on this being the case[4]. A severely abused woman, who has endured frequent assaults by a bullying husband, may therefore be denied the plea of provocation unless she loses her self-control immediately after a bout of violence. This result demonstrates the potential harshness of having an undifferentiated crime of murder. Such women are not morally guilty to the same extent as those who kill for gain or for some other base motive. The doctrine of provocation, like that of diminished responsibility, provides a means of curtailing the rigours of the law in this area, but its efficacy is questionable.

1 (May 1979, unreported), HCJ; *Gane and Stoddart*, p 526.
2 2002 JC 1, 2001 SLT 953, 2001 SCCR 551.
3 1991 SCCR 180.
4 In certain other jurisdictions, the courts have been readier to reach a finding of provocation in such cases; alternatively the situation may be viewed as one in which self-defence is justified. Recent cases in England include *R v Thornton (No 2)* [1996] 2 All ER 1023.

10.21   The response must be proportionate. The accused's response to the provocation must be in proportion to the seriousness of the deceased's provocative act. This effectively means that a serious assault will generally be required for murder; the only circumstances in which a minor assault will justify homicidal retaliation are where the accused has made a reasonable mistake as to the nature of the deceased's attack on him[1].

Formerly if, in the light of the deceased's conduct, the response of the accused amounts to a 'cruel excess', the plea of provocation is excluded. This rule was endorsed in *Lennon v HM Advocate*[2], an assault case, in which the accused made use of an iron bar in his assault on the victim, but ultimately disapproved of in *Gillon v HM Advocate*[3]. The court said that there should be some equivalence between the retaliation and the provocation, so that the violence used by the accused is not disproportionate to the evidence constituting the provocation. The words 'cruel excess' should be confined to cases of self-defence. Essentially, there must be a comparison between the provoking violence and the retaliatory violence; the fact that death was caused did not mean that it was necessarily disproportionate. The court concluded by favouring the formulation set out in *Robertson v HM Advocate*[4], where the Lord Justice Clerk said at paragraph [22] 'It is by now well established that loss of control is not the only element in provocation. Although provocation does involve the loss of control, there must be a reasonably proportionate relationship between the violent conduct offered by the victim and the reaction of the accused.'

There is no Scottish authority on the question of whether subjective factors may be taken into account in assessing proportionality[5] although in *Duffy v HMA*[6], the High Court considered that:

'Whether the use of a knife in what appeared to be a fist fight is disproportionate will generally, in our view, depend upon the particular facts of the case. There may be circumstances in which a reasonable jury might conclude that the use of a knife was not grossly disproportionate, and accordingly that if the other three elements of provocation (namely physical attack, loss of self-control, and immediate retaliation) were proved to their satisfaction, the rider of provocation should be added. It is very much a question for the jury ... It is our opinion that only if a court were able to conclude that no reasonable jury could, on the evidence, reach the view that there was provocation, should directions on provocation be omitted.'

That appears to refine the test to be applied; it is not a question of whether there was reasonably proportionate response. Unless the response can be characterised as 'grossly disproportionate', provocation may apply.

In *Gillon* the court expressly rejected the test (suggested by counsel for the accused) which was 'Whether the accused acted in the circumstances as an ordinary man would have done?' Counsel sought support from the decision in *Drury* for that submission. The court favoured the test in *Robertson* described above, holding that no real assistance could be derived from *Drury* because it dealt with the 'unfaithfulness exception'.

However, in a case where a plea of provocation **is** taken based on the 'unfaithfulness exception', it was held in *Drury* that, assuming a relationship in which sexual fidelity was to be expected, the killing must have been as a result of immediate loss of self-control on discovery of the infidelity. In that case, the accused's actings were to be tested against the reactions of the ordinary person faced with that situation.

1 *Jones v HM Advocate* 1989 SCCR 726, 1990 SLT 517.
2 1991 SCCR 611.
3 2007 JC 24, 2006 SLT 799, 2006 SCCR 561.
4 1994 JC 245, 1994 SLT 1004, 1994 SCCR 589.
5 See '*Gillon v HM Advocate*: provocation, proportionality and the ordinary person', article by Juliet Casey 2006 SLT (News) 193, for an assessment of the doctrine of provocation.
6 2015 SCL 544.

Chapter 11

Sexual offences

CRIMINAL LAW AND SEXUAL FREEDOM

11.1   The extent to which the criminal law attempts to interfere in the sexual conduct of consenting adults is strictly limited. The libertarian ideal – that the law should intervene only if conduct causes unwanted harm to another – is now largely realised in this area, allowing adults to lead the sexual life of their choice. Most sexual offences arise therefore where there is a victim – one who either does not consent to the conduct in question or who does not have the capacity to give a proper consent. There remain, however, certain significant restraints which have nothing to do with consent. Consensual adult incest is still illegal. The possession of child pornography and extreme pornography is illegal, as is the importation or distribution of obscene material in general. There are also prohibitions against indecent displays and other forms of conduct which the public might find sexually shocking. Sexual freedom is therefore conditional upon the recognition of certain social limits, the contours of which may not always be clear and which develop with the views and mores of society.

Sexual offences in Scots law are both statutory and non-statutory, and there is a degree of overlap between the two categories, but the Sexual Offences (Scotland) Act 2009 changed the landscape.

The Sexual Offences (Scotland) Act 2009

11.2   This Act became law on 1 December 2010. It made fundamental changes to the framework of sexual offences in Scotland; it arose from what was described as widespread public professional and academic concern that the Scots Law on rape and other sexual offences was out of date, unclear and derived from a time when sexual attitudes were very different from those of contemporary society[1]. The Scottish Law Commission prepared a report[2] and, after consultation, the Act came into being. The purpose of the Act was to consolidate and clarify the law on sexual offences. The Act makes use of the terminology of the Sexual Offences Act 2003, describing offences with reference to 'a person "**A**" as the perpetrator and 'a person "**B**"; as the victim', the effect of which can be confusing and has been subject to criticism[3].

The effect of the Act is to abolish the common law offences of rape, clandestine injury, lewd indecent or libidinous practices and sodomy[4]; significantly it provides a definition of consent as 'free agreement'. But its provisions apply only to offences committed after it comes into force. The common law and existing statutory provisions will continue to apply to offences committed prior to that date: The Act does not provide a comprehensive treatment of all sexual crimes; for example the common law crime of assault aggravated by indecency and offences relating to prostitution remain. Nevertheless, the common law decisions which preceded the introduction of the Act are likely to inform interpretation[5].

Part One of the Act creates a number of new statutory offences *inter alia* of rape, sexual assault by penetration, sexual assault, sexual coercion, coercing a person to be present during sexual activity, coercing a person to look at an image of sexual activity, communicating indecently, sexual exposure, voyeurism, and administering a substance for sexual purpose.

Part Two of the Act introduces the statutory definition of consent. Consent is defined in s 12 as 'free agreement'; s 13 provides circumstances where free agreement is absent. It further provides that consent to conduct does not of itself constitute consent to any other conduct and that consent may be withdrawn at any time[6].

Part Three makes provision in relation to the capacity of persons with a mental disorder to consent to conduct.

Part Four of the Act introduces what are described as 'protective offences' dealing with potential sexual predators. The age of consent remains sixteen. Separate offences arise in respect of young children (under thirteen years of age) and older children (from thirteen to sixteen years of age). Sexual intercourse and oral sex between under sixteens remains illegal.

Part Five deals with sexual abuse of trust. It is an offence for someone in a position of trust over a child (in this case under eighteen), or a person with a mental disorder to engage in sexual activity with that child or person.

It is proposed to deal briefly with the principal offences.

1 Reflecting the Lord Justice Clerk's observations in *Webster v Dominick* 2005 1JC 65, 2003 SLT 975 at para [58] in relation to the offence of public indecency.
2 Report on Rape and Other Sexual Offences (Scot Law Com No 209, 2007).
3 See Professor JR Spencer article 'The drafting of criminal legislation; need it be so impenetrable?' [2008] CLR 585, where he describes the English Act as impenetrable and ineffective; and E Clive 'Drafting the law on sexual offences'2006 JR 55.
4 Section 52.
5 See, for example, *Drummond v HMA* 2015 SCL 533, where the Lord Justice Clerk said, albeit *obiter* 'The court reserves its opinion on whether, in that state of the evidence, the Crown requires to produce material to negative a state of affairs which does not arise. This was not needed at common law. Notwithstanding the *dictum* in McKearney ... concerning proof in common law rape cases, which proceeded upon a concession by the Crown, it would be surprising if the reforms to the law of rape had intended to introduce such an additional onerous requirement'.
6 Section 14, Reflecting Baroness Hale's words in *R v C* [2009] UKHL 42 at para [27] '... it is difficult to think of an activity which is more person- and situation-specific than sexual relations. One does not consent to sex in general. One consents to the act of sex with the person at this time and this place, Autonomy entails the freedom and the capacity to make a choice of whether or not to do so'.; see also 'Two problems in the Sexual Offences (Scotland) Bill' article by James Chalmers 2009 SCL 553.

11.3   Rape is defined as penetration by the penis of the vagina, anus or mouth, without consent and without reasonable belief of consent, Accordingly rape is extended from the common law offence; it is no longer restricted to vaginal intercourse and can now be perpetrated by male on male. 'Penetration', 'penis' and 'vagina' are all defined[1].

Sexual assault by penetration occurs if the perpetrator penetrates sexually (using part of his body or anything else) the vagina or anus of the victim without consent and without reasonable belief of consent. There must be either an intention to do so, or a recklessness about whether there is penetration[2]. The cases previously referred to in relation to recklessness so far as it affects rape are likely to inform court decisions in relation to these provisions.

Sexual assault covers a variety of conduct deemed to constitute assault, including penetration, reckless or intentional touching, sexual activity which involves physical contact, and the intentional or reckless emission of some bodily fluids. Again the offence is only committed if there is no consent and no reasonable belief of consent[3].

1 Section 1.
2 Section 2.
3 Section 3.

Consent

11.4   Consent is defined as 'free agreement'. Section 13 of the Act sets out factual situations where the law deems there to be no consent at all. These are not evidential presumptions; the section prescribes certain factual situations which, if proved, legally exclude the possibility of valid consent or 'free agreement' existing between the parties. These include where the conduct occurs at a time when the complainer is incapable because of the effect of alcohol or any other substance of consenting to it; or where the complainer agrees or submits to the conduct because of violence or threats of violence used against the complainer or; unlawful detention, or deception. Section 14 provides that 'a person is incapable, while asleep or unconscious, of consenting to any conduct.'

The Act provides further guidance as to particular issues concerning consent or the lack thereof. Section 15 provides that 'consent to conduct does not, of itself, imply consent to any other conduct' and that 'consent to conduct may be withdrawn at any time before, or in the case of continuing conduct, during, the conduct.' It also provides that 'if the conduct takes place, or continues to take place, after consent has been withdrawn, it takes place, or continues to take place, without consent[1].'

The Act provides guidance as to what is meant by 'reasonable belief'; it provides that when a determination is being made by the court or jury as to whether an accused's belief in a complainer's consent or knowledge was reasonable, 'regard is to be had as to whether the person took any steps to ascertain whether there was consent or, as the case may be, knowledge; and if so, what those steps were.' It is likely that the previous common law in relation to consent and reasonable belief will inform the interpretation of the new statutory provisions.

Section 9 introduces the offence of voyeurism; this was not part of the Scottish Law Commission report, but was introduced by the Scottish Government during the passage of the Bill into law. The provisions are broadly similar to the provisions of ss 67 and 68 of the Sexual Offences Act 2003, although arguably less accessible[2]. The section is designed to catch a variety of conduct within the definition of voyeurism. That will include observing a private act of another party, operating equipment with the intention of enabling himself or others to observe such a private act, recording such a private act, and installing equipment or adapting a structure to enable such acts to be observed, or recorded. The conduct must be done with the purpose of obtaining sexual gratification, or humiliating, distressing or alarming the victim.

1 See *Mutebi v HMA* 2014 SCL 5 for one reported case where consent was purportedly withdrawn.
2 See 'Two problems in the Sexual Offences (Scotland) Bill' article by James Chalmers 2009 SCL 553 for a robust critique of these provisions, in which the language is described as 'tortuous'.

OFFENCES AGAINST PUBLIC MORALITY

11.5   Public morality offences are those offences which might not involve a victim in the normal sense of the term, but which nonetheless entail criminal liability on the grounds that they cause offence to the community at large. This is obviously a controversial area, and it is in respect of these offences that the greatest disagreement is likely to occur between the advocates of legal moralism and those who disfavour any regulation of consensual adult sexual behaviour. As the law stands at present in Scotland, prosecutors have a range of weapons to use against public indecency of various sorts, but the potential of these weapons is considerably limited by increased public tolerance and by changing notions of what is indecent.

Obscene material

11.6   Subject to the exceptions of child pornography and extreme pornography[1], it is not an offence merely to possess obscene material (for example, an obscene book, magazine, or video cassette)[2], even if there is an intention ultimately to supply the material to the public. It is an offence, however, to display such items in such a position that it can be seen by a member of the public, or to publish, sell or distribute obscene material[3]. The publication or distribution of obscene material was formerly prosecuted at common law, as a form of shameless indecency[4]; the offence was committed even if the material was kept hidden, so long as it was in immediate readiness for sale and would be displayed to members of the public on request[5]. However, in *Webster v Dominick*[6] (discussed below in the context of public indecency), the court determined at paragraph [56] that, 'The crime [of public indecency] does not extend to consensual sexual conduct committed in private; nor to the private showing of indecent films and videos; nor to the selling of indecent publications. Nor does it extend to conduct witnessed only by persons who wish to see it … except perhaps where the conduct is such as to offend even members of a consenting audience. On this view, indecent exposure … which was found to have offended some of those present, would continue to be criminal.' Accordingly the issue is whether offence is caused, and the extent of that offence. There are no modern Scottish precedents involving the prosecution of publishers purely of the written word on grounds of obscenity; the causes célèbres of English law, such as the *Lady Chatterley's Lover* trial, have not had their counterpart in Scotland. Although the individual may possess almost all forms of pornography, access to it is legally restricted. The importation of obscene articles is an offence under customs legislation[7], and it is also an offence to send obscene matter through the post[8]. Under s 127 of the Communications Act 2003, it is an offence to send by means of a public electronic communications network a message that is grossly offensive or of an indecent, obscene or menacing character.

1 The Civic Government (Scotland) Act 1982, ss 51A–51C criminalises the possession of extreme pornography, being pornography which explicitly and realistically depicts an act taking life, or resulting in severe injury, or rape, or sexual activity with a corpse or an animal.
2 *Sommerville v Tudhope* 1981 JC 58, 1981 SLT 117.
3 Civic Government (Scotland) Act 1982, s 51.
4 As to which see below. Cf, however, *Sommerville v Tudhope* 1981 JC 58, 1981 SLT 117, which suggests that 'trafficking' in obscene material may also be an offence at common law.
5 *Scott v Smith* 1981 JC 46.
6 2005 1 JC 65, 2003 SLT 975, 2003 SCCR 525.
7 Customs Consolidation Act 1876, s 42.
8 Postal Services Act 2000, s 85.

Child pornography

11.7   The growing use of children in pornography is a social evil which is widely regarded with particular abhorrence, and this category of pornography is now totally illicit. The use of internet, file sharing software and social media mean that the dissemination of such material is easier. Under s 52 of the Civic Government (Scotland) Act 1982 it is an offence to take or permit to be taken or make[1] an indecent photograph or pseudo photograph[2] of any child under the age of eighteen[3], to distribute or show such a photograph, to have with a view to distribution or showing such a photograph, or to publish an advertisement for it. It is a defence if the accused proves that he had a legitimate reason for distributing or showing or having the photograph in his possession, or that he was unaware of its nature. Section 52A of the Civic Government (Scotland) Act 1982 provides that it is an offence to have in one's possession an indecent photograph of a child under eighteen. It is a defence to that charge for the accused to prove that he had it legitimately, that he had not seen the photograph and did not know or suspect it was indecent, or that it was sent to him without prior request and he had not kept it for an unreasonable time; the latter defence means that a person receiving such an item must dispose of it. The *mens rea* is that the act of taking or making should be a deliberate act with knowledge that the image made is, or is likely to be indecent[4].

The context in which a photograph was taken is relevant to whether it was taken deliberately or accidentally; the context will not inform the decision about whether it is decent or indecent[5]. The legislation does not define indecency, and this will therefore be determined by the court[6]. The Crown will normally have to lead expert evidence to establish that the subject of the photograph is under the age of eighteen[7].

The Protection of Children and Prevention of Sexual Offences (Scotland) Act 2005[8] made specific provisions to criminalise the causing or inciting provision by a child of pornography[9], the controlling of a child involved in pornography[10] or the arranging or facilitating provision of child pornography[11].

1 'To make' is to be given its ordinary meaning; see *Smart v HM Advocate* 2006 JC 119, 2006 SCCR 120 at para [19].
2 A pseudo-photograph is an image 'whether produced by computer graphics or otherwise howsoever, which appears to be a photograph' (s 52(2A)); all subsequent references to photographs include reference to pseudo-photographs.
3 The age was formerly sixteen until substituted by Protection of Children and Prevention of Sexual Offences (Scotland) Act 2005; there are special provisions dealing with children aged sixteen and seventeen at s 52B.
4 *Smart v HM Advocate* 2006 JC 119, 2006 SCCR 120 at paras [20]–[22].
5 *Bruce v McLeod* 1998 SCCR 733.
6 Expert evidence on the matter is unlikely to be allowed: see *Ingram v Macari* 1983 JC 1, 1982 SCCR 372.
7 *Griffiths v Hart* 2005 JC 313, 2005 SCCR 392 at para [19].
8 Otherwise the Protection of Children etc (Scotland) 2005.
9 Section 10.
10 Section 11.
11 Section 12.

Public indecency

11.8　　The proposition that 'all shamelessly indecent conduct is criminal' appears in *Macdonald*[1], and was repeated with approval by judges in a number of cases[2]. The nature of shameless indecency as a crime was challenged in *Watt v Annan*[3]. The proprietor of a hotel allowed members of a private club to meet at his hotel where they viewed a film described by the sheriff as 'of a degree and nature liable to deprave and corrupt'. The High Court, relying on dicta in *McLaughlan v Boyd*[4] concluded that any form of conduct could be shamelessly indecent, depending on the nature of the conduct, the circumstances in which it took place and the necessary criminal intent. The scope of that offence left a great deal to the discretion of the court in individual cases. Standards of decency change, and the imprecise nature of this offence caused understandable concern amongst civil libertarians who argue that the only proper test of criminality in this context should be whether any person has been involuntarily harmed by the conduct in question.

1 Page 150.
2 Eg by Lord Clyde in *McLaughlan v Boyd* 1933 SLT 629; *R v HM Advocate* 1988 SCCR 254, 1988 SLT 623.
3 1978 JC 84, 1978 SLT 198.
4 1934 JC 19, 1933 SLT 629.

11.9　　Despite concerns, shameless indecency formed the basis for a variety of offences; the crime could take the form of the provision of some sort of sexually stimulating spectacle or article, or the performance of an indecent act with another person.

For example, in *HM Advocate v RK*[1], the judge repelled a plea to the relevancy of a charge of shameless indecency alleging that the accused had sexual intercourse with a girl who had been his foster daughter; the allegation was that the intercourse took place when she was between sixteen and eighteen years of age. Lord Mclean held that such conduct would be repugnant to society until the complainer was eighteen, or had left the family home whichever was later. In *Carmichael v Ashrif*[2], the accused was charged with conducting himself in a shameless and indecent manner towards two school girls to whom he showed a pornographic film.

The uncertain limits caused some judicial concern; in *Paterson v Lees*[3], the Lord Justice General said:

'The term "shamelessly" has been glossed in ways which take it beyond its normal meaning and hence beyond the meaning which, one might suppose, *Macdonald* would have intended it to bear when he framed his proposition in 1866. As a result, the crime which the adverb is meant to define has become amorphous, with any limits being hard to discern'.

1 1953 JC 16, 1953 SLT 67.
2 1985 SCCR 461.
3 1999 JC 159 at 161, 1999 SCCR 231 at 232.

11.10   Finally, in the important case of *Webster v Dominick*[1], a bench of five judges took the opportunity to survey and review the law, concluding that the decisions in *McLaughlan* and *Watt* had created a crime that 'rested on unsound theory, has an uncertain ambit of liability and lays open to prosecution some forms of private conduct the legality of which should be a question for the legislature[2]'. That paragraph concludes 'It is time that this court put it right'.

The Lord Justice Clerk in the first place determined that indecent conduct directed against a specific victim who is within the class of persons whom the law protects falls within the crime of lewd, indecent and libidinous practices. Where the indecent conduct involves no individual victim, it is criminal only 'where it affronts public sensibility'. Such a crime is properly described as public indecency. The *actus reus* has two elements; the act itself and the effect of it on the minds of the public. He gives as an example indecent exposure; the conduct need not be committed for sexual gratification (although that may inform sentencing).

The test is not whether the conduct occurs in a public place in any technical sense; it could take place on a private occasion if it occurred in the presence of unwilling witnesses, or on private premises but visible to the public.

The crime of public indecency does not extend to consensual sexual conduct committed in private; nor to the private showing of indecent films, nor the selling of indecent publications, nor to conduct witnessed only by persons willing to see it.

Whether a particular act is indecent depends on the circumstances judged by social standards that may change; it should be judged by the standards applied by the average citizen in contemporary society[3].

1 2005 1 JC 65, 2003 SLT 975.
2 Webster at para [43].
3 Webster at paras [51]–[58].

Lewd and libidinous practices

11.11   The corollary of the decision in *Webster* which defined public indecency, is that behaviour deemed to be indecent but taking place other than in
public will now be covered by the offence of lewd and libidinous practices.
This was put beyond doubt by the observations of the Lord Justice Clerk at
paragraph [49] as follows:

> 'In the modern law, where indecent conduct is directed against a specific victim
> who is within the class of persons whom the law protects, the crime is that of
> lewd, indecent and libidinous practices. It may be committed by indecent physi-
> cal contact with the victim, but it need not. It may be committed by the taking of
> indecent photographs of the victim (*HM Advocate v Millbank*[1]); or by indecent
> exposure to the victim (*Lockwood v Walker*[2]); or by the showing of indecent pho-
> tographs or videos to the victim; or by other forms of indecent conduct carried
> out in the presence of the victim. It may be committed, in my opinion, by means
> of a lewd conversation with the victim, whether face to face or by a telephone
> call, or through an internet chat-room. In each case, the essence of the offence is
> the tendency of the conduct to corrupt the innocence of the complainer.'

Clearly, there can be no comprehensive description of the type of behaviour
which might constitute lewd and libidinous practice; some further examples
may assist. To engage in indecent conduct in the presence of a child may constitute the offence[3]. A 'french kiss' of a school girl by her teacher was held to
show a tendency to corrupt the victim's innocence[4].

1 2002 SLT 1116, 2003 SCCR 771.
2 1910 (J) SC 3.
3 *Robertson v HM Advocate* 1987 SCCR 387; see *Anderson v HM Advocate* 2001 SLT 1265, 2001
   SCCR 738 where the court held that appearing dressed only in boxer shorts before a child is not
   lewd and libidinous practice.
4 *Moynagh v Speirs* 2003 SLT 1337, 2003 SCCR 765.

SEXUAL ASSAULTS

11.12   Some sexual assaults will now be covered by the Sexual Offences
(Scotland) Act 2009. But the common law remains relevant because the Act
is not retrospective and deals only with offences from 1 December 2010.
Against a background of decreasing crime, the reporting of sexual assaults has
increased, including historical crimes, dating back many years[1]. The case law
will also help to inform interpretation of the new statutory regime.

The category of sexual assaults is a not a formal one, but it usefully groups
together those offences in which there is a non-consensual intrusion into the
sexual integrity of another. A sexual assault may involve considerable violence
or very little; the assault element is to be found in the wrongful sexual contact
rather than in incidental force used by the perpetrator.

1 According to Scottish Government statistics 'Sexual crimes increased by 12%, from 7,693 in
   2012–13 to 8,604 in 2013–14. Sexual crimes have been on an upward trend since 2008-09, however this increase is likely due to an increase in reporting, including reporting of historic crimes,
   as victims find the courage to come forward and report such crimes to the police.' See http://
   news.scotland.gov.uk/News/Recorded-Crime-in-Scotland-2013-14-129d.aspx#downloads.

Rape

11.13   Rape is recognised to be one of the most serious sexual offences. It is committed when a man has sexual intercourse with a woman by means of the overcoming of her will. In most jurisdictions it is defined as being sexual intercourse with a woman who does not consent, but this definition, although it has crept into Scots usage, did not reflect the crime of clandestine injury; in Scots law a sleeping or unconscious woman was held not to have been raped if a man has intercourse with her without her consent as she was deemed incapable of consent.

For offences occurring prior to the Sexual Offences (Scotland) Act 2009, rape requires penetration of the woman *per vaginam*. Penetration must be by the male organ. Oral or anal penetration amount to indecent assault, but do not constitute rape in the legal sense[1]. Who is capable of committing common law rape? Any male over the age of criminal responsibility may be guilty of rape. A woman cannot commit rape herself but may be art and part guilty of rape, as in a case where she assists a man to commit rape on another woman. The rule that a husband cannot be guilty of the rape of his wife, other than by being guilty art and part of such a rape by a third party, was stated by *Hume* and accepted by later commentators. But in *Stallard v HM Advocate*[2], the High Court upheld the relevancy of a charge of rape where the husband was cohabiting with the wife at the time. In this case the court observed that attitudes had changed considerably since *Hume*'s time, and that wives are no longer bound to suffer excessive sexual demands on the part of their husbands. The court acknowledged that it may be harder to prove where the parties are still living together, but the principle that the wife need not have intercourse forced upon her remained applicable in such a case. The court said[3]: 'There is no doubt that a wife does not consent to assault upon her person and there is no plausible justification for saying today that she nevertheless is to be taken to consent to intercourse *by assault* (emphasis added)'. The accused in *Stallard v HM Advocate* used very considerable violence – in such circumstances it will be difficult for a husband to convince the court that he believed that his wife was consenting; the issue of the use of force is discussed below.

1 Compare with the Sexual Offences (Scotland) Act 2009 at para 11.2.
2 1989 SCCR 248, 1989 SLT 469.
3 *Stallard* at 473.

11.14   The *actus reus* of rape.   Rape is committed where a man has intercourse with a woman through the overcoming of her will. This requirement is stated by *Hume* in the following terms: 'The knowledge of the woman must … be against her will, and by force'[1]. This emphasis on force had unfortunate implications in the past in that it had been interpreted as requiring physical resistance on the part of women, which has been translated in due course into an emphasis on injury sustained in the course of this resistance. Gradually, the law developed so that the importance of 'force' diminished. For example in *Barbour v HM Advocate*[2], the court stressed that the amount of resistance put up is not the important matter; what really counts is that the woman remained an unwilling party throughout. Resistance, therefore, is significant only in that it is evidence of unwillingness[3]. The matter was put beyond doubt by a bench of seven judges in *The Lord Advocate's Reference (No 1 of 2001[4])*. The accused had accepted that intercourse took place but argued that in the absence of evidence of force, there could be no conviction for rape. The trial judge upheld a submission of no case to answer, holding that the Crown had to establish that the accused had used force to overcome the will of the complainer, relying to some extent upon Hume's observations and the case law which followed thereon. In allowing the appeal and rejecting force as a prerequisite, the Lord Justice General said:

'In my view this court should hold that the general rule is that the *actus reus* of rape is constituted by the man having sexual intercourse with the woman without her consent ... and *mens rea* on the part of the man is present where he knows that the woman is not consenting or at any rate is reckless as to whether she is consenting.[5]'

The use of threats to secure the victim's compliance amounts to rape[6]. Threats will usually be threats of physical violence; in *Barbour v HM Advocate[7]* the trial judge's charge included the following:

'What [the victim] was indicating was that she did not resist, she said she did not resist but she allowed these things to happen to her, but she emphasized ... that she did not voluntarily agree and was not a willing participant. Now, there is nothing all that unusual about a rape where the victim does not resist physically as, for example, a case in this very courtroom a year ago where a girl submitted to intercourse without struggle because she had been menaced with a knife. That was a clear case of rape.'

Standing the decision in *The Lord Advocate's Reference*, there seems no reason in principle why a threat of another nature, if serious enough, should not have the effect of overcoming the victim's will. For example, a threat to dismiss an employee who relies on her job to support a large family, and who faces financial ruin if dismissed, could have the effect of overcoming her will to resist[8].

It is rape to administer drink or drugs to a woman with a view to overcoming her resistance and to having sexual intercourse as a result[9].

1 I, 302.
2 1982 SCCR 195.
3 See also *C v HM Advocate* 1987 SCCR 104, a case involving a charge of statutory rape.
4 2002 SLT 466, 2002 SCCR 435.
5 At para [44].
6 *Hume* I, 302, *Alison* I, 212; *Macdonald* p 121.
7 1982 SCCR 195.
8 See also Criminal Law (Consolidation) (Scotland) Act 1995, s 7(2)(a): procuring or attempting to procure unlawful sexual intercourse through the use of threats or intimidation.
9 *HM Advocate v Logan* 1936 JC 100, 1937 SLT 104. That case also determined that the nature of the drink or drugs must be concealed from her if it is to be rape; a man who gives drink to a woman, who knows that what she is taking is intoxicating drink, and who then has sexual intercourse with her when she is so drunk as to be unable to form the inclination to resist, does not commit rape. Similarly, a man who encounters a woman who is intoxicated and who has intercourse with her in the knowledge that the only reason she is doing so is because she is too drunk to know what she is doing, does not commit rape. These conclusions probably reflect the mores of the time and are unlikely to be given weight in the twenty-first century.

11.15   There was an offence of clandestine injury to woman, an offence committed by a man who has sexual intercourse with a sleeping or unconscious
woman[1]. *The Lord Advocate Reference* overruled *Sweenie*, effectively abol-
ishing the crime of clandestine injury whereby a man did not commit rape in
such circumstances because a woman in this state is held to have no will to be
overcome. This rule was open to criticism, as the wrong done to a woman who
is raped while conscious and one who has non-consensual sexual intercourse
inflicted on her while she is asleep or unconscious is difficult to distinguish. It
is now to be accepted that an assault involving penetration is rape, although the
Crown may still charge such an offence as assault. In *Spendiff v HM Advocate*[2]
the charges included one of clandestine injury. In *McNairn v HM Advocate*[3],
Sheriff Gordon's commentary said, '[This case] provides a clear statement of
the proposition that evidence that the complainer was asleep at the relevant
time is evidence from which a lack of belief in consent can be inferred; it is difficult to see the need to maintain the distinction in the common law [between
rape and clandestine injury]'.

Where the man deceives the woman as to the nature of the act of sexual intercourse, there may be rape, on the grounds that there is no true consent to the
act. This is a situation unlikely to arise in practice but which, nonetheless, arose
in *R v Williams*[4], a case in which a singing teacher convinced his female pupil
that intercourse was, in fact, treatment designed to improve her singing voice.

It is the offence of rape for a man to induce a married woman to permit him
to have sexual intercourse with her by impersonating her husband[5]. In general, however, inducing a woman to have sexual intercourse on the basis of a
fraudulent misrepresentation does not amount to rape[6]. It is not rape if a man
obtains intercourse on the basis of a false promise to marry[7], nor will misrepresentations as to a man's circumstances negate consent. In the English case of
R v Linekar[8] it was held that there is no rape where consent to intercourse was
given on the strength of a fraudulent promise to pay for that intercourse.

1 *Sweenie* (1858) 3 Irv 109; *HM Advocate v Grainger and Rae* 1932 JC 40, 1932 SLT 28; *Sweeney
   v X* 1982 SCCR 509.
2 2005 1 JC 338, 2005 SCCR 522.
3 2005 SCCR 741.
4 [1923] 1 KB 340.
5 Criminal Law (Consolidation) Scotland Act 1995 s 7(3).
6 *Fraser* (1847) Arkley 280. It may, however constitute the statutory offence set out in the Criminal Law (Consolidation) (Scotland) Act 1995, s 7(2)(b).
7 This point was considered in the well-known Australian case of *R v Papadimitropolous* (1957)
   98 CLR 249. The accused misrepresented to a woman that he and she had gone through a marriage ceremony. Sexual intercourse based on her belief that she was married did not amount to
   rape.
8 [1995] QB 250, [1995] 3 All ER 69, CA.

11.16   Rape is committed if a man has sexual intercourse with a girl under
the age of twelve years. This is termed constructive rape, and the offence is
committed irrespective of whether the girl is a willing party or not. Section
311 of the Mental Health (Care and Treatment) (Scotland) Act 2003 makes it
an offence to engage in a sexual act with a mentally disordered person if at the
time of the act the person does not consent or was incapable of consenting[1].

The *mens rea* requirement in rape. No area of the law relating to sexual offences has been so controversial as the question of the *mens rea* requirement. The fundamental legal proposition is clear enough: the *mens rea* of rape is the intention to have sexual intercourse through the overpowering of the will, or recklessness as to the possibility that the act is performed against the woman's will[2]. If, therefore, a man believes that the woman consents to intercourse, then the *mens rea* of rape is absent. In *Spendiff v HM Advocate*[3], the court considered the effect of the *Lord Advocate's reference* on *mens rea* in rape reflecting that it was there said '*Mens rea* on the part of the man [is] constituted by his knowledge that the woman is not consenting or at any rate by his subjective recklessness as to whether the woman is consenting' determining at paragraph [25], rather tersely that 'The *mens rea* of rape was not changed nor, indeed, was it illuminated by the decision, nor were the means by which that could be determined so illuminated.

In *McKearney v HM Advocate*[4] the Lord Justice Clerk said at paragraph [34]:

'Although the jury had clear evidence that the complainer did not consent to the intercourse and was frightened, even terrified, because of the [accused's] behaviour, there was ample evidence, including that of the complainer herself, that she said and did nothing to indicate to the [accused] that she was not consenting to intercourse. Thus there was clearly room for the jury to form the view that, although the complainer did not consent to the intercourse, and that therefore the *actus reus* was established, nonetheless the possibility that the [accused] acted in the belief that she was consenting was not excluded; the evidence led did not exclude that possibility. If he had acted in that belief then he would not have possessed the *mens rea* that is essential to the commission of the crime of rape.'

The difficulty with this otherwise simple proposition is that of misinterpretation on the part of the man of the woman's attitude. In the English case of *DPP v Morgan*[5] the House of Lords affirmed that an error on the man's part is a defence to a charge of rape, even if the error is one which no reasonable man would have made. In this case the accused alleged that they were told by a woman's husband that any attempt on her part to resist sexual intercourse would not signify real resistance but was merely an aspect of sexual enjoyment on her part. The fact that no reasonable man would have believed this was relevant in deciding whether the accused really believed the woman was consenting, but was not, in itself, grounds for excluding the defence.

In *Meek v HM Advocate*[6] the High Court endorsed this view of unreasonable error, although earlier authorities had consistently required that an error be reasonable before it is capable of being accepted as a defence[7]. In practice juries will be unlikely to believe that a man really made an error as to consent if the error is one which no reasonable man would have made; indeed a jury may be directed that the absence of reasonable grounds for a belief in consent may be relevant to the question of whether the belief was actually held, as in *Jamieson v HM Advocate*[8]. It was held that a direction as to honest belief in consent is not necessary in every case, but only where the issue is raised by the evidence[9]. However *McKearney* established that in any rape case in which there is no evidence of the use or threat of force at the time of, or immediately preceding, the sexual penetration, and the evidence provides some proper basis upon which the jury might hold that the accused believed that the woman was consenting to intercourse, specific directions on *mens rea*, including direction about actual, honest belief, will be required.

1 Originally the Mental Health (Scotland) Act 1984, s 102.
2 'The crime of rape consists in the carnal knowledge of a woman forcibly and against her will. It involves that the act of the accused is consciously and intentionally or recklessly done against the woman's will': *Meek v HM Advocate* 1982 SCCR 613, 1983 SLT 280, per Lord President Emslie.
3 2005 1 JC 338, 2005 SCCR 522.
4 2004 JC 87, 2004 SLT 739, 2004 SCCR 251.
5 [1976] AC 182, [1975] 2 All ER 347.
6 1982 SCCR 613, 1983 SLT 280.
7 Eg *Crawford v HM Advocate* 1950 JC 67, 1950 SLT 279.
8 1994 SCCR 181.
9 *Doris v HM Advocate* 1996 SCCR 854, 1996 SLT 996.

11.17 The *Lord Advocate's Reference* also dealt with the issue of recklessness. They approved the dicta in *Jamieson* at page 92 as follows: 'This is because the question is whether he genuinely or honestly believed that the woman was consenting to intercourse. It will not do if he acted without thinking or was indifferent as to whether or not he had her consent. The man must have genuinely formed the belief that she was consenting to his having intercourse with her. But this need not be a belief which the jury regards as reasonable, so long as they are satisfied that his belief was genuinely held by him at the time'. Thereafter, the opinion continued:

> 'It may be noted that the implication of the court's decision in *Jamieson* was to distinguish between the man who failed to think about, or was indifferent as to, whether the woman was consenting (which might be described as subjective recklessness); and the man who honestly or genuinely believed that the woman was consenting but had failed to realise that she was not consenting when there was an obvious risk that this was the case. The latter might be described as objective recklessness,' concluding at paragraph [44], 'Standing the decision in *Jamieson* and in the absence of discussion of this topic in the present reference, "reckless" should be understood in the subjective sense to which I have referred earlier in this opinion'.

Accordingly, recklessness in rape will be established if the perpetrator failed to think about, or was indifferent to, whether the woman consented. There is still a difficulty; the logic of *Meek* suggests that a man who forms a positive belief that the woman is consenting cannot be guilty of rape, no matter how unreasonable that belief may be in the circumstances; a man who fails to advert to or think about the risk of non-consent in circumstances which would raise doubt in the mind of the reasonable man, may, on this view, be convicted. It is arguable, however, that the former is at least as culpable as the latter. Therefore, if recklessness is a sufficient *mens rea* for rape, then arguably a point must be reached where the belief becomes so unreasonable that it is arrived at recklessly. Certainly it is easy to figure cases in which a belief in consent is arrived at without adverting to an obvious risk that the woman is not consenting. A conviction may be possible, even in the presence of an actual belief in consent, whatever *Meek* may say[1]. There is no difficulty, moreover, about the man who has intercourse with a woman 'willy-nilly'[2], not caring whether she consents or not. He is clearly guilty of rape.

Notwithstanding the apparent clarification afforded by the Lord Advocate's Reference, the issue remains a difficult one for both practitioners and the courts[3].

1 See generally J Temkin 'The limits of reckless rape' [1983] Crim LR 5.
2 As Lord Hailsham memorably put it in *DPP v Morgan* [1976] AC 182 at 215, [1975] 2 All ER 347 at 362.
3 See 'Distress as corroboration of *mens rea*' article by James Chalmers 2004 SLT (News) 141, 'Redefined rape and the difficulties of proof' article by Margaret Scott QC 2005 SLT (News) 65; 'Sexual crimes and the problems of proof' article by Peter Ferguson QC 2007 SCL 1; the concerns were foreshadowed in the dissenting opinions of Lord McCluskey and Lord Marnoch in *The Lord Advocate's Reference (No 1 of 2001)*.

Indecent assault

11.18   An indecent assault is an assault which is aggravated by indecency in the manner of its commission[1]. The normal requirements of assault must be present, namely, physical touching or the threat of physical touching, and there must also be the necessary evil intent (which constitutes the *mens rea* of assault). An indecent assault may be committed by either sex on a member of the same or opposite sex. Consent to the touching is a defence, and it may be a defence for the accused to show that he believed that the other person consented. It appears that, as in rape, there is no need for the belief to be based upon reasonable grounds[2]. It is undecided in Scots law whether consent would constitute a defence where actual physical harm is inflicted in a sexual context[3].

An assault is indecent if the part of the body touched is a sexual part or a part contiguous to a sexual part. The touching of buttocks, breasts, or sexual organs is indecent, but other parts may be involved if the surrounding circumstances are indecent. Thus, the touching of a woman's arm accompanied by the use of suggestive language may be an indecent assault. The conduct in question must be objectively indecent; an assault may have the quality of indecency irrespective of the accused's intention or motive. The Crown need not prove that the offence was committed for the purpose of sexual gratification[4]. In the context of a consensual sexual relationship, there will be no assault unless there is an intention to cause physical harm[5]. Outwardly indecent contact might be rendered innocent by virtue of the circumstances in which it occurs. In *Stewart v Thain*[6] the accused, a schoolmaster, disciplined a partly naked boy, requiring him to expose his buttocks for chastisement. The court held that this did not amount to an indecent assault, given the right of the schoolmaster to punish the boy: no indecent motive was proved, although such a defence would almost certainly fail in the twenty-first century, even if there was right to administer punishment[7].

1 *Grainger v HM Advocate* 2006 JC 141, 2005 SLT 184, 2005 SCCR 175 at para [17].
2 In *Young v McGlennan* 1991 SCCR 738 the accused was convicted of indecently assaulting a woman by lightly touching her breasts. It was argued on his behalf that there was no evil intent, but he was nonetheless convicted. The question of whether his belief in consent would require

to be based on reasonable grounds was not addressed. In *Marr v HM Advocate* 1996 SCCR 696, 1996 SLT 1035, however, the High Court adopted the reasoning in *Jamieson v HM Advocate* 1994 SCCR 181, 1994 SLT 537 as representing the law in relation to indecent assault.
3   Although it seems unlikely that it would. It is clearly no defence to a charge of common assault – see *Smart v HM Advocate* 1975 JC 30 and cf the English sadomasochism cases *R v Brown* [1994] 1 AC 212, [1993] 2 All ER 75 and *Stewart v Nisbet* 2013 SCL 209.
4   *Grainger* at para [17].
5   *McDonald v HM Advocate* 2004 SCCR 161 at para [23].
6   1981 JC 13, 1981 SLT (Notes) 2.
7   See *Barile v Griffiths* 2010 SLT 164.

INCEST AND RELATED OFFENCES

11.19   Under the Criminal Law (Consolidation) (Scotland) Act 1995, the offence of incest is committed by any person, male or female, who has sexual intercourse with a person with whom he or she has a relationship listed in the statutory table[1]. The relationships, which are all ones of consanguinity or adoption are: a man's mother, daughter, grandmother, grand-daughter, sister, aunt, niece, great-grandmother, great-grand-daughter, adoptive mother or former adoptive mother, and adopted daughter or former adopted daughter. The equivalent relationships apply in the case of a woman. Relationships of the half blood are included: it is therefore incest for a man to have intercourse with a woman who shares one parent with him.

1   Criminal Law (Consolidation) (Scotland) Act 1995, s 1.

11.20   The offence is committed by a male or female who has sexual intercourse with a person to whom he or she is related within the prohibited degrees. Proof of sexual intercourse is as in cases of rape. The prosecution does not have to prove that the accused knew of the relationship existing between him and the other person; the onus of proving that he did not know that he was related within the prohibited degrees therefore rests upon the accused person. It is also a defence if intercourse took place without consent or if the parties were married at the time of the offence (as might be the case if a marriage recognised in Scotland as valid had taken place abroad).

The offence of incest is restricted to those cases where sexual intercourse takes place. Sexual activity between persons within the prohibited degrees may also be prosecuted as lewd and libidinous practices, as demonstrated by the decision in *R v HM Advocate*[1], interpreted having regard to *Webster*. This case involved sexual activity between a father and daughter, which excites particular social disapproval. In terms of s 2, sexual intercourse between step-parent and step-child is an offence if the child is under the age of twenty-one at the time at which intercourse takes place, or had at any time before reaching the age of eighteen years lived in the same household as the step-parent and had been treated by him as a child of the family. Defences to this offence are listed in s 2 of the 1995 Act. The Incest and Related Offences (Scotland) Act 1986 had also introduced a new offence of sexual abuse of trust[2]. This offence is committed by a person over the age of sixteen years who enters into a sexual relationship with a child under the age of sixteen years of age in respect of whom he occupies a position of trust and who is a member of the same household.

Such persons are already protected by other provisions of the criminal law; this offence, however, provides for a potentially more severe penalty than would otherwise be available. It is arguable that such conduct might also amount to lewd and libidinous practices in certain circumstances[3]. The matter of persons in a position of trust is dealt with in the Sexual Offences (Scotland) Act 2009.

1 1988 SCCR 254, 1988 SLT 623.
2 Now the Criminal Law (Consolidation) (Scotland) Act 1995, s 3.
3 See *HM Advocate v K* 1994 SCCR 499; *Batty v HM Advocate* 1995 SCCR 525, 1995 SLT 1047.

Part III

SOCIAL PROTECTION OFFENCES

Chapter 12

Social offences

MISUSE OF DRUGS

12.1 The use of drugs for recreational purposes was not illegal in the nineteenth century, and it is only in the earlier years of the twentieth century that many countries began to introduce criminal sanctions directed against the marketing and possession of certain abused drugs. In the case of the United Kingdom, the first important piece of legislation was the Dangerous Drugs Act 1920. This formed the model for subsequent legislation, of which the Misuse of Drugs Act 1971, referred to below as the MDA, is the current representative. This legislation now regulates the importation, production, possession and supply of a wide range of controlled drugs. In addition, there is a large body of subsidiary legislation, in the form of statutory instruments made under the authority of the MDA, which specifies controlled drugs and regulates incidental matters such as secure storage. The government takes advice from an advisory body which monitors the categorisation of the illegal drugs and advises whether new drugs should be added to the prescribed lists. There is other important legislation in this area: the Customs and Excise Management Act 1979, sets out a number of offences relating to importation[1], while the Proceeds of Crime Act 2002 contains offences relating to the acquisition, possession and use of any proceeds of drug trafficking, as well as failure to provide information about money laundering, and hindering investigations into such operations. There is, moreover, an extensive body of law relating to the confiscation of the proceeds of drug-trafficking and forfeiture of property used in relation to such offences. This is beyond the scope of this work, however, which deals only with the main offences commonly charged under the MDA.

1 Particularly s 170, as to which see eg *Monies v HM Advocate* 1990 SCCR 645 and *R v Doran* [2015] EWCA Crim 384.

Controlled drugs

12.2 The MDA divides controlled drugs into three categories: class A, class B, and class C[1]. Class A encompasses the following commonly abused drugs:

(1) The opiates (heroin, morphine, methadone etc). These may be naturally derived from the opium poppy or produced artificially. A feature of their use is both psychological and physical dependence.
(2) Cocaine and its derivatives. Cocaine comes from the coca leaf and is a stimulant. Cocaine itself causes mainly psychological dependence; however its derivate, 'crack', produces intense physical addiction.

(3)   Hallucinogens. The most notorious of these is LSD, although other forms are widely used. These drugs have a profound psychological effect, and their impact on the chemistry of the brain can be significant. The 'dance drug' MDMA or ecstacy also falls into this category.

Class B drugs include amphetamines (stimulants), and cannabis and its derivatives (although for a period cannabis was recategorised as a class C drug, before returning to class B in May 2008). Certain derivatives of cannabis fall into class A.

Class C drugs include minor stimulants, tranquillisers such as temazepam ('jellies'), and diazepam. Other drugs which may be abused, and which are regulated to the extent that they are available only on prescription, fall outwith the scope of the MDA. There has been increasing concern about the effects of so-called 'legal highs' where the MDA has no effect because of the classification of controlled drugs. The Psychoactive Substances Bill, introduced in May 2015 aims to prohibit and disrupt the production, distribution, sale and supply of new psychoactive substances (NPS) in the UK.

1 MDA, Sch 2.

Controlled drug offences

12.3   Offences connected with controlled drugs fall into three main categories: importation and exportation offences; production and supply offences; and possession offences. The seriousness of the penalty in each case will depend on the nature of the drug involved. The supply of a class A drug, for example, will attract a more severe penalty than the supply of a class B or C drug.

Importation and exportation.   Most offences in this category will in practice be concerned with the importation of drugs. This offence is created by the combined effect of s 3(1) of the MDA (which prohibits the importation of controlled drugs) and s 170(2) of the Customs and Excise Management Act 1979[1].

A person is knowingly concerned with the importation of a controlled drug when he is aware of the fact that a substance with the importation of which he is concerned is, in fact, a controlled drug. If **A** thinks that he is bringing currency into the country, and believes (wrongly) that this is a criminal offence, he does not commit the offence of being knowingly concerned in the importation of a controlled drug even if it transpires that the package he is carrying contains heroin[2]. If, however, **A** believes that he is importing a controlled drug, whereas he is in fact bringing in a harmless powder, he commits the offence[3].

The courts have interpreted this provision widely, enabling a person to be convicted of such an offence even if the part he plays in importation comes well before, or well after, the actual importation[4]. Liability may be imposed even where the accused's part in importation has been performed entirely abroad[5]. Similarly, the performance in Scotland of any act intended to breach the provisions of corresponding law abroad is an offence punishable in Scotland[6]. There have been few convictions for such offences, the majority of controlled drugs coming into Scotland from England, but see *Gant v HM Advocate*[7] for an example. Importation offences are among the most serious of the offences under the anti-drugs regime, and sentences tend to be extremely heavy[8].

1 See eg *Montes v HM Advocate* 1990 SCCR 645.
2 *R v Taaffe* [1983] 2 All ER 625, [1983] 1 WLR 627.
3 *R v Shivpuri* 1987 AC 1, [1986] 2 All ER 334. See also *Docherty v Brown* 1996 JC 48, 1996 SCCR 136, 1996 SLT 325.
4 *R v Wall* [1974] 2 All ER 245, (1974) 59 Cr App Rep 58, *R v Jakeman* (1982) 76 Cr App Rep 223.
5 *R v Wall*, above. See also *MacNeil v HM Advocate* 1986 SCCR 288.
6 MDA, s 20; *R v Evans* (1976) 64 Cr App Rep 237.
7 2010 SC 95, 2009 SCCR 929.
8 Eg in *Howarth v HM Advocate* 1992 SCCR 525, sentences of fifteen and twenty-five years for being involved in the importation of cocaine were upheld by the High Court.

12.4   Production and supply.   It is an offence under s 4 of the MDA to produce or supply a controlled drug. Production is defined in s 37(1) and includes cultivation and laboratory production. Cultivation embraces any act which is intended to encourage the growth of a plant in which a controlled drug occurs. In *Tudhope v Robertson*[1] a cannabis plant was found in a bedroom, placed near a window, and the court held that the placing of the plant near the window (in order to encourage photosynthesis) amounted to cultivation. It is not cultivation to leave untouched a plant found growing in one's garden, but cultivation would occur if the plant were to be watered or moved. There has been an increasing incidence of cultivation of cannabis on a large scale and commercial basis; as with importation, sentences have tended to be high to reflect the seriousness of such offences.

Supply offences include actual supply of controlled drugs, being concerned in their supply, and offering to supply. It has been held that the word 'supply' should be given its ordinary natural meaning, and that the term includes sale, exchange, gift, barter; it connotes the parting of possession; it includes the distribution of drugs among a number of 'joint possessors'[2] as well as the return of drugs by a temporary custodian to a possessor[3]. What is important is the transfer of physical control of the drugs – 'questions of transfer of ownership or legal possession of [the] drugs are irrelevant'[4].

The offence of offering to supply is committed even if the accused does not have in his possession the drugs offered and even if he has no means of obtaining them[5]. What is required is some participation in a process having as its aim the supplying of material and knowledge that one is involved in such an operation[6]. It is not necessary that the person knows that what is supplied is controlled drugs; it is enough to have supplied a substance that turns out to be a controlled drug[7]. The accused may have a defence under s 28 of the MDA, which places the onus on him to show that he had no knowledge of the nature of the substance supplied[8].

The corollary of that is if a person offers to supply a harmless substance to another, erroneously believing it to be a controlled drug, he nevertheless commits an offence under s 4 of the MDA in spite of his error as to the nature of the substance[9].

1 1980 JC 62, 1980 SLT 60.
2 *R v Holmes* [1976] Crim LR 125.

3 See *Donnelly v HM Advocate* 1984 SCCR 419; *R v Maginnis* [1987] AC 303, HL. These cases are both concerned with the offence of possession with intent to supply (MDA, s 5(3)), but the principle would appear to apply to supply offences under s 4. See also *Salmon v HM Advocate* 1999 SLT 169, and the reference to the trial judge's charge.
4 *R v Delgado* [1984] 1 All ER 449.
5 *HM Advocate v Ferreira* (April 1976, unreported), Glasgow Sh Ct; discussed by K Bovey *Misuse of Drugs* (1986), p 22.
6 *Salmon* above at pp 772F–773B.
7 *Dickson v HM Advocate* 2001 JC 203; 2001 SCCR 397; at para [31], approving the directions by Temporary Judge Sir Gerald Gordon.
8 *Tudhope v McKee* 1987 SCCR 663, 1988 SLT 153.
9 *Haggard v Mason* [1976] 1 All ER 337, [1976] 1 WLR 187.

Being concerned in the supply of drugs

12.5   Being concerned in the supply requires the accused's active involvement in the supply chain. That can take many forms, from the drugs 'barons' to the street dealers, covering financiers, couriers, go-betweens, look-outs, advertisers, those who store drugs, those who divide them into deals, or package them, and suppliers of single deals. It covers supply itself, or any link in the chain of distribution from producer to ultimate consumer. It can relate to drugs supplied to, or supplied by, the accused.

The words 'concerned in' carry with them the requirement for an accused to have a degree of knowledge. One cannot be concerned in the supplying a controlled drug without awareness of being so concerned; being concerned implies a degree of participation and that in turn implies knowledge. The Crown must prove that the accused knew he was involved in the supply of something and that what he was concerned in supplying was the controlled drug libelled in the charge. Section 4(3)(b) of MDA was enacted to cover a wide variety of activities. No actual supply need take place[1].

Possession and possession with intent to supply.   It is an offence under s 5 of the MDA to be in possession of a controlled drug, or, more seriously, to be in possession of such a drug with intent to supply it to another. It is under this section that the vast majority of drug prosecutions are brought. Possession for these purposes requires both a mental and physical element: the physical element is that of control, yet even if there is control, a person is not in possession of a substance unless he knows that he has it in his control and unless he knows the general nature of the substance. A person who does not know that what he has in his possession is a controlled drug does not commit an offence under s 5[2], but conviction does not require that he should know the exact nature of the drug. If **A** has in his possession a substance which he believes to be heroin, but which is in reality cocaine, he may be convicted of possession under s 5 irrespective of his error as to the nature of the drug.

Knowledge of the existence of a drug will not be enough to secure a conviction where the accused did not have control over it. Whether an inference can be drawn in a particular case that the accused had the requisite degree of knowledge and control is very much a matter of fact and circumstance[3]. A number of cases in this area involve the issue of the presence of controlled drugs in shared accommodation: if drugs are found in a shared house or flat are all the occupants deemed to be in possession of them? The courts have indicated that something more than knowledge will be required in such a case. Access to the drug will be a factor, as indicated in *Allan v Milne*[4]. A somewhat more restrictive view was taken by Lord Cameron in *Mingay v Mackinnon*[5], in which he stated that even though cannabis smoking clearly took place on a large scale in a shared flat, the prosecution still had to prove in relation to the appellant that 'cannabis resin, or some of it, was in the possession and control of the appellant'[6]. It is probably not enough, for example, that drugs are on open view in a house in which the accused is staying. In *Bain v HM Advocate*[7], it was held that there was insufficient evidence of possession where the accused was staying temporarily in a house occupied by his girlfriend, even although in the circumstances he must have known of the presence of the drugs. On the other hand, where drugs were hidden in an accused person's room with the consent of that accused, it was held that there was a sufficient degree of control to found an inference of possession[8]. And in *Davidson v HM Advocate*[9] the accused's 'control' of the drugs was inferred from the fact that he escaped through the window of a room occupied by his girlfriend, when the police came to search that room.

1 *Salmon v HM Advocate* 1999 SLT 169, 1998 SCCR 740.
2 *McKenzie v Skeen* 1983 SLT 121. See the discussion of *Warner v Metropolitan Police Commissioner* [1968] 2 All ER 356 below, however.
3 See eg *Wali v HM Advocate* 2007 JC 111 at para [11]; 2007 SCCR 106; although this case relates to firearms the principle is identical; there has to be knowledge of the item and control of the item; see also *Bain v HM Advocate* 1992 SCCR 705, 1992 SLT 935.
4 1974 SLT (Notes) 76.
5 1980 JC 33.
6 At 35.
7 1992 SCCR 705, 1992 SLT 935.
8 *Murray v MacPhail* 1991 SCCR 245.
9 1990 SCCR 699.

12.6   The question of whether a person can be said to be in possession of the contents of a container which he possesses was addressed in *Warner v Metropolitan Police Commissioner*[1]. The Scottish courts followed the *Warner* approach. In *McKenzie v Skeen*[2], Lord Justice General Emslie said that:

'The proper interpretation to be placed upon the word "possession" as used in [the MDA] was authoritatively decided in the important case of *R v Warner* and the House of Lords held that in proof of possession it was necessary for the prosecutor to establish that the "possessor" had knowledge of the fact that he had the article which turned out to be a prohibited drug, though it was not necessary to prove that he was aware that the article or substance was a drug, far less the prohibited drug libelled .... The decision of the House of Lords was in a case arising out of an English prosecution but it was a decision upon the construction of a penal statute of United Kingdom application, and while it is technically not binding on this court, I respectfully think it is a decision which should be adopted and followed'.

However, *Warner* was not regarded as an unimpeachable statement of the law; the MDA was passed with a view to addressing some of the problems which arose from the speeches in *Warner* (see *R v McNamara* 1988 87 Cr App R

344). Scots Law was clarified by *Salmon v HM Advocate*[3]. In Salmon the court decided that it was sufficient in a case involving possession of drugs in a container, for the Crown to prove that the accused knew he had the container and that there was something in it, even if he did not know that they were controlled drugs. Once that was established, a conviction followed unless the accused could establish that he did not know or suspect that the contents were controlled drugs.

In *Amato v Walkingshaw*[4], the accused had posted a package of drugs to himself. The drugs were intercepted before they reached him. He argued that he did not possess the drugs because they had been removed from his control. The court rejected that argument.

Further problems in possession include the question of whether the possession of a minute quantity of a drug amounts to possession. The smoking of cannabis, for example, may leave traces of the drug in a pipe used for this purpose, as may the storage of a drug in a receptacle. The taking of a scraping from the pipe or receptacle may permit analysis to reveal traces of the drug, even if these traces amount to little more than a few micrograms. In *Booking v Roberts*[5] it was held that the test in such a case should be that of usability, and that there would be no possession where the quantity was so small that it could not be used by the accused. This test was disapproved, however, in *Keane v Gallacher*[6] where the court opted for the test of whether the drug could be identified in an acceptable manner. The only limitations, therefore, are those inherent in the scientific tests available, and it becomes possible for a person to be in possession of a controlled drug long after he had thought that the drugs had been disposed of or consumed, particularly as scientific developments allow for identification of smaller quantities.

1 [1968] 2 All ER 356.
2 1983 SLT 121.
3 1999 SLT 169
4 1990 JC 45, 1990 SLT 399, 1989 SCCR. 564. See Bovey 'Mens Rea in possession' Crim LB 2010 108 and *R v Doran* [2015] EWCA Crim 384, where the fact that goods were under surveillance did not give the Customs officers 'control'.
5 [1974] QB 307, [1973] 3 All ER 962. See also *R v Carver* [1978] QB 472, [1978] 3 All ER 60.
6 1980 JC 77, 1980 SLT 144.

12.7   A similar result may be achieved in a case where the accused has forgotten that he has a controlled drug in his possession. In *Gill v Lockhart*[1] cannabis was found in the accused's golf bag, having allegedly been placed there some years previously and forgotten. It was argued on the accused's behalf that the fact that he had forgotten the presence of the cannabis meant that he could no longer be said to be in possession of it, but this argument was rejected. Possession, the court said, did not require constant awareness of an object; otherwise one would not be in possession of those items of one's property which one does not have in mind at any particular time. This is undoubtedly the case, and yet a case might be made out for stating that a point will come at which it will seem counter-intuitive to say that forgotten property is still in one's possession. This might be so with property which has been forgotten for a period a number of years.

It will be a defence to a charge of possession to prove that controlled drugs were taken from another in order to prevent the commission of an offence and that all reasonable steps have been taken to ensure that the drugs were destroyed or handed over to a person lawfully entitled to take custody of them, or to prove that the drugs were received solely for the purposes of handing them over to the authorities[2]. Possession of a controlled drug for a very brief period of time will not amount to an offence provided that the contact is no more than fleeting[3].

The other offence commonly charged under s 5 is possession with intent to supply. Intention to supply may be, and usually is, inferred from the actings of the accused in general or from the quantity of the drug which is found in his possession[4]. The presence of scales, and other instruments for measuring and parcelling out drugs, may well be evidence of possession with intent to supply. A person who intends merely to return drugs to a person who gave them over for safekeeping is guilty of an offence under this section, as is a person who holds drugs bought jointly and who intends merely to give that person their 'share' of the 'stash'[5]. So the offence covers both commercial and social supply.

1 1987 SCCR 599, 1988 SLT 189.
2 MDA, s 5(4).
3 *R v Wright* [1976] Crim LR 248; *Mackay v Hogg* (11 May 1973, unreported), HCJ, discussed by K Bovey *Misuse of Drugs* (1986), p 78.
4 *Morrison v Smith* 1983 SCCR 171. See on this RS Shiels 'Possession of controlled drugs with intent to supply' (1984) 89 SCOLAG 23.
5 *Donnelly v HM Advocate* 1984 SCCR 419; *R v Maginnis* [1987] 2 WLR 765.

BREACH OF THE PEACE

12.8 Breach of the peace was one of the most commonly charged criminal offences, capable of covering a wide range of conduct which may be considered socially disruptive or offensive. A breach of the peace may actually have caused a disturbance, as in a case where the accused shouted or brawled in the street[1], or it may just be *likely* to do so, as in a case where a person shouts a slogan which could cause a fracas but which does not do so, owing to the self-restraint of others. A clear statement of both of these aspects of the offence was originally provided by Lord Dunpark in *Wilson v Brown*[2] in which he observed:

'It is well settled that a test which may be applied in charges of breach of the peace is whether the proved conduct may reasonably be expected to cause any person to be alarmed, upset or annoyed or to provoke a disturbance of the peace. Positive evidence of actual alarm, upset, annoyance or disturbance created by reprisal is not a prerequisite of conviction'.

The circumstances in which the conduct occurs will determine whether or not a breach of the peace has been committed. Behaviour which is harmless in one context may be inflammatory in another, as was demonstrated by the decision in *McAvoy v Jessop*[3]. In this case the accused was in charge of a marching Orange band which he ordered to strike up when it approached a Catholic church in front of which a priest was greeting parishioners. This was held to constitute a breach of the peace, although the playing of sectarian tunes out of sight and earshot of the church might have been quite innocent conduct.

1 This is the 'classic' instance of a breach of the peace. See eg *Derrett v Lockhart* 1991 SCCR 109.
2 1982 SCCR 49 at 51, 1982 SLT 361 at 362. For a full discussion of the offence, see M Christie *Breach of the Peace* (1990).
3 1989 SCCR 301.

12.9   The essence of the offence is the causing of alarm in the minds of the lieges. This alarm has been variously defined and refined over the years by courts. This culminated in the decision of a five-judge bench in *Harris v HM Advocate*[1], where the opinion of the court emphasised that the true nature of breach of the peace as a crime has, at the least, a public element. The opinion of the court approved *Paterson v HM Advocate*[2], wherein disturbance of even a small group of individuals in a private house may suffice, if there is a reasonable risk of such conduct being discovered (by being heard from the street for example), and *Smith v Donnelly*[3], where the court affirmed the need for conduct 'severe enough to cause alarm to ordinary people *and* threaten serious disturbance to the community'[4]. The fact that the conduct itself occurs on private property is not a decisive feature of the crime[5]. There is no need to prove *actual* alarm in such a charge, provided that the conduct is objectively likely to cause alarm[6], the converse is also true: even if a person is actually alarmed, there is no breach of the peace unless, objectively, the conduct would cause alarm to the ordinary or reasonable person.

Harris determined authoritatively that a breach of the peace cannot arise as a result of purely private conduct (it may give rise to a separate offence)[7]. A requirement that alarm be actually or potentially caused to members of the public would appear to have excluded this, in any event but in a small number of cases the courts had held that a breach of the peace could be committed even when only one or two persons (apart from the accused) are present. In *Young v Heady*[8] the accused was convicted of a breach of the peace in respect of improper suggestions he had made to boys. The suggestions were made in the presence of only one boy at a time, but the court held that this was a special case in which it was justified in holding that a breach of the peace had occurred. Notwithstanding the fact that it had remained law for almost fifty years, the court in *Harris* determined that *Young* did not reflect the law as it did not take into account the public element. The delay in such realisation can in part be attributed to the examination of the crime through the prism of the European convention on human rights, and for the need for any law creating a criminal offence to meet a standard of clarity and comprehensibility (*Smith* at p 68; p 1009). The assessment of how the 'public element' test is met was considered in *McIntyre v Nisbet*[9]. The court held that a disturbance taking place in a private flat could amount to a breach of the peace. The accused was convicted of breach of the peace by shouting and swearing at the occupant of a flat and paramedics who had attended. The High Court refused the appeal, concluding at paragraph [12]:

'[I]t is clear from the findings that the conduct complained of occurred in a flat in an urban area, namely Perth. Although the sheriff did not make specific findings addressing this issue … it is reasonable to suppose that there would be persons passing by the flat and living in the surrounding flats. Some may have observed the ambulance parked at the scene. In that context, were any member of the public to hear shouting and swearing, of the nature and duration found by the sheriff, being apparently directed towards the occupant of the flat where the paramedics were in attendance or towards the paramedics themselves, then he would be likely to be genuinely alarmed. Such conduct would threaten serious disturbance to the community.'

So, despite that fact that there was no finding that any member of the public had heard, far less been upset by, the shouting and swearing, the High Court allowed reasonable supposition to fill that gap, upholding the conviction.

1 2010 SLT 1078.
2 2008 SLT 465.
3 2002 JC 65, 2001 SLT 1007.
4 Lord Coulsfield at p 71; p 1011. This is described as 'the conjunctive test'.
5 *Macdonald v HM Advocate* 2008 JC 262 at 263; see also *McIntyre v Nisbet* [2009] HCJAC 28.
6 See eg *Wyness v Lockhart* 1992 SCCR 808.
7 See *Harris* at para [26].
8 1959 JC 66, 1959 SLT 250.
9 2009 HCJAC 28, 2009 SCL 829.

12.10   The use of abusive language to the police may be a breach of the peace even if no members of the public hear it. In *Norris v Macleod*[1] the accused was convicted of a breach of the peace when he swore at the police in a sustained fashion. In *Saltman v Allan*[2], the court held that 'it is not the law that if upon the evidence it appears that the only persons present at the scene were police officers, there can be no breach of the peace, nor is it the law that a police officer is not to be regarded as a person liable to be affected by disorderly conduct'.

It may be possible to plead self-defence in the context of a charge of breach of the peace, although that may depend on whether the libel includes taking part in a fight[3].

In addition to the common law offence of breach of the peace, which has shown remarkable flexibility[4], minor breaches of public order are covered by the provisions of the Civic Government (Scotland) Act 1982[5].

1 1988 SCCR 572. See also *Stewart v Jessop* 1988 SCCR 492.
2 1988 SCCR 640 at 644; see also *Kinnaird v Higson* 2001 SCCR 427; *McDonald v Heywood* 2002 SCCR 92.
3 *Derrett v Lockhart* 1991 SCCR 109.
4 See 'Breach of the peace and the ECHR' article by Pamela R Ferguson 2001 Edin LR 145 for a comprehensive list of examples of the flexibility.
5 Particularly ss 46–56, covering matters such as drunkenness, urinating in public and displaying obscene material. Although s 48 has been superseded by the Dog Fouling (Scotland) Act 2003.

Section 38 of the Criminal Justice and Licensing (Scotland) Act 2010

12.11   As a consequence of the decision in *Harris*, the requirement of a public element in the crime of breach of the peace, and a general recognition of the need to re-examine the law[1], the Government enacted s 38 of the Criminal Justice and Licensing (Scotland) Act 2010; if an offender behaves in a threatening or abusive manner, and the behaviour would be likely to cause a reasonable person fear or alarm and it is either intended to cause such fear and alarm or the perpetrator is reckless as to whether that result ensues, then the offence is committed. Behaviour includes things said, or communicated, as well as things done, and can include a single act or a course of conduct, recognising that the cumulative effect of minor behaviour could breach the threshold.

Despite Young having governed the test for breach of the peace until *Harris*, a period of fifty years or so, the interpretation of s 38 caused difficulty, culminating in the convening of a five-judge bench to resolve the difficulty. A huge number of cases were marked for prosecution after the introduction of s 38, so the identification of the correct approach was of considerable interest.

Rooney v Brown[2] was initially seen as authority for the proposition that there was no requirement for any person to suffer actual fear or alarm – the behaviour had only to be likely to cause such a reaction in a reasonable person. However in the case of *Jolly v HMA*[3], the court held that *Rooney* was not authority for that proposition, as it had focused on the nature of the behaviour and could be distinguished on its facts. The judges in *Jolly* said, '… [I]t is clear to us that what has been legislated for In terms of s 38 … are circumstances where real fear and alarm has been suffered by a real complainer.'

That decision caused confusion and uncertainty in both the prosecution and determination of such cases. The matter was authoritatively determined in *Patterson v Harvie*[4], where the five-judge bench restored the *Rooney* approach. The Lord Justice General said:

> '… I do not agree that there is any ambiguity in s 38(1). Section 38(1) sets out three clear and concise constituents of the offence. Paragraphs (a) and (b) define the *actus reus* of the offence. Whether the accused has behaved in a threatening or abusive manner and whether that behaviour would be likely to cause a reasonable person to suffer fear or alarm are straightforward questions of fact. Paragraph (c) sets out the *mens rea* that is required. It seems to me that the question under paragraph (b) is not whether the complainer suffered actual fear or alarm. If it had been the intention of the Parliament that the complainer must have suffered actual fear or alarm, paragraph (b) could have said exactly that. On the contrary, paragraph (b) sets an objective test. It provides that the requirement of the subsection is made out if the behaviour would be likely to cause a reasonable person to suffer fear or alarm. A reasonable person is someone who is not of abnormal sensitivity. If a reasonable person would have suffered fear or alarm, it follows on the objective test that it is no defence if the behaviour causes no fear or alarm to the individual complainer, who might be, for example, an intrepid Glasgow police officer. In my view, the essence of the statutory offence is that the accused's conduct is to be judged by an objective test in which the actual effect of the threatening or abusive behaviour on those who experience it is irrelevant. If the requirements of paragraphs (a) and (c) are made out, the crime is complete if the accused's behaviour would be likely to cause fear or alarm to the hypothetical reasonable person.'

Accordingly, after a flurry of case law, it has been established that there is no requirement for an identified victim for the offence to be committed.

Section 38(2) provides a defence that the behaviour was reasonable. The defence of self-defence, arguable available in breach of the peace (above) is not available. In *Urquhart v HMA*[5] the High Court said the following:

'First, it seems to us inevitable that if a person conducts themselves in a manner which accords with the descriptions in parts (i) and (ii) and the reason for him doing so was that he was acting in self-defence in the sense that he genuinely thought he was in danger, he is bound to have intended to cause fear and/or alarm to his assailant. However cogent the case of self-defence might be, it could not, accordingly, prevent part (iii) being established. Secondly, the statutory defence afforded by s 38(2) is plainly wide enough to cover all and anything that an accused person may wish to advance to the effect that he was in fact acting in self-defence. Further, when doing so, it would not be necessary for the accused to meet all the requirements of self-defence that apply when pled as a special defence. The availability of a reasonable alternative means of escape from the danger would not, for instance, deprive him of the defence. There would be no prejudice to the accused in directing him to s 38(2) if he seeks to raise any issue of self-defence. He may in fact be in a better position than if he were constrained by the requirements of the special defence. We are satisfied that the relevant statutory intention clearly was that that is where any such issue should be raised.'

1 See *Breach of the Peace* by Pamela S Ferguson EUP 2013, reviewed by Fiona Leverick 2014 *Edin LR* 157.
2 2013 SCL 615, 2013 SCCR 334.
3 2014 JC 171, 2013 SLT 1100, 2013 SCL 832, 2013 SCCR 511.
4 2015 JC 118, 2014 SLT 857, 2014 SCL 606, 2014 SCCR 521.
5 [2015] HCJAC 101. See also the observation in *Patterson v Harvie* at paragraphs [27]-[29].

Offensive weapons

12.12   The carrying of weapons in public was originally dealt with by the Prevention of Crime Act 1953; the offences relating to the carrying of offence weapons are now found in the Criminal Law (Consolidation) (Scotland) Act 1995 at s 47 which makes it an offence to carry on one's person, in public, an offensive weapon[1] without lawful authority or reasonable excuse. (There are particular provisions made for knives; these are discussed below.) Offensive weapons are divided into three categories: (1) weapons made for the purposes of causing injury to others (bayonets, guns[2] etc); (2) weapons which are adapted for such a purpose (a sharpened steel comb, for example); and (3) items which could be weapons such as hunting knives, shotguns or other items such as a hammer, or baseball bat, which have normal uses not related to use as a weapon which have an innocent purpose. In the case of weapons in classes (1) and (2), the onus is upon the accused to prove that he had the weapon under lawful authority or with a reasonable excuse. In the case of weapons in class (3), the Crown must show that the accused had the weapon on him with the intention of causing personal injury to another.

1 See generally RS Shiels *Offensive Weapons* (W Green Essential Legislation 2013).
2 These are offensive weapons *per se*. Cf *Tudhope v O'Neill* 1982 SCCR 45 (flick knife) with *Woods v Heywood* 1988 SCCR 434 (machete, which also has an innocent use). See also the Firearms Act 1968, s 16; the offence of carrying a firearm with intent to endanger life or cause serious injury to property.

12.13   It is a defence to a charge of possession of an offensive weapon to have lawful authority, or a reasonable excuse, for having the weapon (s 47(1)). Proof of such lawful authority, or reasonable excuse, lies with the accused. A fear of crime does not justify the carrying of an offensive weapon. Thus, a taxi driver who carried with him in his taxi a piece of rubber hose with metal in the end of it was convicted of an offence under the Act in spite of his contention that the risk which a taxi driver runs at night justified the carrying of such a weapon[1]. Members of the public who run no more than the normal risks of violence common to all have no reasonable excuse for the carrying of a weapon. Fear of future violence is not an excuse. For example, it would not be legal for a person fearing sexual or other attack to carry a canister of tear gas spray. In *Lunn v HMA*[2], the accused argued that a reasonable excuse for her possession of a broken bottle arose because of the threat of an attack upon her. The sheriff directed the jury that fear of an attack was not a reasonable excuse. The High Court allowed the appeal, on the concession of the Crown, saying the following:

> '… [W]e understand the Crown's position to be that taking possession of an offensive weapon in anticipation of or fear of future violence would not constitute a reasonable excuse (cf the Lord Justice Clerk in *Grieve v McLeod* 1967 JC 32 at page 36). However matters would be different where a person took possession of a weapon during an incident where he or she was under attack, for the purpose of preventing or discouraging further violence. in the circumstances of the present case … it was for the jury to decide whom to believe and whom to disbelieve, and at least one of the versions of events which was put before the jury in the course of the trial suggested that the appellant, when under attack and *in extremis*, had come into possession of the bottle and used it solely to attempt to prevent further attack (cf dicta of Lord Carloway at paragraph [7] of *Donnelly v HMA* 2009 SCCR 512).'

So, the possession of an offensive weapon may be reasonable if the accused is under attack and had come into possession of a weapon during an incident to be used solely to prevent further attack; the possession cannot be prospective, in anticipation of an attack. The availability of that defence is likely to be of very limited application.

The issue of reasonable excuse was also considered in *Frame v Kennedy*[3]. The accused had weapons with him as part of a police uniform which he wore for his work as a stripper; the court held that there was evidence to support the finding that the accused had a reasonable excuse.

1 *Grieve v Macleod* 1967 JC 32, 1967 SLT 70. On reasonable excuse, see also *Hemming v Annan* 1982 SCCR 432 (Nunchaca sticks).
2 2015 HCJAC 103.
3 2008 HCJAC 25.

Possession of knives or bladed articles in a public place

12.14   Concern over the use of knives in assaults has resulted in legislation aimed specifically at their being carried in public. The Carrying of Knives etc (Scotland) Act 1991 made it an offence, subject to certain defences, to have on one in a public place, without good reason or lawful authority, a knife or blade other than a folding pocket knife with a blade under three inches in length. This was re-enacted in s 49 of the Criminal Law Consolidation Scotland Act 1995. Again a defence exists if the person charged can prove that he had good reason, or lawful authority, for having the article with him. *McGuire v Higson*[1] determined that taking a recently purchased and wrapped knife home from the place of purchase constituted a good defence. The Knives Act 1997 deals with the marketing of 'combat knives' and is designed to control efforts to advertise and sell knives in a way which portrays them as suitable for violent use.

1 2003 SCCR 440; 2003 SLT 890; see also *Frame v Kennedy* above.

Chapter 13

Road traffic offences

13.1   Road traffic law in Scotland is now primarily based on two statutes: the Road Traffic Act 1988 (RTA) (as amended), and the Road Traffic Offenders Act 1988 (RTO). These Acts replace much, although not all, of the previously existing legislation, including the whole of the Road Traffic Act 1972, which previously contained the bulk of road traffic provisions. This chapter deals only with the main offences contained in ss 1 to 5 of the RTA 1988, as already amended by the Road Traffic Act 1991, and includes consideration of the changes introduced by the Road Safety Act 2006.

SOME DEFINITIONS

Driving

13.2   The Acts apply to both England and Scotland, and while English decisions are generally regarded as being relevant in Scottish cases, and vice versa, the two jurisdictions have sometimes differed in their approach to the legislation in more or less identical situations. The interpretation of the word 'driving' provides a good example. A pushes his car along the street, controlling the steering wheel through an open window. Is he 'driving' the car, for the purposes of the RTA? In Scotland the answer appears to be 'yes'. In *Ames v McLeod*[1] it was held that when one is 'in a substantial sense controlling the movement and direction of the car'[2], one is 'driving' for the purposes of the Road Traffic Acts. It is not essential in Scotland that the engine be running, or the accused actually sitting in the car. The opposite conclusion was reached in the English case of *R v McDonagh*[3], in which the Court of Appeal approved the *Ames v McLeod* test, but added to it the rider that 'it is still necessary to consider whether the activity in question can fall within the ordinary meaning of the word "driving"'[4], in order to prevent absurdities. There was an unsuccessful attempt in *McArthur v Valentine*[5] to import this further requirement into Scots law. In that case the court said that absurdity was avoided by giving due weight to the words 'in a substantial sense', and on the facts, followed *Ames v McLeod*. There must be both elements to the control (that is, movement *and* direction). In *Lockhart v Smith*[6], a milk-boy, on instruction released the handbrake on a milk-float, but did not touch the steering wheel. He was held not to have been 'driving'. The 'substantial control' criterion means that it is possible for two people to be 'driving' a car at one time, for example where a driving instructor uses dual controls to assist a learner driver.

There was an ingenious attempt to elide the decision in *Ames* in *Hoy v McFadyen*[7]. The accused had been sitting in the driving seat of a car in which the handbrake was broken. He had started the car, disengaged the gears and put the footbrake on. He argued that 'driving' required motion. The court held that his actions had gone beyond preparation for driving. Driving involved the control of movement and direction of a vehicle and there had been active intervention, even if that was to prevent movement and direction. In a situation where a person merely steers a vehicle which is being towed, such a person has only limited control over the movement and direction of the vehicle, and may not, in terms of the case law be convicted of reckless driving[8]. It has been held in England that a passenger who seizes the steering wheel of the car in which he is travelling, causing the car to swerve into pedestrians, is not 'driving' and cannot therefore be convicted of offences of dangerous or careless driving under the current legislation[9]. Standing *Ames v McLeod* it may be doubted whether this decision would be followed in Scotland.

1 1969 JC 1.
2 At 3, per Lord Justice-General Clyde.
3 [1974] QB 448, (1974) 59 Cr App Rep 55. Cf *Gunnell v DPP* [1994] RTR 151 in which it was held that a person sitting astride a moped and propelling it with his feet *was* driving, distinguishing *McDonagh*.
4 [1974] QB 448 at 452, per Lord Widgery CJ.
5 1990 JC 146, 1989 SCCR 704.
6 1979 SLT (Sh Ct) 52.
7 2000 JC 313, 2000 SLT 1060, 2000 SCCR 875.
8 *Wallace v Major* [1946] KB 473. Doubts have been expressed about this case (for example, in *R v McDonagh* (1974) 59 Cr App Rep 55); a person in this situation can certainly be convicted of driving while disqualified: *McQuade v Anderton* [1980] 3 All ER 540, [1989] 1 WLR 154.
9 *DPP v Hastings* [1993] RTR 205.

Driving and automatism

13.3   Following the decision of the High Court in *Ross v HM Advocate*[1], there was now a limited defence of non-insane automatism in Scots law. However, the decision in *Ross* was in terms that automatism negates *mens rea*. Many driving offences are offences of strict liability for which proof of *mens rea* is unnecessary.

The matter was further considered in the context of a drink driving offence in *Finegan v Heywood*[2]. The accused had been convicted of a drink driving offence committed whilst in a state of parasomnia (sleep disorder). He appealed arguing that he should have been acquitted on the grounds of non-insane automatism. He relied on the decision in *Ross*. The court dismissed the appeal, holding that such a defence was not available where the parasomnia had been induced by alcohol, and the accused knew from previous experience that his condition was preceded by the consumption of alcohol. The Lord Justice General said:

'The defence of automatism cannot in our view be established upon proof that the appellant was in a transitory state of parasomnia which was the result of, or indeed induced by, deliberate and self-induced intoxication. In that regard the decision in *Ross* is distinguishable since it dealt only with those cases where there was no disease of the mind and where the factor which had caused the impairment was not self-induced'[3].

Thus, provided the accused's automatic state was due to some external cause, such as a blow to the head, or the ingestion of drugs, for which the accused was not himself responsible, and the effect of which he was not bound to foresee[4], automatism may be a defence even to absolute driving offences. In cases where the accused knows that he has some condition, such as diabetes, which may result in unconscious 'behaviour', it seems that it will be difficult or impossible for him to establish the defence, since in *Ross* terms, he is bound to foresee his state of automatism[5]. In a case of careless driving, therefore, the lack of 'due care and attention' rests on his knowledge *prior to the driving*, that he might become unconscious while driving. Indeed, it would appear to the case that a charge of dangerous driving would be relevant under such circumstances[6].

1 1991 SCCR 823, 1991 SLT 564.
2 2000 JC 444, 2000 SLT 905, 2000 SCCR 460.
3 *Finegan* at p 451 para 10, in turn quoting Ross at p 213.
4 See *Ross v HM Advocate* 1991 SCCR 823, 1991 SLT 564.
5 See *McLeod v Mathieson* 1993 SCCR 488, Sh Ct, in which *Farrell v Stirling* was distinguished on the grounds that in the latter case, the accused had been affected by his first hypoglycaemic attack and was therefore not bound to foresee its occurrence.
6 *R v Marison* [1996] Crim LR 909.

Attempting to drive

13.4   Whether there has been an attempt to drive is largely a question of fact, but one which looks primarily to the actions and intentions of the driver. It is, for example, irrelevant that the attempt was doomed to failure, because the vehicle had broken down, had been clamped, or because the driver was using the wrong key[1].

Mechanically propelled vehicle

13.5   'Motor vehicle' is defined as 'a mechanically propelled vehicle intended or adapted for use on the roads'[2]. Thus, if a vehicle is not intended for use on the public highway, it may fall outwith the definition. This may lead to anomalous results. In *McLean v McCabe*[3], for example, it was held that 'dumper trucks' used in the construction industry are not motor vehicles, since not intended for use on the roads, while in *Woodward v James Young (Contractors) Ltd*[4], the opposite conclusion was reached in respect of agricultural tractors since they are intended for occasional use on the highways. In Grant v McHale[5], the definition was refined. The High Court, in looking at the provenance of a mini-motorbike, concluded that it was clear that it was mechanically propelled, and was capable of carrying an adult driver, and that no more was required to satisfy the statutory definition. The definition emphasises the construction of the vehicle, rather than the way in which it is used. A vehicle remains a mechanically propelled vehicle even if it is being pedalled or pushed along a road[6]. A vehicle will not fall within the definition if it has reached 'such a state of mechanical or structural decrepitude' that it would be nonsense to describe it as a mechanically propelled vehicle[7]. However, a vehicle which has broken down is still a mechanically propelled vehicle and depending on its condition, may still fall within the definition[8]. In *Newbury v Simmonds*[9] it was held that a car even remains a 'motor vehicle' when its engine has been removed, although it would be different if there was evidence that the engine had been permanently removed or could not easily be replaced.

1 See eg *Kelly v Hogan* [1982] RTR 352; *R v Farrance* [1978] RTR 225, [1978] 67 Cr App Rep 136. This is, in any event, simply an application of the general rule that factual impossibility is no bar to a conviction for attempt: see *Docheny v Brown* 1996 JC 48, 1996 SCCR 136, 1996 SLT 325.
2 RTA, s 185(1). This has been amended by s 4 of the RTA 1991, so that in some offences, it is enough for a vehicle to be 'mechanically propelled'; this captures off road or 'toy' vehicles which have not, in fact, been intended for use on the road.
3 1964 SLT (Sh Ct) 39.
4 1958 JC 28, 1958 SLT 289.
5 2005 SLT 1057, 2005 SCCR 559.
6 See eg *McEachran v Hurst* [1978] RTR 462.
7 *Tudhope v Every* 1976 JC 42.
8 *McEachran v Hurst*, above.
9 [1961] 2 QB 345, [1961] 2 All ER 318.

Road or other public place

13.6   The term 'road' is defined in the Roads (Scotland) Act 1984, s 151), as being any way over which there is a public right of passage, and includes verges, bridges and tunnels, and the RTA, s 192(1) which adds 'and any other way to which the public has access'[1]. The particular definition which applies will need to be considered because different circumstances will give rise to different definitions. The road need not be a public road, but the extent to which private roads fall within the definition is likely to turn on the particular circumstances of the case. In *Hogg v Nicholson*[2] it was held that a road on a private estate, and marked 'Private Road' was nevertheless a road within the statutory definition, since some members of the public, such as traders and the police, had access to it. That case was however decided under a definition of 'road' couched in terms of access[3] rather than 'public right of passage', and it may be that the courts will now take a different view of this type of situation[4].

Brown v Braid[5] defined 'road or other public place' as a place 'on which members of the public might be found, and over which they might be expected to be passing, or over which they are in use to have access'. Fields and other pieces of ground used for parking[6], hotel driveways[7], lay-bys[8], garage forecourts[9], and even school playgrounds[10] have all been held to be public places under the definition. In *Young v Carmichael*[11], however, it was pointed out that a place is not a public place merely because some members of the public have access to it. There must be evidence to show that members of the public in general had access to the place in the sense that they 'normally resorted to it and so might be expected to be there'. Thus, if signs make it clear that only residents are permitted in a car park, it is probably not a public place. The same position was adopted in *Yates v Murray*[12]. The accused had been convicted of drunk driving. He appealed, arguing that the locus in question was not a road or public place. The High Court held that locus had to be used 'by the public generally', rather than by individual members accessing the few houses served by it. The onus was on the Crown to establish the nature of the road in question. In *Rodger v Normand*[13], the accused was charged with careless driving in a school playground. However, although it was local authority policy that the public should not have access to the place, no steps were in fact taken to exclude them, and it was clear on the evidence that children and other members of the public regularly used it for various purposes. It was therefore held to be a public place within the meaning of the legislation.

Accident

13.7 Whether or not an accident has occurred may be of importance in a number of situations, for example where a driver fails to stop after an accident[14]. It is very much a question of fact in each case whether an accident has occurred, and rather than formulating a precise definition, the courts have preferred to apply a 'common sense' approach. In particular, it seems that the term is not to be confined to cases where there has been an 'adverse physical result'. In *Pryde v Brown*[15], for example, it was held that where pedestrians walking on a main road had been forced to jump out of the way of a speeding car, an accident had occurred. The court concluded at page 315:

> 'The appellant, by his driving unlawfully, forced them to do something they otherwise would not have done. We do not think that, if they had been injured in taking such avoiding action – say by spraining an ankle – it could be said that an accident had not occurred. This indeed was conceded by counsel for the appellant. The mere fact that in taking this avoiding action no injury was suffered, cannot in our view make any difference. We are of the opinion that it is not advisable to attempt to give an all-embracing definition of "accident" in this context, which would cover every variety of circumstance.'

Furthermore, an incident may be described as an 'accident' even where it results from a deliberate act[16].

1   See Andrew Brown QC, *Wheatley's Road Traffic Law in Scotland* (5th edn, 2014) Bloomsbury Professional.
2   1968 SLT 265.
3   Road Traffic Act 1960, s 257(1).
4   See *Young v Carmichael* 1991 SCCR 332, discussed below, and cf *Wheatley* at para 1.8:1.
5   1984 SCCR 286, 1985 SLT 37 at 38.
6   *Paterson v Ogilvy* 1957 JC 42, 1957 SLT 354; *McDonald v McEwen* 1953 SLT (Sh Ct) 26.
7   *Dunne v Keane* 1976 JC 39.
8   *MacNeill v Dunbar* 1965 SLT (Notes) 79.
9   *Brown v Braid* 1985 SLT 37, 1984 SCCR 286.
10 *Rodger v Normand* 1994 SCCR 861.
11 1991 SCCR 332.
12 2004 JC 16, 2003 SLT 1348.
13 1994 SCCR 861, 1995 SLT 411.
14 An offence under s 170 of the RTA.
15 1982 SCCR 26, 1982 SLT 314.
16 *Staffordshire Chief Constable v Lees* [1981] RTR 506.

Using, causing or permitting

13.8 The phrase 'using, causing or permitting' is encountered in relation to contraventions of the licensing requirements, and construction and use regulations. Liability for 'use' offences seems to be strict, and knowledge of the contravention is irrelevant[1]. Offences involving the 'causing' or 'permitting' of some contravention, on the other hand, require some degree of knowledge of the circumstances giving rise to the contravention[2]. Wilful blindness may suffice however[3].

THE MAIN OFFENCES

13.9   The main offences are contained in ss 1 to 5 of the RTA, as amended.

Section 1: Causing death by dangerous driving

In a prosecution under s 1, it is necessary to show that the accused drove in a dangerous manner, and thus caused the death of some person. 'Dangerous driving' is defined in s 2A of the Act[4] which states:

'(1)   … a person is to be regarded as driving dangerously if (and, subject to subsection 2 below, only if):

(a)   the way he drives falls far below what would he expected of a competent and careful driver, and

(b)   it would be obvious to a competent and careful driver that driving in that way would be dangerous.

(2)   A person is also to be regarded as driving dangerously for the purposes of ss 1 and 2 above if it would be obvious to a competent and careful driver that driving the vehicle in its current state would be dangerous'[5].

1 For a review of the authorities, see *Valentine v MacBrayne Haulage Ltd* 1986 SCCR 692.
2 *Smith of Maddiston v Macnab* 1975 JC 48, 1975 SLT 86. Cf *Lockhart v National Coal Board* 1981 SLT 161.
3 See eg *Carmichael v Hannaway* 1987 SCCR 236. See also para 2.24, and Wheatley para 1.10
4 Inserted into the RTA 1988 by the RTA 1991, s 1.
5 See *HM Advocate v Campbell* 1993 SCCR 765, 1994 SLT 502. While under the un-amended legislation it may have been that the accused actually had to have known of the state of the vehicle, it seems clear that under the s 2A definition, the test is once again wholly objective. It should be noted that where the alleged dangerousness of the driving rests upon the state of the vehicle, it is possible that a person responsible for the state of the vehicle, but who is not the driver, may be guilty art and part with the person who actually drives it: see *R v Loukes* [1996] 1 Cr App Rep 444.

13.10   The danger in question is danger to any person or serious damage to property. Awareness of danger is assessed objectively, but it is significant that s 2A allows a court to take into consideration any circumstances shown to have been within the knowledge of the accused[1]. Thus special knowledge (such as knowledge that young children are apt to be in a particular part of a road) may impose a duty to take particular care.

Causation.   Where an accused is charged under s 1 it is vital to establish a causal link between the dangerous driving and the victim's death. In doing so, it is enough that the accused's driving was a 'material' or operative cause of the death. Thus, there may be a conviction under s 1 even if the victim is contributorily negligent. In *Watson v HM Advocate*[2], for example, the victim drove through a junction without waiting for a filter signal. The accused was also adjudged to have been reckless however, and was convicted of the s 1 offence.

For the purposes of s 1, it seems that the 'person' killed as a result of the driving need not be in life at the time of the accident. There was a conviction under the section in *McCluskey v HM Advocate*[3], where a fetus was *in utero* at the time the accident occurred, was born alive by caesarian section, but died shortly thereafter as a result of the injuries sustained by his mother[4]. In reaching this conclusion, the court followed the English view that there is manslaughter where a child who has been born alive, dies as a result of injuries sustained while *in utero*[5]. Scots law on this point is unsettled, although it seems likely that in such a case a future court would follow the general approach taken in *McCluskey*[6].

1 RTA, s 2A(3).
2 (1978) SCCR Supp 192. See also *R v Hennigan* [1971] 3 All ER 133, (1971) 55 Cr App Rep 262.
3 1988 SCCR 629, 1989 SLT 175.
4 The civil law takes a similar view. In *Hamilton v Fife Health Board* 1993 SLT 624, IH, it was held that for the purposes of the Damages (Scotland) Act 1976, a 'person' may include a fetus *in utero* at the time injuries are sustained.
5 See *West* (1848) 2 Cox CC 500; *Kwok Chak Ming* (No 1) [1963] HKLR 226, 349.
6 See discussion at para 10.1 above.

Section 1A: Causing Serious Injury by Dangerous Driving

13.11   This provision was introduced by the Legal Aid, Sentencing and Punishment of Offenders Act 2012, although the matter which it concerns might have been addressed by looking at sentencing powers. It makes it an offence to cause serious injury (which means severe physical injury) by driving dangerously. The same test outlined above applies in relation to the definition of dangerous driving. There are no reported Scottish cases on s 1A; all the English reported cases relate to sentencing[1].

1 For example *R v Jenkins (Nathan)* [2015] EWCA Crim 105; [2015] 1 Cr App R (S) 70; [2015] RTR 16; [2015] Crim. LR 467 (CA (Crim Div)).

Section 2: Dangerous driving

13.12   Dangerous driving is an offence *per se*, even if no fatality, or indeed any other adverse consequence, results from the driving[1]. The test to be applied is the statutory one outlined above. The move from 'reckless' to 'dangerous' driving made by the Road Traffic Act 1991, was undertaken to allay fears that the requirement for recklessness placed too much emphasis on the behaviour of the driver rather than the quality of the driving. But the test for reckless driving in Scotland was always objective. Indeed, so objective was the test that reckless driving might be inferred purely from the abnormal behaviour of the vehicle in question[2]. In *Allan v Paterson*[3], the High Court said that a person drives recklessly when the quality of the driving:

'fell far below the standard of driving expected of the competent and careful driver and that it occurred either in the face of obvious and material dangers which were or should have been observed, appreciated and guarded against, or in circumstances which showed a complete disregard for any potential dangers which might result from the way in which the vehicle was being driven'.

The test for dangerous driving under the new provisions, outlined above, is therefore strikingly similar to the test for recklessness under the old legislation, and seems likely to produce similar results. In *Abbas v Houston*[4], the accused drove at 108 miles per hour along a straight stretch of motorway in good driving conditions. His conviction under s 2 was nevertheless upheld on the basis that the grossly excessive speed could of itself be described as dangerous[5]. The same result was reached, in similar circumstances, in relation to the superseded offence, in the case of *Frame v Lockhart*[6]. Accordingly, it seems that the new provisions will make little difference to the outcome in cases involving very bad driving, and old cases on reckless driving remain relevant to cases brought under the amended s 2. In *Fraser v Lockhart*[7], for example, there was a conviction for reckless driving where the accused drove at speed while being pursued by the police, and, without signalling, skidded into a farm road in an attempt to escape. Again, in *Rattray v Colley*[8], a champion go-kart racer performed a 'display manoeuvre' in a public street. In spite of the accused's prowess as a driver, he was convicted of reckless driving since it could be inferred that he had disregarded the danger to himself, his passenger, and to vehicles entering the street from either direction.

1 See *O'Toole v McDougall* 1986 SCCR 56.
2 *Wheatley* para 2.3:4, and cf *Pagan v Ferguson* 1976 SLT (Notes) 44.
3 See *Allan v Paterson* 1980 JC 57.
4 1993 SCCR 1019.
5 While the courts have consistently held that the matter is one of fact and degree in each case, and there may be cases where all potential dangers can be excluded in circumstances such as these, it will nevertheless be extremely difficult to argue against a conviction under s 2 where the accused was travelling much in excess of the statutory speed limit. See *inter alia Trippick v Orr* 1994 SCCR 736, 1995 SLT 272; *Brown v Orr* 1994 SCCR 668. Cf *Brunton v Lees* 1993 SCCR 98, in which the accused was acquitted of careless driving under s 3 where he had driven some 20–30 miles per hour over the prescribed limit, but at 3 am.
6 1985 SLT 367.
7 1992 SCCR 275.
8 1991 GWD 1–71; cf *O'Toole v McDougall* 1986 SCCR 56 at 59, per Lord Justice-General Emslie.

Section 2B: Causing death by careless or inconsiderate driving

13.13   The Road Safety Act 2006 created the new offence of causing death by careless or inconsiderate driving. It deals with the perceived gap in the law, demonstrated by cases such as *McCallum v Hamilton*[1], where the court held that the word 'fatally' describing the injuries sustained by victims of a road traffic accident should be deleted when the charge was one of careless driving; this was on the basis that there was no offence of causing death by careless driving, and that it had no bearing on the sentencing exercise.

Careless driving is now defined by s 3ZA of the RTA[2]. This provision has effect for the purposes of the offences of causing death by careless driving (s 2B), causing death by careless driving when under the influence of drink or drugs (s 3A)[3], and careless driving.

Section 3ZA(2) provides that a person drives without due care and attention if 'the way he drives falls below what would be expected of a competent and careful driver'; there is a curious qualification to this in s 3ZA(3) providing that regard must be had 'not only to the circumstances of which [the hypothetical driver] could be expected to be aware, but also to any circumstances shown to have been within the knowledge of the accused'.

This distinction has been criticised[4] as undermining the objective nature of the test of carelessness.

Section 3ZA(4) provides that a person is driving without reasonable consideration for others only if 'those persons are inconvenienced by his driving', a provision which arguably imports the English interpretation into Scots Law[5].

1 1986 JC 1, 1986 SLT 156.
2 Inserted by s 30 of the Road Safety Act 2006.
3 Inserted by s 3 of the 1991 Act.
4 'Road traffic law reform'; article by Peter W Ferguson 2007 SLT 27.
5 See *Wheatley's Road Traffic Law in Scotland* (5th edn 2014, Bloomsbury Professional) at para 2.10.

Section 3A: Causing death by careless driving when under influence of drink or drugs

13.14   Section 3A, inserted by s 3 of the 1991 Act, created a specific new offence which is committed by a person who causes death while driving without due care and attention, or without reasonable consideration for other persons, and who is, at the time, unfit to drive through drink or drugs, who has more than the prescribed limit of alcohol in his system, or who refuses to provide a specimen within the statutory time limit when required to do so[1].

1 Refusal to provide a specimen may also be a ground for conviction of this offence.

Section 3: Careless and inconsiderate driving

13.15   Section 3 contains two separate offences – driving without due care and attention, and driving without reasonable consideration for other road users[1]. Although each element is now subject to a statutory definition, the cases which have developed the law are useful in assessing the interpretation of the new definition. These cases must be read with the caveat that they preceded the introduction of s 3ZA. In *Allan v Patterson*[2], the court appeared to accept a Crown submission that 'driving "recklessly" accordingly, is driving which demonstrates a gross degree of carelessness in the face of dangers'.

(i) Driving without due care and attention. As in ss 1 and 2, the test for careless driving is an objective one, based on the standard of the competent and careful driver[3]. It seems that the driving must also be judged with reference to the reasonably experienced driver – no concession is made to the learner driver whose driving falls below the required standard[4]. The emergency services like-

wise have no immunity in this regard[5]. As with the previous sections, sub-standard driving may be inferred from the facts and circumstances proved, and it is unnecessary to have any eye-witness to the driving in question. In *Pagan v Ferguson*[6], Lord Justice-Clerk Wheatley said:

'Looking to the stark facts that this car, for no reason that has been explained, left the road on a perfectly straight stretch, travelled 120 feet along the verge, and then collided with a rock face, is in itself sufficient to raise a prima facie inference of negligence'.

1 Although it may be that where driving is said to be inconsiderate, it must also be careless: see *Wilson v Macphail* 1991 SCCR 170.
2 1980 JC 57.
3 See *Simpson v Peat* [1952] 2 QB 24, [1952] 1 All ER 447; *Wilson v Macphail* 1991 SCCR 170.
4 *McCrane v Riding* [1938] 1 All ER 157.
5 See eg *Marshall v Osmond* [1983] QB 1034, [1983] 2 All ER 225; *DPP v Harris* [1995] 1 Cr App Rep 170, which holds that the emergency services have no defence of necessity *qua* emergency services.
6 1976 SLT (Notes) 44.

13.16   The court must, however, take all the circumstances into account, in deciding whether or not the driving has fallen below the required standard. Thus, a finding of careless driving is not inevitable merely because the driver made a mistake. If, for example, a driver is confronted with an emergency, his driving will be judged in the light of the situation, and will not necessarily be adjudged careless (or dangerous) merely because, with hindsight, it is obvious that he did the wrong thing[1]. There must, however, be a genuine emergency. There was, for example, no emergency in *Stebbings v Westwater*[2], where the accused, without stopping, attempted to swat a fly on his windscreen. Failure to observe the Highway Code, while not conclusive of the question, may be one factor tending to establish that driving was careless or dangerous[3].

Driving 'without due care and attention' covers a very wide range of conduct, from the everyday error of the person who turns without signalling, to the seriously negligent driving of one who, perhaps, causes a major accident, but which falls short of the test for dangerous driving. As with dangerous driving, there may be a conviction of careless driving where an accident has occurred partly as a result of another's carelessness[4].

1 [1952] 2 QB 24 at 28, [1952] 1 All ER 447 at 449, per Lord Goddard CJ.
2 1991 GWD 1–55.
3 See RTA, s 38 (7), and *McCrone v Normand* 1989 SLT 332.
4 *Tail v Lees* 1991 GWD 2–122.

13.17   *(ii) Driving without reasonable consideration for others.*   The offence of driving without reasonable consideration is similarly wide in scope, and no list of possible examples can hope to be exhaustive.

'Typical cases of driving without reasonable consideration for other persons using the road may include ... the driving of a vehicle too close to the driver in front ...; driving with full beam headlights at night ...; driving needlessly in the outside lane of a motorway or dual-carriageway, or overtaking in the inside lane; ... or driving deliberately at high speed through pools of water causing pedestrians to be splashed ...'[1].

There was some doubt, however, as to whether in such cases it is necessary to prove that the driving complained of resulted in any actual inconvenience or hazard to other road users, a doubt dispelled by s 3ZA. There is English authority to the effect that in the absence of evidence of inconvenience to others, there could be no conviction under this leg of s 3, which appears to have informed the provisions of s 3ZA[2].

The common law. The RTAs did not abolish the common law offence of 'recklessly or furiously driving a vehicle (or riding a cycle) to the danger of the lieges'[3]. While this offence is uncommon in practice[4], the common law remains available to the prosecutor in unusual situations. In *Macphail v Clark*[5], for example, a farmer burned straw in a field next to the A9. The smoke drastically reduced visibility on the road, and a serious accident occurred. The farmer was tried and convicted of recklessly endangering the lives and safety of the lieges. Similarly in *Robertson v Klos*[6], the High Court directed the sheriff to return a verdict of guilty of culpable and reckless conduct, in relation to a charge of driving in excess of the speed limit whilst using a mobile telephone. The original charge of dangerous driving could not succeed because of a failure to serve the appropriate notice. The sheriff had not convicted of the alternative *inter alia* because of a lack of notice and because he held that there was no evidence of actual danger caused. The High Court in allowing the appeal, held that it was not necessary to show evidence of actual danger in order to found a charge of culpable and reckless conduct. In the instant case, there was adequate evidence that the accused had acted deliberately in the face of potential danger without regard to the consequences.

1 *Wheatley* para 2.10:3.
2 *Dilks v Bowman-Shaw* [1981] RTR 4, described by Ormrod LJ as a 'very unusual' case, and doubted by *Wheatley* at para 2.10:3 who submits that it might not be followed in Scotland. Cf the case of *Wilson v MacPhail* 1991 SCCR 170.
3 See *Quinn v Cunningham* 1956 JC 22, 1956 SLT 55.
4 It may be resorted to where the driving did not take place on a 'road': see *Wheatley* para 2.4
5 1982 SCCR 395, 1983 SLT (Sh Ct) 37.
6 2006 SCCR 52, [2005] HCJAC 136 applying *HM Advocate v Harris (Andrew)* 1993 JC 150.

Section 4(1): Driving or attempting to drive while unfit through drink or drugs

13.18   The offence under s 4(1) is committed only if the driving, or the attempt to drive, takes place on a 'road or other public place'[1]. 'Drink' means alcoholic drink[2], and 'drugs' includes 'any intoxicant other than alcohol'[3]. By far the most common intoxicant is alcohol, and for the purposes of this section the actual amount of alcohol found in the accused's body is irrelevant. The test, set out by s 4(5) of the RTA, is whether the accused's ability to drive was for the time being impaired, and medical evidence will usually be decisive in making out that test[4]. Where the accused is medically examined, for example by a police surgeon, and provided he has 'sufficient command of his faculties to appreciate his position and to behave with reasonable intelligence'[5], the procedural guidelines laid down by a full bench in *Reid v Nixon*[6] should be followed. Failure to do so must be justified[7]. Even if a test is exculpatory, the court is entitled to rely on the evidence of police officers about impairment[8].

1 As to which, see above.
2 *Armstrong v Clark* [1957] 2 QB 391 at 394, [1957] 1 All ER 433 at 435, per Lord Goddard CJ.
3 RTA, s 11(2). This definition will include medicines taken for both therapeutic and non-thera-
  peutic reasons.
4 Lay evidence, usually from police officers, may be enough however, and if need be, the courts
  will look at all the circumstances to find evidence of unfitness: see eg *Kenny v Tudhope* [1984]
  SCCR 290; *Wallace v McLeod* 1986 SCCR 678.
5 *Reid v Nixon* 1948 JC 68 at 72, per Lord Justice-General Cooper.
6 1948 JC 68.
7 At 73. For a commentary on the guidelines, and a review of subsequent cases, see *Wheatley* para
  3.5:1.
8 *McEwan v Higson* 2001 SCCR 579.

13.19 Because it is the accused's fitness to drive which is relevant under
this section, and not the amount of alcohol he has consumed, it is possible for
an accused to be pronounced fit to drive for the purposes of s 4(1), in spite of
having more than the prescribed limit of alcohol in his blood[1]. Conversely, an
accused might have consumed less than the prescribed maximum, and yet still
be found unfit to drive. The fact that the accused has in fact driven a vehicle in a
straight line does not necessarily mean that he is fit to drive. But if the accused
does drive 'sufficiently far and under such conditions as to demonstrate that
his skill, alertness and judgement as a driver were unaffected, that would be a
factor to be weighed along with the other evidence as to his condition'[2].

Section 4(2): Being in charge of a motor vehicle while unfit

13.20 Where a person was neither driving nor attempting to drive a motor
vehicle, that person may nevertheless be convicted under s 4(2) of being 'in
charge' of a motor vehicle while unfit through drink or drugs. Whether or not
someone was 'in charge' of a vehicle is a question of fact, and, at least in Scotland, the test applicable is whether the accused was 'responsible for the control
or driving of the car'[3]. The requirement of de facto control links the offence
under s 4(2) with that in the preceding subsection:

> 'We know quite well what is meant by referring to a person who is driving
> or attempting to drive a car, and when the section goes on to refer also to
> a person "in charge of" a car, the reference must be to a person in de facto
> control, even though he may not be at the time actually driving or attempt-
> ing to drive. Any other reading or any attempt to include the owner merely
> because he was present, or because he had possession of [the] ignition key
> of a car which he had arranged should be driven by [another] would lead to
> extravagant results'[4].

In *Crichton v Burrell*[5], the case from which this statement comes, the accused
had arranged for someone to drive him home, and was waiting beside his car
with the ignition keys in his pocket for that person to arrive. He was found not
to be 'in charge' of his car. The result of this case might well have been different in England. The facts of *Haines v Roberts*[6] were essentially similar to those
in *Crichton v Burrell*. In the English case, however, Lord Goddard CJ said:

> 'How can it be said that in those circumstances the respondent was not in
> charge of the [vehicle]. He had not put it into anybody else's charge. It may

be that if a man goes to a public house and leaves his car outside or in the car park and, getting drunk, asks a friend to look after the car for him or take the car home, he has put it in somebody else's charge, but if he had not put it in charge of somebody else he is in charge of it until he does so. His car is away from home on the road or in the car park – it matters not which – and he is in charge'[7].

Crichton was applied in the case of *Kelso v HM Advocate*[8]. In that case the accused had been in the passenger seat as his wife drove. She had stopped the car and left him sleeping with the keys in the ignition and the heater running. He was convicted of being drunk 'in charge'. On appeal, the High Court held that there was no point at which he could have said to have assumed control of or responsibility for the vehicle. In *Cartmill v Heywood*[9] the accused was found in the driver's seat of his own car with the keys in his hand. In the circumstances, the High Court held that the sheriff had been entitled to convict of being drunk 'in charge', as the circumstances were sufficient to distinguish *Kelso*.

1 See eg *McNeill v Fletcher* 1966 JC 18.
2 *Murray v Muir* 1950 SLT 41 at 43, per Lord Justice-General Cooper.
3 *Crichton v Burrell* 1951 JC 107 at 111, per Lord Keith.
4 At 111 per Lord Justice-General Cooper.
5 1951 JC 107.
6 [1953] 1 All ER 344.
7 At 345, per Lord Goddard CJ.
8 1998 SLT 921; 1998 SCCR 278.
9 2000 SLT 779.

13.21 So in England the driver is in charge of his vehicle until he hands it over to someone else's charge, or abandons it completely. Abandonment is not easy to establish. In *Woodage v Jones (No 2)*[1] the accused left his car in a garage forecourt (a public place), and walked away. He was arrested when about half a mile from the car, and was found still to be in charge of it. His counsel tried to persuade the court to follow *Crichton v Burrell* but the court declined to do so[2].

The English approach implies just what the Lord Justice-General in *Crichton v Burrell* thought should not be implied: that the owner of a vehicle may be convicted 'because he might in strict legal theory have taken action which he is not proved to have intended to take, much less to have put into practice'[3]. Thus, it is unlikely in Scotland that a driver will be convicted under the subsection if he was not in the car at the relevant time[4], unless there is clear evidence of control[5]. A person need not be in the driving seat to be in control of a vehicle however. A driving instructor, for example, may be 'in charge' of a vehicle even though a learner is driving[6].

1 [1975] RTR 119, (1975) 60 Cr App Rep 260.
2 See [1975] RTR 119 at 124, 125, per James LJ.
3 *Crichton v Burrell* 1951 JC 107 at 111, per Lord-Justice General Cooper.
4 See eg *Adair v McKenna* 1951 SLT (Sh Ct) 40.
5 Cf the English case of *Leach v Evans* [1952] 2 All ER 264, which may in any event be a product of the stricter English approach.
6 *Clark v Clark* 1940 SLT (Sh Ct) 68. This seems consistent with the view that more than one person can be driving at the same time: *Langman v Valentine* [1952] 2 All ER 803, [1952] 2 TLR 713. Cf *Winter v Morrison* 1954 JC 7 which came to the opposite conclusion in similar circumstances.

Section 4(3): Defence

13.22   Section 4(3) provides a defence for the accused who can prove that 'at the material time the circumstances were such that there was no likelihood of his driving [the vehicle] so long as he remained unfit to drive through drink or drugs'. This is a question of fact in all the circumstances, including the accused's intentions. The court must be satisfied, on a balance of probabilities[1], not only that the accused did not intend to drive the car while unfit, but also that there was no likelihood that his intentions would be departed from[2].

In *Neish v Stevenson*[3] the accused and a companion missed the last bus to their lodgings after an evening's drinking. Since it was raining heavily, they decided to spend the night in the cab of the accused's lorry. The ignition keys were sitting on the dashboard when they were found by the police. It was held that the court was entitled to be satisfied on a balance of probabilities that the exception had been made out.

Section 5: Driving or being in charge of a motor vehicle with more than the prescribed concentration of alcohol in the body

13.23   A person who drives, or is in charge of a motor vehicle on a road or other public place, having consumed so much alcohol that the proportion of it in his breath, blood or urine exceeds the prescribed amounts is guilty of an offence[4]. The normal method of determining the proportion of alcohol in the body of the accused is by means of a breath test, administered where a uniformed constable has reasonable cause to suspect the accused of a s 5 offence[5]. Where a specimen is provided, it is presumed that the proportion of alcohol in the accused's breath, blood or urine at the time of the alleged offence was not less than the reading given by the specimen[6]. The Crown Office had renounced the right to prosecute in cases where the breath test reading does not exceed 40 microgrammes of alcohol[7], but after the breath alcohol limits was lowered in December 2014 (from 35 to 22 microgrammes), no such undertaking was forthcoming in relation to the lower levels[8].

1 See *Neish v Stevenson* 1969 SLT 229.
2 *Morton v Confer* [1963] 1 WLR 763, [1963] 2 All ER 765.
3 1969 SLT 229.
4 RTA, s 5(1). At present the prescribed limits, set out in s 11(2) of RTA are: breath – 35 mcg of alcohol per 100 mls; blood – 80 mgs per 100 mls; urine – 107 mgs per 100 mls.
5 RTA, s 6(1), (2). This preliminary breath test is not essential to a conviction under s 5, and testing may be carried out at a police station under powers given by s 7. The rules and procedures governing this complex area of the law are fully discussed in *Wheatley* Chapter 4.
6 Section 15(2).
7 See *Benton v Cardle* 1987 SCCR 738, 1988 SLT 310; *McConnachie v Scott* 1988 SCCR 176, 1988 SLT 480. The latter case may be authority for the view that where the lower of two breath specimens shows less than 30 mcg, it is incompetent for the police to proceed on the basis of a blood sample, under s 8(2).

8 Figures showed that in Scotland there was a 17% reduction in drink driving offences from January to March 2015 (997) compared to the same period in 2014 (1,209). See www.scotland. police.uk/whats-happening/news/2015/may/summer-drink-drive-campaign-2015-launched.

DEFENCES

(1) No likelihood of driving

13.24   As with the offence of being in charge of a vehicle while unfit through drink or drugs under s 4(1), it is a defence for a person charged under s 5(1) (b)[1] to show that there was no likelihood of his driving whilst the proportion of alcohol in his body remained likely to exceed the prescribed amount[2]. The rules applicable to the s 4(3) defence apply with equal force to that under s 5(2).

(2) Post incident drinking – the 'hip flask' defence

13.25   The so-called 'hip flask' defence applies to proceedings under both ss 4 and 5 of RTA. As was seen above, where a specimen is provided for analysis, it is presumed that the proportion of alcohol in the accused's blood, breath or urine at the time of the offence was the same as that given by the specimen. However, this presumption can be rebutted if the accused can prove, first, that he consumed alcohol after he ceased to drive and before he provided the specimen, and second, that but for this post-incident consumption of alcohol, he would not have been over the limit[3]. It is clear that the persuasive or legal onus is upon the accused in such cases to prove the matters required by the section before the defence can be made out. It has been held, however, that in order to do so, the accused need not lead corroborated evidence[4], in effect returning the burden on the accused in such cases to the evidential one imposed on an accused before the defence was placed on a statutory footing[5]. The accused need no longer prove that 'an ascertainable and definite amount of alcohol was consumed subsequent to the event, and between the event and the test'[6], and it is now possible for the court to proceed on the basis of an approximation as to the amount consumed, provided that that approximation is capable of raising a reasonable doubt as to the amount of alcohol in the accused's body at the time of the incident[7].

1 Being in charge of a vehicle while the proportion of alcohol in one's body exceeds the pre-scribed amounts.
2 Section 5(2).
3 Road Traffic Offenders Act 1988, s 15(2).
4 *King v Lees* 1993 JC 19, 1993 SCCR 28, 1993 SLT 1184. See '*Hip flasks and burdens*', article by David Sheldon 1993 SLT (News) 33–37.
5 See Transport Act 1981, Sch 8 and *Campbell v McKenzie* 1982 JC 20, 1981 SCCR 341.
6 *Campbell v McKenzie*, above.
7 *Hassan v Scott* 1989 SCCR 49, 1989 SLT 380.

(3) Necessity

13.26   For many years there was some doubt as to whether a defence of necessity at common law may be open to a person charged with an offence

221

under s 5, or indeed any of the offences discussed here. These are offences of more or less strict liability, and it may be doubted whether a defence of necessity can affect not merely *mens rea*, but also *actus reus*[1]. In *Tudhope v Grubb*[2], a sheriff court decision, it was held that the defence was available where the accused had driven while over the limit of alcohol in order to escape from a threatened assault. The necessity to escape from the violence rendered the accused's actions involuntary, and meant that there was indeed no *actus reus*. The High Court cast some doubt on the soundness of the decision in *Grubb* in *McLeod v McDougall*[3]. There the court refused to approve the former case, holding that in the circumstances there was no need to rule on the question of whether the defence of necessity is available in Scots law, since at the material time, there was clearly no necessity for the accused to drive. They did hold, however, that in the circumstances there were special reasons for not disqualifying the accused from driving[4]. In *McNab v Guild*[5] the court was again asked to consider the defence of necessity, and again made no decision as to its availability. In the case of *Moss v Howdle*[6], however, the High Court finally recognised the existence of the defence in circumstances where the accused can show that he acted under threat of death or serious injury to himself or some other person[7], and made clear that the defence was available in relation to relatively minor offences, and not simply 'atrocious crimes' as the old authorities appeared to indicate. It remains to be seen whether the defence can apply to all of the offences in the Act, including those which involve truly strict liability. The matter was considered in *MD v Procurator Fiscal Falkirk*[8], where the court affirmed that the driver has to act under immediate danger of death, or serious bodily harm; immediate danger of a sexual assault also qualified. However, any reasonable alternative to the offending behaviour must be taken[9].

1 See the discussion of driving and automatism, above, and *Farrell v Stirling* 1975 SLT (Sh Ct) 71.
2 1983 SCCR 350.
3 1988 SCCR 519, 1989 SLT 151.
4 Road Traffic Offenders Act 1988, s 34: see *Wheatley* Chapter 8 for procedure where special reasons are advanced.
5 1989 SCCR 138.
6 1997 SCCR 215. See PW Ferguson 'Duress and necessity in Scots law' 1997 SLT (News) 127 for a review of the authorities.
7 See also *Morrison v Valentine* 1991 SLT 413, and cf *R v Conway* [1989] QB 290, [1989] RTR 35, a case on 'duress of circumstances'.
8 2009 HCJAC 37.
9 2009 HCJAC 37 para [4].

Part IV
PROPERTY OFFENCES

Chapter 14

Theft/Reset

THEFT

14.1   The popular view of the crime of theft generally involves the clan-destine removal of goods from their owner's possession, but in Scots law it is not confined to that situation. There is theft whenever someone wrongfully appropriates the property of another, with the intention permanently to deprive that other of possession. This was not always the case. *Hume* confined theft to the popular idea of 'the felonious taking and carrying away of the property of another, for lucre'[1]. Since theft was at that time a capital offence, it is perhaps unsurprising that *Hume* wished to define the crime as narrowly as possible. His definition excluded from the scope of the crime those who appropriated property with which they had been entrusted. *Hume* characterised their offence as one of breach of trust, a crime akin to embezzlement[2]. For *Hume*, a lawful possessor of goods could not be guilty of theft.

The courts found *Hume's* definition unduly restrictive, and soon began to modify it. In *George Brown*[3] a watchmaker was charged with the theft of nine watches, which he had undertaken to repair. The charge was held relevant, even although the accused had not taken the watches but had been entrusted with them by their owners. In *John Smith*[4], Lord Meadowbank said: 'It is of no consequence of what character the original possession of the property is. The moment the intention of appropriating the property of another is formed, then the theft is committed'.

Theft thus came to be based on the idea not of removal, but of appropriation – the application of another's property to the appropriator's own use. The crime could be committed as soon as the intention to appropriate was formed.

1 *Hume* I, 57.
2 See section on Embezzlement in Chapter 17 below.
3 (1839) 2 Swin 394.
4 (1838) 2 Swin 28.

14.2   In *Herron v Diack & Newlands*[1], for example, a large and 'very grand' steel coffin, containing the remains of an American writer, was committed to the care of the two accused, who were funeral directors. The accused removed the deceased from the coffin and placed him in a chipboard container for burial at sea. There were difficulties with the burial and Newlands later had the body replaced in the original casket, which was successfully committed.

The pair were duly charged with the theft of the steel casket. Diack was convicted, even although he was quite properly in possession of the casket at the time of the 'theft', and even although the casket was eventually used for its intended purpose. Their possession of the coffin, originally lawful, became theftuous when the decision was made to appropriate it to their own use. At that moment, the crime was committed, and could not be 'undone' by their eventual decision to use the original casket.

In cases where the accused has had lawful possession of the goods, it may be difficult to prove the presence of an intention to appropriate them. The law tends, therefore, to rely on the conduct of the accused to show that theftuous intent was present. In *Diack and Newlands*, the use of the chipboard coffin for burial in the face of clear instructions to use the steel casket was strong evidence of appropriation.

What sort of property can be stolen?

Anything which is both corporeal and moveable may be stolen. This includes money, and, as Sheriff Gordon points out[2], 'theft of notes to the value of £x ... is theft of £x and not merely a number of pieces of paper'.

1 1973 SLT (Sh Ct) 27.
2 At para 14–12.

Corporeal property

14.3   Generally, the prosecution must be able to point to some physical or tangible object which the accused has stolen. Incorporeal property, such as information or a legal right cannot form the subject of a theft charge in Scotland. A person may be charged with the theft of a thing containing the information or right, such as a file, or a contract, but not with the theft of the incorporeal contents of the document. In *HM Advocate v Mackenzies*[1] a man was accused of stealing a book containing secret recipes. This was held to be a relevant charge of theft, but an additional charge of copying the secret recipes was not. Two points may be made about this case: first, there could probably now be a relevant charge of theft, even if it were alleged that the accused had simply taken the book for the purpose of copying the secrets it contained, and with the intention of returning it later[2]. Secondly, while the accused was relevantly charged only with the theft of the book, and not the information it contained, the court took the contents of the book into account in assessing the seriousness of the charge. 'It is quite evident', said Lord Justice-Clerk Macdonald, 'that a book of no real value in itself may be of great value because of what is written in it'[3].

An accused person may therefore be charged with the theft of a document which is valuable because of the information it contains. But it is not theft (or any other crime) to memorise secret information, or to make copies of documents containing such information. This is so even where information is 'taken' with the intention of selling it 'for lucre'. The accused in *Grant v Allan*[4], made copies of print-outs from his employers' computer, 'detained' these copies, and offered to sell the information they contained to rivals of his employers. He was charged with an innominate offence on the basis of this conduct. The High Court held that the charge disclosed no crime known to the law of Scotland, and the court declined to exercise its declaratory power to make it so. Lord Justice-Clerk Ross said:

'For the appellant clandestinely to make copies of computer print-outs belonging to his employers may well have breached an express or implied obligation owed to his employers by him not to disclose confidential information obtained in the course of his employment, but it is quite another thing to proceed to categorise such behaviour as criminal'[5].

1 1913 SC (J) 107, 1913 SLT 48.
2 This is hinted at by Lord Justice-Clerk Macdonald in *McKenzies* 1913 SC (J) 107 at 110, and see now *Milne v Tudhope* 1981 JC 53, 1981 SLT (Notes) 42 discussed below and cf *HM Advocate v Dewar* (1777); *Burnett* 115; *Hume* I, 75.
3 1913 SC (J) 107 at 110, 1913 2 SLT 48 at 50. See also *Gordon* para 14–14.
4 1987 SCCR 402, 1988 SLT 11.
5 1988 SLT 11 at 14.

14.4   Whether or not energy may be classified as corporeal or tangible, charges of theft of electricity are common[1]. Similarly, non-solid things, such as water or oxygen may be stolen[2].

Moveable property

Property must be moveable in order to be stolen. But 'moveable' in this context is not to be understood in the technical sense known to Scots lawyers. It simply means 'capable of being moved'[3]. Thus, many items of heritable property may be stolen – fruit growing on a tree, turnips in a field[4], or slates from a roof. That the current definition of theft is restricted to corporeal property might be seen to be out of step with the digital age, where, for example the Consumer Rights Act 2015 defines and deals with digital content, has been the subject of comment[5].

Another's property

One cannot steal one's own property[6]. Nor can one steal ownerless property, although the scope of this category is very limited. Wild animals are considered to be *res nullius*, and ownership is acquired by the first person to capture or confine them[7]. Once captured or confined however, wild animals may be stolen. A person who removed salmon from beach nets, for example, would be guilty of theft. Living, adult human beings cannot be 'stolen'[8], but children under the age of puberty are considered in law to be the 'property' of their parents, and as such can form the subject of a theft charge. This type of theft is known as *plagium*[9]. Human remains may be stolen prior to burial – thereafter the relevant crime is that of violation of sepulchres[10].

1 See *Gordon* para 14–16.
2 *Gordon* para 14–15.
3 See *Gordon* para 14–20.
4 *Alex Robertson* (1867) 5 Irv 480.
5 Christie, 'Should the law of theft extend to information', *J Crim L* 2005 69(4).
6 *Hume* I, 77. A charge of attempting to steal one's own property would arguably now be relevant, however, in view of the decision in *Docherty v Brown* 1996 JC 48, 1996 SCCR 136, 1996 SLT 325.
7 Poaching is a separate offence based on incorporeal rights of the Crown or the landowner – but a poacher becomes the owner of the game he traps or kills. See eg *Scott v Everitt* (1853) 15 D 288.
8 Although they can, of course, be abducted. As can children; see *B v HMA* 2015 HCJAC 56.

9 See *Downie v HM Advocate* 1984 SCCR 365; *Hamilton v Mooney* 1990 SLT (Sh Ct) 105; *Hamilton v Wilson* 1993 SCCR 9, and JM Fotheringham 'Plagium' (1990) 35 JLSS 506, but see *Orr v K* 2003 SLT (Sh Ct) 70; 2003 Fam. LR 26 for limitation of offence to natural parents. The court in *B v HMA* 2015 HCJAC 56 stated that it was generally desirable that breach of a court order be dealt with in the context of civil proceedings.
10 *Dewar v HM Advocate* 1945 JC 5.

14.5   Property which has been abandoned falls to the Crown, and appropriation of such property is probably theft[1]. Lost property may be stolen, but it is unclear whether appropriation of such property is always theft[2].

In some situations, it may be unclear who owns an item of property. The question of ownership is determined by the civil law. For example, a firm of builders are constructing a house on land owned by A. They supply double glazing and central heating, and these are duly incorporated into the house. Payment for the construction of the house is by instalment, and when defects in the construction emerge, A withholds further instalments. To force A to resume payments, the builders remove the double glazing and central heating from the house, and take it back to their premises. When these items were incorporated into the house, they became the property of A. The builders may well be guilty of theft[3].

Difficulties may arise where, for example, a buyer removes goods from a shop without paying for them, but at a time when ownership had passed to him[4]. If this was a credit sale, clearly there was no theft. If not, then a charge of theft might relevantly be brought, provided the necessary theftuous intent could be proved[5]. A charge of fraud might also be possible if the 'buyer' obtained the goods by means of a false pretence.

The *actus reus* of theft

Although theft is now defined in terms of appropriation, most cases of theft involve the straightforward taking of another's property. As we noted above, the appropriation of lost property may also form the basis of a theft charge. This mode of theft is considered under the heading of theft by finding. No matter which of these three possible modes of theft – taking, finding, or appropriation – is in issue, problems of distinguishing *actus reus* from *mens rea* loom large. If property can be stolen while lawfully in the thief's possession, it may be difficult to point to any positive act which might constitute the *actus reus*.

1 See *Lord Advocate v University of Aberdeen* 1963 SC 533, 1963 SLT 361 and *Gordon* para 14–41.
2 See *Angus McKinnon* (1863) 4 Irv 398; *Campbell v MacLennan* (1888) 1 White 604; *Gordon* para 14–22, and the discussion of theft by finding below.
3 See eg *Milne v Tudhope* 1981 JC 53, 1981 SLT (Notes) 42.
4 *Gordon* paras 14–31 and 14–32.
5 See eg *Clyne v Keith* (1887) 1 White 356, 14 R (J) 22.

Theft by taking

14.6   'Any amotion of the goods from what is considered as their proper place of keeping, and which clearly evinces the purpose of the taker, is a carrying away, and a sufficient completion of the act'[1].

Amotio is the term used to describe the physical taking away of a thing. According to *Burnett*, there must be *amotio*, and this 'removal' or 'carrying away'[2] must be such as to demonstrate the intentions of the taker. Simply to take hold of goods, or even to move them around within their 'proper place of keeping' would hardly be enough to constitute the *actus reus* of theft, since it would be difficult to interpret such actions as showing theftuous intent. In *Black and Penrice v Carmichael*[3] the necessity for *amotio* was discussed and rejected. This case related to 'wheel clamping'. The accused had immobilised vehicles. They were charged *inter alia* with theft. That charge was held irrelevant by the sheriff, but on appeal, the High Court held that the facts libelled were sufficient to constitute theft. The essential feature of the physical act necessary to constitute theft was appropriation by which control and possession of the thing was taken away from its owner or custodier. *Amotio* in the sense of moving or taking away was not necessary. The accused were charged with taking possession of the car by clamping its wheel, and with appropriating it because only they could remove the clamp. It was the owner's loss and not the appropriator's gain which was important. The deliberate nature of the act of appropriation in knowledge of its consequences was sufficient to justify the inference of *mens rea*. In most cases, the appropriation will be demonstrated by *amotio*. In *Cornelius O'Neil*[4], the accused stood outside an open window, and used a hook to pull towards him objects inside the room; it was held that there was sufficient amotion to justify a theft charge[5]. Thus, the question of sufficient amotion will depend on the particular circumstances. While any degree of movement may demonstrate an intent to steal a car parked on the street, it would probably be necessary to show that goods in a shop were taken beyond the check-out point before an intent to steal could be demonstrated[6].

Theft by appropriation

As was noted above, *Hume* did not regard as theft the appropriation of goods by their lawful possessor. *Hume* required an actual taking of possession before a charge of theft could be made[7]. Thus, where an owner of goods voluntarily handed over possession to another, that other could not steal the goods since there could be no physical removal of the goods from their owner's possession. This led to the growth of an artificial distinction between a possessor of goods, and a mere custodier[8]. A custodier could be found guilty of theft, but a possessor could not. As the modern law developed however, it became clear that a lawful possessor of goods could quite competently be charged with their theft[9]. Thus, in *O'Brien v Strathern*[10], in which it was held that a soldier could steal his kilt, Lord Justice-General Clyde said that 'looking to the course which the law has taken ... I think there is no doubt ... that the appropriation of goods by the person to whom they have been entrusted for a limited and specified purpose constitutes theft'[11].

1 *Burnett* 121. It has recently been held that actual movement of the goods is unnecessary, provided that there is appropriation. See *Black and Penrice v Carmichael* 1992 SCCR 709, 1992 SLT 897, a case in which the accused were convicted of theft having used a wheel clamp to immobilise a car.
2 See *Gordon* para 14–10.
3 1992 SLT 897.
4 (1845) 2 Broun 394.

5   This type of conduct would probably now be charged as attempted theft, a charge unknown to
    the law at this time.
6   See *Gordon* paras 14–11. Cf also *Black and Penrice v Carmichael* 1992 SCCR 709, 1992
    SLT 897.
7   *Hume* I, 57.
8   *Hume* I, 63–65. A custodier was defined as one who holds goods only for a 'limited and speci-
    fied purpose', while a possessor was one who had some right to use the goods on his own
    behalf. See also *Gordon* para 14–03.
9   See *George Brown* (1839) 2 Swin 394 and *John Smith* (1838) 2 Swin 28.
10 1922 JC 55, 1922 SLT 440.
11 1922 JC at 57.

14.7   In *Dewar v HM Advocate*[1], the manager of Aberdeen crematorium
was charged with the theft of more than 600 coffin lids. On receipt of the coffins for cremation, Dewar saved the lids and retained them for use in other
cremations, for firewood, or for use in some other 'economic way'. There was
no evidence that he made a profit from this practice. Dewar claimed that coffins
sent for cremation had been abandoned by their owners, and that accordingly
they were 'completely under his jurisdiction for disposal'. It was held, however, that the coffins were sent to him for the sole purpose of destruction, and
that by preserving and re-using the coffins, he was appropriating them to his
own use. He was therefore guilty of theft.

In such cases, it is difficult, if not impossible, to distinguish *mens rea* and *actus
reus*, since the prosecution can point to no physical act removing the property
from the owner's possession. Indeed the thief in such cases is authorised to possess and to carry out certain acts using the property. It may be necessary therefore to examine carefully the conduct of the accused to determine the moment of
appropriation[2] – the point at which the *mens* became *rea*, and at which the crime
was committed[3]. Thus in *Dewar*, the moment of appropriation and theft was the
moment when Dewar saved the coffin lids from destruction, and in *Herron v
Diack & Newlands*, above, when the two accused removed Mr Groom from his
princely casket, and placed him in the chipboard cut-price coffin. O'Brien's act
of appropriation was the sale of his kilt to a fellow soldier, and at that moment
he committed theft. These cases suggest that to constitute appropriation, the
accused's conduct must amount to an assertion of an unlimited right of disposal
– of the rights of the owner, in other words. Sale or destruction of goods are the
main examples of such conduct[4]. It seems, however, that any unauthorised act
inconsistent with the rights of the true owner may amount to appropriation[5].
Indeed, it seems that merely to deprive the owner of the *use* of his property,
even only partially, may constitute a sufficient *actus reus*. In *Black and Penrice
v Carmichael*[6], the accused were employees of a security firm who used a wheel
clamp to immobilise the complainer's car, and demanded a sum of money in
return for its release. The defence argued that there had been no appropriation,
since the car was not taken away or even moved; nor was there any suggestion
that the purpose of the clamping was to allow the accused to use the car for their
own purposes. On appeal, the relevance of the charge of theft[7] was upheld by
the High Court. Lord Justice-General Hope said[8]:

'The essential feature of the physical act necessary to constitute theft is the
appropriation, by which control and possession of the thing is taken from
the owner or custodier. In principle therefore, the removal of the thing does

not seem to be necessary, if the effect of the act which is done to it is its appropriation by the accused ... [In this case] the physical act of appropriation is clearly present, in my opinion, since the purpose and effect of the wheel clamp was to immobilise the vehicle and to deprive the motorist of his possession and use of it as a motor vehicle'.

1 1945 JC 5.
2 Cf *Morris (David)* [1983] QB 587, [1983] 2 All ER 448, CA; [1984] AC 320, [1983] 3 All ER 288, HL.
3 See Lord Meadowbank's *dictum* from *John Smith* (1838) 2 Swin 28.
4 See *Gordon* para 14–10 for further examples.
5 See *Smith and Hogan*, p 493.
6 1992 SCCR 709, 1992 SLT 897.
7 And extortion. See the discussion below and in Chapter 17.
8 1992 SCCR 709 at 719.

14.8   Thus, it seems that appropriation may be constituted by acts depriving the owner of *possessory* rights, not merely rights of ownership, or by acts which assert some degree of control over the article, albeit not the full 'right' to dispose of it. There is, moreover, no need for the thief to gain from the act, provided that the owner loses the enjoyment or use of the article.

Theft by finding

Theft by finding may be considered as a type of theft by appropriation. A person does not steal goods merely by finding them, even if he retains the goods for some time after the discovery. Such a person may, for a reasonable time, be presumed to possess the goods with the intention of returning them to their true owner[1]. Once that reasonable time has elapsed, however, it may be presumed that the finder has appropriated the goods to his own use, and at that point, theft has occurred.

In *MacMillan v Lowe*[2], a man claimed to have found a cheque book and card in a telephone box. These items clearly bore the owner's name and that of his bank. The accused retained the items for at least four hours without making any attempt to return them to the owner, and when initially apprehended and searched by the police, he attempted to conceal the items. It was held that there was enough evidence to justify a conviction for theft[3].

Once again, the conduct of the accused is vital to the question of whether there has been appropriation. A finder may be found guilty of theft if he pawns the goods shortly after finding them and without attempting to trace the owner[4]. Similarly, there may be theft if a farmer puts his own brand on sheep which he has found straying[5].

There is, however, some doubt as to whether every appropriation of found goods is theft. In *Campbell v MacLennan*[6] Lord Young said[7]: 'A man of large property may find money in the street, and may give it in the way of alms to the next beggar; that is undoubtedly appropriation. Yet who would call it theft, even if the finder had denied having found it?' In *Angus McKinnon*[8], Lord Justice-Clerk Inglis took the view that a finder might innocently retain property while he tried to locate the owner, and that any subsequent appropriation would not be a 'grievous violation of moral right'. This view certainly accords with common sense, but it is hardly consistent with cases such as *John Smith*[9], and *MacMillan v Lowe*.[10] Sheriff Gordon argues that it may be a defence to a charge of theft to show that the finder took all reasonable steps to locate the owner before making the decision to retain the goods[11]. The argument would be the stronger if the goods in question are of 'no great value'[12].

1   Cf *Hume* I, 62.
2   1991 JC 13; 1991 SCCR 113.
3   Cf *Angus McKinnon* (1863) 4 Irv 398 at 405, per Lord Ardmillan.
4   *McLaughlin v Stewart* (1865) Macq 32.
5   *Paterson v HM Advocate* (1901) 3 Adam 490, 4 F (J) 7.
6   (1888) 1 White 604, 15 R (J) 55.
7   (1888) 1 White 604 at 608.
8   (1863) 4 Irv 398.
9   (1838) 2 Swin 28.
10 1991 SCCR 113.
11 See *Gordon*, para 14–23.
12 See *Angus McKinnon* (1863) 4 Irv 398 at 402, per Lord Justice-Clerk Inglis.

14.9   But this argument undermines the idea that finding coupled with appropriation amounts to theft[1], and it may be better to regard the appropriation of articles in such circumstances as a matter for prosecutorial (and personal) discretion, rather than as an exception to the substantive law. In any event, a person who finds any article is obliged by the Civic Government (Scotland) Act 1982[2] to take reasonable care of it, and within a reasonable time to deliver it or report its finding to a police officer or to the owner or occupier of the premises on which the article is found. Failure to do so constitutes an offence in itself[3], and might well demonstrate an intention to appropriate the article such as to form the basis of a theft charge[4].

The owner's consent

Consent is generally no defence to a criminal charge in Scots law[5], but certain crimes specifically include a lack of consent as an essential part of their definition. Rape is one such crime. Theft has traditionally been thought to be another[6]. Appropriation occurs when a person acts in such a way as to assert a right of ownership or control over property in fact owned by another. Theft is committed only if the property is appropriated without the owner's consent. Since appropriation is, in general, an act assertive of ownership, any consent must be to the transfer of ownership of the property – if the owner has consented only to the transfer of possession, any subsequent appropriation will amount to theft. Perhaps surprisingly, this point does not appear to have been considered in *Black and Penrice v Carmichael*[7], in which the rights asserted by the accused were not those of ownership or disposal, but only those of possession or control. Signs were displayed in the place where the complainer parked his car which warned that cars parked without authorisation would be clamped. Arguably, by parking his car in the face of such signs, the complainer could be taken to have consented to the clamping, and impliedly, to the assertion by the accused of those (limited) rights. In the English case of *Lloyd v DPP*[8], it was accepted that a person whose car was clamped in circumstances similar to those in *Black and Penrice v Carmichael* had no right to damage the clamp in order to remove it, because of his implied consent to the clamping. Theft was not an issue in *Lloyd*, and there remains the point that what is generally required to avoid a theft charge is consent to the transfer of *ownership*.

1 See *John Smith* (1838) 2 Swin 28 at 51–52, per Lord Meadowbank.
2 Sections 67–75.
3 Section 67(6).
4 See *Gordon* para 14–24.
5 See *Smart v HM Advocate* 1975 JC 30; *Khaliq v HM Advocate* 1984 JC 23; *Sutherland v HM Advocate* 1994 SCCR 80, 1994 SLT 634; *Stewart v Nisbet* 2013 SCL 209.
6 See *Gordon* paras 14–36 to 14–38.
7 1992 SCCR 709, 1992 SLT 897.
8 [1992] 1 All ER 982. This was another wheel-clamping case involving the same security company as that involved in *Black and Carmichael's* case. In this case, however, it was the owner of the car who was charged (with criminal damage) and not the clampers. The contrast in approach between the English and the Scottish cases is an interesting one. See also *Arthur v Anker* [1996] 2 WLR 602, [1996] RTR 308.

14.10 It is the absence of the owner's consent to the transfer of property which distinguishes theft from fraud[1]. For example, **A** steals a cheque book belonging to **B**. He represents to **C**, who is selling his car, that he is **B**, and forges **B**'s signature on a cheque from the stolen cheque-book. **C** accepts the cheque and gives **A** the keys to his car. He drives away. In this case **B** has consented to the transfer of ownership in his car to **A**. His consent was induced by **A**'s fraudulent use of **B**'s cheque-book. But there is no theft in this situation. Consent induced by fraud is consent nevertheless[2]. The significance for the criminal law of the distinction between theft and fraud is greatly reduced by Schedule 3, paragraph 8, of the Criminal Procedure (Scotland) Act 1995, which provides *inter alia* that a person charged with theft may be convicted of fraud, and vice-versa. The distinction retains considerable importance in the civil law of property however. A person who has obtained goods from their true owner by fraud may competently pass ownership to a third person – a person who has stolen goods can never do this. This means that a victim of theft is entitled to recover his property even from innocent third-party purchasers of stolen property[3]; the victim of fraud is entitled only to damages[4].

The *mens rea* of theft

At the start of this chapter theft was defined as the appropriation of the property of another, with the intention permanently to deprive that other of possession[5]. What was required was an intention to detain the goods from the owner on a permanent basis, whether or not the thief kept the goods for himself[6], and whether or not the goods were in fact returned to their owner[7]. If goods are appropriated with the intention permanently to deprive the owner, the crime is complete, and cannot be 'undone' by any subsequent event[8].

Following the case of *Milne v Tudhope*[9], however, the above definition has been qualified. In *Milne v Tudhope*, the High Court accepted that theft generally requires an appropriation of property with the intention permanently to deprive the owner of possession. But the court held that, in 'exceptional circumstances', an intention to deprive the owner of the property on a temporary basis might suffice: '... A clandestine taking, aimed at achieving a nefarious purpose, constitutes theft, even if the taker intends all along to return the thing taken when his purpose has been achieved'[10].

1 See *Alison* I, 259.
2 *Hume* I, 57.
3 See eg *Macdonald v Provan Ltd* 1960 SLT 231.
4 See *Macleod v Ken* 1965 SC 253, 1965 SLT 358, and cf *Wm Wilson* (1882) 5 Coup 48.
5 That once represented a complete definition. For example, the second edition of *Gordon* stated that 'it is clear that Scots law requires an intention to deprive the owner permanently of his goods', para 14–65, but this is now qualified in the third edition at 14–50.
6 See *Hume* I, 75, and *Gordon* para 14–63. The goods are 'detained' even if they are destroyed, given away or merely abandoned.
7 *Hume* I, 79.
8 Cf *Herron v Diack & Newlands* 1973 SLT (Sh Ct) 27. *Dicta* in *Cameron v HM Advocate* 1971 JC 50 at 53, 1971 SLT 202 at 204, per Lord Cameron, to the effect that 'Whether the intent be permanent or only temporary appropriation, the clandestine or felonious taking of the article constitutes the crime', seem to be based on a misunderstanding of this rule.
9 1981 JC 53, 1981 SLT (Notes) 42.
10 Sheriff Fiddes adopted by Lord Justice-Clerk Wheatley in *Milne* 1981 JC 53 at 56.

14.11   This statement[1] has 'effected a radical alteration in the law of theft'[2]. It is based largely on a passage in *Macdonald*[3] to the effect that there is theft 'if the owner of property is clandestinely deprived of possession of it even although the deprivation be temporary'. This statement in turn is based largely on a *dictum* of Lord Macdonald himself in the *Mackenzies* case[4]:

> 'The indictment seems to hint at the book having been taken, not to appropriate the actual article itself, but in order to obtain the opportunity of copying part of its contents for an illegitimate purpose. That such a taking, although there is no intention to retain the article, may be theft is, I think, clear. The article is taken from its owner for the serious purpose of obtaining something of value through the possession of it ... In this case the prosecutor charging the accused with stealing a book described fulfils all the requirements of relevancy, and he can make out by the evidence that the book was taken, and taken with a nefarious purpose, he may be able to obtain a direction in law from the judge at the trial that what was done constituted a theft of the book'.

Lord Macdonald was, however, the only judge explicitly to mention the idea of temporary taking for a nefarious or illegitimate purpose, and Lord Salvesen in particular seemed to regard the case as a straightforward example of theft by taking. Moreover, all that the indictment in *McKenzies* said in relation to the theft charge was that McKenzie 'did steal a book containing recipes of value ...'. Any 'hint' as to the purpose for the theft is to be found in the second charge on the indictment, that of copying secret recipes, a charge specifically held to be irrelevant[5]. But while there may be considerable doubts as to the basis for the 'temporary taking' rule in theft, the decision in *Milne v Tudhope* has been assimilated as part of Scots criminal law. The difficulty lies in the interpretation of the rule.

Milne carried on business as a builder, and in 1978 entered into a contract to renovate and modernise a cottage in Newarthill. The work was nearing completion and the contract price had been paid when a dispute arose about the quality of the work. The owner of the cottage delivered to Milne a list of defects which required to be put right. Milne refused to carry out the remedial work unless he received further payment. The owner refused to make such payment, and Milne and three others went to the cottage while the owner was out, and removed 24 doors, 10 radiators, 11 windows, a boiler, and a quantity of tiles. The owner was informed that the items would be returned if Milne was allowed to complete the contract, and receive additional payment. Milne and his accomplices were convicted of theft and appealed to the High Court.

1 Referred to hereafter as the *Milne v Tudhope* rule.
2 *Gordon's* commentary to *Sandlan v HM Advocate* 1983 SCCR 71 at 96.
3 Page 20.
4 1913 SC (J) 107 at 110, 1913 SLT 48. See also *Gordon* para 14–72 and his commentary to *Sandlan*, above.
5 See 'What sort of property can be stolen?' above.

14.12   The High Court accepted without amplification the sheriff's view that temporary appropriation was sufficient to form the basis of a theft charge, and disapproved Sheriff's MacPhail's decision in *Herron v Best*[1] that 'an intention to deprive permanently' is essential. Applying the law to the instant facts, they held that the conviction was good.

(i)   The taking had been 'clandestine'[2]. Milne's counsel argued that to satisfy this requirement, the taking had to be accomplished in secret, whereas Milne had removed the items in broad daylight. The court held that the taking was sufficiently clandestine if it was done without the owner's knowledge, and so the requirement of 'clandestinity' adds little to the definition of the new rule.

(ii)   The purpose of the taking was 'nefarious'. The High Court was clearly of the opinion that Milne's scheme to obtain payment was unlawful, but added that for the purposes of the appeal it was irrelevant whether 'nefarious' meant 'criminal' or merely 'unlawful'. Sheriff Fiddes (the sheriff at first instance) commented that Milne was in effect 'holding the articles to ransom'. This may have been an echo of Gordon's earlier comment[3] that 'where **A** takes **B**'s property with the intention of returning it if and only if he is paid a ransom for it', there is clearly extortion[4], and probably theft[5]. In such a case, **A** may have an intention to return the article, but it is a conditional intention, based on an unlawful (because extortionate) condition. It is accordingly equivalent to an intention permanently to deprive the owner, because, if the condition is not fulfilled, the goods will never be returned.

1 1976 SLT (Sh Ct) 80.
2 *Macdonald* p 20.
3 *Gordon* para 14–48.
4 See the section on *Extortion* in Chapter 17 below and especially the case of *Black and Penrice v Carmichael* 1992 SCCR 709, 1992 SLT 897, in which employees of a security company immobilised a vehicle parked on private ground and refused to release it unless the vehicle's owner paid a sum of money.
5 Cf *R v Coffey* [1987] Crim LR 498, a case interpreting s 6(1) of the Theft Act 1968.

14.13   Is it possible to argue, therefore, that the *Milne v Tudhope* rule is confined to cases in which the temporary appropriation itself forms part of the *actus reus* of extortion? In *Kidston v Annan*[1], the accused was asked to give an estimate of the cost of repairing a television. Acting beyond his instructions, he repaired the television and refused to return it unless the owner paid him for the work. His conviction for theft was upheld under reference to *Milne v Tudhope*. *Black and Penrice v Carmichael*[2], discussed above, was another 'ransom' case, and indeed one in which extortion was specifically libelled. However, in *Sandlan v HM Advocate*[3] there was no suggestion of extortion or 'ransom'. The accused was a company director who removed records and stock from company premises to avoid disclosure of stock deficiencies, intending to return the items later. Lord Stewart directed the jury in terms of the rule in *Milne v Tudhope*, that an intention to appropriate goods on a temporary basis will suffice to bring home a charge of theft, if the appropriation is for a 'nefarious' purpose. He referred to the removal of the items as a 'manoeuvre to save Sandlan's face', but it seems clear on the evidence that it formed part of a conspiracy to defraud the auditors and shareholders of the company[4]. Accordingly, a modified view of the *Milne v Tudhope* 'rule' might be that there is theft whenever a temporary appropriation forms part of the *actus reus* of some other crime, extortion or fraud providing examples of 'other crimes' from the case law.

Gordon points out, however, that in *Milne v Tudhope*, the court 'approved a general reference to taking for a nefarious purpose'[5]. Accordingly, any unauthorised 'borrowing' of property may constitute theft whether or not it forms part of the *actus reus* of another offence, if the article is to be used to further a 'nefarious' purpose. That purpose must be an unlawful one, but not necessarily criminal[6]. On this view, it would clearly be theft to borrow a house-key in order to commit housebreaking[7], and, presumably, in order to facilitate the commission of any other offence. It is unclear, however, what other forms of unlawful conduct may be encompassed by the rule. Would it be theft, for example, temporarily to appropriate property for use in conduct which amounted to a deliberate breach of contract? Sheriff Fiddes' view that the rule applies only in 'exceptional cases'[8] makes it seem unlikely, but because *Milne* provides so little guidance as to the meaning of 'nefarious', it is impossible to define the limits of the rule with any precision. A further problem is that *Milne* further obscures the distinction between theft and unauthorised borrowing[9]. If it is accepted that temporary appropriation ought to constitute theft[10], we need a more satisfactory definition of such appropriations than that contained in *Milne*. One way to do this consistently with the case law might have been to make clear that a 'nefarious' purpose means a criminal purpose. Confusion arises from the use of terms 'illegitimate', 'nefarious', 'unlawful' and 'criminal' and the reluctance to define these terms.

1 1984 SCCR 20, 1984 SLT 279.
2 1992 SCCR 709, 1992 SLT 897.
3 1983 SCCR 71.
4 See *Gordon's* commentary at 96.
5 *Gordon* paras 14–48 to 14–49.
6 *Milne v Tudhope* 1981 JC 53 at 57, per Lord Justice-Clerk Wheatley.
7 See *Gordon* 14–48 to 14–49, and Lord Justice-Clerk Macdonald in *McKenzies* 1913 SC (J) 107 at 111. See para 14.21 below on house-breaking.
8 1981 JC 53 at 55. In any event, it may that the rule no longer applies only in 'exceptional cases'. See the further discussion of *Black and Penrice* below.
9 As to which see para 14.16 below.
10 See Glanville Williams 'Temporary appropriation ought to constitute theft' [1981] Crim LR 129.

14.14   The court in *Black and Penrice* did not take the opportunity to equiperate 'nefarious' with 'criminal'. Indeed, following the decision in that case, it is by no means clear that a nefarious purpose is required at all. Lord Justice-General Hope accepted in that case that an intention temporarily to deprive is sufficient in theft, and indeed that the case was one of temporary taking rather than one involving a conditional or impliedly permanent intention to deprive. However, his judgment did not depend upon the presence of a nefarious purpose, although such a purpose may be implied from the related extortion charge, which had clear parallels with *Milne*. It is arguable that he seems to have accepted the Crown's view that where the accused has deliberately deprived the complainer of his property, or the use of it, a nefarious purpose may be implied simply by that fact[1], but in the context of the extortion charge, the nefarious purpose can perhaps be read into his assessment of the theft element. The alternative, that no such purpose was necessary, gives rise to the conclusion that, from the inflexible rule that the intention of the accused must be to deprive the owner permanently of the goods, the law has moved in short order to the position that in 'certain exceptional cases' a temporary deprivation may be sufficient, and finally to the position that, apparently, any temporary deprivation of use will do; it is submitted that such a conclusion goes too far.

Finally, there remains the strange case of *Fowler v O'Brien*[2]. In that case, the accused took the complainer's bicycle without permission, and later abandoned it. He had not told the complainer where to look for it. His conviction for theft was upheld on the basis that he had an intention to deprive the owner of the bicycle neither temporarily nor permanently, but 'indefinitely' (although that might be seen as synonymous with permanent). On the facts, there are striking similarities between this case and that of *Kivlin v Milne*[3]. In the latter case, a young man took a car without the owner's consent and then abandoned it in a place where it was not likely to be found. The High Court held that the sheriff was entitled to draw the inference that there had been an intention to deprive the owner permanently, and therefore that there was theft. In spite of the similarities between the cases, the Court in *Fowler v O'Brien*, appeared to take a rather different view:

'In our opinion, on a proper reading of the findings, the justice was not entitled to conclude that there was an intention to deprive the owner permanently of his bicycle, but he does not suggest that that was the view he took of the facts. Nor, in our view, was this an example, in the true sense, of a taking of an article temporarily from its owner, because it was at no point indicated to the complainer when or on what conditions the bicycle would be returned to him. It appears to us that it would be more accurate to say that the owner was deprived of his bicycle indefinitely, since it was not made clear to him whether, and if so, when it would be returned to him. In these circumstances, there was no need for any clandestine or nefarious purpose to be established. There was no need for any exceptional circumstance. The question is simply whether the necessary criminal intention was present for the taking away of the bicycle to amount to theft. We are persuaded in the light of the findings, that the justice was entitled to reach that view and to regard this as an act of stealing the bicycle'.

1 1992 SCCR 709 at 719, 720.
2 1994 SCCR 112.
3 1979 SLT (Notes) 2.

14.15   Arguably, there may accordingly be as many as four different possible types of *mens rea* which are sufficient for theft: an intention permanently to deprive: an intention to deprive temporarily for a nefarious purpose; an intention to deprive temporarily, but without the need for a nefarious purpose to be explicitly libelled; and an intention to deprive indefinitely. However, as indicated above, to distinguish between an intention to deprive permanently and an intention to deprive indefinitely is to perpetuate a distinction without there being a difference. The concept of temporary deprivation without nefarious purpose is derived from *Black and Penrice*, but must be read in the context of the co-existing extortion charge and is, it is submitted, similarly unsupportable. If an intention to deprive temporarily is sufficient, then it is sufficient only in 'exceptional cases'. It is submitted that only those cases which involve what *Gordon* has described as a conditional intention – that is an intention to deprive permanently, *unless* some condition is fulfilled – are exceptional. This view would account for all of the 'temporary taking' cases except for *Sandlan*[1], the appropriate charge in that case being one of fraud. Such a view would additionally preserve the traditional position that only an intention to deprive permanently will do.

Theft and borrowing

Prior to the decision in *Milne v Tudhope*, it was thought that mere borrowing of property could never amount to theft. 'If the goods are taken with the intention only of using them for a time this is not theft although it may constitute another crime'[2]. The 'other crime' is that of 'clandestinely taking and using'[3] which is considered later[4]. Following *Milne v Tudhope* and the other temporary taking cases, the relationship between theft and borrowing is altogether less clear.

Authorised borrowing. This is relatively safe ground. If property is taken with the owner's consent, there is no theft. It is always a defence to a theft charge to argue that one genuinely believed that the owner was consenting to the removal of the property, or that he would have consented had he been aware of the circumstances[5]. But borrowing may become theft even if initially authorised by the owner.

1 1983 SCCR 71.
2 *Gordon* (2nd edn) para 14–65. See also *Burnett* p 115, *Hume* I, 73.
3 See *Strathern v Seaforth* 1926 JC 100, 1926 SLT 445.
4 See para 14.18 below.
5 See *Gordon* para 14–54 and cf Road Traffic Act 1988, s 178(2)(b).

14.16   **A** borrows a book from the public library. He reads the book, and places it on his bookshelf, intending to return it later. In fact, he forgets about the book, and the library reports the matter to the police. At this stage, no theft has occurred, since **A** lacks the appropriate *mens rea*. However: **A** borrows a book from the library. He reads it, places it on his bookshelf intending to return it later, and forgets about it. The library sends him a reminder that the book is overdue. He sees that a substantial fine is due on the book, and decides not to return it at all[1].

A theft has been committed since **A** has now formed the requisite *mens rea*. Appropriation has taken place. **A**'s retention of the book in spite of the reminder would probably provide adequate evidence of this[2].

Unauthorised borrowing. It is not necessarily theft to take property without the owner's consent. Provided that the property was truly taken with the intention to return it to the owner in due course, and was not done in furtherance of a nefarious purpose, then it appears that there can be no theft[3]. As we saw above, there is no theft if property is borrowed in the genuine belief that the owner would have given consent, had he known the circumstances[4].

Presumption of intent to steal

These defences are obviously open to abuse, and accordingly the law presumes that where someone takes property from its owner without the owner's consent, there was an intention to steal[5]. *Gordon* argued that this is a rebuttable presumption[6], and in principle this must surely be right, for otherwise there would be no need for the *Milne v Tudhope* rule[7], since every taking of property without consent would be theft. In *Kivlin v Milnes*[8], the accused took a car without the owner's consent, drove it around, and then abandoned it in a place where the owner was unlikely to find it. It was held that the sheriff was entitled to infer from the accused's conduct that he intended permanently to deprive the owner, and his theft conviction was upheld[9]. The court did accept, however, that whether or not such an inference could be drawn would depend on the individual circumstances of the case. Accordingly, the conduct of the accused will be very important in determining whether or not theft was committed.

1 Cf Glanville Williams [1981] Crim LR 129 at 132.
2 Cf *Morris (David)* [1983] QB 587, [1983] 2 All ER 448, CA; [1984] AC 320, [1983] 3 All ER 288, HL. *Smith and Hogan* (p 493) suggest that the simplest test for appropriation is to inquire whether what the accused did was authorised by the owner.
3 *Milne v Tudhope* 1981 JC 53. See, however, the discussion of *Black and Penrice v Carmichael* 1992 SCCR 709, 1992 SLT 897, above.
4 See *Gordon* para 14–54.
5 *Hume* I, 76.
6 *Gordon* (2nd edn) para 14–79.
7 Although *McLeod v Mason* 1981 SCCR 75, 1981 SLT (Notes) 109 casts some doubt on this conclusion: see *Gordon's* commentary at 1981 SCCR 78.
8 1979 SLT (Notes) 2.
9 Cf *Fowler v O'Brien* 1994 SCCR 112, which, it is submitted above, was correctly decided, but for the wrong reasons.

14.17   Consumption and destruction. The presumption of theftuous intent will be strengthened if the accused uses the property as if it were his own. In *Kivlin v Milne* the accused 'borrowed' a car for a joyride. However, the fact that he then abandoned the car in an unlikely place gave rise to the inference that he intended to deprive the owner of the car permanently. Similarly, if a person takes property, and consumes it or destroys it, it is clear that appropriation has taken place, whether or not the accused intended to return the property[1].

In Scotland, it would certainly be theft to 'borrow' an article and return it having 'used up' its usefulness, since 'consumption or destruction constitutes appropriation'[2]. A person who 'borrows' a season ticket for the opera, uses it until the end of the season, and then returns it, is certainly guilty of theft. He has 'treated the thing as his own to dispose of regardless of the owner's rights'. But it may also be theft to 'borrow' consumable goods, use them, and to replace them with goods of equivalent value. For example, **A** is late for a lunch date, and discovers that he has no cash. He takes the cash from the petty cash box, fully intending to replace the money after lunch once he has visited a cash machine. He knows that he is not entitled to take money for this purpose. Technically, this may amount to a theft, since the money taken has been used up, and the owner deprived of it permanently.

1 See *Gordon* para 14–68.
2 *Gordon* para 14–68.

14.18
Taking and using

If property is 'borrowed' without consent, and used for a 'nefarious' purpose, then according to *Milne v Tudhope*, there is theft, even if the 'borrower' fully intends to return the property when his purpose has been accomplished. But even if the purpose for which the property was taken was not nefarious, the taker may be guilty of the crime of 'clandestinely taking possession and using'. *Burnett* had long ago suggested that temporarily to appropriate a thing, use it, and then return it to its owner, was not theft, but was nevertheless 'an irregular and punishable act'[1]. It was not until 1926, however, that the High Court clearly adopted this view[2], in what was arguably an exercise of the declaratory power[3].

In *Strathern v Seaforth*[4], Seaforth was charged with clandestinely taking possession of, and driving a car, knowing that he had not received permission from the owner, and that permission would have been refused had he requested it. The sheriff-substitute upheld a plea to the relevancy of this charge, and the prosecutor appealed to the High Court. Lord Alness said that although he was convinced that the authorities supported the relevance of the charge, he would have held Seaforth's conduct to be criminal even without such authority.

> 'The matter may be tested by considering what the contention for the respondent involves. It plainly involves that a motor car, or for that matter any other article, may be taken from its owner, and may be retained for an indefinite time by the person who abstracts it and who may make a profit out of the adventure, but that if he intends ultimately to return it, no offence against the law of Scotland has been committed'[5].

1 *Burnett* p 115.
2 Cf *Dewar* (1777) at *Burnett* p 115.
3 See Chapter 1 above.
4 1926 JC 100, 1926 SLT 445.
5 *Strathern v Seaforth* at 102 per Lord Justice-Clerk Alness.

14.19 Lord Alness thought this an 'absurd' argument, and sustained the relevancy of the complaint. It is interesting to compare his reasoning with that in the English unauthorised borrowing cases, decided under s 6(1) of the Theft

Act. In *R v Lloyd*[1], for example, two film projectionists removed films from the cinema where they worked, copied them for a 'pirate' company, and returned them to the cinema before they were missed. It was held that this was not theft, in spite of the fact that huge profits were being made by pirate companies from such copying, because the films had not lost any of their value.

The crime created in *Strathern v Seaforth* has not proved popular with prosecutors however. The only other reported example of the offence is the case of *Murray v Robertson*[2], in which an Ardrossan fish merchant was charged with clandestinely taking possession of some fish boxes, and using them to transport fish to Glasgow. His conviction was quashed, because there was no evidence that he had taken possession of the boxes 'clandestinely' – Lord Justice-Clerk Alness regarded 'clandestine possession as an essential element in the charge'[3]. As in *Milne v Tudhope* however, it may be that 'clandestinely' means no more than 'without the owner's knowledge'[4].

In *Strathern*, the court placed much emphasis on the mischief which would result if the conduct complained of was not declared criminal[5]. It is arguable, therefore, that the offence created in *Strathern* was largely the result of the pressing need to protect car owners from joyriders, and can now be regarded as a legal museum piece. If, as *Gordon* argues, 'the effect of *Murray v Robertson* has been to discourage any extension of *Strathern v Seaforth* beyond vehicles like boats or cycles'[6], then the scope of the crime is certainly very narrow, since there are now statutory provisions forbidding the unauthorised borrowing of motor cars[7]. In any case where it is unclear whether the accused had the intention to steal a car, or merely to take it and drive it away, it seems that an intention to steal will be presumed[8].

1 [1985] 2 All ER 661, (1985) 81 Cr App Rep 182 – although note the doubts which have been expressed about this case: see JC Smith's commentary to *R v Bagshaw* [1988] Crim LR 321.
2 1927 JC 1, 1927 SLT 74.
3 1927 JC 1 at 4–5.
4 See *Gordon* para 15–30.
5 See *Strathern v Seaforth* 1926 JC 100 at 102, per Lord Justice-Clerk Alness.
6 *Gordon* para 15–31.
7 Road Traffic Act 1988, s 178: considered more fully in Chapter 13.
8 Indeed *must* be presumed: see *McLeod v Mason* 1981 SCCR 75, 1981 SLT (Notes) 109.

Error

14.20 **Identity and consent.** '... If the [accused] takes, believing that what he is taking is his own, or that he has the owner's concurrence, he is not guilty of theft'[1]. **A** takes **B**'s umbrella in the belief that it is his own. This is not theft. **A** asks **B** if he can have some item of property. **B** says 'no' but **A** miss-hears and thinks that he has said 'yes'. **A** takes the item of property. This is not theft either.

If in the examples above, however, **A** realises that the umbrella may belong to **B**, or that **B** may have said 'no', and takes the items nevertheless, he is probably guilty of theft[2]. Furthermore, it seems likely that in the first example at least, **A**'s mistaken belief would have to be an honest and reasonable [one], based on colourable grounds', before it could be accepted as a defence[3]. Doubt in the case of the second example arises from the decision of the High Court in *Meek v HM Advocate*[4]. In *Meek* the court indicated that an unreasonable though honest belief in a woman's consent to intercourse is a defence to a rape charge. Since lack of consent is an essential element in theft as well as rape[5], it may be that an honest but unreasonable belief in the consent of the owner to the removal of his property constitutes a defence to a theft charge[6].

Claim of right. An error as to legal entitlement to property is probably a good defence. There is very little authority on the question, but the question typically arises because of erroneous interpretations of the law of succession[7]. For example, **A** has been cohabiting with **B**, who has just died intestate. In the mistaken belief that one cohabitant's property falls to the other on death, he pawns **B**'s diamond ring. This probably is not theft.

1 *Macdonald* p 18.
2 See *Gordon* paras 14–53.
3 *Dewar v HM Advocate* 1945 JC 5 at 8, per Lord Justice-Clerk Cooper.
4 1982 SCCR 613, 1983 SLT 280.
5 See Lord Hailsham in *R v Morgan* [1976] AC 182 at 214 E–G, [1975] 2 All ER 347.
6 See Chapter 11 for a full discussion of *Meek*.
7 See *Gordon* paras 14–55 to 14–56.

Aggravated thefts

Theft by housebreaking

14.21   Certain modes of theft are considered to aggravate the offence. The most common of these modes is theft by housebreaking. This is something of a misnomer however, since 'Scots law does not distinguish among different types of building, and housebreaking can take place against any roofed building'[1]. Since housebreaking is the mode by which the theft is accomplished, it must precede the theft. **X** enters a house through an open window on the ground floor, steals a valuable painting, and then breaks out through a locked door. There is clearly theft, but not theft by housebreaking. Housebreakings (and attempts to open lockfast places) are not criminal *per se*[2]; they must be done with intent to steal. There can be no charge of, for example housebreaking with intent to commit assault or rape[3].

'Housebreaking' is to be interpreted loosely – while it is clearly housebreaking to force open locked doors or windows, it is also housebreaking to enter a house using a stolen[4] or even a found key to unlock doors or windows[5]. It may be housebreaking to use a key which is lawfully in one's possession to gain unauthorised entry to premises. In *Farquarson*[6], an employee was given the keys of business premises to take to the owner after the premises were locked for the night. Instead of doing so, he returned to the premises, and used the key to gain entry. This was held to be housebreaking. Note, however, that a person authorised to use a key to gain entry to premises would not commit the aggravation if he steals from the premises after using the key to gain entry[7]. Nor is it housebreaking to unlock a door by turning a key found in the lock[8].

1 *Gordon* para 15–03.
2 Although they may form the basis of a charge of malicious mischief; see Chapter 18.

3 *HM Advocate v Forbes* 1994 SCCR 163.
4 *Hume* I, 98.
5 *Alex Macdonald* (1826) *Alison* I, 282.
6 (1854) 1 Irv 512.
7 *Gordon* para 15–10.
8 *Peter Alston and Alex Forrest* (1837) 1 Swin 433.

14.22   Entering by unexpected or unusual means may also constitute the aggravation[1] – entering by a window is probably housebreaking, even if the window is unlocked, or open[2]. Indeed, it may be the case that it is housebreaking to enter premises by any route other than the conventional one. Thus it is housebreaking to enter premises by means of chimneys, sewers, openings in the roof, or trap-doors[3]. It is housebreaking to insert implements, or parts of the body into a house through a window or door, in order to steal things inside – in *O'Neil*[4], the accused used a hook to 'fish' for property through an open window. If any unusual mode of entry to premises is in fact commonly used by the owner or occupier of the premises, it may not be housebreaking if a thief also enters by that method[5], but even in such a case, the aggravation may be made out if it is proved that no-one else would be expected to enter by that method[6].

Finally, gaining entry by means of trickery might be regarded as housebreaking[7]: **A** induces **B** to open his door by pretending to be a representative of an electricity company. He then pushes past **B** and steals a number of items. In this situation, **A** might well be charged with robbery, however, since the theft was accomplished by the use of force, albeit of a very minor degree[8].

Opening lockfast places

Opening a locked room in a building does not constitute housebreaking[9], but it does constitute the separate aggravation of opening lockfast places. For example **X** and **Y** have separate bedrooms in a shared flat. When **Y** is out, **X** picks the lock on his door and steals his hi-fi. **X** can be charged with theft by opening lockfast places.

1 *Alison* I, 282.
2 See *Wm Anderson* (1840) Bell's Notes 199.
3 See eg *Rendal Courtney* (1743) *Hume* I, 99; *John Carrigan and Thos Robinson* (1853) 1 Irv 303; *Angus Sutherland* (1874) 3 Coup 74.
4 (1845) 2 Broun 394.
5 *Jas Davidson* (1841) 2 Swin 630.
6 *Angus Sutherland*, above.
7 See *Hume* I, 100; *Macdonald* p 25; *Alston and Forrest* (1837) 1 Swin 433 at 470, per Lord Moncreiff.
8 See *Alison* I, 287, and *O'Neill v HM Advocate* 1934 JC 98, 1934 SLT 432.
9 See *Alison* I, 287, and eg *Gilchrist and Hislop* Bell's Notes 34.

14.23   Rooms within buildings, safes, drawers, cupboards, motor cars and boxes may all be 'lockfast places', and to open any of them by breaking, picking locks, or using stolen or found keys constitutes the aggravation[1]. Again, it must be shown that the theft was achieved by the opening of a lockfast place. The aggravation is not invoked where a box or safe is stolen and opened elsewhere[2].

The use of explosives to open lockfast places acts as an aggravation of the aggravation, and is regarded by the courts as particularly serious.

Theft by drugging – and other aggravations

Theft by drugging the victim and then stealing from him is in theory an aggravation of theft[3]. In modern practice, housebreaking and opening lockfast places are the only commonly libelled aggravations of theft[4]. Other aggravations, such as stealing articles of high value, theft by a known thief, and theft by those in a position of trust, will probably now be regarded as relevant only to the question of sentence.

Preventive offences

14.24   Housebreaking with intent to steal, and opening lockfast places with intent to steal are distinct offences, and in spite of early doubts[5], are commonly encountered in modern practice[6]. That intention will usually be inferred from the circumstances however.

Civic Government (Scotland) Act 1982 s 57(1)

This section provides that 'Any person who … is found in a building so that in all the circumstances, it may be reasonably inferred that he intended to commit theft there, shall be guilty of an offence'[7]. The accused must be found in the particular place; the rest of the charge deals with the matter of inference to be drawn from the circumstances of the presence[8]. Even if the accused's explanation is not believed, the court must nonetheless examine all the remaining circumstances in order to assess whether they are sufficient to prove beyond reasonable doubt an intention to commit theft[9].

1 See *Gordon* para 15–15.
2 *Gordon* para 15–17.
3 *Macdonald* p 31. This situation is regarded as theft and not robbery: see eg *Stuart* (1829) Bell's Notes 22 and Chapter 14.
4 See *Gordon* paras 15–20 to 15–25.
5 See eg *Allan Lawrie* (1837) 2 Swin 101 and cf *Macdonald* p 51.
6 See eg *McLeod v Mason* 1981 SCCR 75, 1981 SLT (Notes) 109.
7 There must be no lawful authority, and 'building' extends to other premises, enclosed or not, curtilage, vehicle or vessel (s 57(1)).
8 *Frail v Lees* 1997 SCCR 354.
9 *McBurnie v McGlennan* 1991 SCCR 756; *Wilson v PF Aberdeen* [2009] HCJAC 30.

COMMON LAW RESET

14.25   Reset is in essence the handling of ill-gotten goods or gains. The crime is committed when a person retains possession of goods obtained by theft, robbery, fraud, or embezzlement, with the intention of keeping the goods from their true owner. It is probably the case that reset can be committed only in respect of the dishonestly acquired goods themselves. On this view[1] receipt of the proceeds of stolen goods is not reset.

1 As to which see *Gordon* para 20–07.

14.26   It is important to distinguish between a thief or an accomplice to a theft on the one hand, and a resetter on the other, since a person involved in the theft of goods, actor or art and part, cannot be convicted of their reset[1]. It may not be easy to determine which is which however. In *Robert v Agnes Black*[2] Mrs B found a pocket book and took it home to her husband. Both were convicted of theft on the ground that the intention to appropriate the book had been formed in concert after Mrs B had taken it home. Had she appropriated it herself and then brought it home that would have been a completed theft, and Mr B could have been guilty only of reset[3]. Thus, in this type of situation a conviction for reset will depend largely on the question of when and by whom appropriation took place[4].

The *actus reus* of reset

14.27   'It is the fundamental circumstance in the description of this crime that the stolen goods are received into the offender's possession'[5]. *Hume* took the view that possession of the goods, in the broad sense of having control of them, should be a requirement for conviction of reset. Thus, a person who keeps stolen goods in his warehouse, or in a safety deposit box in a bank to which he has the key, has sufficient 'possession' for the purposes of this offence. This is so even if the goods are put there by some other person. *Macdonald* extended this idea somewhat, saying that 'If the [thief] with [the resetter's] knowledge hide the property, even in a hole in a wall, and [the resetter] connive at this, he is guilty'[6]. *Gordon* agrees 'provided the goods are hidden there for [the resetter] and not for the thief'[7]. For *Gordon* it is crucial that the resetter have some degree of control over the goods. The problem with *Macdonald's* statement lies in its use of the word 'connive', which seems to imply that a person is guilty of reset who merely knows the whereabouts of stolen goods.

1 *Hume* I, 116; *Gordon* para 20–15 and see eg *Backhurst v McNaughum* 1981 SCCR 6; *Druce v Friel* 1994 JC 182.
2 (1841) Bell's Notes 46.
3 *Gordon* para 20–15. It may be that Mr B could not be convicted even of reset. See discussion of *Smith v Watson* 1982 JC 34, below.
4 As to which see above on theft. Note also that where an accused is charged with theft, he can be convicted of reset, but not vice versa: Criminal Procedure (Scotland) Act 1995, Sch 3, para 8(2).
5 *Hume* I, 110.
6 *Macdonald* p 68.
7 *Gordon* para 20–02.

14.28   In *HM Advocate v Browne*[1], Macdonald, who at the time was Lord Justice-Clerk, developed this idea, holding that 'reset consists of being privy to the retaining of property that has been dishonestly come by'[2]. Thus, in Macdonald's view, reset is possible where the accused has had neither actual nor constructive possession of stolen property, but where he has simply 'connived' at the retention of the property from its true owner. The precise meaning of this expression continues to exercise the courts. In *Gilbert McCawley*[3], it was held, following *Browne*, that a passenger who knew that the car in which he was being driven had been stolen, was guilty of reset, while in *McNeil v HM Advocate*[4] it was found that a person present when thief was introduced to resetter, was similarly guilty.

In the earlier case *of Clark v HM Advocate*[5], the Criminal Appeal Court had expressed doubts about *Browne* and the views of Lord Justice-Clerk Macdonald, which they had difficulty in reconciling with the views of *Hume* and *Alison* that 'it is fundamental to the crime of reset that the goods be received into the accused's possession'[6]. They did not overrule the offending case, but were clearly of the opinion that 'mere inactivity' cannot constitute 'connivance' for the purposes of reset[7].

The accused in *Clark* was present when 1,000 stolen cigarettes were handed over to a resetter in a pub, but apparently took no active part in this transaction or in the accompanying conversation. The court nowhere defines precisely what 'connivance' means, but in quashing the accused's conviction for reset seemed to imply that some 'overt act' on the part of the accused is required[8]. On its facts, *Clark* is clearly inconsistent with *McCawley* and *McNeil*. But the latter case post-dates *Clark*, and in *McNeil* Lord Justice-General Clyde described the observations made by the court in *Clark* as *obiter*, placed emphasis on the views of the court in *McCawley*, and re-iterated the view expressed in *Browne* that reset can be committed by one who is merely privy to the retention of the stolen goods. Again no further assistance was given as to the meaning of connivance.

1 (1903) 6 F(J) 24, 11 SLT 353.
2 (1903) 6F(J) 24 at 26.
3 (July 1959, unreported), HCJ.
4 1968 JC 29, 1968 SLT 338.
5 1965 SLT 250.
6 *Hume* I, 110; see *Clark v HM Advocate* 1965 SLT 250 at 252, per Lord Justice-Clerk Grant, and at 253 per Lord Strachan.
7 See *Clark* per Lord Justice-Clerk Grant at 252.
8 It seems that counsel were agreed that this was the proper interpretation of *Browne*: see *Clark* at 252, per Lord Justice-Clerk Grant.

14.29 In *McNeil*, the accused was in a car when the thief of certain goods, which were also in the car at the time, was introduced to the resetter. In *Hipson v Tudhope*[1], on the other hand, the accused was a passenger in a stolen car. His conviction for reset was quashed since, when stopped by the police, he made no attempt to get away, and said nothing to the investigating officers. Again, the implication of the case is that silence or inactivity in the presence of stolen goods is insufficient to justify a conviction for reset, since there is no 'connivance' with the thief. However, the grounds for the decision were purely evidential – on the evidence, the court were simply unconvinced that the accused knew that the car was stolen. On the one hand the case refers with approval to *Clark*, while on the other, it suggests, consistently with *McNeil*, that a person may be 'privy to the retention' of stolen goods provided only that he knows the origin of the goods. Lord Wheatley said that: 'the situation falls clearly into the category that was recognised in *Clark v HM Advocate* as being a situation where an inference of guilty knowledge could not be garnered from the mere silence of the accused'[2]. In *Friel v Docherty*[3] the accused was convicted of reset of six HGV test certificates. He had obtained them through a third party who had purportedly repaired and tested the six vehicles. The normal timescale between application and test was four to ten weeks. That process for the accused took place within five days. The sheriff found as a matter of fact that the accused had either known that the certificates had not been issued properly by a testing station or deliberately accepted that possibility in the hope that their validity would not be questioned. The High Court held that the sheriff was entitled on the evidence to come to the conclusion that the appellant, although not actually aware how the third party acquired the certificates, blatantly shut his eyes to the possibility that these had been misappropriated and there was no genuine transaction. Gordon's commentary concludes as follows: 'It may be noted that this was not a case of someone coming into possession of a single suspicious article, but of the deliberate pursuit of a course of conduct in circumstances clearly indicative of criminality'[4].

There is no doubt that knowledge of the theftuous origin of the goods is required for a conviction. But more is required than mere knowledge. In *Clark* Lord Strachan said that 'I cannot hold that the crime of reset may be committed by merely refraining from reporting to the police that stolen property is being disposed of'[5]. *Hume* did use the words 'privity and connivance'[6] in relation to reset, but he was referring to the situation where stolen goods are placed in the accused's house with his knowledge and approval. For *Hume*, the accused's knowledge of the presence of the goods is necessary in order to show his possession of them. In consciously allowing the goods to be brought into his house, the accused has performed an 'overt act' showing his connivance with the thief, and his intention to retain the goods from the true owner[7]. Active connivance with the thief is required, not because it demonstrates that the accused knew that the goods were stolen, but because it shows that the accused had a sufficient degree of control over the goods to allow an inference of possession to be drawn. In so far as *Browne* is inconsistent with this analysis, and this is by no means clear, it is submitted that that case was wrongly decided and now requires to be overruled. The older authorities are adamant that possession is required before a conviction for reset can follow[8], and that view seems to be in accordance with the principle that mere knowledge that a crime has been committed does not infer criminal complicity.

1 1983 SCCR 247, 1983 SLT 659.
2 1983 SLT 659 at 660.
3 1990 SCCR 351.
4 1990 SCCR 351 at p 354
5 1965 SLT 250 at 253.
6 *Hume* I, 114.
7 See *Clark*, above at 252, per Lord Justice-Clerk Grant.
8 *Hume*, I 110; *Alison* I, 328; *Burnett* p 155.

The mens rea of reset

14.30 There are two essential elements in the *mens rea* of reset – guilty knowledge that the goods are stolen, and an intention to retain the goods from their true owner.

Guilty knowledge

To bring home a conviction for reset it is necessary for the prosecutor to prove that the accused knew that the goods were stolen. 'Bare suspicion' is not enough. In *Shannon v HM Advocate*[1] the accused concealed his possession of a 'sawed-off' shotgun, and made off when the police came to search his home. However, the accused's possession of an illegal weapon was not enough to justify the inference that the accused knew that the weapon was stolen.

If on the evidence it is clear that the accused must have known the origins of the goods[2], a conviction will be possible, and for this purpose 'wilful blindness' as to the facts is probably sufficient[3]. Where there is evidence that the accused knew the goods to be stolen, very little in the way of corroboration will be required. In *Nisbet v HM Advocate*[4] the thief testified that the accused had such knowledge. For corroboration, the Crown successfully relied on the fact that Nisbet had told an 'awkward story of the way of getting the goods' – in effect that the goods had fallen off the back of a lorry! Again, where the possession of goods is in itself suspicious, the accused's inability to explain satisfactorily his possession of the goods may be regarded as sufficient evidence of guilty knowledge[5].

1 1985 SCCR 14.
2 See *Alison* I, 330.
3 See *Herron v Latta* (1968) 32 JCL 51, (1967) SCCR Supp 18.
4 1983 SCCR 13.
5 See eg *Forbes v HM Advocate* 1994 SCCR 471, 1995 SLT 627, a case about the reset of a Lowry painting stolen from Glasgow Art Gallery. See also *Friel v Docherty* 1990 SCCR 351.

14.31   The latter case emphasises the importance of 'criminative circumstances' in proving reset, and in particular, in proving *mens rea*. Where stolen goods are possessed in circumstances consistent with an innocent possession of the goods, a conviction is unlikely. In *Hamilton v Friel*[1], for example, the prosecution foundered because the stolen goods – a boat and trailer – were kept quite openly in the accused's driveway, in full view of the public.

Intention to retain the goods from their true owner

Provided there is an intention to 'conceal and withhold' the goods from their true owner[2], it is not necessary to show that the goods were retained for a lengthy period, or that the resetter intended to keep the goods for himself. If someone hides goods, perhaps only for a matter of minutes while the police search the thief's house, there is reset. There can be no conviction in the absence of such an intention, for example where someone finds stolen goods and is apprehended when conveying them back to the owner or to a police station.

The husband and wife rule

14.32   It used to be the case that 'A wife is not in the ordinary case held guilty of reset if she conceal property to screen her husband, without proof of active participation'[3]. Thus, a woman could not be convicted of reset solely by reason of her receipt of stolen goods from her husband[4]. In *Smith v Watson*[5] it was said that 'the doctrine is a relic of an age when wives were expected as a matter of course to submit to their husbands and could therefore be presumed to have done wrong *ex reverentia mariti'*. In modern conditions the rule was positively archaic, particularly in view of the number of cohabiting couples and civil partnerships who presumably do not enjoy its protection to any extent. The Marriage and Civil Partnership (Scotland) Act 2014 repealed that protection in terms of s 7. So it no longer a defence to a charge of reset for a wife to contend that the stolen goods she received, or concealed, had been stolen by her husband.

1 1994 SCCR 748.
2 *Hume* I, 113.
3 *Macdonald* p 68.
4 *Gordon* thought that the rule would also be held to apply to a husband who received stolen property from his wife: para 20–05. Cf *Alison* I, 339.
5 1982 SCCR 15, 1982 JC 34.

Chapter 15

Robbery

15.1   Robbery may be regarded as a form of aggravated theft, involving the use of personal violence or threatening behaviour[1]. However, in robbery the taking is achieved by violence or threats, and accordingly there can be no robbery by appropriation of property lawfully obtained, as in theft. This difference apart, the rules regarding *actus reus* and *mens rea* in theft are applicable, and defences to a theft charge, such as error or claim of right, are likewise defences to a charge of robbery[2].

PERSONAL VIOLENCE

Robbery is in essence the taking of goods by force or the threat of force. When goods are forcibly taken from their owner, there may be a preceding assault, or the act of taking may itself be of such violence as to constitute robbery[3]. In *O'Neill v HM Advocate*[4] for example, the accused knocked the victim's head against a wall and grabbed her handbag. It is unnecessary to prove an assault in order to obtain a conviction. In *O'Neill* Lord Justice-Clerk Aitchison said:

> 'It is well settled that in robbery there must be violence. On the other hand, it is not necessary to robbery that there should be actual physical assault. It is enough if the degree of force used can reasonably be described as violence'[5].

The accused in *O'Neill* was charged with assault and robbery. The jury found the assault not proven, but it was held that it was competent nevertheless to find the accused guilty of robbery. Thus, it is a question of circumstances in each case whether there has been violence sufficient to constitute robbery. The cases suggest that the degree of violence required may be slight, although it must not be *de minimis*.

1 Although technically it is a separate offence: see *Gordon* para 16–02. See also *Allan v HM Advocate* 1995 SCCR 234.
2 Although not, of course, to any charge of assault arising out of the incident.
3 See *Harrison v Jessop* 1991 SCCR 329, where the court approved definitions by Macdonald and Hume.
4 1934 JC 98, 1934 SLT 432.
5 1934 JC 98 at 101.

15.2   In *Cromar v HM Advocate*[1], for example, the robber approached the victim from behind, took hold of a bag which the victim was holding, and tried to pull it away. The victim held onto the bag, but its handle snapped and the robber made off. The jury were directed in terms of *O'Neill* and found the accused guilty of robbery. There must, however, be *some* violence. In *Flynn v HM Advocate*[2] the indictment alleged that the accused took the complainer's wallet having seized him by the throat, punched him and knocked him

251

to the ground. The jury found the accused guilty of robbery under deletion of the specific averments of violence. On appeal his conviction was quashed on the ground that the verdict made no sense – the taking was said to have been achieved by means of certain specific acts of violence; if no such violence took place, there could be no conviction for robbery.

However, deletion of the specific averments need not be fatal to a conviction. In *Morrison v HMA*[3] the High Court dealt with an appeal where the jury had deleted all the elements of assault in a robbery charge. It was argued that the robbery charge could not succeed in the absence of the elements of assault libelled. In refusing the appeal the High Court said.

> 'It is undoubtedly true that the jury rejected the allegation that the appellant assaulted the complainer "and did trip him and force him to the ground, repeatedly kick and repeatedly strike him on the head with your hands to his injury". Standing that decision, in our view the question for us is whether, leaving aside those actions, which the jury held not to be proved, there was sufficient evidence of personal violence used for the purpose of appropriation of the property of the complainer.'

After reviewing the evidence, which included the complainer using the words 'scuffle' and 'mugging', the opinion concludes, 'In our view, these descriptions of the incident, found in the complainer's evidence, demonstrate violence on the part of the appellant which cannot be seen as *de minimis*. Plainly it involved scuffling between the appellant and the complainer, as the latter lay on the ground, and was used for the purpose of appropriating his property. The complainer endeavoured to resist the appellant's actions in seeking to withdraw his property from his pockets, but was unsuccessful in that. In these circumstances we conclude that violence was used by the appellant to obtain control of the complainer's property. Whether that violence did or did not amount to an assault was never an issue in the case, because the Crown, in their averments of assault, did not libel those particular actions as such. Since we conclude that that violence was sufficient as an ingredient in the crime of robbery, we see nothing inconsistent in the jury's verdict to convict of robbery at the same time as acquitting of the allegation made in the particular averments of violence libelled by the Crown.' It is, moreover, essential that the taking be achieved *by means* of the violence[4]. If a thief uses force to escape having once removed the goods, there is no robbery, but only a theft followed perhaps by an assault[5]. It should be noted, however, that even though the thief uses no violence initially, it is robbery if he later resorts to force to overcome resistance from the victim[6]. In *Cameron v HM Advocate*[7] the court held that an accused could be convicted of robbery if he was previously involved in planning a theft at which the use of violence was reasonably foreseeable, even if he were not present at the robbery.

Where the taking is preceded by an assault, the assault is usually subsumed by the robbery, since it is regarded simply as the mode by which the robbery is committed. But not every taking preceded by an assault will constitute robbery. If the assault is not connected with the taking, because either the two acts were performed by different, unconnected people[8], or because the original motive for the attack was not theft, then there is no robbery[9]. The second of these possibilities would of course be very difficult to establish and it is probably the case that in these circumstances it would be presumed that the attack was made with intent to rob[10].

1 1987 SCCR 635.
2 *Flynn v HM Advocate* 1995 SCCR 590, 1995 SLT 1267.
3 2010 JC 174.
4 Or threats of violence: see below.
5 See *Gordon* para 16–07.
6 See eg *Cromar* 1987 SCCR 635; and *Hume* I, 105.
7 2008 SCCR 669.
8 As to which see *Flynn v HM Advocate* 1995 SCCR 590, 1995 SLT 1267.
9 See *Gordon* para 16–08. Cf *Burnett* p 150, and *Alison* I, 238, who both take the view that there can be robbery even though the intention to steal arises after the assault has taken place.
10 *Gordon* para 16–08.

THREATS

15.3   The classic case of armed robbery is where the robber points a gun at the victim and threatens, expressly or by clear implication, to shoot the victim should he fail to provide the goods or money sought. Thus, actual violence is unnecessary to constitute robbery – it is enough that there is 'such behaviour as justly alarms for the personal and immediate consequences of resistance or refusal'[1]. *Gordon* says that:

'The development from violence to intimidation is clear – it is robbery to shoot **B** and steal from him; it is also robbery, because it is technically an assault, to present a weapon at **B** and intimidate him into handing over his goods; and from there it is but a short step to say that it is robbery to threaten to shoot **B** without actually producing a weapon'[2].

It is not clear, however, whether the threat must be such as to overcome the resistance of a reasonable person, or that the alarm felt by the complainer for 'the personal and immediate consequences of resistance or refusal' must be based on reasonable grounds. In *Gilmour v McGlennan*[3], the accused pointed a toy gun at the complainer, who apparently believed it to be real. The High Court upheld his conviction of assault and robbery, holding that since the complainer had in fact been placed in fear and alarm for his safety by the accused, the crime had been committed. The court did not go on to consider whether a reasonable person would have been placed in such fear by the actions of the accused. It is the result that is material; if the victim is induced to part with the property as a result of the threat, then the issue of whether a reasonable person would have done so is immaterial.

Where the threat does not constitute an assault (that is, where neither gun, knife nor fist is presented at the victim), it can become very difficult to distinguish robbery from extortion[4]. According to *Gordon*, 'robbery by threats is distinguished from extortion by the immediacy of the threat and the obtaining of the money'[5]. The older authorities suggest that violence, actual or threatened, is of the essence in robbery[6], and while it is unnecessary to establish that any menaces used themselves constituted an assault, it is submitted that a requirement for 'threats of present injury and not merely of some future wrong'[7] seems necessary to distinguish robbery from extortion. Thus, menaces which 'appear in the weapons shown, in the number and combination of the assailants, or in their words, gestures and carriage, if in the whole circumstances of the situation they may reasonably intimidate and overawe, are therefore a proper description of violence, to found a charge of robbery'[8].

Scots Law also recognises the existence of a crime in the common law of threats. In *Harris v HM Advocate*[9], the court determined that threats made in private, without the prospect of being overheard or indirectly observed, could not constitute an offence of breach of the peace. The Lord Justice General concluded that such conduct might have given rise to a different charge observing, 'The common law of threats might possibly also have been invoked'[10]. The matter was examined in a little more detail in *Baillie v HMA*[11]. The court confirmed that, 'First, a threat to do serious injury to a person, whether oral or written, is criminal in itself. This was ... the view taken in James Miller (1862) 4 Irv 238, where the Lord Justice Clerk explained ... that there were two classes of threats: first, those which involved "grievous bodily harm, or to do any serious injury to his property ...", and, secondly, those in a "much larger class" which contemplated lesser or vaguer harms. Only the former were criminal per se, while the latter might acquire criminal status if they were used for an unlawful purpose, such as extortion.'

So not every threat can give rise to criminal responsibilities, but as with the elements of assault, a seemingly minor threat in the context of a robbery would acquire criminal status.

1 *Hume* I, 107.
2 *Gordon* para 16–12.
3 1993 SCCR 837.
4 As to which see section on *Extortion* in Chapter 17 below.
5 *Gordon* para 16–14.
6 See *Hume* I, 107; *Macdonald* p 41. Cf *Alison* pp 231–233, and see *Jones and Christie* para 10–49.
7 *Macdonald* p 41.
8 *Hume* I, 107.
9 2009 SLT 1078.
10 At para [26]
11 2013 SCL 550; 2013 SCCR. 285.

Chapter 16

Fraud/uttering

16.1 In Scotland, fraud remains largely a common law offence[1]. What is important in the Scottish law of fraud is essentially proof of dishonest conduct which produces some concrete practical result, and a causal link between the pretence and the result. It is a test which is simple to apply in practice and which seems to accord well with popular perceptions or moral intuitions as to what constitutes the offence[2].

1 Although there are numerous statutory frauds, such as: bankruptcy frauds; weights and measures frauds; company frauds; trades descriptions frauds; food and drugs frauds and so on. These are beyond the scope of a work of this nature, but are dealt with in some detail by *Gordon* in Chapter 19. Note that some such frauds may also be frauds at common law, eg bankruptcy frauds. Cf *HM Advocate v Livingston* (1888) 1 White 587, 15 R (J) 48.
2 Although there are clearly limits: in the case of *Macdonald v HM Advocate* 1996 SLT 723 the sheriff's description of the offence as essentially 'fiddling' was held to be a misdirection.

COMMON LAW FRAUD (SIMPLE FRAUD)

16.2 It is of the essence of the crime of fraud that a false impression should be conveyed to the victim[1], with the deliberate aim of achieving some practical, and to the victim, usually prejudicial, result. It is also essential that the false pretence should have brought about this desired result[2]. It is not necessary that the accused should have gained any item of property through his false pretence. There may indeed be fraud where the victim has not been deprived of any item of property.

The false pretence

The false pretence may take a variety of forms. It has been said that it is enough that there is '... any deception by which one man makes another believe to the latter's injury, something that really does not exist. It may be done by direct assertion or by a suggestion, not amounting to a direct assertion, of something which was untrue'[3].

However, the emphasis in Scots law is not so much on the idea of deception – the active creation of a false belief in the mind of the victim[4] – as on the facts that a false pretence has been made, and that some practical result is brought about by the pretence[5]. Thus, it is not necessary in Scotland to show that anyone was in fact deceived, provided that the causal link between false pretence and result is proved[6].

1 See *Guild v Lees* 1994 SCCR 745, 1995 SLT 68, in which the secretary of a curling club drew on the club's bank account in order to pay personal bills. This was said to be an example of embezzlement (as to which, see Chapter 17 below) and not fraud, since no misrepresentation had been made to the bank, the club or the payee.

2 *Gordon* para 18–02. See also *Macdonald v HM Advocate* 1996 SLT 723.
3 *HM Advocate v Livingstone* (1888) 1 White 587 at 592, per Lord Fraser.
4 See *Re London and Globe Finance Corpn* [1903] 1 Ch 728 at 732, per Buckley J, and cf *Welham v DPP* [1961] AC 103 at 133, per Lord Denning.
5 See *Macdonald* p 52.
6 Cf eg *DPP v Ray* [1974] AC 370, [1973] 3 All ER 131, considered below.

16.3   The pretence may be about any relevant matter, the only proviso being that the pretence must bring about the practical result. Thus, for example **A** falsely represents to **B** that she is the daughter of **C**, a person known by **B** to be of good credit. **B** hands over goods to **A** in the belief that **C** will pay him later. **A**, who is never seen again, commits fraud[1].

Again, **A** says to **B** that he can sell him a fragment of Burns' original handwritten manuscript of 'Tam O'Shanter'. The manuscript is a clever but worthless forgery, a fact well known to **A**, but not to **B** who pays a very large sum for the manuscript. **A** commits fraud[2].

A wishes to purchase **B**'s large house. He wishes to convert the house for office use, but is aware that **B** will not sell the house except for residential purposes. He tells **B** that he intends to use the house as a residence for himself and his family, and **B** sells him the house on that basis. **A** commits fraud[3].

Implied representations

It is not necessary that the accused should have made a false statement however. It is enough that he has acted in such a way as to create a false impression about any of the matters referred to above. In the English case of *Barnard*[4], for example, a townsman walked into an Oxford shop dressed as an undergraduate and obtained goods on credit thanks to the false impression he had thus created. At no time did Barnard explicitly claim to be an undergraduate: he was nevertheless convicted of fraud.

In the extraordinary case of *James Paton*[5], the accused inflated the skins of his cattle to make them look fatter, and fixed false horns on to them. He wanted to win a prize at a cattle show, but instead was charged with fraud. Although he was acquitted on other grounds, it was held that the false impression created by his 'window dressing' was sufficient to form the basis of a fraud charge.

1 Cf *Morrison v Robertson* 1908 SC 332, (1908) 15 SLT 697.
2 Cf *Frank v HM Advocate* 1938 JC 17, 1938 SLT 109.
3 See eg *Richards v HM Advocate* 1971 JC 29; *Steuart v Macpherson* 1918 JC 96, 1918 2 SLT 125.
4 (1837) 7 C & P 784.
5 (1858) 3 Irv 208.

Silence as a false pretence

16.4   In some circumstances, a false impression may be created by remaining silent about the true facts. Thus, where a person has a contractual or statutory duty to disclose certain facts to another, and fails to do so, that person may commit common law fraud[1]. Gill expresses the view[2] that where (a) disclosure of the undisclosed fact would have caused the victim to act otherwise than he did, and (b) the accused intended that the victim should not have acted other-wise than he did, fraud is committed. He derives some support for this view from the case of *HM Advocate v Livingston*[3], a prosecution under the Bank-ruptcy Acts, in which the accused obtained a loan without revealing his status as an undischarged bankrupt. Lord Fraser directed the jury that the accused's failure to reveal his state of bankruptcy constituted a relevant false pretence – the accused 'knew perfectly well that if he had told that fact he would not have got credit for a single sixpence'[4]. This may be too wide a view, however. Unless there is a duty to reveal a particular fact, there can be no fraud. To hold otherwise would be to render liable to prosecution those who withhold, for example, commercial information when they are perfectly entitled to do so. Thus, while it has been held that there is a duty to reveal the fact that one is an undischarged bankrupt when seeking credit[5], or to correct inaccuracies in a company prospectus which one has published[6], it seems that there may be no duty to correct a mistake, provided the mistake was not induced by anything the accused said or did.

1 See eg *Strathern v Fogal* 1922 JC 73, 1922 SLT 543; *HM Advocate v City of Glasgow Bank Directors* (1879) 4 Coup 161, 6 R (J) 19.
2 In 'The crime of fraud: a comparative study' (unpublished PhD thesis, Edinburgh University 1975), at p 69n.
3 (1888) 1 White 587, 15 R (J) 48. See also *Patterson v Landsberg* (1905) 7 F 675, 13 SLT 62; *HM Advocate v Pattisons* (1901) 3 Adam 420.
4 *HM Advocate v Livingstone* (1888) 1 White 587 at 592.
5 *HM Advocate v Livingstone*, above.
6 *HM Advocate v Pattisons* (1901) 3 Adam 420.

16.5 In the English case of *Dip Kaur v Chief Constable of Hampshire*[1], goods in a supermarket were mispriced. The accused, who clearly realised what had happened, presented the goods at the cash desk and obtained them at the lower price. Lord Lane CJ held that the accused had practised no deception, nor made any false pretence[2]. Had the shop-assistant known the truth, no doubt he would have acted differently; nevertheless, there was no fraud[3]. Similarly, sellers of goods have no general duty to reveal defects[4], although someone sell-ing reconditioned goods which appear to be new has a duty to reveal their true nature[5].

Whether or not there is a duty to disclose may depend on the relationship of the parties. Although the accused in *Kaur* clearly knew that the goods were mispriced, she was entitled to rely on the cashier's authority to sell the goods at a lower price[6]. But where a customer expresses a mistaken view of the price, nature or quality of certain goods the seller is probably obliged to correct that view[7]. Again, the position is different if the accused has taken active steps to conceal the truth – if Ms Kaur had herself placed the wrong price on the goods, for example – and then remains silent, her conduct would have amounted to a misrepresentation[8].

Of course, the distinction between conduct amounting to a misrepresentation, and non-fraudulent silence is not an easy one to draw. In *HM Advocate v Patti-sons*[9], the accused published a company prospectus containing accounts which had been prepared from the company books. Those books contained material omissions which the accused failed to disclose. It was held that the presentation of the books to the accountants without explanation amounted to a misrepresentation that they were accurate and complete[10]. But unless the accused had a duty to make full disclosure of their company's finances to potential investors, their presentation of the books to the accountants may not amount to such a misrepresentation.

In *Cummings v HM Advocate*[11], the High Court dealt with an appeal against conviction for fraud on an art and part basis. The appellant had called uninvited at the victims' homes, said that roofing work was required, and had then undertaken the work for a reasonable price. He had, the court held, created the circumstances where there was a return visit purportedly for an inspection, which gave his co-accused the opportunity to make fraudulent representations about the remedial work still required. The conviction was upheld although the appellant had restricted involvement in the misrepresentations made.

1   [1981] 2 All ER 430, [1981] 1 WLR 578, CA.
2   See [1981] 1 WLR 578 at 583D, per Lord Lane CJ. Kaur was charged with theft, so Lord Lane's *dictum* was *obiter*, and the crucial question in the case was whether Kaur's dishonesty over the price had vitiated the contract. If it had, then ownership remained with the shop, and her removal of the goods from the shop would have amounted to theft. *Kaur* has since been doubted (on the theft point), by Lord Roskill in *Morris (David)* [1984] AC 320 at 334, and that doubt has itself been doubted, by *Smith and Hogan* p 494.
3   But cf JC Smith *The Law of Theft* (4th edn, 1979) p 88, and cf the cases of *Charles* and *Lambie*, which seem inconsistent with *Kaur*.
4   See eg *Smith and Hogan* p 547. There are, of course, numerous statutory provisions designed to protect the consumer.
5   See *Gibson v National Cash Register Co Ltd* 1925 SC 50, 1925 SLT 377, and cf *Patterson v Landsberg* (1905) 7 F 675, 13 SLT 62.
6   See *Kaur* [1981] 1 WLR 578 at 583C, [1981] 2 All ER 430.
7   Cf *With v O'Flanagan* [1936] Ch 575; *Indedon v Watson* (1862) 2 F&F 841.
8   *Kaur* [1981] 1 WLR 578 at 58ID and 583F.
9   (1901) 3 Adam 420.
10 (1901) 3 Adam 420 at 470.
11 [2009] HCJAC 55, 2009 SCL 1195.

Representations of intention

16.6   Can a statement of intention, and in particular, a statement of intention to pay[1], form the basis of a fraud charge[2]? Such statements present problems for the criminal law, since people frequently break promises, or fail to pay their debts. In such cases, the promisor or debtor has failed to carry out his intention[3], but not all such people ought to be treated as criminals. There are some promises with which the law ought not to become involved, and business people who genuinely intend to meet their obligations may become unable to do so. Even wilful failure to pay a debt is not necessarily treated as criminal, as a visit to any small claims court will demonstrate.

Although the older cases[4] suggested that only a misrepresentation of past or present fact is relevant to a fraud charge, there can now be no doubt, following the case of *Richards v HM Advocate*[5], that a false statement of intention can form the basis for such a charge. Richards wished to buy a property in Edinburgh from the local authority. He was aware that the authority would sell the property only if it was to be used as a private residence, and accordingly he represented to the authority that he intended to use the property as his family home. In fact he had no such intention, and he was convicted of fraud. The court refused to recognise the distinction drawn in the nineteenth century case of *John Hall*[6] between misrepresentations of fact, and misrepresentations of intention, saying that '… a man's present intention is just as much a fact as his name or his occupation, or the size of his bank balance'[7].

1 *See John Hall* (1881) 4 Coup 438, 8 R (J) 28.
2 See *Gordon* para 18–12 to 18–13.
3 Note the problems of classification here: see *Gordon* para 18–13.
4 Such as *John Hall*, above.
5 1971 JC 29.
6 (1881) 4 Coup 438, 8 R (J) 28.
7 *Richards v HM Advocate* 1971 JC 29 at 32, per Lord Justice-Clerk Grant.

16.7   Particular problems have arisen where a person orders goods or services with the initial intention of paying for them, but later changes his mind, and defaults on his obligation.

In the English case, *DPP v Ray*[1], a group of young men ordered a meal in a Chinese restaurant, fully intending to pay for it. After they had consumed the meal they changed their minds and left the restaurant without paying. The House of Lords treated their initial representation of intention to pay as a continuing one[2], which was falsified by their later change of mind.

Ray gave rise to a number of problems[3], not the least of which was that by treating representations of intention to pay as continuing ones, the House of Lords seemed to imply that there is a duty to disclose that the representation has become false. Such an approach is to run the risk of 'treating every defaulting debtor as guilty of fraud where it can be shown that but for his non-disclosure of his change of mind the creditor would have taken steps to try to secure payment'[4]. In Scotland, following *Richards*[5], a charge of obtaining goods or services 'without paying and without intending to pay' is clearly relevant[6]. However, if it is accepted, as it was in *Ray*, that the initial intention of the fraudster was to pay for the goods, and that only at some later stage, after the goods were handed over, did he form the intention to withhold payment, it may in Scotland be very difficult to frame an appropriate charge, since the goods were not obtained by means of any false pretence[7]. But an alternative charge of theft may be available.

Statement of opinion

Statements of opinion generally cannot form the basis of a fraud charge, since such statements cannot easily be shown to be 'true' or 'false'. It might be shown, however, that the maker of the statement did not really hold the opinion claimed, or that he knew of facts tending to negate the opinion, and on that basis a fraud charge might be held relevant[8].

1 [1974] AC 370, [1973] 3 All ER 131.
2 Or possibly as containing a further implied representation that they would not later change their minds: see [1974] AC 370 at 386A, per Lord Morris.
3 As to which see GH Gordon 'Two recent developments in English criminal law' (1975) 20 JLSS 4.

4 *Gordon* para 18–12.
5 1971 JC 29.
6 See also *Gordon* para 18–13, n 78. It should be noted, however, that in the particular circumstances of *Ray*, there might well have been an acquittal in Scotland because of problems of causation.
7 Cf GH Gordon 'Two recent developments' (1975) 20 JLSS 4 at 7.
8 See *Smith and Hogan* pp 510–511.

16.8   Manufacturers and retailers of goods frequently make extravagant or even false claims about their products. Provided, however, that such claims amount only to statements of opinion about the goods, and are not false statements of fact, there is no fraud[1]. In *Tapsell v Prentice*[2], Lord Ardwall referred to statements which were 'just the ordinary lies which people tell when they want to induce credulous members of the public to purchase goods, or to do something for them'[3]. In drawing the line between statements of fact and statements of opinion, advertisers are given considerable freedom. Few people believe the claims which some manufacturers make for their products in their advertising campaigns. Nevertheless, such statements are not generally regarded as fraudulent[4]. It is likely to be regarded as a matter of fact and degree whether more outrageous examples of such statements represent relevant false pretences[5]. Where goods are advertised or sold in the course of a business, the application of a false description to the goods would in any event render the advertiser or seller liable to prosecution under the Trade Descriptions Act 1968[6]. The most likely route for a party disappointed by a description of goods or services would be a civil action, rather than the reporting of a perceived fraudulent act.

The result

Fraud is popularly perceived as an offence by which the perpetrator gains possession of some item of the victim's property, or makes some gain at the victim's expense. In England, for example, an offence is committed by any person who 'by any deception dishonestly obtains property belonging to another'[7]. *Hume* seems to have regarded fraud in this light – he defines fraud as a false pretence made 'for the purpose of obtaining goods or money, or other valuable thing, to the offender's profit'[8], and *Alison* refers to 'All those falsehoods and frauds by which another is deprived of his property'[9]. During the nineteenth century, however, fraud seems to lose the requirement of economic loss to the victim, or indeed gain for the accused. This extension of the offence seems to have been due to the incompetency at that time of a charge of attempted fraud, and acts came to be regarded as fraudulent which involved little or no actual economic prejudice to the victim, but which merely exposed the victim to a risk of such prejudice. Thus, in *James Paton*[10], in which the accused inflated the skins of his cattle beasts in order to win a prize at an agricultural show, it was enough that the accused won the competition, and thus obtained a right to a prize. The lack of any averment that the prize was actually paid was not fatal to the relevancy of the indictment[11].

1 See *Gordon* para 18–09.
2 (1910) 6 Adam 354, 1911 SC (J) 67.
3 (1910) 6 Adam 354 at 357.

4 Some advertisements may, however, give rise to complaints to the Advertising Standards Authority.
5 See *Gordon* para 18–09.
6 Section 1(1). See *Gordon* paras 19–25 to 19–50.
7 If he has the intention permanently to deprive the other of his property: see the Theft Act 1968, s 15(1).
8 *Hume* I, 172.
9 *Alison* I, 362.
10 (1858) 3 Irv 208.
11 See also *Hood v Young* (1853) 1 Irv 236.

16.9 The classic modern statement of the result requirement in fraud is to be found in the case of *Adcock v Archibald*[1]. In that case, Lord Justice-General Clyde said that 'It is … a mistake to suppose that to the commission of a fraud it is necessary to prove an actual gain by the accused, or an actual loss on the part of the person alleged to be defrauded. Any definite practical result achieved by the fraud is enough'[2]. This statement was approved in the later case of *HM Advocate v Wishart*[3]. Wishart was a solicitor who entered into a complex scheme with a stockbroker whereby the latter's accounts were made to appear healthier than was in fact the case. There was no averment that anyone had suffered loss because of the scheme, and the only result was that the stockbroker's auditors were induced to report to the Stock Exchange as genuine, accounts which were inaccurate and misleading[4]. Lord Macdonald held that economic loss is unnecessary in fraud, and found the charge to be relevant.

Fraud in Scots law is therefore a crime wide in scope. It does not even appear from the opinions delivered in *Adcock* that the result need be prejudicial to the victim. While it may be accepted that prejudice does not necessarily imply economic loss[5], to do away altogether with the requirement of prejudice to the victim may lead to absurd results – on this view, there would be fraud if a person was induced by false pretences to accept some benefit[6]. What does seem clear is that the victim must have been induced actually to do some act, rather than simply to believe a lie. Mere deception is not enough[7]. *Gordon* submits that the result must not only be prejudicial but that the prejudice must be more than merely trivial[8]. In support of that contention he cites the case of *HM Advocate v Camerons*[9].

1 1925 JC 58, 1925 SLT 258.
2 1925 JC 58 at 61.
3 1975 SCCR Supp 78.
4 Cf *HM Advocate v Pattisons* (1901) 3 Adam 420.
5 See the examples given by *Gordon* at para 18–21.
6 *Gordon* para 18–19.
7 Cf *Welham v DPP* [1961] AC 103.
8 Cf the pre-Theft Act English law, which did not require economic loss in fraud, but did require that the result of the pretence be prejudicial to the dupe.
9 (1911) 6 Adam 456, 1911 SC (J) 110.

16.10 The Camerons wrote a letter to their insurance firm in which they fabricated a claim in respect of some jewellery, which they claimed was stolen from them. The insurers sent the accused a claim form but the matter went no further than that. Although the insurers had been induced to part with a sheet of paper, and the cost of posting the form to the accused, the charge was one of attempted fraud only.

The result, although definite and practical, was clearly considered too minor to warrant a fraud charge. But although the Crown saw fit to charge the Camerons only with the inchoate offence, there is no legal reason to suppose that a charge libelling the completed crime would not have been held relevant. As *Gordon* recognises[1], there is no *de minimis* rule in Scotland, and the 'practical result' accepted in *Adcock v Archibald* was of no more significance than the result of the Camerons' false pretence[2].

In *Adcock*, the accused was a miner who put his own marker on a hutch of coal mined by another. His employers were thus induced to make an entry in their books signifying that it was he who had mined the coal and not his colleague. This book entry was the only practical result however, since Adcock had failed to extract enough coal to qualify for a productivity bonus.

In theory then, it appears that fraud may be committed where the victim is induced to do something [he] would not otherwise have done'[3], and that that 'something' may be extremely trivial. *Gordon's* view that the result must involve some 'legally significant prejudice' seems, at least in theory, open to debate.

1 See *Gordon* para 18–19, n 8.
2 *Gordon* argues (at para 18–19) that while the *dicta* expressed in *Adcock v Archibald* may have been sound, their application to the facts of the case was not.
3 Lord Hunter in *Adcock* 1925 JC 58 at 61.

16.11   In *McKenzie v HM Advocate*[1], the accused made false statements to solicitors in Edinburgh, and thereby induced them to raise unfounded civil actions against Caley Fisheries of Peterhead. A charge of *attempting* to defraud the fishing company was found to be relevant, although the facts of the case support the view that there might have been a completed fraud on the accuseds' solicitors. False representations made by the accused to their solicitors led to a definite practical result – the raising of the actions against Caley Fisheries[2]. Support for the view that this could have been charged as a completed fraud may be found in *Adcock* where Lord Hunter says, somewhat obscurely, that fraud may consist in inducing someone to 'become the medium of some unlawful act'[3]. On the basis of *Adcock*, it might therefore have been averred that the prejudicial result here lay in the fact that the solicitors became the innocent agents of a fraudulent scheme, and that a completed fraud on the solicitors was committed as soon as the spurious actions were raised[4]. Another result which might in theory have formed the basis of a fraud charge was the simple fact that the solicitors were induced to spend valuable time on a fool's errand. In relation to this possibility, however, an analogy may be drawn with cases such as *Kerr v Hill*[5], and *Robertson v Hamilton*[6], which indicate that the making of false reports to the police, whereby they are induced to spend time making investigations, is not a form of fraud.

Physical prejudice has on occasion also been regarded as a relevant result in fraud. It is, for example, fraud to induce a woman to consent to intercourse by means of a false pretence to be the woman's husband[7]. There are limits to the relevance of physical injury in a fraud charge however. A person who causes injury by means of false pretence may well be guilty of a crime involving real injury, rather than fraud[8], and to allow this as a relevant result in fraud would be to blur the distinction between these two diverse areas of the criminal law.

1 1988 SCCR 153, 1988 SLT 487.
2 See opinion of the court at 1988 SCCR 156, 1988 SLT 489H.
3 *Adcock v Archibald* at 82 – Lord Hunter may also have had in mind the situation in which the dupe renders himself liable to prosecution – see *Gordon* para 18–25.
4 This was the moment when the scheme became an attempted fraud on the fishing companies – see the opinion of the court at 156, 489H.
5 1936 JC 71, 1936 SLT 320. Such conduct is a separate common law offence, however; see Chapter 20.
6 1987 SCCR 477, 1988 SLT 70.
7 *Wm Fraser* (1847) Arkley 280.
8 See Chapter 9 above, and cf CS Kenny *Kenny's Outlines of Criminal Law* (19th edn, 1965) para 377.

The causal link

16.12   The third requirement of a relevant fraud charge is that there must be a causal connection between the false pretence and the result[1]. The result must have been brought about by the false pretence, and it is a defence to a charge of fraud to show that the false pretence did not influence the victim in his actings[2]. Thus, if someone obtains goods from a seller, and later hands to the seller a cheque which is dishonoured, there is no fraud, since the seller did not deliver the goods as a result of any false pretence that the cheque would be honoured in due course[3]. For the same reasons, false statements as to 'collateral' matters cannot form the basis of a fraud charge.

In *Tapsell v Prentice*[4], a woman falsely represented to a shopkeeper that she was a member of a band of gypsies encamped in the area who would buy provisions from his shop. No doubt in anticipation of future custom from this travelling band, the shopkeeper bought a rug from her, and the woman was charged with fraud, by inducing the shopkeeper to 'purchase a rug in excess of its proper value'. The court dismissed the charge as irrelevant. In the first place, the sale of an article in excess of its value was 'a thing that is done any day and is not a criminal offence'[5]. Secondly, the representations were 'not directly connected with the rug, which may have been a perfectly good one … There can be no crime in such a sale as [was] here alleged unless the fraudulent misrepresentations relate directly to the articles to be sold'[6]. The 'collateral representations' rule in relation to the sale of goods seems to some extent anomalous. No doubt it is intended to avoid rendering advertisers liable for over-selling goods. Nevertheless, it is arguable that if a misrepresentation in fact induces a sale there ought to be liability for fraud, regardless of whether the representation is about the goods or about some other matter. The rule seems to create a category of representations which in law simply cannot form a causal connection with the result, whatever the factual situation.

1 See generally *Gordon* paras 18–26 to 18–29.
2 *Gordon* para 18–26.
3 *Mather v HM Advocate* (1914) 7 Adam 525, 1914 SC (J) 184.
4 (1910) 6 Adam 356, 1911 SC (J) 67. See also *Strathern v Fogal* 1922 JC 73, 1922 SLT 543.
5 6 Adam 356 at 356, per Lord Justice-Clerk Macdonald.
6 Lord Ardwall at 357.

The *mens rea* of fraud

16.13   The *mens rea* requirement in fraud may be split into two elements: the *mens rea* required in relation to the false pretence; and that in relation to the result.

(a)   The false pretence

Clearly a representation made in the knowledge of its falsity is enough to satisfy this requirement. However, a reckless belief in the truth of a representation may also suffice, or at least a realisation that the statement may be false. In this context it is thought that the form of recklessness required would probably have to be advertent recklessness, rather than the gross carelessness of cases like *Allan v Paterson*[1]. It is 'unlikely that a situation in which [the accused] does not apply his mind at all to the truth or falsity of the statement would be regarded as fraudulent'[2].

(b)   The result

Whether the accused made the false statement recklessly or knowingly, he must have intended thereby to bring about the result. Fraud cannot be committed by accident.

1 1980 JC 57.
2 *Gordon* para 18–31.

Articles for use in fraud

In the Criminal Justice and Licensing Act 2010, s 49 provides for two new criminal offences relating to fraud in an attempt to address the increasingly sophisticated environment in which frauds are perpetrated. Section 49(1) makes it an offence for a person to possess, or have within their control, an article for use in, or in connection with, the commission of fraud. It will have to be established that the accused possessed or had control of the article and that the article was to be used in the course of or in connection with fraud. Section 49(3) makes it an offence to make, adapt, supply or offer to supply, an article knowing either that the article is designed or adapted for use in, or in connection with, the commission of fraud, or intending the article to be used in, or in connection with, the commission of fraud. Section 49(5) provides that an 'article' within the section includes more than simply a physical object, and can be a program, or data, held in electronic form so could cover lists of credit card details or addresses held on a computer.

UTTERING OF FORGED DOCUMENTS

16.14   Forgery – the manufacture of falsely authenticated documents – is not in itself a crime[1]. Anyone may while away his or her time perfecting counterfeit signatures without becoming liable to the sanctions of the criminal law. Nor does the forgery become criminal if forged documents are stumbled upon by accident. The crime is committed only when a document is intentionally uttered as genuine[2], in the knowledge that it is false[3]. Although fraudulent schemes may thereby be arrested at an early stage of their development, the introduction of the crime of attempted fraud[4], has considerably reduced the scope of this crime. Subject to the *mens rea* elements just mentioned, the prerequisites for a charge of uttering are two:

(1)   The uttering must be carried out with the intention of deceiving the person to whom the document is uttered[5].

(2)   The uttering must be 'towards' the prejudice of the victim. In *Macdonald v Tudhope*[6] the treasurer of a club forged the signature of a third party on certificates recording the amounts of money withdrawn from the club's gaming machines. He was convicted, and appealed on the grounds that there was no averment that anyone was prejudiced by the uttering, and in particular, no allegation that the certificates were anything other than a true record of the monies withdrawn from the machines. His appeal was dismissed on the grounds that ... It was not necessary that actual prejudice should ensue: what was essential was that the uttering should be towards the prejudice of the intended recipient'[7]. The fact that the recipient of the certificates accepted them as genuine documents to be recorded as such in the club's accounts was regarded as sufficiently prejudicial in this case.

If one regards the presentation of a forged document as a false pretence, and looks to the result or potential result which may ensue, it is easy to classify such actions as fraud or attempted fraud, rather than uttering. *Gordon* regards it as a matter of convenience only, whether uttering or fraud is the offence charged in such cases[8].

1   See eg *Alison* I, 402.
2   See eg *Macdonald* p 65; *Jas Devlin* (1828) *Alison* I, 402.
3   *Hume* I, 154.
4   In the Criminal Procedure (Scotland) Act 1887, s 61.
5   See *Gordon* para 18–52.
6   1983 SCCR 341, 1984 SLT 23.
7   At 1984 SLT 23.
8   See *Gordon* para 18–35. Cf *HM Advocate v Hardy* 1938 JC 144, 1938 SLT 412.

The modes of forgery

16.15   A forged document is one which falsely purports to be authenticated by a particular person[1]. It is forgery to sign a document with a fictitious name, at least in circumstances where the recipient of the document 'will be led to believe that the document is the document of some person other than its maker'[2]. If it is forgery to sign a fictitious name, it is even more so to imitate the signature of a real person and append it to a document[3]. However, it appears that the forged signature need not resemble the genuine one[4], a logical conclusion once it is accepted that fictitious signatures will suffice.

'As there were two ways in which Mahomet and the mountain might he brought together, so there are two ways in which a forged bond may be made, either by signing a false name below the bond, or by writing the bond above the genuine signature without permission ...'[5]. Accordingly, there may be forgery where a genuine signature has in some manner been attached to a false deed. Similarly, a deed genuine in all respects may become a forgery by the making of unauthorised additions or alterations to it[6]. The alterations must be such as to affect the essential character of the deed, or significantly to alter its meaning[7].

It is not forgery merely to make a false statement in a deed, however. In *Simon Fraser*[8], a sheriff officer persuaded a colleague to subscribe as a witness to an execution of citation. The citation never took place, and the officer was accused of uttering the execution of citation as genuine. The charge was held to be irrelevant. Lord Justice-Clerk Inglis drew a theological analogy:

> 'In the scientific study of the evidences of Christianity, one becomes familiar with the distinction between the genuineness and the authenticity of the books of the New Testament – the term "genuineness", as applied to them expressing merely the fact that they were written by the persons whose names they bear, apart altogether from any question as to the truth or credibility of their contents. For a writing, though genuine, may contain nothing but falsehoods'[9].

But although false documents which are genuinely authenticated are not forgeries, it might well be fraud or attempted fraud to utter such documents as genuine[10].

There is no doubt that the capabilities of software and of the modern computer, scanner, printer and copier allow documents to be reproduced in a way that can make the copy indistinguishable from an original; however the essence of the crime of uttering remains the intentional uttering of a document as genuine, when the perpetrator knows it to be false.

1 *Hume* I, 140; *Macdonald* p 59.
2 *Gordon* para 18–40. See also *Macdonald* p 63, and eg *Jas Hall* (1849) Shaw 254. Cf *Griffen v HM Advocate* 1940 JC 1, 1940 SLT 175.
3 See eg *John Henderson* (1830) 5 Deas & And 151.
4 *Hume* I, 141; *Macdonald* p 59.
5 *Simon Fraser* (1859) 3 Irv 467 at 494, per Lord Neaves.
6 *Hume* I, 159–160.
7 *Wm Mann* (1877) 3 Coup 376; *Thos Mackenzie* (1878) 4 Coup 50.
8 (1859) 3 Irv 467.
9 Lord Justice-Clerk Inglis at 475.
10 See Lord Justice-Clerk Inglis at 476.

The modes of uttering

16.16 To utter a forged document is to present it or deliberately to display it as a genuine document. There must therefore be an intention to utter the document; involuntary uttering is not an offence. In *Jas Devlin*[1], for example, the trial was stopped when it became apparent that the forged document, which Devlin had clearly intended to utter at some point, had fallen from his hand before he could present it[2].

Uttering may therefore be committed by presenting the document to a particular person, but it is also uttering to 'present' the document to the public at large, as when someone purporting to be a qualified lawyer hangs his forged practising certificate in the waiting room of his chambers, or simply to place the document beyond the utterer's control[3]. To post a letter is therefore to utter it[4], as is the presentation of a document to a third party with instructions to utter it. *Alison* takes the view that in these circumstances it is necessary to prove that the third party in turn presented the document to the victim[5]. *Gordon* takes the opposite view, but while the weight of authority appears to be in his favour[6], it is arguably contrary to principle to allow a charge of uttering in circumstances where the accused could still intervene to prevent his agent from presenting the document to the intended victim[7].

False articles and 'practical cheating'

Occasionally, a clever painter reproduces the style of an Old Master, and presents it to the public, or at least to the art world, as the genuine article. Such conduct is popularly categorised as forgery, and it would seem logical to assume that the presentation of the work is an uttering, and a crime as such. This is particularly so where the painting has been 'signed' by the forger in the name of the original artist[8]. Uttering seems however, to be a crime confined to the presentation as genuine of falsely authenticated documents. An analogy might be drawn between the case of the forged painting and a 'forged' historical or literary work. In *HM Advocate v Smith*[9], the accused sold a number of letters under the pretence that they were written by Burns and Scott. He was charged with fraud and not uttering[10].

The idea that the tendering of false articles may be a form of 'practical cheating' stems from the (rather obscure) case of *Alex Bannatyne*[11]. In that case the accused sold a mixture of oatmeal, barleymeal and bran as pure oatmeal. The account for the supply of this mixture was not paid. Although Bannatyne was charged with and convicted of fraud, 'the delivery of an article which is dis-conform to contract is not a 'definite practical result', nor is it in itself a crime'[12]. According to *Gordon*, the crime consists in disguising an article to make it appear genuine[13]. Three points may be made about this case, however:

(i)   The court in *Bannatyne* did not purport to be creating or dealing with any offence other than fraud.

(ii)   To induce a buyer to accept as genuine adulterated or 'disguised' goods which would not otherwise be acceptable, might well be regarded as sufficient to constitute fraud[14].

(iii)   The circumstances of *Bannatyne* would no doubt be treated now as attempted fraud.

1   (1828) *Alison* I, 402.
2   *Gordon* states that this might now be charged as attempted uttering.
3   See *Gordon* para 18–55.
4   See eg *Daniel Taylor* (1853) 1 Irv 230.
5   *Alison* I, 403–405.
6   See eg *Wm Jeffrey* (1842) 1 Broun 337; *John Smith* (1871) 2 Coup 1.
7   Cf the law of attempt and eg *Samuel Tumbleson* (1863) 4 Irv 426.

8   See *Gordon* para 18–49.
9   (1893) 1 Adam 6.
10 See also *Frank v HM Advocate* 1938 JC 17, 1938 SLT 109. According to *Gordon* 'the fact that the successful use of the letters was charged as fraud does not mean that it could not have been charged as uttering' (para 18–44).
11 (1847) Arkley 361.
12 *Gordon* para 18–50.
13 Para 18–50.
14 See p 278 above.

Chapter 17

Embezzlement/extortion and bribery

17.1

'Perhaps there is no part of our law which is more involved in obscurity, as propounded by our elementary writers, than the distinction between breach of trust and theft'[1].

EMBEZZLEMENT AND THEFT

Embezzlement is the dishonest appropriation of property which is in the possession of the accused as trustee, agent, factor or other administrator, or which is in his possession with a view to his becoming beneficial owner in certain circumstances[2], or held on behalf of another to whom he owes a duty to account, and on whose behalf he is in the process of carrying out a course of dealing with money[3]. Theft is not confined to the situation where property is clandestinely taken and carried away[4]. A person who is lawfully in possession of goods, and holds them of consent, may be guilty of theft if he subsequently appropriates them to his own use. In looking for evidence of such appropriation, the courts must usually have regard to actions of the accused which suggest an assumption of the rights of the owner – the sale or pledge of the goods, for example. But what if the possessor is authorised by the owner to deal with and to dispose of the goods? In such cases, it cannot be said that the goods are appropriated merely because the possessor has assumed some of the rights of the owner. Solicitors, accountants, fund managers and certain types of mercantile agents are frequently entrusted with property which they have no obligation to return to the owner in its original form. It is the function of such agents to deal with the property for the benefit of their principal, and to account to him or her for their intromissions with the property. Where the property thus administered is diverted to the agent's own use, embezzlement may be committed. How then is this crime to be distinguished from that of theft? *Hume* said that 'The trespass lies … in the short accounting, and concealment of [the] receipts, not in the withdrawing of the species or corpus'[5]. The crucial point here is not simply that the accused was entrusted with the property, for a person in such a position can clearly be convicted of theft[6]. In *HM Advocate v Smith & Wishart*[7], for example, two bank tellers were relevantly charged with the theft of money which was in their care. Lord Medwyn said that 'a party may undoubtedly steal a subject entrusted to him'[8], but much was made of the limited extent to which the tellers were entrusted with the money, and in particular of the fact that a 'teller has no power of administration, his duties being simply to pay and receive the money of the bank'[9]. Lord Craighill stated in *HM Advocate v John Smith*[10] that 'the fact that a man is a manager does not prevent him stealing'. In *Smith* £50 was handed to the accused in payment of an account. He appropri-

269

ated the money and his conviction for theft was upheld on appeal. The court observed that:

> 'It depends entirely on the facts as they may arise whether the crime is embezzlement or theft. It is embezzlement if the manager ought to account for money received, and fails to do so; and it is theft if it was his duty to hand over to his employers the very sums he received and instead of doing so he kept them'[11].

Thus, it seems that the essentials of an embezzlement charge are, first, the accused's power to administer the property of another, and second, his subsequent failure to account for dealings with that property in the exercise of his power of administration. Where, on the other hand, the accused's duty is to hand over a particular thing or sum of money, there will be theft if he fails to do so.

1 *Watt v Home* (1851) Shaw 519 at 521, per Lord Colonsay. The term 'embezzlement breach of trust' was the old name for the crime now known simply as 'embezzlement'. There are some suggestions however, that breach of trust may be a distinct offence: see *Gordon's* commentary to *Grant v Allan* 1987 SCCR 402 at 411.
2 *Criminal Law*, Macdonald (5th edn) pp 45–48.
3 *Stair Encyclopaedia* vol 7 paras 350–356.
4 See Chapter 14 above.
5 *Hume* I, 60.
6 See eg *HM Advocate v John Smith* (1887) 1 White 413; *Smith & Wishart* (1842) 1 Broun 342.
7 (1842) 1 Broun 342.
8 (1842) 1 Broun 342 at 350.
9 Lord Medwyn at 350; see also Lord Justice-Clerk Hope at 351.
10 (1887) 1 White 413 at 415.
11 Ibid.

The question of authority

17.2   Another possible way to distinguish the two crimes is by looking at the extent of the accused's authority to enter into the transaction in question. *Kent v HM Advocate*[1], concerned the disposal of a large quantity of apple puree, and turned on the question of whether or not the disposal was authorised. The accused was convicted of embezzlement on the basis that the sale was authorised, but that conviction was set aside, there being no evidence of authorisation. On the facts, the court held that the appropriate charge was one of theft. But on one view, *Kent* threatens the basis of the working definition set out above. 'It is at least logically possible to disentangle the facts of even the most complicated embezzlement and consider each incident separately, and if this is done it will be clear that in every case the accused dealt with his principal's property in an unauthorised way'[2]. On this view, every appropriation of another's property would amount to theft, since every such appropriation would involve an unauthorised act, such as the paying of another's money into the accused's bank account, and the crime of embezzlement would disappear[3]. However, in many cases, it will be impossible to identify any particular unauthorised act, or any particular thing which has been appropriated, and the only evidence of misappropriation will be a discrepancy in a set of accounts, or a failure to pay over an expected sum at the end of a period of administration, or a failure to account when called upon to do so, from which it may be inferred that the accused is withholding money dishonestly[4].

Of course, the Scottish courts clearly do recognise the crime of embezzlement. However, in *HM Advocate v Wishart*[5], Lord McDonald implied that the question of authority is not the decisive one in determining whether or not there has been embezzlement – 'a charge of embezzlement or theft can arise immediately as soon as a solicitor does an unauthorised act concerning the funds of his client'. It is not clear that the case on which Lord McDonald based that dictum will bear the interpretation which he placed on it, however.

The case was that of *Wormald*[6], in which a solicitor was instructed to obtain a heritable security for a client, and a sum of money was placed on deposit-receipt to enable him to do so. Before he obtained a security, and thus when unauthorised to do so, the accused uplifted and appropriated the money. Although no objection was taken to a charge of embezzlement, it seems that the court in *Wormald* regarded the case as one of theft by taking, and not by appropriation, since the accused had not even begun to administer the client's money and had no authority to uplift it[7].

1 1950 JC 38, 1950 SLT 130.
2 *Gordon* para 17–23. *Gordon* describes *Kent* as an exceptional case in that only one transaction was involved 'so that it was easy to disentangle the facts and point to what had been stolen and to when and where it had been stolen'.
3 See also *HM Advocate v Wormald* (1876) 3 R (J) 24.
4 See eg *Edgar v McKay* 1926 JC 94, 1926 SLT 446. and *Criminal Law*, Macdonald (5th edn), p 47.
5 (1975) SCCR Supp 78.
6 (1876) 3 R(J) 24.
7 Cf *Alex Gilruth Fleming* (1885) 5 Coup 552. Note *Gordon*'s comments on this case at para 17–19.

17.3 On the assumption that the question of the accused's authority is a relevant factor in embezzlement, there remains the theoretical problem posed by *Kent*. If the accused acts without authority, surely any appropriation by him is theft? A possible means of reconciling these views is to say that there is theft if appropriation takes place during a transaction which is itself unauthorised, but that if the appropriation takes place during the course of an authorised transaction, there will be embezzlement. The fact that the act of appropriation is itself unauthorised does not assist in the making of the distinction, since in any case there is no crime if the appropriation is by consent of the owner. It is by no means clear that the case law supports this view however.

For example, a charge of embezzlement was found to be relevant in *HM Advocate v Wishart*[1] in which a solicitor drew cheques on his clients' accounts which he paid to a stockbroker friend in return for a cheque for an identical sum. The purpose of these transactions was not to appropriate the clients' money, but to enhance the stockbroker's balance sheet at the end of the financial year. These payments were clearly not part of any authorised transaction, yet the relevancy of the charge was upheld[2].

In *Laing*[3] the accused received money from a client in order to discharge a bond, and instead of doing so simply paid some of the money straight into his own bank account. He was convicted of embezzlement, in spite of the fact that he had not yet entered into any authorised transactions.

The decision does however seem a strange one in the light of cases like *HM Advocate v Smith*[4], and both cases highlight what Sheriff Sir Gerald Gordon has described as the 'sociological aspect of the distinction between theft and embezzlement'[5]. In practice, juries can seem reluctant to convict of theft those 'responsible' people – lawyers, accountants, and company directors, for example – who appropriate property entrusted to them.

1 (1975) SCCR Supp 78.
2 *Wishart* may not be consistent with the previous case law, however. See comments on *Wormald*, above.
3 (1891) 2 White 572.
4 (1887) 1 White 413.
5 *Gordon* para 17–06.

17.4   So what seems to identify embezzlement is not whether the goods have been entrusted to the accused, nor even the extent of the accused's authority to enter any particular transaction, but rather the accused's misappropriation of property over which he has a power of administration[1]. It may be that for this reason, a charge of embezzlement is irrelevant where the accused has not yet begun to administer the property, or where the administration has come to an end[2], the appropriate charge in such a case being one of theft. It should be noted that the distinction between theft and fraud is not of crucial importance in most cases, since it is competent to convict of embezzlement on a theft charge, and vice versa[3]. There may still be some situations, however, where differentiation will be required. The court in *Kent v HM Advocate*[4], for example, declined to substitute a conviction for theft for the discredited embezzlement conviction, since the jury were never asked to consider the evidence in relation to theft[5].

The *actus reus* of embezzlement

Thus, where the accused diverts property to his own use while carrying out the instructions of or exercising authority to administer property given to him by his principal, there will be embezzlement[6]. Actual appropriation, still less permanent appropriation, may not be required. Where there is a fiduciary relationship between the accused and the victim, as for example between solicitor and client, it will amount to embezzlement to employ the victim's funds in any way contrary to the trust[7]. In *Wishart*[8], because the cheques were handed over simultaneously, the clients' funds never left the bank. Nevertheless, the court said that the potential risk to the clients' money created by the transaction was 'appropriation in the sense necessary to found a charge of embezzlement'[9]. In one of the older cases it was said that 'There seems no doubt that if an agent receives money on behalf of a client, and uses it for his own purposes, he is guilty of theft or embezzlement, whether he lodges it in his bank account, or employs it in his business, or pays it on account of other clients'[10]. In *Moore v HM Advocate*[11] the High Court reaffirmed the position. The accused, as sole director of a company, had charge of its funds; he secured the transfer of funds from the company, to whom he had a fiduciary duty, into his personal account. No security was given, nor repayment terms agreed; the Lord Justice General said 'That these transfers were made was amply established and no question arises but that the *actus reus* of embezzlement (appropriation) was proved. The circumstances that the sums transferred were, in some instances, repaid, is immaterial. The transfers, especially given the use to which the appellant put the funds, put them at risk'[12].

1   See eg *Alex Gilruth Fleming* (1885) 5 Coup 552; *Gordon* para 17–22.
2   *Alex Mitchell* (1874) 3 Coup 77. But cf *Edgar v Mackay* 1926 JC 94, 1926 SLT 446, and *Laing* (1891) 2 White 572.
3   Criminal Procedure (Scotland) Act 1995, Sch 3, para 8(3), (4).
4   1950 JC 38, 1950 SLT 130.
5   See also *O'Brien v Strathern* 1922 JC 55, 1922 SLT 440, which may imply that a person cannot be convicted of reset of theft when it is shown that the goods were embezzled.
6   See eg *Guild v Lees* 1994 SCCR 745, 1995 SLT 68.
7   *HM Advocate v Lawrence* (1872) 2 Coup 168.
8   (1975) SCCR Supp 78.
9   Lord McDonald at 84.
10 *HM Advocate v Laing* (1891) 2 White 572 at 574, per Lord Kincairney.
11 2010 SCL 483.
12 Paragraph 4, referring to Lawrence and Wishart.

17.5   In some circumstances it may be very difficult to prove any specific act of appropriation, because of the degree of the embezzler's control over the property in question. In such cases, it may be that the only evidence of appropriation is a failure to account to the victim within a reasonable time of a demand for such an accounting. In *Edgar v Mackay*[1], for example, the accused failed to account to the complainer for a sum of money, and only paid it over on the day of his arrest. These facts were sufficient to justify an inference of appropriation.

The *mens rea* of embezzlement

In order to bring home a charge of embezzlement, the Crown must prove a 'dishonest and felonious intention' to appropriate the property[2]. Thus, as in theft, a belief in the consent of the owner to the acts in question is a good defence to an embezzlement charge.

In *Allenby v HM Advocate*[3] the accused was a fish salesman who acted for a number of different trawler owners. Proceeds from fish sales were paid into a common fund out of which the various owners were paid their share. Allenby was in the habit of making loans to the various owners out of this fund, and because of this practice he was charged with embezzlement. There was evidence that he kept strict records of all his intromissions, but the sheriff directed the jury that to use the common fund in this way amounted to embezzlement. There was a direction that a belief in entitlement to act in this way might be a defence, but in the absence of a direction that evidence of dishonesty was necessary, his conviction was quashed. In addition to a defence of belief in consent, a defence of claim of right, as opposed to a mere denial of dishonesty, may be relevant in embezzlement cases[4]. *Allenby* has been described as a special case, as there was evidence that it was common practice to act in that way in the fishing industry but the legacy of the decision was one of leaving the law 'in rather a vague state'[5].

In *HM Advocate v City of Glasgow Bank Directors*[6], the court held that the act complained of is raised into a crime only if there is some element of 'bad faith, some corrupt motive, some guilty knowledge, some fraudulent intent'[7]. This case *inter alia* was considered in *Moore v HM Advocate*[8]. Mr Moore was the director of a company who had intromitted with company funds for his own benefit. He was convicted of embezzlement by a jury at Cupar Sheriff Court. He argued on appeal that there was insufficient evidence of the *mens rea* of embezzlement. The Lord Justice General said the following:

'The Crown relied for proof of the requisite mental element in this charge on, in the first place, a statement which the appellant had allegedly made to the insolvency practitioner appointed by the Trustee in Bankruptcy to manage his sequestrated estate, that he "was determined that his estranged wife would receive nothing, not a penny from him". That intent – to strip the company of its funds with a view to the interest of the other shareholder in it being rendered valueless – was clearly a "corrupt motive", something done in bad faith. Independently of that statement there was undisputed evidence as to the significant amounts withdrawn and the frequency of these withdrawals, pointing, in the absence of any *bona fide* explanation, to a dishonest intent. It was undisputed that the funds were withdrawn and used for the appellant's personal purposes of gambling and speculative investment – a use which was consistent with an intention to deprive the company and through it the other shareholder of the monies withdrawn. If, as Lord Wark opined, dishonest intention may be evidenced by reckless acts (upon which it is unnecessary for present purposes to express a view) the reckless purpose for which the funds were withdrawn may be an additional pointer to dishonesty. Further, although the withdrawals were recorded in the company's books – as "loans" – there was an absence of security and terms of repayment, and the practice of repaying shortly before the year end, and again withdrawing shortly after it, was consistent with a measure of concealment on the appellant's part. In these circumstances there was, in our view, sufficient evidence of dishonesty in these transactions'[9].

1 1926 JC 94, 1926 SLT 446.
2 See Lord Kincairney's charge to the jury in *Laing* (1891) 2 White 572.
3 1938 JC 55, 1938 SLT 150.
4 See *Gordon* para 17–33.
5 *Stair Encyclopaedia* para 348.
6 1879 4 Couper 161.
7 At p 187.
8 2010 SCL 483.
9 At para [8].

EXTORTION

17.6   Where goods are obtained by the use of violence or threats of immediate violence, robbery is committed[1]. If the threat is one of future violence, or some other type of threat, the relevant charge is one of extortion or blackmail[2]:

'There is the element of force or fear applied – that is the 'threat'; there is the element of intention, the intention being to overcome the reluctance of the victim, and there is the element of so 'extorting' – forcing out – a benefit to oneself which the victim would otherwise have refused to afford or to pay'[3].

In *Crawford (Alex M)*, the Lord Justice Clerk said: 'The crime consists in using threat to concuss a person into paying a demand which he intends to resist; and the crime, the use of the threat for that purpose, is the same, whether the party using the threat thinks his demand good or bad[4].'

The threat

The use of certain types of threat is in itself criminal – threats to kill or injure, to do serious damage to property, or seriously to damage someone's 'fortune or reputation' fall into this category[5]. Where such threats are attached to demands for money or for some other advantage, the relevant charge is one of extortion. It is of the essence of extortion that threats are used to back up the demands of the accused.

In *HM Advocate v Donoghue*[6], five paintings were stolen, and the thief sent a letter to the owner explaining that for £1,200 he was in a position to secure their return. A charge of extortion was held to be irrelevant, for lack of an averment that any threat, such as a threat to destroy the paintings, was made to enforce the demand for money[7].

The paradigm case of extortion is where the gangster offers the shopkeeper or businessman 'protection' against the future destruction of his property, in return for a regular payment. It is not necessary that the threat be one of future violence, however, either to the person or the property of the victim[8]. Another common case is where the blackmailer threatens to make some damaging revelation about the victim. The allegation may be one of dishonesty, crime[9], or sexual immorality[10], and a charge of extortion is relevant regardless of whether the facts alleged are true or false[11].

1   See Chapter 14 above.
2   *Hume* I, 108.
3   *Silverstein v HM Advocate* 1949 JC 160 at 165, 1949 SLT 386 at 388, per Lord Mackay. See also *Black and Penrice v Carmichael* 1992 SCCR 709, 1992 SLT 897.
4   (1850) Shaw 309 at p 322.
5   *Jas Miller* (1862) 4 Irv 238. Although *Gordon* submits (at para 21–05) that the latter category of threats is too widely expressed. See also *WM v HM Advocate* [2010] HC JAC 75 and *HMA v Baillie* [2012] HCJAC 158.
6   1971 SLT 2.
7   What seems to be required is that the threat should be one to alter the victim's position for the worse, and in *Donogue,* there was no such threat, only an offer to help. See *Gordon* para 21–14. See also *Kenny v HM Advocate* 1951 JC 104, 1951 SLT 363.
8   In *Henderson and Marnoch v HM Advocate* [2005] HCJAC 47, the threats were to 'wipe out' the family of the recipient of the call.
9   *Crawford (Alex M)* (1850) Shaw 309.
10   *Marion Macdonald* (1879) 4 Coup 268.
11   *Crawford (Alex M),* above.

17.7   Almost any threat will suffice provided it creates 'in the victim fear that unless he yields, his position will be altered for the worse'[1]. It is probably the case, however, that there is no extortion unless the threats used were objectively such as to overbear the will of the victim[2]. If the victim is unduly timid, there will be no extortion where he accedes to threats which are mild or vague. In the English case of *Harry*[3], for example, it was held that a threat of 'inconvenience' to shopkeepers who failed to buy immunity from the organisers of a student charity campaign was insufficient to overcome the will of an 'ordinary person of normal stability and courage'[4].

In addition, the accused must have intended that the threat should overcome the reluctance of the victim to confer the required benefit[5]. Extortion cannot be committed carelessly. However, it is almost certainly not, as it is in England[6], a defence for the accused to show that he believed that the threat was a proper means of enforcing his demand[7]. In *Black and Penrice v Carmichael*[8], a case which looked at the practice of wheel clamping, the court were satisfied that a notice left advising a car owner that the vehicle would be immobilised until payment of a fee was a threat.

There may be extortion even though the threatened conduct would in some circumstances be regarded as perfectly legitimate. In seeking payment of a debt or performance of some obligation, the law regards as permissible certain types of pressure – for example a threat to resile from a contract, raise an action in court, or do diligence on a court decree[9]. However, where such a threat is used to achieve an illegitimate end, extortion is committed. In *Silverstein v HM Advocate*[10], the accused was the managing director of a landlord company. He informed tenants that unless a sum of money was paid to him as an individual, he would arrange to have them evicted. His conviction for extortion was upheld on appeal, in spite of an acceptance by the Crown of the argument that a landlord has the right to use threats to evict his tenants should they fail to agree a higher rent:

'... the threat to use one's own position and influence as a lever to alter the position of another to his detriment, unless that other buys immunity, is a relevant ground of charge. What brings about this result is that the payment demanded is not a payment to which the claimant has any right arising out of his legal relationship to the victim'[11].

1   *Silverstein v HM Advocate* 1949 JC 160 at 163, 1949 SLT 386 at 387, per Lord Justice-Clerk Thomson.
2   1949 JC 160 at 165, 1949 SLT 386 at 388, per Lord Mackay.
3   [1974] Crim LR 32.
4   Sellers LJ in *R v Clear* [1968] 1 All ER 74 at 80.
5   See Lord Mackay's dictum in *Silverstein* at 165, 388, above.
6   Theft Act 1968, s 21.
7   See *Gordon* para 21–15, and cf *Crawford (Alex M)* (1850) Shaw 309 at 324, per Lord Justice-Clerk Hope and generally *Black and Penrice v Carmichael* 1992 SCCR 709, 1992 SLT 897.
8   1992 SLT 897.
9   See *Silverstein v HM Advocate* 1949 JC 160 at 163, 1949 SLT 386 at 387, per Lord Justice-Clerk Thomson. These categories are not exhaustive of the types of pressure the law will regard as legitimate.
10 1949 JC 160, 1949 SLT 386; considered in *Black and Penrice v Carmichael* 1992 SLT 897.
11 *Silverstein* at 163, 387, per Lord Justice-Clerk Thomson.

17.8   Silverstein would (at that time) have been entitled to make such threats in order to secure a more favourable result for his employers[1], but not entitled to seek any benefit for himself. For this reason, threats to report someone to the police unless a sum of money is paid would be regarded as extortionate, whether or not the alleged crime has really been committed[2]. Such threats are not, of course, criminal in themselves, and there had been some doubt as to whether there will be extortion if the thing demanded of the victim confers no benefit on the accused. However, the matter was clarified in *Black*, where the Lord Justice General said:

'It is not a necessary element in the crime of extortion that the person who makes the threat or issues the demand should be alleged to have been seeking an advantage for himself. ... [He] who robs another in order to give to charity is guilty of the crime of robbery, and so it is with extortion.'

In *Hill v McGrogan*[3] the accused threatened to report a cleaner to the police for theft from her employers unless she quit her job. The charge of extortion was held to be irrelevant, since it was not alleged that the threats were used for an improper purpose, such as the pursuit of personal enrichment or malice. The sheriff-substitute said[4] that he could not 'see that it is wrong in law to do what you are entitled to do without warning or that it makes it worse to add that if the person attacked chooses to put the matter right to your satisfaction you will not pursue her'.

This case suggests that there will be no extortion where the accused gives the 'victim' an opportunity to put right some wrong, provided that the remedy does not involve conferring some benefit on the accused. However, while it is always open to the victim of a theft to refrain from reporting the matter to the police, and perhaps even to make it a condition of that abstention that the thief returns the property[5], or, where the thief is an employee, that he should resign, it is not, it is submitted, open to others to make such 'bargains'. If the owner of stolen goods has any such rights, they arise out of his legal rights over the goods, or his legal relationship to the employee. In the absence of such a legal framework, any use of the word 'unless' in relation to such threats would be extortionate[6]. This would mean that the theft victim could not demand payment for the goods in return for his failure to report the matter to the police. In this situation both threat and demand are legitimate, but there is extortion because there is no legally acceptable link between the two. The only legitimate threat in that case would be one to raise a civil action for the return of the goods, or for damages[7].

1 Where, in addition to rent, a premium is demanded by a landlord in return for the renewal, or assignation of a lease, a crime is committed: Rent (Scotland) Act 1971, ss 101, 102. The Rent (Scotland) Act 1984, s 22(2) also makes it an offence to harass tenants in such a way as to interfere with their peaceful enjoyment of the lease.
2 See eg *Crawford (Alex M)* (1850) Shaw 309 at 326, per Lord Justice-Clerk Hope.
3 1945 SLT (Sh Ct) 18.
4 At 19.
5 See *Gordon* para 21–10.
6 See *Silverstein* 1949 JC 160 at 165, per Lord Mackay, and cf Lord Justice-Clerk Thomson's dictum at 163.
7 Cf the unreported case of *Samuel Smith*, the complaint in which is narrated by *Gordon* para 21–10, n 30.

The demand

17.9   While threats of legitimate behaviour will be regarded as extortion if they are linked to an illegitimate demand, the converse – that illegal threats render legitimate demands extortionate – is also true. Whether or not a debt is due, a creditor cannot enforce payment by threats of violence to the debtor, his family or his property[1], and it matters not that the creditor genuinely believes in the justice of his claim[2]. While the demand is usually for money, or for some other benefit to the accused, it seems that any demand will suffice if it is to the 'detriment'[3] of the victim and provided there are accompanying threats which are not linked to the demand in the appropriate way. Thus, a demand that the victim resign from his job would be enough[4], or even, perhaps, that the victim should donate a sum of money to charity. In *Black and Penrice v Carmichael*[5] the High Court held that the practice of wheel clamping could result in relevant charges of extortion (or attempted extortion) and theft. In such cases there is an illegitimate threat to the owner of the vehicle that his property will not be returned to him unless he pays the sum demanded. The court stressed that the proper method for the recovery of sums owed was by means of the legal process: resort to other methods was not permissible.

1 *Crawford (Alex M)* (1850) Shaw 309.
2 (1850) Shaw 309 at 324, per Lord Justice-Clerk Hope. Cf the subjective approach taken in England which excuses a blackmailer who believes (a) that there are reasonable grounds for his demand and (b) that the use of menaces is a legitimate way of enforcing the demand: Theft Act 1968, s 21(1). See the contrasting views of this provision expressed in [1966] *Crim LR* 467–480 by Sir Bernard MacKenna and Brian Hogan.
3 See dictum of Lord Justice-Clerk Thomson in *Silverstein*, above.
4 But see the discussion of *Hill v McGrogan* 1945 SLT (Sh Ct) 18, and cf the English position which requires that the demand be one which confers a benefit on the defendant, or causes loss to the victim, and that the benefit or loss must be in money or property: Theft Act 1968, s 34.
5 1992 SCCR 709, 1992 SLT 897. For an interesting discussion in a civil context see *Ronald v Duke of Buccleuch* [2014] CSOH 101.

BRIBERY

17.10   In Scotland it was a crime both at common law and at statute. Hume noted that it is a crime to bribe and to attempt to bribe a judicial officer and for the officer himself to take a bribe[1]. However, the crime was more usually prosecuted under statutory law.

The Public Bodies Corrupt Practices Act 1889, and the Prevention of Corruption Acts of 1906 and 1916 extended the scope of the crime from the public sector.

Despite the age of these Acts, the crime of bribery in Scotland continued to be regulated by them[2]; the whole area of the crime of bribery was subject to adverse comment, as failing to comply with international law requirements for its investigation and prosecution[3]. The state of the law was described as 'untidy and unsatisfactory'[4]. These concerns gave rise to a Law Commission report *Reforming Bribery* (2008), Law Com No 313 which in turn led to new legislation.

1 Hume Commentaries vol 1 407–408.
2 See for example *Campbell v HM Advocate* 1942 JC 86; *Carmichael v Kennedy* 1991 JC 32.
3 See article 'The crime of bribery in Scotland' by Dr Paul Arnell 2009 SLT (Notes) 1.
4 [2010] *Crim LR* 6, 439.

The Bribery Act 2010

17.11 This Act came into force on 1 July 2011[1]. The Act creates separate offences of bribing another person (s 1), being bribed (s 2), bribery of a foreign public official (s 6), and failure of a commercial organisation to prevent bribery (s 7). The Act abolished the common law offence of bribery, and the Public Bodies Corrupt Practices Act 1889 and the Prevention of Corruption Acts 1906 and 1916 were repealed.

In terms of ss 1 and 2 of the Act, the person paying a bribe will commit an offence if he offers, promises, or gives a financial or other advantage to another person, intending the advantage to be an inducement, or reward, for the improper performance by another person of a 'relevant function or activity'. The person who receives a bribe will commit an offence if he requests, agrees to receive, or accepts, a financial or other advantage, as an inducement or as a reward, for the improper performance of a relevant function or activity. The function or activity will be performed improperly if it is performed in breach of an expectation that it will be performed in good faith, or impartially, or according to the person's position of trust in its performance. The test of whether there is an 'expectation' is a test of what a reasonable person in the United Kingdom would expect in relation to the performance of the type of function or activity concerned. There is provision where the performance of the function, or activity, is outside UK jurisdiction, effectively excluding reliance on local custom or practice.

The offence in s 6 is of bribery of a foreign public official.

Section 7 creates a new offence of failure of an organisation to prevent bribery. It will be committed where a person associated with the organisation bribes another person, intending to obtain or retain business for it, or obtain or retain an advantage in the conduct of their business[2].

Section 13 provides for a defence of necessity, in that it will be a defence for a person charged with certain bribery offences to prove that his conduct was 'necessary for the proper exercise of any function of an intelligence service, or the proper exercise of any function of the armed forces when engaged on active service'.

In contrast with the law which preceded the Act, there is no requirement to establish a dishonest intention; so that if steps taken induce improper performance, even if there no element of corruption or fraud in the provision of a financial advantage, an offence is committed. An example would be the provision of facilitation payments[3].

The Act is still in its infancy, and the precise effects are still to be monitored; there has been some concern that the Act has not achieved its supposed purpose – notable prosecutions and convictions of bodies' corporate[4].

---

1 See article [2009] Crim LR 61.
2 Section 7 is notable for having given rise to the first deferred prosecution agreement (DPA) in England and Wales under the Crime and Courts Act 2013, s 45. See *SFO v Standard Bank plc* EWHC Crim 30 November 2015. The court approved the DPA, holding that the bank had failed to prevent bribery, although there was no suggestion of knowing participation in a bribery

offence. The offence was limited to an allegation of inadequate systems to prevent associate persons from committing an offence of bribery.

3 See *SFO v Standard Bank plc* (above); and Anwar and Deeprose 'The Bribery Act 2010', 2010 SLT 125.
4 Arnell and Evans, 'The effect of the Bribery Act 2010', 2015 JR 61.

Chapter 18

Malicious mischief

18.1   Traditionally, malicious mischief was a crime involving physical damage to property, and was regarded by *Hume* as one additionally requiring an element of civil disorder:

'It may be affirmed generally, with respect to every act of great and wilful damage to the property of another, and whether done from malice, or mis-apprehension of right, that it is cognisable with us as a crime at common law; if it is done, as ordinarily happens, with circumstances of tumult and disorder, and of contempt and indignity to the owner'[1].

Hume then gives a number of examples to illustrate this statement, such as the casting down of houses, the destruction of the sluices or aqueducts of a mill, or the burning of boats and nets at a fishery. As the law developed, the crime retained its character as a crime of violence against property, but lost the element of riot or public disorder; *Gordon* previously described the crime as consisting 'simply in the destruction or damage of the property of another whether by destroying crops, killing or injuring animals, knocking down walls or fences, or in any other way'[2] but now recognises the causing of economic loss, provided it is caused by unauthorised interference by way of a positive act (rather than an omission).

Accordingly the crime includes actions (and possibly omissions) in respect of property, which result only in patrimonial loss to the owner. It is the crime of intentionally or recklessly damaging or destroying another person's property, without permission, resulting in physical damage or economic loss. Physical damage, of itself, an apparent prerequisite of Hume, is no longer necessarily required. The authority for this is the case of *Wilson v HM Advocate*[3], in which a disgruntled employee at Hunterston 'B' power station activated an emergency stop button bringing to a halt one of the turbines, causing a temporary loss of generating capacity which had to be replaced at a cost of £147,000. In holding that the actions of the accused amounted to malicious mischief, Lord Justice-Clerk Wheatley said[4] that 'it was not suggested, nor could it be, that if the turbine had been stopped not by pressing the emergency stop button by hand, but by hitting the button with a hammer in such a way as to stop the turbine, the crime of malicious mischief would not have occurred'. The Lord Justice-Clerk then went on to say, having consulted the 'Shorter Oxford English Dictionary', that while the older cases all involved physical damage to property, the word 'damage' had a wider connotation, and could include situations where there was financial loss only. 'To interfere deliberately with the plant so as to sterilise its functioning with a resultant financial loss such as is libelled here is in my view a clear interference with another's property which falls within Hume's classification of malicious mischief'.

1 *Hume* I, 122.
2 *Gordon* para 22–01 in the second edition, now revised to recognise the economic loss element.

3 1983 SCCR 420, 1984 SLT 117.
4 1984 SLT 117 at 119.

18.2   *Hume* talked of 'interference' with property as being a sufficient basis
for a charge of malicious mischief, a phrase which taken in isolation might
well be capable of supporting the interpretation which the court placed on it in
Wilson. It is also true that *Hume* regarded fire-raising as an act intended generally to do patrimonial injury[1]. But the whole context in *Hume* suggests that
'interference' is to be read as a synonym for violence or civil disturbance. The
case in which the question of 'interference' arose was one in which a dam-dyke
was pulled down[2]. There was additionally in that case a 'tumultuous intrusion
into the possession of the pursuer's lands', and thus the question arose of the
accused's interference with the possessory, as opposed to proprietary, rights of
the victim. 'It is grounded in the same reason, namely, the due regard to the
order and tranquillity of society, that the pannel shall equally be convicted,
whether he interfere with the property of another, or with his state only of
peaceable and lawful possession'[3].

1 *Hume* I, 125. *Hume* regarded fire-raising as one of the most important, and serious, forms of
   criminal damage to property. See also *Stewart and Walsh* (1856) 2 Irv 359, and the discussion of
   fire-raising below.
2 *Monro of Auchinbowie, Hume* I, 122.
3 *Hume* I, 123.

18.3   Following *Wilson* it is, of course, no longer a distinction which the
law makes. One case might support the conclusion in *Wilson*. The case is that
of *David Monro*[1], in which the accused deliberately removed the bung from
a barrel of oil, causing the oil to escape. The analogy seems a close one, particularly if one were to imagine that Wilson had not stopped the generator,
but had disconnected it from the grid, thus wasting the electricity generated.
The analogy is not exact however, and the indictment in *Monro* averred that
the oil ran out, and was 'wasted and lost or otherwise destroyed', while in
Wilson, although generating capacity was lost, and in that sense 'damaged',
there was no physical damage to any corporeal property. The majority, and
particularly Lord McDonald, also placed some reliance on the case of *Miller*[2],
in which the accused wilfully, maliciously and unlawfully placed a stone on
a railway line 'in a manner calculated to and intended to obstruct trains and
endanger the lives or safety of the passengers'. The stone was removed before
the train arrived, and no damage or injury occurred. This charge, the relevancy
of which was not challenged was said to be 'so obviously an example of conduct amounting to malicious mischief, albeit without actual physical damage,
as to be beyond dispute'[3]. However, this case does not seem like a completed
example of malicious mischief at all, having more in common with the crime
of recklessly endangering the lives or safety of the lieges[4].

1 (1831) Bell's Notes 48; *Alison* I, 451; *Macdonald*, p 84.
2 (1848) Arkley 525.
3 *Wilson* 1984 SLT 117 at 120, per Lord McDonald.
4 See eg *John Murdoch* (1849) Shaw 229, and the commentary to *Wilson* at 1983 SCCR 429.

18.4   As a result of *Wilson*, whenever there is a deliberate interference with
the property of another, and that interference results in financial loss, then

a charge of malicious mischief can be made out, regardless of the question of physical damage[1]. The law was clarified by the case of *Bett v Brown*[2]. An accused was charged with malicious mischief by moving a surveillance camera outside a bank so that it pointed in such a way as to miss the area it was designed to show; the sheriff refused to dismiss the complaint as irrelevant, on the ground that the act resulted in a financial loss as running costs were incurred with no benefit. The accused appealed and the High Court held that malicious mischief required a wilful intent to cause injury which could be either physical damage or patrimonial loss; however they also held that on the particular charge, no such loss was libelled and allowed the appeal on that basis. However, it is clear that patrimonial loss is sufficient to constitute a charge.

The case of *Wilson* also raises the question of whether the crime may be committed by an omission to interfere with property. All the previous cases appeared to deal with positive acts on the part of the accused, which brought about damage to the complainer's property. In *Wilson,* however, the Lord Justice-Clerk reserved his opinion on 'what the position might be in a case where the initial act [sic] was of a negative and not a positive nature'[3], and that reservation of opinion has led to a school of thought to the effect that an omission could be enough to constitute the 'act' which gave rise to the damage. The court's use of the word 'interference' may militate against the inclusion of omissions as relevant to the *actus reus* of this offence, since that word seems to imply some positive act on the part of the accused. But the logic of the court's extension of the law in this area seems to be that where the actions of the accused have 'set in train' damage to property, whether physical or financial, then there is criminal liability for those actions. Logically, omissions to act are equally capable of setting such damage in train, and on this view it would be but a short step to extend the *actus reus* of the crime to include such omissions. There are, after all, situations where a person has a duty to act, whether through contract, or because they have themselves created some danger[4], and where failure to perform that duty may result in physical damage or economic loss. However, as presently constituted, case law supports the notion that it remains a crime of commission, not omission and that any damage or loss must be caused by a positive act by the accused.

1 Physical damage to property will of course remain a relevant ground of charge on the basis of the previous law.
2 1997 SLT 1310.
3 1984 SLT 117 at 120, per Lord Wheatley.
4 See eg *MacPhail v Clark* 1982 SCCR 395, 1983 SLT (Sh Ct) 37.

THE REQUIRED *MENS REA*

18.5   The very name of this crime – malicious mischief – seems to imply that there must be a 'deliberate wicked intent to injure another in his property'[1]. This is not the case. It is enough that 'the damage[2] is done by a person who shows a deliberate disregard of, or even indifference to, the property or possessory rights of others'[3].

The latter statement was made in the case of *Ward v Robertson*[4], in which the accused and two companions walked across grazing land, trampling the grass, and rendering it unfit for grazing. It was held that in the absence of evidence that the accused knew, or should have known that in crossing the field he was doing or was likely to do damage to the grass, his conviction for malicious mischief could not stand.

The situation might have been different had the accused trampled an ordinary growing crop, or had by walking in circles or taking more steps than necessary deliberately set out to cause damage. In the circumstances, however, his behaviour did not display the type of indifference required to constitute the offence. Such indifference might be present even where the accused believes the property damaged to be his own, if his belief is arrived at recklessly[5]. Where the accused's belief is not that the property is his own, but that he is entitled to damage the property of another, it seems that his belief, however genuine, is not a defence to a charge of malicious mischief.

The *mens rea* of the crime was considered in *The Lord Advocate's Reference (no 1 of 2000)*[6]. This case involved a deliberate attack on a submarine; the accused (who were acquitted) had argued that their actions were justified since the deployment of trident nuclear weapons was in breach of Scots Law. The court held at paragraph [30] that:

> 'The modern crime of malicious damage has been defined as the intentional or reckless destruction or damage of the property of another whether by destroying crops, killing or injuring animals, knocking down walls or fences, or in any other way. The *mens rea* of the crime in the case of intentional damage, which is the only relevant head in the present case, consists in the knowledge that the destructive conduct complained of was carried out with complete disregard for, or indifference to, the property or possessory rights of another. ...

> The traditional formulation of the *nomen juris* may be potentially misleading. But there is no room for doubt as to the formal requirements of proof of the offence. "Malice" does not require proof of spite or any other form of motive. The constituent parts of the crime are few. The property in question must have belonged to, or have been in the possession of, another. That property must have been damaged intentionally or recklessly. There must have been knowledge, or facts from which knowledge can be inferred, that the conduct complained of would cause damage to a third party's patrimonial rights in the property in question. In our opinion the admitted facts in the present case show that the respondents set out deliberately to cause damage, including the damage which they did inflict, and there is no substance whatsoever in the argument that they lacked the *mens rea* required for proof of malicious damage. The only substantial issue relates to the contention that they were justified in inflicting that damage'.

1 Lord Justice-Clerk Aitchison in *Ward v Robertson* 1938 JC 32 at 36, 1938 SLT 165. Cf *Gordon* para 22–04 on the older authorities which required proof of spite in order to establish the offence.
2 Or presumably, in the light of *Wilson,* economic loss.
3 Lord Justice-Clerk Clerk Aitchison in *Ward v Robertson*, above, at 36. Cf *Stewart and Walsh* (1856) 2 Irv 359 on the *mens rea* required for fire-raising.
4 1938 JC 32, 1938 SLT 165.

5 See *Gordon* para 22–06 and cf *R v David Smith* [1974] 1 QB 354, [1974] 1 All ER 632, in which
   it was held that the accused's honest belief that the property was his was a defence to a charge
   of causing criminal damage, regardless of whether the belief was justifiable so long as it was not
   reckless.
6 2001 JC 143, 2001 SLT 507, 2001 SCCR 296.

18.6   But although 'vindication' or protection of the accused's property
rights may not excuse him from criminal liability, it may serve as mitigation in
much the same way as provocation may mitigate sentence in an assault case[1].

DEFENCES

It is doubtful whether the accused could argue that he was entitled to act as
he did in order to vindicate some right of his own, unless his actings were in
accordance with general principles of self defence or necessity[2].

VANDALISM

The Criminal Justice (Scotland) Act 1980, s 78, created the new offence of
vandalism, which is now found in s 52 of the Criminal Law (Consolidation)
(Scotland) Act 1995. Under that section, any person who, without reasonable
excuse, wilfully or recklessly destroys or damages any property belonging to
another shall be guilty of the offence of vandalism[3]. The section excludes fire-
raising from the ambit of the offence[4]. On the face of it, this statutory offence
looks very much like malicious mischief. The High Court has held however,
that the offences are distinct.

In *Black v Allan*[5] it was said that:

> 'The Crown interest in this appeal is simply to guard against the risk that
> any support should be given for the view that the offence created by s 78(1)
> [of the 1980 Act] is simply an echo of the common law crime of malicious
> mischief. If anyone thought that it was such an echo, then the sooner they
> disabuse themselves of that notion the better'.

Both offence and crime involve damage to property, although it remains to be
seen how the courts will interpret the concept of 'damage' in relation to the
statutory offence; both can be committed intentionally, and both can be committed with some degree of recklessness. It was on the issue of recklessness
that the High Court appears to have rested their distinction, saying that where
recklessness was in issue, the Crown had to show recklessness of the type
required in *Allan v Patterson*[6] – the conscious and deliberate courting of material risks, or failure to notice obvious risks by reason of gross inattention – in
order to bring home a statutory vandalism charge. The implication is that this
is a higher standard than that applicable to malicious mischief, a 'deliberate
disregard, or even indifference to, the property or possessory rights of others'.
Essentially vandalism is seen to raise an issue of recklessness, malicious mischief an issue of *mens rea*.

1 See eg *Andrew Steuart* (1874) 2 Coup 554.
2 Lord Advocate's Reference (No 1 of 2000) above at para [34]–[55].

3 On the question of what may constitute a reasonable excuse see *MacDougall v Yuk-Sun Ho* 1985 SCCR 199; *Murray v O'Brien* 1994 SLT 1051.
4 Malicious mischief, on the other hand, may be committed by setting fire to property.
5 1985 SCCR 11 at 12–13, per Lord Justice-General Emslie.
6 1980 JC 57, 1980 SLT 77.

FIRE-RAISING

18.7   For an offence of relative rarity, the crime of fire-raising in Scots law gives rise to disproportionate complexity. For long regarded as one of the most serious of criminal damage offences[1], fire-raising is an offence in its own right[2], and consists in the deliberate or reckless burning of another's property[3]. In the first place, one must distinguish between, on the one hand, wilful fire-raising, and on the other, culpable and reckless fire-raising.

Wilful fire-raising

Wilful fire-raising was a capital crime which could only be charged where certain objects – buildings, corn, growing timber, and mine-shafts were set alight[4]. Where any other object or item was set on fire, the appropriate charge was the lesser one of culpable and reckless fire-raising. In 1887, however, the death penalty for fire-raising was abolished[5], and the distinction between the offences was often considered to be of limited practical importance[6]. However, the distinction was confirmed in *Byrne v HM Advocate*[7], a full bench decision, at page 164:

> 'We recapitulate our conclusions on the law. There are two distinct crimes of fire-raising: wilful fire-raising and culpable and reckless fire-raising. The crime of wilful fire-raising may be committed in respect of any form of property. Before an accused can be convicted of wilful fire-raising in respect of any particular item of property in the charge, the Crown must establish beyond reasonable doubt that he intended to set fire to that item of property. Where the jury is not so satisfied in respect of any of several items averred in the charge, they should delete it. The jury may infer the necessary intention from all the relevant circumstances, but there is no room for any doctrine of transferred intent. Nor can any form of recklessness be treated as equivalent to intent'.

Wilful fire-raising is, accordingly 'a separate species of criminal activity'[8]. As its name suggests, the offence can only be committed if the accused acts with the intention to burn one of the specified types of object. In *Blane v HM Advocate*[9], a case referred to in *Byrne*, the accused set fire to some bedding in his hostel room, ostensibly for the purpose of committing suicide by inhaling the smoke produced. However, the fire spread to the fabric of the building and a substantial amount of damage was caused. The accused, having failed to take his own life, was charged with wilful fire-raising on the basis that, having intentionally set fire to his bedding, he had by his own deliberate act brought about the damage to the property. It was held, however, that there was no such thing as transferred intent in wilful fire-raising. Intention to set fire to the bedding was not enough to show an intention to set fire to the building. To bring home liability for the offence, it had to be shown that the accused set fire to his bedding with the intention of burning the *building*, or at any rate in such circumstances of indifference and recklessness as to the consequences of his actions as to give rise to an inference of such an intention. Lord Justice-General Hope said that:

'... Proof of intention may present difficulties, especially in regard to the consequences of the initial deliberate act. But since the matter must be approached objectively, I think that it is open to inference, where the accused is shown to have acted with a reckless disregard for the likely consequences of what he does, that he intended those consequences to occur'[10].

1   See eg *Hume* I, 125.
2   Although malicious mischief could include fire raising within its ambit: see *Gordon* para 22–28.
3   It is a defence to a fire-raising charge for the accused to show that the property was his own: *Gordon* para 22–31. But if an accused set fire to his own property and the fire spreads to another's property, then in presence of the requisite *mens rea*, a charge of fire-raising may be held relevant. A person who sets fire to their own property with the intention of, eg, recovering insurance monies may, of course, be guilty of other offences, such as fraud or even culpable homicide: see eg *Sutherland v HM Advocate* 1994 SCCR 80, 1994 SLT 634.
4   *Hume* I, 131.
5   By the Criminal Procedure (Scotland) Act 1887, s 56.
6   See *Angus v HM Advocate* (1905) 13 SLT 507 at 508, per Lord Justice-General Dunedin.
7   2000 JC 155; 2000 SCCR 77; 2000 SLT 233.
8   *Blane v HM Advocate* 1991 SCCR 576 at 583, per Lord Justice-General Hope.
9   1991 SCCR 576.
10 1991 SCCR 576 at 581, per Lord Justice-General Hope.

18.8   Since in *Blane* the jury had not been properly directed as to the accused's intentions, he could not be convicted of wilful fire-raising. But it was clear that he had deliberately set fire to the bedding, and accordingly the court quashed the conviction for wilful fire-raising, and substituted a conviction of setting fire to the bedding wilfully.

There were some suggestions among the older writers that wilful fire-raising may be committed recklessly, for example where a person intentionally sets fire to his own property, and the fire spreads to the property of someone else[1]. However, in principle, one might have thought that the charge should be brought only where the fire was caused deliberately[2], and that view, implied in *Blane*, has been adopted explicitly in more recent case law. In *Carr v HM Advocate*[3], the Crown, this time taking no chances, brought alternative charges of wilful fire-raising and culpable and reckless fire-raising. The accused had entered a church hall, almost certainly for the purpose of stealing whatever he could find, and, in spite of the presence of electric lights, lit a ball of paper towels to use as a torch. When this began to burn his fingers he threw it down and went to the toilet. On his return, he found that the curtains in the hall had caught fire, and at this point, he left. The sheriff directed the jury that while wilful fire-raising could only be committed intentionally, intention could be inferred from conduct of the accused which demonstrated an utter disregard for the consequences of his actions. He was convicted of wilful fire-raising, and argued on appeal that this direction confused intention and recklessness, but the High Court approved of the sheriff's approach, and in particular of the idea that the test for intention in this context, as in other areas of Scots criminal law, is an objective one.

1 See eg *Hume* I, 130; *Alison* I, 433; Anderson *The Criminal Law of Scotland* (2nd edn, 1904), p 212.
2 Cf *Gordon* para 22–26.
3 1994 SCCR 521.

Causing death by wilful fire-raising

Petto v HMA[1] is an important case in the context of the law of murder; the accused set fire to his flat with a view to destroying evidence of an earlier killing. The fire spread to the flat above and as a result another resident of the block of flats was killed. The accused pled guilty to murder but sought to withdraw the plea on the basis that he had not intended to cause harm to anyone; the motivation had been to destroy his flat. The appeal was rejected by a bench of five judges. The court concluded that where a person started a major fire on the ground floor of a tenement building, he did so in the certain knowledge that those who were in the building would be at risk of being killed or seriously injured, and while he may have neither intended nor wished to harm others, the knowledge of the virtual certainty of such a risk, and the acceptance of it, should be rightly equated with intention that such consequences should occur. The court was not persuaded that wilful fire-raising which caused death was truly an exception to the general rule that the mens rea of murder required an intention to cause injury. The court accepted that there could be a case where someone who deliberately set fire to a building had no reason to know that there was anybody inside, In such a case, Scots law should not recognise an exception to the general principles of mens rea on which *HMA v Purcell*[2] was considered, that there required to be intention to cause injury or wicked recklessness.

Culpable and reckless fire-raising

18.9   From *Byrne*, the definition of culpable and reckless fire raising was given as follows:

> 'The crime of culpable and reckless fire-raising can also be committed in respect of any form of property. In that respect it is similar to wilful fire-raising. The difference from wilful fire-raising lies in the *mens rea*. Mere negligence is not enough: the property must have been set on fire due to an act of the accused displaying a reckless disregard as to what the result of his act would be.

> Contrary to what has sometimes been suggested, the distinction between the crimes remains important since the degree of blameworthiness will be relevant to penalty. A charge of wilful fire-raising does not contain an implied alternative charge of culpable and reckless fire-raising. So, where the only charge is one of wilful fire-raising, the judge may not direct the jury that they can return a verdict of culpable and reckless fire-raising. Nor may this

court substitute a verdict of culpable and reckless fire-raising in an appeal against a conviction of wilful fire-raising.

On the other hand it is open to the Crown to aver wilful fire-raising and, in the alternative, culpable and reckless fire-raising. On an indictment so framed, it will, of course, be open to the jury either to convict of wilful fire-raising or to convict of culpable and reckless fire-raising. Of course, there may be cases in which an accused deliberately sets fire to paper, rubbish or discarded property of no value, but the fire spreads and burns down premises and their contents. In such cases, the lighting of the paper or rubbish may really only be the source of the fire which constitutes the substance of the charge. In such cases, care may be required in framing the indictment to avoid the unwelcome complexity which might arise if the indictment were so framed that, for instance, a jury might have to convict the accused of wilful fire-raising in respect of the rubbish but of the alternative of culpable and reckless fire-raising in respect of the premises and contents'.

The accused in *Blane* could not be convicted of the nominate offence of wilful fire-raising, since it was not shown that he had intended to set fire to the hostel in which he lived. He was nevertheless convicted of the offence of 'setting fire to his bedding wilfully'. It is unclear whether the offence committed was a separate, innominate, offence, or whether it was a variety of the established offence of culpable and reckless fire-raising. There seems to be little doubt that culpable and reckless fire-raising may be charged in all cases other than those which were formerly capital, whether the fire is started recklessly or intentionally – 'it would really be absurd to say that what would amount to a crime if it were done culpably and recklessly is not a crime if it is done wilfully'[3]. It is, moreover, competent to charge culpable and reckless fire-raising where the object set on fire was one formerly reserved for wilful fire-raising charges[4]. In practice, it seems that charges of wilful and culpable and reckless fire-raising must now be laid as alternatives, thus avoiding the difficulty which arose in *Blane*[5].

1 2012 JC 105, 2011 SLT 1043, 2011 SCL 850, 2011 SCCR 519.
2 [2007] HCJ 13, 2008 JC 131, 2008 SLT 44, 2008 SCL 183, 2007 SCCR 520.
3 *Angus v HM Advocate* (1905) 13 SLT 507 at 508, per Lord Justice-General Dunedin. See also *Blane v HM Advocate* 1991 SCCR 576 at 584, per Lord Justice-General Hope.
4 *Geo Macbean* (1847) Arkley 262.
5 See eg *Carr v HM Advocate* 1994 SCCR 521.

18.10 The crime of culpable and reckless fire-raising cannot be committed solely by reason of the fact that the starting of the fire occurred while the accused was 'engaged in some illegal act'[1]. Fire-raising that was merely accidental does not demonstrate the requisite *mens rea* for the crime. It is not a crime and cannot be rendered criminal by the subsequent acts or omissions of the accused. The *mens rea* is determined by reference to the act of starting the fire, not behaviour.

Mere carelessness is clearly not sufficient. **A** is walking along a country lane. He pauses to light his pipe, and throws the match, still lit, over his shoulder, where it ignites some dry grass and in the resulting fire a whole plantation of trees is burned down. This is probably *not* culpable and reckless fire-raising.

Provided that adequate directions are given as to the standard to be applied, however, the question whether the accused's actions are sufficiently culpable is fundamentally a question of fact.

1 *McCue v Currie* 2004 JC 73 2004 SLT 858, 2004 SCCR 200.

Intentional fire-raising

18.11   Although wilful fire-raising may be committed only where certain specified objects are set alight, it is a criminal offence intentionally to set any object on fire which belongs to another[1]. The older authorities are equivocal as to whether this offence is a variant of culpable and reckless fire-raising, or is an offence in its own right[2]. It is thought that given the analysis in *Byrne*, there is no longer any live offence of intentional fireraising[3]. Whether there is any practical need for such an innominate offence seems doubtful, given that culpable and reckless fire-raising may be charged in any case where the technical requirements of wilful-raising are not met[4]. But there seems to be little doubt that the offence was at one stage an established part of the law in this area, and it arguably had the advantage of avoiding confusion in cases where 'non-specified' objects are intentionally set alight, as in *Blane*.

1 See *Blane v HM Advocate* 1991 SCCR 576.
2 See *Blane*, above; and cf *Angus v HM Advocate* (1905) 4 Adam 640; and *Wither v Adie* 1986 SLT (Sh Ct) 32.
3 See article in 2000 SLT 7 by James Chalmers.
4 *Angus v HM Advocate* (1905) 13 SLT 507 at 508; *Gordon* para 22–28.

Part V

OFFENCES AGAINST THE STATE AND ADMINISTRATION OF JUSTICE

Chapter 19

Offences against the state

TREASON

19.1   The Scots law of treason is based wholly on English law[1], and there is no recent Scottish case law. The 1708 Act does make specific provision that it is High Treason to 'slay any of the Lords of Session Lords of Justiciary sitting in judgement in the exercise of their office within Scotland.'

Who may be guilty of treason?

Treason is a breach of allegiance to the Crown, and only a person who owes such allegiance can be guilty of treason in United Kingdom law. Thus, British citizens are subject to the law of treason no matter where in the world the treasonable acts take place. Such a person cannot escape liability by changing his nationality – indeed, to become the naturalised citizen of an enemy state is itself a treasonable act[2]. British subjects who are not British citizens can be charged with treason only in respect of acts taking place within the United Kingdom[3], or its non-self-governing colonies. The same rule applies to aliens, the theory being that while in the United Kingdom they also owe allegiance to the Crown. An alien who holds a valid British passport and who has not surrendered it, nor taken any other overt step towards withdrawing his allegiance at the time of the relevant acts may also be guilty of treason, even if all the treasonable acts take place outwith the realm[4].

1 Treason Act 1708, s 1. For a fuller treatment of the subject, see *Stair Memorial Encyclopaedia* para 566 et seq.
2 *R v Lynch* [1903] 1 KB 444.
3 British Nationality Act 1948, s 3.
4 And even if the passport is obtained by false pretences: *Joyce v DPP* [1946] AC 347. The case turned on the notion that while holding the passport, Joyce was entitled to the protection of the Crown. This ground of decision has been strongly criticised: see eg SC Biggs (1947) 7 *Univ Tor LJ* 162; Glanville Williams (1948) 10 *Camb LJ* 54.

The forms of treason

19.2   The ways in which treason may be committed are still governed by the Treason Act 1351. The prohibited acts which remain of importance are:

(1)   Compassing or imagining the death of the sovereign, or of his Queen, or of their eldest son and heir

On the face of it, the first of these provisions is extremely wide, but in practice requires more than mere 'imaginings'. Some overt act is required, which, as

293

well as acts and conspiracies of a violent nature, may include words spoken or written and published which compass the death of the sovereign[1].

(2)   Levying war against the sovereign in the realm

A plot to levy war on the sovereign would not be covered by this provision, but would be regarded as a compassing of the death of the sovereign[2]. The levying of war against the sovereign is said to be of two types – direct and constructive. It would clearly be regarded as levying war to engage in a direct campaign or uprising against the authority of the sovereign, but it is not necessary that acts of violence take place – the mere recruitment and marching of a rebel force would be enough[3], and for this purpose, the size of the force is irrelevant[4].

There may be a constructive levying of war where armed force is directed not against the sovereign, but used 'for the purpose of effecting innovations of a public and general nature'[5]. Thus it would be a levying of war to raise an armed force to achieve the repeal of a particular statute, improve the general level of wages, or even, it seems, to attempt to destroy the places of worship of a particular religious group[6]. There is no levying of war where there is a demonstration of force on a purely local issue, and such a case would be dealt with as one of mobbing and rioting[7], or perhaps breach of the peace[8]. Cases involving armed mobs, demonstrating even on national issues are generally now treated in a similar way[9].

1 Smith and Hogan, p 827.
2 Hume I, 515.
3 *R v Vaughan* (1696) 13 St Tr 485; John Baird (1820) Hume I, 522. Where no fighting takes place, treason is probably not committed unless the group is armed: Hume I, 523.
4 See 3 Coke's Institutes 9.
5 Smith and Hogan, p 828.
6 See eg *R v Dammaree and Purchase* (1710) 15 St Tr 52.
7 *R v Andrew Hardie* (1820) 1 St Tr (Notes) 609.
8 See eg John Duncan (1843) 1 Broun 512.
9 See Smith and Hogan, p 778.

(3)   Being adherent to the sovereign's enemies in the realm, giving them aid and comfort in the realm, or elsewhere

19.3   In recent times, the most common form of treason has been the offence of adhering to the enemies of the sovereign. It is this provision which is used to prosecute acts of assistance to the enemy during wartime[1]. The assistance may be practical, material, or moral, as in the cases where the defendants took part in enemy propaganda broadcasts. In those cases, as in the following one, there was some doubt as to whether, being outwith the realm at the time of the broadcasts, they were subject to the law of treason. In *R v Casement*[2] an officer in a German prisoner of war camp tried to persuade Irish prisoners to fight for the Irish Brigade against the British. He argued that only acts committed within the realm were relevant to a charge under this provision, and that the words 'or elsewhere' referred not to the acts giving aid and comfort to the enemy, but to the effect of those acts. That argument was rejected, and Casement was convicted. A British citizen will be convicted of giving assistance to an enemy no matter where the assistance is given[3].

For a conviction under this heading, there must be proof of an 'evil' intention to give aid and comfort to the enemy. Thus, the accused's belief that he was entitled to perform the acts in question may be a relevant defence[4]. Similarly, if the accused was compelled to act by threats[5], either to himself or his family, it may be impossible to prove the necessary intention[6].

1 The certificate of the Secretary of State is conclusive evidence that a state of war exists between the United Kingdom and the 'enemy' state: *R v Bottrill, Ex parte Kuechenmeister* [1947] KB 41.
2 [1917] 1 KB 98.
3 See also *Joyce v DPP* [1946] AC 347.
4 See eg *R v Ahlers* [1915] 1 KB 616.
5 Against his life: *R v MacGrowther* (1746) 18 St Tr 391.
6 *R v Steane* [1947] KB 997, [1947] 1 All ER 813: *Steane* was not a case involving the defence of coercion, and it has been strongly argued that *Steane* was wrongly decided. See Glanville Williams *The Mental Element in Crime* (1965) para 21–22; *Gordon* para 7–19.

19.4   Misprision of treason remains a separate offence, and consists in the 'concealment or keeping secret of treason'[1], or possibly a treasonable plot[2], from the authorities.

SEDITION

The crime of sedition consists in words written or spoken which are 'calculated to excite popular disaffection, commotion, and violence and resistance to lawful authority'[3]. In extreme cases, because of its connection with constitutional matters, seditious conduct occurring during a public assembly may be treasonable[4]. In modern conditions, it is thought that the words used would have to be very extreme to justify a sedition charge. What is required is that the accused be:

'made out not to be exercising his right of free discussion for legitimate objects, but to be purposely, mischievously, without regard to his allegiance, and to the public danger, scattering burning firebrands, calculated to stimulate and excite such effects as I have mentioned – reckless of all consequences'[5].

This 'right of free discussion' is now somewhat wider than it was in 1793 when Lord Braxfield described the British constitution as the best in the world, and implied that any proposal for the reform of that constitution was necessarily seditious[6]. It has been said in an English case[7] that 'it is in the highest degree essential that nothing should be done in this court to weaken the liberty of the press', and it seems likely that the same view would prevail in Scotland[8].

To bring home a sedition charge, there must be proof that the relevant words were published intentionally. Once there is such proof, however, it is unnecessary to prove that the accused intended to bring about any of the effects referred to above. Recklessness as to the consequences is sufficient, provided that the words were objectively 'calculated' to have seditious effect[9].

Sedition and treason appear to overlap in the area of conspiracies to alter the constitution by force. There is a constructive levying of war, since there is a conspiracy to effect changes of a 'public and general nature', and there is probably sedition if the conspirators publish their intentions[10]. In recent times, charges of conspiracy to further the aims of terrorist groups, such as the IRA have been brought[11], but such cases are now likely to be dealt with under the Prevention of Terrorism Acts or Terrorism legislation[12].

1   *Sykes v DPP* [1962] AC 528 at 555, per Lord Denning.
2   CS Kenny *Kenny's Outlines of Criminal Law* (1965), para 421.
3   Indictment in *HM Advocate v Aldred* (June 1921, unreported), Glasgow High Court. *Gordon* para 39–01 reported on another point.
4   See *Chas Sinclair* (1794) 23 St Tr 777 at 800, per Lord Justice-Clerk Braxfield, since it may involve the levying of war against the sovereign.
5   *John Grant* (1848) 17 Shaw 50 at 80, per Lord Justice-Clerk Hope.
6   See his summing-up in *Thomas Muir's* case (1793) 23 St Tr 118 at 229.
7   *Caunt* (1947, unreported). See *Smith and Hogan* p 786.
8   See eg Lord Keith in *Lord Advocate v Scotsman Publications Ltd* 1989 SLT 705 at 709, [1990] 1 AC 812, HL.
9   *John Grant* (1848) 17 Shaw 50. There is no need for the words to produce any actual effect.
10 *See John Grant* above, especially Lord Wood at 50.
11 See eg *HM Advocate v Walsh* 1922 JC 82, 1922 SLT 443; *HM Advocate v MacAlister* (November 1953, unreported), HCJ; *Gordon* para 37–26.
12 See below.

THE OFFICIAL SECRETS ACTS

Spying and sabotage

19.5   Section 1 of the Official Secrets Act 1911[1] prohibits the collecting of information from, or being on or around a 'prohibited place'[2], for any purpose prejudicial to the safety or the interests of the state.

The test for conduct prejudicial to the interests of the state is an objective one, and it is not necessary to prove any particular act tending to show a purpose prejudicial to the interests of the state[3]. Motive and the presence or absence of 'evil intention' are irrelevant to a charge under s 1. In *Chandler v DPP*[4] the defendants were campaigners for nuclear disarmament. They were charged with conspiring to gain entry to an American Air Force base in England, and to prevent operations taking place. They argued that far from being a purpose prejudicial to the interests of the state, their purpose was the highly beneficial one of preventing the outbreak of a nuclear war. It was held that no matter what their ultimate intention or desire, the offence was committed, since one of their subordinate purposes was the obstruction of aircraft operations. 'The accused both intended and desired that the base should be immobilised for a time, and I cannot construe purpose in any sense that does not include that state of mind'[5]. Judged by the policies of the democratically elected government of the day, that was a prejudicial purpose, and the defendants were convicted.

Although the section is referred to in the sidenote as relating to spying, other 'prejudicial purposes' are covered by s 1. An obvious example is sabotage, as well as the type of conduct encountered in *Chandler*.

1   As amended by the Official Secrets Act 1920.
2   'Prohibited place' is comprehensively (and widely) defined in s 3 of the 1911 Act (as amended), and includes not only MOD establishments but railways, roads and other public works.

3 Section 1(2).
4 [1964] AC 763, [1962] 3 All ER 142.
5 Lord Reid at 790.

Divulging confidential information

19.6   Section 2 of the 1911 Act made it an offence to communicate, use,
wrongfully to retain, or to fail to take reasonable care of confidential information relating to affairs of state. Again the motive for the disclosure was
irrelevant – if information was deliberately disclosed, it mattered not that the
accused thought that his action was likely to be beneficial to the interests of the
state[1]. The nature and importance of the information was also irrelevant. In *R
v Crisp & Homewood*[2] for example, documents relating to contracts between
the War Office and the army's clothing suppliers were passed on to the director
of a tailoring firm. It was held that the disclosure of this vital information was
an offence under s 2. It was also irrelevant that the information would be of no
value to an enemy[3].

Section 2 has now been repealed and replaced by the provisions of the Official
Secrets Act 1989. Section 1 of this Act deals with the disclosure of information
about the security and intelligence services[4]. Under s 1, the nature and content
of the information communicated remains irrelevant where the communicator
is or has been a member of the security or intelligence services[5]. Where the
communicator is a Crown servant or government contractor, it is necessary to
show that the disclosure of the information is, or is likely to prove, damaging
to the security services[6]. It is a defence for a person charged under this section
to show that he did not know, nor had reasonable grounds to believe, that the
information related to security or intelligence matters, and for a Crown servant[7] to show that he did not realise, nor have reason to believe, that the disclosure would be damaging[8]. The Act contains similar provisions relating to the
disclosure of defence information[9], and information relating to international
relations[10].

1   *R v Fell* [1963] Crim LR 207.
2   (1919) 83 JP 121.
3   Cf s 1, which prohibits the making of sketches, plans, or models, and the collecting of informa-
    tion which may be of use to an enemy, and for the purposes of the section, 'enemy' includes
    potential enemies: *R v Parrot* (1913) 8 Cr App Rep 186.
4   'Security or intelligence' services are defined in s 1(9), and presumably includes MI5, MI6,
    and intelligence gathering stations such as GCHQ.
5   Official Secrets Act 1989, s 1(1).
6   Official Secrets Act 1989, s 1(3), (4).
7   But not a member of the security services.
8   Official Secrets Act 1989, s 1(5).
9   Ibid, s 2.
10 Ibid, s 3.

19.7   The offence of receiving confidential information was abolished[1].
However, s 5 provides that where information is received by a person who
knows, or has reasonable cause to believe, that it is protected by the provisions
of the Act, and disclosure of the information would be damaging, then that
person commits an offence if he discloses the information[2].

Other offences under the Acts include the obstruction of the forces of the Crown in the execution of their duties in relation to a prohibited place[3]; the harbouring of a person or persons who have committed or are about to commit an offence under the Acts[4]; gaining admission to a prohibited place by fraud, forgery or impersonation[5]; and attempts to commit, or the aiding and abetting of the commission of offences under the Acts[6].

1 Official Secrets Act 1911, s 2(2).
2 Ibid, s 5(2).
3 1920 Act, s 3.
4 1911 Act, s 7 (as amended).
5 1920 Act, s 1.
6 1920 Act, s 7.

TERRORISM

19.8   The first Prevention of Terrorism Act was passed in 1974 as a reaction to the IRA's mainland bombing campaign of that year. Since then, the legislation has been re-enacted with modifications from time to time and then expanded including the Terrorism Acts of 2000 and 2006, the Counter Terrorism Act 2008 and the Counter Terrorism and Security Act 2015. The focus of concern has by and large shifted from domestic terrorism to international terrorism, albeit manifested within the UK. The Terrorism Act 2000 as amended gives power to proscribe organisations *inter alia* which (a) commit or participate in acts of terrorism, (b) prepare for terrorism, (c) promote or encourage terrorism, or (d) are otherwise concerned in terrorism.

The 2000 Act *inter alia* proscribes the possession of articles in circumstances which give rise to a reasonable suspicion that possession was connected with the commission, preparation for, or instigation of an act of terrorism[1]. The 2006 Act *inter alia* proscribes the encouragement of terrorism and the dissemination of terrorist publications[2].

The legislation was subject to scrutiny by the High Court in *Siddique v HM Advocate*[3]. This was an appeal by Mr Siddique in connection with convictions under ss 54 and 57 of the 2000 Act and s 2 of the 2006 Act. He was convicted by a jury and appealed. The High Court had to consider a number of aspects of the crime, and the evidence which supported the crimes libelled. A full analysis is beyond the scope of this book but the court held that, for any conviction in relation to s 57, the accused must not only possess the items, but the Crown must prove that the circumstances in which he possessed the items give rise to a reasonable suspicion that the possession was connected with a prospective act of terrorism; it is not the possession itself, but possession in those circumstances. The phrase 'act of terrorism' is not a synonym for 'terrorism'[4].

It is an offence to be a member of a proscribed organisation, although it is a defence to show that membership predated the prescription of the organisation and that there has been no active membership since[5]. Public displays of support for proscribed organisations, such as the wearing of particular items of dress, or the carrying of any particular article are also an offence under the Act[6]. In *O'Moran v DPP*[7] it was held that the wearing of dark glasses, a black beret, and dark clothing at an IRA funeral was the wearing of a uniform, and the wearing of such clothing would almost certainly constitute a public display of support, contrary to the provisions of the Act, as would the wearing or carrying even of single items such as badges or flags[8]. In *Rankin v Murray*[9] the accused was convicted of an offence under s 13 of the 2000 Act as a consequence of wearing jewellery including a ring that gave rise to a reasonable suspicion that he was a member of the UVF.

1 See ss 54–58A for terrorist offences.
2 Sections 1 and 2; see the whole act for the prescribed activities.
3 2010 HCJAC 7.
4 Paragraphs [71]–[77].
5 Terrorism Act 2000 s 11.
6 Sections 11–13.
7 [1975] 1 All ER 473, [1975] QB 864.
8 *O'Moran* at 480. See also *Smith and Hogan* p 795.
9 2004 SLT 1164.

Funding of terrorism

19.9   The 2000 Act also makes it an offence to raise funds for prescribed organisations[1], to use or possess funds or other property which is intended to be used, or has reasonable cause to suspect will be used for the purposes of terrorism[2]. It is an offence to be involved in the arrangement of funding, as a result of which funding is made available to another, if the funder knows, or has reason to suspect, it is for the purposes of terrorism[3]. The law also provides that a person commits an offence if he enters into, or becomes concerned in, an arrangement which facilitates the retention or control by, or on behalf of, another person of terrorist property: (a) by concealment, (b) by removal from the jurisdiction, (c) by transfer to nominees, or (d) in any other way, although it is a defence for a person charged with an offence under subsection (1) to prove that he did not know, and had no reasonable cause to suspect, that the arrangement related to terrorist property[4].

1 Section 15.
2 Section 16.
3 Section 17.
4 Section 18.

Disclosure of information

19.10   Section 19 of the 2000 Act imposes a duty on certain classes of persons to disclose suspicions about their belief that another person has committed an offence under ss 15–18, and information provoking this suspicion came during the course of his trade business or profession, or his employment[1]. Where a bank official or other person in a position of financial responsibility suspects or believes that money or other property with which he is dealing is derived from terrorist funds, that official may disclose his suspicions to the police, regardless of any contractual duty of confidentiality[2].

1 There are some exceptions including information disclosed to legal advisors or to a business in the 'regulated sector'; see Schedule 3A.
2 Terrorism Act 2000, s 20.

Other orders

19.11   The Prevention of Terrorism Act 2005 provided for an order called a control order restricting the freedoms of persons suspected of being involved in terrorist activities; the Counter Terrorism Act 2008 makes provision for notification requirements for persons suspected. The Terrorism Prevention and Investigation Measures (TPIM) Act 2011 was introduced to meet concerns about the nature and effects of control orders. The Act enables the Secretary of State to impose specified terrorism prevention and investigation measures on an individual by means of a 'TPIM' notice. Again the detailed analysis of what has been a sustained legislative assault on terrorism is beyond the scope of this work.

Chapter 20

Offences against the administration of justice

PERJURY

20.1   *Hume* described perjury as 'the judicial affirmation of falsehood on oath'[1]. Macdonald said that a person commits perjury who wilfully and unequivocally makes a false statement on oath or by affirmation in any judicial proceedings[2]. It is of the essence of the crime that an 'absolute falsehood be explicitly and wilfully affirmed'[3] while the accused is giving evidence on oath in some judicial proceeding[4]. Ambiguities in the accused's testimony will be resolved in his favour, and it is only very clear falsehoods which will justify a perjury charge[5]. Accordingly, a failure to tell 'the whole truth' probably does not amount to perjury[6]. In any event, it is necessary to prove that the accused intentionally affirmed the falsehood, in the knowledge of its falsity[7], and this would be difficult where his evidence was merely ambiguous or incomplete.

The perjured evidence must have been given in the course of evidence both competent and relevant, and provided that it is so given, it does not matter that the falsehood is trivial or seemingly insignificant[8]. Evidence which goes merely to credibility, and not to any specific issue in the case is relevant evidence for the purposes of a perjury charge[9].

1 *Hume* I, 366. Note that a person who does not take the usual form of oath, because he is an atheist, for example, but merely affirms that he will tell the truth is still liable to a perjury charge: False Oaths (Scotland) Act 1933, s 7(1)(b) (as amended) although the Criminal Justice and Licensing (Scotland) Bill 2009 proposes the repeal of the 1933 Act at Schedule 5.
2 *Criminal Law*, Macdonald (5th edn), p 164.
3 *Hume* I, 366.
4 Provided that the tribunal can and does administer the oath to witnesses: see *Gordon* para 47–03.
5 *Gordon* para 47–03.
6 But see *Gordon* para 47–11.
7 *Hume* I, 368. Or perhaps not believing it to be true: see *Simpson v Tudhope* 1987 SCCR 348.
8 See *Lord Advocate's Reference (No 1 of 1985)* 1986 JC 137, 1986 SCCR 329, 1987 SLT 187 in which it was held that *Hume's* reference to the need for the falsehood to be 'material' (*Hume* I, 368–369), simply meant that the falsehood must relate to relevant evidence.
9 See eg *Elizabeth Muir* (1830) *Alison* I, 469–470; *HM Advocate v Smith* 1934 JC 66, 1934 SLT 485.

20.2   The relevancy requirement was addressed by the Lord Justice General Emslie in *Lord Advocate's Reference*[1] at p 145; he said that: 'All that is required is that it should be clearly understood that a charge of perjury will not lie unless the evidence alleged to be false was both competent and relevant at the earlier trial either in proof of the libel or in relation to the credibility of the witness'.

The relevancy requirement is a matter of law to be determined by the judge and not by a jury. It was a feature of the case *HMA v Coulson*[2]. The accused had given evidence in a perjury trial. He was then himself charged with perjury. After the Crown case a submission of no case to answer was made, on the basis that his evidence in the original trial was not relevant, and therefore the offence of perjury could not be committed. Lord Burns upheld the submission. He adopted the test of relevance from *CJM v HMA*[3], where the Lord Justice Clerk said *inter alia* at paragraph [28]:

> 'The starting-point for a decision on whether this evidence is admissible is the general principle that evidence is only admissible if it is "relevant" ... Evidence is relevant when it either bears directly on a fact in issue (ie the libel) or does so indirectly because it relates to a fact which makes a fact in issue more or less probable ... The determination of whether a fact is relevant depends very much upon its context and the degree of connection between what is sought to be proved, or disproved, and the facts libelled. It is a "matter of applying logic and experience to the circumstances of the particular case" ... The question is one of degree: "the determining factor being whether the matters are, in a reasonable sense, pertinent and relevant and whether they have a reasonably direct bearing on the subject under investigation" ...'

Lord Burns, adopting the test from the *Lord Advocate's Reference* continued, 'I consider that if the witness gave relevant evidence in causa he can be guilty of perjury even if the perjured evidence related only to his credibility ... Evidence is relevant if it bears directly on a fact in issue or indirectly because it relates to a fact which makes a fact in issue more or less probable. Relevancy depends on its context and the degree of connection between what is sought to be proved or disproved and the facts libelled.'

Lord Burns considered that the false evidence alleged in this indictment was not relevant evidence at the original trial and the charge of perjury in the indictment was irrelevant.

The competency requirement means that a falsehood affirmed in the course of evidence which should have been disregarded as incompetent, cannot ground a perjury charge, and the matter of competency is one which can be reviewed in subsequent perjury proceedings by the trial judge[4], or exceptionally, by the jury[5]. A particular aspect of the competency requirement is that the Crown cannot rely on statements made in precognitions in order to establish a perjury charge. Such statements are inadmissible, even for the purpose of attacking a witness's credibility, and cannot be relied upon[6]. It is the function of the trial judge at the perjury trial to determine whether the words attributed to the person were part of a precognition or a statement[7]. Furthermore, it is not enough for the Crown merely to prove that the accused has sworn contradictory oaths on different occasions. 'The Crown must be able to prove that either **X** or not **X** is the case, they cannot merely show that [the accused] must have committed perjury on one or other occasion'[8]. Finally, it is no defence to a perjury charge that the false testimony was given at the witness's own trial on some other charge. In *HM Advocate v Cairns*[9] the accused was acquitted of murder, but subsequently convicted of perjury in respect of his evidence at the trial that he did not assault and stab the deceased, the truth being that he did indeed carry out the attack.

Subornation of perjury

A person who induces another to commit perjury is himself guilty of subornation of perjury[10]. It is not necessary that the witness be intimidated or bribed into giving perjured evidence, although intimidation or bribery will suffice. Simple persuasion is enough[11]. It is necessary, however, that the witness should actually give the perjured evidence[12] – if the witness does not in fact give evidence, resists the inducement to commit perjury[13], or informs on the accused at or before the trial[14], there can be a conviction only of attempted subornation. An attempt to procure false evidence from a witness may also constitute contempt of court[15], or an attempt to pervert the course of justice[16].

1 1986 JC 137; 1987 SLT 187.
2 2015 SCL 606.
3 2013 SCCR 215.
4 *HM Advocate v Smith*, above.
5 *Low v HM Advocate* 1988 SLT 97, 1987 SCCR 541.
6 See eg *Low v HM Advocate*, above.
7 *Low v HM Advocate* 1987 SCCR; *Thompson v Crowe* 1999 SLT 1434.
8 *Gordon* para 47–18.
9 1967 JC 37, 1967 SLT 165.
10 *Hume* I, 381.
11 *Gordon* para 48–21.
12 *Angus v HM Advocate* 1935 JC 1, 1934 SLT 501.
13 See *Hume* I, 382.
14 *Robert Stirling* (1821) Alison, 487.
15 See below.
16 See *Gordon* paras 47–3940, 51–13.

CONTEMPT OF COURT

20.3   The person accused of contempt of court is in the peculiar position of having committed a punishable offence, but not a crime in Scots law. Contempt of court

'... is the name given to conduct which challenges or affronts the authority of the court or the supremacy of the law itself, whether it takes place in or in connection with civil or criminal proceedings. The offence of contempt of court is an offence *sui generis* and, where it occurs, it is peculiarly within the province of the court itself, civil or criminal as the case may be, to punish it under its power which arises from the inherent and necessary jurisdiction to take effective action to vindicate its authority and preserve the due and impartial administration of justice'[1].

It was a feature of the law in this area that where someone was held to be in contempt of court, the judge was able to deal with the matter immediately, without the need for formal charge or trial, and the person in contempt could be imprisoned or fined then and there. In relation to some types of contempt, for example where a witness prevaricates in order to avoid answering a competent and relevant question, judges will generally give the witness a chance to purge his contempt before making use of the sanctions available to them[2]. The whole issue of contempt of court and the machinery for dealing with the alleged contemnor was examined by a full bench in the cases of *Robertson v HM Advocate* and *Gough v HM Advocate* which were heard together[3]. The High Court dealt with a combination of bills of suspension and a petition to the *nobile officium* in respect of two different, and unrelated parties. Mr Gough had obtained a degree of notoriety throughout Scotland under the nickname of 'The Naked Rambler'. His complaint was that he had been found in contempt of court on a number of occasions because of his insistence in appearing naked in court. The procedure followed in contempt matters which could lead to a sentence of imprisonment, although initiated by the court *ex proprio motu* was challenged. This followed from a decision of the European Court of Human Rights in *Kyprianou v Cyprus (No 2)*[4] which many commentators felt rendered the Scottish procedure incompatible with the ECHR requirements.

The opinion of the court emphasised the interests which a court had in enforcing standards of decorum in behaviour and in the eliciting of truthful evidence, recognising the need for procedural safeguards. The court also distinguished between contemptuous conduct directed at the judge or judges personally, and that directed at the administration of justice; in the former, the judges should remit the matter to another court to determine if contempt is made out. Where a witness is giving evidence for the defence in a criminal trial, it may constitute a miscarriage of justice in relation to the accused if the judge deals with the witness's contempt in open court[5].

1 *HM Advocate v Airs* 1975 SLT 177 at 179, 180, per Lord Justice-General Emslie.
2 See eg *Wylie v HM Advocate* 1966 SLT 149.
3 2007 SLT 1153, 2008 SC 1.
4 (2007) 44 EHRR 27.
5 See eg *Royle v Gray* 1973 SLT 31.

What types of conduct will result in a person being found to be in contempt?

20.4   It should be noted that the jurisdiction of the court to deal with wilful challenges should be used sparingly. In *Robertson*, the Lord Justice Clerk said:

'It should be exercised only out of necessity to protect the integrity of the court's procedures, and preferably only after time for reflection. In all questions of this kind, judges should be cautious in their approach and keep a sense of proportion. Words spoken in heat are sometimes best ignored'[1].

Intention is an essential element for a common law contempt. The behaviour must be wilful and deliberate[2]. The test of wilfulness is a high one, not met if the behaviour might be categorised as careless or negligent[3]. The following gives some guidance of the type of behaviour likely to initiate contempt procedures:

(a) Conduct which challenges or affronts the authority of the court. At common law, the conduct must be such as to demonstrate a neglect of the duty to uphold the dignity of the court, or a wilful or reckless interference with the course of justice[4]. Thus, drunken or disorderly conduct in court will almost certainly constitute contempt[5]. Slandering, or murmuring of judges is also contempt of court[6], as well as being a common law crime[7]. Criticism of judges and the law is not of itself contemptuous, however. In *R v Commissioner of Metropolitan Police, ex parte Blackburn*[8], Salmon LJ said that '… no criticism of a judgment, however vigorous, can amount to contempt of court, providing it keeps within the limits of reasonable courtesy and good faith'. Even where there is some indication that the criticism falls outwith those limits, the courts have said:

> 'over and over again that the greatest restraint and discretion should be used by the court in dealing with contempt of court, lest a process, the purpose of which is to prevent interference with the administration of justice, should degenerate into an oppressive or vindictive abuse of the court's powers'[9].

In addition, it may be the case that abusive statements about judges would not be treated as contempt unless they related to a particular case or cases[10]. In *Anwar, Respondent*[11], a solicitor who represented an accused convicted of terrorism charges was subject to a remit from the trial judge to the High Court on an issue of possible contempt; the solicitor had made a public statement after conviction, but prior to sentencing, which had troubled the trial judge. The High Court held that it was possible to conceive of language so extreme that it challenged or affronted the authority of the court, or the supremacy of the law itself, particularly if the integrity or honesty of a particular judge, or the court generally was attacked, whether it related to ongoing proceedings or not; the court also held that jurors had to be expected not only to do their duty, but also to be robust in the face of any subsequent criticism.

The court declined to make a finding of contempt, describing the statement as embodying 'angry and petulant criticism' of the outcome of the trial, but determining that the authority of the courts and the supremacy of the law had been neither challenged nor damaged by it[12].

Witnesses who prevaricate or refuse to answer competent and relevant questions[13], or who perjure themselves[14], may also be held in contempt, as may anyone who interferes with witnesses or other evidence[15]. Unauthorised or improper absence or lateness from court proceedings by solicitors, jurors, or witnesses may also constitute contempt[16], provided that there is no reasonable excuse for the absence[17]. Wilful failure to attend may also be charged as an attempt to pervert the course of justice[18]. In general it seems that conduct must be wilful in order to constitute a contempt of court[19], although there are indications that in some cases, recklessness may suffice[20].

1　Page 1167, para I.
2　*Mayer v HM Advocate* 2005 JC 121 at para [12]; see also *B v R* 2010 SLT (Sheriff Court).
3　For example *Scott v Dunn* [2014] HCJAC 134.
4　See eg *Pirie v Hawthorn* 1962 JC 69, 1962 SLT 291; *Mackinnon v Douglas* 1982 SCCR 80, 1982 SLT 375. *HM Advocate v Tarbett* 2003 SLT 1288, cf *Butterworth v Herron* 1975 SLT (Notes) 56.
5　*Hume* II, 138; *Gordon* para 50–02. See eg *Dawes v Cardel* 1987 SCCR 135.
6　See eg *Milburn* 1946 SC 301, 1946 SLT 219.
7　Judges Act 1540; *Hume* I, 406, although the last reported case was *HM Advocate v Robertson* (1870) Coup 404.
8　[1968] 2 QB 150 at 155, [1968] 2 All ER 319.

9 *Milburn* 1946 SC 301 at 315, per Lord President Normand.
10 Cf *Gordon* para 51–03.
11 2008 SLT 710.
12 Paragraphs [40]–[44].
13 *Hume* I, 380. *Robertson and Gough* above; Robertson had been found guilty of contempt for prevarication.
14 *Gordon* para 50–03.
15 *Hume* II, 140.
16 See eg *Muirhead v Douglas* 1979 SLT (Notes) 17. Cf *Macara v Macfarlane* 1980 SLT (Notes) 26.
17 Cf *Mackinnon v Douglas* 1982 SCCR 80, 1982 SLT 375. *HM Advocate v Tarbett* 2003 SLT 1288.
18 See *HM Advocate v Mannion* 1961 JC 79; *Gordon* para 48–41.
19 *Pirie v Hawthorn* 1962 JC 69; *Cameron v Orr* 1995 SCCR 365; *Ferguson v Normand* 1994 SCCR 812, 1994 SLT 1355. *HM Advocate v Dickie* 2002 SLT 1083, 2002 SCCR 312.
20 *Muirhead v Douglas* 1979 SLT (Notes) 17; *McKinnon v Douglas* 1982 SCCR 80 and cf *Orr v Annan* 1987 JC 38.

20.5   (b) Conduct which challenges the supremacy of the law[1]. It has sometimes been argued that certain classes of witness – for example doctors and journalists – may refuse to answer questions on the grounds of professional confidentiality. It is true, of course, that certain witnesses are entitled to refuse to answer questions relating to professional communications – the confidentiality attaching to communications between solicitor and client is a good example. Unless the witness falls into one of the recognised exceptions however, it will be contempt if he fails to answer a competent and relevant question, such failure being regarded as challenge to the supremacy of the law itself, whatever the motive for the witness's silence[2]. The court has a residual discretion to excuse a witness from answering such a question on the grounds of conscience, but *HM Advocate v Airs*[3] strongly suggests that no such relief will be available to journalists, in criminal proceedings at least[4]. Further, there is no requirement that the question which the witness fails to answer must be 'useful'. If it is competent and relevant it must be answered, and in any event 'it is hard to figure any circumstances in which a relevant question could, in the course of a trial or proof, be judged unnecessary or not useful …'[5].

1 See *Anwar, Respondent*, above.
2 *HM Advocate v Airs* 1975 SLT 177 at 183, per Lord Justice-General Emslie.
3 1975 SLT 177.
4 The Contempt of Court Act 1981, s 10 provides that journalists and others need not disclose the source of information unless disclosure is deemed by the court to be necessary 'in the interests of justice or national security or for the prevention of disorder or crime'. It is not enough, however, that the information would be relevant to the determination of an issue before the court, since that would mean that disclosure could be required in respect of all admissible evidence. The disclosure must further be 'necessary' in the technical sense of being necessary in the interests of the administration of justice in the course of court proceedings: *Maxwell v Pressdram Ltd* [1987] 1 All ER 621, [1987] 1 WLR 298. This provision probably would not have assisted Mr Airs, who was in possession of information about a terrorist group.
5 *HM Advocate v Airs*, 1975 SLT 177 at 180, per Lord Justice-General Emslie.

The Contempt of Court Act 1981

20.6   It is a contempt of court to prejudice the possibility of a fair trial, or the administration of justice generally[1], by publishing information or opinions likely to lead to pre-judgement of the issues[2]. Contempt generally requires some degree of *mens rea*, in the form of a wilful or reckless disregard of the authority of the court[3]. In relation to pre-trial publicity however[4], the Contempt of Court Act 1981 provides that liability for contempt is strict, and is incurred whenever a publication, be it speech, writing, broadcast or any other form of communication addressed to the public at large, creates 'a substantial risk that the course of justice in the proceedings in question will be seriously impeded or prejudiced'[5]. The Act was passed in order to bring the law of the United Kingdom into conformity with the interpretation of Article 10 of the European Convention of Human Rights; the Convention is now part of domestic law. It must be interpreted in such a way as to comply with the rights arising from the Convention. To incur liability under the Act, it is a further requirement that the proceedings be 'active', a requirement which covers not merely the duration of the trial itself, but the entire period when the person concerned is under the 'care of the court and within its protection'[6]. Thus, a case becomes 'active' when a suspect is arrested[7], or, in a civil case, in the case of an ordinary action in the Court of Session or in the sheriff court, when the Record is closed, in the case of a motion or application, when it is enrolled or made, and in any other case, when the date for a hearing is fixed or a hearing is allowed[8].

Section 3 of the Act creates a defence for publishers or distributors of contemptuous material who, having taken all reasonable care to avoid liability, do not know or have reason to suspect that the proceedings are active, or that the material is contemptuous. The Act further provides that fair and accurate reports of public legal proceedings, published contemporaneously with those proceedings, and in good faith, do not constitute contempt[9]. However, the court can order the postponement of publication of such reports where the risk of prejudice would be 'substantial'[10]. Publications which in good faith discuss public affairs or matters of general public interest and which incidentally cause a risk of prejudice to particular legal proceedings[11], are also protected. In the latter case, the onus is on the Crown to prove that the risk of prejudice to the particular legal proceedings was (a) more than merely remote, and (b) that it was not merely incidental to the matter under discussion[12].

1 *Atkins v London Weekend Television Ltd* 1978 JC 48, 1978 SLT 76; *Hall v Associated Newspapers Ltd* 1979 JC 1, 1978 SLT 241. *AG v MGN Limited and Others [1997] 1 All ER 456*, described as providing a 'useful index of the various matters to be borne in mind' in *HM Advocate v The Scotsman and others* 23 April 1998.
2 *Glasgow Corpn v Hedderwick & Sons* 1918 SC 639, 1918 2 SLT 2; *Stirling v Associated Newspapers* 1960 JC 5, 1960 SLT 5. Publication may include publication of material on the internet *HM Advocate v Beggs (opinion no 2) 21 September 2001*, where the court ultimately decided that the material, including material published on a website, did not give rise to 'a substantial risk'.
3 See *Mackinnon v Douglas* 1982 SCCR 80, 1982 SLT 375.
4 Contempt of Court Act 1981, s 2(1).
5 Ibid, s 2(2). See *PF Edinburgh v Riordan* at www.scotcourts.gov.uk/opinions/2007004186.html.
6 *Hall v Associated Newspapers Ltd* 1979 JC 1 at 12, per Lord Justice-General Emslie.
7 *Hall v Associated Newspapers Ltd*, above. Or perhaps even where a suspect has been detained under statutory powers. Cf *Gordon* para 50–16.
8 Contempt of Court Act 1981, Sch 1, para 14. See eg *Young v Armour* 1921 1 SLT 211.

9 Contempt of Court Act 1981, s 4.
10 Ibid, s 4 (2). See eg *Keane v HM Advocate* 1986 SCCR 491.
11 Contempt of Court Act 1981, s 5.
12 *Attorney General v English* [1983] 1 AC 116, [1982] 2 All ER 903.

MAKING FALSE REPORTS TO THE POLICE

20.7   It has for a long time been a criminal offence to falsely accuse someone of a crime[1]. Simply to waste the time of the police is now a separate crime at common law. The essence of the crime consists in the making of false reports to the police, such that they are 'deliberately set in motion by a malicious person by means of an invented story'[2]. In *Kerr v Hill*[3], the accused was charged that he falsely claimed to have seen a pedal cyclist struck by a bus, thus wasting police time on an unnecessary investigation, and rendering certain bus drivers liable to suspicion and accusations of reckless driving. It would be easy to regard such a charge as one of fraud, particularly in view of the breadth of the result requirement of that crime in Scots law[4]. In the subsequent case of *Robertson v Hamilton*[5] the accused falsely claimed to have been bitten by a police dog during their arrest on other charges, thus rendering the police-dog handler liable to suspicion and possible disciplinary action. At first instance, the sheriff held that the complaint relevantly disclosed a species of fraud. On appeal, however, the High Court expressed no concluded opinion on the question of fraud, and rested their conclusions entirely on *Kerr v Hill*[6].

Both *Kerr v Hill* and *Robertson v Hamilton* involved specific accusations made against others. However, it seems that specific allegations are unnecessary to the commission of this crime. It is enough that false information is conveyed to the authorities, causing them to embark upon a fruitless investigation. In *Bowers v Tudhope*[7] the accused falsely represented to the police that he had lost his giro cheque. Relying on dicta from *Kerr v Hill*, the High Court rejected the argument that a false accusation is a necessary element in the crime[8]. '[If] a person maliciously makes a statement, known to be false, to the police authorities, with the intention and effect of causing them to make inquiries into it, he commits a criminal offence'[9]. It is not, however, a crime merely to tell lies to the police[10], or, presumably, to induce another to tell lies to the police[11].

1 *Hume* I, 341–342.
2 *Kerr v Hill* 1936 JC 71 at 75, per Lord Justice-General Normand.
3 1936 JC 71, 1936 SLT 320.
4 See Chapter 16 above on fraud and Gordon's commentary to *Bowers v Tudhope* 1987 SCCR 77 at 79.
5 1987 SCCR 477, 1988 SLT 70.
6 1936 JC 71, 1936 SLT 320, and in particular Lord Justice-General Normand's dictum quoted above.
7 1987 SCCR 77, 1987 SLT 748.
8 The interpretation of *Kerr v Hill* adopted in *Bowers v Tudhope* has been criticised (see 'Forensis' (1987) 32 JLSS 353), although *Kerr* was followed in *Robertson v Hamilton* 1987 JC 95, 1988 SLT 70, 1987 SCCR 477.
9 *Kerr v Hill* 1936 JC 71 at 76, per Lord Fleming.
10 See *Curlett v McKechnie* 1938 JC 176 at 179, per Lord Fleming and *Gordon* para 48–40.
11 But see *Dalton v HM Advocate* 1951 JC 76, 1951 SLT 294.

ESCAPING FROM LAWFUL CUSTODY

20.8   When a person is lawfully confined to prison, under a valid warrant applicable to him, he commits the common law offence of prison-breaking if he escapes[1]. It is not necessary that violence should be used to effect the escape – even if a prisoner simply walks out of a door which has been carelessly or deliberately left open, prison-breaking is committed[2]. The specific offence of prison-breaking only applies where the accused was held in a public prison, and cannot be charged where the accused was held in some place of temporary custody, such as a police cell[3]. If the accused was not in a public prison, or was not in any place of custody at all, though still a prisoner, the relevant charge is one of defeating or attempting to defeat the ends of justice by escaping from lawful custody. Such was the charge in *HM Advocate v Martin*[4], for example, where the accused was a member of a 'chain-gang' working outside the prison where he was being held. A person assisting the escape of another, whether from prison or from any other place, is also likely to be charged with hindering or defeating the ends of justice[5].

1 *Hume* I, 401–402; *Gordon* paras 49–01, 49–03, but see para 20.9 below.
2 *Hume* I, 402; *Gordon* para 49–05.
3 *Hume* I, 404; *Gordon* para 49–02.
4 1956 JC 1, 1956 SLT 193.
5 See eg *HM Advocate v Martin*, above; *Turnbull v HM Advocate* 1953 JC 59.

ATTEMPTS TO DEFEAT THE ENDS OF JUSTICE

20.9   There are, as described in this chapter, a number of nominate crimes against the administration of justice. There has arisen in practice, where there has been alleged interference with the course of justice, but where the actings do not amount to one of the nominate crimes, a tendency to charge a person with an attempt to defeat or pervert the course of justice. It has coalesced into a crime in its own right and has been charged as an offence in a number of circumstances. So, escaping from legal custody will usually now be charged as an attempt to defeat the ends of justice[1].

In *Harris v HM Advocate*[2] the High Court determined that a threat to a police officer, made in private with no prospect of being overheard or even indirectly observable could not amount to a breach of the peace. However, in his opinion, the Lord Justice General concluded as follows:

'It would be wrong to leave this case without observing that … the conduct here complained of might, with some elaboration, have given rise to a relevant charge of a different kind in particular of an attempt to pervert the course of justice. The common law of threats might possibly also have been invoked'[3].

Accordingly there is explicit approval for the concept of a charge of attempting to defeat the ends, or pervert the course of, justice. The essence of such a crime is as much the hindering or obstruction of justice as it is in the actual defeat or perversion. The offence must be committed intentionally[4].

In *Wade and Coats v HMA*[5], examples of the kind of behaviour which can form the basis of defeating the ends of justice were given, in the context of an appeal against conviction and sentence which was refused; *inter alia* the indictment charged the accused and others with washing and cleaning a flat, applying bleach, lifting and removing a carpet, laying new floorboards, setting fire to and destroying physical, biological and telecommunication evidence implicating them in the crime libelled and to avoid detection, arrest, prosecution and conviction intending to defeat the ends of justice.

There can now be no doubt of the existence of a nominate crime, of attempting to defeat the ends of justice, given the explicit approval in *Harris* and the acceptance by the appeal court of the legitimacy of the charges in cases such as *Wade*.

1 *HM Advocate v Martin* 1956 JC 1, 1956 SLT 193; *Salmon v HM Advocate* 1991 SCCR 628.
2 2009 SLT 1078.
3 At para [26].
4 *Kenny v HM Advocate* 1951 JC 104; 1951 SLT 363.
5 [2014] HCJAC 88.

Index

[references are to paragraph numbers]

A

Abandonment
  attempts, and, 7.7–7.8
  omissions, and, 2.12–2.13
Abortion
  homicide, and, 10.1
Abuse of trust
  sexual offences, and, 11.2
Accident
  road and traffic offences, and, 13.7
Accomplices
  parties to a crime, and, 6.2
'Act' of God
  novus actus interveniens, and, 5.8
Act of third party
  novus actus interveniens, and
    generally, 5.9–5.10
    malregimen, 5.10–5.12
Act of victim
  novus actus interveniens, and
    'escape' cases, 5.15
    feckless conduct, 5.16
    generally, 5.13
    suicide, 5.16
    'supply' cases, 5.13–5.14
Acting in concert
  parties to a crime, and, 6.1
Actus reus
  automatism, 2.5–2.9
  coincidence with mens rea, 2.27–2.28
  generally, 2.2
  introduction, 2.
  omissions
    abandonment of victim, 2.12–2.13
    categories of liability, 2.12
    close relationships between accused
      and person suffering the harm,
      2.14–2.15
    contractual obligations, 2.15
    control of dangerous things, 2.13
    dependent relationships, 2.14–2.15
    duty to prevent commission of
      crime, 2.10
    failure to perform duty, 2.15
    failure to warn, 2.13
    generally, 2.10–2.15

Actus reus – *contd*
  omissions – *contd*
    life-guards, and, 2.14
    previous dangerous actings, 2.12–
      2.14
    status of accused is such that he has
      duty to act, 2.14
  reflex action on the part of the
    accused, 2.4–2.5
  somnambulism, 2.5
  status offences, 2.4
  unconscious acts, 2.5–2.9
  voluntary act
    automatism, 2.5–2.9
    external events beyond the control
      of the actor, 2.3–2.4
    introduction, 2.1
    reflex action on the part of the
      accused, 2.4–2.5
    somnambulism, 2.5
    status offences, 2.4
    unconscious acts, 2.5–2.9
Administration of noxious substances
  generally, 9.12–9.13
Adultery
  provocation, and, 10.19
Age of consent
  sexual offences, and, 11.2
Aggravated theft
  drugging the victim, 14.23
  housebreaking, 14.21–14.22
  opening lockfast places, 14.22–14.23
  robbery, 15.1
Alcohol
  intoxication defence, and, 8.10
Amotio
  theft, and, 14.6
Ancillary responsibility
  parties to a crime, and, 6.1
Appropriation
  theft, and, 14.6–14.8
'Art and part' guilt
  assisting perpetrator in commission of
    crime, 6.15–6.16
  associate liability, 6.5–6.7
  bilateral regulatory offences, 6.9

'Art and part' guilt – *contd*
circumstances in which liability
occurs, 6.10–6.16
common plan, 6.19
counselling an offence, 6.12
'doing nothing', 6.10–6.11
forms, 6.4–6.7
innocent agency, 6.4
instigating an offence, 6.12
introduction, 6.1
joint commission, 6.4
justification, 6.2–6.3
'mere presence' cases, 6.10–6.11
regulatory offences, 6.9
scope, 6.19–6.20
statutory offences, 6.21
supply of materials or information,
6.12–6.15
unintended consequences, and,
6.19–6.20
victim, and, 6.8
withdrawal by participant, 6.17–6.18
Assault
aggravated offences, 9.8
chastisement, 9.3
consent, and, 9.6–9.7
defence, 9.6–9.7
generally, 9.1–9.2
lawful force
chastisement, 9.3
defence of self, others or of
property, in, 9.4
introduction, 9.3
prevention of crime, in, 9.4
restraint of other, in, 9.4
self-defence, in, 9.4
mens rea, 9.5
mitigation, 9.9
reasonable belief in consent, 9.7
**Assisting perpetrator in commission
of crime**
'art and part' guilt, and, 6.15–6.16
Associate liability
'art and part' guilt, and, 6.5–6.7
Attempt
abandonment, 7.7–7.8
generally, 7.1
impossibility, 7.11–7.15
'last act' theory, 7.4–7.6
meaning, 7.2
mental element, 7.8–7.10
preparatory acts, 7.3–7.7
punishment, 7.1

Attempt – *contd*
relevant conduct, 7.2–7.5
statutory offences, 7.10–7.11
suicide, and, 10.2
'thought' crimes, 7.3
Attempting to drive
defence, 13.22
generally, 13.4
while unfit through drink or drugs
defence, 13.22
generally, 13.18–13.19
Attempts to defeat the ends of justice
generally, 20.9
Automatism
road and traffic offences, and, 13.3
voluntary act, and, 2.5–2.9

B
Being concerned in the supply of drugs
generally, 12.5–12.7
Being in charge of motor vehicle
while unfit
defence, 13.22
generally, 13.20–13.21
with more than the prescribed
concentration of alcohol in the
body
defences, 13.24–13.26
generally, 13.23
'hip flask' defence, 13.25
necessity, 13.26
no likelihood of driving, 13.24
post-incident drinking, 13.25
Bladed articles
offensive weapons, and, 12.14
Borrowing
theft, and, 14.15–14.19
Breach of the peace
generally, 12.8–12.10
threatening or abusive behaviour,
12.11
Bribery
generally, 17.10
offences, 17.11

C
Careless and inconsiderate driving
road and traffic offences, and, 13.15
Causation
'act' of God, 5.8
act of third party
generally, 5.9–5.10
malregimen, 5.10–5.12

Causation – *contd*
  act of victim
    'escape' cases, 5.15
    feckless conduct, 5.16
    generally, 5.13
    suicide, 5.16
    'supply' cases, 5.13–5.14
  conclusions, 5.17
  'escape' cases, 5.15
  existing conditions, 5.6
  feckless conduct, 5.16
  generally, 5.1–5.2
  medical treatment, 5.10–5.11
  novus actus interveniens
    'act' of God, 5.8
    act of third party, 5.9–5.12
    act of victim, 5.13–5.16
    introduction, 5.7
    malregimen, 5.10–5.11
  parties to a crime, and, 6.3
  sufficient legal causation
    existing conditions, 5.6
    introduction, 5.3
    'sufficient in itself', 5.4–5.5
  suicide, 5.16
  'supply' cases, 5.13–5.14
Causing
  road and traffic offences, and, 13.8
  strict liability, and, 3.10
Causing death
  careless driving, by
    generally, 13.13
    when under influence of drink or
      drugs, 13.14
  dangerous driving, by, 13.9
  inconsiderate driving, by, 13.13
Causing or risking injury to others
  administration or supply of noxious
    substances, 9.12–9.13
  generally, 9.10–9.11
**Causing serious injury by dangerous
  driving**
  generally, 13.11
Chastisement
  assault, and, 9.3
Child pornography
  public morality offences, and, 11.7
Children
  sexual offences, and, 11.2
Classification of crimes
  generally, 1.11
Coercion
  generally, 8.33–8.36

Common law
  corporate liability, 4.6–4.7
  fraud, 16.2
  reset
    actus reus, 14.27–14.29
    generally, 14.25–14.26
    guilty knowledge, 14.30
    husband and wife rule, 14.32
    intention to retain goods from their
      true owner, 14.31
    mens rea, 14.30–14.31
  road and traffic offences, 13.17
  sexual offences, 11.2
Common plan
  'art and part' guilt, and, 6.19
Complicity in crime
  parties to a crime, and, 6.1
Consent
  assault, and, 9.6–9.7
  sexual offences, and
    definition, 11.4
    generally, 11.4
    guidance, 11.4
    introduction, 11.2
  theft, and, 14.9–14.10
Conspiracy
  inchoate offences, and, 7.16
Consumption
  theft, and, 14.17
Contempt of court
  generally, 20.3
  relevant conduct, 20.4–20.5
  statutory framework, 20.6
Contractual obligations
  omissions, and, 2.15
Control of dangerous things
  omissions, and, 2.13
Control orders
  terrorism, and, 19.11
Controlled drugs
  exportation, 12.3
  generally, 12.2
  importation, 12.3
  production, 12.4
  supply, 12.4
Corporate homicide
  generally, 4.8
Corporate liability
  common law offences, 4.6–4.7
  directors, and, 4.9
  firms, and, 4.3
  generally, 4.1–4.2
  homicide, 4.8

Corporate liability – *contd*
indictment, on, 4.3
managing directors, and, 4.3
manslaughter, 4.8
mens rea, and, 4.5
partners, and, 4.9
partnerships, and, 4.3
'permitting' offences, 4.5
purpose, 4.1–4.2
statutory offences
common law, at, 4.6–4.7
'permitting', of, 4.5
requiring mens rea, 4.5
strict liability, 4.4
strict liability offences, 4.4
summary complaint, on, 4.3
Corporate manslaughter
generally, 4.8
Corporeal property
theft, and, 14.3–14.4
Counselling an offence
'art and part' guilt, and, 6.12
Crimes against property
and see **Property offences**
classification of crimes, and, 1.11
Crimes against the person
and see **Offences against the person**
classification of crimes, and, 1.11
Crimes against the state
and see **Offences against the state**
classification of crimes, and, 1.11
Culpable homicide
generally, 10.13
involuntary, 10.13–10.116
involuntary lawful act homicide,
10.15–10.116
omissions, 10.15
provocation, and
act must follow upon, 10.19–10.20
adultery, 10.19
cumulative provocation, 10.20
generally, 10.17
physical attack, 10.18
proportionality of response, 10.21
requirements, 10.18–10.21
unfaithful spouses, 10.19
unlawful acts other than assault,
10.14
voluntary, 10.17–10.21

D
Dangerous driving
generally, 13.12

Dangerous things
omissions, and, 2.13
Death
homicide, and, 10.4
Declaratory power
sources of law, and, 1.7–1.9
Defences
alcoholic intoxication, 8.10
assault, and, 9.6–9.7
coercion, 8.33–8.36
consent, 9.6–9.7
drug-related intoxication, 8.10
errors
fact, of, 8.6–8.9
introduction, 8.1
law, of, 8.2–8.5
method, as to, 8.7
object of the crime, as to, 8.6
errors of fact
irrelevant, 8.6–8.7
method, as to, 8.7
object of the crime, as to, 8.6
relevant, 8.8–8.9
errors of law
generally, 8.2
irrelevant, 8.3–8.4
relevant, 8.5
'hip flask', 13.25
insanity
connection between abnormality of
the mind and crime, 8.17–8.18
criteria, 8.19–8.25
diminished responsibility, 8.22–
8.24
generally, 8.14
informal measures, 8.17
mental abnormality, 8.15–8.18
nonage, 8.25
plea in bar of trial, 8.17–8.18
psychiatric conditions, 8.16
special defence, as, 8.18
intoxication
critique of the law, 8.12–8.13
generally, 8.10–8.11
malicious mischief, 18.6
necessity
generally, 8.33–8.36
road and traffic offences 13.26
no likelihood of driving, 13.22, 13.24
nonage, 8.25
road and traffic offences, and
'hip flask' defence, 13.25
necessity, 13.26

Defences – *contd*
  road and traffic offences, and – *contd*
    no likelihood of driving, 13.22,
      13.24
    post-incident drinking, 13.25
  robbery, 15.1
  self-defence
    generally, 8.26
    killing, and, 8.27–8.30
    lawful force, and, 8.31
    property, of, 8.32
  self-defence to killing
    erroneous belief life is threatened,
      8.28
    force used must not be excessive,
      8.29–8.30
    generally, 8.27
    imminent danger to life, 8.27
    inescapable danger, 8.29
  strict liability, and, 3.7–3.8
Dependent relationships
  omissions, and, 2.14–2.15
Destruction
  theft, and, 14.17
Digital content
  theft, and, 14.4
  Diminished responsibility
  and see **Insanity**
  generally, 8.22–8.24
Directors
  corporate liability, and, 4.9
Driving
  attempts, 13.4
  automatism, and, 13.3
  generally, 13.2
  while unfit through drink or drugs
    defence, 13.22
    generally, 13.18–13.19
  with more than the prescribed
    concentration of alcohol in the
    body
    defences, 13.24–13.26
    generally, 13.23
    'hip flask' defence, 13.25
    necessity, 13.26
    no likelihood of driving, 13.24
    post-incident drinking, 13.25
  without due care and attention, 13.15–
    13.16
  without reasonable consideration for
    others, 13.17
Drugging the victim
  aggravated theft, and, 14.23

Drugs offences
  being concerned in the supply of
    drugs, 12.5–12.7
  controlled drugs
    exportation, 12.3
    generally, 12.2
    importation, 12.3
    production, 12.4
    supply, 12.4
  export of controlled drugs, 12.3
  import of controlled drugs, 12.3
  intent to supply controlled drugs,
    12.5–12.7
  intoxication defence, and, 8.10
  misuse of drugs
    being concerned in the supply of
      drugs, 12.5–12.7
    controlled drugs, 12.2–12.4
    generally, 12.1
  possession of controlled drugs,
    12.5
  production of controlled drugs,
    12.4
  supply of controlled drugs, 12.4

E
Embezzlement
  actus reus, 17.4–17.5
  authority, 17.2–17.4
  generally, 17.1
  mens rea, 17.5
Error
  theft, and, 14.20
Errors
  fact
    irrelevant, 8.6–8.7
    method, as to, 8.7
    object of the crime, as to, 8.6
    relevant, 8.8–8.9
  introduction, 8.1
  law, of
    generally, 8.2
    irrelevant, 8.3–8.4
    relevant, 8.5
  method, as to, 8.7
  object of the crime, as to, 8.6
'Escape' cases
  novus actus interveniens, and, 5.15
Escaping from lawful custody
  generally, 20.8
**European Convention on Human
  Rights**
  sources of law, and, 1.10

Existing conditions
sufficient legal causation, and, 5.6
Export
controlled drugs, and, 12.3
Extortion
demand, 17.9
generally, 17.6
threat, 17.6–17.8

F
Failure to perform duty
omissions, and, 2.15
Failure to warn
omissions, and, 2.13
False reports to the police
generally, 20.7
Feckless conduct
novus actus interveniens, and, 5.16
Finding
theft, and, 14.8–14.9
Fire-raising
causing death by, 18.8
culpable and reckless, 18.9–18.10
generally, 18.7
intentional, 18.11
wilful, 18.7–18.8
Firms
corporate liability, and, 4.3
Forgery
false articles, 16.16
generally, 16.14
mens rea, 16.14
modes, 16.15
practical cheating, 16.16
uttering, 16.14
Fraud
articles for use, 16.13
common law, at, 16.2
causal link, 16.12
false pretence
generally, 16.2–16.4
mens rea, 16.13
implied representation, 16.3
introduction, 16.1
mens rea, 16.13
representations of intention, 16.6–16.7
result
generally, 16.8–16.11
mens rea, 16.13
silence, 16.4–16.5
statement of opinion, 16.7–16.8
'Free agreement'
sexual offences, and, 11.2

H
Handling ill-gotten goods or gains
actus reus, 14.27–14.29
generally, 14.25–14.26
guilty knowledge, 14.30
husband and wife rule, 14.32
intention to retain goods from their
true owner, 14.31
mens rea, 14.30–14.31
'Hip flask' defence
road and traffic offences, and, 13.25
Homicide
abortion, and, 10.1
categories
culpable homicide, 10.13
introduction, 10.5
murder, 10.6–10.12
non-criminal, 10.5
corporate liability, and, 4.8
culpable homicide
generally, 10.13
involuntary, 10.13–10.116
involuntary lawful act homicide,
10.15–10.116
omissions, 10.15
provocation, 10.17–10.21
unlawful acts other than assault,
10.14
voluntary, 10.17–10.21
'death', 10.4
introduction, 10.1
murder
definition, 10.6
generally, 10.6
intention to inflict harm, 10.9–10.10
intentional killing, 10.6
robbery, and, 10.11–10.12
wicked recklessness, 10.6–10.10
non-criminal, 10.5
provocation, and
act must follow upon, 10.19–10.20
adultery, 10.19
cumulative provocation, 10.20
generally, 10.17
physical attack, 10.18
proportionality of response, 10.21
requirements, 10.18–10.21
unfaithful spouses, 10.19
self-defence, and
erroneous belief life is threatened,
8.28
force used must not be excessive,
8.29–8.30

Homicide – *contd*
self-defence, and – *contd*
generally, 8.27
imminent danger to life, 8.27
inescapable danger, 8.2
strict liability, and, 3.7–3.8
'self-existent' human life, 10.1
suicide, 10.2–10.3
Housebreaking
aggravated theft, and, 14.21–14.22
Human Rights Act 1988
sources of law, and, 1.10

I
Import
controlled drugs, and, 12.3
Impossibility
attempts, and, 7.11–7.15
Incest
sexual offences, and, 11.19–11.20
Inchoate crimes
attempt
abandonment, 7.7–7.8
generally, 7.1impossibility, 7.11–
7.15
'last act' theory, 7.4–7.6
meaning, 7.2
mental element, 7.8–7.10
preparatory acts, 7.3–7.7
punishment, 7.1
relevant conduct, 7.2–7.5
statutory offences, 7.10–7.11
'thought' crimes, 7.3
conspiracy, 7.16
incitement, 7.17
introduction, 7.1
Incitement
inchoate offences, and, 7.17
Indecency
public morality offences, and, 11.8–
11.10
Indecent assault
sexual offences, and, 11.18
Indictment
corporate liability, and, 4.3
Innocent agency
'art and part' guilt, and, 6.4
Insanity
connection between abnormality of the
mind and crime, 8.17–8.18
criteria, 8.19–8.25
diminished responsibility, 8.22–8.24
generally, 8.14

Insanity – *contd*
informal measures, 8.17
mental abnormality, 8.15–8.18
nonage, 8.25
plea in bar of trial, 8.17–8.18
psychiatric conditions, 8.16
special defence, as, 8.18
Instigating an offence
'art and part' guilt, and, 6.12
Intent to steal
theft, and, 14.24
Intent to supply
controlled drugs, and, 12.5–12.7
Intervening acts
'act' of God, 5.8
act of third party
generally, 5.9–5.10
malregimen, 5.10–5.12
act of victim
'escape' cases, 5.15
feckless conduct, 5.16
generally, 5.13
suicide, 5.16
'supply' cases, 5.13–5.14
'escape' cases, 5.15
feckless conduct, 5.16
introduction, 5.7
malregimen, 5.10–5.11
suicide, 5.16
'supply' cases, 5.13–5.14
Intoxication
critique of the law, 8.12–8.13
generally, 8.10–8.11

J
Joint commission
'art and part' guilt, and, 6.4

K
Knives
offensive weapons, and, 12.14

L
'Last act' theory
attempts, and, 7.4–7.6
Lawful force
chastisement, 9.3
defence of self, others or of property,
in, 9.4
introduction, 9.3
prevention of crime, in, 9.4
restraint of other, in, 9.4
self-defence, in, 8.31, 9.4

Lewd and libidinous practices
public morality offences, and, 11.11
Life-guards
omissions, and, 2.14
Look outs
parties to a crime, and, 6.2

M
Making false reports to the police
generally, 20.7
Malicious mischief
defences, 18.6
fire-raising
causing death by, 18.8
culpable and reckless, 18.9–18.10
generally, 18.7
intentional, 18.11
wilful, 18.7–18.8
generally, 18.1–18.4
mens rea, 18.5–18.6
vandalism, 18.6
Malregimen
novus actus interveniens, and, 5.10–5.11
Managing directors
corporate liability, and, 4.3
Manslaughter
corporate liability, and, 4.8
Mechanically propelled vehicle
road and traffic offences, and, 13.5
Medical treatment
novus actus interveniens, and, 5.10–5.11
Mens rea
assault, and, 9.5
coincidence with actus reus, 2.27–2.28
constituent elements, 2.22–2.26
corporate liability, and, 4.5
differing requirements of individual crimes, 2.18
dole, and, 2.17
generally, 2.16
intention, 2.22–2.24
introduction, 2.1
knowledge, 2.23–2.24
motive, and, 2.19–2.21
negligence, 2.25–2.2
recklessness, 2.24–2.25
strict liability, and, 3.1–3.2
Mental abnormality
and see **Insanity**
generally, 8.15–8.18

'Mere presence' cases
'art and part' guilt, and, 6.10–6.11
Misuse of drugs
being concerned in the supply of drugs, 12.5–12.7
controlled drugs, 12.2–12.4
generally, 12.1
Mitigation
assault, and, 9.9
Morality
sources of law, and, 1.16–1.17
Moveable property
theft, and, 14.4
Murder
definition, 10.6
generally, 10.6
intention to inflict harm, 10.9–10.10
intentional killing, 10.6
robbery, and, 10.11–10.12
wicked recklessness, 10.6–10.10

N
Necessity
generally, 8.33–8.36
road and traffic offences, and, 13.26
No likelihood of driving
road and traffic offences, and, 13.22, 13.24
Nonage
generally, 8.25
Non-performance of duty
omissions, and, 2.15
Novus actus interveniens
'act' of God, 5.8
act of third party
generally, 5.9–5.10
malregimen, 5.10–5.12
act of victim
'escape' cases, 5.15
feckless conduct, 5.16
generally, 5.13
suicide, 5.16
'supply' cases, 5.13–5.14
'escape' cases, 5.15
feckless conduct, 5.16
introduction, 5.7
malregimen, 5.10–5.11
suicide, 5.16
'supply' cases, 5.13–5.14
Noxious substances
supply, 9.12–9.13

O

Obscene material
public morality offences, and, 11.6
Offences against the administration of justice
attempts to defeat the ends of justice, 20.9
contempt of court
generally, 20.3
relevant conduct, 20.4–20.5
statutory framework, 20.6
escaping from lawful custody, 20.8
making false reports to the police, 20.7
perjury
generally, 20.1–20.2
subornation, 20.2
Offences against the person
administration of noxious substances, 9.12–9.13
assault
aggravated offences, 9.8
consent, and, 9.6–9.7
defence, 9.6–9.7
generally, 9.1–9.2
lawful force, 9.3–9.4
mens rea, 9.5
mitigation, 9.9
reasonable belief in consent, 9.7
causing or risking injury to others
administration or supply of noxious substances, 9.12–9.13
generally, 9.10–9.11
classification of crimes, and, 1.11
lawful force
chastisement, 9.3
defence of self, others or of property, in, 9.4
introduction, 9.3
prevention of crime, in, 9.4
restraint of other, in, 9.4
self-defence, in, 9.4
risking injury to others
administration or supply of noxious substances, 9.12–9.13
generally, 9.10–9.11
supply of noxious substances, 9.12–9.13
threats, 9.14
Offences against the state
being adherent to the sovereign's enemies in the realm etc, 19.3
classification of crimes, and, 1.11

Offences against the state – *contd*
compassing the death of the sovereign etc, 19.2
imagining the death of the sovereign etc, 19.2
levying war against the sovereign in the realm, 19.2
misprision of treason, 19.4
official secrets, and
divulging confidential information, 19.6–19.17
spying and sabotage, 19.5
sedition, 19.4
terrorism
control orders, 19.11
disclosure of information, 19.10
funding, 19.9
generally, 19.8
terrorism prevention and investigation measures, 19.11
treason
forms, 19.2–19.3
introduction, 19.1
misprision, 19.4
persons liable, 19.1
Offensive weapons
bladed articles, 12.14
generally, 12.12–12.13
knives, 12.14
Official secrets
divulging confidential information, 19.6–19.17
spying and sabotage, 19.5
Omissions
abandonment of victim, 2.12–2.13
categories of liability, 2.12
close relationships between accused and person suffering the harm, 2.14–2.15
contractual obligations, 2.15
control of dangerous things, 2.13
dependent relationships, 2.14–2.15
duty to prevent commission of crime, 2.10
failure to perform duty, 2.15
failure to warn, 2.13
generally, 2.10–2.15
life-guards, and, 2.14
previous dangerous actings, 2.12–2.14
status of accused is such that he has duty to act, 2.14
Opening lockfast places
aggravated theft, and, 14.22–14.23

P
Parties to crime
  accomplices, and, 6.2
  acting in concert, 6.1
  ancillary responsibility, 6.1
  'art and part' guilt
    assisting perpetrator in commission
      of crime, 6.15–6.16
    associate liability, 6.5–6.7
    bilateral regulatory offences, 6.9
    circumstances in which liability
      occurs, 6.10–6.16
    common plan, 6.19
    counselling an offence, 6.12
    'doing nothing', 6.10–6.11
    forms, 6.4–6.7
    innocent agency, 6.4
    instigating an offence, 6.12
    introduction, 6.1
    joint commission, 6.4
    justification, 6.2–6.3
    'mere presence' cases, 6.10–6.11
    regulatory offences, 6.9
    scope, 6.19–6.20
    statutory offences, 6.21
    supply of materials or information,
      6.12–6.15
    unintended consequences, and,
      6.19–6.20
    victim, and, 6.8
    withdrawal by participant, 6.17–
      6.18
  causation, and, 6.3
  complicity in crime, 6.1
  introduction, 6.1
  look outs, 6.2
  regulatory offences, 6.9
  succession to crime, 6.1
Partners
  corporate liability, and, 4.9
Partnerships
  corporate liability, and, 4.3
Perjury
  generally, 20.1–20.2
  subornation, 20.2
Permitting
  corporate liability, and, 4.5
  road and traffic offences, and, 13.8
  strict liability, and, 3.10
Plagium
  theft, and, 14.4
Plea in bar of trial
  insanity, and, 8.17–8.18

Possession
  bladed articles, 12.14
  controlled drugs, 12.5
  knives, 12.14
Preparatory acts
  attempts, and, 7.3–7.7
Prevention of crime
  lawful force, and, 9.4
  omissions, and, 2.10
Preventive offences
  theft, and, 14.24
Previous dangerous actings
  omissions, and, 2.12–2.14
Principles of liability
  actus reus
    coincidence with mens rea, 2.27–
      2.28
    generally, 2.2
    introduction, 2.1
    omissions, 2.10–2.15
    status offences, 2.4
    voluntary act, 2.3–2.9
  introduction, 2.1
  mens rea
    coincidence with actus reus, 2.27–
      2.28
    constituent elements, 2.22–2.26
    differing requirements of individual
      crimes, 2.18
    dole, and, 2.17
    generally, 2.16
    intention, 2.22–2.24
    introduction, 2.1
    knowledge, 2.23–2.24
    motive, and, 2.19–2.21
    negligence, 2.25–2.26
    recklessness, 2.24–2.25
Production
  controlled drugs, and, 12.4
Prohibition of retrospective imposition
  of criminal liability
  sources of law, and, 1.10
Property
  self-defence, and, 8.32
  theft, and
    abandoned property, 14.5
    another's property, 14.4
    corporeal property, 14.3–14.4
    digital content, 14.4
    introduction, 14.2
    moveable property, 14.4
    plagium, 14.4
    wild animals, 14.4

Property offences
aggravated theft
drugging the victim, 14.23
housebreaking, 14.21–14.22
opening lockfast places, 14.22–
14.23
handling ill-gotten goods or gains
actus reus, 14.27–14.29
generally, 14.25–14.26
guilty knowledge, 14.30
husband and wife rule, 14.32
intention to retain goods from their
true owner, 14.31
mens rea, 14.30–14.31
intent to steal, 14.24
property
abandoned property, 14.5
another's property, 14.4
corporeal property, 14.3–14.4
digital content, 14.4
introduction, 14.2
moveable property, 14.4
plagium, 14.4
wild animals, 14.4
reset
actus reus, 14.27–14.29
generally, 14.25–14.26
guilty knowledge, 14.30
husband and wife rule, 14.32
intention to retain goods from their
true owner, 14.31
mens rea, 14.30–14.31
theft
actus reus, 14.5–14.10
aggravated offence, 14.21–14.
amotio, 14.6
appropriation, by, 14.6–14.8
borrowing, and, 14.15–14.19
consent of owner, 14.9–14.10
consumption, 14.17
destruction, 14.17
drugging the victim, by, 14.23
error, 14.20
finding, by, 14.8–14.9
generally, 14.1–14.2
housebreaking, by, 14.21–14.22
intent to steal, 14.24
mens rea, 14.10–14.15
opening lockfast places, by, 14.22–
14.23
plagium, 14.4
presumption of intent to steal,
14.16–14.18

Property offences – *contd*
theft – *contd*
preventive offences, 14.24
property, 14.2–14.5
taking, by, 14.6
taking and using, 14.18–14.19
unauthorised borrowing, 14.16
violation of sepulchres, 14.4
Property-related crimes
classification of crimes, and, 1.11
Protective offences
sexual offences, and, 11.2
Provocation
act must follow upon, 10.19–10.20
adultery, 10.19
cumulative provocation, 10.20
generally, 10.17
physical attack, 10.18
proportionality of response, 10.21
requirements, 10.18–10.21
unfaithful spouses, 10.19
Psychiatric conditions
and see **Insanity**
generally, 8.16
Public indecency
public morality offences, and, 11.8–
11.10
Public morality offences
child pornography, 11.7
classification of crimes, and, 1.11
indecency, 11.8–11.10
introduction, 11.5
lewd and libidinous practices,
11.11
obscene material, 11.6
public indecency, 11.8–11.10
Public order offences
classification of crimes, and, 1.11

R
Rape
actus reus, 11.14–11.16
generally, 11.13
introduction, 11.3
mens rea, 11.16–11.17
'Real crimes'
strict liability, and, 3.5
Regulatory offences
'art and part' guilt, and, 6.9
classification of crimes, and, 1.11
parties to a crime, and, 6.9
Regulatory provisions
strict liability, and, 3.4

Reset
actus reus, 14.27–14.29
generally, 14.25–14.26
guilty knowledge, 14.30
husband and wife rule, 14.32
intention to retain goods from their
true owner, 14.31
mens rea, 14.30–14.31
Restraint of other
lawful force, and, 9.4
**Retrospective imposition of criminal
liability**
sources of law, and, 1.10
Risking injury to others
administration or supply of noxious
substances, 9.12–9.13
generally, 9.10–9.11
Road and traffic offences
accident, 13.7
attempting to drive
defence, 13.22
generally, 13.4
while unfit through drink or drugs,
13.18–13.19
attempting to drive while unfit through
drink or drugs
defence, 13.22
generally, 13.18–13.19
automatism, and, 13.3
being in charge of motor vehicle while
unfit
defence, 13.22
generally, 13.20–13.21
being in charge of motor vehicle
with more than the prescribed
concentration of alcohol in the body
defences, 13.24–13.26
generally, 13.23
'hip flask' defence, 13.25
necessity, 13.26
no likelihood of driving, 13.24
post-incident drinking, 13.25
careless and inconsiderate driving,
13.15
causing, 13.8
causing death by careless driving
generally, 13.13
when under influence of drink or
drugs, 13.14
causing death by dangerous driving,
13.9
causing death by inconsiderate driving,
13.13

Road and traffic offences – *contd*
causing serious injury by dangerous
driving, 13.11
common law, at, 13.17
dangerous driving, 13.12
defence
'hip flask' defence, 13.25
necessity, 13.26
no likelihood of driving, 13.22,
13.24
post-incident drinking, 13.25
definitions, 13.2–13.8
driving
attempts, 13.4
automatism, and, 13.3
generally, 13.2
driving a motor vehicle with more than
the prescribed concentration of
alcohol in the body
defences, 13.24–13.26
generally, 13.23
'hip flask' defence, 13.25
necessity, 13.26
no likelihood of driving, 13.24
post-incident drinking, 13.25
driving while unfit through drink or
drugs
defence, 13.22
generally, 13.18–13.19
driving without due care and attention,
13.15–13.16
driving without reasonable
consideration for others, 13.17
introduction, 13.1
mechanically propelled vehicle, 13.5
permitting, 13.8
road or other public place, 13.6
under influence of drink or drugs,
13.14
unfit through drink or drugs, 13.18–
13.19
using, 13.8
without due care and attention, 13.15–
13.16
without reasonable consideration for
others, 13.17
Robbery
actus reus, 15.1
aggravated theft, as, 15.1
defences, 15.1
introduction, 15.1
mens rea, 15.1
murder, and, 10.11–10.12

Robbery – *contd*
personal violence, 15.1–15.2
threats, 15.3

S
Sabotage
generally, 19.5
Sedition
generally, 19.4
Self-defence
generally, 8.26
killing, and
erroneous belief life is threatened,
8.28
force used must not be excessive,
8.29–8.30
generally, 8.27
imminent danger to life, 8.27
inescapable danger, 8.29
strict liability, and, 3.7–3.8
lawful force, and, 8.31 , 9.4
property, of, 8.32
Sepulchres
theft, and, 14.4
Sexual assault
generally, 11.12
indecent assault, 11.18
introduction, 11.3
rape, 11.13–11.17
Sexual offences
abuse of trust, 11.2
age of consent, 11.2
children, 11.2
common law, at, 11.2
consent
definition, 11.4
generally, 11.4
guidance, 11.4
introduction, 11.2
'free agreement', 11.2
incest, 11.19–11.20
indecent assault, 11.18
introduction, 11.1
perpetrator, 11.2
protective offences, 11.2
public morality, and
child pornography, 11.7
indecency, 11.8–11.10
introduction, 11.5
lewd and libidinous practices,
11.11
obscene material, 11.6
public indecency, 11.8–11.10

Sexual offences – *contd*
rape
actus reus, 11.14–11.16
generally, 11.13
introduction, 11.3
mens rea, 11.16–11.17
sexual assault
generally, 11.12
indecent assault, 11.18
introduction, 11.3
rape, 11.13–11.17
sexual assault by penetration, 11.3
statutory framework, 11.2
terminology, 11.2
victim, 11.2
Social protection offences
being concerned in the supply of
drugs, 12.5–12.7
breach of the peace
generally, 12.8–12.10
threatening or abusive behaviour,
12.11
controlled drugs
exportation, 12.3
generally, 12.2
importation, 12.3
production, 12.4
supply, 12.4
export of controlled drugs, 12.3
import of controlled drugs, 12.3
intent to supply controlled drugs,
12.5–12.7
misuse of drugs
being concerned in the supply of
drugs, 12.5–12.7
controlled drugs, 12.2–12.4
generally, 12.1
offensive weapons
bladed articles, 12.14
generally, 12.12–12.13
knives, 12.14
possession of bladed articles, 12.14
possession of controlled drugs, 12.5
possession of knives, 12.14
production of controlled drugs,
12.4
supply of controlled drugs, 12.4
Somnambulism
voluntary act, and, 2.5
Sources of law
classification of crimes, and, 1.11
declaratory power of the High Court,
1.7–1.9

Sources of law – *contd*
European Convention on Human
Rights, 1.10
Human Rights Act 1988, 1.10
introduction, 1.1–1.5
morality, and, 1.16–1.17
prohibition of retrospective imposition
of criminal liability, 1.10
statutes, 1.6
temporal scope, and, 1.14
territorial scope, and, 1.12–1.13
Spying
generally, 19.5
Status offences
voluntary act, and, 2.4
Statutes
sources of law, and, 1.6
Statutory offences
'art and part' guilt, and, 6.21
attempts, and, 7.10–7.11
corporate liability, and
common law, at, 4.6–4.7
'permitting', of, 4.5
requiring mens rea, 4.5
strict liability, 4.4
strict liability, and, 3.1–3.2
Strict liability offences
causing offences, 3.10
corporate liability, and, 4.4
defences, 3.7–3.8
generally, 3.1–3.2
mens rea, and, 3.1–3.2
permitting offences, 3.10
statutes silent as to mens rea
effectiveness argument, 3.6
inability to avoid occurrence of an
actus reus, 3.6
introduction, 3.4
'real crimes', 3.5
regulatory nature of provision,
3.4
statutes using words implying mens
rea, 3.3
vicarious liability, 3.9–3.10
'wilfully', 3.3
Succession to crime
parties to a crime, and, 6.1
Sufficient legal causation
existing conditions, 5.6
introduction, 5.3
'sufficient in itself', 5.4–5.5
Suicide
novus actus interveniens, and, 5.16

Summary complaint
corporate liability, and, 4.3
Supply
controlled drugs, and, 12.4
novus actus interveniens, and, 5.13–
5.14
noxious substances, 9.12–9.13
Supply of materials or information
'art and part' guilt, and, 6.12–6.15

T
Taking
theft, and, 14.6
Temporal scope of criminal law
generally, 1.14
Territorial scope of criminal law
generally, 1.12–1.13
Terrorism
control orders, 19.11
disclosure of information, 19.10
funding, 19.9
generally, 19.8
terrorism prevention and investigation
measures, 19.11
Theft
actus reus, 14.5–14.10
aggravated theft
drugging the victim, 14.23
housebreaking, 14.21–14.22
opening lockfast places, 14.22–14.23
amotio, 14.6
appropriation, by, 14.6–14.8
borrowing, and, 14.15–14.19
consent of owner, 14.9–14.10
consumption, 14.17
destruction, 14.17
drugging the victim, by, 14.23
embezzlement, by
actus reus, 17.4–17.5
authority, 17.2–17.4
generally, 17.1
mens rea, 17.5
error, 14.20
finding, by, 14.8–14.9
generally, 14.1–14.2
housebreaking, by, 14.21–14.22
intent to steal, 14.24
mens rea, 14.10–14.15
opening lockfast places, by, 14.22–
14.23
plagium, 14.4
presumption of intent to steal, 14.16–
14.18